W9-BGZ-001

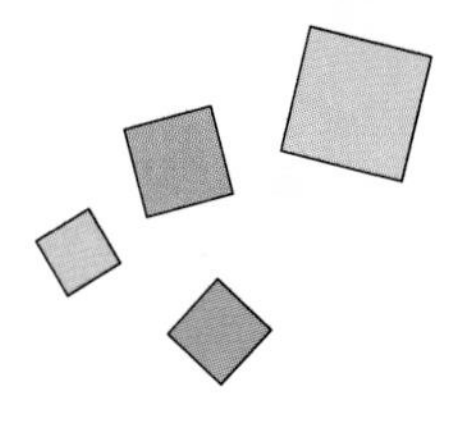

Rendez-vous

AN INVITATION TO FRENCH

Third Edition

Judith A. Muyskens
UNIVERSITY OF CINCINNATI

Alice Omaggio Hadley
UNIVERSITY OF ILLINOIS, URBANA-CHAMPAIGN

Claudine Convert-Chalmers

Michèle Sarner
CONTRIBUTOR

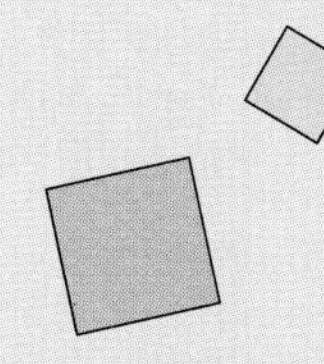

McGraw-Hill Publishing Company
New York · St. Louis · San Francisco · Auckland · Bogotá · Caracas
Hamburg · Lisbon · London · Madrid · Mexico · Milan
Montreal · New Delhi · Oklahoma City · Paris · San Juan
São Paulo · Singapore · Sydney · Tokyo · Toronto

This is an EBI book.

Rendez-vous: An Invitation to French

3 4 5 6 7 8 9 0 VNH VNH 9 4 3 2

Library of Congress Cataloging-in-Publication Data:

Muyskens, Judith A.
Rendez-vous: an invitation to French / Judith A. Muyskens, Alice C. Omaggio, Claudine Chalmers.—3rd ed., Instructor's ed.
p. cm.
ISBN 0-07-540871-6 (Instructor's ed.).—ISBN 0-07-540867-8 (Student ed.)
1. French language—Textbooks for foreign speakers—English.
2. French language—Grammar—1950– I. Omaggio, Alice C.
II. Chalmers, Claudine, 1948– III. Title.
PF2129.E5M87 1990 89-13252
448.2'421—dc20 CIP

Developmental editor: Eileen LeVan
Copyeditor: Xavier Callahan
Editing supervisor: Jan deProsse
Text and cover designer: Albert Burkhardt
Art editor: Edie Williams, Vargas/Williams/Design
Illustrators: Katherine Tillotson, Axelle Fortier
Photo researcher: Judy Mason
Production supervisor: Pattie Myers
Compositor: Graphic Typesetting Service
Printer and binder: Von Hoffmann Press

Text and Art Credits

Cover art Pierre Auguste Renoir, *Déjeuner des canotiers* (Luncheon of the Boating Party), from the Phillips Collection, Washington, D.C. **Chapter-opening Photographs** *page 1* © Beryl Goldberg; *13* © Henebry Photography; *45* © Chip & Rosa Maria Peterson; *76* © Bruno Maso / PhotoEdit: *107* © 1987 Charles Gupton / Stock, Boston; *136* © 1983 Peter Miller; *169* © Henebry Photography; *201* © Chip & Rosa Maria Peterson; *235* © Hartman-De Witt; *269* © 1989 Comstock, Inc.; *300* © Stuart Cohen; *329* © Henebry Photography; *358* © Henebry Photography; *387* © Owen Franken / Stock, Boston, *413* © Alan Oddie / PhotoEdit; *448* © 1987 Charles Gupton; *481* © Fay Torresyap / Stock, Boston; *507* © Peter Gonzalez; *535* © Daniel Simon / Gamma-Liaison

Realia and Cartoons *page 9* © *Vos Études; 28* © *Vos Études; 49* © Agfa Gevaert, S.A.; *70* illustration by Simé from *The French* by Theodore Zeblin, Éditions André Balland; *81* from "En Route," reprinted with permission of Air Canada; *90* © *Vital; 101* Copyright © C. Charillon-Paris; *128* © McDonald's Corporation; *132* Copyright © C. Charillon-Paris; *140* © *Gault-Millau Magazine; 148* Vittel label produced by Vittel, France & reprinted with permission; *152* © *Jacinte; 196* © *Clin d'oeil; 216* ad reprinted with permission of Rossignol Ski Co., Inc.; *220* © *Forbes Magazine; 226* © Claude Verrier, Intermonde-Presse; *228* © Club Med; *232–233* © *Vital; 236* (Air Canada logo) reprinted with permission of Air Canada; *236* (Air Afrique logo) © Air Afrique; *236* (Air France logo) reprinted courtesy of Air France; *236* (Sabena logo) © Sabena, Belgian World Airlines; *236* (Air Algérie logo) © Air Algérie;

(continued on p. 610)

Table des matières

CHAPITRE 18

La société contemporaine: lectures et activités 535

Appendices 547

Lexiques

Index 607

Preface

Rendez-vous is a complete first-year college and university French program designed for the proficiency-oriented classroom. Emphasizing vocabulary before grammar, grammar within a cultural context, and a communicative approach to learning that gives students useful language for everyday life, *Rendez-vous* aims to develop the four language skills (listening, speaking, reading, and writing) and to introduce students to the diversity of the French-speaking world.

Organization of the Third Edition

Rendez-vous is composed of eighteen chapters preceded by an introductory chapter. With the true beginner in mind, the preliminary chapter has been shortened in this edition. Chapter 18 has been revised to serve as a review of essential first-year skills.

The third edition includes five new review sections, called *Communication et vie pratique*. Each contains a sketched scene from everyday life, followed by questions that review vocabulary and grammar from the preceding chapters. There is also a writing section that focuses both on general writing skills and on functional topics.

All chapters except the preliminary chapter and Chapter 18 have the same structure. The contents are as follows:

Étude de vocabulaire

This section presents and offers practice of vocabulary, which is based on broad cultural themes. Chapter themes were determined according to the principle that students should first learn to use words they will encounter in a French-speaking culture (for example, vocabulary for making purchases, ordering and buying food, traveling, and so on). Sketches, photographs, realia, and varied reinforcement activities enable students to use the new vocabulary without recourse to translations.

Étude de grammaire

A "slice of life" dialogue introduces new grammar inductively. A brief set of follow-up questions calls attention to the new structure, as used in context, before students study it as a "grammar point." Grammar explanations in English are concise and are often accompanied by charts and other visual supports. Each exercise is built around a coherent context; series of exercises are sequenced from controlled response to open response. Open-ended activities usually encourage students to express their own ideas and opinions; many call for paired and group work.

Étude de prononciation

Basic pronunciation information, accompanied by drills, appears through Chapter 5. Practice of individual sounds and speech patterns continues in the laboratory program.

Situation

Focusing on conversation and culture, this section features a dialogue with accompanying role-playing exercises and activities. A vocabulary section, *A propos,* gives functional expressions needed for carrying out typical everyday tasks (*comment critiquer un film, comment donner des conseils, comment exprimer l'admiration ou l'indignation,* and so on). A *Commentaire culturel* treats an aspect of French or francophone culture; it often includes photos or other authentic materials.

Mise au point

A set of recombinant exercises reviews the chapter's core vocabulary and grammar. It concludes with *Interactions,* role-playing exercises for the novice- and intermediate-level French student that are based on guidelines published by the American Council on the Teaching of Foreign Languages (ACTFL).

Intermède

Optional readings include photo essays (in the early chapters), readings written specifically for *Rendez-vous* and based on information from the popular press, a few simple literary pieces, and unedited excerpts from magazines and newspapers, brochures, and other authentic sources. In the context of the comprehension activities that follow them, all these materials are easily accessible to the beginning student. The first eleven readings are preceded by a section (*Avant de lire*) that teaches reading skills, such as skimming for the gist and contextual guessing. In the final seven chapters, reading strategies precede only those readings for which students may need special guidance (for example, poetry).

Major Changes in the Third Edition

- Realia and authentic materials appear in exercises and reading sections, to expose students to French in real-life contexts and to enhance the cultural content of the course.
- Functional expressions are introduced when the situation demands them (*Mots-clés*). Functional language in *A propos* has been expanded to increase students' "survival" vocabulary.
- All exercises are contextualized, and some of the more mechanical exercises from the second edition have been moved to the marginal notes in the Instructor's Edition or to the *Instructor's Manual.* Many activities that involve paraphrasing, interviews, partners, role playing, and problem solving have been added to all parts of the chapters.
- Review and reentry have been expanded, especially in the new *Communication et vie pratique* sections, with an emphasis on creative language use.
- The language has been made more natural in all dialogues, offering authentic, spontaneous discourse for students to imitate and expand on.
- Whenever possible, grammar topics are presented in terms of what students can do with the language: talking about the past, expressing desires and requests, and so on. Some material (*je voudrais..., j'aimerais...,* for example) is introduced when the situation demands it, although the entire paradigm (in this case, the conditional) may not be presented until later in the text.
- The number of grammar points presented in each chapter has been reduced, and the practice of certain difficult points, such as the past conditional, now requires only recognition or low-level production. Thus, students become familiar with a concept without being expected to master it. Certain sections, such as the one on pronominal verbs, have been rewritten so that the material will be easier to present and practice.
- Pre-reading and pre-writing sections (*Avant de lire* and *Avant d'écrire*) emphasize building skills in reading and writing.
- There is an increased focus on the francophone world throughout the book, in exercises, realia, and readings.
- Updated cultural information reflects the contemporary francophone world. Starting in Chapter 9, cultural readings are now in French.
- ACTFL "situations" (in *Interactions*) review chapter functions.
- Five color maps showing francophone countries and regions throughout the world precede the *Premier Rendez-vous.* Activities throughout the text refer students back to these maps.

Rendez-vous *and Developing Language Proficiency*

The authors of *Rendez-vous* believe that the primary goal of a language course is to enable students to *use* the language they are studying. Grammar and vocabulary are not introduced as ends in themselves, as materials for students to master; rather, they are seen as a means to communication and self-expression. For that reason, grammar is presented in English, to eliminate the need for lengthy explanations during class. Although students are exposed to the range of grammar and vocabulary that is usual in a first-year course, those structures that students most need to express their ideas are frequently emphasized and reviewed. Realia, exercises built around authentic situations, and notes on cultural phenomena aim to raise students' awareness of the link between language and society. The text emphasizes the skills students are learning, rather than a body of material, and follow-up exercises call on students to use their knowledge in creative ways. Paired and group activities encourage students to communicate with one another, as well as with their instructor.

One of the organizing principles of *Rendez-vous* is the concept of proficiency, described in the ACTFL guidelines and based on standards long used by the United States government and armed services. The guidelines use five major descriptive labels to gauge levels of linguistic development: Novice (Low, Mid, High), Intermediate (Low, Mid, High), Advanced, Advanced Plus, and Superior. The proficiency guidelines can be used to appraise speaking, reading, writing, and listening, and they are built into the structure of *Rendez-vous.* For example, those functions that novice- and intermediate-level speakers can be expected to master are emphasized and reviewed often; by contrast, functions appropriate to an advanced speaker are presented for recognition, with only low-level practice. The ACTFL guidelines helped us set priorities for the information presented and allowed us to emphasize skill building along with mastery of concepts. We hope that, rather than leaving their introductory course only vaguely familiar with French grammar and vocabulary, students will be able to *use* French at the high-novice to intermediate levels of proficiency.

Supplementary Materials for the Third Edition

- The *Workbook* complements the student text. Focused exercises provide thorough written practice of the theme vocabulary and grammatical structures presented in the corresponding chapters of the text. The third edition of the workbook has been revised to emphasize practice in real-life contexts. It includes personalized and realia-based exercises. Study hints give students specific advice on acquiring language skills.
- The *Laboratory Manual and Tape Program* has been simplified and rerecorded with the aim of making it more accessible to students. The third edition also contains more sketch-based exercises, and its personalized focus should make it more interesting. Students are given guidance in numerous listening-comprehension tasks. (A tapescript and cassette tapes are provided free to institutions that adopt *Rendez-vous.* Cassette tapes are also available for students to purchase, and reel-to-reel tapes are available for duplication.)
- A separate *listening-comprehension tape,* for use in the classroom, provides recorded passages keyed to chapter themes. These passages expose students to everyday conversations in French and teach listening-comprehension skills. An accompanying manual provides scripts and follow-up activities. See the audiocassette symbol in the marginal notes of the Instructor's Edition for suggestions about how to use the tapes.

- The *Instructor's Edition* has been enriched to provide additional on-page suggestions for practice of new material, listening-comprehension practice, development of speaking skills, and variations on text materials.
- The *Instructor's Manual* offers an introduction to teaching techniques, suggestions for constructing a course syllabus, ideas for lesson planning, guidelines for testing, dictations, composition topics, and conversation cards.
- The *Testing Program* reflects the revisions of the student text.
- The *Computerized Testing Program* contains all the material in the *Testing Program,* and is available for IBM, IBM-compatible and Apple Macintosh computers.
- Two types of *computer-assisted instructional programs* are available with this edition: an interactive program with a game format that emphasizes communication skills in French, *Jeux communicatifs,* and a program featuring all the single-response grammatical exercises in the text, *McGraw-Hill Electronic Language Tutor* (*MHELT*).
- A *video program,* consisting of nineteen tapes keyed to chapter themes, is available through the University of Illinois, Urbana–Champaign.
- Another video program, *Pleins Feux sur la Révolution,* tells the story of the French Revolution through historical and artistic documents.
- The *Instructor's Resource Kit* contains supplementary realia and activities, as well as transparency masters of the sketches in the main text.
- A set of *slides* of the francophone world, with commentary and questions by Claudine Chalmers, offers visual reinforcement of the cultural themes presented in the text.

Acknowledgments

The publishers and authors would like to thank those instructors who participated in the surveys that proved indispensable in the development of the third edition of *Rendez-vous* and to thank again those who participated in the surveys conducted for the first and second editions. Many instructors who have used *Rendez-vous* have offered invaluable insights.

Many other individuals deserve our thanks. Michèle Sarner contributed a wealth of new ideas to the third edition. Gilberte Furstenberg of the Massachusetts Institute of Technology read the manuscript for linguistic and cultural accuracy.

The production staff at McGraw-Hill shepherded the manuscript, along with its complex art program, through its various stages. Special thanks to Jan deProsse, editing supervisor, Jamie Brooks, design manager, and Marie Deer, for work that is always excellent.

Leslie Berriman directed the development of the third edition. Her good judgment about content and fine sense of structure inspired us; her encouragement kept us going. Eileen LeVan was the editor of this new edition. Her creative involvement and constant editorial guidance shaped this book through all stages of writing and development. A final word of thanks to Eirik Børve and Thalia Dorwick, as always, for their support, enthusiasm, and good ideas.

LE GROENLAND
LE CANADA
L'AMÉRIQUE DU NORD[f]
le Québec
St-Pierre-et-Miquelon[f] (Fr.)
l'Île du Prince-Édouard[f]
la Nouvelle-Écosse
le Nouveau-Brunswick
la Nouvelle-Angleterre
la Louisiane
L'OCÉAN PACIFIQUE[m]
LES ANTILLES FRANÇAISES[f]
HAÏTI[m]
la Guadeloupe
la Dominique
la Martinique
la Guyane
L'AMÉRIQUE DU SUD[f]
les Îles Marquises[f] (Fr.)
les Îles Tuamotu[f] (Fr.)
Tahiti[f]
LA POLYNÉSIE FRANÇAISE
Vanuatu
la Nouvelle-Calédonie
Les régions francophones du monde
0 1000 2000 3000 4000 MILLES
0 1000 2000 3000 4000 5000 6000 KILOMÈTRES
m = masculin f = féminin

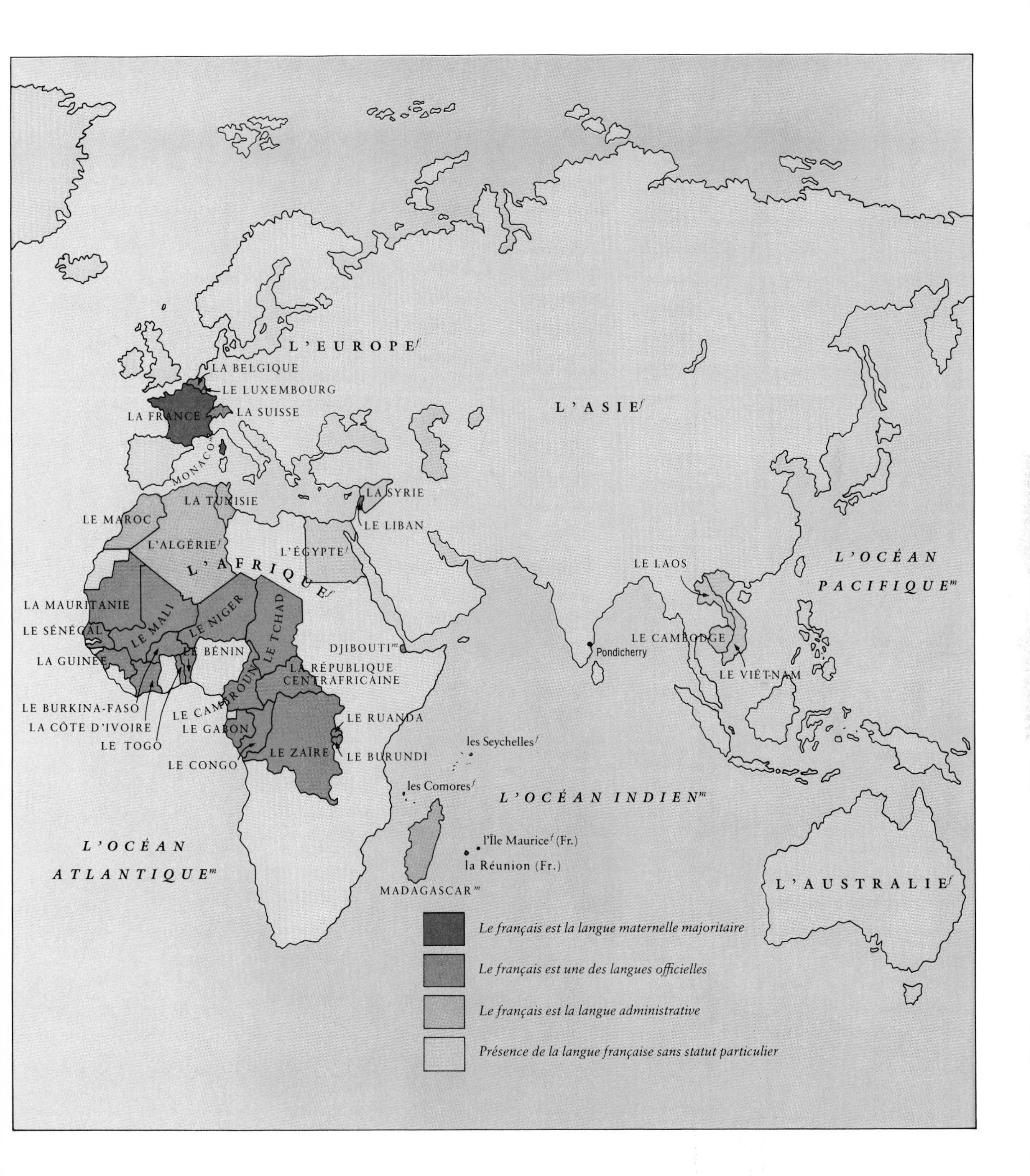
L'EUROPE[f]
LA BELGIQUE
LE LUXEMBOURG
LA FRANCE
LA SUISSE
MONACO
L'ASIE[f]
LA SYRIE
LA TUNISIE
LE MAROC
LE LIBAN
L'ALGÉRIE[f]
L'ÉGYPTE[f]
L'AFRIQUE[f]
LE LAOS
L'OCÉAN PACIFIQUE[m]
LA MAURITANIE
LE MALI
LE NIGER
LE TCHAD
LE SÉNÉGAL
DJIBOUTI[m]
LE CAMBODGE
Pondicherry
LA GUINÉE
LE BÉNIN
LA RÉPUBLIQUE CENTRAFRICAINE
LE VIÊT-NAM
LE BURKINA-FASO
LE CAMEROUN
LE RUANDA
LA CÔTE D'IVOIRE
LE GABON
LE TOGO
les Seychelles[f]
LE ZAÏRE
LE BURUNDI
LE CONGO
les Comores[f]
L'OCÉAN INDIEN[m]
L'OCÉAN ATLANTIQUE[m]
l'Île Maurice[f] (Fr.)
la Réunion (Fr.)
L'AUSTRALIE[f]
MADAGASCAR[m]
Le français est la langue maternelle majoritaire
Le français est une des langues officielles
Le français est la langue administrative
Présence de la langue française sans statut particulier

L'ANGLETERRE f
Dunkerque
Calais
Boulogne
Lille
LA BELGIQUE
L'ALLEMAGNE f
LA MANCHE
la Picardie
Dieppe
Amiens
LE LUXEMBOURG
Cherbourg
Le Havre
Rouen
la Seine
Caen
Reims
Verdun
la Normandie
Paris
la Champagne
la Lorraine
Brest
Versailles
l'Île-de-France f
Nancy
Strasbourg
LES VOSGES f
Chartres
la Bretagne
Rennes
l'Alsace f
le Rhin
Orléans
la Loire
la Loire
Angers
Tours
Blois
Dijon
Besançon
Nantes
la Touraine
LA SUISSE
Bourges
la Bourgogne
la Vendée
la Saône
LE JURA
La Rochelle
L'OCÉAN ATLANTIQUE m
le Poitou
Limoges
Clermont-Ferrand
Lyon
la Savoie
L'ITALIE f
l'Auvergne f
Grenoble
LE MASSIF CENTRAL
LES ALPES f
Bordeaux
la Garonne
le Dauphiné
le Rhône
Avignon
Nîmes
Arles
la Provence
Nice
MONACO m
Biarritz
Toulouse
Montpellier
Aix-en-Provence
Cannes
Marseille
St-Tropez
Carcassonne
LES PYRÉNÉES f
le Languedoc
Perpignan
L'ESPAGNE f
la Corse
L'ANDORRE f
Ajaccio
La France
0 50 100 150 MILLES
0 50 100 150 200 250 KILOMETRES
LA MER MÉDITERRANÉE
m = masculin f = féminin

L'Europe[f]
0 50 100 200 300 400 500 MILLES
0 100 200 400 600 800 KILOMÈTRES
m = masculin f = féminin
Le français est la langue maternelle majoritaire
Le français est une des langues officielles
Le français est la langue administrative
Présence de la langue française sans statut particulier
Reykjavik
L'ISLANDE[f]
LA SUÈDE
LA FINLANDE
LA NORVÈGE
Oslo
Helsinki
Leningrad
Stockholm
L'ÉCOSSE[f]
L'IRLANDE DU NORD[f]
LE DANEMARK
LA GRANDE-BRETAGNE
L'IRLANDE[f]
Dublin
Copenhague
LA MER BALTIQUE
Moscou
LA MER DU NORD
L'U.R.S.S.[f]
LE PAYS DE GALLES
L'ANGLETERRE[f]
Londres
Amsterdam
LA RÉPUBLIQUE DÉMOCRATIQUE ALLEMANDE
Berlin-Est
LES PAYS-BAS[m]
Varsovie
LA POLOGNE
Bruxelles
LA BELGIQUE
Jersey[f]
Bonn
LE LUXEMBOURG
Luxembourg
Prague
L'OCÉAN ATLANTIQUE[m]
Paris
LA RÉPUBLIQUE FÉDÉRALE D'ALLEMAGNE
LA TCHÉCOSLOVAQUIE
LA FRANCE
Vienne
Berne
Lausanne
Genève
LA SUISSE
L'AUTRICHE[f]
Budapest
LA HONGRIE
le Val d'Aoste
LA ROUMANIE
L'ITALIE[f]
LA YOUGOSLAVIE
Belgrade
Bucarest
LA MER NOIRE
LE PORTUGAL
L'ANDORRE[f]
MONACO[m]
Lisbonne
Madrid
la Corse
LA BULGARIE
Ajaccio
Sofia
L'ESPAGNE[f]
Rome
Istanbul
Tirana
L'ALBANIE[f]
LA GRÈCE
LA TURQUIE
LA MER MÉDITERRANÉE
Athènes
L'AFRIQUE[f]

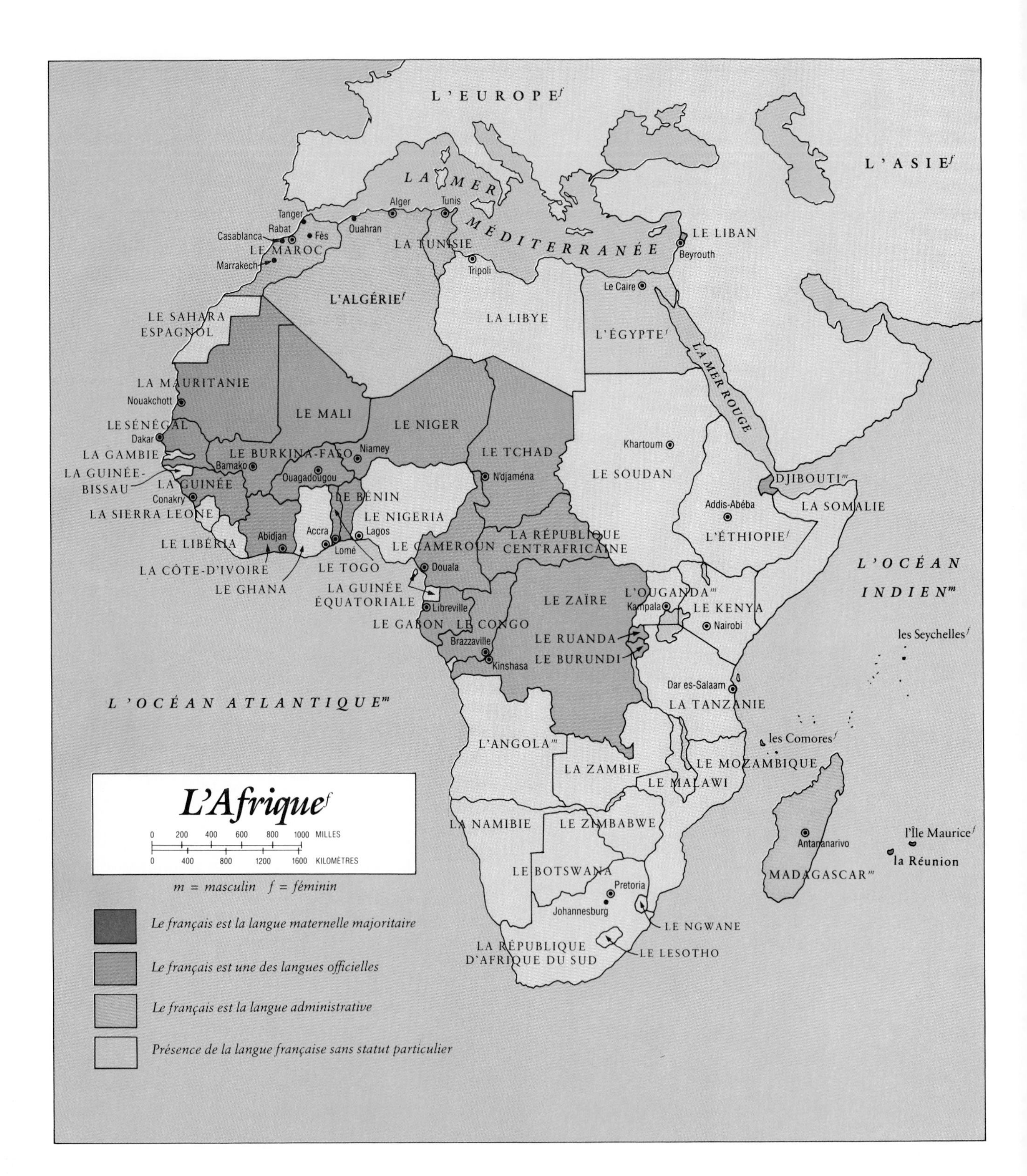

L'EUROPE^f
L'ASIE^f
LA MER MÉDITERRANÉE
LA MER ROUGE
L'OCÉAN ATLANTIQUE^m
L'OCÉAN INDIEN^m
L'Afrique^f
0 200 400 600 800 1000 MILLES
0 400 800 1200 1600 KILOMÈTRES
m = masculin f = féminin
Le français est la langue maternelle majoritaire
Le français est une des langues officielles
Le français est la langue administrative
Présence de la langue française sans statut particulier
LE MAROC
Tanger
Rabat
Casablanca
Fès
Marrakech
Alger
Ouahran
Tunis
LA TUNISIE
Tripoli
L'ALGÉRIE^f
LA LIBYE
LE LIBAN
Beyrouth
Le Caire
L'ÉGYPTE^f
LE SAHARA ESPAGNOL
LA MAURITANIE
Nouakchott
LE MALI
LE NIGER
LE TCHAD
LE SÉNÉGAL
Dakar
LA GAMBIE
LA GUINÉE-BISSAU
LA GUINÉE
Conakry
LA SIERRA LEONE
LE LIBÉRIA
LA CÔTE-D'IVOIRE
Abidjan
LE GHANA
Accra
LE TOGO
Lomé
LE BÉNIN
LE BURKINA-FASO
Bamako
Ouagadougou
Niamey
LE NIGERIA
Lagos
N'djaména
Khartoum
LE SOUDAN
DJIBOUTI^m
Addis-Abéba
L'ÉTHIOPIE^f
LA SOMALIE
LE CAMEROUN
Douala
LA RÉPUBLIQUE CENTRAFRICAINE
LA GUINÉE ÉQUATORIALE
Libreville
LE GABON
LE CONGO
Brazzaville
Kinshasa
LE ZAÏRE
L'OUGANDA^m
Kampala
LE KENYA
Nairobi
LE RUANDA
LE BURUNDI
Dar es-Salaam
LA TANZANIE
les Seychelles^f
les Comores^f
L'ANGOLA^m
LA ZAMBIE
LE MOZAMBIQUE
LE MALAWI
LA NAMIBIE
LE ZIMBABWE
LE BOTSWANA
Pretoria
Johannesburg
LE NGWANE
LE LESOTHO
LA RÉPUBLIQUE D'AFRIQUE DU SUD
MADAGASCAR^m
Antananarivo
l'Île Maurice^f
la Réunion

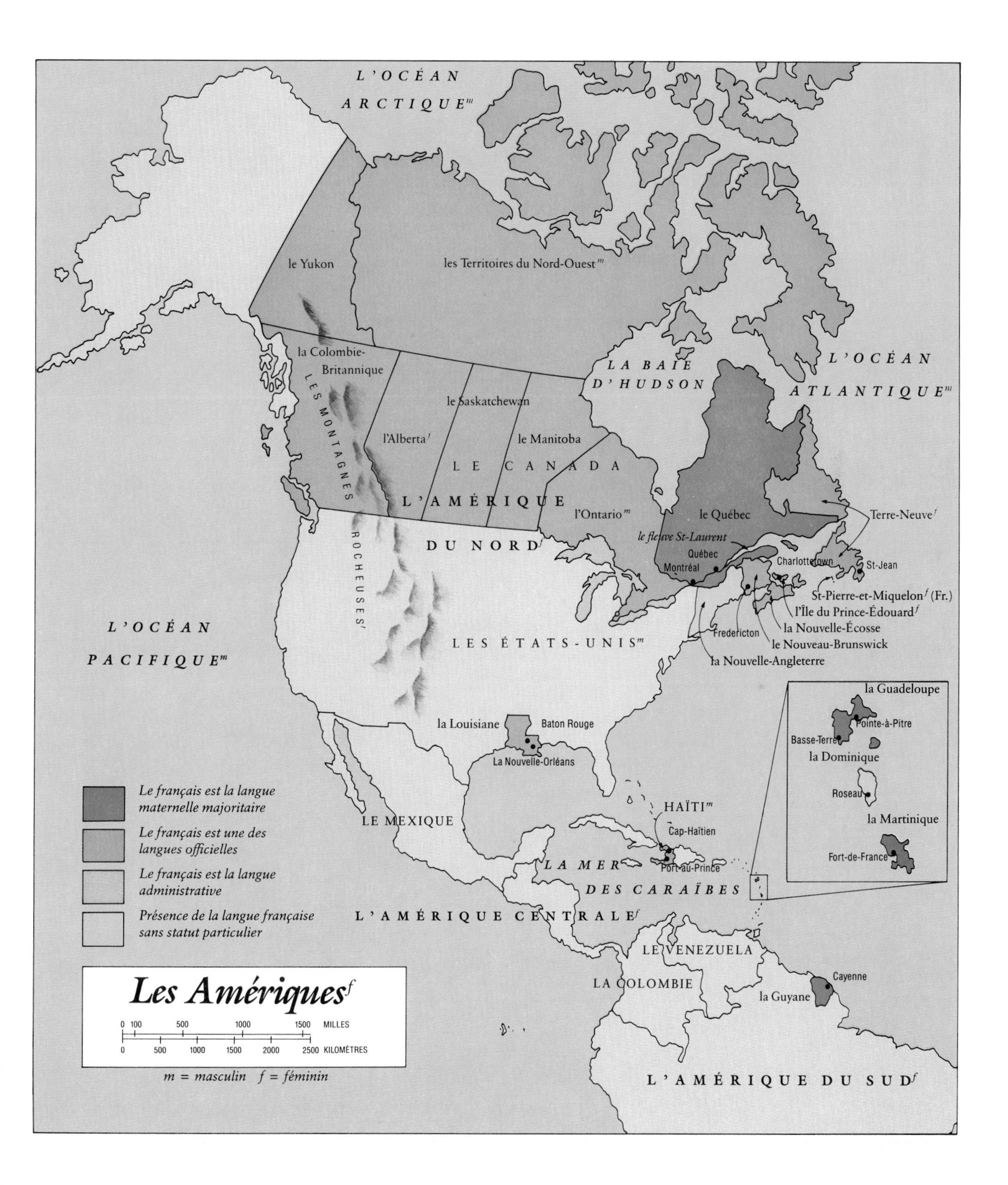
L'OCÉAN ARCTIQUE[m]
le Yukon
les Territoires du Nord-Ouest[m]
la Colombie-Britannique
LES MONTAGNES ROCHEUSES[f]
le Saskatchewan
l'Alberta[f]
le Manitoba
LE CANADA
L'AMÉRIQUE DU NORD[f]
LA BAIE D'HUDSON
L'OCÉAN ATLANTIQUE[m]
l'Ontario[m]
le Québec
le fleuve St-Laurent
Québec
Montréal
Charlottetown
St-Jean
Terre-Neuve[f]
St-Pierre-et-Miquelon[f] (Fr.)
l'Île du Prince-Édouard[f]
la Nouvelle-Écosse
le Nouveau-Brunswick
Fredericton
la Nouvelle-Angleterre
L'OCÉAN PACIFIQUE[m]
LES ÉTATS-UNIS[m]
la Louisiane
Baton Rouge
La Nouvelle-Orléans
la Guadeloupe
Pointe-à-Pitre
Basse-Terre
la Dominique
Roseau
la Martinique
Fort-de-France
HAÏTI[m]
Cap-Haïtien
Port-au-Prince
LE MEXIQUE
LA MER DES CARAÏBES
L'AMÉRIQUE CENTRALE[f]
LE VENEZUELA
LA COLOMBIE
la Guyane
Cayenne
L'AMÉRIQUE DU SUD[f]
Le français est la langue maternelle majoritaire
Le français est une des langues officielles
Le français est la langue administrative
Présence de la langue française sans statut particulier
Les Amériques[f]
0 100 500 1000 1500 MILLES
0 500 1000 1500 2000 2500 KILOMÈTRES
m = masculin f = féminin

Premier rendez-vous

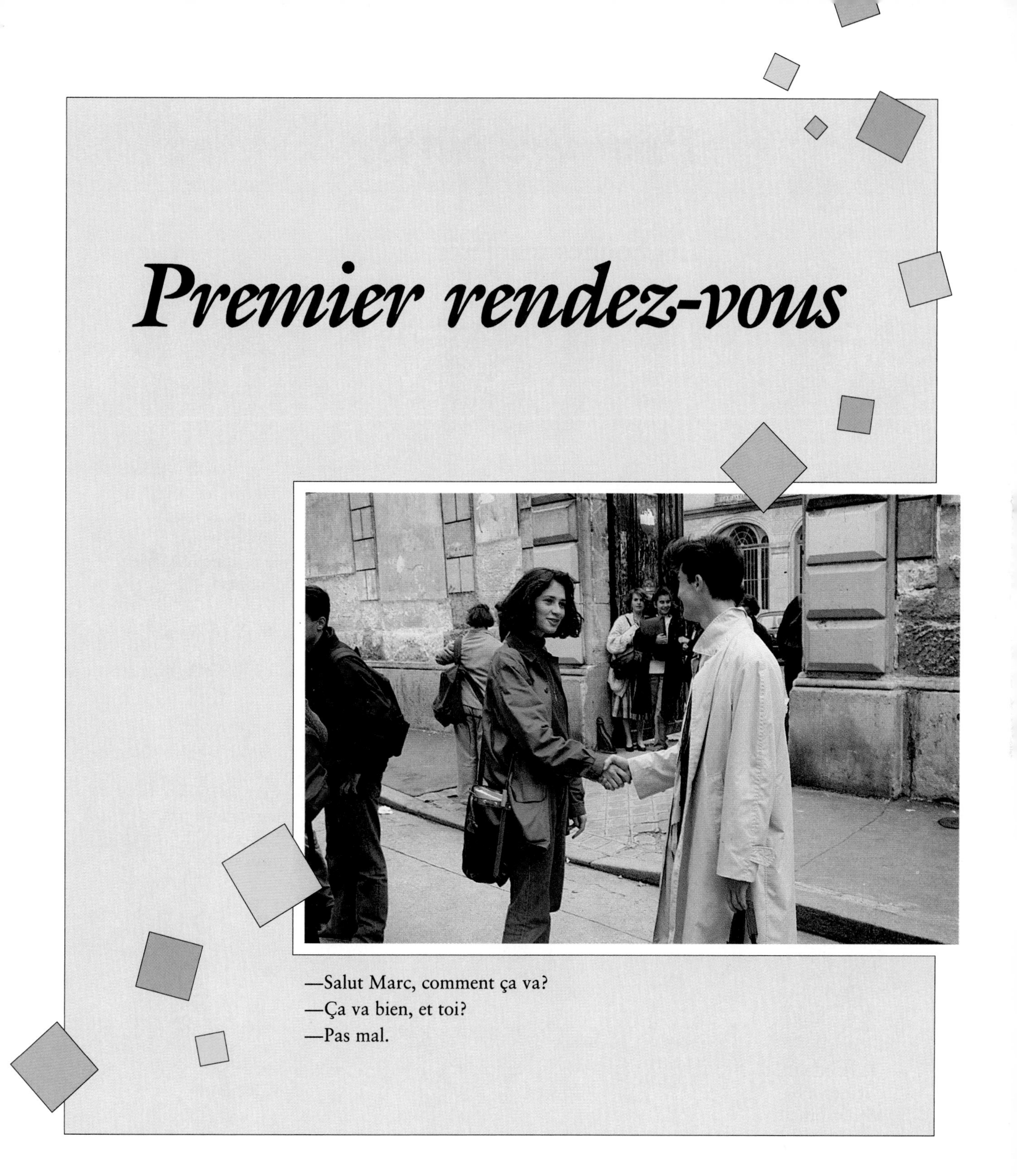

—Salut Marc, comment ça va?
—Ça va bien, et toi?
—Pas mal.

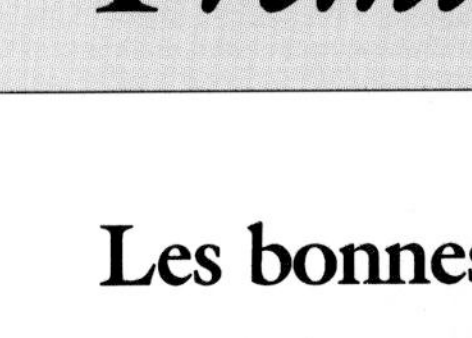

Première partie

Les bonnes manières

1. —Bonjour, Mademoiselle.*
   —Bonjour, Madame.

2. —Bonsoir, Monsieur.
   —Bonsoir, Madame.

3. —Je m'appelle Marcel Martin. Et vous, comment vous appelez-vous?
   —Je m'appelle Marie Dupont.

4. —Comment allez-vous?
   —Très bien, merci. Et vous?
   —Pas mal, merci.

5. —Salut, ça va?
   —Oui, ça va bien. Et toi?
   —Comme ci, comme ça.

6. —Comment? Je ne comprends pas. Répétez, s'il vous plaît.

7. —Oh, pardon! Excusez-moi, Mademoiselle.

8. —Merci beaucoup.
   —De rien.

9. —Au revoir!
   —A bientôt!

---

*Abréviations: Mademoiselle = Mlle Monsieur = M. Madame = Mme

MAINTENANT A VOUS

A. Répondez, s'il vous plaît.

1. Je m'appelle Maurice Lenôtre. Et vous, comment vous appelez-vous?
2. Bonsoir! 3. Comment allez-vous? 4. Merci. 5. Ça va? 6. Au revoir!
7. Bonjour.

B. Donnez (*Give*) une expression pour chaque (*for each*) situation.

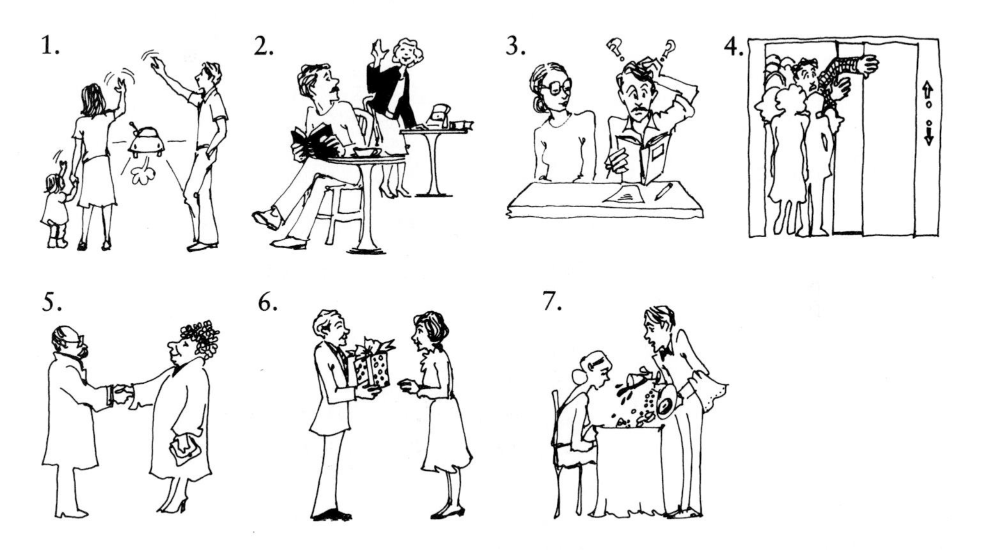

Commentaire culturel

Greetings. There is almost always some sort of physical contact when French-speaking people greet each other. Casual acquaintances or co-workers shake hands briefly when they meet, even if they see each other every day. Friends and relatives exchange two, three, or four kisses on the cheek; the number varies from region to region. Men generally shake hands rather than exchange kisses (**faire la bise**). In conversation, the French tend to stand or sit closer together than the British or Americans do.

Les nombres de 0 à 20

0	zéro	7	sept	14	quatorze
1	un	8	huit	15	quinze
2	deux	9	neuf	16	seize
3	trois	10	dix	17	dix-sept
4	quatre	11	onze	18	dix-huit
5	cinq	12	douze	19	dix-neuf
6	six	13	treize	20	vingt

MAINTENANT A VOUS

A. Combien? (*How many?*) Donnez (*Give*) le nombre correct.

1. 卌 卌 |||
2. ||
3. 卌 ||
4. 卌 卌 ||
5. 卌 卌 卌 ||
6. 卌 卌
7. 卌 卌 卌 ||||
8. ||||
9. 卌 ||||
10. 卌 卌 ||||

B. Problèmes de mathématiques.

+ **plus** / **et**	− **moins**	× **fois**	= **font**

MODÈLES: $4 + 3 = ? \rightarrow$ Quatre et trois font sept. (Quatre plus trois font sept.)

$4 - 3 = ? \rightarrow$ Quatre moins trois font un.

1. $2 + 5 = ?$
2. $6 + 8 = ?$
3. $5 + 3 = ?$
4. $10 + 1 = ?$
5. $9 + 8 = ?$
6. $5 - 5 = ?$
7. $15 - 9 = ?$
8. $13 - 12 = ?$
9. $20 - 18 = ?$
10. $19 - 15 = ?$

11. $10 \times 2 = ?$
12. $11 \times 1 = ?$
13. $8 \times 2 = ?$
14. $6 \times 3 = ?$
15. $5 \times 4 = ?$

La communication en classe

Donnez l'équivalent anglais de chaque expression française.

1. Répondez.
2. En français, s'il vous plaît.
3. Oui, c'est exact.
4. Non, ce n'est pas juste, ça.
5. Est-ce que vous comprenez?
6. Non, je ne comprends pas.
7. Bravo! Excellent!
8. Je ne sais pas.
9. Comment dit-on «Cheers!» en français?
10. Écoutez et répétez!
11. Vive le professeur!
12. A bas les examens!
13. Attention!
14. J'ai une question.

a. Great! Excellent!
b. Do you understand?
c. How do you say "Cheers!" in French?
d. I have a question.
e. In French, please.
f. Listen and repeat!
g. Yes, that's correct.
h. Long live (Hurray for) the professor!
i. No, that's not right.
j. Pay attention! (Be careful!)
k. Answer (Respond).
l. No, I don't understand.
m. I don't know.
n. Down with exams!

MAINTENANT A VOUS

Donnez une réaction personnelle, en français, s'il vous plaît.

1. You don't understand what the instructor said.
2. You want to know how to say "help!" in French.
3. The exam for the day has been canceled.
4. You have a question.
5. The stack of books on your instructor's desk is about to fall onto the floor.
6. A classmate mentions that Marseilles is the capital of France.

Commentaire culturel

The French-speaking world. More than one hundred million people in the world speak French, either as their native language or as a second language used in business or in the workplace. French-speaking countries or regions are found on five continents. Look at the world map at the beginning of the book and find

- the four European countries where French is one of the principal languages
- three regions on the American continents where French is spoken
- two francophone island nations
- three major North African francophone countries
- five francophone nations on the West African coast
- the largest Central African nation where French is spoken
- three French-speaking Asian nations.

Besides the countries shown on the map, French-speaking populations are found in pockets all over the globe. In the United States alone, more than thirteen million people are descendants of French or French-Canadian emigrants. Most live in Louisiana or New England. Many of these Americans still speak or understand French; in numerous ways—through music, food, family customs, habits of thought—their everyday lives reflect their francophone heritage.

© HENEBRY PHOTOGRAPHY

© D.H. HESSELL / STOCK, BOSTON

© RICHARD LUCAS / THE IMAGE WORKS

© BERYL GOLDBERG

Dans la salle de classe

MAINTENANT A VOUS

A. Qu'est-ce que c'est? (*What is it?*) Avec un(e) camarade de classe, identifiez les personnes et les objets sur le dessin précédent.

MODÈLE: VOUS: L'objet numéro un, qu'est-ce que c'est?*
UN(E) CAMARADE: C'est un (une)... (*It's a . . .*)

B. Combien? Regardez la salle de classe ci-dessus avec un(e) camarade de classe.

*The intonation of the voice should drop slightly at the end of this question.

MODÈLE: étudiantes → UN(E) CAMARADE: Il y a combien d'étudiantes?*
VOUS: Il y a quatre étudiantes.†

1. portes 2. fenêtres 3. professeurs 4. étudiants 5. cahiers 6. livres 7. chaises 8. stylos

Les nombres de 20 à 60

Presentation of numbers: Model pronunciation, followed by choral response. *Suggestion for listening comprehension:* Students write the numbers they hear: 24, 35, 49, 23, etc.

Suggestions: (1) Use flash cards with numbers, arranged in random order. Student says number as it appears. (2) Ask students to count from 2 to 60 by 2's, from 3 to 60 by 3's, etc. Call on students individually in random order for this exercise.

20	vingt	25	vingt-cinq	30	trente
21	vingt et un	26	vingt-six	40	quarante
22	vingt-deux	27	vingt-sept	50	cinquante
23	vingt-trois	28	vingt-huit	60	soixante
24	vingt-quatre	29	vingt-neuf		

MAINTENANT A VOUS

A. Problèmes de mathématiques

+ { **plus** / **et** — **moins** × **fois** = **font**

1. 18 + 20 = ?	5. 43 − 16 = ?	9. 2 × 10 = ?
2. 15 + 39 = ?	6. 60 − 37 = ?	10. 3 × 20 = ?
3. 41 + 12 = ?	7. 56 − 21 = ?	11. 25 × 2 = ?
4. 32 + 24 = ?	8. 49 − 27 = ?	12. 15 × 3 = ?

B. Les numéros de téléphone. French telephone numbers are said in groups of four two-digit numbers. On this map of France (see facing page) published in the magazine *Vos études*, French universities are listed with the telephone numbers of the registrar's office. Practice saying some of these phone numbers with a classmate.

MODÈLE: —L'université de Nantes?
—40.29.07.39

C. Association. Donnez un chiffre (de 1 à 60) que vous associez avec ____.

1. la superstition 2. l'âge minimum d'un adulte 3. l'alphabet 4. une minute 5. Noé et le déluge dans la Bible 6. les mousquetaires

---

*The intonation of the voice should rise slightly on **combien,** then drop at the end of the sentence.
†**Il y a** can mean *there are* as well as *there is.* The **s** that makes a word plural is not pronounced.

La carte de France des C.I.O.

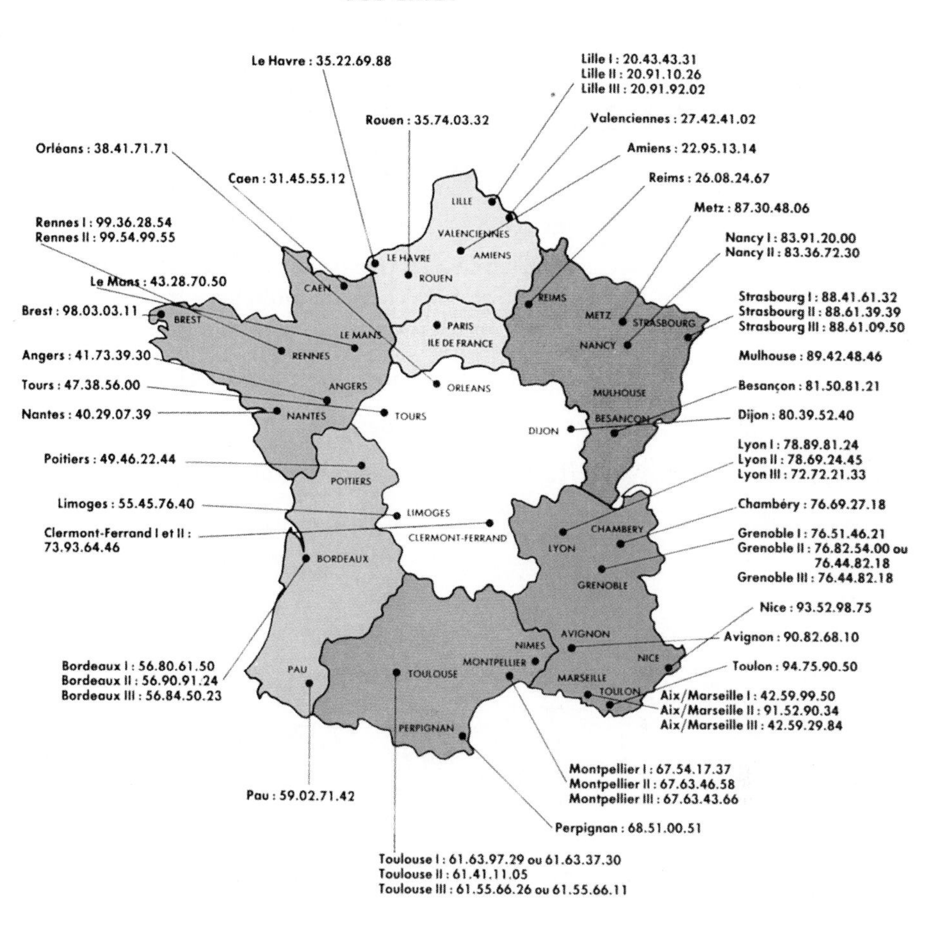

Quel jour sommes-nous?

La semaine (*week*) de Claire

lundi	examen de biologie
mardi	examen de chimie
mercredi	chez le dentiste
jeudi	tennis avec Vincent
vendredi	laboratoire
samedi	théâtre avec Vincent
dimanche	en famille

In French, the days of the week are not capitalized. The week starts on Monday on the French calendar.

Quel jour sommes-nous (aujourd'hui)?	*What day is it (today)?*
Nous sommes mardi.	*It's Tuesday.*

MAINTENANT A VOUS

A. La semaine de Claire. Quel jour est-ce? (Voir le dessin, page 9.)

MODÈLE: Claire est au laboratoire. → Nous sommes vendredi.

1. Claire va au théâtre avec Vincent. 2. Claire est chez (*at*) le dentiste. 3. Claire a un cours de biologie. 4. Claire est en famille. 5. Claire joue au tennis avec Vincent. 6. Claire a un examen de chimie.

B. Votre semaine. (*Your week.*) Quel jour sommes-nous?

MODÈLE: Vous êtes (*You are*) en famille. → Nous sommes dimanche.

1. Vous êtes au cours de français. 2. Vous êtes au restaurant. 3. Vous êtes au cinéma. 4. Vous êtes au laboratoire. 5. Vous êtes au match de football (*soccer*).

Étude de prononciation

The International Phonetic Alphabet

In English, each letter often represents several sounds. Note the sounds made by the letter *o* in these six words: *cold, cot, corn, love, woman, women.* The same is true in French; the **o**, for example, is pronounced differently in the words **rose** and **robe.** Conversely, in both languages, a single sound can often be spelled in several different ways. Notice, for example, how the sound [f] is spelled in the words ***f**ish, al**ph**abet,* and *tou**gh**.* Similarly, in French the sound [e], for example, can be spelled in many ways: universit**é**, appel**ez**, cahi**er**.

The discussion of sounds and pronunciation is simplified by the use of the International Phonetic Alphabet (IPA), which assigns a symbol, given in brackets [ ], to each sound in a language. These symbols are used in dictionaries to show pronunciation; they will appear in the pronunciation sections of *Rendez-vous* and the accompanying laboratory program. The IPA appears in its entirety in the Appendix.

Articulation in French

Articulation. The articulation of French is physically more tense and energetic than that of English. French sounds, generally produced at the front of the mouth, are never slurred or swallowed.

Prononcez avec le professeur.

1. Bonjour, ça va?
2. Oui, ça va bien.
3. Comment vous appelez-vous?
4. Je m'appelle Marcel Martin.
5. Je ne comprends pas.
6. Répétez, s'il vous plaît.

Cognates and New Sounds. French and English have many cognates (**mots apparentés**), that is, words spelled similarly with similar meanings. Even though two words may look alike in French and English, they generally do not sound the same; many consonant and vowel sounds are quite similar in English and French, but others are very different. Indeed, some sounds will be altogether new to a native speaker of English. You will learn the sounds and intonation patterns of French most easily through attentive listening and imitation.*

Prononcez avec le professeur.

1. l'attitude
2. la police
3. la balle
4. le bracelet
5. la passion
6. la conclusion
7. l'injustice
8. la côtelette

English diphthongs. A diphthong consists of two vowel sounds pronounced together within the same syllable, such as in the English word *bay*. There is a tendency in English to prolong almost any vowel into a diphthong. In such English words as *rosé, café,* and *entrée,* the final vowel is drawn out into two separate vowel sounds: a long *a* sound and an *ee* sound. In French, each vowel in the words **rosé, café,** and **entrée** is pronounced with a *single,* pure sound, regardless of the length of the syllable.

Prononcez avec le professeur.

1. entrée café matinée blasé rosé frappé
2. cage page sage table fable câble sable
3. beau gauche parole rouge

*Several other general aspects of French pronunciation are treated in this chapter and in Chapters 1 through 5 of *Rendez-vous*. Pronunciation is presented and practiced more extensively in the Laboratory Program.

Vocabulaire

Bonnes manières

A bientôt. See you soon.
Au revoir. Good-bye.
Bonjour. Hello. Good day.
Bonsoir. Good evening.
Ça va? How's it going?
Ça va bien. Fine. (Things are going well.)
Ça va mal. Things are going badly.
Comme ci, comme ça. So so.
Comment. What? (How?)
Comment allez-vous? How are you?
Comment vous appelez-vous? What's your name?
Et vous? And you?
Excusez-moi. Excuse me.
Je m'appelle... My name is . . .
Je ne comprends pas. I don't understand.
Madame (Mme) Mrs. (ma'am)
Mademoiselle (Mlle) Miss
Merci. Thank you.
Monsieur (M.) Mr. (sir)
Pardon. Pardon (me).
Pas mal. Not bad(ly).
Répétez. Repeat.
Salut! Hi!
S'il vous plaît. Please.
Très bien. Very well (good).

Dans la salle de classe

un bureau a desk
un cahier a notebook
une chaise a chair
une craie a stick of chalk
un crayon a pencil
un étudiant a (male) student
une étudiante a (female) student
une fenêtre a window
un livre a book
une porte a door
un professeur a professor, instructor
une salle de classe a classroom
un stylo a pen
une table a table
un tableau a blackboard

Les nombres

un, deux, trois, quatre, cinq, six, sept, huit, neuf, dix, onze, douze, treize, quatorze, quinze, seize, dix-sept, dix-huit, dix-neuf, vingt, vingt et un, vingt-deux, etc., trente, quarante, cinquante, soixante

Les jours de la semaine

Quel jour sommes-nous? Nous sommes... (lundi, mardi, mercredi, jeudi, vendredi, samedi, dimanche).

Mots divers

aujourd'hui today
beaucoup very much, a lot
c'est un (une)... it's a . . .
combien de how many
il y a there is/are
il y a... ? is/are there . . . ?
non no
oui yes
qu'est-ce que c'est? what is it?
voici here is/are
voilà there is/are

CHAPITRE UN

La vie universitaire

—Est-ce que tu as un cours de maths aujourd'hui?
—Non, mais j'ai un cours de physique et de chimie.
—Moi, je déteste la chimie!

Étude de vocabulaire

Les lieux

Voici l'amphithéâtre.

© BRUNO MASO / PHOTOEDIT

Voici la cité universitaire (la cité-u).

© MATT JACOB / THE IMAGE WORKS

Voici le restaurant universitaire (le restau-u).

© ULRIKE WELSCH

Voici la bibliothèque.

© OWEN FRANKEN / STOCK, BOSTON

A. Une visite. Où trouvez-vous ces choses? (*Where do you find these things?*)

MODÈLE: Un examen de français? → Dans un amphithéâtre.
Dans le _____.
Dans la _____.
Dans l'_____.

1. un dictionnaire? 2. une radio? 3. un café? 4. un livre? 5. une télévision? 6. un cours de français? 7. un sandwich? 8. une encyclopédie?

B. Bizarre ou normal?

MODÈLE: Un match de football dans le restaurant universitaire... → Un match de football dans le restaurant universitaire, c'est bizarre!

1. Un cours de français dans un amphithéâtre...
2. Une radio dans la bibliothèque...
3. Un examen dans la cité universitaire...
4. Un café dans l'amphithéâtre...
5. Un dictionnaire dans la bibliothèque...

Les matières

A la Faculté des Lettres et Sciences Humaines, on étudie (*one studies*) la littérature, la linguistique, les langues étrangères, l'histoire, la géographie, la philosophie et la sociologie.

© ULRIKE WELSCH

A la Faculté des Sciences, on étudie les mathématiques (les maths), la physique, la chimie et les sciences naturelles (la géologie et la biologie).

© ULRIKE WELSCH

A. Les études et les professions. Imaginez les études nécessaires pour les professions suivantes (*following*).

MODÈLE: pour la profession de diplomate →
On étudie les langues étrangères.

1. pour la profession de psychologue 2. pour la profession de professeur de langues 3. pour la profession de physicien 4. pour la profession d'historien 5. pour la profession d'ingénieur

B. Les cours à l'université. Regardez (*Look at*) la liste suivante et dites quelles matières vous étudiez ce (*this*) semestre et quelles matières vous aimez étudier (n'aimez pas étudier) en général.

1. J'étudie...
2. J'aime étudier (Je n'aime pas étudier)...

l'espagnol	l'histoire	la géographie	la philosophie
la sociologie	les maths	la physique	la chimie
la biologie	l'informatique	la musique	le dessin
le droit	la psychologie	le marketing	le commerce
l'anglais	le français	la littérature	la linguistique

Maintenant dites (*now say*) quel est votre (*your*) programme d'études idéal. Donnez la liste des matières.

C. Et vos camarades? Posez les questions à (*to*) un(e) camarade.

1. Qu'est-ce que tu étudies maintenant (*now*)? (J'étudie...)
2. Tu aimes étudier le français? les maths? ... ? (Oui, j'aime / Non, je n'aime pas étudier...)

Maintenant comparez les matières que vous avez (*have*) en commun ce trimestre (semestre) avec vos (*your*) camarades.

Commentaire culturel

The French educational system. The educational system in France differs greatly from that of the United States. Most university-bound students start to narrow their fields of specialization when they enter the **lycée,** at fifteen or sixteen years old. At that point, they focus on an area of studies such as humanities (**philo-lettres**), social sciences (**économique et social**), or mathematics and science (**mathématiques et sciences de la nature/et techniques/et sciences physiques**). They start early to prepare for the comprehensive exam (**le Baccalauréat** or **le Bac**) required for entrance to the university. The **Bac** is difficult; those who fail often decide to follow other career paths rather than take the exam again.

At the university, students immediately begin specialized programs in their areas of interest. French universities offer degrees in technological fields, in health-related fields such as medicine, pharmacology, and dentistry, and in law (**droit**), as well as in traditional disciplines.

Students may also undertake advanced professional studies at a variety of private institutes and schools offering programs in fields such as architecture, military science, business administration, and nursing. The top students in secondary school may decide to compete for admission to the **Grandes Écoles.** Most of the **Grandes Écoles** prepare students for careers in engineering and business. The following chart shows the various **Grandes Écoles** and their specializations. The names of the branches of government with which they are allied appear in blue.

TABLE D'ORIENTATION DES GRANDES ÉCOLES

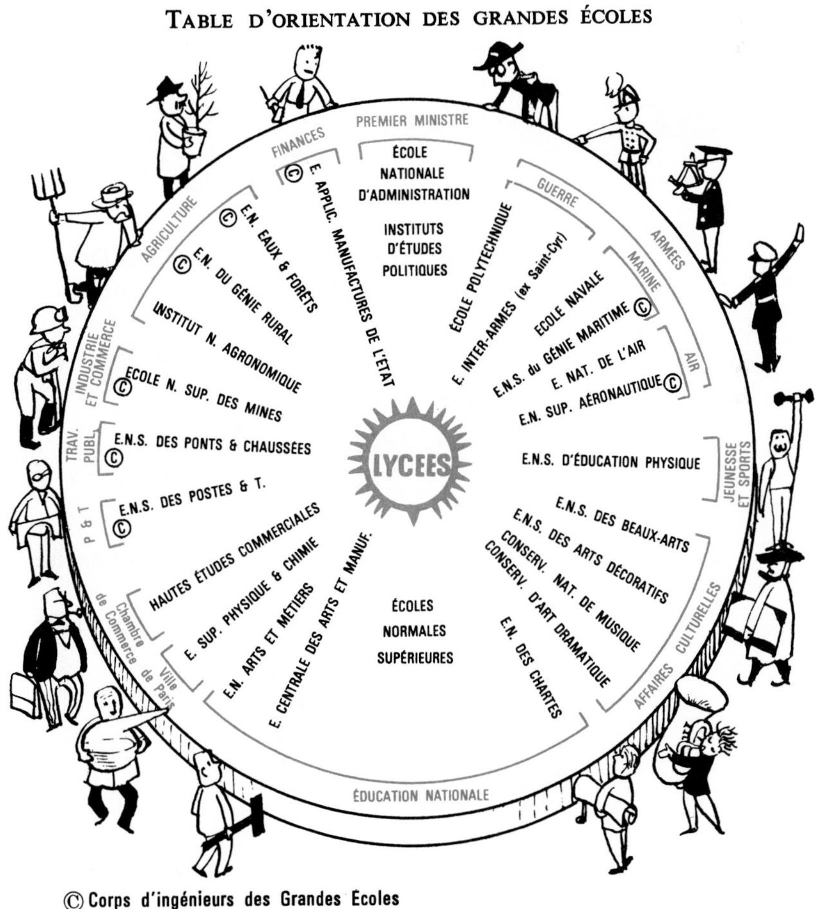

© Corps d'ingénieurs des Grandes Écoles
EN BISTRE : les ministères dont elles dépendent

Les pays et les nationalités

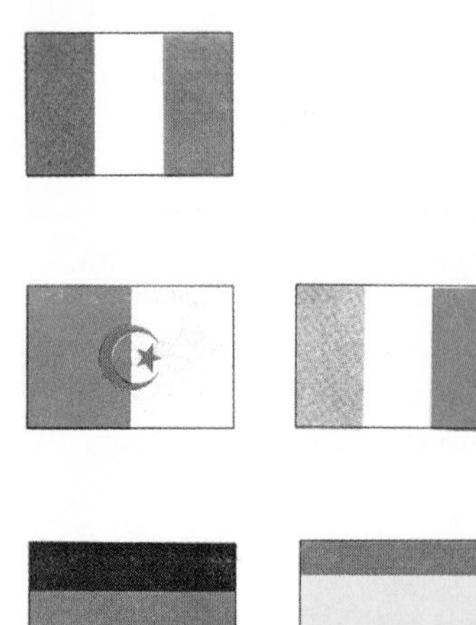

la France	Français/Française*
l'Angleterre	Anglais/Anglaise
l'Espagne	Espagnol/Espagnole
l'Italie	Italien/Italienne
l'Allemagne	Allemand/Allemande
la Suisse	Suisse
l'URSS	Russe
la Belgique	Belge
l'Algérie	Algérien/Algérienne
le Maroc	Marocain/Marocaine
la Tunisie	Tunisien/Tunisienne
le Liban	Libanais/Libanaise
le Zaïre	Zaïrois/Zaïroise
la Côte d'Ivoire	Ivoirien/Ivoirienne
le Sénégal	Sénégalais/Sénégalaise
les États-Unis	Américain/Américaine
le Canada	Canadien/Canadienne
le Québec	Québécois/Québécoise
le Mexique	Mexicain/Mexicaine
la Chine	Chinois/Chinoise
le Japon	Japonais/Japonaise

A. Les villes (*Cities*) et les nationalités. De quelle nationalité sont les personnes suivantes? Posez les questions à un(e) camarade.

MODÈLE:

Karim / Tunis

VOUS: Karim habite Tunis. De quelle nationalité est-il?

VOTRE CAMARADE: Il est tunisien.

1. Gino / Rome

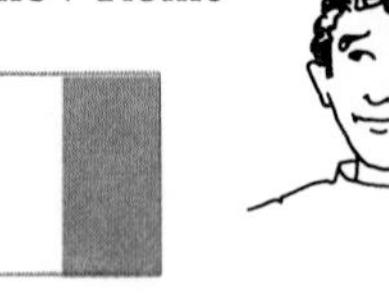

2. Kai / Kyoto

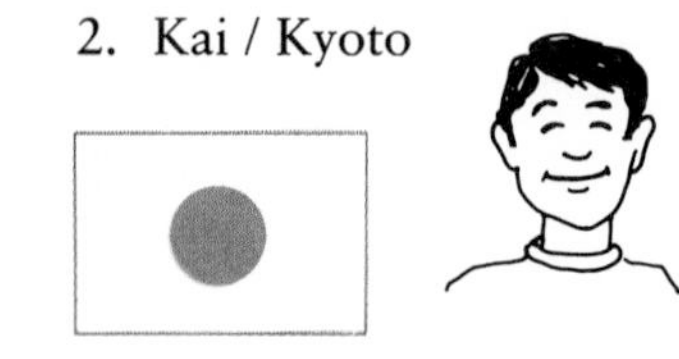

*The adjective formed from these nouns is identical to the noun except that it is written in lower case. Example: **Un étudiant anglais; une étudiante italienne.**

3. Mme Roberge / Montréal

4. Évelyne / Beirut

5. Léopold / Dakar

6. Françoise / Bruxelles

7. Salima / Casablanca

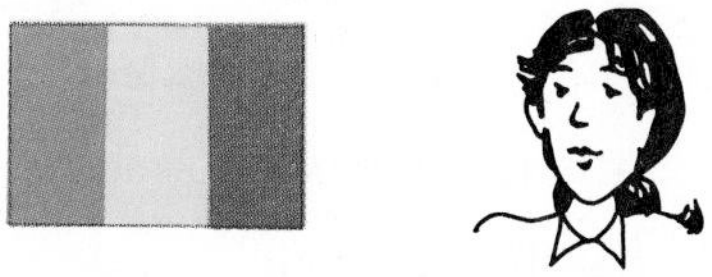

8. Claudine / Genève

B. Quelle langue parlent-ils (*they*)? Maintenant, regardez la liste des langues ci-dessous (*below*). Selon la nationalité des personnes, décidez avec un(e) camarade quelle(s) langue(s) ils parlent probablement.

MODÈLE: Karim parle arabe et français.

1. Gino
2. Kai
3. Mme Roberge
4. Évelyne
5. Léopold
6. Françoise
7. Salima
8. Claudine

a. italien
b. français
c. arabe
d. anglais
e. allemand
f. flamand
g. japonais

C. Réponses personnelles. Complétez les phrases suivantes avec une réponse personnelle.

1. Mon (*My*) professeur de français parle ____ et ____.
2. Mon père (*father*) parle ____.
3. Ma mère (*mother*) parle ____.
4. Mon cousin parle ____.
5. Ma cousine parle ____.
6. Mon professeur de ____ parle ____, et ____.
7. Je parle ____, et ____.

Les distractions

LA MUSIQUE	LE SPORT	LE CINÉMA
la musique classique	le tennis	les films d'amour
le rock	le jogging	les films d'aventure
le jazz	le ski	les films de science-fiction
la musique country	le basket-ball	les films d'horreur
	le football américain	

A. Préférences. Qu'est-ce qu'ils aiment?

MODÈLE: Rémi? → Rémi aime le rock.

1. Et Geneviève? 2. Et Odile? 3. Et Paulette? 4. Et François? 5. Et Charles? 6. Et Marc? 7. Et Claudette?

B. Trouvez quelqu'un qui... Find someone in class who likes or dislikes each of the following activities. Make a list of six questions, then interview as many classmates as possible. Note students' names next to the activities they like and dislike.

MODÈLE: skier →
VOUS: Tu aimes skier?
UN(E) CAMARADE: Non, je n'aime pas skier.
(*ou*) Oui, j'aime skier.

Suggestions: étudier, danser la salsa, écouter la radio, parler au téléphone, manger à McDonald's, observer la nature, voyager en autobus, visiter Manhattan, Chicago ou Los Angeles, ?*

*Throughout *Rendez-vous,* a question mark in an activity indicates that you are to add an item of your own creation.

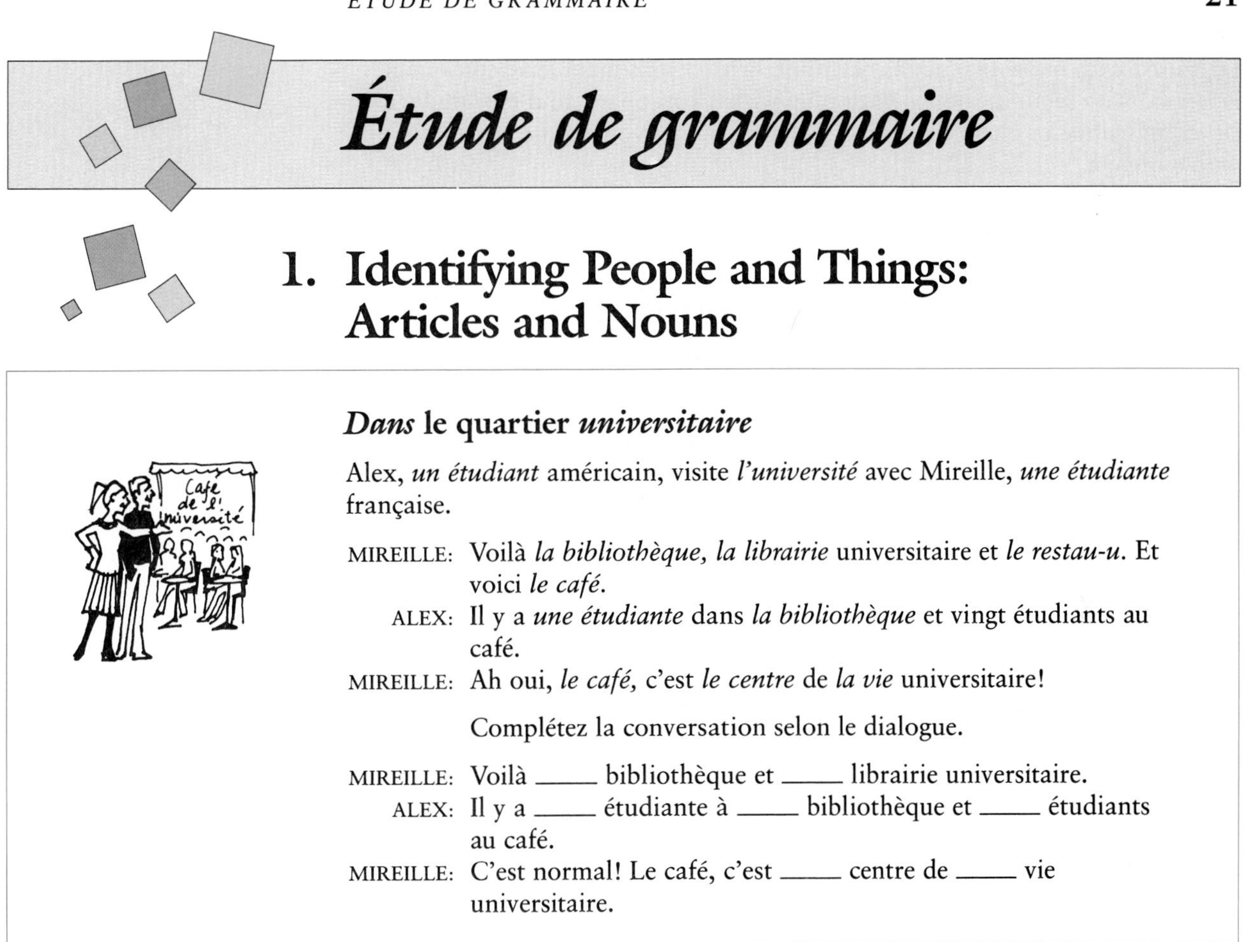

Étude de grammaire

1. Identifying People and Things: Articles and Nouns

Dans le quartier *universitaire*

Alex, *un étudiant* américain, visite *l'université* avec Mireille, *une étudiante* française.

MIREILLE: Voilà *la bibliothèque, la librairie* universitaire et *le restau-u.* Et voici *le café.*
ALEX: Il y a *une étudiante* dans *la bibliothèque* et vingt étudiants au café.
MIREILLE: Ah oui, *le café,* c'est *le centre* de *la vie* universitaire!

Complétez la conversation selon le dialogue.

MIREILLE: Voilà ____ bibliothèque et ____ librairie universitaire.
ALEX: Il y a ____ étudiante à ____ bibliothèque et ____ étudiants au café.
MIREILLE: C'est normal! Le café, c'est ____ centre de ____ vie universitaire.

A. Gender and Forms of the Definite Article

In French, all nouns are either masculine (**masculin**) or feminine (**féminin**) in gender, as are the definite articles that precede them. This applies to nouns designating objects as well as people.

There are three forms of the singular definite article (**le singulier de l'article défini**) in French, corresponding to *the* in English: **le, la,** and **l'.**

MASCULINE		FEMININE		MASCULINE OR FEMININE BEGINNING WITH A VOWEL OR MUTE **h**	
le livre	*the book*	**la** femme	*the woman*	**l'**ami	*the friend (m.)*
le cours	*the course*	**la** table	*the table*	**l'**amie	*the friend (f.)*
				l'homme	*the man (m.)*
				l'histoire	*the story (f.)*

Le is used with masculine nouns beginning with a consonant (**une consonne**), **la** is used with feminine nouns beginning with a consonant, and **l'** is used with either masculine or feminine nouns beginning with a vowel (**une voyelle**) or with a mute **h.***

The definite article is used, as in English, to indicate a specified or particular person, place, thing, or idea: **le livre** (*the book*). The definite article also occurs in French with nouns used in a general sense.

le ski	*skiing (in general)*
la vie	*life (in general)*

B. Forms of the Indefinite Article

MASCULINE		FEMININE	
un ami	*a friend (m.)*	**une** amie	*a friend (f.)*
un bureau	*a desk*	**une** librairie	*a bookstore*
un homme	*a man*	**une** histoire	*a story*

The singular indefinite article (**le singulier de l'article indéfini**), corresponding to *a* (*an*) in English, is **un** for masculine nouns and **une** for feminine nouns. **Un/Une** can also mean *one,* depending on the context.

Il y a **une** étudiante.	*There is one student.*
Voilà **un** café.	*There's a café.*

C. Identifying the Gender of Nouns

Since the gender of a noun is not always predictable, it is best to learn the gender along with the noun. For example, learn **un livre** rather than just **livre.** Here are some general guidelines to help you determine gender.

1. Nouns that refer to males are usually masculine. Nouns that refer to females are usually feminine.

l'homme	*the man*
la femme	*the woman*

---

*In French, **h**'s are either *mute* (*nonaspirate*) or *aspirate.* In **l'homme,** the **h** is called *mute,* which means simply that the word **homme** "elides" with a preceding article (**le** + **homme** = **l'homme**). Most **h**'s in French are of this type. However, some **h**'s are aspirate, which mean there is no "elision." **Le héros** (*the hero*) is an example of this. However, in neither case is the **h** pronounced. The **h** is always silent in French.

2. Sometimes the ending of a noun is a clue to its gender. Some common masculine and feminine endings are:

MASCULINE		FEMININE	
-eau	le bureau	**-ence**	la différence
-isme	le tourisme	**-ion**	la vision
-ment	le département	**-ie**	la librairie
		-ure	la littérature
		-té	l'université

3. Nouns that have come into French from other languages are usually masculine: **le jogging, le tennis, le Coca-Cola, le jazz, le basket-ball.**

4. The names of languages are masculine. They correspond to the masculine singular form of the nouns of nationality, but they are not capitalized.

l'anglais	*(the) English (language)*
le français	*(the) French (language)*

5. Some nouns that refer to people can be changed from masculine to feminine by changing the noun ending. The feminine form often ends in **-e.**

un ami *a friend (m.)*	→ une ami**e** *a friend (f.)*
un étudiant *a student (m.)*	→ une étudiant**e** *a student (f.)*
un Américain *an American (m.)*	→ une Américain**e** *an American (f.)*
un Allemand *a German (m.)*	→ une Allemand**e** *a German (f.)*
un Français *a Frenchman*	→ une Français**e** *a French woman*

Final **t, n, d,** and **s** are silent in the masculine form. When followed by **-e** in the feminine form, **t, n, d,** and **s** are pronounced.

6. The names of some professions and many nouns that end in **-e** have only one singular form, used to refer to both males and females. Sometimes gender is indicated by the article:

le touriste	*the tourist (m.)*
la touriste	*the tourist (f.)*

Sometimes even the article is the same for both masculine and feminine.

une personne	*a person (male or female)*
Madame Brunot, **le** professeur	*Mrs. Brunot, the professor*

MAINTENANT A VOUS

A. Le, la ou l'? Devinez! (*Guess!*)

1. appartement 2. division 3. allemand 4. tableau 5. Coca-Cola 6. biologie 7. chaise 8. aventure 9. préférence 10. personne 11. tourisme 12. professeur de français

B. Qu'est-ce que c'est?

MODÈLE: → C'est une table.

1. 2. 3. 4.

5. 6. 7. 8.

C. A l'université. Faites des phrases avec les mots suivants. Puis faites une autre phrase en changeant le lieu.

MODÈLE: étudiante / salle de classe →
Il y a une étudiante dans la salle de classe.
Il y a une étudiante dans la librairie (*bookstore*).

1. tableau / salle de classe
2. meeting / amphithéâtre
3. télévision / laboratoire
4. cahier / bureau
5. radio / salle de classe
6. Américaine / restaurant
7. dictionnaire / bibliothèque
8. dictionnaire français / librairie

D. A l'école (*school*) de musique. Voici l'histoire de Jean, un ami de Marc, et de son professeur, Monsieur Dupré. Changez l'histoire pour parler de Marie et de son professeur, Madame Dumont.

L'ami de Marc est américain. C'est un étudiant en musique. Monsieur Dupré, le professeur de musique moderne, est canadien, de Montréal. C'est une personne excentrique mais amusante et enthousiaste.

Maintenant corrigez les phrases incorrectes.

1. L'amie de Marc est excentrique.
2. Le professeur de musique est américain.
3. L'amie de Marc étudie le français.

Mots-clés

Working with a partner: As you have seen, many of the activities in *Rendez-vous* ask you to work with a partner. You probably did the preceding partner activity with the person sitting next to you. This time, when your instructor says **Trouvez un partenaire,** find a different partner. Here are some useful phrases to use.

—As-tu un(e) partenaire?	*—Do you have a partner?*
—Pas encore.	*—Not yet.*
—Tu veux travailler ensemble?	*—Do you want to work together?*
—Oui, bien sûr.	*—Yes, of course.*

E. Interview. Avec un(e) camarade de classe, posez la question et répondez selon vos préférences.

MODÈLE: café →
VOUS: Est-ce que tu aimes le café (*coffee*)?
UN(E) CAMARADE: Oui, j'aime le café. Vive le café!
(*ou*) Non, je déteste le café. A bas le café!

1. jazz
2. jogging
3. littérature
4. philosophie
5. professeur
6. cinéma
7. conformisme
8. cours de français
9. chimie

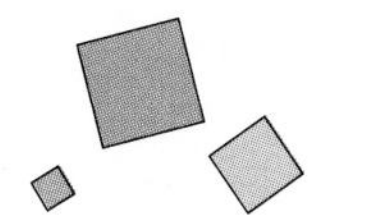

2. Expressing Quantity: Plural Articles and Nouns

Un professeur excentrique

LE PROFESSEUR: Voici le système de notation:
zéro pour *les imbéciles*
quatre pour *les médiocres*
huit pour *les génies*
et dix pour le professeur
Il y a *des questions*?

Expliquez le système de notation du professeur: dix pour... ? huit pour... ? quatre pour... ? zéro pour... ?

	DEFINITE ARTICLES		INDEFINITE ARTICLES	
	Singular	*Plural*	*Singular*	*Plural*
Masculine	**le** touriste →	**les** touristes	un étudiant →	**des** étudiants
Feminine	**la** touriste →		une étudiante →	**des** étudiantes

A. Plural Forms of Definite and Indefinite Articles

1. The plural form (**le pluriel**) of the definite article is always **les.**

le livre, **les** livres	*the book, the books*
la femme, **les** femmes	*the woman, the women*
l'examen, **les** examens	*the exam, the exams*

2. The plural indefinite article is always **des.**

un ami, **des** amis	*a friend, some friends, friends*
une question, **des** questions	*a question, some questions, questions*

3. Note that in English a plural noun frequently has no article: *friends, questions.* In French, however, a form of the article is almost always used with plural nouns: **les amis, des questions.**

B. Plural of Nouns

1. Most French nouns are made plural by adding an **s*** to the singular, as seen in the preceding examples.
2. Nouns that end in **s**, **x**, or **z** in the singular stay the same in the plural.

le cour**s**, les cour**s**	*the course, the courses*
un choi**x**, des choi**x**	*a choice, some choices*
le ne**z**, les ne**z**	*the nose, the noses*

3. Nouns that end in **-eau** or **-ieu** in the singular are made plural by adding **x.**

le tabl**eau**, les tabl**eaux**	*the board, the boards*
le bur**eau**, les bur**eaux**	*the desk, the desks*
le l**ieu**, les l**ieux**	*the place, the places*

*A final s is usually not pronounced in French: **les touristes.** When the final **s** of an article is followed by a vowel sound, it is pronounced [z] and begins the following syllable: **des‿étudiants** [de-ze-ty-djɑ̃], **des‿hommes** [de-zɔm]. This is called **liaison** (*f.*).

4. Nouns that end in **-al** or **-ail** in the singular usually have the plural ending **-aux.**

un hôpit**al**, des hôpit**aux**	*a hospital, hospitals*
le trav**ail**, les trav**aux**	*the work, tasks*

5. To refer to a group that includes at least one male, French uses the masculine form.

 un étudiant et sept étudiantes → des étudiants
 un Français et une Française → des Français

MAINTENANT A VOUS

A. Suivons (***Let's follow***) **le guide!** Le tour de l'université. Donnez le pluriel.

MODÈLE: Voilà la salle de classe. → Voilà les salles de classe.

1. Voilà la bibliothèque.
2. Voilà l'amphi(théâtre).
3. Voilà le professeur.
4. Voilà l'étudiant.
5. Voilà le laboratoire de langues.
6. Voilà le bureau.

Le tour du quartier (*neighborhood*).

MODÈLE: un Français → Voilà des Français.

7. un hôpital
8. un Anglais
9. une touriste
10. une librairie
11. un restaurant
12. une salle de gymnastique

B. Description. Décrivez la salle de classe.

MODÈLE: Dans la salle de classe, il y a des chaises.

Maintenant, décrivez votre (*your*) salle de classe.

C. **Les études en France.** Skim the following announcement taken from the French magazine *Vos études* to find out in general what it is about. You do not need to understand every word to do this. Now look at the highlighted words and try to guess their gender. Use them with **un** or **une.** Since most of them are cognates, you should be able to guess their meanings as well. Discuss with the rest of the class the reasons for your choices. Can you find other cognates in the announcement?

MODÈLE: université → une université

Université de Montpellier I

BP 1017, 34006 Montpellier cedex. Tél. : 67 41 20 90.
Président : Jacques Mirouze.

L'UNIVERSITE EN CHIFFRES

Montpellier 1, c'est 17 012 étudiants, c'est 7 disciplines : droit, AES, sciences économiques gestion-comptabilité, médecine, odontologie, pharmacie, Staps. C'est 4 instituts : institut supérieur de l'Entreprise de Montpellier, institut de Recherche et d'Etudes pour le Traitement de l'Information Juridique et l'institut régional des études économiques et l'institut de préparation à l'administration générale.

LES INNOVATIONS

Le président Mirouze n'a pas été prolixe sur notre questionnaire, ces réponses sont brèves. « Innovations à trois niveau[a] : médecine - droit des affaires[b] et relations avec les pays européens. »

LES RELATIONS AVEC L'INDUSTRIE

Le président insiste sur « les nombreux contrats de recherche qui lie[c] les entreprises à l'université. »

L'OUVERTURE[d] INTERNATIONALE

Là également, peu de bavardage : « nombreuses conventions et participations aux programmes Erasmus et Comett ».

a. *levels* (should be **niveaux**)
b. *business*
c. *link*
d. *opening*

3. Expressing Actions: *-er* Verbs

© BERYL GOLDBERG

Rencontre d'amis à la Sorbonne

XAVIER: Salut, Françoise! *Vous visitez* l'université?
FRANÇOISE: Oui, *nous admirons* la bibliothèque maintenant. Voici Paul, de New York, et Mireille, une amie.
XAVIER: Bonjour, Paul, *tu parles* français?
PAUL: Oui, un petit peu.
XAVIER: Bonjour, Mireille, *tu étudies* ici?
MIREILLE: Oh non! Je *travaille* ici!

Trouvez (*Find*) la forme correcte du verbe dans le dialogue.

1. Vous _____ l'université?
2. Nous _____ la bibliothèque.
3. Tu _____ français?
4. Tu _____ ici?
5. Je _____ ici!

A. Subject Pronouns and *parler*

The subject of a sentence indicates who or what performs the action of the sentence: ***L'étudiant* visite l'université.** A pronoun is a word used in place of a noun: ***Il* visite l'université.**

SUBJECT PRONOUNS AND **parler**					
Singular			*Plural*		
je	parle	*I speak*	nous	parlons	*we speak*
tu	parles	*you speak*	vous	parlez	*you speak*
il	parle	*he, it (m.) speaks*	ils	parlent	*they (m., m. + f.) speak*
elle	parle	*she, it (f.) speaks*	elles	parlent	*they (f.) speak*
on	parle	*one speaks*			

1. **Tu** and **vous**: These are the two ways to say *you* in French. **Tu** is used when speaking to someone you know well—a friend, fellow student, relative, child, or pet. **Vous** is used when speaking to a person you don't know well or when addressing an older person, someone in authority, or anyone else with whom you wish to maintain a certain formality. The plural of both **tu** and **vous** is **vous.** The context will indicate whether **vous** refers to one person or to more than one.

Michèle, **tu** parles espagnol?	*Michèle, do you speak Spanish?*
Maman! Papa! Où êtes-**vous**?	*Mom! Dad! Where are you?*
Vous parlez bien français, Madame.	*You speak French well, madame.*
Pardon, Messieurs (Mesdames, Mesdemoiselles), est-ce que **vous** parlez anglais?	*Excuse me, gentlemen (ladies), do you speak English?*

2. **Il**(s) and **elle**(s). The English pronouns *he, she, it,* and *they* are expressed by **il**(s) (referring to masculine nouns) and **elle**(s) (referring to feminine nouns). **Ils** is used to refer to a group that includes at least one masculine noun.

3. **On.** In English, the words *people, we, one,* or *they* are often used to convey the idea of an indefinite subject. In French, the indefinite pronoun **on** is used, always with the third person singular of the verb.

   Ici **on** parle français. — *One speaks French here.* / *People (they, we) speak French here.*

   On is also used frequently in colloquial French instead of **nous.**

   Nous parlons français? → **On** parle français?

B. Present Tense of *-er* Verbs

Most French verbs have infinitives ending in **-er: parler** (*to speak*), **aimer** (*to like, to love*), for example. To form the present tense of regular **-er** verbs, add to the stem of the verb, **parl-/aim-** (the infinitive minus the ending **-er**), the endings **-e, -es, -e, -ons, -ez, -ent.***

PRESENT TENSE OF **aimer** (*to like, to love*)			
j'	aime†	nous	aim**ons**
tu	aim**es**	vous	aim**ez**
il / elle / on	aime	ils / elles	aim**ent**

1. Other verbs conjugated like **parler** and **aimer** include:

adorer	*to love, to adore*	**étudier**	*to study*
aimer mieux	*to prefer (to like better)*	**habiter**	*to live*
		regarder	*to watch, to look at*
chercher	*to look for*	**rêver**	*to dream*
danser	*to dance*	**skier**	*to ski*
détester	*to detest, to hate*	**travailler**	*to work*
		trouver	*to find*
donner	*to give*	**visiter**	*to visit (a place)*
écouter	*to listen to*		

*As you know, final s is usually not pronounced in French. Final **z** of the second-person plural and the **ent** of the third-person plural verb form are also silent. Thus, in the spoken language, **parler** has only three forms: [parl], [parlɔ̃], [parle].

†When a verb begins with a vowel, the pronoun **je** becomes **j': j'aime.**

2. Note that the present tense (**le présent**) in French has three equivalents in English.

Je **parle** français.	*I speak French.* *I am speaking French.* *I do speak French.*

3. Some verbs, such as **adorer, aimer,** and **détester,** can be followed by an infinitive or a noun.

J'**aime écouter** la radio quelquefois.	*I like to listen to the radio sometimes.*
Je **déteste regarder** la télévision.	*I hate to watch television.*
J'**aime** la musique.	*I like music.*

Mots-clés

Telling how often you do things: Use the following adverbs to tell how often you perform an activity. They usually follow the verb.

toujours	*always*	**quelquefois**	*sometimes*
souvent	*often*	**rarement**	*rarely*

Je regarde **souvent** la télévision.
Annie et moi, nous dansons **quelquefois** à la discothèque.

MAINTENANT A VOUS

A. Passe-temps. Décrivez les activités des personnes suivantes. Faites des phrases complètes.

MODÈLE: Olivier / visiter / Marseille → Olivier visite Marseille.

1. Claire / écouter / la radio
2. Vous / travailler / beaucoup
3. Philippe et Annie / regarder / la télé
4. Annie et moi, nous / danser quelquefois / à la discothèque
5. Tu / parler / très bien français
6. Je / étudier souvent / le français
7. On / organiser quelquefois / une soirée (*party*)
8. Paul et Monique / visiter / les États-Unis

B. Tu ou vous? Complétez les phrases suivantes avec le pronom correct et la forme correcte du verbe entre parenthèses.

1. Madame, _____ _____ (habiter) New York?
2. Papa, _____ _____ (chercher) la voiture?
3. Paul et Jacqueline, _____ _____ (visiter) le campus aujourd'hui?
4. Salut, Jeanne! _____ _____ (étudier) le français?

C. Eric, étudiant à la Sorbonne. Complétez l'histoire d'Eric avec la forme correcte des verbes.

A la Sorbonne on ____[1] beaucoup. En classe, les étudiants ____[2] le professeur attentivement mais quelquefois ils ____[3] de vacances. Après les cours, ils ____[4] à la bibliothèque. Moi, j' ____[5] étudier dans ma chambre.	rêver aimer mieux étudier écouter travailler
Mes camarades et moi, nous ____[6] à la cité universitaire. En général, le soir, on ____[7] de nos cours. Puis (*Then*) Chantal ____[8] un film à la télé, Marc ____[9] de la musique classique et moi, je ____[10] à ma petite amie (*girlfriend*), qui étudie à Lausanne, une ville suisse.	regarder parler habiter écouter téléphoner

Vrai ou faux? Now tell if the statements are true (**vrai**) or false (**faux**), according to what Eric says.

1. ____ Eric étudie à la bibliothèque.
2. ____ Chantal regarde la télé.
3. ____ Marc aime le rock.
4. ____ Les étudiants travaillent beaucoup.
5. ____ Ils rêvent des examens.

D. Portraits. Donnez les préférences des personnes suivantes.

MODÈLE: Mon (*My*) cousin... →
Mon cousin aime bien le football, mais (*but*) il aime mieux le basket. Il adore le rock et il déteste le travail!

Je...	aimer bien	le tennis
Mon (Ma) camarade...	aimer mieux	les grandes (*big*) villes
Mes parents...	adorer	le jogging
Tu...	détester	le cinéma
Le professeur...		la littérature
?		les maths
		la physique
		?

E. Une interview. Maintenant, interviewez votre professeur.

MODÈLE: aimer mieux danser ou skier →
Vous aimez mieux danser ou skier?

1. aimer mieux la télévision ou le cinéma 2. adorer ou détester regarder la télévision 3. aimer mieux le rock ou la musique classique 4. aimer mieux la musique ou le sport 5. skier ou regarder le ski à la télévision 6. aimer mieux les livres ou l'aventure

F. Interview. Et vos camarades, qu'est-ce qu'ils aiment? Posez à tour de rôle (*taking turns*) les questions suivantes à un(e) camarade.

1. Tu aimes mieux quels cours? Tu détestes quels cours? Tu rêves en classe quelquefois? 2. Tu aimes quel sport? 3. Tu regardes quel programme à la télé? 4. Tu écoutes quelle musique, d'habitude? 5. Qu'est-ce que tu détestes? 6. Qu'est-ce que tu adores? 7. ?

Dites maintenant quelle réponse vous trouvez (*find*) originale, bizarre.

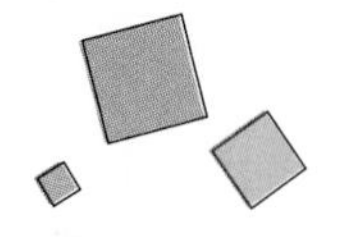

4. Expressing Disagreement: Negation using *ne... pas*

La fin d'une amitié?

BERNARD: Avec Martine ça va comme ci, comme ça. Elle aime danser, je *n'aime pas* la danse. J'aime skier, elle *n'aime pas* le sport. Elle est étudiante en biologie, je *n'aime pas* les sciences...

MARTINE: Avec Bernard ça va comme ci, comme ça. Il *n'aime pas* danser, j'aime la danse. Je *n'aime pas* skier, il aime le sport. Il est étudiant en lettres, je *n'aime pas* la littérature...

1. Martine aime danser? et Bernard?
2. Martine aime le sport? et Bernard?
3. Martine aime la littérature? et Bernard?
4. Martine aime les sciences? et Bernard?

Maintenant posez ces questions à un(e) camarade. (Tu aimes... ?)

To make a sentence negative in French, **ne** is placed before a conjugated verb and **pas** after it.

> Je **parle** chinois. → Je **ne parle pas** chinois.
> Elles **regardent** quelquefois la télévision. → Elles **ne regardent pas** la télévision.

Ne becomes **n'** before a vowel or a mute **h.**

> Elle aime skier. → Elle **n'aime** pas skier.
> Nous habitons ici. → Nous **n'h**abitons pas ici.

If a verb is followed by an infinitive, **ne** and **pas** surround the conjugated verb.

> Il aime étudier. → Il **n'aime pas** étudier.

MAINTENANT A VOUS

A. La fin d'une amitié: Portrait de Bernard. Voici plus de (*more*) détails sur Bernard.

Bernard habite à la cité universitaire et, en général, il étudie à la bibliothèque. Après les cours, il parle avec ses amis au café. Le soir (*In the evening*), il écoute la radio, il aime beaucoup le jazz. Il adore le sport, il skie très bien et le week-end, il regarde le match de football à la télé.

Et Martine? Maintenant dites ce que Martine n'aime pas et ne fait pas (*doesn't do*). Remplacez **il** par **elle** dans le paragraphe ci-dessus (*above*). Martine...

Qui est-ce? Martine ou Bernard? Cherchez l'information ci-dessus et dans le dialogue, *La fin d'une amitié.*

1. Cette personne n'aime pas le jazz. C'est ____.
2. Cette personne n'aime pas les sciences. C'est ____.
3. Cette personne regarde le sport à la télé. C'est ____.
4. Cette personne adore danser. C'est ____.
5. Cette personne ne skie pas. C'est ____.
6. Cette personne n'étudie pas à la cité universitaire. C'est ____.

B. Interview. Posez les questions suivantes à un(e) camarade. Il/Elle donne une réponse personnelle.

1. Tu parles italien? russe? chinois? espagnol? anglais?
2. Tu habites quelle ville? à Paris? à New York? à Los Angeles? à Cincinnati?
3. Tu étudies la littérature? la linguistique? les langues étrangères? la géologie?
4. Tu aimes les examens? les films de science-fiction? les films d'amour? le jazz? la musique country?
5. Le week-end (*On weekends*), tu regardes la télé? Tu écoutes la radio? Tu parles avec tes amis? Tu manges au restaurant?
6. Tu aimes le sport? le football américain? le basket-ball? le base-ball?
7. Est-ce que tu skies? Est-ce que tu danses bien? Est-ce que tu cuisines (*cook*)?

Maintenant dites à la classe cinq activités que votre camarade ne fait pas ou n'aime pas faire.

C. Et vous? Donnez vos (*your*) préférences. Complétez les phrases.

1. J'aime ____, mais je n'aime pas ____.
2. J'adore ____, mais je déteste ____.
3. J'écoute ____, mais je n'écoute pas ____.
4. J'aime ____, mais j'aime mieux ____.
5. Je n'étudie pas ____. J'étudie ____.

French Vowel Sounds: Oral Vowels

Some French vowel sounds are represented in the written language by a single letter: **a** and **u,** for example. Other vowel sounds have a variety of spellings: the sound [o], for example, can be spelled **o, au, eau,** or **ô.**

Prononcez avec le professeur.

	IPA SYMBOL	MOST COMMON SPELLING(S)
1. ami agréable madame bravo salle classe	[a]	a
2. ici hypocrite typique dîner vive ski	[i]	i î y
3. aussi radio beaucoup chose faux drôle	[o]	eau au ô o
4. objet homme notation normal encore snob	[ɔ]	o
5. utile université musique bureau flûte rue	[y]	u û
6. écouter excusez télévision répéter cité cahier	[e]	é er ez
7. être aimer fenêtre question treize très examen	[ɛ]	e è ê ei ai
8. Eugène Europe neutron bœufs sérieuse eucalyptus	[ø]	eu œu
9. bœuf déjeuner jeunesse heure jeune professeur	[œ]	eu œu
10. où ouverture tourisme courageux coûte outrage	[u]	ou où oû

French Vowel Sounds: Nasal Vowels

When the letter **n** or **m** follows a vowel or a combination of vowels, it frequently affects the pronunciation of the vowel, giving it a nasal quality. Such vowels are called nasals. The **n** or **m** itself is not pronounced.

Prononcez avec le professeur.

	IPA SYMBOL	MOST COMMON SPELLING(S)
1. amphithéâtre employer plan attendez français centre	[ɑ̃]	an am en em
2. onze oncle combien bonjour bon nombre	[ɔ̃]	on om
3. impatient intéressant synthèse sympathique peintre américain	[ɛ̃]	im in yn ym ein ain aim

Note that the vowel is not nasal if the **n** or **m** is followed by a vowel. The **n** or **m** is then pronounced: **banane, fine.** The same is true if the **n** or **m** is doubled and then followed by a vowel: **comme, Anne.**

Prononcez avec le professeur.

1. un / une
2. dans / Anne
3. Italien / Italienne
4. brun / brune
5. Américain / Américaine
6. fin / fine

Situation

Rendez-vous

Contexte *Michel et Julien aiment parler ensemble, mais ils étudient dans des sections° différentes de la Faculté des Lettres.* — *departments*

Objectif *Michel donne rendez-vous à Julien au° café.* — *at the*

MICHEL: Tiens! Salut, Julien. Comment ça va?
JULIEN: Pas mal. Et toi°? — *you*
MICHEL: Bof, ça va. Tu travailles à la bibliothèque cet° après-midi? — *this*
JULIEN: Oui, je prépare une dissertation.° — *paper, report*
MICHEL: Eh bien alors,° rendez-vous au Métropole à cinq heures°? — Eh... *Well, then* / cinq... *five o'clock*
JULIEN: D'accord.° — *okay, agreed*
MICHEL: A tout à l'heure.° — A... *See you later.*
JULIEN: Salut.

VARIATIONS

1. Jouez (*Act out*) le dialogue.
2. Jouez une scène similaire avec un(e) camarade, mais changez le lieu du rendez-vous.

A propos

Comment saluer (to greet) *les amis*

Salutations (*Greetings*):	**Réponses:**
Salut!	Salut!
Comment ça va? Comment vas-tu? (*How are you?* *How's it going?*)	Très bien, merci. Et toi (*you*)? Comme ci, comme ça. (*So so.*) Ça va à peu près. (*Fairly well.*) Pas mal. (*Not bad.*) Ça ne va pas du tout. (*Very bad.*)
Quoi de neuf? (*What's new?*)	Rien de nouveau. (*Nothing new.*) Pas grand-chose. (*Not much.*)
Au revoir.	Au revoir. A bientôt. (*See you soon.*)
Salut!	Salut!

Jeu de rôles. Refaites le dialogue, mais cette fois utilisez les expressions de l'*A propos* pour saluer vos amis. Changez aussi le lieu du rendez-vous à chaque fois (*each time*).

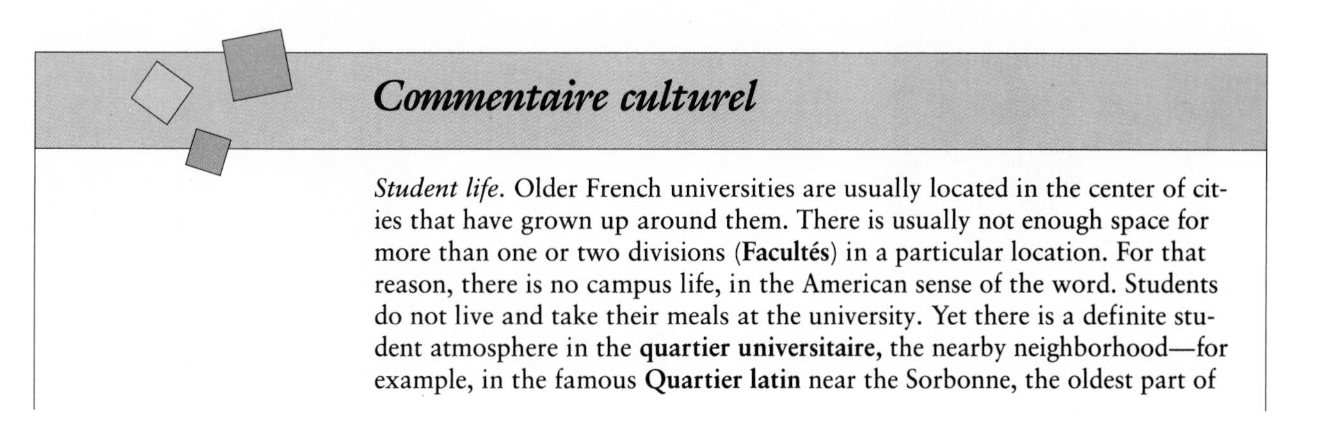

Commentaire culturel

Student life. Older French universities are usually located in the center of cities that have grown up around them. There is usually not enough space for more than one or two divisions (**Facultés**) in a particular location. For that reason, there is no campus life, in the American sense of the word. Students do not live and take their meals at the university. Yet there is a definite student atmosphere in the **quartier universitaire,** the nearby neighborhood—for example, in the famous **Quartier latin** near the Sorbonne, the oldest part of the **Université de Paris.** Students gather to talk in neighborhood **cafés,** which are animated from early morning until well past midnight.

Newer **campus universitaires** in the suburbs (**la banlieue**) resemble American campuses somewhat more. Some residential housing (**la cité universitaire**) is provided on university grounds. There are, however, few facilities for recreation and socializing. Students still prefer to meet at neighboring **cafés** rather than in the university-run **cafétérias** and self-service restaurants.

French universities are state-owned and come under the centralized jurisdiction of the Ministry of Education. Tuition is not charged, and the students pay only a nominal fee of approximately $30.00 a year. Students with a **baccalauréat** degree theoretically have the right to admittance at any university they like, although in reality certain schools have more applicants and are necessarily more competitive.

The French educational system is quite strenuous. Highly competitive exams administered at the end of the first year of a university program allow fewer than half the students to go on to the second year. The others must pass a second exam in the fall or start the first year over again. Those students who make it into the second year have more exams waiting for them before advancement into the third year, at the end of which successful students will earn a **licence,** similar to an American bachelor of arts or bachelor of science degree. They can complete a master's degree (**la maîtrise**) in the fourth or fifth year and may then choose to pursue one of several types of doctoral degrees (**le doctorat**) in succeeding years.

Some French universities have arranged special courses for foreigners (**cours pour étrangers**). Such courses are designed for students whose special interest is the study of French language, literature, and culture.

L'université de Jussieu à Paris

Mise au point

A. La vie d'une étudiante. Composez des phrases complètes.

MODÈLE: Julia / étudier / les langues étrangères →
Julia étudie les langues étrangères.

1. elle / étudier / français / et / allemand
2. elle / ne... pas / aimer / restaurants universitaires
3. elle / ne... pas / regarder / télévision
4. elle / ne... pas / parler / avec / camarades / après / cours
5. elle / travailler / à / bibliothèque

Probable ou peu probable?

MODÈLE: Julia parle bien français. → C'est probable.

1. Julia aime les sciences.
2. Julia parle bien allemand.
3. Julia aime les restaurants élégants.
4. C'est une personne sérieuse.

B. Interview en désordre. Voici une interview avec Jean-Louis, un étudiant français. Trouvez la réponse correcte à chaque (*each*) question.

Questions

1. Tu étudies à l'Université de Toulouse?
2. Tu aimes étudier ici?
3. Tu étudies l'anglais?
4. Tu travailles?
5. Tu aimes les films d'amour?
6. Tu aimes le sport?

Réponses

J'adore le sport... à la télévision.
Oui, j'étudie les sciences.
Non, mais j'aime les films de science-fiction, par exemple, *Les extra-terrestres, Alien, E.T., Rencontres du troisième type.*
J'aime mieux vagabonder. J'aime l'évasion, par exemple, les voyages, le cinéma.
Oui, je travaille à la Librairie La Plume.
Non, j'étudie l'allemand.

Maintenant, interviewez un(e) camarade de classe. Adaptez les questions précédentes ou inventez des questions.

C. Amis par correspondance. This is a brochure from Quebec for students looking for pen pals. Fill it out with as much information as you can. Guess the categories you are unsure of. Pay special attention to the section that asks for **goûts** (*tastes*) **et intérêts particuliers.** Name at least two things you like and two you particularly dislike, using **J'aime... / Je n'aime pas...**

CORRESPONDANCE
SCOLAIRE
INDIVIDUELLE

Québec

NOM ....
PRÉNOM ....
ADRESSE ....
no rue ou route appartement
....
village ou ville comté
....
code postal
TÉLÉPHONE ....
SEXE .... ÂGE ....
ÉCOLE[a]:
Nom ....
Adresse ....
....
ANNÉE OU NIVEAU[b] D'ÉTUDES ....
....
GOÛTS OU INTÉRÊTS PARTICULIERS
....
....

CORRESPONDANT(E) DÉSIRÉ(E)

SEXE .... ÂGE ....

Dans l'impossibilité d'obtenir le correspondant ou la correspondante de ton choix, accepterais-tu indifféremment un garçon ou une fille?
oui .... NON ....
PAYS[c] 1er choix ....
2e choix ....
3e choix ....

Si tu ne peux obtenir un correspondant ou une correspondante des pays ou régions mentionnés, en accepterais-tu un de n'importe quel[d] pays ou région?
oui .... NON ....

LANGUE(S) DE CORRESPONDANCE
....
....
....

a. *school*
b. *level*
c. *nation*
d. n'importe... *just any*

Interactions

In the first chapter of *Rendez-vous,* you learned how to talk about various aspects of campus life and about your likes and dislikes, as well as how to express actions. Now act out the following situations, using the vocabulary and structures from this chapter.

1. **Rendez-vous.** You run into a friend on campus. Greet him or her. Tell him or her about the courses you like and do not like. Arrange to meet later.

2. **Interprète.** You have been asked to be an interpreter for an exchange student from Africa (your partner). He or she speaks French and Swahili. Introduce yourself. Tell the student that you speak French but not Swahili. Give him or her a tour of the campus. Ask the student what classes he or she would like to visit. Get to know the student by telling him or her what you enjoy doing. Ask about his or her likes and dislikes.

Vocabulaire

Verbes

adorer to love, adore
aimer to like, love
aimer mieux to prefer (like better)
chercher to look for
danser to dance
détester to detest
donner to give
écouter to listen to
étudier to study
habiter to live
parler to speak
regarder to look at; to watch
rêver to dream
skier to ski
travailler to work
trouver to find
visiter to visit

Substantifs

l'ami(e) friend
l'amphithéâtre (*m.*) lecture hall
la bibliothèque library
le café café; cup of coffee
le cinéma movie theater
la cité universitaire (la cité-u) university dormitory
le cours course
le dictionnaire dictionary
l'examen (*m.*) test, exam
la faculté division (*academic*)
la femme woman
le film film
l'homme (*m.*) man
la librairie bookstore
le lieu place
la musique music
le quartier quarter, district
la radio radio
le restaurant restaurant
la soirée party
le sport sport; sports
la télévision television
le travail work
l'université (*f.*) university
la vie life
la ville city
la visite visit

Mots divers

à at, in
après after
avec with
d'accord okay; agreed
dans in
de of, from
en in
et and
ici here
maintenant now
mais but
ou or
pour for, in order to
quelquefois sometimes
rarement rarely
souvent often
toujours always

Nationalités

l'Allemand(e), l'Américain(e), l'Anglais(e), le/la Chinois(e), l'Espagnol(e), le/la Français(e), l'Italien(ne), le/la Japonais(e), le/la Russe

Les matières

la biologie, la chimie, le droit (law), **la géographie, la géologie, l'histoire, l'informatique** (*f.*) (computer science), **les langues étrangères, la linguistique, la littérature, les mathématiques (les maths)** (*f.*), **la philosophie, la physique, la psychologie, la sociologie**

Expressions utiles

As-tu un(e) partenaire? Do you have a partner?
Pas encore. Not yet.
Veux-tu travailler avec moi? Do you want to work with me?

INTERMÈDE 1

Lecture

AVANT DE LIRE (*Before Reading*)

Contextual guessing: When you read a text in your own language, you often guess the meanings of unfamiliar words from the context. This is equally true when you read a foreign language. Read the following sentence and see if you can guess its meaning.

> **En général, il n'y a pas de campus dans une université française traditionnelle.**

The construction **il n'y a pas de** is new to you, but since you know the expression **il y a** and the negation of verbs with **ne pas**, you probably guessed the meaning of the sentence: *In general, there is no campus in a traditional French university.*

You can apply this strategy to reading French by being aware of cognates (**les mots apparentés**). In the preceding sentence, there are several cognates: **en général, campus, université, traditionnelle. Le campus** is an exact cognate since it is identical to the corresponding English word. What do the underlined words in the following sentence mean?

> **A Paris, le quartier universitaire évoque le prestige du passé.**

In reading "Les universités françaises," you will notice that the cognates and constructions you have not already seen or learned are underlined the first time they appear.

Before you begin to read, look at the photos. If you remember to look carefully at the title, lead lines, photographs, and sketches that often accompany a text, you will usually find important clues about the content of the passage. Anticipating content helps you recognize the main ideas in the passage as you read.

Les universités françaises

En France, les universités anciennes sont dans les villes. Les étudiants habitent, en général, près des Facultés. Le quartier universitaire est toujours très animé avec ses restaurants, ses cafés, ses librairies, ses cinémas et ses galeries d'art.

Marion étudie la philosophie à la Sorbonne, à l'Université de Paris. Elle habite à côté de sa Faculté dans le Quartier latin. Quel nom bizarre pour un quartier! Quand on fonda (*founded*) la Sorbonne en 1257, les cours étaient (*were*) en latin. Voilà l'origine du nom.

Alain est étudiant en physique à Grenoble. Son université est moderne et elle n'est pas en ville. Le campus est très grand. Le campus moderne, isolé de la ville, est un phénomène récent en France.

COMPRÉHENSION

Find passages in the reading that either support or refute the following statements.

1. En France, les universités anciennes sont dans les villages.
2. Les étudiants habitent dans des quartiers près des bâtiments universitaires.
3. Il y a beaucoup (*much*) d'activité dans les quartiers universitaires.
4. L'Université de Grenoble est au centre-ville.
5. Le Quartier latin est le quartier universitaire à Marseille.

Par écrit

Une autobiographie. Write a short autobiographical sketch consisting of three paragraphs by answering the following three sets of questions. Add any information you can. Or interview another student and write the sketch about him or her.

Paragraphe 1

1. Comment vous appelez-vous?
2. Qu'est-ce que vous étudiez?
3. Vous aimez les cours à l'université?
4. Vous aimez (adorez, détestez) le français?

Paragraphe 2

1. Vous habitez à la cité universitaire? dans un appartement? dans une maison (*house*)?
2. Vous aimez les distractions? le sport?
3. Vous regardez la télévision? Vous écoutez la radio?
4. Vous aimez la musique classique? le jazz? le rock?

Paragraphe 3

1. Qu'est-ce que vous aimez faire avec des amis?
2. Vous aimez discuter au café? flâner (*stroll*) sur le campus? explorer les bibliothèques? hanter (*to haunt*) les _____?

CHAPITRE DEUX

Descriptions

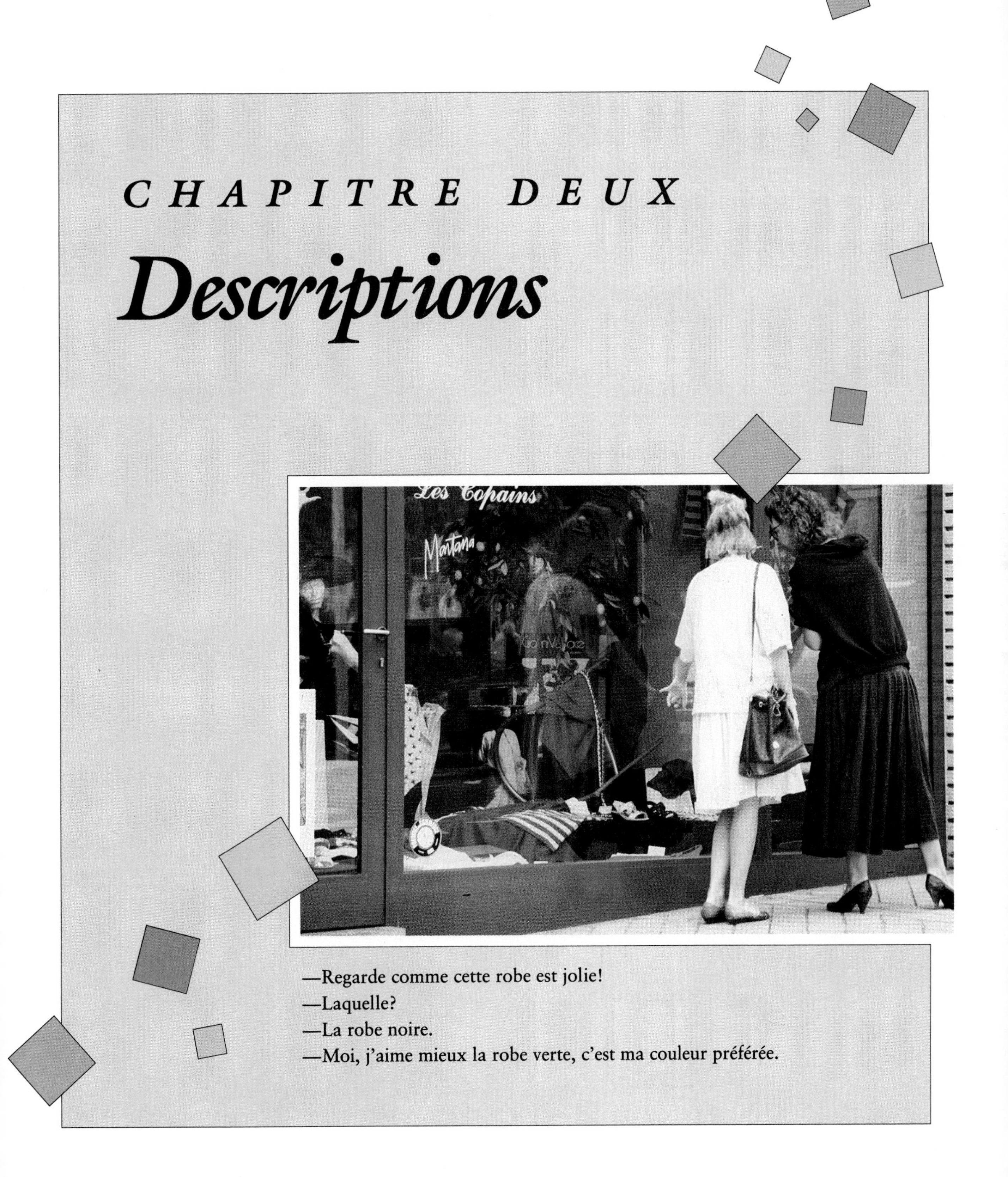

—Regarde comme cette robe est jolie!
—Laquelle?
—La robe noire.
—Moi, j'aime mieux la robe verte, c'est ma couleur préférée.

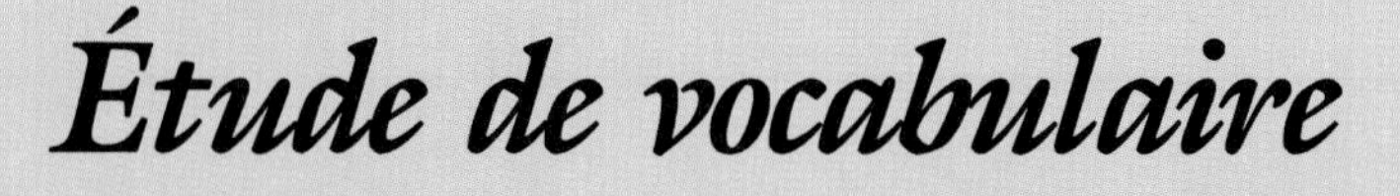

Étude de vocabulaire

Quatre personnalités différentes

Claude est un jeune homme { enthousiaste. / idéaliste. / sincère.

Michèle est une jeune fille { sociable. / sympathique. / dynamique.

Solange est une jeune fille { calme. / réaliste. / raisonnable.

Jean est un jeune homme { individualiste. / excentrique. / drôle.

A. Qualités. Donnez la qualité correspondante.

MODÈLE: Michèle aime parler avec des amis. → C'est une jeune fille sociable.

1. Claude parle avec sincérité. 2. Solange n'aime pas l'extravagance. 3. Jean est amusant. 4. Michèle aime l'action. 5. Claude parle avec enthousiasme. 6. Jean n'est pas conformiste. 7. Solange regarde la vie avec réalisme. 8. Jean aime l'excentricité. 9. Solange n'est pas nerveuse.

B. Question de personnalité. D'après vous, comment sont les personnes suivantes? Utilisez trois adjectifs dans votre description. **Autres adjectifs possibles:** hypocrite, conformiste, altruiste, antipathique, absurde, optimiste, pessimiste, insociable, calme, égoïste, sincère, modeste, matérialiste...

votre meilleur ami (meilleure amie) (*best friend*)
votre père
votre mère
le maire de votre ville (*city*)
le président américain
Ann Landers
votre camarade de chambre (*roommate*)
Joe Montana
votre professeur de français
?

Il/Elle est...

Et vous? Comment êtes-vous? Maintenant décrivez-vous (*yourself*). Begin your sentence with **Je suis** (*I am*)... **mais je ne suis pas** (*I'm not*)...

Mots-clés

How to qualify your description: When you first learn a foreign language, you inevitably exaggerate a little because you do not yet know the words to give nuances to your descriptions. The following adverbs may be useful.

très	*very*	**peu**	*hardly*
assez	*somewhat*	**un peu**	*a little*

Jeanne est **très** calme mais Jacques est **un peu** nerveux.
Mon chien (*dog*) est **peu** intelligent mais il est **assez** drôle.

C. Interview. Posez des questions à un(e) camarade.

MODÈLE: Es-tu sociable ou insociable? → Je suis sociable.

1. sincère ou hypocrite? 2. excentrique ou conformiste? 3. individualiste ou altruiste? 4. sympathique ou antipathique? 5. calme ou dynamique? 6. réaliste ou idéaliste? 7. raisonnable ou absurde? 8. optimiste ou pessimiste?

Maintenant, donnez une qualité et un défaut de votre camarade.

Les vêtements

A. Qu'est-ce qu'ils portent? Décrivez les vêtements des personnes suivantes.

1. Albert porte ______________.
2. Mme Dupuy porte __________.
3. Alice porte ______________.
4. M. Martin porte ___________.

En général, quels vêtements sont seulement pour les hommes? pour les femmes? pour les hommes et pour les femmes?

B. Un vêtement pour chaque (*each*) occasion. Décrivez avec beaucoup de détails ce que vous portez pour aller (*to go*)...

1. à un match de football américain 2. à un concert de rock 3. à une soirée (*party*) 4. à un restaurant élégant 5. à l'université 6. à la plage (*beach*)

C. Description. Maintenant décrivez aux autres étudiants ce que vous portez aujourd'hui (*today*). Puis décrivez ce que portent un(e) de vos camarades et votre professeur de français. Ensuite, parlez de vos préférences.

1. Aujourd'hui je porte...
2. Mon/Ma camarade porte...
3. Mon professeur porte...
4. Le week-end, j'aime mieux porter...
5. Pour une soirée, je préfère porter...

Les couleurs

A. Association. Quelles couleurs associez-vous avec ______?

MODÈLE: Halloween? → Le noir et l'orange.

1. le ski?
2. l'écologie?
3. le pessimisme?
4. l'amour?
5. le jour de la Saint-Valentin?
6. Noël?

B. Préférences. Donnez une opinion personnelle. Utilisez les verbes **aimer, ne pas aimer, aimer mieux** ou **détester.** Ensuite, demandez (*ask*) l'opinion d'un(e) camarade ou du professeur.

MODÈLE: Je n'aime pas le vert. J'aime mieux le bleu. Et toi? (Et vous, Monsieur/Madame?)

Christine, Michel et la voiture

1. Christine est **à côté de** la voiture.

2. Michel est **sur** la voiture.

3. Christine est **dans** la voiture.

4. Michel est **devant** la voiture.

5. Michel est **derrière** la voiture.

6. Christine est **sous** la voiture. Elle est **par terre.**

A. Oui ou non? Regardez les images et corrigez les phrases inexactes.

1. Michel est à côté de la voiture.
2. Christine est sur la voiture.
3. Christine est dans la voiture.
4. Michel est derrière la voiture.
5. Michel est devant la voiture.
6. Christine est sous la voiture.
7. Michel est par terre.

B. Désordre. Décrivez la chambre d'Alain. Utilisez **sur, sous, devant, derrière, dans** et **par terre.**

MODÈLE: Il y a deux livres sous la chaise.

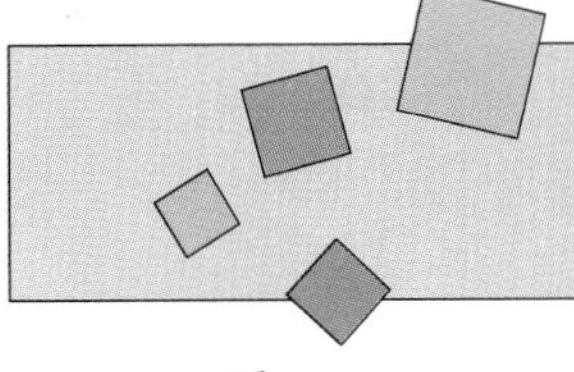

Étude de grammaire

5. Identifying People and Things: The Verb *être*

Le génie de Roger

ROGER: Eh bien, je **suis** prêt à travailler!

MARTINE: Moi aussi, mais où **sont** les livres et le dictionnaire?

ROGER: Euh... ah oui, regarde, les voilà. Le dictionnaire **est** sous le chapeau et les cahiers **sont** sur le blouson. Maintenant, nous **sommes** prêts.

MARTINE: Tu sais, Roger, tu **es** très bon en littérature, mais pour l'organisation, tu **es** nul!

ROGER: Peut-être, mais le désordre, c'**est** un signe de génie!

Complétez les phrases d'après le dialogue.

1. La chambre de Roger est **en ordre / en désordre.**
2. Martine et Roger sont étudiants **en lettres / en sciences.**
3. Martine **admire / critique** les talents de Roger en littérature.

PRESENT TENSE OF **être** (*to be*)			
je	**suis**	nous	**sommes**
tu	**es**	vous	**êtes**
il, elle, on	**est**	ils, elles	**sont**

A. The Uses of *être*

The uses of **être** closely parallel those of *to be.*

Paul **est** de New York.	*Paul is from New York.*
Est-ce que Solange **est** sociable?	*Is Solange sociable?*
Nous **sommes** d'accord.	*We agree.*
Jacques et Marie **sont** dans la bibliothèque.	*Jacques and Marie are in the library.*

In describing someone's nationality, religion, or profession, no article is used with **être.**

—Je **suis anglais. Tu es protestant?**	*—I am English. Are you (a) Protestant?*
—Non, **je suis catholique.** Vous **êtes professeur**?	*—No, I am (a) Catholic. Are you a teacher?*
—Non, je **suis étudiant.**	*—No, I am a student.*

B. *Ce* and *il/elle* Used with *être*

1. The indefinite pronoun **ce** (**c'**) is an invariable third-person pronoun. **Ce** has various English equivalents: *this, that, these, those, he, she, they,* and *it.*

- The expression **c'est** (along with its plural, **ce sont**) is used before modified nouns (*always with an article*) and proper names; it usually answers the questions **Qui est-ce?** or **Qu'est-ce que c'est?**

—Qui est-ce?	*—Who is it?*
—C'est Maxime. C'est un étudiant belge.	*—It's Maxime. He is a Belgian student.*
—Ce sont des Français?	*—Are they French?*
—Non, ce sont des Italiens.	*—No, they are Italian.*
—Qu'est-ce que c'est?	*—What is that?*
—C'est un chandail.	*—That's (it's) a sweater.*
—Et ça, qu'est-ce que c'est?	*—And what is that?*
—Oh ça, ce sont des bottes.	*—Oh, those are boots.*

- **C'est** can also be followed by an adjective, to refer to a general situation or to describe something that is understood in the context of the conversation.

  Le français? C'est facile!

2. **Il/Elle est** (and **Ils/Elles sont**) are generally used to describe someone or something already mentioned in the conversation. They are usually followed by an adjective and occasionally by an unmodified noun (*without an article*).

—De quelle couleur est le chandail?	—*What color is the sweater?*
—Il est vert.	—*It's green.*
Voici Paul. Il est étudiant en biologie.	*Here is Paul. He is a biology student.*
—Est-il français?	—*Is he French?*
—Non, il est algérien.	—*No, he is Algerian.*

MAINTENANT A VOUS

A. Complétez le dialogue suivant entre Roger et Martine avec la forme correcte du verbe **être**.

ROGER: Ces livres ______ difficiles!
MARTINE: Pas pour toi, tu ______ un génie!
ROGER: Oui, mais le professeur ______ très exigeant (*demanding*).
MARTINE: Et il dit toujours (*always says*): «Vous ______ une étudiante intelligente, Mademoiselle.»
ROGER: Nous ______ peut-être intelligents, mais moi, je ne ______ pas prêt pour l'examen!

Qui est-ce? Identify each person described below, on the basis of the dialogue.

1. C'est une personne très exigeante. C'est ______________.
2. C'est une étudiante intelligente. C'est ______________.
3. Il n'est pas prêt pour l'examen. C'est ______________.

B. Deux étudiants africains à Paris. Décrivez cet homme et cette femme. Complétez les phrases avec une expression de la colonne de droite. (*Reminder: Use* **c'est** + *modified nouns;* **il/elle est** + *adjectives;* **il/elle** est + *unmodified nouns expressing profession, religion, or nationality.*)

Voici Barthélémy.

C'est...	sénégalais.
Il est...	un jeune homme enthousiaste.
C'est...	aussi (*also*) un peu timide.
Il est...	un étudiant sérieux.

Sa petite amie s'appelle Océanie.

Elle est...	martiniquaise.
C'est...	étudiante en philosophie.
Elle est...	une personne sociable et dynamique.

On the basis of these descriptions, who do you think would have made the following statements, Barthélémy or Océanie?

1. J'aime beaucoup Hégel et Descartes.
2. Je n'aime pas beaucoup les grandes fêtes.
3. Je ne suis pas philosophe, mais mathématicien.
4. Je déteste les problèmes de mathématiques.

C. La France et les Français. Choisissez la réponse correcte. Utilisez **c'est** ou **ce n'est pas** dans votre réponse.

MODÈLE: le sport préféré des Français: le jogging? le football (*soccer*)? → Ce n'est pas le jogging, c'est le football.

1. un symbole de la France: la rose? la fleur de lis? 2. un président français: Chevalier? Mitterrand? 3. un cadeau (*present*) des Français aux Américains: la Maison-Blanche (*White House*)? la Statue de la Liberté? 4. une ville avec beaucoup de Français: La Nouvelle-Orléans? St. Louis? 5. un pays (*country*) avec beaucoup de Français: le Canada? le Mexique? 6. un génie français: Louis Pasteur? Werner von Braun? 7. parler français: difficile? facile?

D. Et vous, comment êtes-vous? Donnez un portrait de vous-même (*yourself*).

Je m'appelle ______________.
Je suis un(e) ______________. (*femme / homme / jeune fille / jeune homme*)
Je suis ______________. (*étudiant[e] / professeur*)
Je suis ______________. (*nationalité*)
Je suis de ______________. (*ville [city]*)
Je suis l'ami(e) de ______________.
______________ et ______________ sont mes (*my*) amis.
Maintenant je suis ______________. (*lieu*)
Je porte ______________. (*vêtements*)

Maintenant, donnez un portrait d'un(e) camarade de classe.

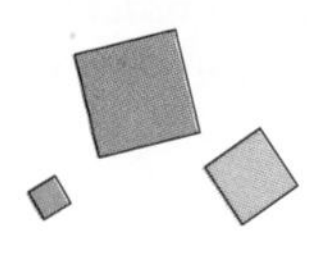

6. Describing People and Things: Descriptive Adjectives

Les annonces matrimoniales—sur ordinateur

Il est sociable,	Elle est sociable,
charmant,	charmante,
sérieux,	sérieuse,
beau,	belle,
idéaliste,	idéaliste,
sportif...	sportive...

Répondez aux questions suivantes.

1. Il cherche (*is looking for*) une femme sportive? réaliste? extravagante?
2. Il est ordinaire? extraordinaire? réaliste?
3. Elle cherche un homme sociable? drôle? réaliste?
4. Elle est ordinaire? extraordinaire? réaliste?
5. La machine est optimiste?

A. Position of Descriptive Adjectives

Descriptive adjectives (**les adjectifs qualificatifs**) are used to describe people, places, and things. In French, they normally *follow* the nouns they modify. They may also modify the subject when they follow the verb **être.**

un professeur **intéressant**	*an interesting teacher*
un ami **sincère**	*a sincere friend*
Elle est **sportive.**	*She is sports-minded (likes sports).*

B. Agreement of Adjectives*

In French, adjectives must agree in both gender (masculine or feminine) and number (singular or plural), with the nouns they modify. Note the different forms of the adjective **intelligent:**

	MASCULINE	FEMININE
Singular	un étudiant intelligent	une étudiante intelligente
Plural	des étudiants intelligents	des étudiantes intelligentes

1. To create a feminine adjective, an **e** is usually added to the masculine form.

Alain est persévérant. → Sylvie est persévérante.†

If the masculine singular form of the adjective ends in an unaccented or silent **-e,** the ending does not change in the feminine singular.

Paul est optimiste. → Claire est optimiste.

*L'accord des adjectifs
†Remember that final **t, d,** and **s,** usually silent in French, are pronounced when **-e** is added.

masculine: **intelligent** [ɛ̃teliʒɑ̃]
feminine: **intelligente** [ɛ̃teliʒɑ̃t]

2. To make an adjective of either gender plural, an **s** is added in most cases.

   Ils sont charmants. Elles sont charmantes.

If the singular form of an adjective already ends in **s** or **x**, the ending does not change in the masculine plural.

L'étudiant est **français.** → Les étudiants sont **français.**
Le professeur est **courageux.** → Les professeurs sont **courageux.**

3. If a plural subject contains one or more masculine items or persons, the plural adjective is masculine.

   Sylvie et François sont **français.** Sylvie et Françoise sont **françaises.**

4. Most adjectives of color have both masculine and feminine forms.

   un chemisier **blanc / bleu / gris / noir / vert / violet**
   une chemise **blanche / bleue / grise / noire / verte / violette**

Adjectives of color that end with a silent **e** have the same form for masculine and feminine.

un pantalon }
une robe } **jaune, rose, rouge**

Two adjectives of color, **marron** and **orange,** are invariable in both gender and number.

les chemisiers { **marron** / **orange**   les chemises { **marron** / **orange**

C. Descriptive Adjectives with Irregular Forms

PATTERN			SINGULAR		PLURAL	
Masc.		*Fem.*	*Masc.*	*Fem.*	*Masc.*	*Fem.*
-eux }	→	**-euse**	courageux	courageuse	courageux	courageuses
-eur }			travailleur	travailleuse	travailleurs	travailleuses
-er	→	**-ère**	cher (*expensive*)	chère	chers	chères
-if	→	**-ive**	sportif	sportive	sportifs	sportives
-il }	→	**-ille**	gentil (*nice, pleasant*)	gentille	gentils	gentilles
-el }		**-elle**	intellectuel	intellectuelle	intellectuels	intellectuelles
-ien	→	**-ienne**	parisien	parisienne	parisiens	parisiennes

Other adjectives that follow these patterns include **paresseux/paresseuse** (*lazy*), **naïf/naïve** (*naïve*), **sérieux/sérieuse** (*serious*), **fier/fière** (*proud*), and **canadien/canadienne** (*Canadian*). The feminine form of **beau** (*beautiful*) is **belle.**

MAINTENANT A VOUS

A. Dans la salle de classe. Complétez les phrases avec les adjectifs appropriés d'après leur sens (*their meaning*) et leur forme.

1. La salle de classe est... (blanche / noir / gentil / orange / petite / chers)
2. Le professeur est... (sérieux / dynamiques / actif / travailleuse / gentils / sportives)
3. Les étudiants sont... (fier / sincères / intelligente / courageux / naturelles / paresseux)
4. Le livre de français est... (longs / intéressant / difficiles / amusant / originale / petites)

B. Le couple idéal. Paul et Paulette sont semblables.

MODÈLE: Paul est français. → Paulette est française aussi.

1. optimiste 2. intelligent 3. charmant 4. fier 5. sérieux 6. parisien 7. naïf 8. gentil 9. sportif 10. courageux 11. travailleur 12. intellectuel

C. Un couple irréconciliable. Mais Louis et Louise sont complètement différents. Comment est Louise?

Louis est travailleur, patient, sincère, sérieux, sympathique, raisonnable, intéressant, agréable.

D. Des amis intéressants? Jean et Catherine parlent des amis de Jean. Que dit Jean? (*What does Jean say?*)

MODÈLE: CATHERINE: Et Marguerite, elle est sportive? (femme)
JEAN: Oui, c'est une femme sportive.

1. Et Jean-Pierre, il est sympathique? (étudiant)
2. Et Margot, elle est intéressante? (jeune fille)
3. Et Mme Lenoir, elle est dynamique? (femme)
4. Et M. Béranger, il est paresseux? (homme)
5. Et Mlle Duval, elle est travailleuse? (personne)
6. Et Claude, il est très sérieux? (garçon)
7. Et Renée, elle est très naïve? (jeune fille)
8. Et Paul, il est courageux? (jeune homme)

E. Les personnes idéales. Complétez les phrases avec des adjectifs.

1. L'homme idéal est ______________.
2. La femme idéale est ______________.
3. Le/La camarade de classe idéal(e) est ______________.
4. Le professeur idéal est ______________.
5. Le chauffeur de taxi idéal est ______________.

F. De quelle couleur? Donnez la couleur des choses (*things*) suivantes.

MODÈLE: Le drapeau (*flag*) américain →
Le drapeau américain est rouge, blanc et bleu.

1. le drapeau français 2. la mer (= l'océan) 3. le lion 4. la violette 5. la neige (*snow*) 6. le tigre 7. le zèbre 8. les plantes (*f.*) 9. les fleurs (*f.*)

G. Vive la mode! Regardez les personnes sur la publicité à la page 62 et décrivez les vêtements qu'ils portent. Indiquez aussi les couleurs. Utilisez le verbe **porter.** Puis dites à la classe quels vêtements vous aimez et quels vêtements vous n'aimez pas.

Maintenant décrivez ce que porte un(e) camarade de classe. Indiquez aussi les couleurs. Les autres (*other*) étudiants vont deviner (*are going to guess*) de qui vous parlez.

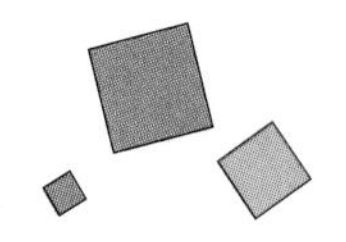

7. Getting Information: *Yes/No* Questions

Discussion entre amis

LE TOURISTE: **Est-ce** un accident?
L'AGENT DE POLICE: Non, ce n'est pas un accident.
LE TOURISTE: **Est-ce que** c'est une manifestation?
L'AGENT DE POLICE: Mais, non!
LE TOURISTE: Alors, c'est une dispute?
L'AGENT DE POLICE: Pas vraiment, c'est une discussion animée entre amis.

Voici les réponses. Posez les questions. Elles sont dans le dialogue.

1. Ce n'est pas un accident.
2. Ce n'est pas une manifestation.
3. Ce n'est pas une dispute.

Questions that ask for new information or facts often begin with interrogative words (*who?*, *what?*, and so on). Other questions simply require a *yes* or *no* answer.

A. *Yes/No* Questions with No Change in Word Order

Like English, French has more than one type of *yes/no* question.

STATEMENT:	Vous êtes parisien.
QUESTION WITH RISING INTONATION:	Vous êtes parisien?
TAG QUESTION WITH **n'est-ce pas:**	Vous êtes parisien, **n'est-ce pas?**
QUESTION WITH **est-ce que:**	**Est-ce que** vous êtes parisien?

1. Questions with rising intonation: the pitch of your voice rises at the end of a sentence to create a vocal question mark.

   —Vous ne parlez pas anglais? — *—Don't you speak English?*
   —Si,* je parle anglais. — *—Yes, I do.*

2. Tag questions: when agreement or confirmation is expected, the tag **n'est-ce pas?** is added to the end of a sentence.

   Il aime la musique, **n'est-ce pas?** — *He loves music, doesn't he?*
   Elle porte un chapeau rouge, **n'est-ce pas?** — *She's wearing a red hat, isn't she?*

3. Questions with **est-ce que:** the statement is preceded by **est-ce que.** This is the easiest and most common way to ask a question in French.

   Est-ce qu'elle étudie l'espagnol? — *Is she studying Spanish?*
   Est-ce qu'il arrive à midi? — *Is he arriving at noon?*

Est-ce que is pronounced as one word. Before a vowel, it becomes **est-ce qu':** **est-ce qu'ils** [ɛskil], **est-ce qu'elles** [ɛskɛl].

B. *Yes/No* Questions with a Change in Word Order

As in English, questions can be formed in French by inverting the order of subject and verb.

1. Questions with pronoun subjects: the subject pronoun (**ce, on, il,** and so on) and verb are inverted and hyphenated. Note that **pas** follows the pronoun in negative questions.

*To say *yes* to a negative question, **si** is used, rather than **oui.**

PRONOUN SUBJECT	
STATEMENT:	Il est touriste.
QUESTION:	**Est-il** touriste?
NEGATIVE QUESTION:	**N'est-il pas** touriste?

Est-ce un match de boxe? — *Is it a boxing match?*
N'aiment-elles pas regarder la télévision? — *Don't they like to watch television?*
N'êtes-vous pas de Paris? — *Aren't you from Paris?*

The final **t** of third-person plural verb forms is pronounced when followed by **ils** or **elles: aiment-elles.** If a third-person singular verb form ends in a vowel, **-t-** is inserted between the verb and the pronoun.

Aime-t-elle la littérature? — *Does she like literature?*
N'aime-t-il pas danser? — *Doesn't he like to dance?*
Parle-t-on français ici? — *Is French spoken here?*

The subject pronoun **je** is seldom inverted. **Est-ce que** is used instead: **Est-ce que je suis en avance?**

2. Questions with noun subjects: the third-person pronoun that corresponds to the noun subject follows the verb and is attached to it by a hyphen. The noun subject is retained.

NOUN SUBJECT	
STATEMENT:	Marc est étudiant.
QUESTION:	**Marc est-il** étudiant?
NEGATIVE QUESTION:	**Marc n'est-il pas** étudiant?

L'étudiante est-elle sympathique? — *Is the student nice?*
Roger habite-t-il à Dijon? — *Does Roger live in Dijon?*
Anne et Marie n'aiment-elles pas le professeur? — *Don't Anne and Marie like the professor?*
Les tee-shirts sont-ils blancs ou noirs? — *Are the T-shirts white or black?*

MAINTENANT A VOUS

A. Bonne mémoire. Lisez attentivement la description de Solange, puis recréez sa description avec un(e) camarade.

Voici Solange. Solange est française. Elle est de Paris. C'est une jeune fille très romantique. Elle est sympathique et intelligente. Elle parle anglais, allemand et français, bien sûr. Elle étudie la biologie à l'université de Grenoble. C'est une étudiante sérieuse mais quelquefois frivole. Elle aime les films d'amour et la musique classique. Elle aime aussi le tennis et la natation (*swimming*). Aujourd'hui, elle porte une jupe blanche, un tee-shirt jaune et des sandales blanches.

Recreate the description of Solange without looking at the text. Ask a classmate questions to check that the facts are accurate as you remember them. Alternate, using the two interrogative forms shown in the model.

MODÈLE: Solange est française?
(*ou*) Est-ce que Solange est française?

Information given in the text:

nationality
city of origin
personality
languages she speaks
subject she studies
university she attends
kind of student she is
movies she likes
music she likes
sports she likes
clothes she is wearing

B. Portrait d'un professeur. Posez des questions à votre professeur sur ses origines, sa personnalité, ses goûts (regardez la liste de l'exercice A) et ses vêtements. Utilisez l'inversion dans vos questions. **Verbes suggérés:** être, aimer, porter, visiter, parler, écouter, habiter, donner, danser, regarder, skier, travailler, étudier...

MODÈLE: Etes-vous français(e)?
Parlez-vous italien?
Aimez-vous les sports?

Maintenant posez trois questions sur l'information donnée par le professeur à un(e) camarade.

MODÈLE: VOUS: Est-ce que le professeur parle espagnol?
VOTRE CAMARADE: Non, il/elle ne parle pas espagnol.
(*ou*) Oui, il/elle parle espagnol.

C. Une interview. Interviewez un(e) camarade de classe. Demandez s'il (si elle)...

MODÈLE: is impatient → Es-tu impatient(e)?
(*ou*) Est-ce que tu es impatient(e)?

1. is optimistic or pessimistic 2. is hardworking or lazy 3. likes sports (tennis, basketball, football) 4. likes to dance 5. speaks Spanish (Italian, Russian, . . .) 6. lives at home (**à la maison**) 7. prefers television or movies 8. ?

Maintenant décrivez votre camarade à la classe.

D. Une publicité. Voici une publicité publiée (*published*) dans le magazine français *20 ans*. Regardez bien la publicité et répondez aux questions.

1. Est-ce que le cardigan est pour homme ou pour femme?
2. Est-ce que le cardigan est en coton ou en acrylique?
3. Est-ce que le jean pour homme est en coton ou en polyester?
4. Est-ce que la veste est pour homme ou pour femme?
5. Est-ce que les mannequins portent des tennis ou des mocassins?

Maintenant posez des questions générales à un(e) camarade. Utilisez les expressions suivantes: en polyester, en coton, en laine (*wool*), en soie (*silk*), en nylon...

MODÈLE: En général, une cravate est-elle en soie ou en coton?

8. Mentioning a Specific Place or Person: The Prepositions *à* and *de*

© PETER MENZEL / STOCK, BOSTON

Pierre et Francine, deux étudiants français typiques

Ils habitent **à la** cité universitaire.
Ils mangent **au** restaurant universitaire.
Ils jouent **au** volley-ball dans la salle de sports.
Le week-end, ils jouent **aux** cartes avec des amis.
Ils aiment parler **des** professeurs, **de l'**examen d'anglais, **du** cours de littérature française et **de la** vie **à** l'université.

Et vous?

1. Habitez-vous à la cité universitaire?
2. Mangez-vous au restaurant universitaire?
3. Jouez-vous au volley-ball dans la salle de sports?
4. Le week-end, jouez-vous aux cartes?
5. Aimez-vous parler des professeurs? de l'examen de français? du cours de français? de la vie à l'université?

Prepositions (**les prépositions**) are words such as *to, in, under, for,* and so on. In French, they sometimes contract with the following article. The most common French prepositions are **à** and **de.**

A. Uses of *à* and *de*

1. **A** indicates location or destination. Note that **à** has several English equivalents.

Pierre étudie **à** la bibliothèque.	*Pierre studies at (in) the library.*
Ils habitent **à** Paris.*	*They live in Paris.*
Ils arrivent **à** Paris.	*They're arriving in Paris.*

*The preposition à expresses location primarily with names of cities. Prepositions used with names of countries are treated in Grammar Section 29.

With verbs such as **parler, donner, montrer** (*to show*) and **téléphoner, à** introduces the indirect object (usually a person).

Pierre **parle à** un professeur.	*Pierre is speaking to a professor.*
Pierre **téléphone à** un ami.	*Pierre is calling a friend.*
Il **montre** une photo **à** une camarade.	*He is showing a photo to a friend.*

The preposition *to* is not always used in English but à must be used in French with these verbs.

2. **De** indicates where something or someone comes from.

Pierre est **de** Casablanca.	*Pierre is from Casablanca.*
Ils arrivent **de** la bibliothèque.	*They are coming from the library.*

De also indicates possession (expressed by *'s* or *of* in English) and the concept of belonging to, being a part of.

Voici le bureau **de** Madame Vernier.	*Here is Madame Vernier's desk.*
J'aime mieux la librairie **de** l'université.	*I prefer the university bookstore (the bookstore of the university).*

When used with **parler, de** means *about.*

Nous parlons de la littérature anglaise.	*We're talking about English literature.*

B. Contractions of *à* and *de* with the Definite Articles *le* and *les*

à + le = au	Pierre arrive **au** cinéma.	**de + le = du**	Pierre arrive **du** cinéma.
à + les = aux	Pierre arrive **aux** courts de tennis.	**de + les = des**	Pierre arrive **des** courts de tennis.
à + la = à la	Pierre arrive **à la** librairie.	**de + la = de la**	Pierre arrive **de la** librairie.
à + l' = à l'	Pierre arrive à l'université	**de + l' = de l'**	Pierre arrive **de l'**université.

C. The Verb *jouer* (to play) with the Prepositions *à* and *de*

Martine
joue au tennis.

Philippe
joue du piano.

When **jouer** is followed by the preposition **à**, it means *to play* a sport or game. When it is followed by **de**, it means *to play* a musical instrument.

MAINTENANT A VOUS

A. Des personnes très actives. Transformez les phrases suivantes.

1. Mireille parle *à la jeune fille.* (touristes, chien, femme)
2. Nous parlons *du Café Flore.* (cours de français, musique zydeco, sports français)
3. Jean-Loup arrive *de New York.* (bibliothèque, cours d'anglais, restaurant universitaire)
4. Vous jouez *au golf.* (le rugby, le violon, la guitare, le hockey)

B. Où (*Where*) sommes-nous?

MODÈLE: Nous visitons la Statue de la Liberté. → Donc, nous sommes à New York.

1. Nous jouons aux cartes. 2. Nous mangeons* un sandwich. 3. Nous regardons un film de Truffaut. 4. Nous admirons la Sorbonne. 5. Nous visitons la Maison-Blanche. 6. Nous cherchons un livre.

Maintenant, donnez trois activités. Vos camarades devinent où vous êtes.

C. Où va-t-on? (*Where do we go?*) Répondez selon le modèle.

MODÈLE: Pour écouter une symphonie? → le concert On va au concert.

1. Pour regarder un film?
2. Pour trouver un livre?
3. Pour jouer au tennis?
4. Pour jouer au volley-ball?
5. Pour écouter le professeur?
6. Pour danser?
7. Pour manger?
8. Pour visiter la Sorbonne?
9. Pour parler avec des amis?
10. Pour écouter un orchestre?

On va ____.

l'amphithéâtre, la discothèque, le Quartier latin, le cinéma, le café, la bibliothèque, les courts de tennis, le concert, la salle de sports, le restaurant universitaire, la maison

D. D'où sont-ils? Lisez les définitions et donnez la ville (*city*) d'origine des personnes suivantes.

MODÈLE: Claudette est française. Elle habite la capitale de la France. (Lyon / Paris) → Elle est de Paris.

---

*Note the spelling change in the **nous** form of **manger: nous mangeons.** (See Appendices.)

1. Robert est québécois. Il habite sur le golfe du Saint-Laurent. (Québec / Toronto)
2. Mohamed est marocain. Le nom de sa ville est aussi le nom d'un film très célèbre. (Marrakech / Casablanca)
3. Mary est américaine. L'appartement de Mary n'est pas loin (*far*) d'un obélisque blanc. (San Francisco / Washington)

Et vous, d'où êtes-vous? Mentionnez un endroit (*place*) célèbre d'une ville. Vos camarades devinent le nom de la ville.

Mots-clés

Linking words: When you first begin to study French, you may think you can speak only in very simple sentences. The following words will help you form more interesting and complicated sentences by linking ideas.

et	*and*	**mais**	*but*
aussi	*also*	**si**	*if*
ou	*or*	**donc**	*therefore*

Note the different impression linking words make in the following sentences.

- Ma cousine étudie l'espagnol. J'étudie le français. →
  Ma cousine étudie l'espagnol **mais** (**et**) j'étudie le français.
- Je n'aime pas danser. Je ne danse pas ce (*this*) week-end. →
  Je n'aime pas danser, **donc** je ne danse pas ce week-end.
- Je ne sais pas (*I don't know*) **si** le professeur aime danser.

E. Trouvez quelqu'un qui... Find someone in the classroom who does each of the following activities. On a separate piece of paper, note down his or her name next to the activity. See who can complete the list the fastest.

MODÈLE: VOUS: Est-ce que tu joues au tennis?
UN(E) CAMARADE: Oui, je joue au tennis.
(*ou*) Non, je ne joue pas au tennis.

jouer de la guitare	aimer les films français
jouer au poker	porter un pantalon vert aujourd'hui
jouer au base-ball	jouer aux dominos
jouer au volley	manger à la cafétéria aujourd'hui
jouer au bridge	aimer le laboratoire de langues

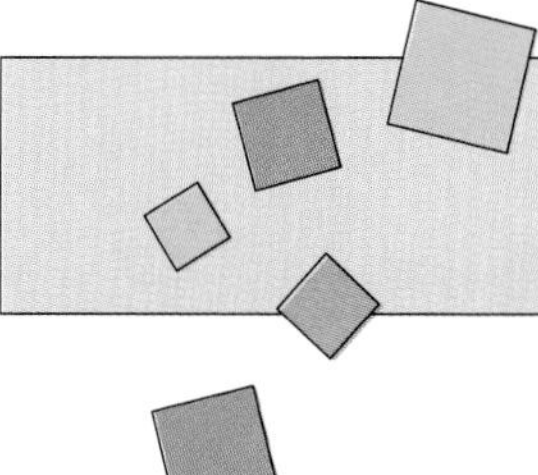

Étude de prononciation

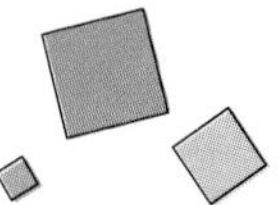

Accent Marks and the French Alphabet

Accent Marks

NAME	MARK	EXAMPLE	PRONUNCIATION
Accent aigu	é	**café**	Letter **é** pronounced [e].
Accent grave	è à, ù	**très** **là, où**	Letter **è** pronounced [ɛ] Does not affect pronunciation. Used to distinguish words spelled alike but having different meanings: **la** (*the*) vs. **là** (*there*); **ou** (*or*) vs. **où** (*where*).
Accent circonflexe	ê â, û ô	**prêt** **âge, flûte** **hôpital**	Letter **ê** pronounced [ɛ]. Does not affect pronunciation. Letter **ô** pronounced [o].
Tréma	ë, ï	**Noël, naïf**	Indicates that each vowel is pronounced independently of the other: [no-ɛl], [na-if].
Cédille	ç	**français**	Letter **c** pronounced [s].

Prononcez avec le professeur. Donnez aussi le nom des accents.

1. à bientôt
2. voilà
3. étudiant
4. Ça va.
5. fenêtre
6. modèle
7. à bas
8. répétez
9. français
10. s'il vous plaît
11. très
12. Noël

The French Alphabet

a	a	[a]	**j**	ji	[ʒi]	**s**	esse	[ɛs]
b	bé	[be]	**k**	ka	[ka]	**t**	té	[te]
c	cé	[se]	**l**	elle	[ɛl]	**u**	u	[y]
d	dé	[de]	**m**	emme	[ɛm]	**v**	vé	[ve]
e	e	[ə]	**n**	enne	[ɛn]	**w**	double vé	[dubləve]
f	effe	[ɛf]	**o**	o	[o]	**x**	iks	[iks]
g	gé	[ʒe]	**p**	pé	[pe]	**y**	i grec	[igrɛk]
h	hache	[aʃ]	**q**	ku	[ky]	**z**	zède	[zɛd]
i	i	[i]	**r**	erre	[ɛr]			

Épelez (*Spell*) en français. Donnez aussi le nom des accents.

1. Paris
2. Georges Brassens
3. excellent
4. vive
5. hôtel
6. épelez
7. je
8. Yves Montand
9. kiosque
10. comprenez
11. Françoise Hardy
12. très bien

Situation

Au restau-u

Contexte *Nous sommes dans un restaurant universitaire d'Aix-en-Provence. Patricia, une étudiante américaine, trouve une place° à la table de Clément.* — seat

Objectif *Patricia fait connaissance avec° des étudiants français et francophones.* — fait... *meets*

CLÉMENT: Bonjour! Comment t'appelles-tu°? — Comment... *What's your name?*
PATRICIA: Je m'appelle Patricia. Et toi°? — *you*
CLÉMENT: Moi, c'est° Clément. Je suis nul en anglais° mais je suis un génie en musique... Voilà Didier. C'est un pianiste. Il est de Dakar. — Moi... *Me, I'm* / Je... *I'm very bad at English*
PATRICIA: Bonjour, Didier.
CLÉMENT: Et voici Christine. Elle est de Genève et joue très bien au tennis.
PATRICIA: Salut, Christine.
CHRISTINE: Salut. Et toi, Patricia, tu es d'où?

VARIATIONS

1. Enact the dialogue. Patricia answers Christine's question and explains what she is studying in Aix-en-Provence.
2. Reenact the dialogue in groups of three students. Base the dialogue on your own identities, or make up new ones.

A propos

Comment présenter quelqu'un

The following expressions will help you to introduce people to each other.

Voici Jim.	*This is Jim.* This expression is used when you are introducing someone informally.
Je te présente Catherine.	*I would like you to meet Catherine.* Used with someone whom you address with **tu.**
Je vous présente Catherine.	Used with someone whom you address with **vous.**

The French usually shake hands when being introduced.

Comment répondre

Bonjour.	*Hello.*
Très heureux. (*male*) **Très heureuse.** (*female*)	*Glad to meet you.*
Enchanté(e).	*Delighted to meet you.*
Je suis très heureux (**heureuse**) **de faire votre connaissance.**	*I am very happy to make your acquaintance.* (This is a very formal expression, often avoided because of its length.)

Jeu de rôles. Gérard is a French student who has just come to your university. Working with several classmates, use the expressions in *A propos* to enact the situations suggested here. Alternate playing the various roles, and ask questions to find out as much as you can from one another.

Introduce Gérard to . . .

your French teacher
Paul, a classmate
your parents

Commentaire culturel

L'esprit critique. The French often describe themselves as a nation of individualists. One facet of this individualism is their **esprit critique,** the French tendency to call almost everything into question, to take nothing for granted.

The **esprit critique** leads to original and creative thought, but it can also be a source of conflict. Conversations among friends may sound brusque and aggressive to foreigners, as if participants were trying to assert their viewpoints for the pure pleasure of it. As a population, the French enjoy discussion immensely, spending hours—usually around a table—debating everything from politics to food. Defending one's opinions with wit and flair is much admired.

In politics, **l'esprit critique** shows up as a spirit of confrontation rather than compromise. If the government proposes an unpopular law, the French will often protest spontaneously and vocally. Demonstrations and strikes are more common than in the United States, because the average French citizen has strong opinions about politics and slightly mistrusts the intentions of politicians—indeed, of any institution or bureaucracy. Criticizing the status quo is a tradition in France. That may account for the popularity of satirical cartoons, which can be found in almost all newspapers and magazines.

What does the following cartoon satirize?

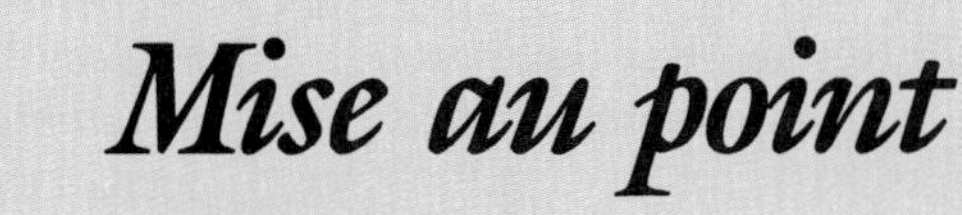

Mise au point

A. Description d'un(e) **camarade.** Faites des phrases complètes avec les éléments donnés.

1. <u>(nom)</u> / être / étudiant(e) / sérieux / intéressant / ?
2. il (elle) / habiter / près de / ?
3. il (elle) / jouer de / ?
4. il (elle) / aimer / jouer à / ?
5. aujourd'hui / il (elle) / porter / ? (de quelle couleur?)

Maintenant, donnez trois adjectifs qui résument le caractère de la personne décrite (*described*).

B. Qui admirez-vous? Demandez l'opinion personnelle d'un(e) camarade de classe. Utilisez des formes interrogatives différentes.

MODÈLE: personne / courageux →

VOUS: Est-ce que tu admires les personnes courageuses?
UN(E) AMI(E): Oui, j'admire les personnes courageuses.

1. professeur / patient
2. étudiante / sérieux
3. jeune fille / sportif
4. étudiant / travailleur
5. personne / naïf

Maintenant, créez d'autres (*other*) questions et réponses avec les noms et les adjectifs suivants: président; homme/femme politique; professeur; musicien(ne); paresseux; excentrique; drôle; individualiste; réaliste

LE SECRET DES PRÉNOMS

MANUEL

L'imagination joue un très grand rôle chez ces garçons. Chez eux, on constate souvent une double personnalité : l'une capable d'idées[a] remarquables, et une autre, capable de les mettre en pratique, ce qui est assez rare. Ils peuvent être difficiles à vivre[b] car[c] on ne sait pas toujours à quelle facette de sa personnalité on a affaire.
Couleur : rouge.

a. *ideas*
b. difficiles... *hard to live with*
c. *because*

C. Le secret des prénoms. This section from the French magazine *Star club* links people's personalities to their first names. Scan what is said about the name *Manuel,* then complete the following sentences correctly.

According to the excerpt . . .

1. men called Manuel have no imagination / a lot of imagination / a little imagination.
2. They have two personalities / no personality / a lot of personality
3. Their color is pink / red / green.

D. Qui est-ce? Décrivez un(e) camarade de classe. Le reste de la classe devine qui c'est.

MODÈLE: Il aime la musique et le tennis, il étudie l'allemand et le français et il n'aime pas danser. Il est de Cincinnati et il habite à la cité universitaire. Il est intelligent, sympathique et sportif. Il porte un pull-over et un jean. Qui est-ce? Son prénom commence par **M.**

Interactions

In Chapter 2, you learned how to ask questions, describe people and things, identify people and things, and talk about where they are. Act out the following situations, using the vocabulary and structures from this chapter.

1. **Journaliste.** You are a reporter for the school newspaper. A classmate plays the role of a visiting celebrity. Find out everything you can about this classmate: likes and dislikes; where she or he likes to go, some personality characteristics.
2. **Emprunt.** (A loan.) Imagine that someone in the class borrowed your French book but you have forgotten his or her name. Describe what he or she was wearing to another classmate, who will try to name the student.

Vocabulaire

Verbes

arriver to arrive
être to be
jouer à to play (*a sport or game*)
jouer de to play (*a musical instrument*)
manger to eat
porter to wear; to carry
téléphoner à to telephone

Substantifs

le garçon boy
la jeune fille girl, young lady
le jeune homme young man
la personne person
la voiture automobile

Adjectifs

cher, chère expensive
drôle funny, odd
facile easy
fier, fière proud
gentil(le) nice, pleasant
paresseux (-euse) lazy
sportif (-ive) *describes someone who likes sports*
sympa(thique) nice
travailleur (-euse) hardworking

Adjectifs apparentés

amusant(e), calme, courageux (-euse), conformiste, (dés)agréable, différent(e), difficile, dynamique, enthousiaste, excentrique, idéaliste, (im)patient(e), important(e), individualiste, (in)sociable, intellectuel(le), intelligent(e), intéressant(e), naïf (naïve), nerveux (-euse), optimiste, parisien(ne), pessimiste, raisonnable, réaliste, sérieux (-euse), sincère, snob

Prépositions

à côté de beside, next to
derrière behind
devant in front of
sous under
sur on, on top of

Mots divers

à la maison at home
aussi also
assez somewhat
donc therefore
eh bien,... well, . . . (well, then)
où where
peu not very; hardly
un peu a little
par terre on the ground
quand when
qui... ? who (whom) . . . ?
si if
très very

Les vêtements

le blouson windbreaker
les bottes (*f.*) boots
le chapeau hat
les chaussettes (*f.*) socks
les chaussures (*f.*) shoes
la chemise shirt
le chemisier blouse
le costume (*man's*) suit
la cravate tie
l'imperméable (*m.*) raincoat
le jean jeans
la jupe skirt
le maillot de bain swimsuit
le manteau coat
le pantalon pants
le pull-over sweater
la robe dress
le sac à main handbag
le sac à dos backpack
les sandales (*f.*) sandals
le short shorts
le tailleur woman's suit
le tee-shirt T-shirt
les tennis (*m.*) tennis shoes
la veste sports coat or blazer

Les couleurs

blanc, blanche white
bleu(e) blue
gris(e) gray
jaune yellow
marron (*inv.*) brown
noir(e) black
orange (*inv.*) orange
rose pink
rouge red
vert(e) green
violet(te) violet

INTERMÈDE 2

Lecture

AVANT DE LIRE

Recognizing cognates: You already know that cognates are words similar in form and meaning in two or more languages. The more cognates you recognize, the more quickly and easily you will read French. It will help you to be aware that the endings of many French words correspond to certain English word endings. Here are a few of the most common.

FRENCH	ENGLISH
-ment	*-ly*
-iste	*-ist*
-eux	*-ous*
-ion	*-ion*
-ie, -é	*-y*
-ique	*-ical* or *-ic*

What are the English equivalents of the following words?

1. la caractéristique
2. l'unité
3. la transformation
4. la théorie
5. politique
6. typiquement
7. écologiste
8. courageux

In the following passage, you will also come across a number of examples of **franglais,** English words used in French. Before reading, scan the passage and make two lists, one of the cognates and another of the English words used in French. Remember that in this and subsequent readings, guessable cognates are not glossed. Here, unfamiliar terms that you should be able to guess from context have been underlined.

A bas la mode et vive le look!

Le chic d'Yves Saint-Laurent ou de Pierre Cardin n'intéresse pas les jeunes Français. La mode, pour eux,° c'est le «look». Quelle est la différence? Le look exprime° des idées personnelles. Les ancêtres du look sont les Hippies de '68. Pour ces° groupes de jeunes le style de vie et les vêtements sont des messages. La jeunesse française d'aujourd'hui est divisée en groupes d'intérêts et d'opinions divers. Chaque groupe a° un code, un langage, un look.

them
expresses
these
has

Les punks
Le look: blouson en cuir, cheveux décolorés en crête, lunettes noires, chaîne de vélo
Les idées: nihilistes, anarchistes
Les passions: la laideur (*ugliness*) calculée, l'agressivité, la provocation

Les BCBG (bon chic, bon genre)
Le look: britannique, les mocassins, les foulards Hermès
Les idées: bourgeoises, droite libérale
Les passions: les grands couturiers, le bridge, le golf, le tennis

Les minets (les minettes)
Le look: le jean, le T-shirt
Les idées: américanophiles
Les passions: les États-Unis, le Coca-Cola, les jeeps, le disco

COMPRÉHENSION

Corrigez les phrases inexactes.

1. Les jeunes Français adorent la mode chic.
2. La mode chic exprime des idées personnelles.
3. Les ancêtres du look sont Yves Saint-Laurent et Pierre Cardin.
4. La jeunesse française est unifiée.
5. Le look des BCBG est américain.
6. Les babas portent des tee-shirts Fruit-of-the-Loom.
7. Les minets sont écologistes.

Par écrit

Description. Write two paragraphs describing a friend or acquaintance who fits into one of the groups mentioned in the reading. Use these suggestions as a guide. Replace the underlined words with words relevant to your description. Add as much detail as you can.

Paragraph 1

Julie est une rockeuse. Elle habite à Los Angeles. C'est une jeune fille excentrique mais intéressante. Elle aime parler de musique et de discothèques. Elle n'aime pas parler de cours universitaires. En général, elle porte un chandail noir, un jean et des chaussettes blanches.

Paragraph 2

Julie admire les Talking Heads, Sting et Elvis Costello. Elle déteste les Silicon Valleys. Elle adore danser et écouter la radio. Elle est sociable et optimiste. C'est une personne dynamique.

CHAPITRE TROIS

Le logement

—Il est chouette ton studio!
—Oui, il est tout petit, mais il est à moi!

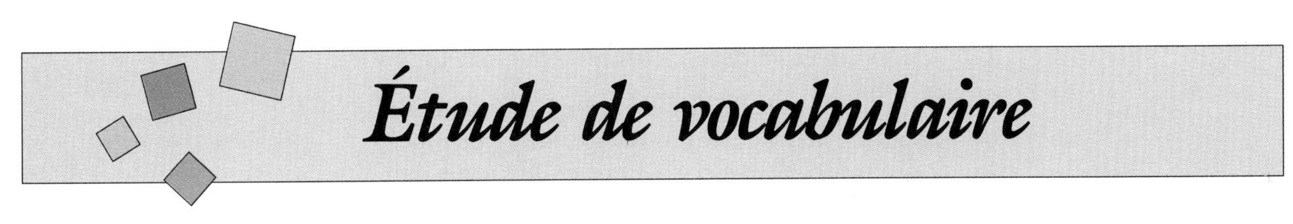

Étude de vocabulaire

Deux chambres d'étudiants

La chambre de Marie-France est en ordre.
Marie-France habite dans une maison.

La chambre de Jacqueline est en désordre.
Jacqueline habite dans un appartement.

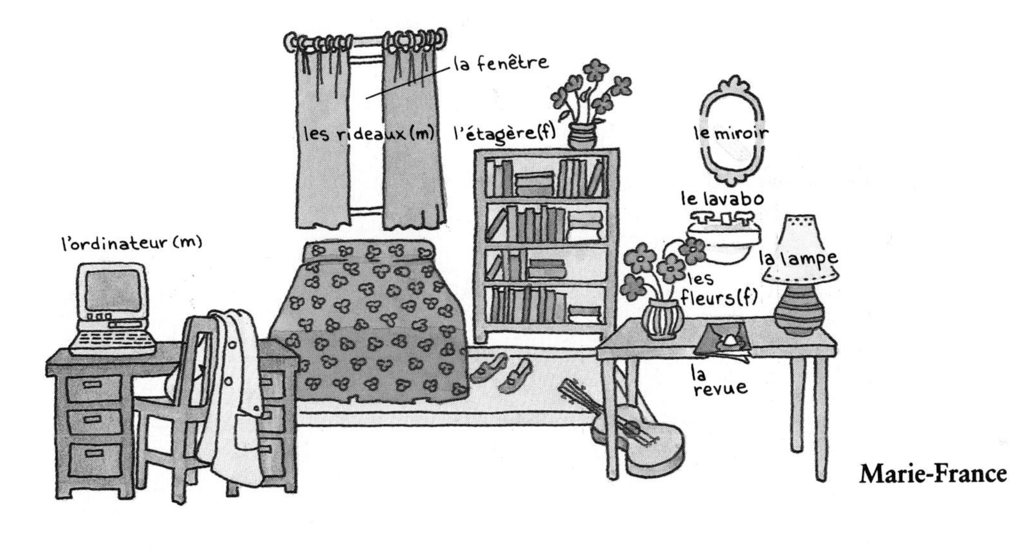

Marie-France

Jacqueline

A. Décrivez les deux chambres. Qu'est-ce qu'il y a...

1. sur le bureau de Marie-France? de Jacqueline?
2. à côté du lit de Marie-France? de Jacqueline?
3. sous la table de Marie-France? de Jacqueline?
4. sur le lit de Marie-France? de Jacqueline?
5. sur l'étagère de Marie-France? de Jacqueline?
6. sous le bureau de Jacqueline?
7. à côté de la radio de Jacqueline?
8. sur le mur de Marie-France? de Jacqueline?
9. par terre dans la chambre de Jacqueline?
10. sur la table de Jacqueline?
11. à côté de l'étagère de Marie-France?
12. sur le tapis de Marie-France? de Jacqueline?
13. derrière les étagères de Marie-France et de Jacqueline?

B. L'intrus. Trois choses semblables (*similar things*), une chose différente. Trouvez l'intrus.

1. lit / commode / armoire / fleur
2. chaîne stéréo / affiche / guitare / disque
3. lavabo / livre / revue / étagère
4. miroir / affiche / rideaux / revue

C. Préférences. Qu'est-ce qu'il y a dans la chambre d'une personne qui aime...

1. étudier? 2. écouter de la musique? 3. parler à des amis? 4. le sport? 5. la mode? 6. le cinéma?

D. La chambre et la personnalité. Une chambre révèle la personnalité de l'occupant. Décrivez la chambre sur la photo. Qu'est-ce qu'il y a dans la chambre? Quels adjectifs (en ordre, en désordre, confortable, calme, simple,...) la décrivent le mieux (*the best*)? Donnez le plus de détails possibles: meubles, objets, couleurs...

© ULRIKE WELSCH

Puis déterminez...

1. Qui habite cette chambre—un homme? une femme?
2. Quelles sont les préférences de cette personne?
3. D'après vous, comment est la personne qui habite cette chambre? Utilisez trois adjectifs pour décrire sa personnalité.

Il/Elle est ____________, ____________ et ____________.

Maintenant décrivez votre chambre. Donnez beaucoup de détails. D'après vous, quels objets dans votre chambre révèlent votre personnalité?

Les amis de Marie-France et de Jacqueline

Lise est petite, belle et dynamique. Elle a (*has*) les yeux verts et les cheveux blonds. (Elle est blonde.)

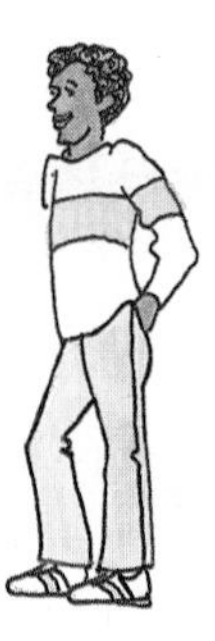

Olivier a les cheveux noirs. Il est beau et très charmant. Il est de taille moyenne.

Chantal est aussi de taille moyenne. Elle a les yeux marron et les cheveux courts et roux. (Elle est rousse.*)

Jacques est très sportif. Il est grand, il a les cheveux longs, châtains† et en désordre.

*redheaded
†marron

A. Erreur! Corrigez les phrases inexactes.

MODÈLE: Olivier a les yeux bleus. →Mais non, il a les yeux noirs.

1. Jacques a les cheveux courts. 2. Chantal a les cheveux longs et châtains. 3. Jacques a les cheveux noirs. 4. Chantal a les yeux noirs. 5. Lise a les cheveux roux. 6. Olivier est très grand. 7. Lise est de taille moyenne. 8. Jacques est petit. 9. Olivier et Lise sont laids (*ugly*). 10. Chantal est blonde et Lise est rousse.

B. Personnalités célèbres. De quelle couleur sont les cheveux des personnes suivantes?

MODÈLE: John Travolta → John Travolta? Il a les cheveux noirs.

1. Jessica Lange 2. Eddie Murphy 3. Annie, la petite orpheline 4. ?

De quelle taille sont les personnes suivantes? Sont-elles petites, grandes ou de taille moyenne?

1. Joan Collins 2. Danny DeVito 3. Bruce Springsteen 4. ?

Maintenant décrivez votre acteur préféré (actrice préférée). Les autres étudiants devinent son nom.

C. Et vos camarades de classe? Décrivez les cheveux, les yeux et la taille de la personne devant ou derrière vous.

MODÈLE: Peter a les cheveux longs et noirs, il a les yeux marron et il est de taille moyenne.

Maintenant faites votre portrait.

MODÈLE: J'ai (*I have*)...
Je suis...

Quelle est la date d'aujourd'hui?

Les mois

décembre	mars	juin	septembre
janvier	avril	juillet	octobre
février	mai	août	novembre

In French, the day is usually followed by the month: **le 21 mars** (abbreviated as 21.3). The day of the month is usually preceded by **le,** meaning *the*. However, the first day of each month is expressed with an ordinal number: **le premier janvier** (**avril, septembre,** etc.). The day of the week and the date can be expressed together, as follows. Here are two ways to give the date.

Aujourd'hui, nous sommes mardi, le 20 avril.
Aujourd'hui, nous sommes le 20 avril.

MAINTENANT A VOUS

A. Fêtes (*Holidays*) américaines. Quels mois associez-vous avec les fêtes suivantes?

Quelle est la date de la fête la plus importante dans votre famille?

B. Quelle est la date d'aujourd'hui?

MODÈLE: 8.7 → Nous sommes le huit juillet.

1. 2.8
2. 7.4
3. 21.12
4. 10.11
5. 31.5
6. 1.6
7. 15.2
8. 11.3
9. 8.1
10. 30.10

C. Le voyageur bien informé. Quand vous voyagez, il est nécessaire de savoir (*to know*) quels sont les jours de fêtes dans les pays que vous visitez. Regardez les listes suivantes et comparez les trois pays.

États-Unis

1er janv.	Nouvel An
20 févr.	Anniversaire de Washington
24 mars	Vendredi saint
29 mai	Jour du Souvenir
4 juill.	Fête de l'Indépendance
5 sept.	Fête du Travail
11 nov.	Fête des Anciens Combattants
23 nov.	Action de Grâce
25 déc.	Noël

France

1er janv.	Nouvel An
27 mars	Lundi de Pâques
1er mai	Fête du Travail
4 mai	Ascension
8 mai	Armistice
15 mai	Lundi de Pentecôte
14 juill.	Fête nationale (Prise de la Bastille)
15 août	Assomption
1er nov.	Toussaint
11 nov.	Jour du Souvenir
25 déc.	Noël

Suisse

1er janv.	Nouvel An
2 janv.	Fête légale
24 mars	Vendredi saint
26 mars	Pâques
27 mars	Lundi de Pâques
4 mai	Ascension
15 mai	Lundi de Pentecôte
1er août	Fête nationale
25 déc.	Noël
26 déc.	Lendemain de Noël

1. Quelles fêtes est-ce qu'on célèbre aux États-Unis qui ne sont pas célébrées en France? en Suisse? Donnez la date de ces fêtes.
2. Y a-t-il plus de (*more*) fêtes religieuses en France et en Suisse qu'aux (*than in the*) États-Unis? Nommez-les et donnez leur date.
3. Donnez les dates des fêtes nationales dans les trois pays.
4. Quel est votre jour de fête préféré? Pourquoi (*Why*)?

Étude de grammaire

9. Expressing Actions: *-ir* Verbs

A bas le bavardage!*

FLORENCE: Tu sais, Pierre **finit par** m'énerver.
ARMAND: Pourquoi?
FLORENCE: Eh bien, parce qu'il **réussit** toujours **à** monopoliser la conversation, et en plus, il ne **réfléchit** pas **à** ce qu'il dit!

Vrai ou faux?

1. Florence trouve Pierre sympathique.
2. Pierre est une personne réservée.
3. Pierre parle sans (*without*) réfléchir.

You have learned the present-tense conjugation of the largest group of French verbs, those whose infinitives end in **-er**. The infinitives of a second group of verbs end in **-ir**. Notice the addition of **-iss-** between the verb stem and the personal endings in the plural.

PRESENT TENSE OF **finir** (*to finish*)			
je	finis	nous	**finissons**
tu	finis	vous	**finissez**
il, elle, on	finit	ils, elles	**finissent**

*A bas... *Down with empty talk*

The **-is** and **-it** endings of the singular forms of **-ir** verbs are pronounced [i]. The double **s** of the plural forms is pronounced [s].

Other verbs conjugated like **finir** include the following.

agir *to act*
choisir *to choose*
réfléchir (à)* *to reflect (upon), to consider*
réussir (à) *to succeed (in)*

J'**agis** toujours avec raison.	*I always act reasonably.*
Nous **choisissons** des affiches.	*We're choosing some posters.*
Elles **réfléchissent aux** questions de Paul.	*They are thinking about Paul's questions.*

The verb **réussir** requires the preposition **à** before an infinitive or before the noun in the expression **réussir à un examen** (*to pass an exam*).

Je **réussis** souvent à trouver les réponses.	*I often succeed in finding the answers.*
Marc **réussit** toujours **à** l'examen d'histoire.	*Marc always passes the history exam.*

The verb **finir** requires the preposition **de** before an infinitive.

En général, je **finis d'**étudier à 8 h 30.	*I usually finish studying at 8:30.*

When followed by **par** plus an infinitive, **finir** means *to end (up) by.*

Florence **finit** toujours **par** être furieuse contre Pierre.	*Florence always ends up by being furious with Pierre.*

MAINTENANT A VOUS

A. En cours de littérature. Complétez les phrases avec une forme d'**agir, choisir, finir, réfléchir** ou **réussir.**

1. Le professeur ______ des textes intéressants.
2. Les étudiants ______ avant de répondre aux questions du professeur.
3. Pierre et Anne ______ toujours les devoirs très vite (*fast*).
4. Nous ______ toujours aux examens.
5. Toi, tu ______ souvent sans réfléchir.
6. Et moi, je ______ toujours par comprendre la leçon.

B. Une interview. Inventez des questions avec les mots suivants et interviewez un(e) camarade de classe.

---

*The verb **réfléchir** requires the preposition **à** before a noun when it is used in the sense of *to consider, to think about,* or *to reflect upon something.*

MODÈLE: réussir / aux examens →

VOUS: Est-ce que tu réussis toujours aux examens?
UN(E) CAMARADE: Oui, je réussis toujours aux examens.
(*ou*) Non, je ne réussis pas toujours aux examens.

1. agir / souvent / sans / réfléchir
2. finir / exercices / français
3. choisir / les cours (difficiles, faciles,...)
4. réfléchir / les problèmes (politiques, des étudiants,...)
5. choisir / camarade de chambre / patient (intellectuel, calme,...)
6. ?

Et vous? Donnez une réponse personnelle aux mêmes (*same*) questions.

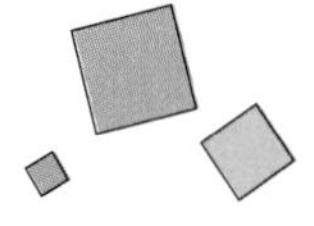

10. Expressing Possession and Sensations: The Verb *avoir*

Camarades de chambre

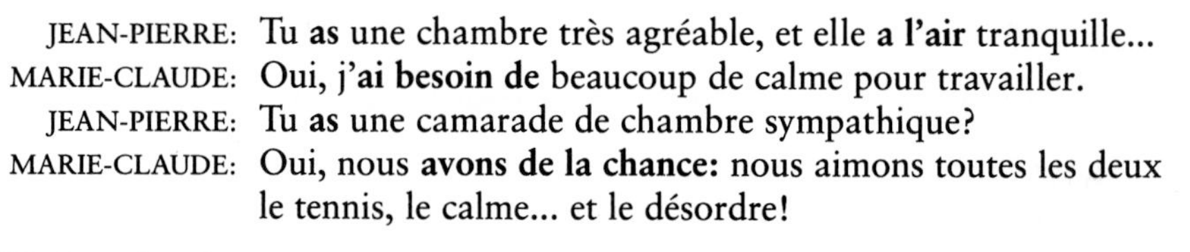

JEAN-PIERRE: Tu **as** une chambre très agréable, et elle **a l'air** tranquille...
MARIE-CLAUDE: Oui, j'**ai besoin de** beaucoup de calme pour travailler.
JEAN-PIERRE: Tu **as** une camarade de chambre sympathique?
MARIE-CLAUDE: Oui, nous **avons de la chance:** nous aimons toutes les deux le tennis, le calme... et le désordre!

Vrai ou faux?

1. La chambre est calme.
2. Marie-Claude aime le calme pour étudier.
3. La camarade de chambre de Marie-Claude est ordonnée.
4. Elles n'aiment pas le tennis.

A. Forms of *avoir* (*to have*)

The verb **avoir** is irregular in form.

PRESENT TENSE OF **avoir**			
j'	**ai**	nous	**avons**
tu	**as**	vous	**avez**
il, elle, on	**a**	ils, elles	**ont**

J'**ai** une maison agréable. — *I have a nice house.*

Avez-vous une camarade de chambre sympathique? — *Do you have a pleasant roommate?*

Oui, elle **a** beaucoup de patience. — *Yes, she has lots of patience.*

B. Expressions with *avoir*

Many concepts expressed in French with **avoir** have English equivalents that use *to be.*

Elle **a chaud,** il **a froid.**

Elles **ont faim,** ils **ont soif.**

Paul, tu **as tort.**
Jacqueline, tu **as raison.**

Claude **a l'air** content.
Il **a de la chance.**

L'immeuble **a l'air** moderne.

Jean **a sommeil.**

Claudette **a besoin d'**une lampe.

Avez-vous envie de danser?

Il **a rendez-vous** avec le professeur.

Il **a peur du** chien.

Elle **a honte.**

Isabelle **a quatre ans.**

Note that with **avoir besoin de, avoir envie de,** and **avoir peur de,** the preposition **de** is used before an infinitive or a noun.

MAINTENANT A VOUS

Mots-clés
Expressing uncertainty: If you are not sure of someone's age, say Il a **environ** quarante ans. *or* Il a **entre** (*between*) trente-cinq et quarante ans.

A. Quel âge ont-ils? Un étudiant (Une étudiante) demande (*asks*) à un(e) camarade quel âge ont les personnes sur les images suivantes.

MODÈLE: L'ÉTUDIANT(E): Quel âge a-t-il?
UN(E) CAMARADE: Il a entre un et trois ans.

B. Qu'est-ce que vous avez? Pour chaque situation, utilisez une expression avec **avoir.**

MODÈLE: Pour moi, un Coca-Cola, s'il vous plaît. → J'ai soif.

1. Je porte un pull et un manteau.
2. Il est minuit (*midnight*).
3. J'ouvre (*open*) la fenêtre.
4. Je mange une quiche.
5. Paris est la capitale de la France.
6. Des amis français m'invitent à Paris.
7. Je gagne (*win*) à la roulette.
8. Attention, un lion!
9. Je casse (*break*) le vase préféré de ma mère.
10. Je vais à la discothèque.
11. Rome est en Belgique.
12. 30 ans? Non, moi...
13. J'ai un examen difficile.
14. Et une bière, s'il vous plaît.

C. Claude cherche une chambre. Formez des phrases complètes avec les éléments donnés.

1. tu / envie de / changer de / chambre?
2. oui, / je / besoin de / chambre / très tranquille
3. nous / avoir / chambre / confortable / près d'ici (*near here*)
4. elle / avoir / deux / fenêtre / un lavabo / et / deux / lit
5. vous / avoir / téléphone?
6. oui, / mais / nous / avoir / envie de / chaîne stéréo
7. Bernard et Henri / avoir / télévision
8. ils / avoir / chance

Et vous? De quoi avez-vous besoin pour votre chambre? De quoi avez-vous envie? Nommez trois objets pour chaque catégorie.

J'ai besoin de/d' ______, ______ et ______.
J'ai envie de/d' ______, ______ et ______.

D. Une chambre vide (***empty***). Imaginez qu'un des étudiants (une des étudiantes) du cours de français loue (*is renting*) une chambre vide. Faites (*Make*) une liste des objets et des meubles (*furniture*) nécessaires.

MODÈLE: UN(E) ÉTUDIANT(E): Cindy a besoin d'une chaise.
UN(E) AUTRE ÉTUDIANT(E): Elle a besoin d'une chaise et aussi d'une table.
UN(E) AUTRE ÉTUDIANT(E): Elle a besoin d'une chaise, d'une table et aussi d'un bureau (etc.).

E. Désirs et devoirs (***duties***). Faites des phrases complètes et logiques avec les éléments des trois colonnes. Attention à la forme d'**avoir.**

Je Mon meilleur ami (Ma meilleure amie) Mes parents Le professeur de français Mon/Ma camarade de chambre ?	avoir besoin de avoir envie de	étudier davantage (*more*) acheter (*to buy*) une voiture visiter l'Europe danser à la discothèque jouer au tennis écouter un concert de rock travailler le week-end ?

F. Conversation. Posez les questions suivantes à un(e) camarade. Puis racontez (*tell*) à la classe quel est le fait (*fact*) le plus surprenant (*surprising*) ou bizarre.

1. De quoi as-tu peur? 2. Quel objet bizarre as-tu dans ta chambre? 3. De quoi as-tu besoin pour préparer ton cours de français? 4. De quoi as-tu envie quand tu as faim? quand tu as soif? 5. De quoi as-tu envie maintenant? 6. ?

11. Expressing the Absence of Something: Indefinite Articles in Negative Sentences

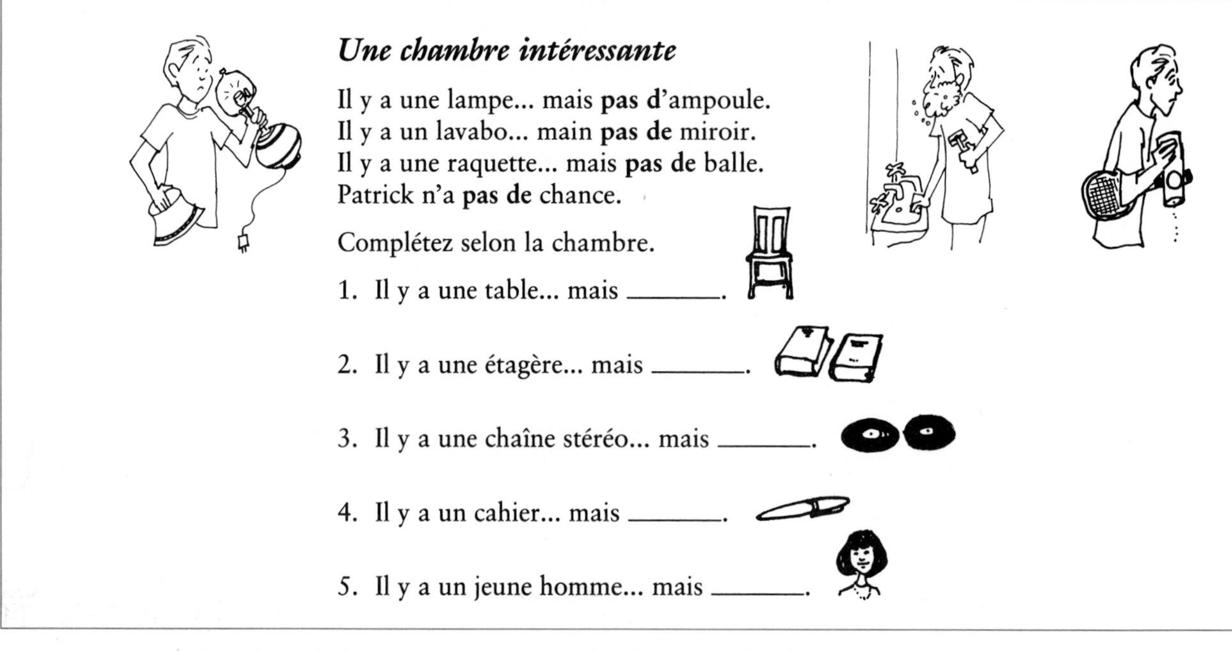

Une chambre intéressante

Il y a une lampe... mais **pas d'**ampoule.
Il y a un lavabo... main **pas de** miroir.
Il y a une raquette... mais **pas de** balle.
Patrick n'a **pas de** chance.

Complétez selon la chambre.

1. Il y a une table... mais ______.
2. Il y a une étagère... mais ______.
3. Il y a une chaîne stéréo... mais ______.
4. Il y a un cahier... mais ______.
5. Il y a un jeune homme... mais ______.

In negative sentences, the indefinite article (**un, une, des**) becomes **de** (**d'**) after **pas.**

Il a une amie.

Elle a un ballon.

Il y a des voitures dans la rue.

Il n'a pas d'amie.

Elle n'a pas de ballon.

Il n'y a pas de voitures dans la rue.

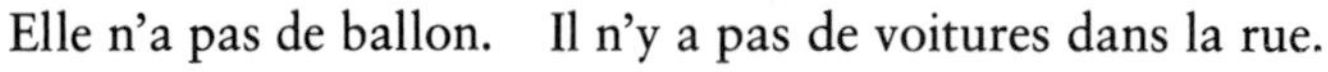

Il y a **un livre** sur la table.	Il n'y a **pas de livre** sur la table.	*There is no book on the table.*
Il y a **des livres** sur la table.	Il n'y a **pas de livres** sur la table.	*There aren't any books on the table.*

In negative sentences with **être**, however, the indefinite article does not change.

C'est un livre? Non, ce n'est pas un livre. (*It's not a book.*)

The definite article (**le, la, les**) does not change in a negative sentence.

Elle a **la** voiture aujourd'hui?
Non, elle n'a pas **la** voiture.

MAINTENANT A VOUS

A. Réponses négatives. Suivez les modèles.

MODÈLES: C'est un livre humoristique, *La Condition humaine?* →
Non, ce n'est pas un livre humoristique.

Avez-vous une biographie de Malraux? →
Non, je n'ai pas de biographie de Malraux.

1. Avez-vous des livres de Marguerite Yourcenar?* 2. *In Cold Blood,* c'est un livre drôle? 3. Y a-t-il des cours de littérature à la Faculté des sciences? 4. Le Dr Kissinger, c'est un professeur d'anglais? 5. Avez-vous un tableau de Picasso? 6. On donne des cours d'art à la Faculté des sciences?

B. Une interview. Interviewez un(e) camarade selon le modèle.

MODÈLE: ami français →
VOUS: As-tu un ami français?
UN(E) CAMARADE: Oui, j'ai un ami français.
(*ou*) Non, je n'ai pas d'ami français, mais j'ai un ami mexicain.

1. amis individualistes, snobs, blonds, roux 2. livre de français, de russe, d'espagnol 3. cours d'anglais, d'art, d'histoire 4. chaîne stéréo, télévision, disques de ____ 5. guitare, piano 6. chat, chien 7. affiches, téléphone, rideaux, armoire 8. appartement, voiture de sport 9. ?

*Novelist, historian, and translator Marguerite Yourcenar was born in Belgium. She lived in Maine for many years, where she died in 1988. She was the first woman to be elected (in 1979) to the **Académie française,** the highest honor bestowed by the French government for literary accomplishment in French.

C. **Sondage: Les Français et la chance.** Voici un sondage (*poll*) publié dans le magazine français *Vital.* Lisez les quatre opinions du sondage, regardez les résultats et choisissez la réponse correcte.

Question : « Diriez-vous qu'en général... ? »

	Ensemble	Hommes	Femmes
	%	%	%
• Vous avez une chance insolente	4	4	2
• Vous avez beaucoup de chance	31	32	31
• Vous n'avez pas tellement de chance	45	45	45
• Vous n'avez pas de chance du tout	11	8	14
• Ne se prononcent pas	9	11	8
	100	100	100

4% des Français ont une chance insolente. 11% n'ont pas de chance du tout. Les femmes croient moins à la chance que les hommes.

1. D'après le sondage, 4% des (hommes / femmes) ont une chance insolente (exceptionnelle).
2. Et (14% / 11%) des femmes n'ont pas de chance.

Maintenant, choisissez la phrase qui vous décrit le mieux (*describes you best*).

D. **De quoi as-tu besoin? De quoi as-tu envie?** Chaque membre du cours nomme (*names*) un objet qu'il n'a pas et qu'il désire, et puis il explique pourquoi il désire l'objet en question.

MODÈLE: Je n'ai pas de chaîne stéréo. J'ai envie d'une chaîne stéréo parce que j'aime la musique.

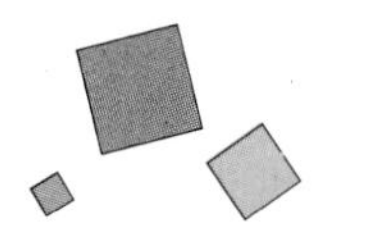

12. Getting Information: *où, quand, comment, pourquoi,* etc.

Yvette cherche une chambre à louer.

MME GÉRARD	YVETTE
Comment vous appelez-vous?	Je m'appelle Yvette Delorme.
D'**où** êtes-vous?	Je suis de Normandie.
Où étudiez-vous?	J'étudie à la Sorbonne.
Qu'est-ce que vous étudiez?	J'étudie la littérature française.
Aimez-vous la musique, les spectacles, les animaux?	Oui, mais je n'ai pas de radio, pas de télévision, pas d'animaux.

Combien d'amis avez-vous? — Beaucoup, mais pas de visiteurs.
Mademoiselle, vous êtes parfaite. **Quand** commencez-vous à louer? — Tout de suite, parce que j'ai besoin de trouver une chambre aujourd'hui!

Vrai ou faux?

1. Yvette est belge.
2. Yvette est étudiante à Paris.
3. Yvette a un chien.
4. Yvette est sociable.
5. Yvette ne loue pas la chambre.

Information questions ask for new information or facts.

A. Information Questions with Interrogative Words

Information questions often begin with interrogative expressions. Here are some of the most common interrogative words in French.

où *where* — **comment** *how* — **combien de** *how much, how many*
quand *when* — **pourquoi** *why*

Information questions may be formed with **est-ce que** or by inverting the subject and verb. The interrogative word is usually placed at the beginning of the question.

1. These are information questions with **est-ce que.**

   Où / **Quand** / **Comment** / **Pourquoi** } **est-ce que** Michel étudie les beaux-arts?

   Combien de langues **est-ce que** Michel étudie?

2. These are information questions with a change in word order.

   Pronoun subject: **Où** / **Quand** / **Comment** / **Pourquoi** } étudie-t-il les beaux-arts?

   Combien de langues étudie-t-il?

   Noun subject: **Où** / **Quand** / **Comment** / **Pourquoi** } Michel étudie-t-il les beaux-arts?

   Combien de langues Michel étudie-t-il?

3. These are information questions with noun subject and verb only. With the interrogatives **où, quand, comment,** and **combien de,** it is possible to ask information questions using only a noun subject and the verb, with no pronoun.

   Où / **Quand** / **Comment** } étudie Michel?

   Combien de langues étudie Michel?

   However, the pronoun is almost always required with **pourquoi.**

   Pourquoi Michel étudie-t-**il**?

B. Information Questions with Interrogative Pronouns

Some of the most common French interrogative pronouns (**les pronoms interrogatifs**) are **qui, qu'est-ce que, que,** and **quoi.**

1. **Qui** (*who, whom*) is used in questions inquiring about a person or persons.

Qui étudie le français?	*Who studies French?*
Qui regardez-vous? **Qui** est-ce que vous regardez?	*Whom are you looking at?*
A qui Michel parle-t-il? **A qui** est-ce que Michel parle?	*Whom is Michel speaking to?*

2. **Qu'est-ce que** and **que** (*what*) refer to things or ideas. **Que** requires inversion.

Qu'est-ce **que** vous étudiez? Qu'étudiez-vous?	*What are you studying?*
Que pense-t-il de la chambre?	*What does he think of the room?*

3. **Quoi** (*what*) also refers to things or ideas but is used as the object of a preposition.

A quoi Corinne réfléchit-elle? **A quoi** est-ce que Corinne réfléchit?	*What is Corinne thinking about?*
De quoi parlez-vous? **De quoi** est-ce que vous parlez?	*What are you talking about?*

MAINTENANT A VOUS

A. La vie à l'université. Exercice de substitution.

1. *Comment* est-ce que vous étudiez le français? (pourquoi, quand, où)
2. *Avec qui* le professeur parle-t-il? (de qui, de quoi, à qui)
3. *Pourquoi* parle-t-il avec les étudiants? (où, comment, quand)

© ANDREW BRILLIANT

Ce studio a l'air bien, on va le voir après les cours?

B. Les activités de Marcel. Trouvez une question qui correspond à chaque réponse.

MODÈLE: 1. De la flûte. → d. De quoi joue-t-il?

1. De la flûte.
2. Au tennis.
3. A la question.
4. Du concert.
5. D'une limonade.
6. D'un stylo.

a. De quoi parle-t-il?
b. A quoi réfléchit-il?
c. De quoi a-t-il envie?
d. De quoi joue-t-il?
e. A quoi joue-t-il?
f. De quoi a-t-il besoin?

C. Les étudiants et le logement. Posez des questions avec **qui** ou **à qui.**

MODÈLE: *Marie* désire un logement. → Qui désire un logement?

1. *Marie* cherche un logement. 2. *Mme Boucher* a une petite chambre à louer dans une maison. 3. Jocelyne et Richard parlent de Mme Boucher à *Marie.* 4. Marie téléphone à *Mme Boucher.* 5. Mme Boucher montre (*shows*) la chambre à *Marie.* 6. *Marie* loue la chambre de Mme Boucher.

D. Une chambre d'étudiant. Voici une conversation entre deux étudiants. D'après les réponses de Julien, imaginez les questions de Laurence. **Suggestions:** comment, où, qu'est-ce que (que), pourquoi, quand, combien de...

MODÈLE: LAURENCE: Comment est la chambre?
JULIEN: La chambre est très agréable.

LAURENCE: ______________________________?
JULIEN: Il y a *des affiches* et *un miroir* sur le mur.
LAURENCE: ______________________________?
JULIEN: La lampe est *à côté de la stéréo.*
LAURENCE: ______________________________?
JULIEN: Il y a *deux* chaises et *une* table.
LAURENCE: ______________________________?
JULIEN: J'ai une stéréo *parce que j'adore la musique.*
LAURENCE: ______________________________?
JULIEN: J'écoute de la musique *quand j'étudie.*
LAURENCE: ______________________________?
JULIEN: La chambre est *petite* mais *confortable.*

Mots-clés

Giving reasons: To answer the question *why* (**pourquoi?**), use **parce que.**

Je travaille **parce que** j'ai besoin d'argent.

Another word used to give reasons is **car.**

La chambre est sombre **car** elle n'a pas de fenêtres.

Car is more formal and is usually used in writing.

E. Une interview. Interviewez un(e) camarade.

1. D'où es-tu? Comment est ta (*your*) ville?
2. Où habites-tu? Dans une maison, un appartement ou une résidence universitaire? Avec qui? Comment est ta chambre?
3. Est-ce que tu aimes l'université? Pourquoi? Combien de cours as-tu ce semestre? Comment sont tes cours?
4. Comment sont tes camarades? Ton/Ta camarade de chambre? Tes professeurs?
5. De quoi parles-tu avec tes amis après les cours? Où?
6. Quand fais-tu du sport? A quoi aimes-tu jouer? Avec qui?

Est-ce que la vie de votre camarade est très différente de votre vie? Qu'est-ce que vous avez en commun? de différent? Expliquez.

F. Êtes-vous curieux (curieuse)? Pourquoi est-ce toujours le professeur qui pose des questions? Profitez de cette (*this*) leçon pour poser des questions au professeur.

MODÈLES: D'où êtes-vous?
Pourquoi aimez-vous le français?
Avez-vous des disques de Sting?

Commentaire culturel

Foreign students in France. Students from all over the world attend French universities for part or all of their higher education. Students from francophone countries in Africa, from Vietnam, and Cambodia (Kampuchea) are especially numerous. The French Ministry of Education maintains an open system of enrollment, in which any student, native or foreign, is admitted to university study as long as he or she holds the **baccalauréat** degree or its equivalent. For American students, this usually means the completion of two years in an accredited college or university.

If you would like general information about French universities and the application process, visit or write to the **Services culturels** of the French embassy or consulate nearest you. You can get more detailed information by writing to the **Bureau de l'Information et de l'Orientation du Ministère de l'Éducation Nationale (Directeur des Enseignements Supérieurs, 61–65, rue Dutot, 75015 Paris).** If you know which French university you would like to enter, write to its **Centre de l'Information et de l'Orientation.**

An important alternative for students wishing to study in France is the **académies** that specialize in teaching French language courses at all levels. For information, write to the **Ministère des Relations Extérieures (34–36, rue La Pérouse, 75016 Paris)** and ask for the brochure published by the **Association pour la Diffusion de la Pensée française.**

Étude de prononciation

Stress, Intonation, and Linking

Stress (*L'accent*). Stress refers to the emphasis given to a syllable. English speakers tend to emphasize syllables within a word and within a sentence. French rhythmic patterns, however, are based on *evenly* stressed syllables. There is a slight emphasis (called **l'accent final**) on the final syllable of each French word.

Prononcez avec le professeur.

1. le bureau
2. le professeur
3. la différence
4. l'attention
5. l'administration
6. le garçon

Intonation. Intonation refers to the variation of the pitch, the rise and fall of the voice (not loudness), in a sentence. Here are three basic French intonation patterns.

1. In *declarative sentences,* the intonation rises within each breath group (group of words produced in one breath) and falls at the end of the sentence, starting with the last breath group.

   Je m'appelle Marcel Martin. Bonjour, Mademoiselle.

   Il est content de quitter l'université à trois heures.

2. In *yes/no questions,* the intonation rises at the end of the question.

   Ça va? Est-ce que c'est un professeur?

3. In *information questions,* the intonation starts high and falls at the end of the question.

   Comment allez-vous? Qu'est-ce que c'est?

Linking (*L'enchaînement*). A sentence or breath group spoken in French can be considered a cluster of syllables that are linked together. The voice does not stop between words in such groupings. Note that most French syllables end with a vowel; in English, most end with a consonant.

Prononcez avec le professeur.

1. Comment vous appelez-vous? [kɔ-mɑ̃-vu-za-ple-vu]
2. Répétez, s'il vous plaît. [re-pe-te-sil-vu-plɛ]
3. Comment allez-vous? [kɔ-mɑ̃-ta-le-vu]

In **liaison** a silent consonant at the end of a word is linked to the next word and pronounced if that word begins with a vowel sound: **C'est un livre. Comment vous appelez-vous?** Liaison occurs between words connected by meaning or function (syntax) in a sentence: **six étudiants** [si-ze-ty-djɑ̃], **huit étudiants** [ɥi-te-ty-djɑ̃]. Liaison is discussed in more detail in Chapter 5.

Prononcez avec le professeur.

1. C'est un cahier.
2. C'est un étudiant.
3. Comment allez-vous?
4. Vive les examens!

Situation

Pardon...

Contexte *C'est le premier jour de Karen, une étudiante américaine, à la cité universitaire d'Orléans. Elle pose des questions à une étudiante française.*

Objectifs *Karen demande des renseignements.°* — *information*

KAREN: Pardon, où est le téléphone, s'il te plaît?
MIREILLE: Dans le foyer.
KAREN: Mmm... qu'est-ce que c'est, le foyer?
MIREILLE: Eh bien, c'est la salle, en bas, où il y une télé, une table de Ping-Pong, un distributeur° de café et de Coca... — *machine*
KAREN: Dis-moi, comment est le restaurant universitaire?
MIREILLE: Ça, je ne sais pas. Moi aussi, je suis nouvelle° ici. On déjeune ensemble°? — *new*; à deux
KAREN: Bonne idée! J'ai très faim!

VARIATIONS

1. Jouez la scène avec vos camarades de classe.
2. Jouez la scène, mais c'est Mireille qui arrive aujourd'hui à votre université et elle vous pose beaucoup de questions.

A propos

Comment demander des renseignements

Pouvez-vous m'indiquer / Peux-tu m'indiquer...	*Can you tell me . . .*
où on trouve...	*where to find (one finds) . . .*
combien coûte (-ent)...	*how much (something) costs . . .*
Pouvez-vous me dire, s'il vous plaît / Peux-tu me dire, s'il te plaît...	*Tell me please . . .*

Savez-vous / Sais-tu...	*Do you know . . .*
J'aimerais savoir...	*I would like to know . . .*
Je ne sais pas...	*I don't know . . .*
s'il y a...	*if there is/are . . .*
quand... etc.	*when*

Jeu de rôles. Utilisez les expressions de l'*A propos* pour poser des questions dans les situations suivantes. Imaginez que vous êtes nouveau (nouvelle) (*new*) à l'université. Jouez les rôles avec un (e) camarade de classe.

1. Vous posez des questions à un professeur pour savoir (*know*):

- où est la bibliothèque
- si on a besoin d'une carte d'étudiant (*student ID card*)
- s'il y a une salle de lecture (*reading room*)
- à quelle heure ferme (*closes*) la bibliothèque

2. Vous posez des questions à un étudiant (une étudiante) qui cherche un(e) camarade de chambre pour savoir:

- où est la chambre à louer
- s'il y a un téléphone ou une télévision
- s'il y a un lavabo ou une douche (*shower*) dans la chambre
- si la chambre est calme
- s'il est possible d'avoir des visiteurs le soir
- si l'immeuble est grand ou petit

Après l'interview, décidez si vous louez la chambre ou non. Expliquez pourquoi.

Commentaire culturel

Student housing. Housing for students is in short supply in French towns and cities. Apartments close to public transportation and to university buildings are in great demand and are very expensive to rent or buy. Every French university provides housing services, however. Some are run by student unions, others by an official social service like the **Centre régional des œuvres universitaires et scolaires** (C.R.O.U.S.). Lists of available apartments and rooms can be consulted free of charge at each housing service. Ads in daily or specialized newspapers are another source of information. They are found under the heading **locations** (*rentals*) or **chambres meublées** (*furnished rooms*).

Some students live in dormitories in the **cités universitaires,** but there are long waiting lists for rooms. Most **cités universitaires** have a definite international flavor. For example, groups of students of many nationalities each have their own houses within the **Cité universitaire de Paris.** An alternative to the **cité universitaire** is a room in a boarding house (**un foyer**), usually run by a private organization.

Many French students live with their families while they are in school. Even those students lucky enough to have rooms in the **cité universitaire** usually spend weekends and holidays at home with their families.

Very few students share apartments or houses with other students. Students unable to find apartments or rooms in a **cité universitaire** or **foyer** often try to find convenient rooms with families. Young couples who have high mortgage payments, or older people who live alone in apartments or houses that have become too expensive for them, often rent rooms to students. Because of the shortage of student housing, owners who rent rooms to students are not required to pay taxes on the rent they receive.

The following guide from the magazine *20 ans* (September 1988) lists useful resources for students looking for lodging.

ETUDIANTS CHERCHENT LOGEMENTS

Débrouillardise et persévérance sont nécessaires, mais pas forcément suffisantes pour dénicher une piaule à Paris. Choisissez votre formule et frappez à toutes les portes susceptibles de vous aider.

Location

La location d'une chambre coûte de 800 à 1 500 f par mois. Celle d'un studio, 1 500 à 2 500 f. Consultez les petites annonces des quotidiens, des facs, des écoles primaires (« Propose logement contre quelques heures de travail »). Tapez sur Minitel 3615 code MNEF, AA ou APBAC.

Ne négligez pas le bouche à oreilles.

Une fois découverte la chambre de vos rêves, n'oubliez pas de vous assurer. Renseignements : MNEF ou SMEREP.

Centre info-Habitat, à Paris sur rendez-vous : 45.49.25.26.

Foyer

Leurs prix sont très variables, de 800 à 3 900 f. En moyenne comptez 1 600 f par mois.

Procurez-vous la liste des foyers à l'Association catholique des services de la jeunesse féminine, 63, rue Monsieur-le-Prince, 75006 Paris. 43.26.92.84.

Renseignez-vous aussi auprès de l'Union nationale des maisons d'étudiants, 15, rue Ferrus, 75014 Paris. 45.89.38.35.

Résidence universitaire

Une chambre coûte entre 520 et 700 f par mois.

S'adresser au service des logements du CROUS avant le mois de mars précédent la rentrée universitaire pour laquelle l'admission est souhaitée.

- Union nationale des étudiants locataires (UNEL), 120, rue Notre-Dame-des-Champs, 75006 Paris, 46.33.30.78.
- Union nationale des étudiants de France (UNEF), 52, rue Edouard-Pailleron, 75019 Paris. 42.45.84.84.
- Mutuelle universitaire du logement (MUL), 7, rue Sarrazin, 44000 Nantes.

Pour tous problèmes concernant les étudiants à Paris, deux organismes à retenir :

- CROUS (Centre régional des œuvres universitaires et scolaires), 39, av. Georges-Bernanos, 75005 Paris. 43.29.12.43.
- CIDJ (Centre d'information jeunesse), 101, quai Branly, 75015 Paris. 45.66.40.20.

Complétez les phrases d'après l'article.

1. Louer une chambre à Paris, c'est *facile / difficile / impossible.*
2. Le prix d'un foyer est en moyenne (*on the average*) *1 600 f / 800 f / 3 900 f* par mois.
3. Pour avoir une chambre en résidence universitaire, il est nécessaire de commencer à chercher *deux / six / dix* mois à l'avance.

Mise au point

A. Une conversation téléphonique. Une amie parle au téléphone. Vous entendez (*hear*) les réponses, mais pas les questions. Quelles sont les questions que vous n'entendez pas? A votre avis, avec qui parle-t-elle?

QUESTIONS	RÉPONSES
?	1. Non, je n'ai pas faim.
?	2. Maintenant? Les maths.
?	3. Avec Jim.
?	4. Parce qu'il est très fort en maths.
?	5. De maths, et aussi de littérature, du cours d'anglais, de la vie à l'université.
?	6. Oui, il est très sympa.

B. Au contraire. Working with one or more students, practice your argumentative skills by contradicting every statement they make in response to these questions. You may start your sentences with **Au contraire... , Moi, je pense que... ,** or **Ce n'est pas vrai** (*true*).

MODÈLE: Comment trouvez-vous la vie universitaire? →

UN(E) ÉTUDIANT(E): La vie universitaire n'est pas très intéressante.

UN(E) AUTRE ÉTUDIANT(E): Au contraire, elle est dynamique et très, très intéressante.

1. De quoi a-t-on besoin pour réussir dans un cours? 2. Où trouve-t-on un restaurant près de l'université? 3. Est-ce que les étudiants ont besoin d'une chaîne stéréo? 4. Pourquoi étudiez-vous le français? 5. De quoi a-t-on envie après un examen difficile? 6. Quand étudiez-vous?

Interactions

In Chapter 3, you have practiced talking about rooms, describing people, telling what you do and do not have, and asking questions. Act out the following situations, using the vocabulary and structures from this chapter.

1. **Camarade de chambre.** You are interviewing a prospective roommate (your partner). You find out the following information about him or her.

    what his or her name is
    how old he or she is
    what he or she is studying
    what time he or she has class
    whom he or she telephones often
    if he or she likes order or disorder

2. **Description.** Someone has just robbed you. Describe the robber physically (and his or her clothes) to a police officer (a classmate). The police officer will draw the individual as you talk. Decide whether the drawing matches your description.
3. **Un appartement.** You are moving into an unfurnished apartment. Next door, two French students (your partners) are moving out. Introduce yourself to them, and engage them in conversation. Describe the things you need for your small apartment, in the hope that you might be able to obtain some of them from your departing neighbors.

–C'est un impulsif. Quand il a sommeil, il ne réfléchit pas, il dort[a]!

a. *sleeps*

Vocabulaire

Verbes

agir to act
avoir to have
choisir to choose
demander to ask (for)
finir de (+ *inf.*) to finish
finir par (+ *inf.*) to end up by . . .
louer to rent
penser (à) to think (of, about)
penser de to think of (to have an opinion about)
poser une question to ask a question
réfléchir à to think (about)
réussir (à) to succeed (at); to pass (*a test*)

Noms

l'affiche (*f.*) poster
le (la) camarade de chambre roommate
le canapé sofa
la chaîne stéréo stereo
la chambre room
le chat cat
les cheveux (*m.*) hair
le chien dog
le choix choice
la commode chest of drawers
le disque record
l'étagère (*f.*) shelf
la fête holiday
la fleur flower
l'immeuble (*m.*) building
la lampe lamp
le lavabo washbasin
le lit bed
le logement lodging(s), place of residence
la maison house, home
le miroir mirror
le mot word
le mur wall
l'ordinateur (*m.*) computer
la revue magazine
le rideau curtain
la rue street
le tapis rug
le téléphone telephone
les yeux (*m.*) eyes

Adjectifs

autre other
beau, belle handsome, beautiful
blond(e) blond(e)
chaque each, every
châtain brown (*hair*)
court(e) short (*hair*)
grand(e) tall, big
long(ue) long
petit(e) small, short
roux red (*hair*)
roux, rousse redheaded
tout, tous, toute, toutes all, every
tranquille quiet, calm

Prépositions

contre against
entre between
par by
près de close to
sans without

Expressions avec avoir

avoir l'air (+ *adj.*); **avoir l'air (de** + *inf.*) to seem; to look
avoir (20) ans to be (20) years old
avoir besoin de to need
avoir chaud to be warm
avoir de la chance to be lucky
avoir envie de to want, to feel like
avoir faim to be hungry
avoir froid to be cold
avoir honte to be ashamed
avoir peur de to be afraid of
avoir raison to be right
avoir rendez-vous avec to have a meeting (date) with
avoir soif to be thirsty
avoir sommeil to be sleepy
avoir tort to be wrong

Expressions interrogatives

combien (de)... ?, comment... ?, pourquoi... ?, que... ?, qu'est-ce que... ?, ...quoi... ?

Mots divers

de taille moyenne of medium height
en désordre disorderly, disheveled
en ordre orderly
parce que because

Les mois

janvier January
février February
mars March
avril April
mai May
juin June
juillet July
août August
septembre September
octobre October
novembre November
décembre December

INTERMÈDE 3

Lecture

AVANT DE LIRE

More on contextual guessing: Another form of guessing you probably use often when you encounter an unfamiliar word in English is to look at the surrounding context to figure out the meaning of the word. It is usually necessary to read ahead. Often the sentences that follow it will clarify the meaning of an unfamiliar phrase or word. Look, for example, at the underlined word in this sentence.

> L'appartement n'est pas grand mais il est clair car il a de grandes fenêtres.

When you encounter the word **clair,** you probably do not know what it means, but if you finish the sentence, you will easily guess that it means *light* or *sunny*. Try the same strategy with the other underlined words in the reading.

Le logement

Pierre et Sophie habitent un joli appartement à Lyon. C'est un trois pièces avec une grande cuisine toute équipée et une terrasse. Il n'est pas très grand, mais il est clair car il a de grandes fenêtres. Comme° beaucoup de Français, Pierre et Sophie sont propriétaires de leur logement.

°*Like*

© PETER MENZEL / STOCK, BOSTON

© MONKMEYER PRESS
© ULRIKE WELSCH

L'immeuble des parents de Pierre est ancien. Mais en France on trouve aussi beaucoup de maisons et d'immeubles modernes, surtout en banlieue.° *suburbs* Dans les villes on construit beaucoup ou on rénove les bâtiments anciens. Souvent, quand l'immeuble est très beau mais en mauvais état, on garde seulement° *only* sa façade et on construit derrière un bâtiment neuf.

Comme beaucoup de personnes qui habitent en ville, Pierre et Sophie ont aussi une maison à la campagne° (≠ en ville) où ils passent leurs week-ends et une partie de leurs vacances. Ils organisent souvent des dîners en famille ou entre amis. Les enfants adorent jouer dans le jardin.° *garden*

COMPRÉHENSION

1. Comment est l'appartement de Pierre et Sophie? Donnez des détails.
2. Où trouve-t-on, en général, des immeubles modernes?
3. Où vont beaucoup de Français le week-end?

Par écrit

Vous cherchez une chambre d'étudiant à Québec. Écrivez une lettre à un foyer. Décrivez en détail ce que vous cherchez et demandez s'il y a des chambres libres (*free*).

MODÈLE: (votre ville), le 18 février, 1990
(votre nom)
(votre adresse)

Madame J. Roberge
9, Rue du Château
G1S 4S8 Québec
Canada

Chère Madame,

Je suis ______. Je cherche ______. J'ai besoin de ______. J'ai aussi envie de ______. Avez-vous ______? ______?

Croyez, chère Madame, à mes sentiments les plus distingués (*traditional closing line*).

Communication et vie pratique 1

ACTIVITÉ

Une soirée. Faites une description détaillée de la scène suivante.

- Qu'est-ce qui se passe? (*What's happening*?) Que fait (*is doing*) chaque personne?
- Comment sont les personnes? Comment est leur (*their*) apparence physique (vêtements, couleurs, nationalités)? Imaginez aussi les préférences et la personnalité de chaque personne—et de Wolfgang!
- Décrivez les objets dans la salle. Quels objets est-ce qu'il y a? Où sont-ils?

EXPRESSION ÉCRITE

«Je m'appelle Rangira Césieu. J'habite au Zaïre. Je suis aux États-Unis pour améliorer mon anglais. Je me spécialise en sciences. Un jour, je veux être médecin comme mon père.»

Situation. You are writing an article for the student newspaper about the new exchange student on campus, Rangira Césieu. Begin by completing the following sentences. Then write two or three other sentences of your own. Make inferences from Rangira's description of herself and invent other plausible details.

Rangira est étudiante en biologie. Elle veut (*wants*)...
Elle a aussi envie...
Elle a l'air...
Elle a ____ ans.
Elle étudie aux États-Unis parce que...
Elle dit...
C'est une jeune fille...
Elle parle...
Elle aime spécialement... mais elle n'aime pas du tout...

Imagine that you have the chance to do a follow-up interview before you finish your article. Write down a few questions to ask Rangira, to get a better idea of what she is like.

Avant d'écrire

Writing lively prose: When you write a description of someone, try to make the subject come alive for your readers. Here are a few ways to do that.

- Include vivid and specific details that suggest something about the person's personality—preferences, appearance, taste in clothing.
- Quote the person, to give an idea of what he or she is like.
- Arrange each sentence so that the most interesting points stand out. Put them at the beginning or the end, or set them off in a brief sentence contrasted with longer ones that surround it.

CHAPITRE QUATRE

Les Français chez eux

—Encore une histoire, s'il te plaît.
—Bon, mais après vous allez au lit, les enfants!

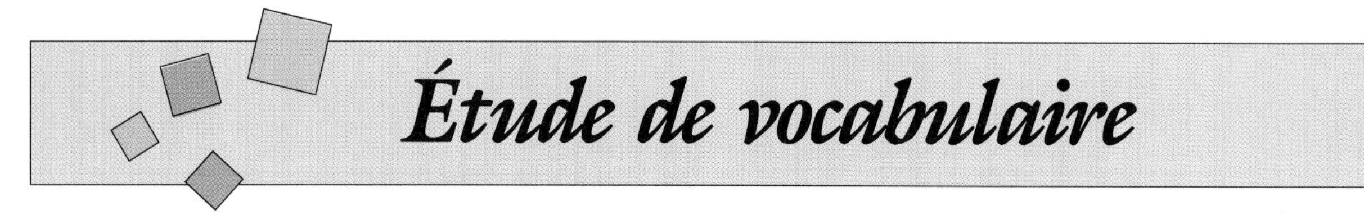

Étude de vocabulaire

Trois générations d'une famille

A. La famille Deschamps. Étudiez l'arbre généalogique de la famille Deschamps et répondez aux questions suivantes.

1. Comment s'appelle la femme d'Édouard?
2. Comment s'appelle le mari d'Isabelle?
3. Comment s'appelle la tante de Marie-France et de Robert? Et l'oncle?
4. Combien d'enfants ont les Lagrange? Combien de filles? Combien de fils?
5. Comment s'appelle le frère de Marie-France?
6. Combien de cousins ont Marie-France et Robert? Combien de cousines?
7. Comment s'appelle la grand-mère de Philippe? Et le grand-père?
8. Combien de petits-enfants ont Édouard et Marie? Combien de petites-filles? Combien de petits-fils?
9. Comment s'appelle la sœur de Philippe?
10. Comment s'appellent les parents de Maurice et de Simone?

B. Masculin, féminin. Donnez le féminin.

MODÈLE: le frére → la sœur

1. le mari 2. l'oncle 3. le père 4. le fils 5. le grand-père 6. le cousin

C. Vrai ou faux? Corrigez les définitions qui ne sont pas exactes.

1. La mère de ma cousine est ma tante.
2. Le père de ma mère est mon oncle.
3. La femme de mon oncle est ma nièce.
4. Le mari de ma grand-mère est mon grand-père.
5. La sœur de mon cousin est ma cousine.
6. Le fils de mon oncle est mon neveu.
7. Le frère de mon père est mon cousin.
8. Le neveu de ma mère est mon cousin.

D. Qui sont-ils? Complétez les définitions suivantes de façon logique.

1. Le frère de mon père est mon ________.
2. La fille de ma tante est ma ________.
3. Le père de ma mère est mon ________.
4. La femme de mon grand-père est ma ________.

Maintenant définissez les personnes suivantes.

5. nièce
6. cousin
7. tante
8. grand-père

E. Conversation: Une famille française. Avec un(e) camarade, décrivez la famille sur la photo. Donnez le nombre de personnes, et essayez de deviner qui ils sont et quel âge ils ont. Puis imaginez leur profession, leurs goûts, leur personnalité. Donnez le plus de détails possible. **Suggestions:** Voici, voilà, c'est, il/elle a, il/elle aime, il/elle est...

© PALMER & BRILLIANT

F. Une famille américaine. Maintenant posez les questions suivantes à votre camarade.

1. As-tu des frères? des sœurs? Combien? Comment s'appellent-ils/elles? (Ils/Elles s'appellent...)
2. As-tu des grands-parents? Combien? Habitent-ils avec la famille? dans une maison? dans un appartement?
3. As-tu des cousins ou des cousines? Combien? Habitent-ils/elles près ou loin (*far*) de la famille?
4. Combien d'enfants (de fils ou de filles) désires-tu avoir? Combien d'enfants y a-t-il dans la famille idéale?

La maison des Chabrier

MAISON A LOUER: 5 pièces—cuisine, salle de bains

A. Les pièces de la maison. Trouvez les pièces d'après les définitions suivantes. 1. la pièce où il y a une table pour manger 2. la pièce où il y a un poste de télévision 3. la pièce où il y a un lavabo 4. la pièce où on prépare le dîner 5. un lieu de passage 6. la pièce où il y a un lit

B. Le Lavandou: appartements à vendre. Regardez la publicité et choisissez la réponse correcte.

1. La publicité montre une résidence *simple/luxueuse.*
2. La résidence est *loin/près* de la mer.
3. Il y a différentes tailles d'appartements. / Les appartements sont tous identiques.
4. A votre avis, quels sont les avantages de ces résidences? Les inconvénients?
5. Trouvez quelque chose (*something*) sur la photo qui n'est pas mentionné dans le texte.

Commentaire culturel

Family life in France. The French family is a strong social unit. In general, divorce is less common than in the United States, although the rate is rising. Extended families, in which grandparents and other family members live near one another and see each other frequently, are slightly more common. For all these reasons, the family has a strong influence on an individual's life. It has been said that in France you may love your family or hate it, you may run away from it, but you cannot be indifferent to it.

The French government provides significant financial support for families. Both mother and father have the right to a substantial paid leave from work when a child is born. Families with more than two children receive governmental subsidies (**allocations familiales**). State-supported day-care centers (**crèches**) make it possible for parents to work outside the home. Children of unmarried parents receive the same protection and benefits as those of married parents; in fact, there are few financial disadvantages in France to living together outside of marriage (**l'union libre**). Nevertheless, most French people continue to marry.

C. **Conversation.** Posez les questions suivantes à des camarades.

1. Dans quelle pièce aimes-tu étudier? dîner? écouter des disques? 2. Dans quelle pièce est-ce que tu regardes la télévision? 3. As-tu une terrasse? un balcon? un couloir? un jardin? des arbres dans le jardin? 4. Où aimes-tu lire (*read*) un livre ou une revue? 5. Où joues-tu aux cartes? d'un instrument de musique? 6. Où es-tu à minuit? 7. Où préfères-tu être quand il fait du soleil? 8. Quelle pièce préfères-tu à toutes les autres? Pourquoi? (Je préfère...)

Étude de grammaire

13. Expressing Possession: *mon, ton,* etc.

La maison, reflet d'une personnalité

Complétez les phrases selon les images.

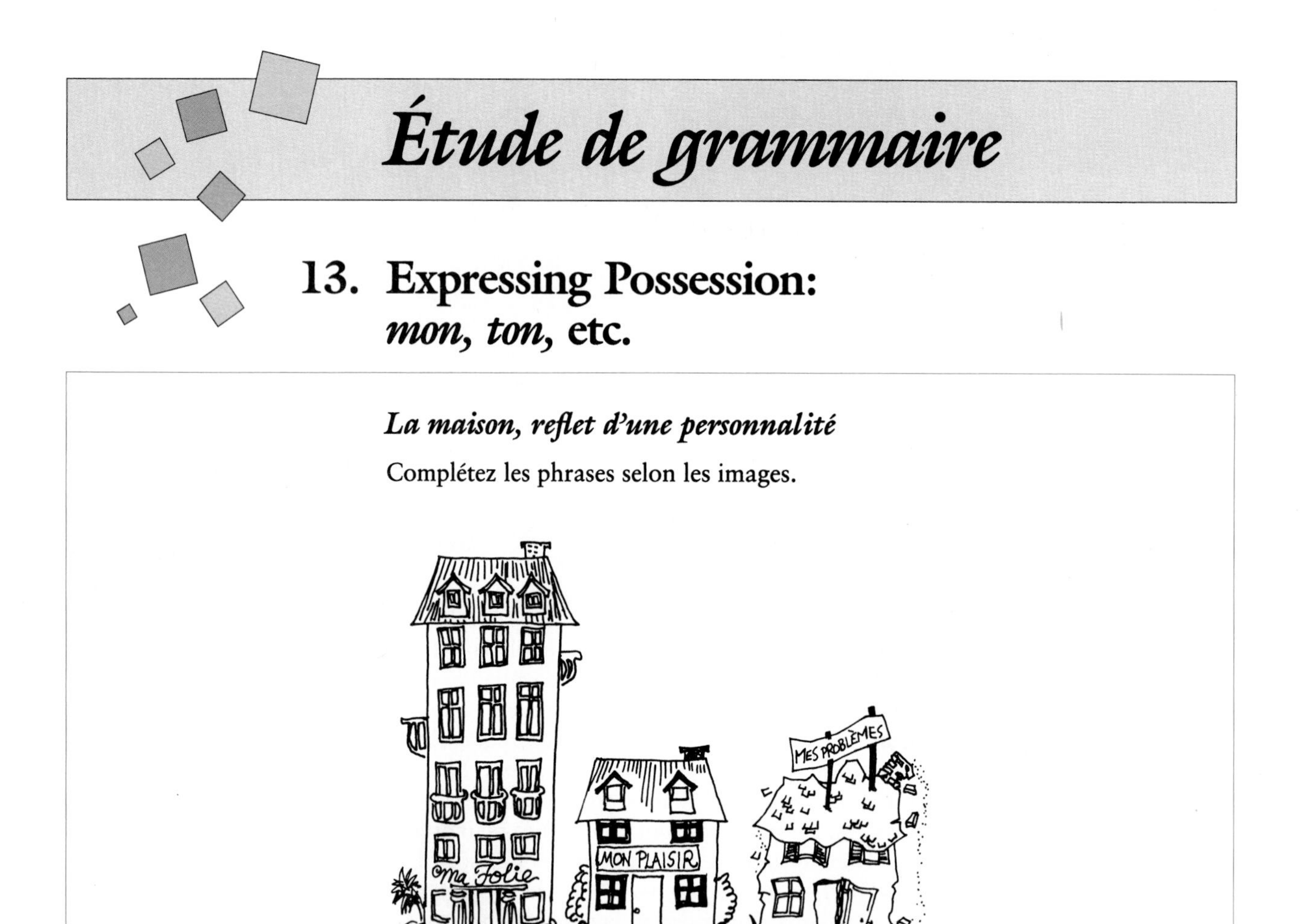

1. La maison à l'air excentrique et riche s'appelle ______.
2. La maison à l'air agréable s'appelle ______.
3. La maison à l'air désordonné s'appelle ______.

One way to indicate possession in French is to use the preposition **de: la maison *de* Claudine.** Another way to show possession is to use possessive adjectives. In French, possessive adjectives agree in gender and number with the nouns they modify.

	SINGULAR		PLURAL
	Masculine	*Feminine*	*Masculine and Feminine*
my your (**tu**) his, her, its, one's	**mon** père **ton** père **son** père	**ma** mère **ta** mère **sa** mère	**mes** parents **tes** parents **ses** parents
our your (**vous**) their	**notre** père **votre** père **leur** père	**notre** mère **votre** mère **leur** mère	**nos** parents **vos** parents **leurs** parents

Mon frère et **ma sœur** aiment le sport. — *My brother and my sister like sports.*
Voilà **notre maison.** — *There's our house.*
Habitez-vous avec **votre sœur** et **vos parents**? — *Do you live with your sister and your parents?*
Ils skient avec **leurs cousins** et **leur oncle.** — *They're skiing with their cousins and their uncle.*

The forms **mon, ton,** and **son** are also used before feminine nouns that begin with a vowel or mute **h**:

affiche (*f.*) → **mon affiche**
amie (*f.*) → **ton amie**
histoire (*f.*) → **son histoire**

Pay particular attention to the use of **sa, son, ses** (*his, her*). While English has two possessives, corresponding to the sex of the possessor (*his, her*), French has three, corresponding to the gender and number of the noun possessed (**sa, son, ses**).

Il / Elle } aime **sa** maison. — *He likes his house. She likes her house.*
Il / Elle } aime **son** chien. — *He likes his dog. She likes her dog.*
Il / Elle } aime **ses** livres. — *He likes his books. She likes her books.*

MAINTENANT A VOUS

A. A qui est-ce? Complétez les dialogues suivants avec des adjectifs possessifs: **mon, ma, mes, ton, ta, tes, son, sa, ses, notre, nos, votre, vos, leur, leurs.** Utilisez chaque adjectif seulement une fois (*only once*). Étudiez bien le contexte avant de choisir l'adjectif.

1. —Paul et Florence adorent les animaux.
   —Oui, ils ont un chien et deux chats (*cats*): ______ chien s'appelle Marius et ______ chats Minou et Félix.
2. —Oh, il pleut (*is raining*)! Est-ce que vous avez ______ imperméable?
   —Non, mais j'ai ______ parapluie (*m.*) et ______ bottes.
3. —Tiens, voilà Pierre. Avec qui est-il?
   —Il est avec ______ parents et ______ amie Laure.
   —Et ______ sœur n'est pas là?
   —Non, elle est en vacances au Maroc.
4. —Salut, Alain!
   —Salut, Pierre. Dis, la jolie fille aux cheveux blonds, c'est ______ cousine belge?
   —Oui. Viens (*Come*). Alain, je te présente ______ cousine Sylvie.
   —Enchanté, Mademoiselle.
5. —Pardon, vous êtes Monsieur et Madame Legrand, n'est-ce pas?
   —Oui.
   —Je suis Monsieur Smith, le professeur d'anglais de ______ enfants.
   —Oh, mais ce ne sont pas ______ enfants, ce sont les fils de mon frère Henri. Voici ______ fils.
6. —Tu as de la chance, tu as une famille super! ______ parents sont très sympa! Est-ce que ______ grand-père habite avec vous?
   —Non, mais il est souvent à la maison.

B. La curiosité. Répondez aux questions suivantes.

MODÈLE: Est-ce que c'est la lampe de Georges? (oui) → Oui, c'est sa lampe.

1. Est-ce que c'est la chambre de Pierre? (oui)
2. Est-ce que c'est la commode d'Yvonne? (non)
3. Est-ce que ce sont les affiches de Jean? (non)
4. Est-ce que c'est le piano de Pierre et de Sophie? (oui)
5. Est-ce que ce sont les meubles (*furniture*) d'Annick? (non)
6. Est-ce que ce sont les bureaux des professeurs? (oui)

C. Casse-tête familial. (*Family puzzle.*) Posez rapidement les questions suivantes à un(e) camarade.

MODÈLE: Qui est le fils de ton oncle? → C'est mon cousin.

1. Qui est la mère de ton père?
2. Qui est la fille de ta tante?
3. Qui est la femme de ton oncle?
4. Qui est le père de ton père?
5. Qui est le frère de ta mère?
6. Qui est la sœur de ta mère?

Mots-clés

Saying how you feel about something: Often in conversation, you just want to express your personal reaction to something. Here are some useful phrases.

Comment tu trouves la nouvelle maison de mon oncle?	*What do you think of my uncle's new house?*
Elle est **formidable**!	*It's great!*
Franchement, elle est **affreuse**!	*Frankly, it's awful!*
Elle est **bien.**	*It's nice.*
Elle n'est **pas mal,** mais je préfère les maisons de style rustique.	*It's not bad, but I prefer rustic houses.*

D. Interview. Posez les questions suivantes à un(e) camarade de classe.

1. Y a-t-il un membre de ta famille (un cousin, une cousine, un neveu, etc.) que tu admires particulièrement? Pourquoi?
2. Comment s'appelle-t-il/elle?
3. Où habite-t-il/elle? Avec qui? Comment est sa maison?
4. Quel est son sport préféré? Sa musique favorite?
5. Quel genre de films aime-t-il/elle?

Maintenant faites le portrait du parent proche préféré de votre camarade.

E. Sondage *Madame Figaro:* Le bonheur (*happiness*) dans le monde; les Européens plutôt heureux. Regardez le tableau, couvrez les résultats et donnez votre opinion. Classez les différents critères du tableau de 1 = le plus (*the most*) à 10 = le moins (*the least*).

Sur le plan du bonheur, quel domaine vous semble le plus important ?

CRITÈRES \ PAYS	FRANCE	BELGIQUE	R.F.A.	ITALIE	ESPAGNE	G.B.	ETATS-UNIS	JAPON
ÉDUCATION ENFANTS	**8,4**	**8,2**	7,8	**8,4**	**8,3**	**7,4**	**7,1**	6,5
SANTÉ	8,1	8,1	**8,4**	8,2	7,9	7,3	7,0	**8,1**
VIE DE FAMILLE	8,0	7,8	7,8	8,0	7,9	7,3	7,1	7,6
QUALITÉ DE VIE	7,0	6,5	6,4	6,0	6,2	6,8	6,8	6,3
JOB	6,8	6,8	6,8	6,8	6,8	6,0	5,9	7,6
VIE AMOUREUSE	6,5	6,7	5,7	7,5	7,1	6,3	6,1	5,7
AMIS	6,2	6,0	5,6	5,8	7,1	6,2	6,5	6,6
NIVEAU DE VIE	6,1	5,7	6,1	5,6	5,4	5,9	5,9	5,8
LOISIRS	5,5	5,7	5,0	5,8	5,7	4,7	5,3	5,2
POLITIQUE	3,8	3,3	5,0	3,2	3,9	4,1	4,5	5,1

N.B. : les notes sont données sur 10.

Selon vous

Le domaine le plus important, c'est ______.
Le domaine le moins important, c'est ______.
Le domaine qui donne le plus de satisfaction, c'est ______.
Le domaine qui donne le moins de satisfaction, c'est ______.

Maintenant regardez les résultats du sondage par catégorie et par pays (= *nation*). Choisissez la réponse correcte.

1. Les Français pensent que le plus (*the most*) important, c'est *la santé / l'éducation des enfants / la vie de famille.*
2. Les Japonais pensent que le plus important, c'est *l'éducation des enfants / la vie de famille / la santé.*
3. Les Américains pensent que *le job / la vie amoureuse / la vie de famille* donne le plus de satisfaction.
4. Les Espagnols pensent que *la vie de famille / l'éducation des enfants / la qualité de la vie* donne le plus de satisfaction.

Comparez vos réponses avec les résultats du sondage et les réponses de vos camarades. Justifiez vos idées.

Le jardinage est un des passe-temps favoris des Français.

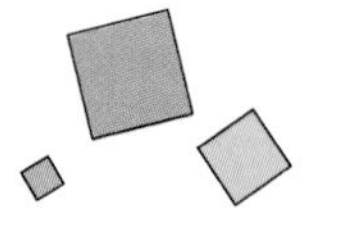

14. Talking About Your Plans and Destinations: The Verb *aller*

Un père exemplaire

SIMON: On joue au tennis cet après-midi?
STÉPHANE: Non, je **vais** au jardin zoologique avec Céline.
SIMON: Alors, demain?
STÉPHANE: Désolé, mais demain je **vais** emmener Sébastien chez le dentiste.
SIMON: Quel père exemplaire!

Vrai ou faux? Corrigez les phrases fausses.

1. Stéphane est le grand-père de Céline et Sébastien.
2. Stéphane va aller au zoo avec Céline.
3. Simon va jouer au tennis avec Stéphane.

A. Forms of *aller* (to go)

The verb **aller** is irregular in form.

PRESENT TENSE OF **aller**			
je	**vais**	nous	**allons**
tu	**vas**	vous	**allez**
il, elle, on	**va**	ils, elles	**vont**

Allez-vous à Grenoble pour vos vacances? — *Are you going to Grenoble for your vacation?*
Comment **va-t-on** à Grenoble? — *How do you go to (get to) Grenoble?*

You have already used **aller** in several expressions.

Comment **allez-vous**? — *How are you?*
Salut, ça **va**? — *Hi, how's it going?*
Ça **va** bien. — *Fine. (Things are going fine.)*

B. *Aller* + Infinitive: Near Future*

In French, **aller** + *infinitive* is used to express a future event, usually something that is going to happen soon, in the near future. English also uses *to go* + *infinitive* to express actions or events that are going to happen soon.

Nous **allons téléphoner** à mon oncle. — *We're going to call my uncle.*
Il **va louer** un appartement. — *He's going to rent an apartment.*

To ask a question or to make a sentence negative, treat the verb **aller** as the main verb in the sentence. The infinitive does not change.

Allez-vous **visiter** la France cet été? — *Are you going to visit France this summer?*
Non, nous n'**allons** pas **voyager.** — *No, we are not going to travel.*
Je **vais** peut-être **visiter** Miami. — *Maybe I'm going to visit Miami.*

MAINTENANT A VOUS

A. Où va-t-on? La solution est simple!

MODÈLE: J'ai envie de regarder un film. → Alors, je vais au cinéma!

*Le futur proche

1. Nous avons faim.
2. Il a envie de parler français.
3. Elles ont besoin d'étudier.
4. J'ai soif.
5. Tu as sommeil.
6. Vous avez envie de regarder la télévision.
7. Nous sommes malades (*sick*).
8. Elle a envie de jouer au tennis.

à l'hôpital, dans la salle de séjour, à la bibliothèque, dans la cuisine, aux courts de tennis, à Paris, au café, dans la salle à manger, dans la chambre

Mots-clés

Saying when you are going to do something:

tout de suite	*immediately*
bientôt	*soon*
demain	*tomorrow*
la semaine prochaine	*next week*
dans quatre jours	*in four days*
ce week-end	*this weekend*
ce soir/matin	*this evening/morning*
cet après-midi	*this afternoon*

B. Des projets pour demain (*tomorrow*).

MODÈLE: tu / regarder / programme préféré →
Tu vas regarder ton programme préféré.

1. je / finir / travail
2. nous / écouter / disques de jazz
3. vous / jouer / guitare
4. Frédéric / trouver / livre de français
5. je / choisir / film préféré
6. les garçons / aller au cinéma / en voiture
7. tu / aller / concert / avec / amis

C. Samedi après-midi. Qu'est-ce que ces gens vont faire? Regardez les dessins et devinez leur intention.

MODÈLE: Monique a sa raquette parce qu'elle (*because she*) **va jouer au tennis.**

D. Quels sont vos projets pour le week-end? Interviewez un(e) camarade de classe. Racontez à la classe les projets de votre camarade. Est-ce que vous faites (*are doing*) les mêmes choses ce week-end? **Suggestions:** rester (*stay*) à la maison, écouter la radio (des disques), préparer un dîner (des leçons), regarder un film (la télévision), travailler à la bibliothèque (dans le jardin), aller dans un restaurant extraordinaire, parler avec des amis, finir un livre intéressant...

MODÈLE: aller au cinéma →

VOUS: Vas-tu aller au cinéma?
UN(E) CAMARADE: Oui, je vais aller au cinéma.
(*ou*) Non, je ne vais pas aller au cinéma.

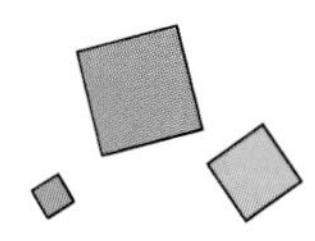

15. Expressing What You Are Doing or Making: The Verb *faire*

Une question d'organisation

SANDRINE: Vous mangez à la cafétéria, ta camarade de chambre et toi?
MARION: Non, Candice et moi, nous sommes très organisées. Elle, elle **fait** les courses et moi, je **fais** la cuisine.
SANDRINE: Et qui **fait** la vaisselle?
MARION: Le lave-vaisselle, bien sûr!

Répondez d'après le dialogue.

1. Qui fait la cuisine?
2. Qui fait la vaisselle?
3. Qui fait les courses?

Et chez vous, en général, qui fait la cuisine? Qui fait la vaisselle? Qui fait les courses?

A. Forms of *faire* (to do, to make)

The verb **faire** is irregular in form.

PRESENT TENSE OF **faire**			
je	**fais**	nous	**faisons**
tu	**fais**	vous	**faites**
il, elle, on	**fait**	ils, elles	**font**

Note the difference in the pronunciation of **fais/fait** [fɛ], **faites** [fɛt], and **faisons** [fəzɔ̃].

Je fais mon lit. — *I make the bed.*
Nous faisons le café. — *We're making coffee.*

B. Expressions with *faire*

The verb **faire** is used in many idiomatic expressions.

faire la connaissance (de)	*to meet (for the first time), make the acquaintance (of)*
faire les courses	*to do errands*
faire la cuisine	*to cook*
faire ses devoirs	*to do (one's) homework*
faire la lessive	*to do the laundry*
faire le marché	*to do the shopping, to go to the market*
faire le ménage	*to do the housework*
faire une promenade	*to take a walk*
faire la vaisselle	*to do the dishes*
faire un voyage	*to take a trip*

Le matin **je fais le marché**, l'après-midi **je fais une promenade** et le soir **je fais la cuisine.** — *In the morning I go to the market, in the afternoon I take a walk, and in the evening I cook.*

Faire is also used to talk about sports: **faire du sport, faire du jogging, de la voile** (*sailing*), **du ski, de l'aérobic...**

MAINTENANT A VOUS

A. Activités du week-end. Qui fait les activités suivantes? Faites des phrases logiques avec les éléments des deux colonnes.

1. Tu...
2. Pierre...
3. Anne et Monique...
4. Mon frère et moi, nous...
5. Benoît et toi, vous...
6. Non, moi le dimanche, je...

a. faisons du jogging dans le parc.
b. ne fais pas le ménage.
c. faites vos devoirs de français.
d. fais la cuisine pour mes amis.
e. font des courses en ville.
f. fait du sport avec ses copains.

B. La solution est simple! Utilisez dans vos phrases une expression avec **faire.**

MODÈLE: J'ai envie de visiter la France. →
Alors, je fais un voyage.

1. J'invite des amis à dîner.
2. J'ai besoin d'exercice.
3. J'ai envie de visiter la Tunisie.
4. J'ai beaucoup de travail pour mon cours de littérature.
5. J'ai envie d'aller au parc.
6. Mon réfrigérateur est vide (*empty*).
7. Ma maison est en désordre.
8. J'ai besoin d'aller à la banque et à la pharmacie.

C. Qu'est-ce qu'ils font? Faites des phrases complètes. Utilisez des expressions avec **faire.**

1. M. Dupont et son chien...
2. M. Henri... de Mlle Gervais.
3. Vous, vous...

4. Mlle Duval... 5. Ma sœur et moi...

6. Et moi maintenant, je...

D. Conversation: Chez vos parents (*At your parents' house*) qui fait quoi? Quand est-ce qu'on le fait?

1. Qui fait le ménage? 2. Qui fait les courses? 3. Qui fait la cuisine? 4. Qui fait la vaisselle? 5. Qui fait le marché?

Mots-clés

Saying how often you usually do things:

tous les jours	*every day*
une fois par semaine (deux/trois fois, etc.)	*once a week* (*twice/three times, etc.*)
le lundi/le vendredi soir	*on Mondays/on Friday evenings*
le week-end	*on weekends*
pendant les vacances	*during vacation*

E. Vive le week-end! Qu'est-ce que vous faites le week-end? Complétez les phrases suivantes.

1. Je fais toujours (*always*) _______.
2. J'aime faire _______.
3. Je suis obligé(e) de faire _______.
4. Je déteste faire _______.
5. J'adore faire _______.

Sondage. Maintenant comparez vos réponses avec celles (*those*) de vos camarades. Faites une liste de toutes les activités mentionnées. Ensuite, rangez-les selon leur popularité.

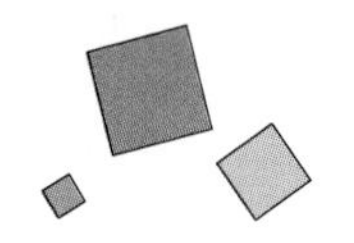

16. Expressing Actions: *-re* Verbs

Beauregard au restaurant

JILL: Vous **entendez**?
GÉRARD: Non, qu'est-ce qu'il y a?
JILL: **J'entends** un bruit sous la table.
GENEVIÈVE: Oh ça! C'est Beauregard... Il **attend** le poulet... et il n'aime pas **attendre**...

Trouvez la phrase équivalente dans le dialogue.

1. Écoutez.
2. Quel est le problème?
3. Il n'aime pas patienter (*wait patiently*).

A third group of French verbs has infinitives that end in **-re,** like **vendre** (*to sell*).

PRESENT TENSE OF **vendre**			
je	vends	nous	vend**ons**
tu	vends	vous	vend**ez**
il, elle, on	vend	ils, elles	vend**ent**

Other verbs conjugated like **vendre** include the following.

attendre	*to wait (for)*
descendre	*to go down (to), to get off*
entendre	*to hear*
perdre	*to lose, to waste*
rendre	*to give back, to return*
rendre visite à	*to visit (someone)*
répondre à	*to answer*

Elle attend le dessert.	*She's waiting for dessert.*
Nous descendons de l'autobus.	*We're getting off the bus.*
Le commerçant rend la monnaie à la cliente.	*The storekeeper gives change back to the customer.*
Je réponds à sa question.	*I'm answering his question.*

In French, the expression **rendre visite à** means to visit a *person or persons.*

Je rends visite à mon ami.

The verb **visiter** is used only with places or things.

> **Les touristes visitent** les monuments de Paris.

MAINTENANT A VOUS

A. Une visite chez oncle Eugène. Qu'est-ce qu'ils font? Faites des phrases complètes avec les éléments donnés.

1. ma sœur / répondre à / téléphone
2. tu / perdre / clés / voiture
3. nous / attendre / dans / voiture
4. mes parents / descendre de / voiture
5. je / entendre / voix (*f.*) (*voice*) / oncle Eugène
6. nous / rendre / visite à / oncle Eugène

Bruxelles
Paris

B. Un week-end à Paris. Complétez l'histoire avec les verbes de la colonne de droite.

Alain et Marie-Lise habitent à Bruxelles. Aujourd'hui ils _______[1] à Paris en train. Ils vont _______[2] visite à leur cousine Pauline. Tous les trois ont toujours beaucoup de projets et ne _______[3] pas une minute quand ils sont ensemble (*together*). Alain et Marie-Lise aiment beaucoup Pauline parce qu'elle _______[4] toujours à leurs lettres. Pauline aussi aime bien ses cousins, et elle _______[5] leur arrivée avec impatience. Elle _______[6] enfin la sonnette (*doorbell*), les voilà!

perdre
rendre
descendre
entendre
attendre
répondre

D'après l'histoire,...

1. Alain et Marie-Lise habitent en *France* / *Suisse* / *Belgique*.
2. Alain, Marie-Lise et Pauline sont *calmes* / *actifs* / *individualistes*.
3. Pauline *déteste* / *aime* écrire des lettres.

C. Perdez-vous souvent patience? Utilisez les questions suivantes pour interviewer un(e) camarade de classe. Il/Elle utilise **souvent, pas souvent** ou **toujours** dans sa réponse. Décidez d'après ses réponses s'il (si elle) est **très patient**(e), **patient**(e), **normal**(e), **impatient**(e), **très impatient**(e).

MODÈLE: VOUS: Tu attends l'autobus. Il n'arrive pas. Est-ce que tu perds patience?
UN(E) CAMARADE: Oui, je perds souvent patience.

1. Tu attends un coup de téléphone. La personne ne téléphone pas. 2. Un(e) ami(e) ne répond pas à tes lettres. 3. Tu perds les clefs de ta voiture ou de ton appartement. 4. Tu es malade. Tu attends le médecin longtemps. Il n'arrive pas. 5. ?

Étude de prononciation

Semivowels and Consonants

Semivowels. The sounds [ɥ], [w], and [j] are called semivowels. They are spelled with the letter groups indicated in the following examples and are pronounced in a single syllable, with no diphthong.

Prononcez avec le professeur.

1. [ɥ] huit fruit cuisine
2. [w] moi moins oui quoi revoir fois
3. [j] bien Marseille science voyage famille

English Plosives. Many French consonant sounds resemble those of English. However, unlike in English, in French the sounds [p], [t], and [k] are not plosives; there is no escape of air from between the lips and teeth.

Prononcez avec le professeur.

1. [p] page pic pâté Patrice
2. [t] table thé Timothé très
3. [k] cours car exact kiosque

French [r] and [l]. The English **r** is formed with the tongue; the French **r** is guttural, produced in the throat, with the tongue in the bottom of the mouth. The French **l** is pronounced in the front of the mouth, with the tongue pressed against the top of the back of the upper teeth.

Prononcez avec le professeur.

1. [r] sports rose arrive soir février
2. [l] livre mademoiselle calme bleu avril

Final Consonants. You have noticed that final consonants are generally silent in French. There are, however, a number of exceptions. The final consonant *is* pronounced, for example, in many words that end in the letters **c, r, f,** and **l: le lac, le soir, le chef, l'hôtel.** This rule itself has numerous exceptions: **le tabac, le dîner, la clef** (*key*), and **gentil** all end in a silent consonant. Learn the pronunciation of final consonants by example or by referring to a dictionary.

Invitation

Contexte *Jennifer et son ami Yannick étudient le marketing à l'université de Montpellier. Yannick et sa famille invitent souvent Jennifer pour le week-end.*

Objectif *Jennifer accepte une invitation.*

YANNICK: Jennifer, tu es libre° dimanche? — *free*

JENNIFER: Oui, pourquoi?

YANNICK: Eh bien, nous allons pique-niquer en famille. Tu veux venir avec nous?

JENNIFER: Oh, oui, avec plaisir! Qu'est-ce que je peux apporter°? — *to bring*

YANNICK: Je ne sais pas, des fruits ou du chocolat... Ah, et n'oublie° pas ton frisbee! — *forget*

JENNIFER: Oui, d'accord. Ça va être sympa!

VARIATIONS

Improvisez! Vous invitez un étudiant français (une étudiante française) à un barbecue avec votre famille. Jouez le dialogue avec un(e) camarade de classe.

A propos

Comment inviter des amis

Tu es libre?/Vous êtes libres?
Viens donc/Venez donc (*Come then*)...
Tu as/Vous avez envie de (d')... ?

} visiter la Faculté
écouter un concert
discuter au café avec nous
jouer au tennis
faire une promenade
voir (*to see*) un film
écouter une conférence (*lecture*)

Comment accepter

Oui, je suis libre.
Quelle bonne idée! (*Good idea!*)
D'accord.
Avec plaisir.
Ça va être sympa(thique)!

Comment refuser poliment

C'est gentil, mais...
C'est dommage (*too bad*), mais...
Désolé(e), mais...

{ je ne suis pas libre
je suis pris(e) (*engaged*)
je ne peux pas (*I can't*)
je suis occupé(e) (*busy*)

A. Où habitent les personnes suivantes? Expliquez leurs préférences.

Superman	la Maison-Blanche
Tarzan et Jane	la jungle
Robinson Crusoë	une île déserte
Louis XIV	une très petite maison dans l'Illinois
le président des États-Unis	l'île du Diable
Abraham Lincoln	Monticello
Papillon	un jardin merveilleux
Thomas Jefferson	le château de Versailles
Adam et Eve	(sur) la planète Crypton

Parmi les endroits indiqués, lequel préférez-vous? Pourquoi?

B. **Qu'est-ce que c'est qu'une maison?** A-t-elle toujours quatre murs? Est-elle toujours bien meublée (*furnished*)? A votre avis, qu'est-ce qu'une maison? Complétez la phrase suivante avec des mots qui décrivent une maison.

La maison est un endroit où ____________________.

C. **Jeu de rôles.** Utilisez les expressions de l'*A propos* pour inviter un(e) camarade de classe à sortir (*to go out*). Parfois il/elle accepte l'invitation, parfois il/elle refuse l'invitation. Regardez les différentes possibilités ci-dessous et invitez votre camarade. Expliquez-lui chaque fois votre choix.

Maintenant dites où vous préférez aller et pourquoi.

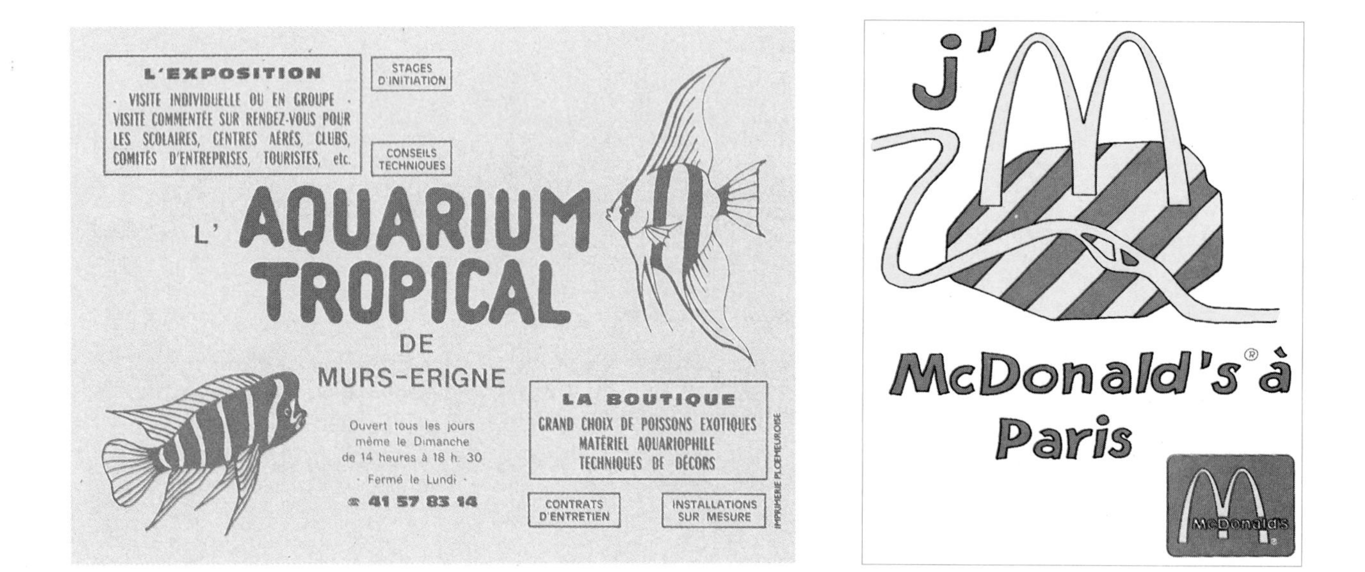

CONCERT de musique de chambre

Jean-Michel PENOT, *Hautbois*
Horia FULEA, *violon*
Jean-Michel VERNIER, *alto*
Jean-Philippe AUDIN, *cello*

HAYDN - MOZART

DIMANCHE 26 JUILLET à 18 h 30
ABBAYE ROYALE DE FONTEVRAUD

PSYCHOLOGIE Espace Mimont
5, rue Mimont

MAI *Jeudi 7* *14 h 30*

*** TOUR DE FAMILLE**
J. ROYER, Psychologue

- Qu'est-ce que des grands-parents ?

Commentaire culturel

French cities. Because most French cities began to grow during the Middle Ages, nearly every street and corner in any city center bears traces of that medieval origin. A church or cathedral dominates the old town center (**le centre-ville**); narrow cobblestoned streets are still lined with buildings six to eight centuries old. Their interiors are now renovated, and they often house small businesses and comfortable apartments. The narrow streets are sometimes closed to cars, to form pedestrian zones.

Unlike most Americans, who have abandoned the city center for suburban life, the French continue to live, work, and shop in the city. Many French families own apartments in the more modern buildings, dating from the nineteenth and early twentieth centuries, that surround the city center. Public transportation is good, and city dwellers tend to use their cars largely to leave town on weekends and holidays. Neighborhoods are self-sufficient; small businesses such as grocery stores, bakeries, dry cleaners, and bookstores can all be found within walking distance.

Modern French cities are surrounded by suburbs (*la banlieue*), which grew up after World War II. Some contain subsidized housing projects, called **HLM** (*Habitations à loyer modéré*), built in response to the postwar housing shortage. Sometimes poorly constructed, **les HLM** are isolated from business and commercial centers. There are also suburban neighborhoods with single-family houses, yards, and local shopping streets.

Commuter trains and buses link the suburbs to the city center. Despite a good system of public transportation, however, French cities are plagued with the same traffic problems as those in other industrialized countries.

Une rue commerçante à St-Malo, en Bretagne

Un quartier moderne à Grenoble

Mise au point

A. Les projets de Martine et de Claudine. Formez des phrases complètes.

1. Martine et Claudine / aller / finir / études
2. elles / aller / faire / voyage / en France
3. elles / travailler / maintenant / pour payer (*to pay for*) / voyage
4. Martine / faire / ménage / pour / tante
5. elles / aller / rendre visite à / tante de Martine / à Paris
6. tante / habiter / près de / Quartier latin
7. elles / aller / être / content / parce que / elles / aller / faire / voyage magnifique

D'après l'histoire, choisissez la réponse la plus logique.

1. Martine et Claudine ont *50 ans / 35 ans / 20 ans.*
2. La tante de Martine parle *allemand / français / latin.*
3. Pour payer le voyage, Martine travaille comme *secrétaire / femme de ménage / vendeuse.*

B. Activités. Qu'est-ce qu'ils font et qu'est-ce qu'ils vont faire? Expliquez.

MODÈLE: le frère de Robert et de Marie-France →
Maintenant, leur frère fait ses devoirs. Après, il va aller au cinéma.

1. les parents de Robert et de Marie-France

2. le père de Robert et de Marie-France

3. l'oncle de Robert et de Marie-France

Vocabulaire

Verbes

accepter to accept
aller to go
aller + *inf.* to be going (to do something)
aller mal to feel bad (ill)
attendre to wait for
changer de to change
descendre à to go down (south) to
descendre de to get down (from), get off
entendre to hear
faire to do; to make
inviter to invite
perdre to lose
préparer to prepare
rendre to give back; to return; to hand in
rendre visite à to visit (*someone*)
répondre à to answer
rester to stay, remain
vendre to sell

Substantifs

l'appartement (*m.*) apartment
l'arbre (*m.*) tree
l'autobus (*m.*) (city) bus
le coup de téléphone telephone call
la famille family
le jardin garden
la lettre letter
le meuble piece of furniture
la pièce room
le plaisir pleasure
le poste de télévision TV set
les projets (*m.*) plans
le temps time
la terrasse terrace
les vacances (*f.*) vacation

Adjectifs

affreux (**-euse**) awful
bien good (*fam.*)
formidable great
libre free (*to do something*)
malade sick
préféré(e) favorite, preferred

Les parents

le cousin cousin (*male*)
la cousine cousin (*female*)
l'enfant (*m., f.*) child
la femme wife; woman
la fille daughter; girl
le fils son
le frère brother
la grand-mère grandmother
le grand-père grandfather
les grands-parents (*m.*) grandparents
le mari husband
la mère mother
le neveu nephew
la nièce niece
l'oncle (*m.*) uncle
les parents (*m.*) parents; relatives
le père father
la petite-fille granddaughter
le petit-fils grandson
la sœur sister
la tante aunt

Les pièces

le couloir hall
la cuisine kitchen
la salle à manger dining room
la salle de bains bathroom
la salle de séjour living room

Expressions avec faire

faire la connaissance de to meet (*for the first time*), make the acquaintance of
faire les courses to do errands
faire la cuisine to cook
faire ses devoirs to do homework
faire le marché to do the shopping, go to the market
faire le ménage to do the housework
faire une promenade to take a walk
faire la vaisselle to do the dishes
faire un voyage to take a trip

Mots divers

alors then, in that case
après after, afterward
chez at the home of
loin de far from
mal badly
peut-être maybe

Expressions utiles

bientôt	*soon*
cet **après-midi** / ce **matin** / ce **soir**	*this afternoon / morning / evening*
demain	*tomorrow*
la semaine prochaine	*next week*
pendant les vacances (*f.*)	*during vacation*
une fois par semaine	*one time (once) per week*
tous les jours	*every day*
tout de suite	*immediately*

INTERMÈDE 4

Lecture

AVANT DE LIRE

Topic sentences: Notice that a sentence has been underlined in each of the first two paragraphs of this passage. These are the topic sentences of the paragraphs. A topic sentence is one that expresses the general idea or the main point of a paragraph. The other sentences elaborate or illustrate what is expressed in the topic sentence. It is usually the first sentence of a paragraph, but not always. After reading the passage, return to the second paragraph and consider why the first sentence would not be identified as the topic sentence. How would you describe its function in that paragraph?

La télévision, une affaire de famille

<u>En France, la télévision est essentiellement un phénomène familial.</u> La majorité des familles françaises accorde° une place d'honneur au téléviseur,° dans la salle de séjour ou dans la cuisine. On organise les meubles autour de lui.° On organise la soirée et les loisirs° aussi autour de lui. Il occupe une place importante dans la famille. Mais est-ce un allié ou un ennemi?

En France les enfants de 10 à 12 ans consomment en moyenne 21 heures de télévision par semaine et les téléspectateurs adultes approximativement 18 heures. Il est possible de parler de lavage de cerveau.° Les parents ont du mal à contrôler l'irruption° des programmes dans la vie familiale. La télé est la rivale du jeu,° de la lecture et de la conversation. On regarde le téléviseur et on cesse de parler. <u>La télévision remplace des activitiés familiales possibles, elle isole chaque membre de la famille dans son monde privé.</u>

Mais à la réflexion, la télé donne aussi un rôle prépondérant à l'institution familiale. Elle rassemble les membres de la famille pour un temps défini, dans un espace défini. C'est une habitude sécurisante.° C'est une occupation commune qui oblige à inventer des règles.° Les enfants organisent leur temps pour finir leurs devoirs avant° leur programme favori. Parents, frères et sœurs négocient le choix du programme de la soirée. La télé crée des rapports° complexes entre les membres de la famille.

Dans l'opinion de beaucoup de spécialistes, sociologues et professeurs, la télévision est un média très bien adapté à l'univers domestique. Elle renforce l'intimité de la famille. Mais certains° pensent qu'elle renforce aussi la coupure° qui existe entre la vie privée et la vie publique de la famille.

donne / poste de télévision
le téléviseur
leisure activities
lavage... *brainwashing*
l'invasion
par exemple, on **joue** aux cartes
habitude... *reassuring habit*
rules
before
relationships
some (people)
la séparation

COMPRÉHENSION

1. Trouvez la «phrase-clé» (*key*) du paragraphe 3.
2. Quels sont les aspects négatifs de la télé? Et les aspects positifs?
3. Est-il possible d'identifier l'attitude de l'auteur (*author*) envers (*toward*) la télévision? Pourquoi? Y a-t-il une phrase qui représente bien l'attitude de l'auteur?

Par écrit

Le samedi chez vous. Expliquez à un correspondant français (une correspondante française) ce que vous faites chez vous le samedi. Ecrivez trois petits paragraphes. Utilisez les expressions suivantes comme guide (**matin** = *morning;* **après-midi** = afternoon; **soir** = evening).

Paragraphe 1: Le matin, je...
Paragraphe 2: L'après-midi, je...
Paragraphe 3: Le soir, je...

Expressions utiles: parler avec ma famille / mes amis, écouter la radio / des disques, danser, faire la vaisselle / le ménage / la cuisine / mes devoirs, répondre aux lettres, étudier, rêver de, regarder les livres, être au lit, regarder la télévision, parler des programmes de télévision.

CHAPITRE CINQ

Les Français à table

—Ce gâteau a l'air délicieux.
—Merci. Il est très facile à faire. Est-ce que tu veux la recette?

Étude de vocabulaire

Les repas de la journée*

Le matin: le petit déjeuner

A midi: le déjeuner

L'après-midi: le goûter†

Le soir: le dîner

---

*Use **la journée** (*the day*) instead of **le jour** when you wish to emphasize the notion of an entire day, or the whole day long, as in the expression "Quelle journée!" (*What a day!*).

†**Le goûter** is an occasional afternoon snack: **pain et chocolat pour les enfants; thé ou café et gâteaux pour les adultes.**

A. Catégories. Ajoutez (*Add*) d'autres aliments dans les catégories mentionnées.

MODÈLE: La mousse au chocolat est *un dessert.* →
Le gâteau, la tarte aux pommes et les fraises sont aussi des desserts.

1. La bière est *une boisson.*
2. La pomme de terre est *un légume.*
3. Le porc est *une viande.*
4. La banane est *un fruit.*

Maintenant, trouvez l'intrus et expliquez votre choix.

1. café / fraise / bière / thé / lait
2. haricots verts / salade / carotte / œuf* / pomme de terre
3. veau / porc / pain / jambon / poulet
4. sel / gâteau / poivre / sucre / beurre
5. vin / banane / pomme / orange / melon

B. Associations. Quels mots associez-vous avec... ?

1. une omelette 2. une salade de fruits 3. un régime (*diet*) 4. un bon repas 5. un sandwich 6. un pique-nique

C. Joyeux Noël! Regardez le dessin et complétez les phrases.

a. *candied chestnuts*

*Pronunciation: **un œuf** [ɛ̃nœf], **des œufs** [dezø].

1. Les ______ et le ______ sont sur la table.
2. M. Huet ouvre (*is opening*) une bouteille de ______.
3. Mme Huet apporte (*is bringing*) la ______.
4. Emilie regarde les ______.

Maintenant comparez le repas de Noël typique en France et aux États-Unis. Quels sont les plats communs? les plats différents? Et chez vous, est-ce que vous célébrez Noël? Quelle autre fête célébrez-vous? Mangez-vous un plat particulier? Décrivez les plats et les boissons que vous prenez.

D. Fiche gastronomique. Demandez à un(e) camarade de classe quelles sont ses préférences et complétez la fiche. Utilisez **quel/quelle** et le verbe **préférer.**

MODÈLE: —Quelle boisson préfères-tu?*
—Je préfère le/la...

boisson ______
viande ______
légume ______
fruit ______
dessert ______
repas ______
plat (*dish*) ______

Maintenant, avec vos camarades de classe, examinez les différentes fiches et déterminez quels sont les plats et les boissons préférés de la classe.

A table

A. L'objet nécessaire. Quels objets utilisez-vous?

MODÈLE: le café au lait →
J'utilise un bol (*wide cup*) pour le café au lait.

1. le vin
2. la viande
3. la soupe
4. la salade
5. le thé
6. la mousse au chocolat

***Préférer:** for **-er** verbs with spelling changes, see Appendix.

B. L'art de la table. Mettre le couvert (*setting the table*) est souvent un art. Regardez cet extrait du magazine *GaultMillau* sur l'Élysée (la «Maison-Blanche» française).

1. Décrivez ce qu'il y a sur la table. Est-ce une table pour un repas simple ou élégant? Quel est l'objet en papier à gauche (*on the left*)? Où sont la salière et la poivrière?
2. A votre avis, pourquoi y a-t-il quatre verres?
3. Et chez vous, qu'est-ce qu'on place sur la table au petit déjeuner? au déjeuner? au dîner? pour un repas spécial?

L'ÉLYSÉE

Reportage photos : YANN LAYMA

TABLE OUVERTE

L'Elysée n'est pas seulement la première table de France — grâce à Marcel Le Servot, en haut, qui fut le maître des cuisines jusqu'en 1984 —, elle est aussi la plus belle : chaque jour, le couvert, choisi parmi les dix mille pièces estampillées RF,[a] est placé dans les plus strictes règles de l'art.

a. République française

Quelle heure est-il?

Il est sept heures. Quel repas Vincent prend-il?

Il est dix heures et demie.* Où est Vincent?

Il est midi. Quel repas prend-il?

Il est deux heures et quart. Où est Vincent?

Il est quatre heures moins le quart. Où Vincent prend-il un café?

Il est huit heures vingt. Qui sert le dîner?

Il est minuit moins vingt. Est-ce que Vincent étudie toujours?

Il est minuit. Vincent dort.

- To ask the time

Excusez-moi, **quelle heure est-il,** s'il vous plaît?	*Excuse me, what time is it, please?*

- To ask at what time something happens

A quelle heure commence le film?	*At what time does the movie start?*
A deux heures et demie. (*ou*)	*At two thirty.*
Vers trois heures.	*Around three.*

- To tell the time

In French, the expression **Il est... heure**(s) is used to tell time on the hour. *Noon* is expressed by **midi,** *midnight* by **minuit.**

Il est une **heure.**	*It is one o'clock.*
Il est deux **heures.**	*It is two o'clock.*
Il est midi/minuit.	*It's noon/midnight.*

---

*To tell the time on the half hour, **et demie** is used after **heure**(s) and **et demi** is used after **midi** and **minuit.**

Il est trois heures **et demie.**	*It's 3:30* (*half past three*).
Il est midi **et demi.**	*It's 12:30* (*half past noon*).

Commentaire culturel

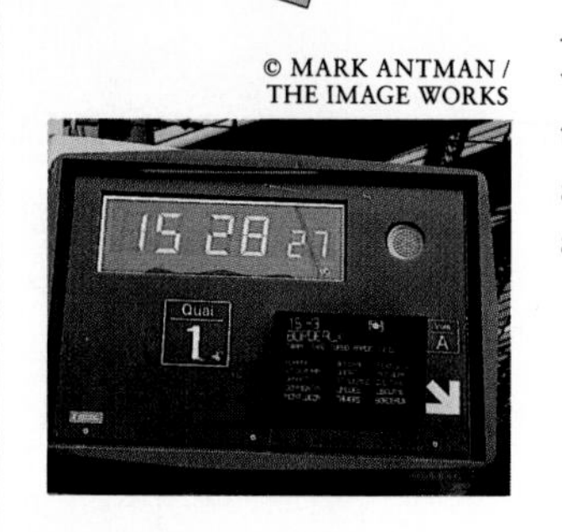

Quelle heure est-il?

A.M. versus P.M. In both English and French, the context often makes it clear whether a speaker is talking about A.M. or P.M. In French, **du matin** is used to specify A.M. To indicate P.M., **de l'après-midi** is used for *in the afternoon,* and **du soir** is used for *in the evening* or *at night* (before midnight). Generally, these expressions are used only to tell the time on the hour.

Il est neuf heures **du matin.**	*It's 9 A.M.*
Il est quatre heures **de l'après-midi.**	*It's 4 P.M.*
Il est onze heures **du soir.**	*It's 11 P.M.*

The twenty-four-hour clock is used in official announcements—such as on TV, on the radio, and in train or plane schedules—to avoid ambiguity. Sometimes it is also used to make appointments.

Il est quinze heures trente.	*It's 3:30 P.M.*
Il est vingt-deux heures quarante cinq.	*It's 10:45 P.M.*

MAINTENANT A VOUS

A. Quelle heure est-il?

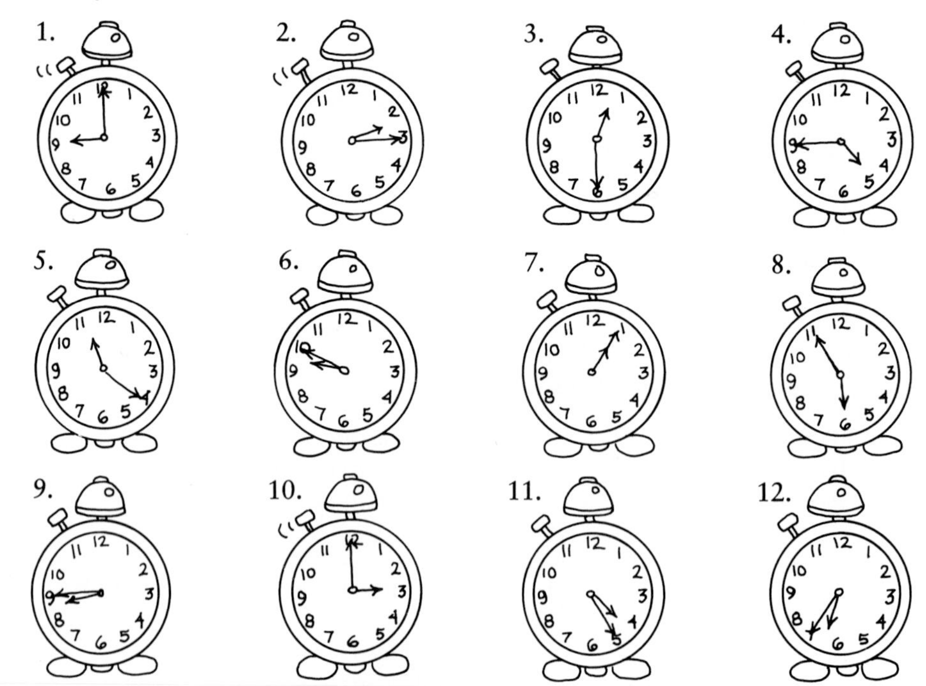

B. Quelle heure est-il pour vous? Qu'est-ce que vous faites?

C. Paris–Genève en TGV. Imaginez que vous êtes à Paris et que vous voulez visiter Genève. Vous décidez de prendre le train. Voici les horaires du TGV (Train à Grande Vitesse).

HORAIRES ET SUPPLEMENTS TGV HORAIRES ET SU

○ TGV sans supplément.
★ TGV avec supplément.

PARIS → GENÈVE

	Nº du TGV		EC 921	EC 923	EC 925	EC 927	EC 929
	Restauration		■	■		■	■ 1/2
	Paris-Gare de Lyon	D	7.35	10.36	14.32	17.42	19.13
	Mâcon TGV	A	9.15		16.13		
	Bourg-en-Bresse	A			16.33		21.11
	Culoz	A			17.21		
	Bellegarde	A	10.37	13.34	17.46	20.43	22.18
	Genève	A	11.08	14.05	18.16	21.13	22.46
SEMAINE TYPE	Lundi		★	○	○	★	★
	Mardi		★	○	○	★	★
	Mercredi		★	○	○	★	★
	Jeudi		★	○	○	★	★
	Vendredi		★	○	○	★	★
	Samedi		○	○	○	○	○
	Dimanche		○	○	○	★	★
JOURS PARTICULIERS	Dimanche 7 juin		○	○	○	○	○
	Lundi 8 juin		○	○	○	★	★
	Samedi 4 juillet		○	★	★	○	○
	Samedi 11 juillet		○	★	★	○	○
	Mardi 14 juillet		○	○	○	★	★
	Samedi 1er août		○	★	★	○	○
	Dimanche 2 août		○	★	○	★	★

A Arrivée D Départ EC Eurocity (voir p. 11)
■ Service Restauration à la place en 1re classe, en réservation.
1/2 Coffrets repas froids ou sandwiches en 1re et 2e classes, sans réservation.
Pour Mâcon TGV, Bourg-en-Bresse et Culoz, voir également le tableau page 30.

1. A quelle heure y a-t-il des départs de Paris–Gare de Lyon pour Genève? A quelle heure ces trains arrivent-ils à Genève?
2. A quelle heure y a-t-il des départs le week-end?
3. Regardez l'itinéraire du TGV 925. A quelle heure part-il de Paris? A quelle heure arrive-t-il dans chaque ville? Utilisez **du matin, de l'après-midi** et **du soir** (14:32 = 2 heures trente-deux, de l'après-midi).
4. Maintenant décidez quel train vous allez prendre et expliquez pourquoi.

Les saisons et le temps: Quel temps fait-il?

En été...
il fait du soleil.
il fait beau.
il fait chaud.

En automne...
il pleut.
il fait mauvais.

En hiver...
il neige.
il fait froid.

Au printemps...
il fait du vent.
il fait frais.

Commentaire culturel

Measuring temperature. Throughout Europe, temperature is measured on the Celsius, rather than the Fahrenheit scale. The following chart gives approximate correspondences between the two scales.

CELSIUS	FAHRENHEIT
100°	212°
37°	98.6°
30°	86°
20°	68°
10°	50°
0°	32°

)US

s **fêtes et le temps.** Donnez la saison et le temps qu'il fait.

DÈLE: Noël → Nous sommes en hiver et il fait froid.

ıes (*Easter*) 2. Thanksgiving 3. la Saint-Valentin 4. le jour de ›ndance américaine 5. Labor Day

météo. Regardez le temps prévu sur toute la France et corrigez les incorrectes.

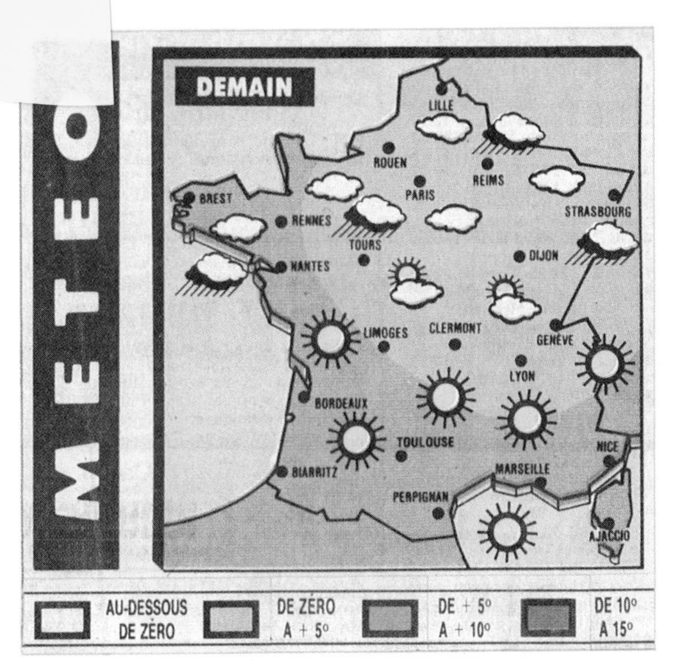

1. Il pleut à Marseille.
2. Il fait du soleil à Paris.
3. Il neige à Strasbourg.
4. Il fait mauvais à Lille.
5. Il fait beau à Lyon.
6. Il fait du soleil à Biarritz.
7. Calculez approximativement la température qu'il fait à Paris et à Marseille en degrés Fahrenheit.

Maintenant décrivez le temps qu'il fait aujourd'hui dans votre ville.

C. **Le temps et les goûts.** Qu'est-ce que vous aimez manger et boire quand... ?

1. il fait très chaud
2. il fait froid et qu'il neige
3. il fait beau et frais
4. il pleut

Étude de grammaire

17. Talking About Food and Drink: *-re* Verbs: *prendre* and *boire*

© CHIP & ROSA MARIA PETERSON

Au restaurant

SERVEUR: Que **prenez**-vous, Messieurs-Dames?
JEAN-MICHEL: Nous **prenons** le veau à la crème et les légumes.
SERVEUR: Et que **buvez**-vous?
JEAN-MICHEL: Je **prends** une bière, et pour mademoiselle une bouteille d'eau minérale, s'il vous plaît.

Maintenant, avec un(e) camarade, faites les substitutions suivantes et jouez à nouveau le dialogue.

le veau à la crème → le poulet froid
les légumes → la salade de tomates
une bière → un verre de vin rouge
une bouteille d'eau minérale → une carafe d'eau

A. *Prendre* (to take) and Verbs Like *prendre*

The verb **prendre** is irregular in its plural forms.

PRESENT TENSE OF **prendre**			
je	prends	nous	pren**ons**
tu	prends	vous	pren**ez**
il, elle, on	prend	ils, elles	pre**nnent**

Verbs conjugated like **prendre** are **apprendre** (*to learn*) and **comprendre** (*to understand*).

Qu'est-ce que **vous prenez**?	*What are you having?*
Je prends la salade verte.	*I'm having the green salad.*
Il apprend l'espagnol.	*He's learning (how to speak) Spanish.*
Est-ce que **tu comprends** presque toujours les autres étudiants?	*Do you almost always understand the other students?*

When an infinitive follows **apprendre,** the preposition **à** must be used also.

Ma sœur apprend à danser.	*My sister is learning (how) to dance.*
Apprenez-vous à skier?	*Are you learning (how) to ski?*

Some common expressions with **prendre** include the following.

prendre un repas	*to eat a meal*
prendre le petit déjeuner	*to have breakfast*
prendre un verre	*to have a drink (usually alcoholic)*
prendre son temps	*to take one's time*

B. *Boire* (to drink)

The verb **boire** is also irregular in form.

PRESENT TENSE OF **boire**			
je	**bois**	nous	**buvons**
tu	**bois**	vous	**buvez**
il, elle, on	**boit**	ils, elles	**boivent**

Je bois de l'eau minérale.	*I'm drinking mineral water.*
Nous buvons de la bière.	*We're drinking beer.*

MAINTENANT A VOUS

A. Des étudiants modèles. Lisez les phrases, puis faites les substitutions suivantes: (1) tu, (2) mon meilleur ami (ma meilleure amie), (3) mon/ma camarade et moi, (4) je, (5) mes camarades de classe. Faites d'autres substitutions si vous voulez (*want*).

1. Vous apprenez le français. 2. Vous comprenez presque toujours le professeur. 3. Pour préparer les examens, vous prenez des livres à la bibliothèque. 4. Pour faire vos devoirs, vous prenez votre temps. 5. Mais malheureusement, vous buvez trop de (*too much*) café.

B. La réponse est simple! Trouvez des réponses aux problèmes suivants. Utilisez les verbes **boire, apprendre, comprendre** ou **prendre** ou des expressions avec **prendre.**

MODÈLE: Je désire parler avec un ami. →
Je prends un verre au café avec un ami.

1. J'ai faim. 2. J'ai soif. 3. Je désire bien parler français. 4. Je désire étudier les mathématiques. 5. Je n'aime pas le vin.

C. Mission impossible? Parmi (*Among*) vos camarades, trouvez quelqu'un qui...

MODÈLE: prend du sucre dans son café →
Est-ce que tu prends du sucre dans ton café?

1. ne prend pas de petit déjeuner
2. prend en général des crêpes au petit déjeuner
3. boit cinq tasses de café ou plus chaque (*each*) jour
4. boit un verre de lait à chaque repas
5. apprend un nouveau sport ce semestre
6. comprend le sens de la vie

Celui qui finit le premier gagne le concours (= compétition).

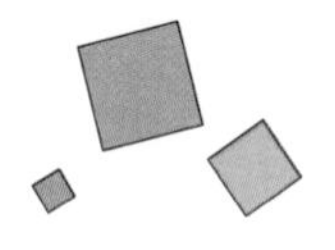

18. Expressing Quantity: Partitive Articles

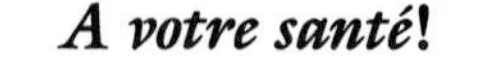

A votre santé!

Voici **l'eau** minérale.

Voici **une eau** minérale française et **une eau** minérale américaine.

Voici **de l'eau** minérale.

1. Aimez-vous l'eau minérale?
2. Est-ce qu'il y a une eau minérale célèbre aux États-Unis? Est-ce que toutes les familles ont de l'eau minérale à la maison?

A. The Partitive Articles

In addition to the definite and indefinite articles, French has a third article, called the partitive (**le partitif**). It has three forms: **du** (*m.*), **de la** (*f.*), and **de l'** (before a vowel or mute h). It agrees in gender with the noun it precedes.

Prenez-vous **du** porc?	*Are you having* (*some*) *pork?*
de la salade?	(*some*) *salad?*
de l'eau minérale?	(*some*) *mineral water?*

The partitive article is used to indicate only a part of an entire quantity, which is measurable but not countable. This idea is sometimes expressed in English by *some* or *any;* usually, however, *some* is not stated directly but only implied. Examples of noncountable nouns (also called *mass nouns*) include **viande, chocolat, lait, sucre, glace, vin,** and **eau.**

Avez-vous **du** thé?	*Do you have tea?*
Je voudrais **du** sucre.	*I would like* (*some*) *sugar.*
Mangez-vous **du** poisson?	*Do you eat fish?*

When the quantity is countable, the indefinite article is used instead.

Je vais préparer **une** tarte aux fraises.	*I'm going to prepare a strawberry tart.*
Elle commande **une** bière.	*She is ordering a beer.*
Elle achète **des** tomates et **des** haricots verts.	*She is buying tomatoes and green beans.*

B. The Partitive versus the Definite Article

The partitive article is used with such verbs as **prendre, boire, acheter,** and **manger,** because they refer to consuming or buying a portion of something. One usually has, drinks, buys, and eats a limited amount or number of things, and not all of them. But, after such verbs of preference as **aimer, aimer mieux, préférer, adorer,** and **détester,** the definite article is used, because these verbs express a preference or an aversion to a general category.

Beaucoup de Français mangent **du** fromage après le repas, mais moi, je déteste **le** fromage.	*Many French people eat* (*some*) *cheese after a meal, but I hate cheese.*

The partitive is also used with abstract qualities attributed to people, while the definite article is used to talk about these qualities in general.

Elle a **du** courage.	*She has* (*some*) *courage.*
Elle admire **le** courage.	*She admires courage.*

C. The Partitive in Negative Sentences

In negative sentences, partitive articles become **de** (**d'**), except after **être.**

Je bois **du** vin. → Je ne bois **pas de** vin.
Tu prends **de l'**eau. → Tu ne prends **pas d'**eau.
Vous mangez **des** carottes. → Vous ne mangez **pas de** carottes.

The expression **ne... plus** (*no more, not any more*) surrounds the conjugated verb, like **ne... pas.**

Je suis désolé, mais nous **n'**avons **plus de** vin. — *I'm sorry, but we have no more wine.*

© ULRIKE WELSCH

Les Français mangent beaucoup de pain.

D. The Partitive with Expressions of Quantity

Partitive articles also become **de** (**d'**) after expressions of quantity.

Elle commande **du vin.**

Combien de vin commande-t-elle?

Elle commande **un peu de vin.**

Elle commande **beaucoup de vin.**

Elle commande **un verre de vin.**

Elle a **assez de vin.**

Elle a **trop de vin.**

MAINTENANT A VOUS

A. A table! Qu'est-ce que vous prenez, en général, à chaque repas?

MODÈLE: Je prends... / Je ne prends pas de...

Au petit déjeuner...	**Au déjeuner...**	**Au dîner...**
du bacon	du poisson	de la soupe
des œufs	des huîtres	un hamburger
des croissants	du poulet	des frites
du café au lait	de la pizza	du fromage
du thé	des spaghetti	du riz
des céréales	de la viande	du veau
du jus d'orange	des légumes	de la dinde
de la confiture	un fruit	de la salade
?	?	?

B. Au supermarché. Vous avez des invités à dîner et vous faites le marché. Qu'est-ce que vous achetez pour préparer les plats suivants? Faites des phrases complètes avec un élément de chaque colonne.

Pour préparer	une soupe une omelette un gâteau au chocolat du poulet à la crème ?	j'achète du/de la/des	carottes (*f.*) oignons (*m.*) lait (*m.*) fromage (*m.*) crème (*f.*) œufs (*m.*) vin blanc (*m.*) farine (*f.*) chocolat (*m.*) beurre (*m.*) sucre (*m.*) champignons (*m.*) tomates (*f.*) ?

C. Une boisson pour chaque occasion. Choisissez votre boisson préférée pour chaque occasion. **Suggestions:** le café (noir, au lait), le thé (glacé), le lait, le vin (blanc, rouge, rosé), le chocolat chaud, le champagne, l'eau minérale, la bière, le Coca-Cola, le jus de fruits (d'orange, de pomme, de tomate, de citron, de raisin...)

MODÈLE: après une journée de ski →
Après une journée de ski, je bois du chocolat chaud ou peut-être un café au lait.

1. au petit déjeuner 2. à midi 3. après les cours 4. pour fêter un anniversaire 5. pour un dîner spécial 6. en période d'examens 7. quand vous êtes au régime 8. ?

D. **Fiche beauté.** Lisez ce «programme d'été pour garder votre poids idéal», publié dans le magazine *Jacinte*. Puis répondez aux questions. (**le poids** = *weight*)

FICHE BEAUTE N° 18 FORME

L'été, ne mangez plus n'importe quoi[a]!

a. n'importe... *just anything*

Programme d'été pour garder votre poids idéal.

■ **Matin**
Un laitage. Un œuf coque ou une tranche de jambon. Un quart de baguette ou deux tranches de pain complet. Un fruit.

■ **Midi sur la plage**
Un sandwich, plutôt jambon ou viande froide que saucisson ou deux œufs durs, moutarde et cornichons. Un laitage : 40 à 50 g de fromage ou 300 g de fromage blanc de 10 à 30 % de matières grasses. Un fruit. De l'eau.

■ **Soir**
Viande ou poisson (150 g). Légumes ou féculents (200 g) trois fois par semaines. 50 g de fromage blanc de 10 à 30 %de matières grasses.

1. Cet extrait (*excerpt*) propose un menu *d'un jour / de plusieurs jours.*
2. D'après le contexte, pouvez-vous deviner ce que veulent dire (*mean*) les mots suivants? Donnez une définition ou un exemple en français si possible.

a. un laitage	c. une tranche	e. un œuf dur
b. un œuf coque	d. du saucisson	f. de la moutarde

3. Maintenant, en petits groupes de trois ou quatre, composez un menu «bonne forme» pour un repas. Vous n'êtes pas limités à la liste proposée par *Jacinte*. Puis présentez votre menu à la classe.

E. Dîner d'anniversaire. Avec un(e) camarade vous préparez un dîner surprise pour fêter l'anniversaire d'un ami (d'une amie). Mais avez-vous tous les ingrédients nécessaires?

MODÈLE: carottes (assez) / (ne... pas) champignons →

VOTRE CAMARADE: Est-ce que tu as des carottes?
VOUS: Oui, j'ai assez de carottes mais je n'ai pas de champignons.

1. vin (3 bouteilles) / (ne.... plus) bière
2. café (un peu) / (ne... plus) thé
3. fraises (beaucoup) / (ne... pas) melon
4. chocolat (trop) / (ne... pas) marrons glacés
5. viande (assez) / (ne... pas) légumes
6. sucre (un bol) / (ne... plus) sel
7. talent pour faire la cuisine (beaucoup) / (ne... pas) patience
8. ?

F. Un pique-nique réussi. Complétez avec l'article défini, indéfini ou partitif.

Aujourd'hui, nous allons pique-niquer. Madame Belleval prépare _______ repas froid avec _______ poulet, _______ haricots verts, _______ melon et ____ salade. Comme dessert, il y a _______ fromage et _______ tarte aux fraises. Monsieur Belleval choisit _______ bouteille de vin blanc. La famille Belleval arrive à la rivière (*stream*). Les enfants préparent _______ table, on mange, on parle, _______ poulet est excellent, _______ melon est parfait. Quelle belle journée! Au dessert, on mange _______ tarte avec une tasse _______ café. Les enfants préfèrent _______ jus de fruits et ils adorent _______ tarte. Tout le monde mange bien, et même (*even*) mange un peu trop... alors, après _______ repas, il reste une chose à faire: chacun (*everyone*) fait la sieste!

Choisissez la bonne réponse, selon l'histoire. Puis répondez à la question.

1. La famille Belleval mange *peu / beaucoup / trop*.
2. Les Belleval boivent du vin *rouge / blanc / rosé*.
3. Les enfants aiment *peu / assez / beaucoup* la tarte.
4. En quoi ce pique-nique est-il différent d'un pique-nique américain?

Mots-clés

More about expressing likes and dislikes: You have been expressing your preferences since the beginning of the course. Here are several simple ways to express *intense* likes and dislikes.

Moi, j'adore ça! Je suis gourmand(e). (*I love to eat.*)
Je n'aime pas du tout le bifteck!
J'ai horreur des escargots.

G. Trouvez quelqu'un qui... Parmi vos camarades de classe, trouvez quelqu'un dans chacune des catégories suivantes. Demandez aussi des renseignements (= information) supplémentaires. Ensuite, présentez les résultats de l'enquête aux autres membres de la classe. Trouvez quelqu'un qui...

1. est végétarien(ne) (Pourquoi?)
2. ne prend jamais de dessert (Pourquoi?)
3. adore faire la cuisine (Spécialité?)
4. mange très peu (Combien de fois par jour?)
5. apprécie la cuisine exotique (Quels plats?)
6. refuse de manger certains aliments (*foods*) (Lesquels et pourquoi?)
7. déteste certains légumes (Lesquels?)
8. aime spécialement certaines viandes (Lesquelles?)
9. est gourmand(e)

19. Giving Commands: The Imperative

L'ennemi d'un bon repas

FRANÇOIS: Martine, **passe**-moi le sel, s'il te plaît... (*Martine passe la salade à François.*)

FRANÇOIS: Mais non, enfin! **Écoute** un peu... je demande le sel!

MARTINE: François, **sois** gentil—**ne parle pas** si fort. Je n'entends plus la télé...

1. Est-ce que François demande la salade?
2. Est-ce que Martine passe le sel à François?
3. Est-ce que Martine écoute François?

A. Kinds of Imperatives

The imperative is the command form of a verb. There are three forms. Note that subject pronouns are not used with them.

tu form	**Parle!**	*Speak!*
nous form	**Parlons!**	*Let's speak!*
vous form	**Parlez!**	*Speak!*

B. Imperative Forms of *-er* Verbs

The imperatives of regular **-er** verbs are the same as the corresponding present-tense forms, except that the **tu** form does not end in **-s.**

INFINITIVE	tu	nous	vous
regarder	**Regarde!**	**Regardons!**	**Regardez!**
entrer	**Entre!**	**Entrons!**	**Entrez!**

Regardez! Un restaurant russe. **Entrons!** — *Look! A Russian restaurant. Let's go in!*

The imperative forms of the irregular verb **aller** follow the pattern of regular **-er** imperatives: **va, allons, allez.**

C. Imperative Forms of *-re* and *-ir* Verbs

The imperative forms of the **-re** and **-ir** verbs you have learned—even most of the irregular ones—are identical to their corresponding present-tense forms.

INFINITIVE	tu	nous	vous
attendre	**Attends!**	**Attendons!**	**Attendez!**
finir	**Finis!**	**Finissons!**	**Finissez!**
faire	**Fais... !**	**Faisons... !**	**Faites... !**

Attends! Finis ton verre! — *Wait! Finish your drink!*
Faites attention! — *Pay attention!* (*Watch out!*)

D. Irregular Imperative Forms

The verbs **avoir** and **être** have irregular command forms.

INFINITIVE	tu	nous	vous
avoir	**Aie... !**	**Ayons... !**	**Ayez... !**
être	**Sois... !**	**Soyons... !**	**Soyez... !**

Sois gentil, Michel, et va au marché. — *Be nice, Michel, and go to the market.*
Ayez de la patience. — *Have patience.*

E. Negative Commands

In negative commands, **ne** comes before the verb and **pas** follows it.

Ne vends pas ta guitare!	*Don't sell your guitar!*
Ne buvons pas trop de café.	*Let's not drink too much coffee.*
N'attendez pas le dessert.	*Don't wait for dessert.*

MAINTENANT A VOUS

A. Les bonnes manières. Vous apprenez* les bonnes manières à un enfant.

MODÈLE: ne pas jouer avec ton couteau →
Ne joue pas avec ton couteau!

1. attendre ton père 2. prendre ta serviette 3. finir ta soupe 4. manger tes carottes 5. regarder ton assiette 6. être sage (*good*) 7. ne pas manger de sucre 8. boire ton verre de lait 9. ne pas demander le dessert

B. Un job d'été. Vous travaillez deux semaines comme serveur (serveuse) dans un café. Voici les recommandations du patron (*owner*).

MODÈLE: faire attention aux clients → Faites attention aux clients.

1. être aimable 2. avoir de la patience 3. écouter les clients 4. répondre aux questions 5. ne pas perdre de temps 6. rendre correctement la monnaie

Imaginez maintenant trois autres recommandations possibles du patron. Soyez créatif (créative)!

C. C'est simple! Votre camarade vous donne plein de conseils (*lots of advice*), mais vous avez toujours une bonne excuse. Jouez les deux rôles.

MODÈLE:
VOUS: J'ai faim.
VOTRE CAMARADE: Alors, prends un casse-croute (*snack*).
VOUS: Mais je suis au régime.

1. J'ai besoin d'exercice.
2. J'ai besoin d'argent (*money*).
3. J'ai envie d'aller en Espagne.
4. J'ai soif.
5. J'ai sommeil.
6. Je ne comprends pas un mot dans mon livre d'anglais.
7. Je cherche un camarade de chambre.

jouer au tennis, aller au lit, vendre sa voiture, faire un voyage, boire un verre d'eau, téléphoner à ses amis, chercher dans le dictionnaire, ?

---

*__Apprendre__ can also mean *to teach*. The person taught is preceded by **à**. The thing taught can be either a noun or a verb. The verb is also preceded by **à: Tu apprends les bonnes manières à un enfant.** (**Tu apprends à l'enfant à avoir de bonnes manières.**)

D. Le robot. Vous avez un robot qui travaille pour vous. La classe choisit un étudiant (une étudiante) pour jouer le rôle du robot. Donnez cinq ordres en français au robot. Il/Elle est obligé(e) d'obéir.

MODÈLE: Va au tableau!
Prends ton livre de français!
Regarde le mur!

Étude de prononciation

Liaison

A consonant that occurs at the end of a word is often "linked" to the next word if that word begins with a vowel sound: les‿amis [lɛ za mi]. This linking is called **liaison.** It occurs between words that are already united by meaning or syntax: Ils‿ont‿un‿ami [il zɔ̃ tɛ̃ na mi].

Liaison is compulsory in the following cases.

between a pronoun and a verb	ils‿ont
between a verb and a pronoun	ont‿ils
between a noun and a preceding adjective	de beaux‿hommes
between short adverbs and adjectives	très‿intéressant
between articles and nouns	un‿exercice
between articles and following adjectives	les‿autres pays
between a one-syllable preposition and its object	sans‿argent
after numbers	huit‿étudiants
after **est**	c'est‿évident

Liaison *does not* take place in the following cases.

after a singular noun	un étudiant / intéressant
after **et**	il parle français et / anglais
before an aspirate **h**	un / Hollandais

Liaison produces the following sound changes.

a final **s** is pronounced [z]	les‿étudiants
a final **x** is pronounced [z]	dix‿étudiants
a final **z** is pronounced [z]	chez‿elle
a final **d** is pronounced [t]	un grand‿homme
a final **f** is pronounced [f] or [v]*	neuf‿ans

*Final **f** is pronounced [v] before the words **an** (*year*) and **heure** (*hour*) only.

Liaison and its uses vary according to language level. For example, in a poetic or dramatic reading, or in other very formal situations, most conventional **liaisons** are made. Fewer and fewer are made as the level of language becomes more informal.

A. Prononcez avec le professeur.

1. un grand appartement 2. les écoles américaines 3. le jardinier anglais 4. les hors-d'œuvre 5. les deux églises 6. Il est ouvrier et artisan 7. Elles étaient à la mairie. 8. Vous êtes sans intérêt. 9. Vont-elles dans le centre-ville? 10. Tu ne m'as pas écouté. 11. C'est horrible! 12. C'est un quartier ancien.

B. Prononcez avec le professeur.

1. Vous allez mettre trois assiettes sur la table. 2. Les deux assiettes blanches sont à la cuisine. 3. Vous achetez des oranges et des œufs, n'est-ce pas? 4. Les nouveaux étudiants français mangent des huîtres pour le repas de Noël.

Situation

Non, merci

Contexte *Ken, un étudiant américain, passe un semestre à Strasbourg, où il habite dans une famille française. Strasbourg est la ville principale d'Alsace, une province où la cuisine est savoureuse et très riche. Les Alsaciens sont aussi très hospitaliers. Ken découvre° les plaisirs et les dangers d'un repas de week-end en famille!* — *discovers*

Objectif *Ken n'arrive pas à refuser un plat avec tact.*

M. GIRARD: Encore un peu de bière, Ken?
KEN: Non, merci.
MME GIRARD: Vous allez bien reprendre un peu de quiche, quand même°? — quand... *all the same*
KEN: Elle est vraiment° délicieuse, mais non, merci. — *truly, really*
MARIE-LINE: Tu es au régime?
KEN: Non, mais j'ai déjà beaucoup mangé.
MARIE-LINE: Ken, la cuisine, c'est une expérience culturelle.
MME GIRARD: Mais oui, Ken, faites un sacrifice culturel et prenez de la tarte aux mirabelles:° c'est ma spécialité! — *plums*
KEN: Alors, je ne peux° pas refuser. — *can*

© ROBERT BRETZFELDER / PHOTOEDIT

Une vue pittoresque du vieux Strasbourg

VARIATIONS

Rejouez la scène, mais elle est maintenant en Amérique, et l'étudiant(e) est un Français (une Française) qui rend visite à une famille américaine.

A propos

A table

The following expressions will be useful when you are eating in a French-speaking area.

Bon appétit!	*Enjoy your meal;* literally, *good appetite.*
Santé! **A votre santé!** **A ta santé!**	This expression, meaning *to your health,* is used as a toast.
Je reprendrais bien un peu de... **Passe-moi... s'il te plaît.**	*May I have another helping of . . . .* Say this when you want someone to pass you something.
En voulez-vous encore? **En veux-tu encore?**	*Do you want some more* (*of a certain dish or drink*)?
S'il vous plaît. Non, merci.	*Yes, please. No, thank you.*
Je n'ai plus faim.	*I'm full. I've eaten enough.*
C'est délicieux! Je me régale.	*It's delicious! I'm having a feast.* Say this to compliment the cook.

A. Jeu de rôles: Un repas entre amis. Avec deux camarades, préparez une conversation à table. Utilisez les expressions de l'*A propos*. Puis jouez la scène devant la classe.

B. Une recette québécoise.* Regardez la recette suivante pour le potage aux épinards (*spinach soup*). La première partie de la recette est en ordre. Essayez de trouver l'ordre correct pour la deuxième (*second*) partie.

MOTS UTILES

boîte de soupe	*can of soup*
le riz	*rice*
c. à table	*tablespoon* (**cuillère à soupe**)
c. à thé	*teaspoon* (**cuillère à café**)
la farine	*flour*
fondre	*to melt* (**faire fondre**)
ajouter	*to add*
brasser	*to mix, stir* (**mélanger**)
cuire en tournant sans arrêt	*to cook, stirring constantly* (**faire cuire en remuant**)
épaisse	*thick*
le tout	*the entire amount*
remettre sur feu doux	*to return to low flame* (**remettre à feu doux**)
jusqu'à ce que	*until*
rectifier l'assaisonnement	*to season to taste*
servir brûlant	*to serve hot* (**servir très chaud**)
garni de filaments de piment doux	*garnished with thin slices of red pepper* (**garni de fines tranches de piment doux**)
le blender	*blender* (**le mixeur**)

POTAGE AUX ÉPINARDS

INGRÉDIENTS

1/4 tasse de beurre
2 tasses de lait
1 boîte de soupe Campbell's poulet et riz
3 c. à table de farine
1/2 livre d'épinards crus (*uncooked*)
1/2 c. à thé de sel
Crème

*This recipe is authentic and illustrates differences between standard continental French and the French spoken in Quebec, **le québécois.** Standard French equivalents are in parentheses after the English translations.

PRÉPARATION

Fondre le beurre.* Ajouter la farine et bien brasser. Cuire en tournant sans arrêt. Ceci (*This*) donne une sauce épaisse.

Quel est l'ordre correct du reste de la préparation?

Ajouter les épinards, la soupe au poulet.
Rectifier l'assaisonnement.
Passer le tout au blender.
Servir brûlant garni de filaments de piment doux.
Ajouter de la crème jusqu'à ce que le potage soit (*is*) de bonne consistance.
Remettre sur feu doux.

Faites-vous la cuisine? Présentez la recette de votre spécialité à la classe.

Réponse à l'Exercice B: Ajouter les épinards, la soupe au poulet. Passer le tout au blender. Remettre sur feu doux. Ajouter de la crème jusqu'à ce que le potage soit de bonne consistance. Rectifier l'assaisonnement. Servir brûlant garni de filaments de piment doux.

Commentaire culturel

French food. French home cooking is probably simpler than most foreign visitors imagine. Its excellence comes partly from the high quality of the ingredients used. French consumers spend significantly more on food than American consumers do, and as a group, they seem willing to pay more for high-quality products.

Breakfast (**le petit déjeuner**) is simple—usually **tartines** (French bread and butter) or croissants with **café au lait.** The noon meal (**le déjeuner**) has traditionally been the main meal, but many people now take less time for lunch and prefer to have a larger evening meal (**le dîner**). Children usually have a snack (**le goûter**) of bread and chocolate when they come home from school around 4:00 or 5:00; adults have tea or coffee with pastry (**une pâtisserie**). Dinner is served around 7:30 or 8:00.

Whether served at noon or in the evening, a French meal begins with either an **hors-d'œuvre** or an **entrée** or both. The **hors-d'œuvre** is always a cold dish, sometimes similar to the light snacks called *hors d'œuvres* in the United States. It may be coldcuts, eggs in mayonnaise, or some variety of **pâté.** An **entrée** is not a main dish but a light, warm dish—trout, mussels, or **quenelles** (*fish dumplings*), for example. It is followed by a meat or fish dish, vegetable, salad, cheese, and fresh fruit. Children often drink water, while the rest of the family may have **vin rouge ordinaire,** sometimes diluted with

*In certain contexts, such as recipes, the infinitive is used to give instructions.

water. After the meal, a small cup of strong coffee is generally served.

Bread is laid directly on the tablecloth, beside each plate; it is broken with the fingers and eaten in small pieces. Each course of a French meal is served separately, usually on the same plate (unless the meal is formal).

Meals take longer in France than in the United States, partly because there are so many courses, but also because they are a time for socializing.

Mise au point

A. Vos plats préférés. Quels plats aimez-vous? Quels plats n'aimez-vous pas? Pourquoi? Faites des phrases complètes.

MODÈLE: J'aime les hot dogs parce qu'ils sont faciles à préparer.
Je n'aime pas le curry indien parce qu'il est épicé (*spicy*).

J'aime... / Je n'aime pas...	**parce que...**	
les «Big Mac»	est	difficile(s) à préparer
le bifteck et les pommes de terre	n'est pas	facile(s) à préparer
le jambon	sont	beaucoup de calories
les soupes de légumes	ne sont pas	peu de calories
les gâteaux au chocolat	a	beaucoup d'ingrédients
les hot dogs	n'a pas	des ingrédients chimiques
les spaghetti	ont	exotique(s)
la pizza	n'ont pas	dégoûtant(e/s) (*disgusting*)
les escargots		cher(s)/chère(s)
le curry indien		très sucré(e/s)
le canard laqué (*Peking duck*)		nutritif(s)/nutritive(s)
le poulet frit à la Kentucky		très snob
les éclairs		très américain(e/s)
les fruits		très français(e/s)
?		?

On est ce qu'on mange. Le/La gourmand(e) aime manger et mange beaucoup. Le gourmet aime manger seulement (*only*) la nourriture (*food*) de qualité et ne mange pas nécessairement beaucoup. Selon vos réponses, êtes-vous gourmand(e) ou gourmet? Pourquoi? A quelles occasions êtes-vous gourmand(e)? A quelles occasions êtes-vous gourmet?

B. La nourriture et les boissons. Complétez le dialogue.

1. qu'est-ce que vous / prendre / dîner?
2. on / prendre / jambon / et / salade
3. manger / vous / assez / fruits?
4. oui, nous / manger / souvent / poires / et / pommes
5. prendre / tu / beaucoup / vin?
6. non / il y a / ne... plus / vin
7. mes amis / boire / eau minérale
8. qui / payer / repas?
9. hélas / souvent / moi

C. Au téléphone. Regardez la recette québécoise à la page 160. Imaginez que vous êtes au téléphone et que vous expliquez la recette à un ami (une amie).

1. Donnez la liste des ingrédients. (Tu as besoin de lait,...)
2. Expliquez la préparation. Mettez les verbes à l'impératif (**remettre** → ***remets***; **servir** → ***sers***).

Mots-clés

Expressing agreement, disagreement, and surprise:

D'accord.	*All right.*
Bien sûr que oui (non).	*But of course. / Of course not.*
Ah bon.	*Oh, really?*
Mais non! Moi, je préfère...	*Of course not! I'd rather . . .*
Au contraire, moi, je..	*On the contrary, I . . .*
Peut-être, mais...	*Maybe, but . . .*

D. Sondage: Préférences gastronomiques. Interviewez cinq camarades. Ensuite décrivez à la classe leurs préférences gastronomiques et comparez vos résultats avec les résultats des autres enquêteurs. Puis décidez qui dans la classe aime le plat le plus original, le plus bizarre; qui mange à des heures inhabituelles; qui préfère une boisson peu commune, un restaurant exotique... Y a-t-il d'autres réponses surprenantes? Expliquez.

Questions suggérées:

1. Quel est ton restaurant préféré? Manges-tu souvent au restaurant?
2. Quel est ton repas préféré? Pourquoi?
3. Au petit déjeuner, préfères-tu prendre du café? du thé? du chocolat? du lait? _______? Prends-tu aussi des œufs? des céréales? _______?
4. Que préfères-tu prendre au déjeuner? un sandwich? une omelette? un repas complet? _______?
5. Qu'est-ce que tu bois au déjeuner? du lait? du vin? du Coca-Cola? de l'eau minérale? du café?

6. Qu'est-ce que tu prends au dîner? du jambon? du rôti de bœuf? du poisson? _______? Qu'est-ce que tu bois?
7. En général, quel dessert préfères-tu? des fruits? du fromage? du gâteau? _______?
8. Manges-tu les mêmes plats toute l'année? Y a-t-il quelque chose que tu aimes particulièrement en chaque saison?

Interactions

In this chapter, you have practiced talking about food and drink, giving commands, and telling time. Act out the following situations, using the vocabulary and structures from this chapter.

1. **Au restaurant universitaire.** While you are eating on campus, you get stuck sitting next to someone (role-played by a classmate) with whom you have nothing in common and whom you do not particularly like. Make small talk about the meal, the weather, the classes, etc. Try to leave as soon as you can.
2. **Conseils.** A young French exchange student is soon going to attend an American college. Give him or her some simple advice on how to succeed in college and have a good time.

Vocabulaire

Verbes

acheter to buy
apprendre to learn
boire to drink
commander to order (*in a restaurant*)
comprendre to understand
dîner to dine, have dinner
employer to use
envoyer to send
espérer to hope
essayer to try
passer to pass, spend (*time*)
payer to pay for
préférer to prefer
prendre to take; to have (to eat; to order)

Substantifs

la boisson drink
la cuisine cooking; kitchen
le déjeuner lunch
le dessert dessert
le dîner dinner
le fruit fruit
le goûter afternoon snack
la journée (whole) day
le légume vegetable
le marché market
la monnaie change (*money*)
le petit déjeuner breakfast
le régime diet
le repas meal
la viande meat

Les provisions

le beurre butter
le bifteck steak
la carotte carrot
le champagne champagne
le chocolat chocolate
la crème cream
le croissant croissant
la dinde rôtie roast turkey
l'eau (minérale) (*f.*) (mineral) water
la fraise strawberry
le fromage cheese
le gâteau cake
les *haricots verts (*m.*) green beans

---

*The initial **h** is aspirate here.

l'huître (*f.*) oyster
le jambon ham
le lait milk
le marron (**glacé**) (candied) chestnut
l'œuf (*m.*) egg
le pain bread
le pâté de foie gras liver pâté
la poire pear
le poisson fish
le poivre pepper
la pomme apple
la pomme de terre potato
le poulet chicken
la salade salade, lettuce
le sel salt
le sucre sugar
la tarte pie
le thé tea
le veau veal
le vin wine

A table

l'assiette (*f.*) plate
le bol wide cup
la bouteille bottle
la carafe carafe
le couteau knife
la cuillère (**à soupe**) (soup) spoon
la fourchette fork
la serviette napkin
la tasse cup
le verre glass

Mots divers

assez de enough
encore another, more; still
moins de less
ne... plus no more
plus de more
presque almost
trop de too much
un peu de a little
vers around (*with time expressions*)
vite quickly

L'heure

Quelle heure est-il? What time is it?
Il est... heure(s). The time is . . . o'clock.
Il est midi. It's noon.
Il est minuit. It's midnight.
...et demi(e) half past (the hour)
...et quart quarter past (the hour)
...moins le quart quarter to (the hour)
...du matin in the morning
...de l'après-midi in the afternoon
...du soir in the evening, at night

Le temps

Quel temps fait-il? How's the weather?
Il fait beau. It's nice (out).
Il fait chaud. It's hot.
Il fait du soleil. It's sunny.
Il fait frais. It's cool.
Il fait du vent. It's windy.
Il fait froid. It's cold.
Il fait mauvais. It's bad (out).
Il neige. It's snowing.
Il pleut. It's raining.

Les saisons

En été...
En automne...
En hiver...
Au printemps...

Expressions utiles

Ah bon.	*Oh, really?*
Au contraire...	*On the contrary . . .*
Bien sûr que oui (non).	*Of course (not).*
J'ai horreur de...	*I can't stand . . .*
Je suis gourmand(e).	*I like to eat.*

INTERMÈDE 5

Lecture

AVANT DE LIRE

Finding the main thought in a sentence: As you know, the normal word order of French syntax is *subject + verb.* Together, the subject and the verb represent the main thought expressed in a sentence. If you are having trouble understanding a long sentence, isolate the subject and the verb in order to grasp the main thought.

Two strategies can help you search out the main thought of a sentence. First, omit words and phrases set off by commas. They are most likely to give information supplementary to the main thought. Second, delete the relative clauses or the clauses introduced by the relative pronouns (for example, **qui** and **que,** meaning *who, whom,* or *that*). You will learn the relative pronouns later, but you should recognize them for the purpose of reading. Try this technique in the following sentence.

> **Au dessert, on mange la bûche de Noël, un gâteau roulé au chocolat en forme de bûche.**

Once you have located the subject and the verb (**on mange**), you can reread the sentence, adding more information. What does one eat? Is there a definition of **la bûche de Noël** in the sentence? Set off by a comma to the right of this term is a phrase including the words **gâteau** and **chocolat,** which you learned in this chapter. Set off by a comma at the beginning of the sentence is the word **dessert.** Without English glossing, you still may not know the literal definition of **la bûche,** but you should have understood that it is a chocolate dessert eaten at Christmas time. And that is sufficient to understand the gist of the sentence.

Apply these strategies to your reading of "*Grandes occasions,*" and remember to scan the glosses and the illustrations first.

Grandes occasions

En France, les jours de fête sont une occasion pour se réunir en famille ou entre amis. Pour chaque fête, on mange des plats typiques qui changent (= varient) parfois° selon les régions. Voici les fêtes les plus gourmandes° du calendrier français.

quelquefois / où l'on mange bien

Pour la fête des rois, le 6 janvier, on achète chez le pâtissier une galette. C'est un gâteau qui contient un petit objet appelé une **fève.** On donne à la

Qui a trouvé la fève?

Je voudrais une crêpe au Grand-Marnier, s'il vous plaît.

personne qui trouve la fève dans son morceau de gâteau une couronne en papier doré. Cette personne est maintenant le roi (ou la reine) et elle choisit sa reine (ou son roi). La famille ou les amis boivent à leur santé.°

health

Pour la Chandeleur, la fête de l'enfant Jésus au Temple, le 2 février, on mange beaucoup de crêpes! On les prépare en famille selon la tradition: Faites sauter des crêpes avec une pièce de monnaie dans la main, et vous serez riche toute l'année...

Pâques° est, bien sûr, la fête du chocolat! C'est aussi un grand jour de réunion familiale, à l'église et à table. On fait un grand repas, et au dessert grands et petits mangent des œufs, des cloches, des poules ou des poissons en chocolat remplis° de bonbons.

Easter

filled

Noël est peut-être la fête des fêtes. Le Réveillon° de Noël est un grand dîner que l'on prend le plus souvent après la messe° de minuit. Au menu: huîtres, foie gras, dinde aux marrons et beaucoup de champagne! Au dessert, on mange la bûche de Noël, un gâteau roulé au chocolat en forme de bûche. Les enfants, bien sûr, attendent avec impatience l'arrivée du Père Noël.

Midnight supper

une cérémonie catholique

COMPRÉHENSION

Match the following quotations with the relevant paragraphs in "*Grandes occasions.*"

1. «Qui a la fève?»
2. «Qu'est-ce que j'ai faim! Il est très tard, mais je ne perds pas patience.»
3. «Moi, je laisse toujours tomber (*drop*) la crêpe par terre (*on the floor or ground*).»
4. «C'est ma fête préférée parce que j'adore les œufs en chocolat.»

Par écrit

A. **Et en Amérique?** Vous êtes journaliste en France et vous écrivez un article qui décrit une fête célébrée en Amérique mais pas en France. Comment les Américains célèbrent-ils la fête en question?

B. **A table.** Ecrivez une lettre à un correspondant français (une correspondante française). Parlez de vos habitudes culinaires. Utilisez les questions comme guide. Commencez par **Cher (Chère)...** Terminez par **Amitiés,...**

1. Combien de repas prenez-vous par jour? 2. Mangez-vous bien ou mal? 3. Que prenez-vous au petit déjeuner? 4. Où mangez-vous à midi? Prenez-vous un repas complet? 5. Mangez-vous pendant l'après-midi? Qu'est-ce que vous mangez? 6. Qui prépare le dîner chez vous? Passez-vous beaucoup de temps à table? 7. Quand invitez-vous vos amis à dîner à la maison?

CHAPITRE SIX

On mange bien en France!

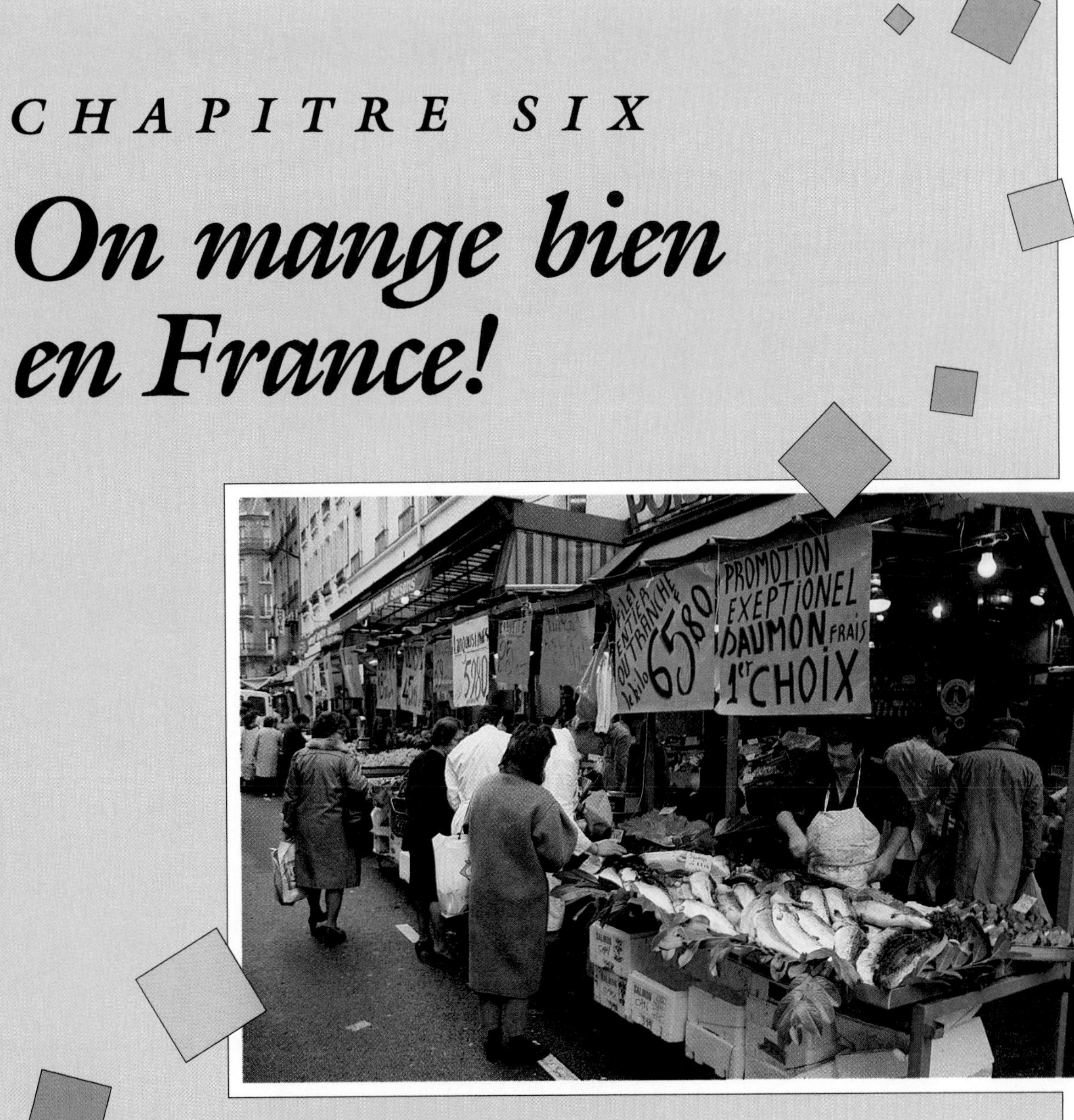

—Bonjour, Madame.
—Bonjour. Je voudrais un kilo de saumon, s'il vous plaît.
—Oui, et avec ceci?
—C'est tout.
—Alors, ça vous fait 65, 80 F.

Étude de vocabulaire

Les magasins d'alimentation

Les magasins du quartier. Où allez-vous pour acheter les produits suivants?

MODÈLE: des côtes de bœuf →
Pour acheter des côtes de bœuf, je vais à la boucherie-charcuterie.*

1. des petits pains au chocolat 2. des pommes de terre 3. du thon (*tuna*) à l'huile 4. du poisson frais (*fresh*) 5. des escalopes de veau 6. une baguette 7. du pâté de canard (*duck*) 8. des crevettes (*shrimp*)

---

*There are also separate stores: **la boulangerie, la pâtisserie, la boucherie, la charcuterie.**

Au restaurant

NOVEMBRE 1989

FORFAIT A 155 FRS

APERITIF, VINS A DISCRETION,
CAFE ET SERVICE COMPRIS.

restaurant la tour de la pelote   pierre ferreux   quai de strasbourg   25000 besançon   tél 81 82 14 58 et 81 81 29 96

L'APERITIF MAISON

L'entrée au choix : SAUMON FRAIS EN PAPILLOTTE
CONFIT DE LAPIN AUX PRUNEAUX
PETITE SALADE DE CAILLE EN GRENOUILLETTE
SOUPE DE POISSON MAISON
CASSOLETTE DE RIS DE VEAU A LA CLAMART

Le plat garni au choix : CIVET DE SANGLIER A LA FRANÇAISE
BARON D'AGNEAU A LA PROVENÇALE
NAVARIN D'AGNEAU AUX PETITS LEGUMES
LE TOURNEDOS A LA BRAISE
FILETS DE PERCHE BELLE MEUNIERE

GARNITURE DE LEGUMES

LE PLATEAU DE FROMAGES

Dessert : A CHOISIR DANS LA CARTE DES DESSERTS

LE CAFE EN MAZAGRAN

L'HIPPO FUTÉ 73,00 F

Salade Hippo
Faux filet grillé (240 g)
sauce poivrade
Pommes allumettes

LES VINS EN PICHET (31 cl)

BORDEAUX ROUGE A.C.	23,00 F
GAMAY DE TOURAINE A.C.	17,00 F

LES ENTRÉES

ASSIETTE DU JARDINIER	29,00 F
TERRINE DU CHEF	27,00 F
COCKTAIL DE CREVETTES	30,00 F
SALADE DE SAISON	13,00 F

LES GRILLADES

avec sauce au choix.

FAUX FILET MINUTE — 59,00 F
Tellement goûteux qu'il plaît aussi à ceux qui l'aiment «bien cuit».

T. BONE — 89,00 F
Tranche à l'américaine, avec le filet et le faux filet de part et d'autre de l'os en T. 2 qualités de viande dans le même morceau d'environ 380 g.

PAVÉ — 69,00 F
Tranché dans le cœur des rumsteaks, c'est une tranche maigre et épaisse (conseillé pour ceux qui aiment «rouge»).

ENTRECÔTE — 69,00 F
Un morceau qui permet à ceux qui aiment «bien cuit» d'apprécier cependant la bonne viande.

CÔTE «VILLETTE» — 184,00 F
Pour 2 affamés d'accord sur la même cuisson. 850 grammes environ.

CÔTES D'AGNEAU — 73,00 F

LES FROMAGES

BRIE DE MEAUX AUX NOIX	23,00 F
FROMAGE BLANC NATURE	15,00 F

LES DESSERTS

MOUSSE AU CHOCOLAT	22,00 F
TARTE AUX FRUITS	29,00 F

LES SORBETS

POIRE	22,00 F
FRUIT DE LA PASSION	22,00 F

A. Au restaurant. Avec un(e) camarade, regardez les deux cartes à la page 171. Imaginez que vous déjeunez (*have a midday meal*) dans l'un des restaurants et que vous dînez dans l'autre. Jouez les rôles du serveur (de la serveuse) et du client (de la cliente). Notez ce que votre camarade commande.

MODÈLE: SERVEUR/SERVEUSE: Qu'est-ce que vous prenez comme entrée? (plat principal, boisson, dessert...)
CLIENT/CLIENTE: Je prends le/la*...

Ensuite décrivez le déjeuner et le dîner de votre camarade à la classe. Commentez ses goûts (*tastes*).

Y a-t-il un plat très populaire parmi vos camarades? Qui dans la classe commande le plat le plus simple? le plus sophistiqué?

B. Faites vos courses. Avec un(e) camarade, imaginez un menu pour chacun (*each*) des repas suivants. Faites une liste de choses (*things*) à acheter. Où achetez-vous les aliments?

1. pour un petit déjeuner français 2. pour un petit déjeuner américain
3. pour un pique-nique 4. pour un dîner très simple entre ami(e)s
5. pour un dîner très élégant

La Tour de la Pelote
XVe SIECLE

C. Conversation. Posez les questions suivantes à des camarades.

1. Préfères-tu manger à la maison ou au restaurant? Quand manges-tu au restaurant? Qu'est-ce que tu préfères: un restaurant simple ou un restaurant élégant? Quels sont les restaurants élégants de ton quartier?

*When ordering from a menu, one often uses the definite article, rather than the partitive.

2. Aimes-tu goûter les cuisines étrangères (*foreign*)? de quels pays (*countries*)? Aimes-tu la cuisine française? Quel est ton plat français favori? Manges-tu souvent dans un restaurant mexicain? chinois? japonais? Où mange-t-on des spaghetti, généralement?
3. Aimes-tu les escargots? les sardines à l'huile? les huîtres? le pâté de campagne?
4. Au restaurant, est-ce que la qualité du service est très importante ou peu importante? Est-ce que tu laisses toujours un pourboire?
5. Préfères-tu «manger pour vivre (*to live*)» ou «vivre pour manger»?

Encore des nombres (60, 61, etc.)

60	soixante	80	quatre-vingts
61	soixante et un	81	quatre-vingt-un
62	soixante-deux	82	quatre-vingt-deux
63	soixante-trois	83	quatre-vingt-trois
70	soixante-dix	90	quatre-vingt-dix
71	soixante et onze	91	quatre-vingt-onze
72	soixante-douze	92	quatre-vingt-douze
73	soixante-treize	93	quatre-vingt-treize
		100	cent

Note that the number 80 (**quatre-vingts**) takes an **-s**, but that numbers based on it do not: **quatre-vingt-un**, and so on.

Note that the **-s** of **cents** is dropped if it is followed by any other number: **deux cent un, sept cent trente-cinq.**

101	cent un	500	cinq cents
102	cent deux, etc.	600	six cents
200	deux cents	700	sept cents
201	deux cent un, etc.	800	huit cents
300	trois cents	900	neuf cents
400	quatre cents	999	neuf cent quatre-vingt dix-neuf
		1 000	mille
		999 999	?

Like **cent, mille** (*one thousand*) is expressed without an article. **Mille** is invariable and thus never ends in **s.**

1 004	**mille quatre**
7 009	**sept mille neuf**
9 999	**neuf mille neuf cent quatre-vingt dix-neuf**

A. Voyage gastronomique. Vous passez trois jours en Bretagne avec des amis. Vous cherchez des restaurants dans un guide.

1. Avec un(e) camarade, regardez la carte et cherchez les villes où se trouvent les restaurants. Choisissez vos deux restaurants préférés, puis expliquez à la classe les raisons de votre choix (spécialités de la maison, type de cuisine, etc.).
2. Téléphonez pour réserver une table. Jouez les rôles du maître d'hôtel et du client (de la cliente). N'oubliez pas d'indiquer le nombre de personnes, le jour et l'heure de votre réservation. Vous pouvez aussi demander le prix du menu s'il n'est pas indiqué.

   MODÈLE: —Allô, c'est bien le 98.70.47.74?
   —Oui, c'est le restaurant...
   —Je voudrais réserver une table pour...

3. Maintenant votre camarade donne à la classe les détails de votre réservation: jour, heure et nombre de personnes. Allez-vous rencontrer d'autres camarades dans un de ces restaurants? Qui?

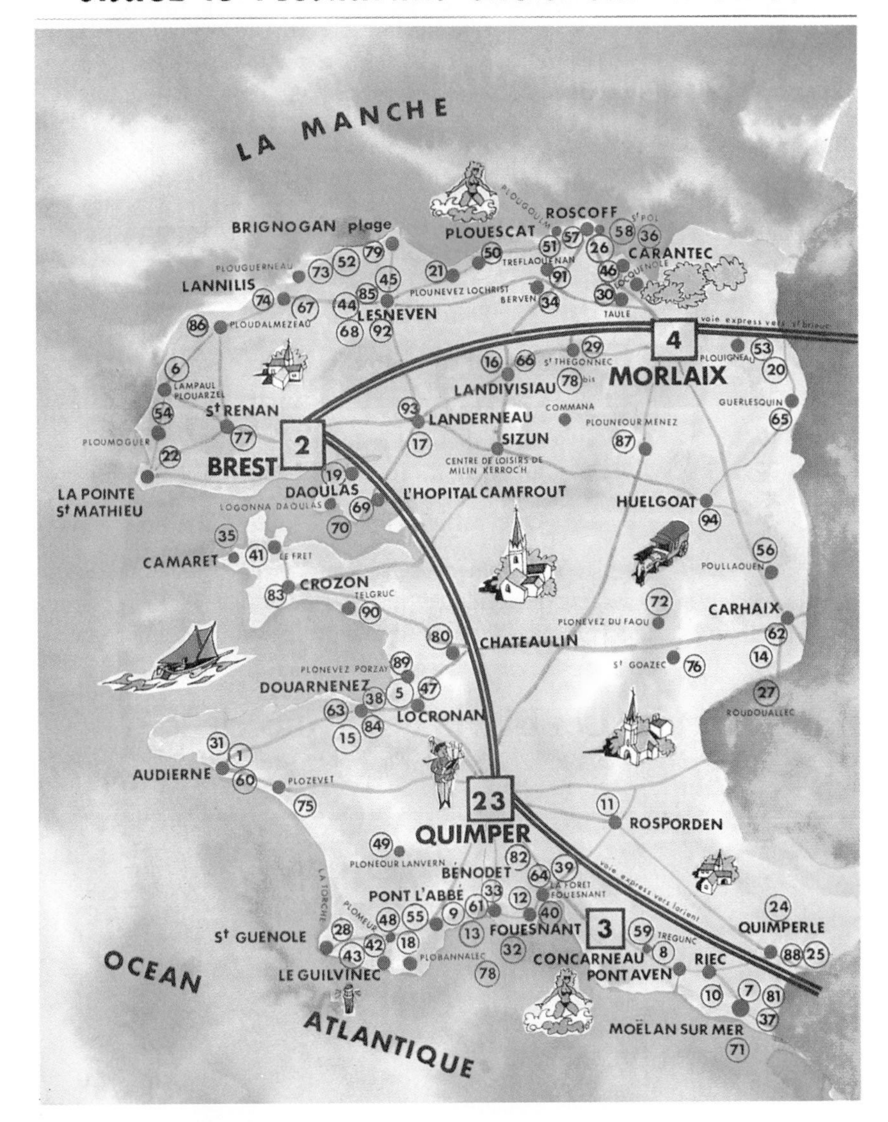

B. Problèmes de mathématiques. Inventez six problèmes selon le modèle, puis demandez à un(e) camarade de les résoudre (*solve them*).

+ {plus / et	− **moins**	× **fois**	= **font**

MODÈLE: $37 + 42 = ?$ $96 - 3 = ?$ $500 \times 24 = ?$

C. L'addition, s'il vous plaît! Avec le/la même camarade, reprenez vos rôles de l'exercice A (page 172). Imaginez que vous finissez votre repas et que vous demandez l'addition. D'après ce que vous avez commandé, le serveur (la serveuse) prépare l'addition et calcule les 15 pourcent (%) pour le service. Combien allez-vous payer chaque repas? Est-ce que vous allez laisser un pourboire? Combien allez-vous laisser?

	L'HIPPOPOTAMUS	LA TOUR DE LA PELOTE
Prix du repas	______________	______________
Service (15%)	______________	______________
Total	______________	______________
Pourboire?	______________	______________

Maintenant comparez les additions.

- Qui dans la classe dépense le plus pour déjeuner? pour dîner?
- Qui est le/la plus économe?
- Qui laisse un pourboire généreux? Qui ne laisse pas de pourboire?

D. Quel est le numéro? Demandez à un(e) camarade les numéros suivants.

1. son numéro de sécurité sociale 2. son adresse 3. le numéro de son permis de conduire (*driver's license*) 4. son code postal 5. le numéro de téléphone d'un ami (d'une amie) 6. le numéro de sa carte d'étudiant

L'argent français: Les billets et les pièces

Les promotions du mois. Ce soir vous faites des courses. Vous allez dans un magasin spécialisé en produits surgelés (*frozen*). Vous achetez un plat principal, des légumes et un dessert. Qu'est-ce que vous allez choisir?

Les promotions du mois chez Picard Surgelés

carte bleue CB

Bifteck bavette Bigard, 130 g env. Sac de 8. Le kg ~~75,70~~ **68,10**

Côtes de porc première et filet Bigard, 140 g. env. (le kg 32,00 F). Sac de 1,3 kg ~~46,30~~ **41,60**

Rôti de veau épaule, sans barde, Bigard, 1 kg environ. Le kg ~~58,20~~ **52,40**

Navarin (assortiment ragoût) Bigard, morceaux 70 g env. Sac de 1 kg ~~41,10~~ **37,00**

Poulet classe A, sans abats, 1,2 kg environ. Le kg ~~20,80~~ **18,70**

Poisson Thaï au lait de coco, avec riz printanier, Thaïlande, (le kg 58,44 F). Boîte de 450 g ~~29,20~~ **26,30**

Chili con carne, bœuf et légumes avec épices fortes à part, Mexique (le kg 61,42 F). Boîte de 350 g ~~23,90~~ **21,50**

Feuilletine de veau à l'orange, sauce porto, M. Guérard (le kg 92,50 F). Boîte de 440 g ~~45,20~~ **40,70**

Cannelloni (le kg 34,44 F). Boîte de 450 g ~~18,20~~ **15,50**

Petits pois doux extra-fins (le kg 10,00 F). Sac de 2,5 kg ~~28,40~~ **25,00**

Haricots mange-tout mi-fins (le kg 7,76 F). Sac de 2,5 kg ~~22,10~~ **19,40**

Epinards hachés, tablettes 6 g environ. Sac de 1 kg ~~8,60~~ **7,60**

Choux-fleurs en fleurettes. Sac de 1 kg ~~12,50~~ **11,00**

Chou vert, 2 plaques de 500 g. Sac de 1 kg ~~13,40~~ **11,80**

Poivrons verts et rouges mélangés en dés, Espagne. Sac de 1 kg ~~13,70~~ **12,10**

Pommes de terre en cubes à rissoler, préfrites Sac de 1 kg ~~9,80~~ **8,60**

Purée de carottes, tablettes de 6 g environ. Sac de 1 kg ~~13,20~~ **11,60**

Eclairs (2 café, 2 chocolat) 60 g, Patigel (le kg 53,75 F). Boîte de 4 ~~15,20~~ **12,90**

Bavaroise aux myrtilles, Niemetz, 530 g, 8 parts (le kg 54,15 F). Pièce ~~33,80~~ **28,70**

Tarte Tatin, Ninon, 450 g, 4 parts (le kg 44,22 F). Pièce ~~23,40~~ **19,90**

Fraises entières, France. Sac de 1 kg ~~23,70~~ **21,00**

Croissants feuilletés, pur beurre, cuits, 40-45 g (le kg 38,75 F). Sachet de 12 ~~21,90~~ **18,60**

Poire Belle-Hélène, Miko, 125 ml (le litre 27,40 F). Boîte de 4 ~~16,10~~ **13,70**

Crème vanille, Mövenpick, crème glacée vanille avec crème. Boîte de 1 litre ~~29,80~~ **25,30**

Composez votre menu.

Maintenant calculez le prix réel de ce que vous allez acheter, le prix en promotion que vous allez payer et combien vous allez économiser (*to save*).

	PRIX AVANT PROMOTION	PRIX APRÈS PROMOTION	DIFFÉRENCE DE PRIX
Plat principal	______	______	______
Légumes	______	______	______
Dessert	______	______	______
Total	______	______	______

Enfin, donnez votre menu et les résultats de vos calculs à la classe. Qui compose le menu le plus cher (*most expensive*)? Le plus original? Qui économise le plus? Combien économise-t-il/elle?

Commentaire culturel

Shopping for food in France. Although the **supermarché** is becoming more common in France, many French people still shop in the traditional way—that is, they walk from store to store in their own neighborhoods, finding the items that are especially fresh and engaging store owners and other customers in conversation. Shopping in this manner is part of the social fabric of the **quartier**, or neighborhood, and it gives city dwellers the same sense of community found in small towns or villages.

For the foreign visitor, shopping in the traditional French way is fun. To get a "cook's tour" of the great variety of specialty dishes that make up French cuisine, go to **le traiteur**, a shop that provides catering service to gourmet dishes, mostly precooked and ready to go. Although **traiteur** means "delicatessen owner," it is also used to designate the store itself.

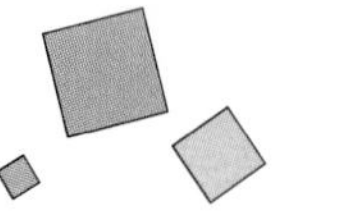

Étude de grammaire

20. Pointing Out People and Things: Demonstrative Adjectives

© GEORGES BELILE / AGENCE VANDYSTADT

Un choix difficile

FERNAND: Bonjour, Madame, est-ce qu'il est possible de goûter **ces** fromages?

L'ÉPICIÈRE: Mais bien sûr, choisissez.

FERNAND: Merci bien. Euh... je voudrais goûter un peu de **cet** emmenthal, et un peu de **ce** fromage-**là**. C'est du brie, n'est-ce pas?

L'ÉPICIÈRE: Oui, mais il est encore un peu jeune. Goûtez plutôt **ce** roquefort. Il est excellent. Alors, vous êtes prêt à choisir?

FERNAND: Oui, donnez-moi de l'emmenthal... là, **ce** morceau-**là**, et un peu de **ce** roquefort, s'il vous plaît.

1. Qu'est-ce que Fernand va goûter?
2. Quel fromage lui recommande l'épicière?
3. Quels fromages achète-t-il?

A. Forms of Demonstrative Adjectives

Demonstrative adjectives (*this/that, these/those*) are used to point out or to specify a particular person, object, or idea. They agree with the nouns they modify in gender and number.

	SINGULAR	PLURAL
Masculine	**ce** magasin **cet** escargot **cet** homme	**ces** magasins **ces** escargots **ces** hommes
Feminine	**cette** épicerie	**ces** épiceries

Note that **ce** becomes **cet** before masculine nouns that start with a vowel or mute **h.**

B. Use of *-ci* and *-là*

In English, *this/these* and *that/those* indicate the relative distance to the speaker. In French, the suffix **-ci** is added to indicate closeness, and **-là,** to indicate greater distance.

—Prenez-vous ce gâteau-ci?
—Non, je préfère cet éclair-là.

MAINTENANT A VOUS

A. Au supermarché. Qu'est-ce que vous achetez?

MODÈLE: une bouteille d'huile → J'achète cette bouteille d'huile.

1. une boîte de sardines 2. un camembert 3. des tomates 4. une bouteille de vin 5. quatre poires 6. une eau minérale 7. des pommes de terre 8. un éclair au café 9. un artichaut

B. Exercice de contradiction. Vous allez faire un pique-nique. Vous faites des courses avec un(e) camarade, mais vous n'êtes pas souvent d'accord! Jouez les rôles.

MODÈLE: pain / baguette → VOUS: On prend ce pain?
UN(E) AMI(E): Non, je préfère cette baguette.

1. saucissons / jambon
2. pâté / poulet froid
3. filets de bœuf / rôti de veau
4. haricots verts / boîte de carottes
5. pizza (*f.*) / sandwich
6. pommes / bananes
7. tarte / éclair
8. gâteau / glace
9. jus de fruit / bouteille de vin
10. boîte de sardines / morceau de fromage

C. Chez le traiteur. Avec un(e) camarade, jouez les rôles du client et du traiteur.

MODÈLE: poulet → LE/LA CLIENT(E): Donnez-moi du poulet, s'il vous plaît.
LE TRAITEUR: Ce poulet-ci ou ce poulet-là?

1. salade
2. rôti
3. légumes
4. pâté
5. pizza (*f.*)
6. saucisses

21. Expressing Desire, Ability, and Obligation: The Verbs *vouloir, pouvoir,* and *devoir*

*Le Procope**

MARIE-FRANCE: Tu **veux** du café?
CAROLE: Non, merci, je ne **peux** pas boire de café. Je **dois** faire attention. J'ai un examen aujourd'hui. Si je bois du café, je vais être trop nerveuse.
PATRICK: Je bois du café seulement les jours d'examen. Ça me donne de l'inspiration, comme à Voltaire!

Répétez le dialogue et substituez les expressions nouvelles aux expressions suivantes.

1. café → vin
2. nerveux (nerveuse) → lent(e) (*sluggish*)
3. Voltaire → Bacchus

A. Present-Tense Forms of *vouloir, pouvoir,* and *devoir*

The verbs **vouloir** (*to want*), **pouvoir** (*to be able to*), and **devoir** (*to owe; to have to, to be obliged to*) are all irregular in form.

	vouloir	pouvoir	devoir
je	veux	peux	dois
tu	veux	peux	dois
il, elle, on	veut	peut	doit
nous	voulons	pouvons	devons
vous	voulez	pouvez	devez
ils, elles	veulent	peuvent	doivent

*In the eighteenth century, Le Procope was the first place in France to serve coffee. Because coffee was considered a dangerous, subversive beverage, only liberals like Voltaire dared to consume it.

Voulez-vous des hors-d'œuvre, Monsieur?	*Do you want some hors d'œuvres, sir?*
Est-ce que nous **pouvons** avoir la salade avant le plat principal?	*Can we have the salad before the entrée?*
Je **dois** laisser un pourboire.	*I must leave a tip.*

B. Uses of *vouloir* and *devoir*

1. **Vouloir bien** means *to be willing to, to be glad to* (*do something*).

Je **veux bien.**	*I'm willing.* (*I'll be glad to.*)
Il **veut bien** goûter les escargots.	*He's willing to taste the snails.*

Vouloir dire expresses *to mean.*

Qu'est-ce que ce mot **veut dire**?	*What does this word mean?*
Que **veut dire** «pourboire»?	*What does* pourboire *mean?*

2. **Devoir** can express necessity or obligation.

Je suis désolé, mais nous **devons** partir.	*I'm sorry, but we must leave.*

Devoir can also express probability.

Elles **doivent** arriver demain.	*They are supposed to arrive tomorrow.*
Marc n'est pas en cours; il **doit** être malade.	*Marc isn't in class; he must be ill.*

When not followed by an infinitive, **devoir** means *to owe.*

Combien d'argent est-ce que tu **dois** à tes amis?	*How much money do you owe* (*to*) *your friends?*
Je **dois** 87 F à Henri et 99 F à Georges.	*I owe Henri 87 francs and Georges 99 francs.*

MAINTENANT A VOUS

A. Une soirée gastronomique. Lisez l'histoire suivante. Puis remplacez les mots en italique par les suggestions de personnes et plats ci-dessous (*below*). Créez à chaque fois une nouvelle histoire. (Attention! Faites toutes les modifications nécessaires pour que le reste de la phrase s'accorde avec les mots que vous remplacez.)

PERSONNES	PLATS
vous	un bœuf bourguignon
Anne et Jean-Loup	un couscous
toi	une soupe de poisson
ma mère	un coq au vin
moi	?

1. Ce soir *nous* voulons préparer *un jambalaya.* 2. *Nous* devons aller au supermarché acheter tous les ingrédients. 3. *Nous* voulons réussir notre dîner, alors nous achetons beaucoup de choses. 4. *Notre jambalaya* est si (*so*) copieux que nous pouvons inviter beaucoup d'amis.

Lequel des plats mentionnés préférez-vous? Nommez quelques (*a few*) ingrédients.

B. Une soirée compliquée. Composez un dialogue entre Christiane et François.

CHRISTIANE	FRANÇOIS
1. je / avoir / faim / et / je / vouloir / manger / maintenant	2. tu / vouloir / faire / cuisine?
3. non... / est-ce que / nous / pouvoir / aller / restaurant?	4. oui, je / vouloir / bien
5. où / est-ce que / nous / pouvoir / aller?	6. on / pouvoir / manger / couscous / Chez Bébert
7. nous / devoir / inviter / Carole	8. tu / pouvoir / inviter / Jean-Pierre aussi
9. ce / soir / ils / devoir / être / cité universitaire?	10. oui, ils / devoir / préparer / un examen
11. un examen? mais / nous / aussi, / nous / avoir / un / examen / demain	12. ce / (ne... pas) être / sérieux / nous / pouvoir / parler / de / ce / examen / restaurant

Maintenant donnez une réponse logique d'après le dialogue.

1. François veut aller dans un restaurant *italien / marocain / antillais.*
2. François pense que ce soir Jean-Pierre et Carole doivent *étudier / travailler / dîner.*
3. A la fin, Christiane et François *veulent / ne veulent pas* dîner au restaurant.

Mots-clés

Other ways to talk about obligations: **Devoir** is generally used to talk about what one or several individuals must do. To talk about necessity in a more general way, use **il faut** with an infinitive.

> **Pour ne pas grossir, il *faut* faire de l'exercice. *Il ne faut pas* manger trop d'aliments riches.**

Il faut can also be followed by nouns referring to objects, to talk about what is needed.

> **Pour faire une soupe à l'oignon, *il faut* des oignons, du consommé de bœuf, du fromage de Gruyère et du pain.**
> ***Il faut* du courage pour goûter des escargots, n'est-ce pas?**

C. **Qu'est-ce qu'il faut?** Répondez aux questions avec un(e) camarade de classe et notez vos conclusions. (Vous pouvez utiliser des infinitifs ou des noms.)

MODÈLE: Qu'est-ce qu'il faut pour faire plaisir (*to please*) à vos parents? → Il faut écrire beaucoup de lettres. Il faut aussi de la patience, parce qu'ils peuvent être difficiles.

1. pour apprendre un nouveau sport? 2. pour réussir à un examen de français? 3. pour s'amuser (*to have fun*) à une soirée? 4. pour avoir beaucoup d'amis? 5. pour avoir un mariage réussi? 6. pour être heureux (heureuse)?

D. **Conversation à trois.** Avec deux autres camarades vous allez préparer un repas pour toute la classe. Qu'est-ce que vous allez préparer? Où pouvez-vous acheter les provisions nécessaires? Comment voulez-vous partager (*to share*) le travail? Utilisez les verbes **pouvoir, vouloir** et **devoir.**

Expressions utiles: vouloir bien, devoir acheter, devoir commander, devoir essayer de préparer un plat français, pouvoir acheter, pouvoir choisir, pouvoir boire du champagne, devoir demander un pourboire

Après votre tête-à-tête (votre conversation), décrivez votre menu à la classe.

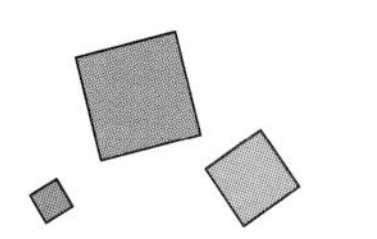

22. Asking About Choices: The Interrogative Adjective *quel*

Qu'est-ce que vous prenez?

Quel vin prenez-vous?

Quelle viande prenez-vous?

Quels légumes prenez-vous?

Quelles pâtisseries prenez-vous?

Avec un(e) camarade de classe, jouez les rôles du serveur et du client. Quelles sont les réponses du client?

A. Forms of the Interrogative Adjective *quel*

You are already familiar with the interrogative adjective **quel** in expressions such as **Quelle heure est-il?** and **Quel temps fait-il? Quel** (**quelle, quels, quelles**) means *which* or *what.* Its function is to elicit more precise information about a noun that is understood or established in context. It agrees in gender and number with the noun to which it refers.*

Quel fromage voulez-vous goûter?	*Which (What) cheese would you like to try?*
A **quelle** heure dînez-vous?	*What time do you have dinner?*
Dans **quels** restaurants aimez-vous manger?	*In what (which) restaurants do you like to eat?*
Quelles boissons préférez-vous?	*What (Which) beverages do you prefer?*

B. *Quel* with *être*

Quel can also stand alone before the verb **être** followed by the noun it modifies.

Quel est le prix de ce champagne?	*What's the price of this champagne?*
Quelle est la différence entre le Perrier et le Calistoga?	*What's the difference between Perrier (water) and Calistoga (water)?*

Mots-clés

Expressing admiration: **Quel** is also used in exclamations.

Quel père exemplaire!	*What an exemplary father!*
Quelle bonne idée!	*What a great idea!*

MAINTENANT A VOUS

A. Préparatifs. Vous organisez une soirée avec un(e) camarade. Formez des questions complètes et indiquez la lettre correspondant à l'adjectif interrogatif utilisé. Votre camarade donne une réponse.

MODÈLE: quel / boisson / apporter / tu? →
Quelle boisson apportes-tu? / (b)

*Note that the pronunciation of all four forms of **quel** is identical, [kɛl], but when the plural form precedes a word beginning with a vowel sound, there is liaison: **quels étudiants, quelles étudiantes,** [kɛl-ze-ty-djɑ̃(t)].

1. quel / viande / préparer / tu ?
2. quel / légumes / préférer / tu ?
3. quel / plat / apporter / tu ?
4. quel / salade / préparer / tu ?
5. quel / fromage / acheter / tu ?
6. quel / fruits / avoir / tu ?
7. quel / dessert / choisir / tu ?
8. quel / amies / inviter / tu ?

a. quel
b. quelle
c. quels
d. quelles

Maintenant, d'après les réponses de votre camarade, décrivez les plats à la classe.

B. Une interview. Interrogez vos camarades sur leurs goûts. Utilisez l'adjectif interrogatif **quel** et variez la forme de vos questions.

MODÈLE: sport → Quel est le sport que tu préfères?
(*ou*) Quel sport préfères-tu?

Voici des suggestions.

1. boisson
2. légume
3. viande
4. repas
5. distractions
6. disques
7. discothèque (*f.*)
8. programme de télévision
9. livres
10. revues
11. couleur (*f.*)
12. matières
13. vêtements
14. films

Quelle est la réponse la plus insolite (*unusual*)? la plus drôle?

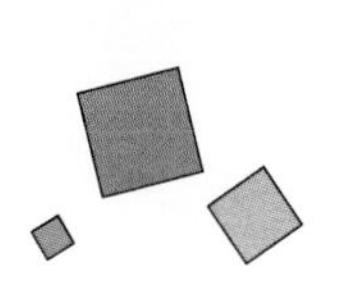

23. Describing People and Things: The Placement of Adjectives

La Tour d'Argent

MARGUERITE: Quel **beau** restaurant! Regarde ces **jolies** tables et ces **grandes** fenêtres qui donnent sur Notre-Dame.

VINCENT: Tu sais, nous sommes dans un **grand** restaurant **parisien.** Ici, **chaque** plat est **délicieux.**

MARGUERITE: Oui, mais il y a un **petit** détail qui manque.

VINCENT: Quoi donc?

MARGUERITE: Il n'y a pas de prix sur la carte!

Corrigez les phrases incorrectes.

1. Vincent et Marguerite dînent dans un petit bistrot.
2. Ce restaurant doit être cher.
3. Le restaurant a de grandes fenêtres qui donnent sur un jardin.

A. Adjectives That Usually Precede the Noun

1. Certain short and commonly used adjectives usually precede the nouns they modify.

REGULAR	IRREGULAR	IDENTICAL IN MASCULINE AND FEMININE
grand(**e**) *big, tall; great*	**beau, belle** *beautiful, handsome*	**autre** *other*
joli(**e**) *pretty*	**bon**(**ne**) *good*	**chaque** *each, every*
mauvais(**e**) *bad*	**faux, fausse** *false*	**jeune** *young*
petit(**e**) *small, little*	**gentil**(**le**) *nice, kind*	**pauvre** *poor; unfortunate*
vrai(**e**) *true*	**gros**(**se**) *large, fat, thick*	
	long(**ue**) *long*	
	nouveau, nouvelle *new*	
	vieux, vieille *old*	

La cuisine est une **grande** tradition pour les Français. — *Cooking is a great tradition for the French.*

La **nouvelle** cuisine est très populaire en ce moment. — *The "new cooking" is very popular right now.*

Antoine est un **vieux** restaurant de La Nouvelle-Orléans. — *Antoine is an old restaurant in New Orleans.*

Les **jeunes** clients aiment bien la propriétaire de La Poule au Pot. — *The young customers like the owner of the Poule au Pot.*

Un restaurant élégant en plein air, en Alsace

2. The adjectives **beau, nouveau,** and **vieux** are irregular. They have two masculine forms in the singular.

SINGULAR		
Masculine	*Masculine before vowel or mute* **h**	*Feminine*
un **beau** livre	un **bel** appartement	une **belle** voiture
un **nouveau** livre	un **nouvel** appartement	une **nouvelle** voiture
un **vieux** livre	un **vieil** appartement	une **vieille** voiture

PLURAL	
Masculine	*Feminine*
de **beaux** appartements	de **belles** voitures
de **nouveaux** appartements	de **nouvelles** voitures
de **vieux** appartements	de **vieilles** voitures

B. Adjectives Preceding Plural Nouns

When an adjective precedes the noun in the plural form, the plural indefinite article **des** generally becomes **de.***

J'ai **des** livres de cuisine.	J'ai **de** nouveaux livres de cuisine.
Commandons **des** desserts!	Commandons **de** bons desserts!

C. Adjectives That May Precede or Follow Nouns They Modify

The adjectives **ancien/ancienne** (*old; former*), **cher/chère** (*dear; expensive*), **grand**(**e**), and **pauvre** may either precede or follow a noun, but their meaning depends on their position. Generally, the adjective in question has a literal meaning when it follows the noun and a figurative meaning when it precedes the noun.

LITERAL SENSE	FIGURATIVE SENSE
C'est un homme très **grand.**† *He's a very tall man.*	C'est un très **grand** chef de cuisine. *He's a very great chef.*
Les clients **pauvres** ne vont pas à la Tour d'Argent. *Poor (not rich) customers don't go to the Tour d'Argent.*	**Pauvres** clients! Il n'y a plus de champagne! *The poor (unfortunate) customers! There's no more champagne!*
Il achète des chaises **anciennes** pour décorer la Tour d'Argent. *He's buying antique (ancient) chairs to decorate the Tour d'Argent.*	M. Sellier est **l'ancien** maître d'hôtel de la Tour d'Argent. *Mr. Sellier is the former maitre d' of the Tour d'Argent.*
C'est un vin très **cher.** *That's a very expensive wine.*	Ma **chère** amie... *My dear friend . . .*

MAINTENANT A VOUS

A. Le bon ordre. Faites des phrases.

MODÈLES: un restaurant / japonais → C'est un restaurant japonais.
une table / long → C'est une longue table.

---

*In colloquial speech, **des** is often retained before the plural adjective: **Elle trouve toujours** ***des beaux*** **fruits.**

†The adjective **grand**(e) is placed *after* the noun to mean *big* or *tall* only in descriptions of people. When it precedes the noun in descriptions of things and places, it means *big, tall, large:* **les grandes fenêtres, un grand appartement, une grande table.**

1. une assiette / vert
2. une serveuse / beau
3. un dîner / cher
4. un maître d'hôtel / gentil
5. un décor / joli
6. un chef de cuisine / nouveau
7. des prix / raisonnable
8. le plat / principal
9. des chaises / ancien
10. un dessert / délicieux

B. On fait la critique. Voici la description d'un nouveau restaurant à New York. Complétez les phrases avec les adjectifs entre parenthèses. Faites attention! Les adjectifs ne sont pas toujours dans le bon ordre.

MODÈLE: Le chef fait la cuisine selon *la tradition*... (français, vieux) →
Le chef fait la cuisine selon la vieille tradition française.

1. Les clients trouvent *une ambiance*... (bon, français)
2. Vous pouvez dîner sur *une terrasse*... (agréable, grand)
3. On peut commander *un vin*... (rouge, bon)
4. Il y a *du pain*... (vrai, français)
5. Les clients paient *des prix*... (raisonnable, petit)
6. Vous allez parler avec *la propriétaire*... (vieux, sympathique)
7. Les étudiants universitaires sont *des clients*... (agréable, jeune)

C. Une bonne table. Lisez ce que le magazine gastronomique *GaultMillau* dit du restaurant l'Auberge du Cheval Blanc à Lembach, en Alsace. Puis remplacez les adjectifs **vieux, opulente** et **large** par les adjectifs **ancien, pittoresque** et **varié.** Faites attention à la position des nouveaux adjectifs.

• LEMBACH

15/20 Auberge du Cheval Blanc
Un vieux relais de poste transformé en opulente auberge au large répertoire culinaire : salade aux crustacés, panaché de foie chaud, turbot aux huîtres. Produits magnifiques, exécution impeccable. Menus de 115 F à 265 F.
4, rue Wissembourg. F. lundi, mardi et du 4 au 22 juil. Jusqu'à 21 h. Tél. : 88 94 41 86.

Maintenant, avec un(e) camarade, faites la description d'un des restaurants dans votre région. Ensuite, présentez votre description devant la classe sans nommer le restaurant. Est-ce que les autres membres de la classe peuvent deviner de quel restaurant vous parlez?

Situation

Déjeuner sur le pouce*

Contexte *Nous sommes dans une croissanterie° du Quartier latin où Sébastien et Corinne, deux étudiants québécois, déjeunent sur le pouce, entre deux cours.*

°un magasin où on vend des croissants

Objectif *Sébastien et Corinne commandent un repas pour emporter* (to take out).

*Déjeuner... Snack lunch (literally, "lunch on the thumb")

LA SERVEUSE: Vous désirez?
SÉBASTIEN: Un croissant au jambon, s'il vous plaît.
CORINNE: Et pour moi, un croque-monsieur.
LA SERVEUSE: C'est tout?
SÉBASTIEN: Non, je voudrais aussi une crêpe au Grand-Marnier.° Et toi, Corinne?
CORINNE: C'est tout pour moi.
LA SERVEUSE: Et comme boisson?
SÉBASTIEN: Deux cafés, s'il vous plaît.
LA SERVEUSE: C'est pour emporter ou pour manger ici?
CORINNE: Pour emporter.
SÉBASTIEN: Ça fait combien?
LA SERVEUSE: Ça fait trente-sept francs trente... Merci.
SÉBASTIEN: Au revoir, merci.

crêpe... *French-style pancake served with Grand Marnier liqueur*

VARIATIONS

Improvisez! Vous et vos camarades êtes dans une crêperie à Paris pour déjeuner sur le pouce. Un étudiant (une étudiante) joue le rôle du serveur (de la serveuse). Voici la carte.

Crêpes

Prix nets

BEURRE ET SUCRE	11,00 F
POMMES (compote)	14,50 F
CITRON	14,00 F
MIEL D'ACADIA	17,00 F
CHOCOLAT CHAUD	17,00 F
CREME DE MARRONS	17,00 F
CONFITURE (fraise, abricot)	16,00 F
CONFITURE (myrtilles)	17,00 F
NOISETTES CHOCOLAT OU CARAMEL	19,50 F
LA CHOCONOIX	20,50 F
COCO CASSIS (noix de coco et crème de cassis)	19,50 F
CHANTILLY	18,00 F
SIROP D'ERABLE	18,00 F
GRAND MARNIER OU RHUM	19,50 F
LA CHATELAINE (Noisettes, chocolat chaud, Chantilly)	23,00 F
CLAFOUTIS Maison	15,50 F
+ Chantilly	17,50 F
CREPE TATIN A LA SAUCE NOUGAT (Pommes morceaux, sauce nougat, Calvados, Chantilly)	23,50 F
L'ARMADA (Poire arrosée de Calvados, chocolat chaud, Chantilly)	23,50 F
COCKTAIL DE FRUITS AU GRAND MARNIER	17,50 F

—Tu veux un hamburger et des frites?

A propos

Au restaurant

Voici d'autres expressions qu'on entend au restaurant.

Le maître d'hôtel, le serveur ou la serveuse:
- Combien de personnes, s'il vous plaît?
- Comment voulez-vous le bifteck?

Les clients:
- ...bleu (*extremely rare*)
- ...saignant (*rare*)
- ...à point (*medium*)
- ...bien cuit (*well done*)
- Je vais prendre...
- Donnez-moi aussi...
- L'addition, s'il vous plaît.
- Je vous dois combien? (*in a café*)
- Le service est-il compris? (*Is the tip included?*)

A. Jeu de rôles. Avec des camarades, utilisez ces nouvelles expressions pour créer une scène de restaurant depuis (*from*) l'arrivée des clients jusqu'à leur départ. Voici une description des rôles à jouer.

- Un membre de votre groupe est très gourmand. Il/Elle aime beaucoup manger et mange beaucoup. Commandez le repas d'un vrai gourmand.
- Un autre est un gourmet qui apprécie la bonne cuisine.
- Un autre a peur de grossir (*to gain weight*). Commandez un repas léger en (*light in*) calories.

Utilisez les cartes à la page suivante. Bon appétit!

B. Cuisine internationale. En groupes de deux ou trois, regardez ces annonces de restaurants parisiens. Choisissez ensemble le restaurant où vous voulez manger. Ensuite, expliquez votre choix aux autres et donnez autant de renseignements (*as much information*) que possible sur le restaurant de votre choix.

MODÈLE: Nous allons au Benkay parce que nous voulons goûter la cuisine japonaise. On peut déjeuner pour environ cent-trente francs. Le numéro de téléphone du restaurant est quarante-cinq, soixante-quinze, soixante-deux, soixante-deux. Il est ouvert (*open*) tous les jours.

Mots utiles: ouvert (*open*), fermé, tous les jours, les spécialités, la vente à emporter, le parking

C. **Question de goût.** Modifiez les noms pour expliquer vos goûts à la classe. Vous pouvez utiliser plusieurs adjectifs par phrase. Attention à la place de l'adjectif.

	Suggestions:
1. J'aime les *restaurants*.	bon / nouveau / cher / intéressant / chinois...
2. Je vais souvent au *restaurant* avec des *amis*.	sympathique / intime / jeune bon / amusant...
3. Nous buvons souvent du *vin et de la bière*.	californien / français / frais / bon / rouge...
4. Nous prenons quelquefois des *repas* ensemble.	cher / bon / long / agréable / gastronomique...

Commentaire culturel

Famous regional French dishes. Although "fast food" is making inroads into French culture, **la grande cuisine** remains one of France's great traditions. This is due less to sophisticated recipes than to the variety and delicacy of French regional products. Regional cuisine is as diverse as French geography, from the endless variety of **crêpes** in Brittany to oysters and rich **pâtés de foie gras** in the Bordeaux region; from the **quiche,** fruit desserts, and brandies of Alsace to the heady flavors of garlic, herbs, and fresh tomato and fish dishes of Provence. Here are some famous regional dishes.

- **Ratatouille provençale:** A vegetable casserole made with sliced eggplant, tomatoes, onions, bell peppers, and zucchini, first fried in olive oil and garlic, then simmered in alternating layers until flavors blend. It can be served hot as an **entrée** or cold as an **hors-d'œuvre.**
- **Salade niçoise:** A salad of cooked vegetables (potatoes, string beans, bell peppers, and tomatoes) garnished with hard-boiled eggs, anchovies, canned tuna, olives, and lettuce. It is served with a garlic flavored **vinaigrette.**
- **Bouillabaisse marseillaise:** A two-course dish consisting of a fish-and-seafood stew served on thick slices of French bread. It is served with a garlic mayonnaise called **ailloli.**

- **Choucroute alsacienne:** Sauerkraut simmered in a white Riesling wine **consommé,** flavored with herbs and spices, amd served with smoked bacon, Strasbourg pork sausages, smoked pork or ham, and potatoes.
- **Tripes à la mode de Caen** (Normandy): A famous casserole dish of tripe (the stomach lining of calf or beef), simmered for ten hours or more in cider with calves' feet, onions, carrots, leeks, herbs, and garlic.

- **Crêpes bretonnes:** Very thin pancakes made of buckwheat flour and filled with roasted sausages, meats, or cheese, or made of wheat flour and filled with jam, honey, or fruit.
- **Cassoulet de Toulouse:** A casserole dish made with dried white beans, simmered for days with ham, bacon, sausage, goose or duck meat, and flavored with tomatoes, herbs, and wine.
- **Escargots à la bourguignonne:** Snails cooked in broth, replaced in their shells, and baked in bubbling hot butter with herbs and spices. It is served at the beginning of a meal.

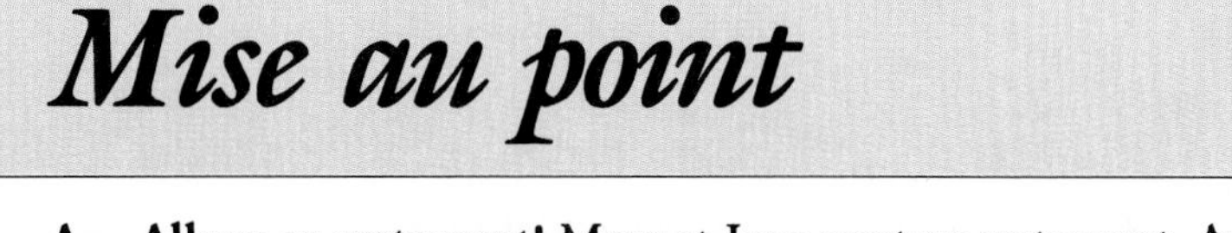

Mise au point

A. Allons au restaurant! Marc et Jean vont au restaurant. Avec un(e) camarade, faites des phrases complètes et jouez le dialogue entre les deux amis.

MARC: je / vouloir / aller / restaurant
JEAN: dans / quel / restaurant / vouloir / tu / aller?
MARC: on / ne... pas / pouvoir / passer / trop / temps / restaurant
JEAN: oui / on / devoir / être / université / à / 2 heures
MARC: alors / nous / pouvoir aller / dans / bistrot
JEAN: je / aller / manger / sandwich
MARC: moi / vouloir / aussi / dessert
JEAN: addition / s'il vous plaît. Mais / je / ne... pas / avoir / argent
MARC: moi / je / aller / payer / addition / et / laisser / pourboire
JEAN: merci / je / te / devoir / trente-cinq / francs

1. Qui veut un dessert?
2. Qui paye l'addition? Pourquoi?

B. Vos impressions. Complétez les phrases suivantes à la forme affirmative ou à la forme négative, selon votre opinion personnelle. Utilisez **devoir, pouvoir** ou **vouloir** + *infinitif* dans chaque phrase.

MODÈLE: Les étudiants ______. →
Les étudiants ne doivent pas étudier jusqu'à minuit tous les soirs.

1. Le professeur ______.
2. Les parents ______.
3. Mes camarades ______.
4. Les hommes ______.
5. Les femmes ______.
6. Je ______.

Interactions

In this chapter, you practiced how to specify, express desire and obligation, and describe people and things. Act out the following situations, using the vocabulary and structures from these chapters.

1. **Au marché.** You are at an open-air food market. Tell the shopkeeper (your partner) what you would like to buy. Be sure to indicate specifically which items you want. She or he is happy to serve you, but you never seem to be satisfied, and you become a little bossy. You change your mind often, and then you leave abruptly.
2. **Au restaurant.** You are out to dinner with a special person. You want everything to be perfect. You make everything clear to the head waiter or waitress (your partner). Tell him or her that you want a small table for two, a good waiter or waitress, and a good wine. Ask what meal is good this evening and which dessert is good. Explain that you have no money (**argent** [m.]). Jokingly ask if you can do the dishes. Ask if the restaurant accepts credit cards (**accepter des cartes de crédit**). Thank him or her for the help.

Vocabulaire

Verbes

apporter to bring; to carry
devoir to owe; to have to, be obliged to
goûter to taste
laisser to leave (behind)
pouvoir to be able
vouloir to want
  vouloir bien to be willing

Substantifs

l'addition (*f.*) bill, check (*in a restaurant*)
l'argent (*m.*) money
la baguette (**de pain**) baguette
le billet bill (*currency*)
la boîte (**de conserve**) can (of food)
la carte menu
le centime 1/100th of a French franc
le crabe crab
la crêpe crepe (*French pancake*)
l'éclair (*m.*) eclair (*pastry*)
l'entrée (*f.*) first course
l'escargot (*m.*) snail
le filet fillet (*beef, fish, etc.*)
le franc franc (*currency*)
la glace ice cream; ice
le *hors-d'œuvre appetizer
le jus (**de fruit**) (fruit) juice
le menu fixed (price) menu
le morceau piece
le pâté de campagne (country) pâté
la pièce coin
le plat course (*meal*)
le porc pork
le pourboire tip
le prix price
le rôti roast
les sardines (**à l'huile**) (*f.*) sardines (in oil)
le saucisson dry sausage
le (**la**) **serveur** (**-euse**) waiter, waitress
la sole sole (*fish*)

Adjectifs

ancien(ne) old, antique; former
bon(ne) good
bon marché cheap, inexpensive
cher, chère dear
faux, fausse false
frais, fraîche fresh
jeune young

joli(e) pretty
mauvais(e) bad
nouveau, nouvel, nouvelle new
pauvre poor; unfortunate
prêt(e) **à** + *infinitive* ready to (do something)
quel, quelle which (*int. adj.*)
vieux, vieil, vieille old
vrai(e) true

Les magasins

la boucherie butcher shop
la boulangerie bakery
la charcuterie pork butcher's shop (delicatessen)
l'épicerie (*f.*) grocery store
la pâtisserie pastry shop; pastry
la poissonnerie fish store

Mots divers

cela (**ça**) this, that
ensuite then, next
même same; even
parfois sometimes
plutôt instead, rather
(**et**) **puis** (and) then, next
si so (very); if

Expressions utiles

J'aimerais (+ *infinitive*)...	*I would like*
Que veut dire... ?	*What does _____ mean?*
Il faut...	*It is necessary to / One needs . . .*

INTERMÈDE 6

Lecture

AVANT DE LIRE

Skimming for the gist: The following article appeared in a magazine from Québec, *Clin d'œil.*

- Glance at the title, the photographs, the lead lines, and the first few sentences. What do you think the article is about?
- Next, skim the article for the major points. Skip over the sections you don't understand. Did you find what you expected? What surprised you?
- Now go back to the passages you found difficult on first reading, and guess their meaning based on the rest of the article.

Skimming is a useful way to approach any new text, particularly in a foreign language. You will usually find it easier to understand more difficult passages once you have a general idea of the overall content. But your aim in reading authentic French texts is never to understand everything; just try to get the gist, then answer the questions that follow the reading.

OBJECTIF MINCEUR

par Janine Renaud

Manger au resto... sans prendre un kilo

Les repas au restaurant ne sont pas nécessairement synonymes de calories en trop. Tout comme à la maison, on peut choisir ses aliments et opter pour la minceur. Par obligation ou par plaisir, à l'occasion ou cinq fois par semaine, vous pouvez manger au restaurant sans engraisser... à certaines conditions!

Ne pas s'affamer

Un estomac vide est plus vulnérable à la tentation, c'est bien connu. Donc...

- Prenez un bon petit déjeuner, sinon vous serez littéralement morte de faim dès 11 heures et prête à vous gaver sans discernement le midi. Si vous avez l'appétit capricieux au lever, prenez une collation légère au milieu de la matinée: un verre de lait écrémé, un muffin au son et un fruit, par exemple.
- Buvez de l'eau en abondance; cela vous coupera l'appétit. Chaque matin, remplissez d'eau une bouteille d'un litre et assurez-vous de l'avoir bue au complet avant d'aller dîner.
- Quinze minutes avant le repas, buvez un jus de légumes. Cela apaisera votre faim et vous pourrez choisir votre menu plus « lucidement ».
- Choisissez votre restaurant la veille, après le souper par exemple, et n'en démordez pas même si la pizzeria vous fait des clins d'oeil insistants vers la fin de la matinée.

Les bons choix

- Les poissons bouillis ou pochés.
- Les grillades maigres (poulet, poisson, boeuf), à condition qu'elles ne soient pas marinées dans l'huile (n'hésitez pas à demander au serveur).
- Les légumes nature, sans beurre, sauce ou vinaigrette.
- Les grains entiers comme le pain de blé et le riz brun.
- L'eau et le café décaféiné (sans calories et sans excitant).
- Les demi-portions ou les entrées de pâtes et de salades, moins copieuses que les plats principaux.

Les mauvais choix

- Les sauces riches – donc presque toutes – et les vinaigrettes.
- Le pain blanc, pauvre en éléments nutritifs mais riche en calories.
- Le beurre, évidemment, sous toutes ses formes.
- Le fromage, hypocrite, qui se glisse dans les salades ou sur les pâtes.
- Les charcuteries, grasses et salées (attention au jambon, il y en a partout!).
- Les fritures et toutes les panures.

De bons menus

GREC
non aux brochettes (marinées dans l'huile);
oui à la salade grecque sans huile.

CHINOIS
non aux pâtés impériaux et aux sauces sucrées;
oui au chow mein et au chop suey au poulet.

ITALIEN
non aux sauces blanches ou au beurre à l'ail;
oui aux pâtes avec sauce tomate et légumes.

JAPONAIS
non au tempura;
oui au sushi.

FRUITS DE MER
non aux crevettes panées;
oui au cocktail de crevettes.

CASSE-CROÛTE
non au sandwich chaud au poulet;
oui au sandwich tomates-laitue-pain de blé.

COMPRÉHENSION

1. A votre avis, quel est le conseil le plus important pour ne pas avoir faim?
2. Donnez deux aliments conseillés et deux à éviter (*avoid*).
3. En suivant ces conseils, imaginez ce que vous pouvez manger dans un restaurant mexicain, dans un restaurant français. Qu'est-ce que vous ne pouvez pas manger?
4. Composez le petit déjeuner, le déjeuner et le dîner idéals pour ne pas grossir.
5. Êtes-vous au régime? Si oui, qu'est-ce que vous ne mangez pas?
6. Est-ce que vous réfléchissez à ce que vous allez commander quand vous êtes au restaurant, ou est-ce que vous choisissez ce que vous aimez?

Par écrit

A. Une conversation au restaurant. Vous êtes au restaurant et vous entendez une partie d'une conversation. Imaginez ce que répond l'autre personne.

LA PERSONNE PRÈS DE VOUS	SON COMPAGNON
1. Et alors, Pascal, tu as très faim? Que veux-tu prendre ce soir comme plat principal?	2. ________...
3. Si tu veux... moi, je préfère le poisson. Et comme boisson? Qu'est-ce que tu veux?	4. ________...
5. C'est une bonne idée. Ce vin-ci est excellent. Et tu prends des légumes?	6. ________...
7. Ah oui? Je déteste ça. Et comme dessert, qu'est-ce que tu prends?	8. ________...
9. Oui, ça va bien avec un bon dîner. Moi, je prends de la tarte aux pommes. Oh, je n'ai pas d'argent! Tu peux payer, n'est-ce pas?	10. (Zut!)...

B. Mon restaurant préféré. Ecrivez un petit mot (*note*) pour inviter un ami (une amie) à dîner avec vous. Pour persuader votre ami(e), faites une description du restaurant. Utilisez les questions suivantes comme guide.

Dans quel restaurant préférez-vous dîner? Est-ce que ce restaurant est célèbre? Est-ce qu'il est fréquenté (*visited*) par beaucoup de clients? Mangez-vous souvent dans ce restaurant? Quand? Est-ce que la carte est simple ou compliquée? Quel est votre plat préféré? Quelle est la spécialité du chef? Qu'est-ce que vous buvez?

Commencez par **Cher** (**Chère**) ________. Terminez par **A bientôt** (*See you soon*)...

Communication et vie pratique 2

ACTIVITÉ

La famille de Daniel Klein. M. et Mme Klein fêtent leur anniversaire de mariage pendant que (*while*) la mère de Mme Klein, Mme Duriez, s'occupe des enfants. Décrivez ce qui se passe (*what's happening*) à la maison pendant leur absence.

- Que fait Daniel? Et ses frères et sœurs?
- Que fait la sœur de Daniel dans la cuisine? (Donnez aussi les ingrédients.)
- Et qu'est-ce qui se passe dans la rue?
- Que fait Mme Duriez pendant ce temps?

EXPRESSION ÉCRITE

Situation: Une lettre de recommandation. Your instructor has been asked to write a confidential letter of recommendation, giving an opinion about your work, your character, your talents, and your future plans. Write the one-paragraph letter you would like to have him or her send.

Avant d'écrire

Topic sentences. In the reading in *Intermède 4,* you looked for the topic sentence in each paragraph. As you structure your letter of recommendation, keep in mind what you discovered about topic sentences. After you have jotted down several things you want to say, write a single sentence that sums up the main point you want to make in your letter. A topic sentence is always an *assertion,* an idea you will support in the rest of your letter. Write a few trial topic sentences before you settle on the final one. Underline the topic sentence before you hand in the letter.

CHAPITRE SEPT

Vive les vacances!

—Que c'est bon, les vacances!
—Oui, on oublie ses problèmes, on peut faire de la voile...
—Et on peut dormir jusqu'à midi!

Étude de vocabulaire

Les vacances en France

A. Où passer les vacances? Quels sont les avantages touristiques des endroits (*places*) suivants? **Autres possibilités:** faire du cheval, de la plongée sous-marine, du ski nautique, du ski de fond, une promenade, une randonnée, pêcher...

1. Qu'est-ce qu'on peut faire dans les montagnes? 2. Dans les lacs? 3. Sur les plages? 4. Sur les routes de campagne? 5. Sur les fleuves? 6. Dans les forêts? 7. A la mer?

Maintenant expliquez où vous voulez passer vos prochaines vacances et quelles activités on peut faire à cet endroit.

B. Activités de vacances. Qu'est-ce qu'ils font?

1. Que fait un nageur (une nageuse)? Où trouve-t-on beaucoup de nageurs?
2. Que fait un campeur (une campeuse)? Où fait-on du camping en France? Aux États-Unis?
3. Que fait un skieur (une skieuse)? Où fait-on du ski en France? Aux États-Unis?
4. Que fait un cycliste? Où fait-on de la bicyclette en France? Aux États-Unis?
5. Combien de nageurs, campeurs, skieurs, cyclistes y a-t-il dans la classe? D'habitude, où passent-ils leurs vacances?

Au magasin de sports

A. Achats. (*Purchases.*) Complétez les phrases selon l'image.

1. Le jeune homme va acheter des ______. Il va passer ses vacances à Grenoble où il veut ______.
2. La jeune femme veut acheter un ______ et des ______. Elle va descendre sur la Côte d'Azur (*French Riviera*) où elle va ______ et ______.
3. La jeune fille a envie d'acheter des ______ de ski, des chaussures de ______ et un ______ de ski. Sa famille va passer les vacances dans les Alpes où elle va ______.
4. L'homme va acheter un ______, un ______ et une ______. Il va ______ dans le nord de la France ce week-end.
5. Le garçon veut acheter un ______. Il va passer l'été dans une colonie de vacances (*summer camp*) où il aime ______ dans le lac.
6. La vieille dame est très sportive. Elle va acheter un ______ et des ______. Ce week-end, elle va ______ avec son mari à Grenoble.
7. Le vieux monsieur perd patience. Il veut acheter un ______.

B. L'intrus. Dans les groupes suivants, trouvez le mot qui ne va pas avec les autres. Expliquez votre choix.

1. le slip de bain / les lunettes de soleil / l'huile solaire / l'anorak
2. la tente / le maillot de bain / le sac de couchage / le sac à dos
3. les gants de ski / le sac à dos / les skis / l'anorak
4. le slip de bain / les chaussures de ski / le short / le maillot de bain

C. Choix de vêtements. Qu'est-ce qu'on porte pour faire les activités suivantes?

MODÈLE: pour aller pêcher (*to go fishing*) →
Pour aller pêcher, on porte un chapeau, un vieux pantalon...

1. pour aller faire du ski nautique 2. pour aller à la montagne 3. pour faire une promenade dans la forêt 4. pour aller faire de la bicyclette 5. pour aller faire du bateau 6. pour faire du ski de fond

Et vous? Décrivez les vêtements que vous portez quand vous faites votre sport favori.

D. Conseils pratiques. Vous préparez un voyage en Tunisie. Voici les vêtements qu'on vous recommande.

Les vêtements

En hiver : quelques pulls, un imperméable et des vêtements de demi-saison.
En été : des vêtements légers en fibres naturelles, maillot de bain, lunettes de soleil, chapeau, chaussures aérées, tenues pratiques pour les excursions. Sans oublier un léger pull pour les soirées et les hôtels climatisés.

1. Selon la brochure, quels vêtements mettez-vous dans votre valise si vous voyagez en hiver? en été? Donnez des exemples.
2. A votre avis, quel temps fait-il en Tunisie en hiver? en été?

Imaginez maintenant que vous travaillez dans une agence de voyages. Quels vêtements allez-vous conseiller à des touristes qui voyagent en Alaska? au Mexique? dans le Grand Canyon? Quels autres achats conseillez-vous?

Des années importantes

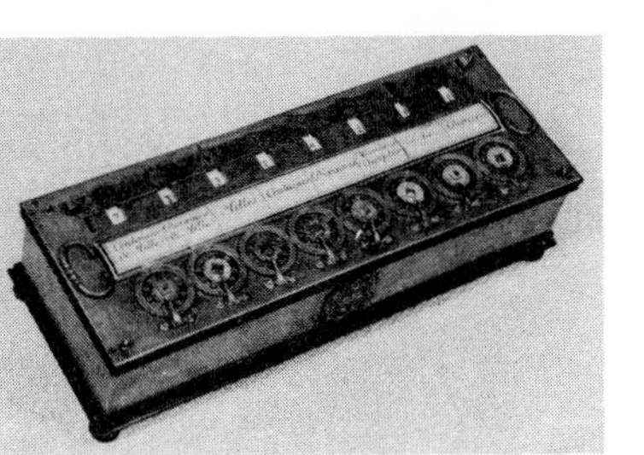
COURTESY OF IBM ARCHIVES

1642 La machine à calculer inventée par Blaise Pascal en seize cent quarante-deux.

1783 Le ballon à air chaud inventé par les frères Montgolfier en dix-sept cent quatre-vingt-trois.

© BETTMANN ARCHIVES

1835 Les procédés de développement des images photographiques inventés par Jacques Daguerre en dix-huit cent trente-cinq.

1946 Le bikini, créé en dix-neuf cent quarante-six par Louis Réard.

In French, years are expressed with a multiple of **cent** or with **mil.***

dix-neuf cents (mil neuf cents)	*1900*
dix-neuf cent quatre-vingt huit (mil neuf cent quatre-vingt huit)	*1988*
seize cent quatre (mil six cent quatre)	*1604*

***Mille** is spelled **mil** when years are spelled out. An exception is the year 1000, **l'an mille,** or 2000, **l'an deux mille.**

The preposition **en** is used to express *in* with a year.

en dix-neuf cent vingt-trois — *in 1923*

Mots-clés

To talk about a decade or an era:

les années ______________ — Pendant les années soixante (*During the sixties*), les étudiants discutaient plus souvent de politique.

A. Un peu d'histoire. Êtes-vous bon(ne) en histoire? Avec un(e) camarade, trouvez la date qui correspond à chaque événement historique.

1. Charlemagne est couronné (*crowned*) empereur d'Occident.	a. 1763
2. Guillaume, Duc de Normandie, conquiert (*conquers*) l'Angleterre.	b. 1944
3. Jeanne d'Arc bat (*beats*) les Anglais à Orléans.	c. 1804
4. Les Français perdent le Canada.	d. 1889
5. Prise de la Bastille.	e. 1066
6. Napoléon est couronné empereur des Français.	f. 1429
7. Alexandre-Gustave Eiffel construit la Tour Eiffel.	g. 1979
8. Débarquement (*landing*) anglo-américain en France.	h. 1789
9. Premier lancement (*launch*) de la fusée Ariane.	i. l'an 800

B. Dates inoubliables. Lisez les dates suivantes. Quel événement correspond à chaque date?

MODÈLE: 28.6.19 →
le vingt-huit juin dix-neuf cent dix-neuf: le Traité de Versailles*

1. 7.12.41	a. Le tremblement de terre à San Francisco
2. 22.11.63	b. L'éruption du Mont Sainte-Hélène (état de Washington)
3. 2.9.45	c. La fin de la Deuxième Guerre mondiale (*WW II*) aux États-Unis.
4. 18.4.06	d. L'attaque de Pearl Harbor
5. 18.5.80	e. L'assassinat de J. F. Kennedy
6. ?	f. Aujourd'hui

*Le Traité de Versailles marque la fin de la Première Guerre mondiale (*World War I*).

C. L'avenir. (*The future.*) Quels sont vos projets d'avenir? Posez les questions suivantes à un(e) camarade. Ensuite, présentez à la classe une observation sur l'avenir de votre camarade.

1. En quelle année vas-tu obtenir (*obtain*) ton diplôme universitaire?
2. En quelle année vas-tu commencer à exercer un métier (une profession)?
3. En quelle année vas-tu prendre ta retraite?

Étude de grammaire

24. Expressing Actions: *dormir* and Similar Verbs; *venir* and *tenir*

Les joies de la nature

JEAN-PIERRE: Où allez-vous passer vos vacances cet été?
MICHÈLE: Cette année nous **tenons** à descendre en Espagne. Nous voulons faire du camping près d'une plage. La mer, les pins, les fleurs sentent si bon en été! **Viens** avec nous, ça va être super! Nous partons le 2 août.
JEAN-PIERRE: Heu... **dormir** sous une tente... je n'aime pas beaucoup ça...
ÉDOUARD: Une tente? Pas question! On **dort** dans la caravane, c'est plus confortable!

Décidez d'après le dialogue si les affirmations suivantes sont probables ou peu probables. Corrigez les phrases improbables.

1. Michèle et Édouard ont peur de dormir sous une tente.
2. Jean-Pierre adore camper.
3. Michèle est romantique.
4. Michèle et Édouard aiment la nature.

A. *Dormir* (*to sleep*) and Verbs Like *dormir*

1. The verbs in the group **dormir** have an irregular conjugation.

PRESENT TENSE OF **dormir**			
je	dors	nous	dormons
tu	dors	vous	dormez
il, elle, on	dort	ils, elles	dorment

Je dors très bien. — *I sleep very well.*
Dormez-vous à la belle étoile? — *Do you sleep in the open air (under the stars)?*
Nous dormons jusqu'à 7 h 30. — *We sleep until 7:30.*

2. Verbs conjugated like **dormir** include the following.

partir *to leave, to depart* — **servir** *to serve*
sentir *to feel; to sense; to smell* — **sortir** *to go out; to take out*

Je pars en vacances. — *I'm leaving on vacation.*
Ce plat **sent** bon (mauvais). — *This dish smells good (bad).*
Nous servons le petit déjeuner à 8 heures. — *We serve breakfast at 8:00.*
A quelle heure allez-vous **sortir** ce soir? — *What time are you going out tonight?*

B. *Partir, sortir,* and *quitter*

Partir, sortir, and **quitter** can all mean *to leave,* but each is used differently. **Partir** is either used alone or is followed by a preposition.

Je pars. — *I'm leaving.*
Elle part de (**pour**) Cannes. — *She's leaving from (for) Cannes.*

Sortir is also used either alone or with a preposition. In this usage, **sortir** implies leaving an enclosed space.

Tu sors? — *You're going out?*
Elle sort de la caravane. — *She's getting out of the camping trailer.*
Sortons de l'eau! — *Let's get out of the water!*

Sortir can also mean that one is going out for the evening, or it can be used to imply that one person is going out with someone else in the sense of seeing him or her regularly.

Tu **sors** ce soir? — *Are you going out tonight?*
Michèle et Édouard **sortent** ensemble. — *Michèle and Edouard are going out together.*

When **sortir** is followed by a direct object, it means *to take out* in the sense of taking something out from an enclosed space.

Elles sortent les vêtements des valises.	*They are taking the clothes out of the suitcases.*
Sortez la clef de votre poche!	*Take the key out of your pocket!*

Quitter, a regular **-er** verb, always requires a direct object, either a place or a person.

Je **quitte Paris.**	*I'm leaving Paris.*
Elle **quitte son ami.**	*She's leaving her friend.*

C. *Venir* and *tenir*

1. The verbs **venir** (*to come*) and **tenir** (*to hold*) are irregular.

venir				tenir			
je	viens	nous	venons	je	tiens	nous	tenons
tu	viens	vous	venez	tu	tiens	vous	tenez
il, elle, on	vient	ils, elles	viennent	il, elle, on	tient	ils, elles	tiennent

Nous **venons** de Saint-Malo.	*We come from Saint-Malo.*
Viens voir les clowns!	*Come see the clowns!*
Voici ma sœur. Elle **tient** ses skis à la main.	*Here's my sister. She's holding her skis in her hand.*

Venir de plus an infinitive means *to have just* (done something).

Je **viens de nager.**	*I have just come from swimming.*
Mes amis **viennent de téléphoner.**	*My friends have just telephoned.*

Tenir à plus an infinitive means *to be eager* or *determined* to do something.

Nous **tenons** beaucoup **à faire** de la planche à voile.	*We are determined to go windsurfing.*

2. Verbs conjugated like **venir** and **tenir** include the following.

devenir	*to become*
obtenir	*to get, to obtain*
revenir	*to come back*

Ils **reviennent** de vacances.	*They're coming back from vacation.*
On **devient** expert grâce à l'expérience.	*One becomes expert with (thanks to) experience.*
Patrick va **obtenir** des renseignements.	*Patrick is going to obtain some information.*

MAINTENANT A VOUS

A. Bon voyage! Complétez l'histoire avec les verbes de la colonne de droite. Puis racontez l'histoire à nouveau en commençant (*beginning*) par «Les Dupont... »

Nous venons de Saint-Malo. Nous voulons visiter les États-Unis. En juin, nous _______[1] un visa au consulat américain et nous _______[2] pour les États-Unis. Nous _______[3] à visiter New York, Washington et La Nouvelle-Orléans.	partir obtenir tenir
Chaque matin nous _______[4] jusqu'à huit heures. Après le petit déjeuner, nous _______[5] l'hôtel pour aller découvrir l'Amérique. Le soir, nous _______[6] dîner au restaurant. En deux semaines nous _______[7] très américains. Mais hélas, c'est la fin des vacances et nous _______[8] en France.	dormir sortir quitter revenir devenir

Maintenant imaginez que c'est vous qui partez en vacances en France. Reprenez le passage, faites tous les changements nécessaires et racontez votre voyage au reste de la classe. Commencez par «Je viens de... »

B. La curiosité. Imaginez ce que ces personnes viennent de faire. Donnez trois possibilités pour chaque phrase.

MODÈLE: Albert rentre d'Afrique. →
Il vient de visiter le Sénégal. Il vient de passer une semaine au soleil. Il vient de faire un safari.

1. Jennifer quitte Paris. 2. Je sors du magasin de sport. 3. Nous revenons de la montagne. 4. Jean-Jacques et Yvon reviennent de la campagne. 5. Marie-Laure rentre du Canada.

C. Conversation. Engagez avec un(e) camarade assis(e) loin de vous une conversation basée sur les questions suivantes. Ensuite, faites un commentaire sur les habitudes (*habits*) ou les attitudes de ce(tte) camarade.

1. Pars-tu souvent en voyage? Où vas-tu? Viens-tu d'acheter des vêtements ou d'autres objets nécessaires pour tes vacances? Qu'est-ce que tu viens d'acheter?

Ski de randonnée en Vanoise, Alpes françaises

2. Sors-tu souvent pendant (*during*) le week-end ou restes-tu à la maison? Sors-tu souvent pendant la semaine? Qu'est-ce que tu portes quand tu sors?
3. Fumes-tu (*Do you smoke*)? Tes amis fument-ils? Est-ce que ton appartement ou ta chambre sent (*smells of*) la fumée? Deviens-tu désagréable si un ami (une amie) fume chez toi (*at your house*)? Sens-tu une différence si un ami (une amie) arrête (*stops*) de fumer? Devient-il (elle) calme ou nerveux (nerveuse)?

D. En français, s'il vous plaît.

1. My family is leaving on vacation today. 2. My cousins are leaving New York. 3. My sister is leaving for Brittany tomorrow at 9:45. 4. My brother has just bought a windsurfer. 5. He's leaving the house with his friend. 6. Why are you leaving? 7. You're going out with my sister now? 8. Let's leave together! 9. I can't go out. I have to work.

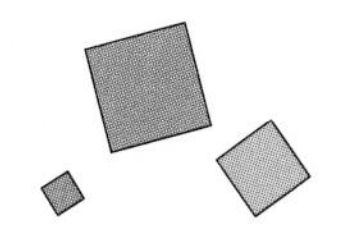

25. Talking About the Past: The *passé composé* with *avoir*

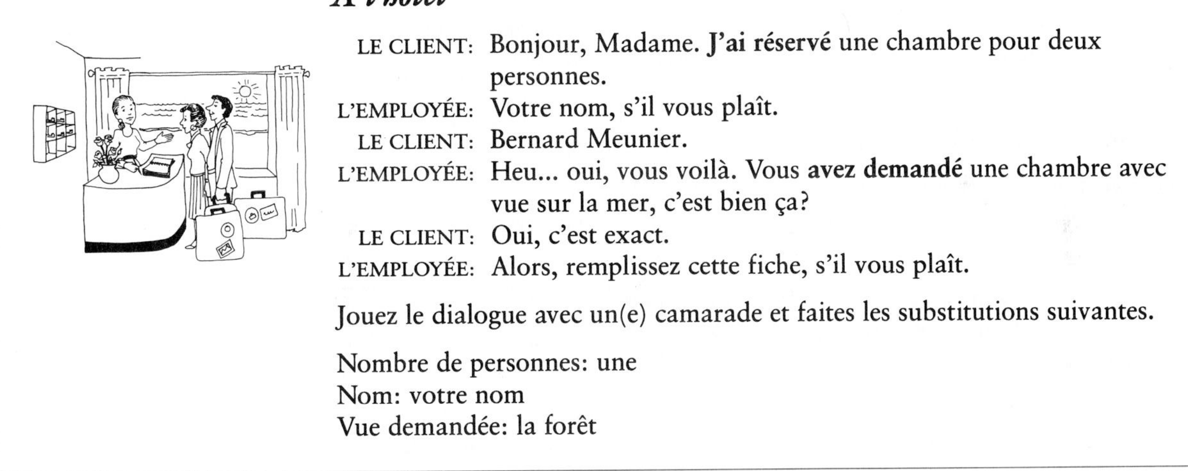

A l'hôtel

LE CLIENT: Bonjour, Madame. **J'ai réservé** une chambre pour deux personnes.
L'EMPLOYÉE: Votre nom, s'il vous plaît.
LE CLIENT: Bernard Meunier.
L'EMPLOYÉE: Heu... oui, vous voilà. Vous **avez demandé** une chambre avec vue sur la mer, c'est bien ça?
LE CLIENT: Oui, c'est exact.
L'EMPLOYÉE: Alors, remplissez cette fiche, s'il vous plaît.

Jouez le dialogue avec un(e) camarade et faites les substitutions suivantes.

Nombre de personnes: une
Nom: votre nom
Vue demandée: la forêt

A. The *passé composé*

As in English, there are several past tenses in French. The **passé composé,** the compound past tense, is most commonly used to indicate simple past actions. It describes events that began and ended at some point in the past. The **passé composé** of most verbs is formed with the present tense of the auxiliary verb (**le verbe auxiliaire**) **avoir** plus a past participle (**le participe passé**).*

*The formation of the **passé composé** with **être** will be treated in Chapter 8.

PASSÉ COMPOSÉ OF **voyager**			
j'	ai voyagé	nous	avons voyagé
tu	as voyagé	vous	avez voyagé
il, elle, on	a voyagé	ils, elles	ont voyagé

The **passé composé** has several equivalents in English. For example, **j'ai voyagé** can mean *I traveled, I have traveled,* or *I did travel.*

B. Formation of the Past Participle

1. To form regular past participles of **-er** and **-ir** verbs, the final **-r** is dropped from the infinitive. For **-er** verbs, an **accent aigu** (´) is added to the final **-e.** For regular past participles of **-re** verbs, the **-re** is dropped and **-u** is added.

acheter → **acheté**	J'**ai acheté** de nouvelles valises.	*I bought some new suitcases.*
choisir → **choisi**	Tu **as choisi** la date de ton départ?	*Have you chosen your departure date?*
perdre → **perdu**	Nous **avons perdu** nos passeports.	*We lost our passports.*

2. Most irregular verbs have irregular past participles.

- Verbs with past participles ending in **-u**

avoir:	**eu**	pouvoir:	**pu**
boire:	**bu**	recevoir:	**reçu**
devoir:	**dû**	tenir:	**tenu**
obtenir:	**obtenu**	vouloir:	**voulu**
pleuvoir (*to rain*):	**plu**		

Nous avons eu peur. — *We got scared.*
Il a bu deux verres de vin. — *He drank two glasses of wine.*
Nous avons obtenu de bons résultats. — *We got (obtained) good results.*

- Verbs with past participles ending in -s

apprendre:	**appris**
comprendre:	**compris**
mettre:	**mis**
prendre:	**pris**

Nous **avons pris** le soleil. — *We sat in the sun (sunbathed).*
Marc **a appris** à faire du ski. — *Marc learned to ski.*

- Verbs with past participles ending in **-t**

décrire:	**décrit**
dire:	**dit**
écrire:	**écrit**
faire:	**fait**

Nous **avons fait** une promenade sur la plage.	*We took a walk on the beach.*
Ce matin j'**ai écrit** six cartes postales.	*This morning I wrote six postcards.*

- The past participle of **être** is **été.**

Mes vacances **ont été** formidables.	*My vacation was wonderful.*

C. Negative and Interrogative Sentences in the *passé composé*

In negative sentences, **ne... pas** surrounds the auxiliary verb (**avoir**).

Nous **n'avons pas** voyagé en Suisse.	*We have not traveled to Switzerland.*
Vous **n'avez pas** porté de chandail?	*Didn't you wear a sweater?*

In questions with inversion, only the auxiliary verb and the subject are inverted.

Marie **a-t-elle demandé** le prix de la robe?	*Did Marie ask the price of the dress?*
As-tu oublié ton passeport?	*Did you forget your passport?*

MAINTENANT A VOUS

A. Des vacances réussies. Laurent a passé ses vacances au Maroc. Qu'est-ce qu'il a fait? **Verbes utiles:** acheter, aimer, apprendre, boire, dormir, faire du jogging, jouer au tennis, manger, nager, prendre des photos, visiter...

(Voir la page suivante.)

B. A Orange. Thierry donne des conseils à ses cousins Chantal et Jean-Claude... mais trop tard. Jouez les rôles avec deux camarades.

MODÈLE: visiter Orange →

THIERRY: Visitez Orange.
CHANTAL OU JEAN-CLAUDE: Nous avons déjà (*already*) visité Orange.

1. faire une promenade dans la vieille ville 2. prendre une photo de l'amphithéâtre romain 3. contempler la vieille fontaine 4. étudier les inscriptions romaines 5. apprendre l'histoire de France 6. acheter des cartes postales 7. envoyer une description de la ville à vos parents

C. Une carte postale de la neige. Complétez la carte postale de Marie. Mettez les verbes au passé composé.

Chère Claudine,

J' _______[1] mes vacances d'hiver une semaine avant Noël. J' _______[2] Rouen avec Christine et nous _______[3] le train jusqu'en Suisse. Nous _______[4] deux semaines à la montagne.

Nous _______[5] de rester à Saint-Moritz. Nous _______[6] du ski et du patin à glace. Nous _______[7] une fondue délicieuse. Au retour, nous _______[8] visite à des amis à Genève. Notre séjour en Suisse _______[9] inoubliable.

Je t'embrasse,
Marie

quitter
prendre
commencer
passer
être
manger
faire
décider
rendre

Mots-clés

Expressing when you did something in the recent past:

avant-hier (*the day before yesterday*)	**Avant-hier,** une amie m'a invité à faire du camping.
hier matin	**Hier matin,** j'ai fait les préparatifs.
hier après-midi, hier soir	Nous avons acheté des sacs à dos **hier après-midi,** et nous les avons perdus **hier soir.**

Use **matinée** and **soirée,** rather than **matin** and **soir,** if you wish to emphasize the duration. They are often used with **toute.**

toute la matinée (**soirée**)	J'ai passé toute la matinée (soirée) à acheter des provisions.

D. Interview. Posez des questions à un(e) camarade sur ses activités d'hier ou du week-end passé. Voici des suggestions.

LE MATIN	L'APRÈS-MIDI	LE SOIR
dormir tard	pique-niquer	étudier une leçon
faire du sport	faire de la bicyclette	finir une dissertation
regarder la télévision	nager	regarder un film
boire du café	faire du bateau	danser
prendre un petit déjeuner copieux (*large*)	skier	dîner dans un grand restaurant
?	travailler	inviter des amis
	rendre visite à des amis	?
	jouer aux cartes	

Puis racontez à la classe ce que votre camarade a fait.

E. Les Jeux olympiques de Calgary. Regardez cette publicité parue dans le magazine *Ski Québec,* puis choisissez la bonne réponse.

Marina Kiehl: Médaillé d'Or en Descente.

1. C'est une publicité pour des *skis / chaussures de ski / vêtements de ski.*
2. Les Jeux olympiques de Calgary ont eu lieu en *1984 / 1988 / 1980.*
3. Selon la publicité, les skieurs avec des skis Rossignol ont gagné *4 / 5 / 6* médailles d'or en six compétitions.

- Est-ce que pour vous l'équipement est important quand vous faites du sport? Quels critères considérez-vous avant d'acheter des tennis, une raquette, des skis, un ballon... ? (le prix, la qualité, la marque [*brand*], l'apparence)
- Avez-vous déjà participé à des compétitions? Dans quel sport? Avez-vous déjà gagné une coupe ou une médaille?
- Avez-vous regardé les derniers Jeux olympiques à la télévision? Quel(s) sport(s) avez-vous suivi(s)?

Commentaire culturel

Finding a hotel room. Here are some phrases to use when looking for a hotel room in France. Note that breakfast (coffee, tea, or hot chocolate with croissants or bread and butter) is included in the price of the room at many French hotels.

Avez-vous une chambre pour deux personnes? une chambre à deux lits?	Oui, Mademoiselle (Monsieur, Madame). Pouvez-vous remplir cette fiche (*fill out this form*)?
Quel est le prix de la chambre?	Elle fait quatre-vingts francs la nuit (*per night*).
Est-ce que le petit déjeuner est compris?	Oui, il est compris.

Est-ce qu'il y a une salle de bains dans la chambre?	Il y a un lavabo. Les toilettes (*toilet*) et la douche (*shower*) sont dans le couloir.
Acceptez-vous les cartes de crédit ou les chèques de voyage?	Nous préférons du liquide (*cash*), mais ça va.

Quand vous sortez de votre chambre, n'oubliez pas de laisser votre clef à la réception (*front desk*), s'il vous plaît!

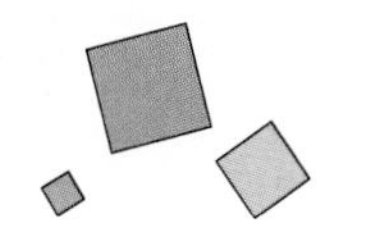

26. Expressing How Long: *depuis, pendant*

Question d'entraînement

MONIQUE: **Depuis quand** participes-tu à des compétitions?
FRANÇOISE: **Depuis** 1985. Et toi, **depuis combien de temps** fais-tu de la planche à voile?
MONIQUE: **Depuis** quinze jours seulement!
FRANÇOISE: Moi, j'ai commencé **il y a** huit ans. Et **depuis que** je fais de la planche à voile, je passe mes vacances à la mer.
MONIQUE: C'est dur, mais c'est formidable! **Hier** j'ai même pu rester sur la planche **pendant** quatre minutes.

1. Depuis quand Françoise participe-t-elle à des compétitions?
2. Depuis combien de temps Monique fait-elle de la planche à voile?
3. Depuis quand Françoise passe-t-elle ses vacances à la mer?
4. Pendant combien de temps Monique a-t-elle pu rester sur sa planche hier?

A. *Depuis* Used with the Present Tense

1. **Depuis quand... ? Depuis combien de temps... ?** These expressions are used with a verb in the present tense to ask how long something has been going on—how long an action that began in the past has continued into the present. Note that English uses a present perfect progressive tense.

Depuis quand est-elle ici?	*How long has she been here?*
Depuis combien de temps jouez-vous au tennis?	*How long have you been playing tennis?*

2. Questions with the above expressions can be answered in the present tense with **depuis** + *a period of time.*

Elle **est** ici **depuis vingt minutes.**	*She's been here for twenty minutes.*
Je **joue** au tennis **depuis deux ans.**	*I've been playing tennis for two years.*

3. Questions might also be answered with **depuis** + *specific point in time:* When **depuis** is used with a specific point in time, rather than with a period or quantity of time, it means *since.*

J'apprends le français **depuis le mois de septembre.**	*I've been learning French since the month of September.*
Nous téléphonons à l'hôtel **depuis vendredi.**	*We've been telephoning the hotel since Friday.*
Ils font de la bicyclette **depuis 1982.**	*They've been bicycling since 1982.*

© PHOTOEDIT

Une randonnée en montagne au printemps

4. **Il y a... que, voilà... que:** When used with the present tense, these expressions have the same meaning as **depuis.** Note the different word orders.

Il y a deux ans **que** je fais du ski. **Voilà** deux ans **que** je fais du ski. Je fais du ski **depuis** deux ans.	*I've been skiing for two years.*

B. *(Pendant) combien de temps...* + Present or Past Tense

This preposition expresses the duration of an habitual or repeated action. **Pendant** can be omitted in some instances.

(**Pendant**) **combien de temps** dormez-vous en cours chaque jour?	*How long do you sleep in class each day?*
Je ne dors pas (**pendant**) une seule minute en cours.	*I don't sleep for one single minute in class.*
(**Pendant**) **combien de temps** ont-ils visité Paris?	*How long did they visit Paris?*
Ils ont visité Paris **pendant** une semaine.	*They visited Paris for a week.*

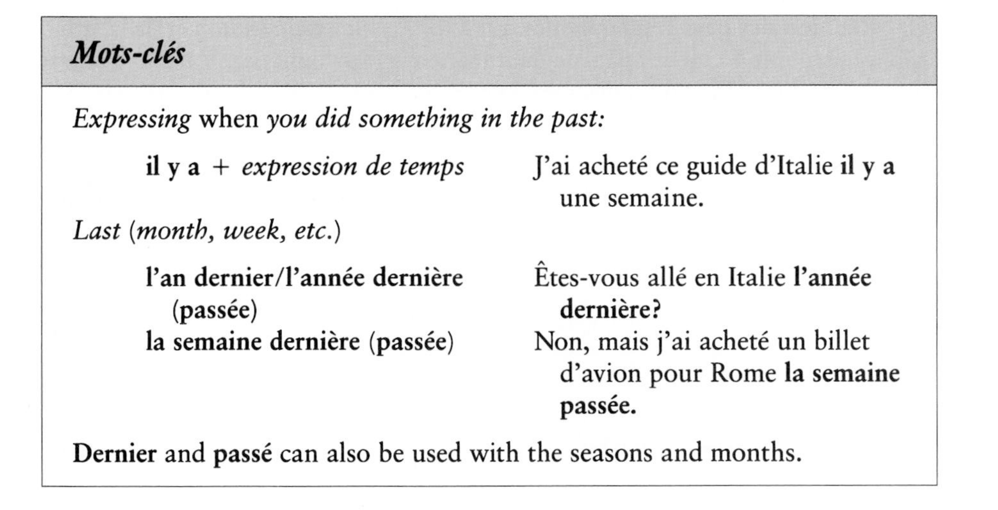

Mots-clés

Expressing when *you did something in the past:*

il y a + *expression de temps*	J'ai acheté ce guide d'Italie **il y a** une semaine.

Last (*month, week, etc.*)

l'an dernier/l'année dernière (passée)	Êtes-vous allé en Italie **l'année dernière?**
la semaine dernière (passée)	Non, mais j'ai acheté un billet d'avion pour Rome **la semaine passée.**

Dernier and **passé** can also be used with the seasons and months.

MAINTENANT A VOUS

A. Les vacances. Les vacances jouent un rôle important dans la vie de famille en France. Décrivez ce rôle en transformant les phrases suivantes.

MODÈLE: Il y a trois ans que les Leblanc passent leurs vacances en Espagne. (depuis) →
Les Leblanc passent leurs vacances en Espagne depuis trois ans.

1. Voilà cinq ans que la famille Rosso va à la montagne pour les vacances de Pâques. (depuis)
2. Il y a un mois que les parents font des préparatifs pour le voyage. (depuis)
3. La famille a acheté un châlet dans les Alpes en 1987. (il y a + *expression de temps*)
4. Cela fait ______ ans qu'ils ne sont plus obligés de trouver une chambre d'hôtel pour leurs vacances. (depuis)
5. Cette année ils vont faire du ski du lundi au vendredi. (pendant)

B. Activités. Demandez à vos camarades depuis quand ou depuis combien de temps ils (elles) font les activités suivantes.

MODÈLE: être étudiant(e) →
—Depuis combien de temps est-ce que tu es étudiant(e)?
—Je suis étudiant(e) depuis...

1. étudier le français 2. pratiquer son sport préféré 3. être à l'université 4. avoir son objet préféré 5. habiter à... 6. ?

C. **Réunion des pays francophones.** En 1987, le Deuxième sommet de la francophonie réunit à Québec plus de quarante pays francophones. Voici une courte description historique d'un des pays invités: le Zaïre.

ZAÏRE

Chef de l'État et du gouvernement : Monsieur Mobutu Sese Seko
Situation géographique : situé en Afrique centrale, le Zaïre est limité au nord par la République centrafricaine et le Soudan, à l'est par l'Ouganda, le Rwanda, le Burundi et la Tanzanie, au sud par l'Angola, à l'ouest par le Congo.
Capitale : Kinshasa
Population : 29,06 millions (1984)
Superficie : 2 345 410 km²
Langues : français, langue officielle ; bantou, batéké, etc.
Produit intérieur brut per capita : 140 $ US (1984)

Le 30 juin 1960, l'ex-Congo belge acquiert son indépendance. Joseph Kasavubu et Patrice Lumumba se partagent le pouvoir.[a] Les premières années d'indépendance sont fort agitées : tentative de sécession du Katanga, meurtre[b] de Lumumba, intervention armée de l'ONU[c] pour mettre fin à la sécession katangaise (1963)... En 1965, le président actuel Mobutu prend le pouvoir avec l'aide des puissances[d] occidentales et fonde en 1967 le Mouvement populaire de la révolution qui devient le seul parti légal en 1979. En 1971, Mobutu lance[e] sa politique de retour à l'authenticité, donne au pays le nom de Zaïre, change le nom du Katanga en Shaba. La politique extérieure du Zaïre est résolument pro-occidentale.

a. se... *share power* b. assassinat c. les Nations unis d. *powers* e. *begins*

- Où se trouve le Zaïre? (Voir la carte d'Afrique.)
- Pourquoi est-ce qu'on y parle français?
- Depuis quand le Zaïre est-il indépendant?
- Depuis combien de temps M. Mobutu est-il président du Zaïre?
- Depuis combien de temps est-ce que le Mouvement populaire de la révolution est un parti légal?
- Quel fait dans la description du Zaïre vous a surpris le plus?

D. Sondage. Posez les questions ci-dessous à trois ou quatre camarades de classe et notez leurs réponses. Ensuite, déterminez qui a les meilleures habitudes parmi les personnes sondées.

1. Combien d'heures dors-tu chaque nuit?
2. Combien de temps passes-tu à la bibliothèque le week-end?
3. Pendant combien de temps est-ce que tu prépares la leçon de français, en général? Pendant combien de temps as-tu preparé la leçon hier soir?
4. Pendant combien de temps as-tu fait de l'exercice la semaine dernière?
5. Combien de repas as-tu pris hier?
6. Combien de tasses de café as-tu bu ce matin?
7. Quand tu téléphones à un ami, pendant combien de temps parles-tu?

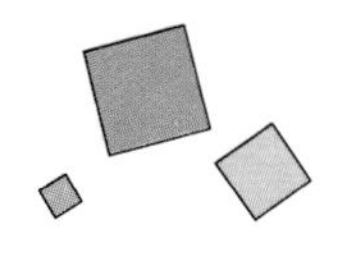

27. Expressing Observations and Beliefs: *voir* and *croire*

Promenade en bateau

GISÈLE: Tu ne prends pas de chandail!
RAOUL: Je ne **vois** pas pourquoi. Il fait si beau.
GISÈLE: Tu as **vu** ce brouillard arriver hier après-midi? Et d'après Monsieur Météo, à la télé...
RAOUL: Bon, d'accord. Je **crois** Monsieur Météo. Mais n'oublie pas ta boussole (*compass*). S'il y a du brouillard...

Trouvez dans le dialogue les synonymes des expressions suivantes.

1. Je ne comprends pas pourquoi.
2. Je fais confiance à Monsieur Météo.

Lequel des deux jeunes est le plus sarcastique? Comment le savez-vous?

The verbs **voir** (*to see*) and **croire** (*to believe*) are irregular.

voir		croire	
je vois	nous voyons	je crois	nous croyons
tu vois	vous voyez	tu crois	vous croyez
il, elle, on voit	ils, elles voient	il, elle, on croit	ils, elles croient
Past participle: vu		*Past participle*: cru	

J'**ai vu** Michèle à la plage la semaine passée. — *I saw Michèle at the beach last week.*
Est-ce que tu **crois** cette histoire? — *Do you believe this story?*

Revoir (*to see again*) is conjugated like **voir.**

Je **revois** les Moreau au mois d'août. — *I'm seeing the Moreau family again in August.*

Croire à* means *to believe in* a concept or idea.

Nous **croyons** à la chance. — *We believe in luck.*

MAINTENANT A VOUS

A. Alpinisme dans le brouillard. Complétez la conversation avec les verbes **croire** et **voir** au présent, sauf quand le passé composé est indiqué.

JULIE: Tu ______[1] où on est?
ALAIN: Non, je ne ______[2] pas cette montagne sur la carte.
YVES: Vous faites confiance à cette vieille carte?
JULIE: Non, nous ______[3] ce que nous a dit le guide.
ALAIN: Elle a beaucoup d'expérience et elle ______[4] que cette route est bonne.
YVES: Moi, je pense qu'elle ______[5] à la chance!
JULIE: Très drôle... mais dis, Alain, tu ______[6] (passé composé) Annick, le guide, quelque part?
ALAIN: Oui, j' ______[7] (passé composé) le guide, mais il y a environ une heure.
YVES: Cette fois, je ______[8] que nous sommes perdus!

B. Conversation. Avec un(e) camarade, parlez d'un voyage qu'il (qu'elle) a fait récemment. Qu'est-ce qu'il (elle) a vu? Qui a-t-il (elle) vu? Qu'est-ce qu'il (elle) veut revoir? Qui veut-il (elle) revoir? Ensuite, racontez à la classe l'expérience la plus intéressante (*most interesting*) de votre camarade.

*An exception is the expression **croire en Dieu,** *to believe in God.*

C. **Interview.** Interrogez un(e) camarade sur ses croyances. Est-ce qu'il (elle) croit à la science? à la médecine? à la chance? à l'amour? au progrès? à la technologie? à une religion? à la perception extra-sensorielle? à _____?... Après l'interview, essayez de définir la personnalité de votre camarade d'après ses réponses. Est-ce qu'il (elle) est sceptique? idéaliste? religieux (religieuse)? réaliste? sentimental(e)? superstitieux (superstitieuse)?

Situation

Une nuit à l'auberge de jeunesse

Contexte *Sean fait un voyage en France depuis deux mois et il dort chaque nuit dans une auberge de jeunesse. L'avantage? Les auberges sont souvent situées près d'une gare,° elles ne coûtent pas cher et l'ambiance° y est très sympathique. Ici, Sean arrive à l'Auberge de Jeunesse de Caen, en Normandie.*

gare: train station; ambiance: atmosphere

Objectif *Sean réserve une place à l'auberge.*

SEAN: Bonjour, madame, est-ce que vous avez encore de la place?
LA DAME: Oui, il y a de la place dans le petit dortoir.°
SEAN: Ça fait combien, pour une nuit? J'ai une carte° de l'American Youth Hostels...
LA DAME: Alors, 19 francs. Vous avez besoin de draps°?
SEAN: Non, j'ai mon sac de couchage.
LA DAME: Nous ne servons pas de repas chauds, mais il y a une petite cuisine au rez-de-chaussée.°
SEAN: Eh bien, c'est d'accord. Voici 19 francs.
LA DAME: Merci. Ah, faites bien attention: l'auberge ferme° à 22 heures. Ne rentrez° pas trop tard!

dortoir: sleeping quarters (dormitory); carte: (membership) card; draps: sheets; rez-de-chaussée: ground floor; ferme: closes; rentrez: return

VARIATIONS

1. Rejouez le dialogue avec l'une des variations suivantes.

- Vous n'avez pas de sac de couchage (8 francs pour les draps).
- Vous n'avez pas de carte de l'American Youth Hostels (50 francs d'inscription).

2. Les vacances... bougez! Regardez la brochure à la page précédente.

- Quelles activités organisent les auberges de jeunesse?
- Peut-on faire ces activités seulement en France ou aussi à l'étranger?
- Quelle(s) activité(s) préférez-vous?
- Que savez-vous à propos des Auberges de Jeunesse aux États-Unis?
- Offrent-elles les mêmes activités?
- Avez-vous déjà été dans une Auberge de Jeunesse? Racontez votre expérience.

A propos

Comment demander de l'aide dans un hôtel

Pardon, mais les toilettes (*the toilet*) / l'ascenseur (*elevator*) / la douche ne **marche**(nt) pas (*doesn't/don't work*).
Excusez-moi, où est la douche? où sont les toilettes? Avez-vous un oreiller (*pillow*), s'il vous plaît?
Je voudrais (*would like*) téléphoner à l'extérieur (*make an outside call*). Le numéro est...
Excusez-moi, mais il y a une erreur dans **la note** (*bill*).

Jeu de rôles. Vous avez une chambre d'hôtel, mais vous n'aimez pas le traversin (*bolster, long pillow*), vous ne pouvez pas trouver la douche, les toilettes ne marchent pas, l'ascenseur ne marche pas et vous avez envie de téléphoner à un ami (une amie). Téléphonez à la propriétaire et expliquez vos problèmes. Voici des expressions utiles pour le (la) camarade qui joue le rôle de la propriétaire.

au fond du couloir	*at the end of the hallway*
réparer	*to repair*
prendre l'escalier	*to take the staircase*
Que voulez-vous?	*What do you expect?*
Ne coupez pas!	*Don't hang up!*
Je suis navré(e).	*I'm very sorry.*

Commentaire culturel

Vacations in France. If you go to France in summer, you will witness an amazing French custom: **les vacances.** Most French people get a minimum of five weeks paid vacation (**congé payé**), and 60 percent of the French take their vacations in August. For this reason, more than half of all French businesses shut down during that month, and there are terrible traffic jams on the highways. It has been said that the **congé** is to the French what **Carnaval** is to the Brazilians: a social phenomenon that contains an element of revolution, a breakdown in the rhythm of society that results in a kind of mass shutdown.

—Pourquoi sont-ils tous partis en même temps que nous? (Tetsu)

Some people stay at home during their vacations, but they are a minority. Most go away to resorts, take organized tours, go camping, or stay in **villages de vacances** (*vacation towns*) or at a **pension de famille** (an inexpensive hotel). Vacations devoted to learning crafts, skills, or even more intellectual subjects are popular; workshops (**stages**) that focus on pottery, painting, music, dance, and so forth are offered in vacation communities.

If *you* need a hotel in France, you might go to a local **syndicat d'initiative,** where you'll find information on hotels, free maps, and lists of places of interest. Or you might purchase the **Guide Michelin,** which provides a reliable rating of hotels and restaurants. In two short lines per entry, **Guide Michelin** tells you everything you need to know about prices, facilities, whether there are views, beaches, tennis courts, and so on.

For young people, of course, sometimes the whole summer is vacation time. Children may go to a government-sponsored **colonie de vacances** (*summer camp*) for a month or more, and young adults may travel the whole summer, camping or staying in **auberges de jeunesse.** Staying in a hostel is an excellent way to meet people of various ages and nationalities. Hostels are inexpensive because they are subsidized by the government, but they are usually spartan, and everyone is expected to help with upkeep.

Mise au point

A. Vacances d'été. Formez des phrases complètes selon les indications.

MARC: où / passer / tu / vacances d'été? (*passé composé*)
PAULE: je / voyager / à la Guadeloupe avec mes parents (*passé composé*) / nous / camper / et / prendre le soleil (*passé composé*)
MARC: nager / vous / beaucoup? (*passé composé*)
PAULE: oui, il y a / plages magnifiques / et / climat / tropical (*présent*) la Guadeloupe / être / vraiment / beau (*présent*)
MARC: manger / vous / bien? (*passé composé*)
PAULE: oui, / nous / manger / petit / restaurants / et nous / essayer / plats créoles (*passé composé*)

Maintenant, décrivez les vacances de Paule.

- Est-ce qu'elle a passé des vacances superbes ou ennuyeuses?
- Où est-ce qu'elle a dormi?
- Qu'est-ce qui l'a impressionnée le plus?

B. En français, s'il vous plaît.

CORINNE: Two days ago, I met Bob, an American. I'm going out with him (**avec lui**) this evening.
SYLVIE: Oh, how long has he been in Paris?
CORINNE: Three days, but he's been traveling in France for four weeks.
SYLVIE: You know (**Tu sais**), I lived in Chicago for a year.
CORINNE: How long did you spend in the United States, in all (**en tout**)?
SYLVIE: Two years. I left the United States in 1985. I would like (**J'aimerais**) to meet a young American.
CORINNE: I'm going to ask Bob if he has a friend.
SYLVIE: Thank you, Corinne.

C. Vos vacances. Interviewez un(e) camarade sur ses vacances les plus (*the most*) intéressantes. Posez les questions suivantes et encore d'autres de votre invention. Puis décrivez ses vacances à la classe.

1. Où as-tu passé tes vacances les plus intéressantes?
2. Combien de temps as-tu passé à cet endroit?
3. Où as-tu logé?
4. Qu'est-ce que tu as fait pendant la journée?
5. Quel temps a-t-il fait?
6. Qu'est-ce que tu as acheté?
7. Qu'est-ce que tu ne vas jamais oublier?
8. As-tu envie de retourner au même endroit l'année prochaine (*next*)?

D. Vacances exotiques au Club Med. Vous allez passer une semaine de vacances au Club Med en Martinique. Voici la brochure du village où vous allez.

MARTINIQUE

les Boucaniers

TOUS LES PLAISIRS DE LA MER DES CARAIBES. COULEURS ET PARFUMS DES TROPIQUES.
RYTHMES DE LA "BIGUINE" ET DOUCEUR DU PARLER CREOLE.

VILLAGE
Au sud de la Martinique, à proximité de Sainte-Anne, un village aux teintes pastel entre une vaste cocoteraie et une plage de sable clair. Bungalows climatisés à 2 lits avec salle d'eau. Voltage : 220.

SPORTS
Voile : 10 Holders, 1 Laser, 1 Mentor. Ski nautique : 4 bateaux. Plongée bouteille : école d'initiation et de perfectionnement. Plongée libre. Planche à voile Tiga : 15 Fun Cup, 7 Speed, 5 Swift, 3 Jibe. Promenades en mer et pique-niques. Tennis : 7 courts en dur dont 6 éclairés. Basket-ball. Volley-ball. Salle de musculation et mise en forme. Aérobic.

ET AUSSI...
Spécialites à la "Maison créole". Boutique Club. Location de voitures. Enfants à partir de 12 ans.

EXCURSIONS
Un programme varié d'excursions vous sera proposé sur place.
C.M. - Les Boucaniers -
97227 Pointe Marin - Sainte-Anne - Tél. 596.76.74.52.

1. Quel est le nom du village? 2. Où allez-vous loger? 3. Essayez d'identifier quelles activités représentent les dessins. 4. Quelles activités aimeriez-vous faire?

Imaginez maintenant que vous venez de rentrer de vacances. Décrivez vos vacances à la classe. Commencez par «J'ai passé une semaine en Martinique... ». **Suggestions:** vêtements, temps, sports, ambiance, repas, jeux...

Interactions

In Chapter 7 you practiced talking about vacations, about events in the past, and about how long you have been doing certain things. Act out the following situations, using vocabulary and structures from this chapter.

- **En vacances.** You are planning a vacation. Visit a travel agent (your partner). Explain what type of vacation to France you would like to take. Talk about the activities that interest you. Decide how long you will stay. The agent will recommend an itinerary and explain why.
- **Qu'est-ce que j'ai fait?** Think of something you did last evening. Your partner will ask you yes/no questions, to guess what it was. Then exchange roles.

Vocabulaire

Verbes

camper to camp
croire to believe
croire à to believe in
devenir to become
dormir to sleep
fermer to close
fumer to smoke
marcher to work (*machine or object*)
nager to swim
obtenir to obtain, get
oublier to forget
partir (à) (de) to leave (for) (from)
quitter to leave (*someone or someplace*)
revenir to return (*someplace*)
revoir to see again
sentir to feel; to sense; to smell
servir to serve
sortir to leave; go out; to take out
tenir to hold
tenir à + *inf.* to be eager; to be determined to (*do something*)
venir to come
venir de + *inf.* to have just (*done something*)
voir to see

Substantifs

l'achat (*m.*) purchase
l'alpinisme (*m.*) mountaineering
l'an (*m.*) year
l'année (*f.*) year
le bateau (à voile) (sail)boat
la bicyclette bicycle
la campagne country(side)
le camping camping
la chose thing
le fleuve (large) river
la forêt forest
le lac lake
la matinée morning
la mer sea, ocean
le mois month
la montagne mountain
la nuit night
le parapluie umbrella
la plage beach
la planche à voile windsurfer
la route road
la semaine week
la soirée evening
le (la) voisin(e) neighbor

Les vêtements et l'équipement sportifs

l'anorak (*m.*) (ski) jacket
le gant (de ski) (ski) glove
les lunettes (*f.*) glasses
...de ski goggles
...de soleil sunglasses
le sac de couchage sleeping bag
le short shorts
le ski ski
le slip de bain swimsuit (*man's*)
les tennis (*m.*) tennis shoes
la tente tent

Expressions utiles

une chambre { pour deux personnes	*a double room*
une chambre { à deux lits	*a room with two beds*
une carte de crédit	*credit card*
des chèques (*m.*) de voyage	*traveler's checks*
je voudrais...	*I would like . . .*

Expressions temporelles

les années (cinquante) the fifties (*decade*)
avant-hier the day before yesterday
depuis since
depuis combien de temps... ? for how long . . . ?
depuis quand... ? for how long . . . ? since when . . . ?
dernier, dernière last
hier yesterday
il y a... ago
passé(e) last

Mots divers

comme like
seulement only
tard late

INTERMÈDE 7

Lecture

AVANT DE LIRE

Reading for global understanding: The poll (*une enquête*) on pp. 232–33 was published in a French women's fitness magazine, *Vital*. It has not been simplified, except for the glosses. Your goal as you read through it should be simply to understand as much as you can, without looking words up in the dictionary. Use the strategies you learned in the preceding chapters. Look for cognates. Read for the gist of each question; you do not need to understand every word. Develop your guessing skills; you will use them often, whenever you read in French.

In particular, the following strategies may help.

- If you don't understand something, read ahead. What follows will often clarify an unfamiliar word or phrase. In this poll, the proposed answers will often tell you what the question is about, or the final answer may make clear what the preceding ones were.
- Think about what you expect the question to be, on the basis of your knowledge of the magazine and the interests of its readers: fitness, sports, diet, well-being.
- Skip questions that you really don't understand. You can figure them out later, during class discussion, or with a classmate.

After your first reading, go back and answer as many questions as you can, on the basis of one of your vacations. Skip questions that do not apply to you. Remember that this poll was written for women; you may need to make certain changes if you are a man.

—En vacances, j'adore faire du vélo sur les petites routes de campagne.

RACONTEZ VOUS VOS

En répondant à ce questionnaire, vous allez pouvoir tester vos vacances, tranquillement, sans vous raconter d'histoires. Et savoir si elles ont bien rempli la mission pour laquelle elles sont faites : vous faire vivre[a] un mois, au plus près du bonheur.[b]

1 Avez-vous pris des vacances cet été ?
oui
non

2 Combien de temps aurez-vous pris cet été ?
Moins d'une semaine
1 semaine
2 semaines
3 semaines
1 mois
plus d'un mois
c'était suffisant
ce n'était pas assez

3 Etes-vous encore[c] en vacances en ce moment ?
oui
non

4 Etes-vous restée[d] au même endroit pendant toutes vos vacances ?
oui
non

5 Si oui, où ?
Mer en France
Montagne en France
Campagne en France
Ville en France
Mer A l'étranger
Montagne A l'étranger
Campagne A l'étranger
Ville A l'étranger
Désert
Pleine mer

6 Si non, pourquoi et comment ?
(Précisez-nous s'il s'agissait d'une décision (ne jamais rester au même endroit), d'une obligation (famille, enfants, opportunités), ou bien d'un périple (itinéraire culturel, aventurier, amical, autres...)

____
____
____

7 Ces vacances étaient[e] :
les mêmes que celles de l'an passé
les mêmes que celles de chaque année
différentes
une innovation

8 Vos vacances, cette année, ont été :
parfaites
plutôt réussies
un petit peu ratées
décevantes
mieux que celles de l'année dernière
moins bien que celles de l'année dernière
les mêmes

9 Est-ce vous qui avez décidées ces vacances, lieu, timing, activité ?
oui
non

10 Les avez-vous préparées longtemps à l'avance ?
non
oui
oui, depuis quand ?

11 Avez-vous vécu :
dans une maison
dans un hôtel
sous une tente
à la belle étoile
sur un bateau
dans un club
entre deux aéroports et quelques six étoiles
chez des copains

12 Etiez-vous :
seule
seule avec lui
avec lui et les enfants
avec les enfants
avec vos parents
dans votre famille
avec des ami (e) s

13 Avez-vous découvert cette année un endroit dont vous êtes tombé amoureux[f] au point :
d'y revenir l'année prochain..oui..non
d'avoir envie d'y acheter une maison oui non
d'avoir envie d'y vivre.. oui ..non

14 La dominante de ces vacances :
Le repos
Le sport
La convivialité
La lecture
La culture (festivals, châteaux, musées...)
Les souvenirs d'enfance
Les affaires (contacts et recontacts)
Les enfants
L'amour
L'aventure
La réflexion

15 Après ces vacances, quoi de neuf[g] ?
Du tonus
De la beauté
Des sentiments
Un cerveau clair
De la santé
De la lucidité
Rien

16 Pendant les vacances, avez-vous ?
minci de...kilos
grossi de...kilos
vous êtes restée stable

17 Trouvez-vous que votre peau[h] est plus :
lisse
ferme
douce
tendue
jeune
ridée
saine

18 Etes-vous ?
très bronzée
bronzée
hâlée
blanche volontairement
blanche pour cause de météo

19 Trouvez-vous que vos cheveux ont :
pris de l'éclat[i]
perdu de l'éclat
éclairci
pris du volume
pris triste mine

20 Pendant ces vacances, avez-vous ?
ri[j] tout le temps
bien ri
assez peu ri

21 En vacances, éprouvez-vous plus que dans l'année un sentiment de :
liberté
santé
séduction
dynamisme
beauté
bien-être
sensualité
vérité

a. *live*
b. *happiness*
c. *still*
d. Êtes... *Did you stay . . . ?*
e. *were*
f. êtes.. *did you fall in love . . . ?*
g. quoi... *what's new?*
h. *skin*
i. *shine*
j. *laughed*

VACANCES

22 En rentrant[k] de vacances, vous vous estimez :
plus jolie
plus performante
plus drôle
plus chaleureuse
plus indulgente
plus détendue
plus amoureuse
plus paisible
plus proche des autres

23 En vacances, vous avez mangé :
plus léger[l]
plus lourd[m]
plus arrosé
plus savoureux
plus rigolo
comme d'habitude

24 Vous avez, en particulier, forcé sur :
le poisson, les fruits de mer
les crudités
les fruits
les produits laitiers
le pain
autre chose, quoi ?

25 Vous avez fait :
trois repas à horaire fixe
des grignotages suivant l'humeur
un grand petit déjeuner et un dîner
des variations chaque jour

26 En vacances, vous avez :
plus faim que pendant l'année
moins faim
le même appétit que d'habitude

27 Avez-vous dormi
plus que d'habitude
moins que d'habitude
mieux[n] que d'habitude
comme d'habitude

28 Pendant ces vacances, avez-vous :
fait quelque chose que vous n'aviez jamais fait[o] et quoi ?
oui
non
quoi

29 Avez-vous :
lu[p]
nagé
couru
dansé
joué au tennis
joué au volley
joué au golf
écrit
fait de la planche à voile
du dériveur
du gros bateau
du deltaplane
de l'escalade
de la marche
joué de la musique
écouté de la musique
brodé
fait de la cuisine

30 Avez-vous fait la sieste ?
oui
non

31 Si vous fumez,[q] avez-vous :
moins fumé ?
davantage ?
autant ?
vous avez arrêté ?

32 Pendant ces vacances, avez-vous rencontré :
un monsieur formidable
une fille sympa
des gens merveilleux

33 Vous profitez des vacances pour vous occuper de :
votre peau, en utilisant soigneusement vos crèmes
vos cheveux, que vous soignez
vos muscles, que vous entraînez
vos ongles que vous manucurez
vos pieds que vous poncez
vous en entier

34 Pendant les vacances, vous consacrez :
deux heures ou plus à votre beauté
entre une et deux heures
moins d'une heure
pas une minute, ce n'est pas la peine en vacances

35 Avez-vous utilisé cet été :
un démaquillant
un produit solaire
un produit après soleil
une crème anti-âge
un shampooing spécial
un produit protecteur des cheveux
un produit amincissant
un lait corporel hydratant

36 Etes-vous allée[r]
chez le coiffeur
chez une esthéticienne
vous faire masser

37 Avez-vous fait une cure style thalasso, et laquelle ?
oui
non

38 Vous êtes-vous
plus maquillée[s] que d'habitude
pas plus mais différemment
moins maquillée
pas maquillée du tout

39 Votre tenue de vacances préférée :
le maillot de bain
la minijupe
le short
des trucs fous
toute nue
le jean
la robe légère
autre

40 Quelle somme faudrait-il vous donner pour que vous acceptiez l'année prochaine de renoncer à vos vacances d'été ?

41 A votre avis, ce qui gâche[t] le plus sûrement les vacances :
le mauvais temps
la mauvaise humeur
le manque de sous
la promiscuité
l'idée de la rentrée
les embouteillages
la foule
la solitude
la monotonie
les accidents
quoi d'autre

42 Lorsque vous rentrez de vacances, vous êtes pleine[u] :
de projets
de regrets
de désirs
de souvenirs

43 Le plus important en vacances :
c'est le soleil
c'est d'être amoureuse
c'est d'être bien avec ceux qu'on aime
c'est d'avoir la paix
c'est d'avoir le temps

44 Attribuez une note de 0 à 20 aux vacances que vous venez de vivre :

45 Une bonne fée[v] vous offre les vacances idéales. Racontez :

____

____

____

k. En... *coming back*
l. *light*
m. *heavy*
n. *better*
o. n'aviez... *had never done*
p. *read*
q. *smoke*
r. Êtes... *Did you go . . . ?*
s. *made up* (with cosmetics)
t. *ruins*
u. *full*
v. *fairy*

COMPRÉHENSION

Comparez vos réponses avec celles de vos camarades.

1. Qui a donné la meilleure (*best*) note à ses vacances?
2. Où sont allés (*went*) les étudiants qui sont restés aux États-Unis? Quels pays ont visités les étudiants qui ont voyagé à l'étranger (*abroad*)?
3. Quel type de logement a été le plus populaire parmi vos camarades?
4. Qu'est-ce que vos camarades ont fait pendant leurs vacances?
5. Y a-t-il eu une réponse que vous avez trouvée particulièrement intéressante? surprenante? bizarre? amusante?

Par écrit

A. Des vacances désastreuses. Vous venez de passer des vacances horribles. Écrivez une lettre à vos parents pour raconter vos vacances. Commencez par «Chère maman/Cher papa». Terminez par «Mille bises,... »

B. Les Américains et les vacances. Écrivez pour un journal français un paragraphe qui décrit les vacances aux États-Unis.

Les évasions préférées des Américains sont ______________. Les Américains aiment (n'aiment pas) les vacances organisées parce que ______________. Ils préfèrent aller ______________ et ils partent en vacances quand ______________. J'aime (Je n'aime pas) les vacances parce qu'(e) ______________. Je prends mes vacances quand ______________.

C. Répondez par écrit à la question 45, de l'enquête précédente.

CHAPITRE HUIT

Voyages et transports

—A quelle heure part ton train pour Marseilles?
—A 19 h 30.
—Si tu veux, je peux te conduire à la gare.
—A cette heure-là? Avec toute la circulation? Non, je vais prendre le métro, il y en a un tous les quarts d'heure.

Étude de vocabulaire

Visitez le monde en avion

1. De quelle nationalité sont ces compagnies aériennes?

2. Quelle compagnie aérienne peut-on prendre pour aller à Montréal, à Bruxelles, à Dakar, à New York, à Tunis, à Alger, à Paris?
3. Avez-vous déjà pris une de ces compagnies? Quels pays avez-vous visités? Si non, quelle compagnie aimeriez-vous prendre? Quel pays aimeriez-vous visiter? Pourquoi?
4. Donnez les noms d'autres compagnies aériennes, leur nationalité et leurs destinations.

A. Bienvenue à bord. Complétez les phrases d'après le dessin.

1. Si on fume, on veut un siège dans la ______________.
2. Le ______________ est le conducteur de l'avion.
3. L'______________ apporte les repas.
4. Les personnes très riches voyagent en ______________.
5. Quand on est dans la ______________, on ne peut pas fumer.
6. Le ______________ sert les boissons.
7. On présente une ______________ pour monter dans l'avion.
8. Les hommes et les femmes d'affaires voyagent en ______________.
9. Les étudiants voyagent en ______________.
10. Le ______________ 512 part à 13 h 50.

B. Vols internationaux. Quels sont les pays de départ et d'arrivée des vols suivants? **Les pays:** la Chine, les États-Unis, l'Algérie, l'URSS,* le Brésil, le Maroc, la Côte d'Ivoire, le Canada, la France, le Zaïre, la Belgique, le Sénégal, la Suisse, le Mexique,† le Japon, la Colombie, la Tunisie, le Viêt-nam.

MODÈLE: Rabat–Paris → C'est un vol entre le Maroc et la France.

1. Pékin–New York
2. Alger–Moscou
3. Rio–Rabat
4. Bogota–Tunis
5. Mexico–Tokyo
6. Montréal–Paris
7. Dakar–Genève
8. Kinshasa–Bruxelles
9. Abidjan–Saigon

C. Quelques pays européens et leurs capitales. Quel pays trouve-t-on _______? Quelle est sa capitale?

MODÈLE: au sud-est‡ de l'Italie →
Au sud-est de l'Italie, on trouve la Grèce. Capitale: Athènes.

PAYS	CAPITALES
1. au nord-est de l'Espagne	Londres
2. à l'est de l'Allemagne de l'ouest	Madrid
3. à l'est de la Belgique	Bruxelles
4. au sud-ouest de la France	Berne
5. à l'ouest de l'Espagne	Bonn
6. au nord-ouest de la France	Rome
7. au sud-est de la France	Lisbonne
8. au nord de l'Italie	Paris
9. au nord de la France	Berlin

Devinez! Maintenant, un(e) de vos camarades décrit la situation géographique d'un pays étranger qu'il (qu'elle) a visité ou d'un pays étranger visité par un ami ou un parent. Essayez de deviner le pays. Puis donnez le nom d'une ville de ce pays.

---

*l'Union (*f.*) des Républiques Socialistes Soviétiques (où **la Russie** est le pays prédominant)
†Mexico = la ville; le Mexique = le pays.
‡In the words **est** (*east*), **ouest** (*west*), and **sud** (*south*), the final consonant is pronounced.

MODÈLE: VOTRE CAMARADE: Ma cousine Betty a visité un pays au nord-ouest de l'Italie.
VOUS: Ta cousine, a-t-elle visité la France?
VOTRE CAMARADE: C'est exact. Elle a visité Lille.

Voici quelques possibilités: l'Irlande, l'Écosse (*Scotland*), le Danemark, la Suède, la Norvège, l'Autriche (*Austria*), la Grèce, l'Égypte, l'Éthiopie, l'Afrique du sud, le Zaïre, Israël, la Jordanie, la Syrie, l'Arabie Saoudite, l'Iraq, l'Iran, l'Australie, l'Argentine, la Colombie, le Vénézuela, le Nicaragua

L'Europe en train

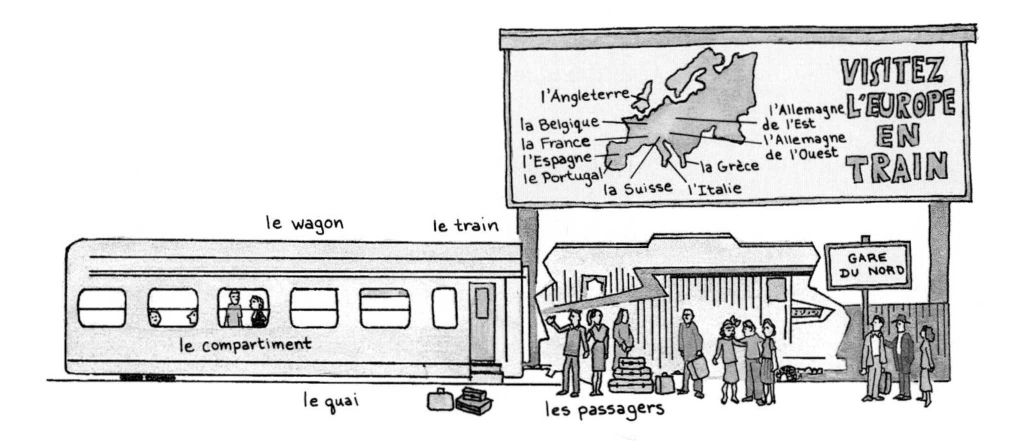

A. Définitions

1. Quel véhicule de transport trouve-t-on dans une gare?
2. Comment s'appelle chaque voiture d'un train?
3. Comment s'appellent les personnes qui voyagent?
4. Comment s'appelle la partie du wagon où les passagers sont assis (*seated*)?
5. Où est-ce que les passagers attendent l'arrivée d'un train?

B. Trains-autos accompagnés. Pour partir en vacances, beaucoup de Français prennent le train. Lisez la publicité de la SNCF (Société Nationale des Chemins de Fer) à la page suivante, puis répondez aux questions.

1. Quel service propose cette publicité?
2. Où se trouve le «coffre» d'une voiture? A quoi sert-il?
3. Quel autre véhicule peut-on transporter en train?
4. Comment sont les compartiments?
5. Est-ce que le petit déjeuner est compris dans le prix du voyage?
6. Combien de temps après l'arrivée retrouve-t-on sa voiture?
7. D'après vous, quels avantages y a-t-il à faire voyager sa voiture avec soi dans le train?

SNCF

TRAINS AUTOS ACCOMPAGNÉES

1 Chez vous ; le coffre est chargé : plus de souci de valises jusqu'à l'arrivée.

2 Vous arrivez tranquillement à la gare de chargement, vous avez jusqu'à 20 h 15 pour remettre votre voiture ou votre moto

3 Le compartiment est climatise, la couchette est confortable, vous vous glissez dans vos draps.

4 C'est le plein sommeil, le train roule, votre voiture ou votre moto vous suit.

5 7 h 45 : vous descendez du train ; le petit déjeuner vous attend, il est gratuit.

6 8 h 30 : en forme, vous retrouvez votre voiture ou votre moto. Bonne route !

Un exemple : Paris - Saint-Raphaël.

C. **Interview.** Demandez à un(e) camarade s'il (si elle) a voyagé en train. A-t-il (elle) mangé dans un wagon-restaurant? A-t-il (elle) dormi dans un wagon-lit? Quelle ville a-t-il (elle) visitée pendant ce voyage? A qui a-t-il (elle) rendu visite? Ensuite, racontez à la classe le voyage de votre camarade.

Commentaire culturel

Trains. Trains are an important form of transportation, much more popular in France than in the United States. Since 1938, French railroads have been controlled by the **Société Nationale des Chemins de Fers Français** (SNCF), a government-regulated monopoly. SNCF's ads to attract passengers emphasize that trains save energy and are environmentally clean; safety and comfort are also stressed. The number of train passengers is steadily increasing. You will find the train system to be the most economical and convenient form of transportation in France. Here are some points to keep in mind.

- For long trips, it is possible to reserve a seat or a berth (**couchette**) in a sleeping compartment. If the station seems crowded, or if you are traveling during a French vacation time, be sure to make such a reservation at the ticket window.

- On the door of each train compartment there is a notice that indicates if the seats inside are reserved. If you cannot find an unreserved seat or if you have reserved a seat in advance, seek help from the conductor taking tickets. One of his or her responsibilities is to help people find seats. The conductor can also sell you a berth if you decide you want one after you have boarded.
- On the platform there is a notice board (**un tableau d'affichage**) that indicates which cars are first class and which are second. You can move from car to car within a given class, but it is often impossible to move from one class to another.

En route

Jean-Pierre **conduit** sa moto à travers les Alpes.

Le camion de M. Michelin **tombe** souvent **en panne** sur l'autoroute.

Annick **roule** toujours très vite. Elle a une voiture de sport toute neuve!

Marianne **fait le plein** d'essence à la station-service.

Martine et Annie **traversent** la France en vélo.

A. Associations. Quels adjectifs associez-vous avec les moyens de transport suivants? Expliquez les raisons de votre choix.

1. l'avion
2. le bateau
3. l'autobus
4. la voiture
5. le train
6. le camion (*truck*)
7. le taxi
8. la moto
9. l'ambulance
10. l'hélicoptère
11. le métro
12. le vélo
13. la mobylette

a. lent
b. cher
c. rapide
d. bruyant (*noisy*)
e. dangereux
f. amusant
g. fatigant (*tiring*)
h. confortable
i. sûr (*safe*)
j. économique
k. silencieux
l. pratique
m. polluant
n. agréable
o. monotone
p. luxueux

Inter-Rail 1988
SNCF

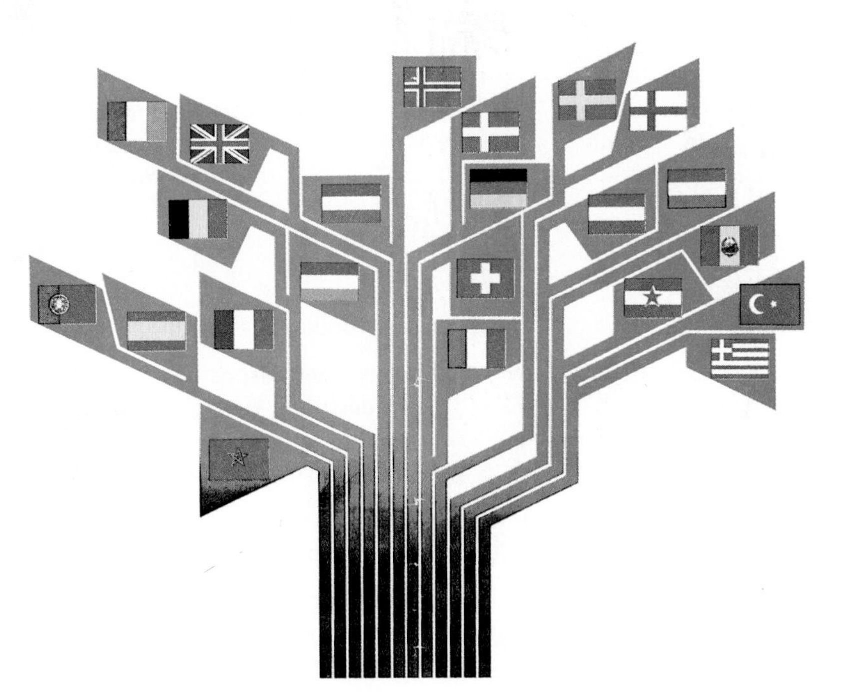

En général, quand et pourquoi utilise-t-on ces moyens de transport? Lesquels avez-vous déjà utilisés? Quand? Quels adjectifs associez-vous avec la marche (*walking*) et l'auto-stop (*hitchhiking*)?

Quel moyen de transport préférez-vous? Pourquoi? Lequel avez-vous? Comment venez-vous au cours? à pied (*on foot*), en voiture, en bus... ?

B. Moyens de transport. Quel véhicule conduit-on dans les situations suivantes?

1. Votre famille déménage (*moves*). 2. La classe fait une excursion. 3. Vous êtes sportif (sportive). 4. Vous aimez conduire vite. 5. Vous passez le week-end avec votre famille. 6. Vous arrivez à l'aéroport d'une ville. 7. Vous voulez faire de l'exercice.

C. Interview. Posez les questions suivantes à un(e) camarade.

1. Comment préfères-tu voyager en vacances? Pourquoi? Est-ce que ça dépend de ta destination?
2. Quels moyens de transport préfères-tu prendre en ville?
3. A ton avis, quel moyen de transport est très économique? très rapide? très dangereux? très polluant? très agréable? Quels problèmes de transport y a-t-il dans ta ville ou dans ta région? Comment peut-on résoudre (*to solve*) ces problèmes?

Pour parler de la conduite: le verbe *conduire* (to drive)

conduire			
je	**conduis**	nous	**conduisons**
tu	**conduis**	vous	**conduisez**
il, elle, on	**conduit**	ils, elles	**conduisent**
Past participle: **conduit**			

All verbs ending in **-uire** are conjugated like **conduire.**

construire	*to construct*	Nous **construisons** une nouvelle ville.
détruire	*to destroy*	On **détruit** le vieux pour construire du neuf.
traduire	*to translate*	**Traduis** cette brochure en espagnol.

Interview. Posez les questions suivantes à un(e) camarade de classe. Ensuite, rapportez le fait le plus intéressant à la classe.

1. Conduis-tu souvent? Quand tu sors avec des copains (= amis), conduisez-vous ou prenez-vous des transports publics?
2. Dans ta famille, qui conduit le plus souvent? Qui ne conduit pas?

3. Aimes-tu conduire? Quelle marque de voiture préfères-tu? Pourquoi? Préfères-tu les voitures américaines ou les voitures fabriquées à l'étranger?
4. Penses-tu que les voitures détruisent les grandes villes? Est-ce qu'on construit trop d'autoroutes aux États-Unis?
5. Que penses-tu des motos? des bicyclettes?
6. A quel âge as-tu eu ton permis de conduire? Conduis-tu prudemment, en général? As-tu déjà eu un accident de voiture? As-tu attrapé une contravention (*traffic ticket*)? Pourquoi?

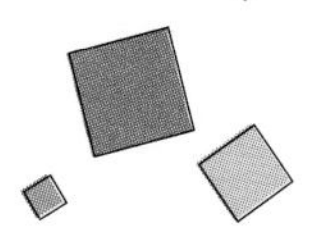

Étude de grammaire

28. Talking About the Past: The *passé composé* with *être*

Accident de voiture

JEAN-FRANÇOIS: ...eh bien, tout à l'heure, je **suis arrivé** au carrefour Magnan, et un camion **est passé** au feu rouge juste devant moi. Je n'ai pas pu l'éviter: je **suis rentré** dedans. Alors, avec l'autre conducteur, nous **sommes descendus** de voiture et nous avons... euh... discuté de priorité...

MICHÈLE: Mais Jean-François, pourquoi n'**es**-tu pas encore **reparti**?

JEAN-FRANÇOIS: Parce que les automobilistes derrière nous **sont restés** pour donner leur avis, et maintenant il y a un embouteillage.

Retrouvez la phrase correcte dans le dialogue.

1. Je viens d'arriver au carrefour.
2. Le camion vient de passer au feu rouge.
3. Je viens de rentrer dedans.
4. Nous venons de descendre de voiture.
5. Les automobilistes derrière nous sont encore ici.

A. The Auxiliary Verb *être*

Most French verbs use a form of **avoir** as an auxiliary verb in the **passé composé.** The **passé composé** of some verbs, however, is generally formed with **être**; one of these verbs is **aller** (*to go*).

PASSÉ COMPOSÉ OF **aller**			
je	suis allé(e)	nous	sommes allé(e)s
tu	es allé(e)	vous	êtes allé(e)(s)
il, on	est allé	ils	sont allés
elle	est allée	elles	sont allées

In the **passé composé** with **être,** the past participle always agrees with the subject in gender and number. The following verbs* take **être** in the **passé composé.** The drawing that follows lists most of these verbs, organized around the "house of **être.**"

aller: allé to go
arriver: arrivé to arrive
descendre: descendu to go down; to get off
devenir: devenu to become
entrer: entré to enter
monter: monté to go up; to climb
mourir: mort to die
naître: né to be born
partir: parti to leave
passer (par): passé to pass (by)
rentrer: rentré to return; to go home
rester: resté to stay
retourner: retourné to return; to go back
revenir: revenu to come back
sortir: sorti to go out
tomber: tombé to fall
venir: venu to come

*When **monter, descendre, sortir,** and **passer** are followed by a direct object, they take **avoir** in the passé composé: elle *a passé* la frontière hier. Nous *avons descendu* la rivière en bateau.

Mme Bernard **est née** en France.	*Mme Bernard was born in France.*
Elle **est allée** aux États-Unis en 1940.	*She went to the United States in 1940.*
Elle **est arrivée** à New York.	*She arrived in New York.*
Elle **est partie** en Californie.	*She left for California.*
Elle **est restée** dix ans à San Francisco.	*She stayed in San Francisco for ten years.*
Ensuite, elle **est rentrée** en France.	*Then she returned to France.*
Elle **est morte** à Paris en 1952.	*She died in Paris in 1952.*

B. Negative and Interrogative Sentences in the *passé composé*

Word order in negative and interrogative sentences in the **passé composé** with **être** is the same as that for the **passé composé** with **avoir.**

Je **ne suis pas** allé en Allemagne.	*I did not go to Germany.*
Sont-ils arrivés à l'heure?	*Did they arrive on time?*
Ne sont-ils pas arrivés à l'heure?	*Didn't they arrive on time?*

MAINTENANT A VOUS

A. Une journée de vacances. Dites où chaque personne est allée selon ses préférences.

MODÈLE: Jessica aime la musique classique. Elle est allée au concert.

mon meilleur ami (ma meilleure amie)	au cinéma
	à l'agence de voyages
toi	à la gare
le professeur	en ville
nous	à la mer
mes parents (cousins...)	à la montagne
	au restaurant
vous	à la campagne
moi	au bord d'un lac

B. Week-end en Suisse. Brigitte et Bernard ont passé le week-end à Genève. Mettez l'histoire au passé composé et faites attention au choix de l'auxiliaire (**avoir** ou **être**).

Bernard vient[1] chercher Brigitte pour aller à la gare. Ils montent[2] dans le train. Ils cherchent[3] leur compartiment. Le train part[4] quelques minutes plus tard. Il entre[5] en gare de Genève à midi. Bernard et Brigitte descendent[6] du train et vont tout de suite à l'hôtel. L'après-midi, ils sortent[7] visiter la ville. Le soir ils dînent[8] dans un restaurant élégant. Dimanche Brigitte va[9] au musée et prend[10] beaucoup de photos de la ville. Bernard reste[11] à l'hôtel. Brigitte et Bernard quittent [12] Genève en fin d'après-midi. Ils arrivent[13] à Paris fatigués mais contents de leur week-end.

Qu'est-ce que Brigitte a fait que Bernard n'a pas fait?

C. Vacances en Afrique. Vous venez de passer dix jours en Côte-d'Ivoire avec deux autres camarades de classe. Voici une brochure de l'endroit où vous êtes allés.

LA TAVERNE BASSAMOISE ★

GRAND BASSAM

Grand Bassam fut la première capitale de la Côte-d'Ivoire. C'est aujourd'hui une petite ville historique chargée de souvenirs d'un passé encore vivant. Elle est située au bord de la mer, à 43 km environ d'Abidjan.
Amateurs de bonne table, d'harmonie, de calme, des vacances sans contrainte dans un établissement qui offre les garanties d'un bon confort dans un cadre agréable, Patrick et Isabelle vous attendent à la Taverne Bassamoise ! C'est une exclusivité AIRTOUR.

FICHE D'IDENTITÉ :
- BP 154 Grand Bassam - Tél. : (225) 30.10.62.
- Capacité : 20 chambres et 5 bungalows.

SITUATION :
Construit directement en bordure de plage, au milieu d'une belle cocoteraie, de la verdure et des fleurs. Grand Bassam est à 1,5 km, l'aéroport à 25 km, Abidjan à 45 km.

A VOTRE DISPOSITION :
- 1 restaurant en terrasse (spécialités européennes et africaines).
- 2 bars.
- 1 salon.
- 1 salon TV vidéo.
- 1 boutique.
- 1 discothèque : « le Mogambo ».
- Piscine, bassin pour les enfants.
- Plage aménagée.

VOTRE CHAMBRE :
Les chambres de plain-pied, construites au milieu de la verdure et des fleurs, sont avec douche, climatisation et terrasse.
Possibilité de logement en bungalows (plus spacieux) avec supplément.

- Demi-pension (dîner obligatoire), pension complète en option.

EXCURSIONS :
- **Exclusif : descente du fleuve Comoe en zodiac** (1 jour/1 nuit) 28 000 CFA environ. Logement sur une île dans un campement simple. La cuisine sera confectionnée par les villageois.
- **1 journée en brousse** en Chevrolet 4/4 climatisée : 22 500 CFA environ pique-nique inclus. Visite des plantations de café, cacao, bananes et ananas. Promenade en pirogue sur le fleuve Comoe. Possibilité de baignade dans le fleuve. Visite de villages typiques.

SPORTS ET LOISIRS :

Gratuits :
- Tennis : 1 court en dur.
- Ping-pong.
- Pétanque.
- Volley-ball.

Payants :
Possibilité de sports nautiques sur la lagune proche de l'hôtel. Soirée folklorique avec repas langouste : 5000 CFA environ.

Choisissez d'abord vos compagnons de voyage. Puis, à l'aide de cette brochure, répondez aux questions suivantes.

1. Où est situé Grand Bassam? 2. Quels sports offre l'hôtel? 3. Que met (*puts*) l'hôtel à votre disposition? 4. Quelles excursions peut-on faire?

Ensuite imaginez ce que vous avez fait tous les trois pendant votre séjour à Grand Bassam. Prenez quelques notes, puis faites une courte présentation au reste de la classe (au passé composé, bien sûr!). Attention au choix de l'auxiliaire. Commencez par «Nous sommes allés à Grand Bassam, en Côte d'Ivoire... » **Voici quelques verbes utiles:** rester, dormir, aller, jouer à, regarder, prendre, manger, visiter, faire, nager, danser, descendre, passer, voir, avoir, être...

D. Départ en vacances. Les Dupont, vos voisins, sont partis en vacances ce week-end. Vous racontez maintenant la scène à vos amis. Complétez l'histoire de façon logique et mettez les verbes au passé composé.

Ce matin, mes voisins les Dupont ____________[1] en vacances. Ils ____________[2] à la mer. A 8 heures, Monsieur Dupont et son fils ____________[3] et ____________[4] de la maison plusieurs fois avec des sacs et des valises. Madame Dupont ____________[5] cinq fois dans la maison pour aller chercher des objets oubliés.

Enfin, trois heures plus tard, toute la famille ____________[6] dans la voiture et elle ____________[7]. Mais pas de chance, une des valises ____________[8] de la galerie. M. Dupont ____________[9] de la voiture pour la remettre sur la galerie et ils ____________[10]. Moi, je ____________[11] chez moi.

sortir
entrer
partir
retourner
aller
descendre
partir
tomber
repartir
monter
rester

E. Souvenirs de vacances. Décrivez les vacances de l'année passée d'un(e) camarade. D'abord (*First*), posez les questions suivantes à votre camarade. Si vous voulez, posez encore d'autres questions. Ensuite, présentez à la classe une description de ses vacances.

1. Quand es-tu parti(e)? Quel moyen de transport as-tu pris? Où es-tu allé(e)? Es-tu resté(e) aux États-Unis ou es-tu allé(e) à l'étranger? As-tu visité un endroit exotique?
2. Es-tu allé(e) voir l'endroit où tes parents sont nés? Où es-tu né(e)?
3. Qu'est-ce que tu as fait pendant les vacances? As-tu rencontré des gens intéressants?
4. Comment es-tu rentré(e)? en avion? par bateau? Es-tu mort(e) de fatigue?
5. Prépares-tu déjà tes vacances de l'année prochaine?

F. Profil psychologique. Posez à un(e) camarade des questions basées sur les éléments donnés. Utilisez le passé composé dans vos questions. Après, faites le portrait psychologique de votre camarade. Justifiez votre profil. **Mots utiles:**

sociable, (ir)responsable, ponctuel(le), négligent(e), nostalgique, courageux (courageuse), aventureux (aventureuse), (im)prudent(e), superstitieux (superstitieuse)...

1. prendre un verre avec des amis hier soir
2. à quelle heure / rentrer
3. à quelle heure / arriver à l'université ce matin
4. entrer dans la salle de classe en retard, à l'heure ou en avance (*early, or in advance*)
5. retourner souvent à l'endroit où il (elle) est né(e)
6. passer la nuit tout(e) seul(e) dans une forêt
7. monter souvent au sommet d'une montagne
8. descendre souvent dans une grotte (*cave*)
9. refuser de passer sous une échelle (*ladder*)

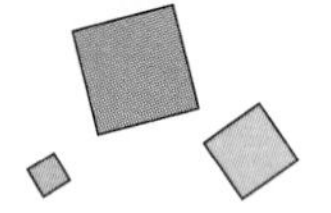

29. Expressing Location: Using Prepositions with Geographical Names

A l'aéroport Charles de Gaulle–Roissy

«Attention, attention! Embarquement immédiat pour les passagers en transit d'Alger et à destination **de Washington,** vol Air France n° 82 avec escale à **Ottawa.**»

MARYVONNE: Voilà, c'est pour nous.
JEAN-LUC: Tu es sûre?
MARYVONNE: Mais oui, elle vient de parler de nous: nous venons **d'Afrique, d'Algérie;** nous sommes restés en transit **en France** quelques heures et nous partons maintenant **en Amérique du Nord, au Canada** d'abord et ensuite **aux États-Unis!**

Répondez aux questions selon les indications.

1. D'où viennent Jean-Luc et Maryvonne? (continent, pays)
2. Où sont-ils en transit? (pays, ville)
3. Quelle est leur destination? (continent, pays)
4. Où vont-ils faire escale? (pays, ville)

A. Gender of Geographical Names

In French, most place names that end in -e are feminine; most others are masculine. Two exceptions are **le Zaïre** and **le Mexique.** The names of the continents are feminine: **l'Europe, l'Afrique, l'Asie, l'Australie,*** **l'Amérique du**

*To refer to the Pacific islands and Australia as a whole, the French use **l'Océanie** (*f.*)

Nord, l'Amérique du Sud. The names of most states in the United States are masculine: **le Kentucky, le Connecticut.** The names of nine states end in -e in French and are feminine: **la Californie, la Caroline du Nord et du Sud, la Floride, la Géorgie, la Louisiane, la Pennsylvanie, la Virginie, la Virginie occidentale.**

B. *To, in,* and *from* with Geographical Names

1. With the names of cities and most islands and groups of islands, use **à** to express *to* or *in* and **de** (**d'**) to express *from.*

Mlle Dupont habite **à Paris.**	*Mlle Dupont lives in Paris.*
Ils sont allés **à Cuba.**	*They went to Cuba.*
Ils sont **de Carcassonne.**	*They are from Carcassonne.*
Elles sont parties **d'Hawaï.**	*They left (from) Hawaii.*

   One exception is the city of New Orleans, whose feminine definite article is used with à or **de: Nous allons *à La Nouvelle-Orléans.* Êtes-vous *de La Nouvelle-Orléans?***

2. With masculine countries, use **au** (**aux**) to express *to* or *in,* and **du** (**des**) to express *from.*

Les Doi habitent **au Japon.**	*The Doi family lives in Japan.*
Ils vont arriver **aux États-Unis** demain.	*They're going to arrive in the United States tomorrow.*
Es-tu jamais allé **au Mexique**?	*Have you ever been to Mexico?*
Quand sont-ils partis **des Pays-Bas**?	*When did they leave the Netherlands (Holland)?*

3. With names of continents, feminine countries and states, and masculine countries beginning with a vowel sound, use **en** to express *to* or *in* and **de** (**d'**) to express *from.*

Le prof d'espagnol voyage **en Amérique du Sud.**	*The Spanish professor is traveling in South America.*
Je vais **en Belgique.**	*I'm going to Belgium.*
Elle est allée **en Israël.**	*She went to Israel.*
Pierre va passer un mois **en Californie.**	*Pierre is going to spend a month in California.*
M. Carter est **de Géorgie.**	*Mr. Carter is from Georgia.*

4. With the names of masculine states, usage varies. Generally, **dans le** (**l'**) is used for *to* or *in* and **du** (**de l'**) for *from.**

Sophie a passé la semaine **dans le Nevada.**	*Sophie spent the week in Nevada.*
Les Smith arrivent **de l'Illinois.**	*The Smiths are arriving from Illinois.*

*Exceptions: The French always say **au Texas.** To distinguish the states of New York and Washington from the cities of the same name, the French say **dans l'état de New York** (**Washington**).

MAINTENANT A VOUS

A. Jeu géographique. Voici quelques villes francophones. Savez-vous dans quels pays elles se trouvent? (Voir les cartes au début du livre.)

MODÈLE: Paris est en France.

1. Brazzaville	a. Madagascar
2. Rabat	b. Haïti
3. Montréal	c. la Belgique
4. Kinshasa	d. la Tunisie
5. Alger	e. la France
6. Dakar	f. le Zaïre
7. Antananarivo	g. le Canada
8. Bruxelles	h. la Suisse
9. Tunis	i. le Maroc
10. Abidjan	j. le Congo
11. Paris	k. la Côte-d'Ivoire
12. Port-au-Prince	l. l'Algérie
13. Genève	m. le Sénégal

Maintenant donnez le nom d'une ville (francophone ou non); le (la) camarade assis(e) à votre droite dit dans quel pays elle est. Puis c'est à son tour de donner une ville et ainsi de suite. **Suggestions:** Tokyo, La Nouvelle-Orléans, Mexico, Athènes, Rio de Janeiro, Pékin, Ottawa, Moscou, San Francisco, Honolulu, Londres...

B. Retour de vacances. Voici un groupe de touristes qui rentre de vacances. D'après ce qu'ils ont dans leurs valises, dites d'où ils arrivent.

MODÈLE: une montre
la Suisse → Ils arrivent de Suisse.

SOUVENIRS	PAYS
1. du parfum	le Cameroun
2. une caméra vidéo ultramoderne	la Hollande
3. une bouteille de Tequila	l'Italie
4. un masque d'initiation	le Mexique
5. des chaussures en cuir	le Japon
6. un pull en cashmere	l'Écosse
7. du chocolat	le Maroc
8. du café	la Colombie
9. un couscoussier (*couscous maker*)	la Belgique
10. des tulipes	la France

C. Un(e) jeune globe-trotter. Votre camarade va faire le tour du monde. Vous lui demandez où il (elle) va aller. **Continents:** l'Afrique, l'Océanie, l'Europe, l'Asie, l'Amérique du Nord, l'Amérique du Sud.

Pays: l'Algérie, l'Allemagne, l'Australie, le Brésil, le Canada, la Chine, le Danemark, l'Égypte, les États-Unis, la Finlande, la Grèce, l'Inde, l'Italie, le Japon, le Maroc, le Mexique, la Polynésie française, la Norvège, le Viêt-nam...

MODÈLE: —Vas-tu en Asie?
—Oui, je vais en Chine (au Japon...).

D. **Interview.** Posez les questions à un(e) camarade de classe. Ensuite, racontez sa réponse la plus surprenante à la classe.

1. D'où viens-tu? de quelle ville? de quel état? Et tes parents?
2. Où habitent tes parents? Et le reste de ta famille?
3. De quel pays est venue ta famille?
4. Dans quels états as-tu voyagé?
5. Est-ce qu'il y a un état que tu préfères? Pourquoi?
6. Est-ce qu'il y a un état que tu n'aimes pas? Pourquoi?
7. Dans quel état est-ce qu'il y a de beaux parcs? de beaux lacs? de belles montagnes? de grandes villes? de grands déserts?
8. A ton avis, où dans le monde y a-t-il de jolies montagnes? de belles plages? des villes pittoresques? d'excellentes autoroutes?
9. Tu es riche. Où vas-tu passer tes vacances?
10. Tu n'as pas d'argent. Où vas-tu passer tes vacances?

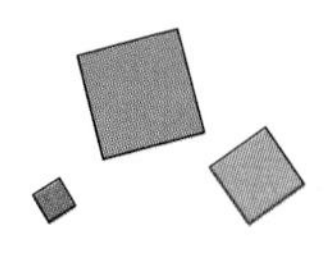

30. Expressing Negation: Affirmative and Negative Adverbs

Le train à grande vitesse

PATRICIA: Je **n'**ai **pas encore** voyagé en TGV... Tu as aimé ça?
FRÉDÉRIC: Oui, c'est formidable! Il est très rapide et très confortable.
PATRICIA: On doit réserver sa place à l'avance, non?
FRÉDÉRIC: Oui, parce qu'il **n'**y a **que** des places assises dans le TGV, alors on **ne** peut **jamais** le prendre sans réservation. Mais le système de réservation est ultra-rapide. On peut encore réserver sa place trois minutes avant le départ!

Trouvez la phrase équivalente dans le dialogue.

1. Je n'ai toujours pas voyagé en TGV.
2. Il y a seulement des places assises dans le TGV.
3. On a toujours la possibilité de réserver sa place juste avant le départ.

A. Ne... jamais, ne... plus, ne... pas encore

1. **Toujours, souvent,** and **parfois** are adverbs that generally follow the verb in the present tense. The expression **ne (n')... jamais,** constructed like **ne... pas,** is the negative adverb (**l'adverbe de négation**) used to express the fact that an action never takes place.

Henri voyage **toujours** en train.* Marie voyage **souvent** en train.* Hélène voyage **parfois** en train.	Je **ne** voyage **jamais** en train. *I never travel by train.*

Other adverbs also follow this pattern.

AFFIRMATIVE	NEGATIVE
encore *still*	**ne (n')... plus** *no longer, no more*
déjà *already*	**ne (n')... pas encore** *not yet*
Le train est **encore** sur le quai. *The train is still on the platform.*	Le train **n'**est **plus** sur le quai. *The train is no longer on the platform.*
Nos valises sont **déjà** là? *Our suitcases are already there?*	Nos valises **ne** sont **pas encore** là. *Our suitcases are not there yet.*

2. As with **ne (n')... pas,** the indefinite article and the partitive article become **de (d')** when they follow negative verbs.

Je vois **toujours des Américains** dans l'autocar. *I always see Americans on the tourist bus.*	Je **ne** vois **jamais de Français** dans l'autocar. *I never see (any) French people on the tourist bus.*
Avez-vous **encore des billets** à vendre? *Do you still have (some) tickets to sell?*	Non, je **n'**ai **plus de billets** à vendre. *No, I have no more (I don't have any more) tickets to sell.*
Karen a **déjà des amis** en France. *Karen already has (some) friends in France.*	Vincent **n'**a **pas encore d'amis** aux États-Unis. *Vincent doesn't have any friends in the United States yet.*

Definite articles do not change.

Je ne vois jamais **le** contrôleur (*conductor*) dans ce train.
Annick ne prend plus **l'**autoroute à Caen.
Éric ne voit pas encore **le** sommet de la montagne.

---

*Sentences whose verbs are modified by **toujours** and **souvent** may also be negated by **ne (n')... pas: Henri ne voyage pas toujours en train. Il voyage parfois en avion. Marie ne voyage pas souvent en train. Elle préfère conduire sa voiture.**

3. In the **passé composé,** the affirmative adverbs are generally placed between the auxiliary and the past participle.

   M. Huet **a toujours** (**souvent, parfois**) pris l'avion.

   Note the negative and interrogative forms of the negative adverbial construction.

—Marie **n'a-t-elle jamais** voyagé en avion?	—*Has Marie never traveled by air?*
—Non, elle **n'a jamais** voyagé en avion.	—*No, she has never traveled by air.*
—Non, elle **n'a pas encore** voyagé en avion.	—*No, she has not yet traveled by air.*

4. **Ne... pas du tout** is used instead of **ne... pas** for emphasis.

—Je **n'aime pas du tout** les avions!	—*I don't like planes at all!*
—As-tu faim?	—*Are you hungry?*
—Pas du tout!	—*Not at all!*

B. Ne... que

The expression **ne (n')... que (qu')** is the equivalent in meaning of **seulement.** It is used to indicate a limited quantity of something.

Je **n'**ai **qu'**un billet.	→	*I have only one ticket.*	←	J'ai **seulement** un billet.
Il **n'**y a **que** trois trains cet après-midi.	→	*There are only three trains this afternoon.*	←	Il y a **seulement** trois trains cet après-midi.

In the **passé composé, que** precedes the word or phrase that it limits.

Hélène **n'**a acheté **que** deux billets.	*Hélène bought only two tickets.*
Je **n'**ai pensé **qu'à** mon voyage.	*I thought only about my trip.*

MAINTENANT A VOUS

A. Préparatifs de voyage. Quand vous partez en voyage, faites-vous les choses suivantes **toujours, souvent, parfois** ou **jamais**?

MODÈLE: arriver à l'aéroport à la dernière minute. →
J'arrive toujours (Je n'arrive jamais) à l'aéroport à la dernière minute.

1. oublier son passeport (sa brosse à dents [*toothbrush*], sa carte de crédit...)
2. prendre son appareil-photo (un guide, une carte...)
3. acheter de nouveaux vêtements (de nouvelles chaussures, de nouvelles lunettes de soleil...)
4. créer un itinéraire (à l'avance, au dernier moment)
5. faire sa valise au dernier moment (la veille [*the day before*], une semaine avant...)
6. ?

Maintenant donnez deux choses que vous faites quand vous êtes en voyage. Utilisez **ne... que,** si possible.

MODÈLE: Quand je suis en voyage...
Je ne prends qu'une valise.
Je n'envoie des cartes postales qu'à mes parents.
J'achète seulement des souvenirs drôles.

B. Personnalités opposées. Voici le portrait de Monique. Faites le portrait de Joseph en suivant le modèle.

MODÈLE: Monique a parfois sommeil en cours. →
Joseph n'a jamais sommeil en cours.

1. Monique a déjà des problèmes avec ses études. 2. Elle a souvent envie de changer de cours. 3. Elle a parfois peur des professeurs. 4. Elle a déjà besoin de vacances. 5. Elle croit encore aux miracles.

D'après ces descriptions, quels adjectifs associez-vous avec Monique? avec Joseph? **Adjectifs:** optimiste/pessimiste, naïf (naïve)/intelligent(e), stable/instable, sérieux (sérieuse)/frivole, courageux (courageuse)/lâche...

C. Voyages exotiques. Interviewez vos camarades.

MODÈLE: camper dans le Sahara →
VOUS: As-tu jamais campé dans le Sahara?
VOTRE CAMARADE: Non, je n'ai jamais campé dans le Sahara.
(*ou*) Oui, j'ai campé dans le Sahara (l'été passé, il y a deux ans, etc.).

1. faire du bateau sur le Nil 2. voir le Sphinx en Égypte 3. faire une expédition dans l'Antarctique 4. passer tes vacances à Tahiti 5. faire de l'alpinisme dans l'Himalaya 6. voir les chutes Victoria (*Victoria Falls*) en Afrique 7. faire de la voile dans les fjords en Norvège 8. faire un safari-photos au Cameroun 9. ?

Qui dans votre classe a fait le voyage le plus exotique?

D. Voyages chez nous. Vous apprenez que votre camarade a très peu voyagé aux États-Unis. Posez des questions selon le modèle.

MODÈLE: voir les chutes du Niagara →

VOUS: As-tu déjà vu les chutes du Niagara?
VOTRE CAMARADE: Non, je n'ai pas encore vu les chutes du Niagara.
(*ou*) Oui, j'ai déjà vu les chutes du Niagara.

1. visiter le Grand Canyon 2. aller à San Francisco 3. voir les Everglades en Floride 4. skier dans les Montagnes Rocheuses (*Rocky Mountains*) 5. visiter La Nouvelle-Orléans 6. voir le geyser «vieux fidèle» de Yellowstone 7. ?

Qui dans votre classe a visité le plus grand nombre de sites extraordinaires en Amérique?

E. Et dans votre région? Pensez aux lieux intéressants de la région où vous habitez et posez des questions à un(e) camarade. Commencez vos phrases par **As-tu jamais vu... , N'es-tu pas encore allé(e) à... , As-tu déjà vu... ,** etc.

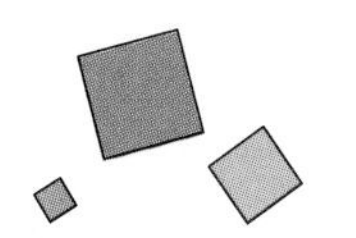

31. Expressing Negation: Affirmative and Negative Pronouns

La consigne automatique

SERGE: Il y a **quelque chose** qui ne va pas?
JEAN-PIERRE: Oui, j'ai des ennuis avec la consigne.
SERGE: Ah, ça! Il n'y a **rien** de plus énervant!
JEAN-PIERRE **Tout le monde** semble toujours trouver une consigne qui marche, sauf moi.
SERGE: Regarde, **quelqu'un** sort ses bagages d'une consigne. Là, tu es sûr qu'elle marche!
JEAN-PIERRE: Excellente idée!

Corrigez les phrases inexactes.

1. Tout va bien avec Jean-Pierre.
2. Il y a quelque chose de plus énervant (*something more exasperating*) qu'une consigne qui ne marche pas.
3. Jean-Pierre et deux autres passagers ne trouvent pas de consigne qui marche.
4. Quand quelqu'un place ses bagages dans une consigne, on est sûr qu'elle marche.

A. Affirmative Pronouns

Quelqu'un* (*someone*), **quelque chose** (*something*), **tout** (*everything, all*), and **tout le monde** (*everybody*) are indefinite pronouns (**des pronoms indéfinis**). All four may serve as the subject of a sentence, the object of a verb, or the object of a preposition.

Il y a **quelqu'un** au guichet maintenant.	*Someone is at the ticket counter now.*
Vous avez vu **quelqu'un** sur le quai?	*Did you see someone on the platform?*
Jacques a parlé avec **quelqu'un** il y a un moment.	*Jacques spoke with someone a moment ago.*
Quelque chose est arrivé.	*Something has happened.*
Marie a acheté **quelque chose** au restaurant de la gare.	*Marie bought something at the station restaurant.*
Elle pense à **quelque chose,** mais à quoi?	*She's thinking about something, but what?*
Tout est possible.	*Everything is possible.*
Tout le monde est prêt?	*Is everybody ready?*

B. Negative Pronouns

Personne (*no one, nobody, not anybody*) and **rien** (*nothing, not anything*) are negative pronouns generally used in a construction with **ne** (**n'**). They can be the subject of a sentence, the object of a verb, or the object of a preposition. As objects of a verb in the **passé composé, rien** precedes the past participle, but **personne** is placed after the past participle.

Personne n'est monté dans ce train.	*No one boarded this train.*
Je **n'**ai vu **personne** sur le quai.	*I didn't see anyone on the platform.*
Jacques **ne** parle avec **personne** maintenant.	*Jacques isn't speaking with anyone right now.*
Rien ne l'intéresse.	*Nothing interests him (her).*
Marie **n'**a **rien** acheté au restaurant de la gare.	*Marie didn't buy anything at the station restaurant.*
Elle **ne** pense à **rien.**	*She's not thinking about anything.*
Rien n'est impossible.	*Nothing is impossible.*
Personne n'est prêt.	*Nobody is ready.*

*__Quelqu'un__ is invariable in form: it can refer to both males and females.

C. *Rien* and *personne*

Like **jamais, rien** and **personne** may be used without **ne** when they answer a question.

—Qu'est-ce qu'il y a sur la voie?	—*What's on the track?*
—**Rien.**	—*Nothing.*
—Qui est au guichet?	—*Who's at the ticket counter?*
—**Personne.**	—*Nobody.*

D. Negative Pronouns with Adjectives

Affirmative and negative expressions with adjectives are formed with **quelque chose/quelqu'un/ne... rien/ne... personne** plus **de** (**d'**) plus a masculine singular adjective.

Y a-t-il **quelque chose de bon** au menu du wagon-restaurant?	*Is there something good on the menu in the restaurant car?*
Il y a **quelqu'un d'intéressant** dans ce compartiment.	*There is someone interesting in this compartment.*
Il **n'**y a **rien d'amusant** dans ce journal.	*There is nothing entertaining in this paper.*
Il **n'**y a **personne d'important** dans la salle d'attente.	*There is no one important in the waiting room.*

MAINTENANT A VOUS

A. A la gare. Vous avez des ennuis avant de partir en voyage. Transformez les phrases suivantes.

MODÈLE: Quelqu'un est prêt! →
Personne n'est prêt!

1. Quelqu'un a acheté les billets. 2. Quelqu'un a apporté nos valises. 3. Tout est prêt. 4. Jean-Claude pense à quelque chose. 5. Éric a tout pris. 6. Claudine parle avec quelqu'un.

B. Mais si! Donnez une réponse affirmative pour chaque phrase négative.

MODÈLE: —Il n'y a personne à la caisse (*cash register*).
—Mais si! Il y a quelqu'un à la caisse.

1. Il n'y a personne dans ce restaurant. Il n'y a rien de bon sur la carte.
2. Il n'y a rien dans ce magasin de sport. Il n'y a rien de joli ici.
3. Il n'y a personne dans cette agence de voyages. Il n'y a rien d'intéressant dans ces brochures.
4. Il n'y a rien de moderne dans ce quartier. Il n'y a rien d'intéressant dans les rues.

C. **Qu'est-ce qui se passe?** (*What's happening?*) Posez des questions à vos camarades pour apprendre ce qui se passe sur votre campus aujourd'hui. **Suggestions:** Y a-t-il quelque chose d'intéressant dans la salle de conférences (*lecture hall*) ce soir? Y a-t-il quelqu'un d'intéressant au ciné-club ce soir? Y a-t-il quelque chose de délicieux au restau-u ce soir? ______________?

En voiture!*

Contexte *Geoffroy est venu faire des études d'optométrie à Nice. Il n'a pas encore eu le temps de visiter le Sud et a décidé de passer le week-end à Avignon pour voir le Palais des Papes° et le vieux pont.° Comme tout le monde, il prend le train.*

Objectif *Geoffroy achète un billet° de train.*

Palais... *Palace of the Popes* / *bridge*
ticket

GEOFFROY: (*au guichet*) A quelle heure est le prochain train pour Avignon, s'il vous plaît?
LE GUICHETIER: Vous avez un train dans vingt minutes et le suivant° est à 22 heures.
GEOFFROY: Combien coûte le billet aller-retour° en deuxième classe?
LE GUICHETIER: 294 francs.
GEOFFROY: Je veux un aller simple,° s'il vous plaît. Je peux régler° par chèques de voyage?
LE GUICHETIER: Oui, s'ils sont en francs. Voilà votre billet. Vous avez une place° dans le compartiment 23, et vous partez du quai numéro 6.
GEOFFROY: Merci.
LE GUICHETIER: Oh, n'oubliez pas de composter.°

le... *the next one*
round-trip
aller... *one-way ticket* / payer
seat
have your ticket punched

*En... *All aboard!*

VARIATIONS

© OWEN FRANKEN / STOCK, BOSTON

—Avec les distributeurs automatiques, on n'a pas besoin de faire la queue au guichet.

1. Rejouez le dialogue avec une des variations suivantes.

- Vous prenez un billet aller-retour.
- Vous allez à Paris et vous prenez une couchette (*berth*); le billet pour Paris coûte 650 F et le supplément couchette coûte 85 F.
- Vous avez une carte inter-rail;* vous payez demi-tarif.

2. **Voyage interplanétaire.** Vous allez réserver une place sur la navette (*shuttle*) interplanétaire. Inventez le dialogue avec l'employé de l'agence de voyages interplanétaires. N'oubliez pas de choisir entre première ou deuxième classe, entre places assises (*seat only*) ou couchettes. Y a-t-il d'autres choix à faire? Peut-être un supplément hibernation? Inventez les tarifs.

© J. L. MANAUD

Maquette de la navette Hermès

*The **carte inter-rail** provides half-price tickets for young people between the ages of 12 and 25. It is valid on all trains, including the TGV, on weekdays other than holidays.

A propos

Expressions utiles en voyage

EN VOITURE

Faites le plein (*Fill it up*), s'il vous plaît.
...de l'essence ordinaire ou du super?
Ma voiture est en panne (*broken down*).
Où y a-t-il une station-service (un garage), s'il vous plaît?

EN TAXI

Quels sont les tarifs (*fares*), s'il vous plaît?
Emmenez-moi à l'Hôtel du Centre, s'il vous plaît.

DANS LE MÉTRO

(Je voudrais) un ticket (de métro), s'il vous plaît.
(Je voudrais) un carnet (*book of tickets*), s'il vous plaît.

EN AUTOBUS

Où est l'arrêt d'autobus (*bus stop*), s'il vous plaît?
(Je voudrais) un ticket (d'autobus), s'il vous plaît.
Quel autobus faut-il prendre pour aller à... ?

A. Sur les routes de France. Pour être un bon conducteur (une bonne conductrice), on doit reconnaître (*recognize*) les panneaux (*road signs*). Devinez ce que ces panneaux représentent.

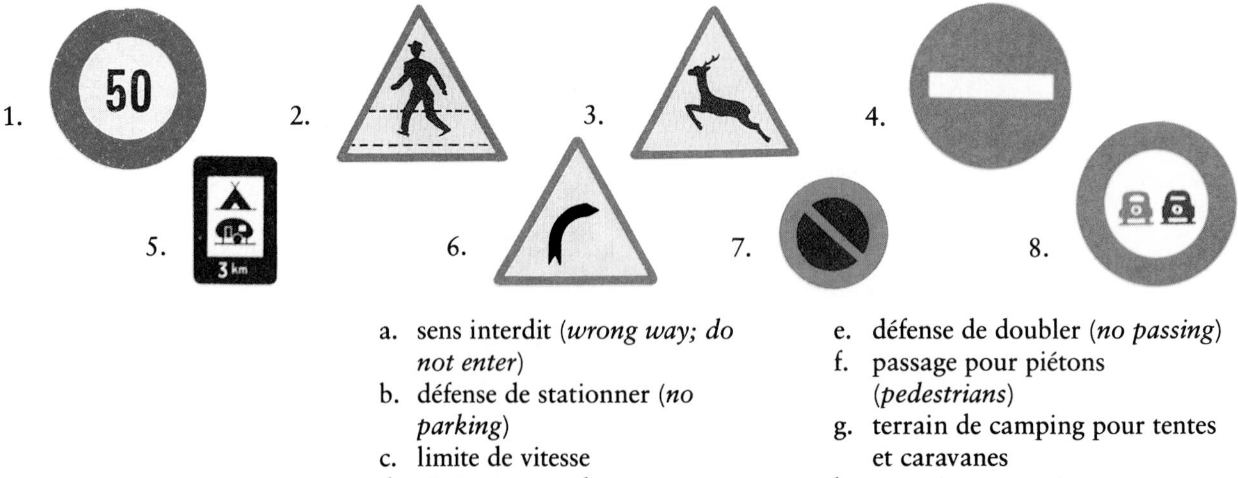

a. sens interdit (*wrong way; do not enter*)
b. défense de stationner (*no parking*)
c. limite de vitesse
d. virage (*curve*) dangereux
e. défense de doubler (*no passing*)
f. passage pour piétons (*pedestrians*)
g. terrain de camping pour tentes et caravanes
h. attention aux animaux sauvages

Avec un(e) camarade, imaginez que vous êtes sur la route. C'est vous qui conduisez. Indiquez quatre des panneaux, l'un après l'autre, à votre camarade. A chaque fois, votre camarade doit vous donner un ordre correspondant au panneau que vous avez indiqué. Ensuite, changez de rôles et faites de même avec les autres panneaux.

Expressions utiles: Attention à ______!
Il est interdit de ______!
Ralentis! (*Slow down!*)
Fais demi-tour!

Mots-clés

Expressing your opinions:

Je (ne) suis (pas) d'accord (que...)	*I do (not) agree (that) . . .*
Vous avez raison.	*You're right.*
Vous avez tort.	*You're wrong.*
A mon avis...	*In my opinion . . .*
Je n'ai pas terminé!	*I haven't finished!*
Laissez-moi terminer!	*Let me finish!*

B. **Pour ou contre?** Organisez un débat. Prenez parti **pour** ou **contre** et défendez votre opinion.

1. Êtes-vous pour ou contre la limitation de vitesse aux États-Unis à cinquante-cinq miles à l'heure? Est-ce qu'elle permet d'économiser de l'essence? Est-ce qu'on respecte cette limitation?
2. Êtes-vous pour ou contre les petites voitures? Sont-elles confortables? Est-ce qu'elles permettent d'économiser de l'essence? Sont-elles sûres (*safe*)?

C. **Jeu de rôles.** Imaginez que vous visitez Paris en voiture. Vous n'avez plus d'essence, et vous vous arrêtez dans une station-service pour faire le plein. Vous repartez, mais peu après votre voiture tombe en panne. Elle ne démarre (*starts*) plus. Jouez la situation avec un(e) camarade. Utilisez les expressions de *l'A propos*.

Commentaire culturel

Une rue animée du centre-ville de Montréal

Quebec and the francophone world. Because it is the largest industrialized francophone region outside of Europe, Quebec has become a leader in the growing international movement toward cooperation among francophone nations.

Since 1967, leaders of French-speaking countries have been working together to promote cultural and technological exchange. Quebec was influential in establishing the **Agence de coopération culturelle et technique** and the **Association internationale des parlementaires de langue française.** In 1987, Quebec hosted the **Deuxième sommet de la francophonie** in Quebec City, bringing together representatives of francophone nations in Asia, Africa, Europe, and the Americas. The aim of these efforts is to promote international economic development and benefit francophone countries. In particular, discussion at the 1987 **Haut conseil de la francophonie** focused on the following areas:

- Political and economic problems within participating countries
- Development of the poorest francophone nations, especially through technological advancements
- Development of a worldwide network of television in French
- Increasing the influence of the French language in the world

The provincial government of Quebec is committed to building solid relations with other French-speaking areas through increased trade, educational exchange programs, and shared technological and scientific developments.

French speakers continue to emigrate to Quebec, as they have done for more than three hundred years. The government encourages immigration. It recognizes that people willing to face the hurdles of adapting to a new world tend to be ambitious and to infuse new skills and different points of view into Canadian society. Immigration also helps maintain population levels, otherwise in decline because of the low birthrate in Canada. Especially during the 1980s, tens of thousands of francophone immigrants from Haiti, the Near East, North Africa, Southeast Asia, and Europe have found a home in Quebec. Their presence gives Montreal and Quebec City a genuinely international flavor.

Mise au point

15 Acadie et Gaspésie

Sur les traces de Jacques Cartier

6ème jour :
PERCÉ

Journée de détente et d'excursions à Percé. Promenade en bateau jusqu'à l'Ile de Bonaventure où les fous de Bassan nichent par milliers. Dîner et logement.

7ème jour :
PERCÉ/CARLETON

Les villages de pêcheurs se succèdent le long de la baie. Arrêt à la Réserve Indienne de Maria. Dîner et logement à Carleton.

8ème jour :
CARLETON/CARAQUET

La route longe la Baie des Chaleurs : vous sentirez la joie de vivre des Acadiens et la volonté qu'ils ont de conserver un patrimoine francophone unique. Dîner et logement à Caraquet.

9ème jour :
CARAQUET

Visite du Village Historique Acadien : hommes, femmes et enfants y vivent comme leurs ancêtres venus de France. A Shippagan, le Musée marin vous dévoilera les secrets de la mer. Dîner.

10ème jour :
CARAQUET/FRÉDERICTON

Vous traverserez une région connue pour les saumons de la Miramachi et les chansons transmises par les bûcherons[a] aux voyageurs. Fin de votre journée à Frédericton, capitale de la province, fondée par les loyalistes en 1783. Dîner et logement.

11ème jour :
FRÉDERICTON/RIVIÈRE DU LOUP

Visite du King's Landing, reconstitution d'un village anglais au 19e siècle. Route de la vallée de la Saint Jean, par Hartland au pont couvert[b] le plus long du monde, Grand Sault et ses chutes, Saint François de Madawaska où la rivière sert de frontière entre le Canada et les États-Unis. Dîner et logement à Rivière du Loup.

12ème jour :
RIVIÈRE DU LOUP/QUÉBEC

Route pour Québec, capitale de la "Belle Province". Arrêt à Saint Jean Port Joli, connue pour la sculpture sur bois. Déjeuner. Arrivée en fin d'après-midi. Dîner et logement à Québec.

13ème jour :
QUÉBEC

Tour guidé de la seule ville fortifiée d'Amérique du Nord. Visite de l'Ile d'Orléans où sera servi le déjeuner. Retour à Québec. Après-midi et soirée libres.

14ème jour :
QUÉBEC/MONTRÉAL

Temps libre, puis route vers Montréal ou vers l'aéroport pour le vol de retour vers l'Europe. Dîner et nuit à bord.

15ème jour :
ARRIVÉE EN FRANCE

Arrivée à Paris après le petit déjeuner servi en vol. Transit et acheminement jusqu'à votre ville de retour.

a. *loggers*
b. pont... *covered bridge*

A. Voyage en Acadie. Voici l'itinéraire proposé par une brochure touristique pour découvrir l'Acadie. **Verbes utiles:** voir, déjeuner, dîner, prendre, visiter, faire, dormir, parler, traverser, découvrir, conduire, quitter, tenir à, revoir, vouloir, pouvoir...

1. Quels noms de ville reconnaissez-vous (*do you recognize*)? Quels noms sont d'origine française? indienne?
2. Qui est Jacques Cartier? Qu'est-ce qu'il a découvert?

Maintenant, imaginez que vous venez de rentrer d'Acadie et que vous racontez votre voyage à un ami (une amie). Choisissez deux étapes (*segments of trip*). Cherchez pour chaque étape une ou deux informations-clés. Puis, à partir de cette information, faites des phrases au passé composé.

MODÈLE: Vol vers Montréal →
Nous avons déjeuné dans l'avion et nous avons vu un film.

B. Êtes-vous un grand voyageur? Où allez-vous pour voir les choses suivantes?

MODÈLE: La fontaine de Trevi →
On va à Rome (en Italie) pour voir la fontaine de Trevi.

1. Carnac	a. la Bretagne (France)
2. le Pont-du-Gard	b. l'Égypte
3. les Pyramides	c. Londres
4. Big Ben	d. l'Afrique
5. L'Amazone	e. l'Asie
6. le Mont Everest	f. l'Amérique du Sud
7. le Sahara	g. l'Allemagne, l'Autriche (*Austria*)
8. le Danube	h. la Provence (France)
9. la Grande Muraille (*wall*)	i. la Chine

Faites le total des réponses correctes. Dans quelle catégorie êtes-vous?

8–9 Très bien! Vous êtes très bien informé(e) et vous aimez les voyages.

5–7 Pas mal, mais vous n'êtes pas un(e) voyageur (voyageuse) très passionné(e).

0–4 Restez à la maison et lisez un livre de géographie avant de partir en voyage.

Maintenant, nommez d'autres choses à voir dans d'autres pays et mettez à l'épreuve (*test*) les connaissances (*knowledge*) géographiques de vos camarades de classe.

Interactions

In Chapter 8, you practiced talking about traveling and transportation, discussing events in the past, expressing location, and making negative comments. Act out the following situations, using the vocabulary and structures from this chapter.

1. **Un mauvais voyage.** You are in France. You are so angry with your travel agent that you call him or her to complain. Among other things, mention the following: the plane left late, your hotel room was not reserved (**réservé**), no one is friendly, there is nothing good to eat, there's so much traffic that it's impossible to drive, the phones don't work, etc.
2. **Devinez.** Describe a trip, telling where you went, when, and with whom. Mention some of your activities and the means of transportation. Your partner will guess if you are telling the truth.

Vocabulaire

Verbes

conduire to drive
construire to construct
coûter to cost
détruire to destroy
entrer to enter
faire le plein to fill it up (*gas tank*)
monter to go up, climb
mourir to die
naître to be born
rentrer to return, go home
rouler to travel (*in a car*)
tomber to fall
tomber en panne to break down (*vehicle*)
traverser to cross

Substantifs

l'aéroport (*m.*) airport
l'arrivée (*f.*) arrival
l'autoroute (*f.*) highway
l'avion (*m.*) airplane
le camion truck
la carte d'embarquement boarding pass
la classe affaires business class
la classe économique tourist class
le compartiment compartment
le (la) conducteur (-trice) driver
la couchette berth
le départ departure
l'endroit (*m.*) place
l'état (*m.*) state
la fois time
la gare train station
le guichet (ticket) window
l'hôtesse de l'air (*f.*) stewardess
la marche walking
le métro subway
le monde world
la motocyclette, la «moto» motorcycle
le (la) passager (-ère) passenger
le pays country (nation)
le pilote pilot
le quai platform (train station)
la section fumeurs/non-fumeurs smoking/nonsmoking section
le steward steward
le train train
la valise suitcase
le vol flight
le wagon train car

Expressions affirmatives et négatives

déjà already
ne... jamais never
ne... pas du tout not at all
ne... pas encore not yet
ne... personne no one, nobody
ne... plus no longer
ne... que only
ne... rien nothing
quelque chose something
quelqu'un someone
tout everything
tout le monde everybody, everyone

Pays

l'Algérie (*f.*) Algeria
l'Allemagne (*f.*) **de l'Est** East Germany
l'Allemagne (*f.*) **de l'Ouest** West Germany
l'Angleterre (*f.*) England
la Belgique Belgium
le Brésil Brazil
le Canada Canada
la Chine China
l'Espagne (*f.*) Spain
les États-Unis (*m.*) United States
la France France
la Grèce Greece
l'Italie (*f.*) Italy
le Japon Japan
le Maroc Morocco
le Mexique Mexico
le Portugal Portugal
la Suisse Switzerland
l'U.R.S.S. (*f.*) U.S.S.R.

Mots divers

à l'est/ouest to the east/west
à l'étranger abroad, in a foreign country
à l'heure on time
à mon avis in my opinion
au nord/sud to the north/south
chacun(e) each, everyone
en retard late, not on time
plusieurs several
prochain(e) next
si yes
tôt early

INTERMÈDE 8

Lecture

AVANT DE LIRE

Anticipating content: Even in your native language, reading is a process of forming expectations and then confirming or changing them on the basis of what you learn as you read on. Suppose you find a clipping from a magazine that quotes the President of the United States, who is vividly describing his hatred of all foreigners. If you think it's a clipping from *The New York Times*, you may worry about the consequences for national security. If you read on and recognize it as a clipping from a magazine of political satire, you may find it highly entertaining. What you expect has a profound influence on what you find when you read.

Especially when you read French, it is useful to focus on and develop your expectations about a reading before you plunge into it. Anticipating content enables you to structure all the unfamiliar elements of the reading. Think of what you already know about the topic, and glance at titles, opening lines, photos, and illustrations before you begin reading. Ask yourself what you know about the author and any other readers of the piece.

Before you read the following unedited excerpt from a brochure about Montpellier, answer the following questions.

- Where is Montpellier? How do you know?
- What kind of place is it? What adjectives come to mind?
- Now read the first sentence. What is the writer's attitude toward the city? What is his relationship to the city? What aspects of the city will he probably describe? For whom do you think he is writing?

Remember, too, as you read this excerpt that your aim is not to understand every word. Try simply to guess the core meaning of most sentences, embodied in the subject-verb-object combinations. Read only for the gist of the piece.

Vieille de sept cents ans, l'université de Montpellier reste l'une des plus prestigieuses de France, surtout dans le domaine médical. Sa Faculté de médicine est la plus ancienne d'Europe.

Montpellier Etoile[a] du Sud

De retour à Montpellier après une longue absence, je suis toujours frappée[b] par l'intensité de la lumière[c] de ma ville natale. Que ce soit le bleu ou l'ocre de la pierre calcaire des maisons, que ce soit le vert tendre des platanes[d] au printemps ou le jaune des genêts, tout est lumineux, comme enveloppé d'un éclat[e] particulier propre aux cités du Sud. L'air aussi a une odeur personnelle, composée de la subtile présence marine et de la garrigue[f] toute proche, riche de mille parfums. Tantôt, lorsque le vent vient de la mer, le souffle du large s'imprègne de la senteur un peu forte des étangs, tantôt le mistral[g] souffle, et c'est l'odeur de thym, de romarin et de fenouil[h] qui envahit les vieilles rues du centre. Montpellier est juste à la limite entre côte et arrière-pays. Ni balnéaire ni paysanne, la ville a exploité au cours de son histoire des matières précieuses mais impalpables : la culture et la science. Vouée[i] depuis sept siècles[j] à la formation des esprits[k], elle s'est taillé une place de choix dans le palmarès des villes universitaires. Aujourd'hui, Montpellier est la cité de la jeunesse[l]. Dans les rues, à la terrasse des cafés, des milliers d'étudiants vivent[m] au rythme du soleil et des examens. Ces jeunes gens viennent d'horizons aussi différents que lointains, attirés[n] par cette belle cité du sud de la France et par l'excellence de son université. Dès[o] les premiers beaux jours, parfois dès février, la ville subit une transhumance quotidienne[p] vers Palavas-les-Flots. 8 kilomètres séparent la cité de ses plages[q], 8 kilomètres que tous les Montpelliérains franchissent aux premiers rayons de soleil. Ils y vont à l'heure du déjeuner, après le travail et, bien sûr, à chaque fin de semaine. C'est un pèlerinage[r] obligatoire que tous, jeunes et moins jeunes, accomplissent régulièrement en hommage à la divinité Soleil. Ici, la pluie et le beau temps restent un sujet de discussion sérieux.

a. *Star*
b. *struck*
c. *light*
d. arbres
e. clarté
f. *stony, sun-drenched hills*
g. *winds blowing from inland*
h. thym... des herbes
i. *Devoted*
j. depuis... *for seven centuries*
k. *minds*
l. *youth*
m. *live*
n. *attracted*
o. *As early as*
p. subit... *experiences a daily migration*
q. *beaches*
r. *pilgrimage*

COMPRÉHENSION

1. L'auteur associe sa ville natale...
   a. à un climat très contrasté
   b. à l'antiquité romaine
   c. à la lumière et aux parfums
2. Montpellier est une ville près de...
   a. la montagne
   b. la mer

3. Montpellier est célèbre aussi grâce à...
   a. ses casinos
   b. son université
   c. ses pistes de ski
4. Ce texte pourrait (*could*) être divisé en deux parties: (a) Montpellier, ville de soleil et de lumière et (b) Montpellier, centre universitaire. Marquez les deux parties en utilisant (a) et (b).
5. Pensez à un endroit que vous avez beaucoup aimé. Quels adjectifs et noms associez-vous à cet endroit? Quelles sensations avez-vous éprouvées (*experienced*) quand vous avez visité cet endroit?

Par écrit

Vous êtes étudiant en écologie, et vous écrivez un article sur les problèmes de transport près de votre campus. Utilisez les questions suivantes comme guide.

1. Quels sont les problèmes de transport sur le campus? Est-ce qu'il est difficile de garer (stationner) une voiture? Y a-t-il trop de voitures? Assez de transports publics? Est-il facile de sortir le soir sans voiture? Peut-on se déplacer à pied sans ennuis?
2. Quel moyen de transport préfère la plupart (= majorité) des étudiants? Êtes-vous d'accord avec ces étudiants? Pourquoi ou pourquoi pas?
3. Proposez quelques réformes pour améliorer les problèmes de transport. (**Il faut que... , On doit...**)

CHAPITRE NEUF

Bonnes nouvelles

—Est-ce que tu as déjà lu le journal ce matin?
—Oui, dans le métro.
—Alors, quoi de neuf?
—Oh, pas grand-chose. Tu sais, je ne lis que les grands titres et la section sportive.

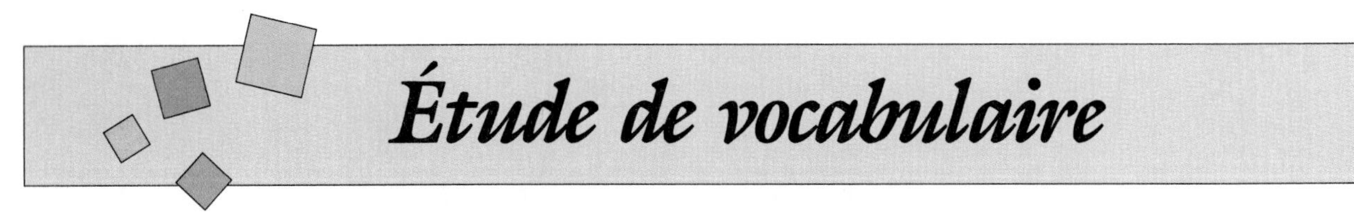

Étude de vocabulaire

La communication et les médias

1. Nous écrivons et nous envoyons*...

Où est la dame sur le dessin? Qu'est-ce qu'il y a, en général, sur une enveloppe? Où trouve-t-on des boîtes aux lettres? Que fait-on quand on veut envoyer (*to send*) un message urgent?

2. Nous lisons...

Où va-t-on pour acheter des journaux? Quand est-ce qu'on regarde les petites annonces? Quels magazines achetez-vous régulièrement? quelles revues?† quels journaux?

---

*For the complete conjugation of **envoyer** and **appeler** (next page), see the Appendix at the back of the book.

†**Une revue** is generally a monthly publication whose articles share a common theme and whose purpose is scholarly or informational. **Un magazine,** on the other hand, contains articles on a wide variety of topics and has many photographs and advertisements.

3. Nous parlons...

D'après ce dessin, comment fait-on pour téléphoner en France? Que doit-on chercher? Comment peut-on payer sa communication? Que dit la personne qui répond?

Quelques chaînes de la télévision française

Télévision Francaise 1 (TF1) les nouvelles

Antenne 2 (A2) la publicité

France-Régions 3 (FR3) un programme de musique

Canal Plus Télévision privée par cable

4. Nous écoutons et nous regardons...

Voici, à la page suivante, un programme de la télévision française. Combien de chaînes y a-t-il? Comment s'appellent-elles? Combien de chaînes retransmettent (*broadcast*) 24 heures sur 24? Quelles émissions vous sont familières? A première vue, y a-t-il des différences entre les programmes français et américains? Lesquelles?

Maintenant imaginez que vous êtes en France et que vous voulez passer une partie de la journée à regarder la télé. Quels programmes allez-vous choisir? Expliquez les raisons de votre choix.

MARDI : HEURE PAR HEURE

				LA CINQ 5	M6	CANAL+
de 5.00 à 9.00	6.27 UNE PREMIÈRE 7.30 CLUB DOROTHÉE 8.27 FLASH 8.30 LE MAGAZINE DE L'OBJET 9.00 HAINE ET PASSIONS 9.40 CLUB DOROTHÉE	6.45 TÉLÉMATIN 8.30 AMOUREUSEMENT VOTRE 9.00 L'ÉTÉ EN BASKETS		5.00 JOURNAL 8.00 DESSINS ANIMÉS 9.02 BELLE RIVE 9.52 VIVE LA VIE	6.00 MATIN CHAUD 8.00 NANS LE BERGER 8.30 SÉBASTIEN ET LA MARY-MORGANE 9.00 PLEIN LES BAFFLES	7.00 CABOU CADIN 8.00 CBS EVENING NEWS 8.25 THROB 8.45 CABOU CADIN 9.00 ALLAN QUATERMAIN ET LES MINES DU ROI SALOMON
10.00	10.45 ET AVEC LES OREILLES			10.18 LES THIBAULT	10.00 BOULEVARD DES CLIPS	10.35 FLASH 10.40 LA VOIE LACTÉE
11.00	11.10 C'EST DEJA DEMAIN 11.35 ON NE VIT QU'UNE FOIS	11.00 AVENTURES-VOYAGES 11.25 GORRI LE DIABLE 11.55 FLASH		11.30 FLASH 11.38 CAPITOL	11.00 GRAND PRIX 11.30 SÉBASTIEN ET LA MARY-MORGANE 11.55 HIT HIT HIT HOURRA !	
12.00	12.00 TOURNEZ... MANEGE 12.30 FLASH 12.35 LE JUSTE PRIX	12.05 KAZCADO 12.30 FLASH 12.35 LES MARIÉS DE L'A2	12.00 ESTIVALES	12.30 JOURNAL	12.05 GRAFFI'6 12.30 JOURNAL 12.45 LA PETITE MAISON DANS LA PRAIRIE	12.30 T.N.T.
13.00	13.00 JOURNAL 13.40 COTE OUEST	13.00 JOURNAL 13.40 LA SONATE PATHÉTIQUE	13.00 40° A L'OMBRE DE LA 3 13.30 CAP DANGER	13.30 MIKE HAMMER	13.30 POIGNE DE FER ET SÉDUCTION 13.55 NANS LE BERGER	13.00 FLASH 13.05 TOP 50 13.30 SOAP
14.00	14.25 DES AGENTS TRÈS SPÉCIAUX	14.05 JEUNES DOCTEURS 14.45 BING PARADE	14.00 40° A L'OMBRE DE LA 3	14.20 LE TRANSFUGE	14.20 POT BOUILLE	14.00 A.I.D.S. TROP JEUNE POUR MOURIR
15.00	15.15 LE GERFAUT	15.40 LES EYGLETIÈRE		16.00 CAPITAINE FURILLO 16.50 DESSINS ANIMÉS	15.15 FAITES-MOI 6	15.25 FILM D'ANIMATION 15.45 WOODY ET LES ROBOTS
16.00	16.30 CLUB DOROTHÉE	16.30 LE CHIRURGIEN DE SAINT CHAD			16.15 CLIP COMBAT 16.55 HIT HIT HIT HOURRA !	
17.00		17.30 QUOI DE NEUF DOCTEUR ? 17.55 FRANCK, CHASSEUR DE FAUVES	17.00 AMUSE 3		17.05 HAWAII POLICE D'ÉTAT	17.10 CINÉMA DANS LES SALLES 17.40 SUPERMAN
18.00	18.10 CHIPS	18.45 DES CHIFFRES ET DES LETTRES	18.00 COLORADO	18.05 RIPTIDE 18.55 JOURNAL	18.00 JOURNAL 18.15 LES ROUTES DU PARADIS	18.05 CABOU CADIN 18.50 TRIP TRAP
19.00	19.00 SANTA BARBARA 19.30 LA ROUE DE LA FORTUNE	19.10 JOURNAL RÉGIONAL 19.35 L'ARCHE D'OR	19.00 JOURNAL 19.53 JOUEZ LA CASE	19.03 L'HOMME QUI VALAIT 3 MILLIARDS 19.58 JOURNAL	19.00 LES TETES BRULÉES 19.54 FLASH	19.00 TOP 50 19.25 FLASH 19.30 STALAG 13 19.58 OBJECTIF NUL
20.00	20.00 JOURNAL TAPIS VERT	20.00 JOURNAL	20.01 LA CLASSE		20.00 CHACUN CHEZ SOI	20.05 STARQUIZZ 20.30 FLASH
20.30	20.30 FILM MONSIEUR PAPA *de Philippe Monnier* *avec Nathalie Baye*	20.35 FILM LES CHARIOTS DE FEU *de Hugh Hudson* *avec Ben Cross*	20.30 FILM LE SCANDALE *de Claude Chabrol* *avec Maurice Ronet*	20.30 FILM LA GROSSE PAGAILLE *de Steno* *avec Rita Pavone*	20.30 FILM TV L'HOMME PAR QUI LE SCANDALE ARRIVE *de Robert Leiberman* *avec Robert Conrad*	20.31 FILM REMO SANS ARME ET DANGEREUX *de Guy Hamilton* *avec Fred War*
de 22.00 à 5.00	22.05 HISTOIRES NATURELLES 23.00 CANNON 23.50 LA SOIRÉE CONTINUE (VOIR P. 25)	22.35 DÉBAT 23.40 JOURNAL 0.00 HISTOIRES COURTES 0.25 JAZZ 0.55 FIN	22.20 JOURNAL 22.40 TÉLÉVISION RÉGIONALE	22.15 MIKE HAMMER 23.10 DE PARFAITS GENTILS HOMMES 0.00 LA SOIRÉE CONTINUE (VOIR P. 29)	22.05 CAGNEY ET LACEY 22.55 DESTINATION DANGER 23.45 LA SOIRÉE CONTINUE (VOIR P. 30)	22.20 FLASH 22.25 L'OR SE BARRE 0.00 LA SOIRÉE CONTINUE (VOIR P. 30) 3.00 FIN

Quelques verbes de communication

Dire bonjour

Lire un journal

Écrire une lettre

Mettre de l'argent

	dire (*to say, to tell*)	lire (*to read*)	écrire (*to write*)	mettre (*to place, to put*)
je	dis	lis	écris	mets
tu	dis	lis	écris	mets
il, elle, on	dit	lit	écrit	met
nous	disons	lisons	écrivons	mettons
vous	dites	lisez	écrivez	mettez
ils, elles	disent	lisent	écrivent	mettent
Past participle:	dit	lu	écrit	mis

Dire, lire, and **écrire** have similar conjugations, except for the second-person plural of **dire** and the **v** in the plural stem of **écrire.** Another verb conjugated like **écrire** is **décrire** (to describe).

A. Lettre aux parents

1. Vous racontez à un(e) camarade ce que vous mettez dans la lettre que vous écrivez à vos parents. Complétez les phrases avec les verbes **décrire, dire, écrire, lire** et **mettre,** au présent. Faites tous les changements nécessaires.

Cet après-midi, je _______ [1] une longue lettre à mes parents. Dans ma lettre, je _______ [2] mes cours et ma vie à l'université. Je donne aussi beaucoup de détails sur mes camarades et mes professeurs parce que mes parents sont très curieux. Ils sont aussi très compréhensifs et je leur _______ [3] toujours la vérité sur mes problèmes. Avant de fermer l'enveloppe, je _______ [4] la lettre une dernière fois (*last time*). Puis je _______ [5] la lettre à la boîte aux lettres.

2. Ensuite, mettez le passage au passé composé. Commencez par «*Hier...*»
3. Racontez la même histoire, mais cette fois commencez par «**mon** (**ma**) **camarade de chambre**», puis par «**Stéphanie et Albane**». Faites tous les changements nécessaires.

B. Interview. Posez les questions suivantes à un(e) de vos camarades, puis inversez les rôles.

1. Est-ce que tu écris souvent des lettres? des cartes postales? A qui écris-tu? D'habitude, pour donner de tes nouvelles à tes amis, préfères-tu écrire ou téléphoner? Appelles-tu* souvent tes parents? ton petit ami (ta petite amie)? As-tu le téléphone ou dois-tu chercher une cabine téléphonique? Envoies-tu parfois des télégrammes?
2. Est-ce que tu aimes lire? Lis-tu le journal tous les jours? Si oui, lequel? As-tu déjà cherché du travail dans les petites annonces? Quel magazine achètes-tu régulièrement? As-tu lu un bon livre récemment? Lequel? En général, quel genre de livre préfères-tu?
3. Est-ce que tu regardes la télévision tous les soirs? Quelles émissions préfères-tu? Que penses-tu de la télévision américaine? A ton avis, y a-t-il trop de publicité à la télévision? Essaies-tu* (*Do you try*) de regarder moins de (*less*) télévision?

D'après ses réponses, que pouvez-vous dire de votre camarade et de ses goûts?

L'ordinateur

A. Définitions. Regardez le dessin et trouvez le mot qui correspond à chaque définition.

1. C'est l'appareil qui écrit le texte sur papier.
2. C'est la partie qu'on regarde.
3. C'est la partie qu'on utilise pour emmagasiner (=stocker) l'information.
4. C'est le système qui fait marcher l'ordinateur.
5. C'est la partie qu'on touche pour taper (*type*) un texte.

*For the complete conjugations of **appeler** and **essayer**, which have slight irregularities, see the verb charts in the Appendices.

B. Les nouvelles technologies. Avec des camarades, discutez des réponses aux questions suivantes. **Mots et expressions utiles:** le photocopieur, le répondeur téléphonique, le magnétophone (la cassette), le compact disk, le magnétoscope (la vidéocassette), la caméra vidéo, la base de donnée (*data*), le traitement de texte (*word processing*), programmer, faire des calculs, des recherches...

1. Avez-vous un ordinateur? Est-ce qu'il a changé votre façon de travailler? Expliquez.
2. Quel logiciel utilisez-vous? Pourquoi?
3. Jouez-vous aussi avec votre ordinateur? Quel jeu préférez-vous?
4. Quelles autres technologies nouvelles utilisez-vous? D'après vous, lesquelles sont indispensables? Expliquez pourquoi.

Étude de grammaire

32. Describing the Past: The *imparfait*

Pauvre grand-mère!

MME CHABOT: Tu vois, quand **j'étais** petite, la télévision n'**existait** pas.
CLÉMENT: Mais alors, qu'est-ce que vous **faisiez** le soir?
MME CHABOT: Eh bien, nous **lisions**, nous **bavardions**; nos parents nous **racontaient** des histoires...
CLÉMENT: Pauvre grand-mère, ça **devait** être triste de ne pas pouvoir regarder «Deux flics à Miami» le soir...

Qui parle dans les phrases suivantes, Mme Chabot ou Clément?

1. La télévision n'existait pas quand j'étais petite.
2. Ça devait être triste de ne pas regarder «Deux flics à Miami».
3. Tu n'avais pas de télévision, mais avais-tu la radio?
4. La télévision existait-elle quand je suis né?
5. Nous n'avions que la radio et les journaux pour avoir les nouvelles.

The **passé composé** is used to relate events that began and ended in the past. In contrast, the **imparfait** is used to describe continuous, repeated, or habitual past actions or situations.* It is also used in descriptions.

*The differences between the **passé composé** and the **imparfait** are presented in detail in the next chapter.

The **imparfait** has several equivalents in English. For example, **je parlais** can mean *I talked, I was talking, I used to talk,* or *I would talk.*

A. Formation of the *imparfait*

The formation of the **imparfait** is identical for all French verbs except **être.** To find the regular imperfect stem, drop the **-ons** ending from the present-tense **nous** form. Then add the imperfect endings.

nous parl~~ons~~	**parl-**	nous vend~~ons~~	**vend-**
nous finiss~~ons~~	**finiss-**	nous av~~ons~~	**av-**

IMPARFAIT OF **parler**			
je	parl**ais**	nous	parl**ions**
tu	parl**ais**	vous	parl**iez**
il, elle, on	parl**ait**	ils, elles	parl**aient**

J'**allais** au bureau de poste tous les matins.	*I used to go to the post office every morning.*
Mon grand-père **disait** toujours: «L'excès en tout est un défaut».	*My grandfather always used to say, "Moderation in all things."*
Quand j'**habitais** avec les Huet, je **mettais** souvent la table.	*When I lived with the Huets, I would often set the table.*

Verbs with an imperfect stem that ends in **-i** (**étudier: étudi-**) have a double **i** in the first- and second-persons plural of the **imparfait: nous étud*ii*ons, vous étud*ii*ez.** The **ii** is pronounced as a long i sound [i:], to distinguish the **imparfait** from the present-tense forms **nous étudions** and **vous étudiez.**

Verbs with stems ending in **ç** [s] or **g** [ʒ] have a spelling change when the **imparfait** endings start with **a: je mangeais, nous mangions; elle commençait, nous commencions.** In this way, the pronunciation of the stem is preserved.

B. *Imparfait* of *être*

The verb **être** (*to be*) has an irregular stem in the **imparfait: ét-.**

IMPARFAIT OF **être**			
j'	**étais**	nous	**étions**
tu	**étais**	vous	**étiez**
il, elle, on	**était**	ils, elles	**étaient**

Quand tu **étais** petit, tu **aimais** bien lire les contes de la Mère l'oie.	*When you were little, you liked to read Mother Goose stories.*
J'**étais** très heureux quand j'**habitais** à Paris.	*I was very happy when I lived in Paris.*
Mes parents **étaient** à l'étranger à ce moment-là.	*My parents were abroad at that time.*

C. Uses of the *imparfait*

In general, the **imparfait** is used to describe actions or situations that existed for an indefinite period of time in the past. There is usually no mention of the beginning or end of the event. The **imparfait** is used in the following situations.

1. In descriptions, to set a scene

C'**était** une nuit tranquille à Paris. Il **pleuvait** et il **faisait** froid. M. Cartier **lisait** le journal. Mme Cartier **regardait** la télévision, et Achille, leur chat, **dormait.**	*It was a quiet night in Paris. It was raining and (it was) cold. Mr. Cartier was reading the newspaper. Mrs. Cartier was watching television, and Achille, their cat, was sleeping.*

2. For habitual or repeated actions

Quand j'étais jeune, j'**allais** chez mes grands-parents tous les dimanches. Nous **faisions** de belles promenades.	*When I was young, I went to my grandparents' home every Sunday. We would take (used to take) lovely walks.*

3. To describe feelings and mental or emotional states

Claudine **était** très heureuse—elle **avait** envie de chanter.	*Claudine was very happy—she felt like singing.*

4. To tell the time of day or to express age in the past

Il **était** cinq heures et demie du matin.	*It was 5:30 A.M.*
C'était son anniversaire; il **avait** douze ans.	*It was his birthday; he was twelve years old.*

5. To describe an action or situation that was happening when another event (usually in the **passé composé**) interrupted it

Jean **lisait** le journal quand le téléphone a sonné.	*Jean was reading the paper when the phone rang.*

Mots-clés

Talking about repeated past actions: Use **tous les** (*m.*) or **toutes les** (*f.*) in the following expressions to indicate habitual actions.

tous les jours	*every day*
tous les après-midi/matins/soirs	*every afternoon (morning/evening)*
toutes les semaines	*every week*

Other useful adverbs with the **imparfait** include the following.

d'habitude	*as a rule, habitually*
en général	*generally*
souvent	*often*

MAINTENANT A VOUS

A. Souvenirs d'enfance. Qui dans votre famille faisait les choses suivantes quand vous étiez petit(e)? **Expressions utiles:** mes parents, mon frère/ma sœur, mon meilleur ami (ma meilleure amie) et moi, je...

1. Qui lisait le journal tous les matins?
2. Qui regardait la télévision après le dîner?
3. Qui aimait écouter la radio le matin?
4. Qui faisait beaucoup de sport?
5. Qui étudiait tous les après-midi?
6. Qui lisait des bandes dessinées (*comics*)?
7. Qui avait beaucoup d'amis?

Maintenant organisez vos réponses et faites une courte présentation à la classe. Commencez par «Quand j'étais petit(e)... ». Ajoutez d'autres détails si vous voulez.

B. Sorties. L'an dernier, vous sortiez régulièrement avec vos amis. Faites des phrases complètes selon le modèle.

MODÈLE: dîner ensemble → Nous dînions ensemble.

1. jouer aux cartes les jours de pluie 2. boire des cafés 3. faire des promenades l'après-midi 4. pique-niquer à la campagne 5. aller à la discothèque tous les week-ends 6. partir en vacances ensemble

C. Créez une atmosphère. Imaginez que vous êtes romancier (romancière) (*novelist*) et que vous commencez un nouveau livre. Vous avez déjà composé le paragraphe suivant: «Il est huit heures du matin. De ma fenêtre, je vois le kiosque de la rue de la République. Les trottoirs (*sidewalks*) sont pleins de gens* (*filled with people*) qui vont au travail. Un groupe d'hommes attend l'autobus. Un autre groupe descend dans la station de métro. Près d'une cabine téléphonique un jeune homme lit le journal et une petite femme met des enveloppes dans une boîte aux lettres. Dans le café, les garçons servent du café et des croissants chauds. Il fait chaud. Je suis content(e). »

Mais non! Vous n'êtes pas satisfait(e). Recommencez. Mettez le paragraphe à l'imparfait: «Il était... .»

Mais vous n'êtes toujours pas satisfait(e). Essayez encore une fois. Créez une atmosphère sombre et mystérieuse. Commencez par: «Il était onze heures du soir... ». Adaptez l'histoire à la nouvelle heure.

D. Conversation. Posez les questions suivantes à un(e) camarade. En 1980...

1. Quel âge avais-tu? 2. Habitais-tu à la campagne? dans une petite ville ou dans une grande ville? Avec qui habitais-tu? 3. Comment était ta maison ou ton appartement? 4. Étais-tu bon(ne) élève (*pupil*) à l'école (*school*)? Aimais-tu tes instituteurs (*teachers*)? Avais-tu des devoirs? 5. Étais-tu content(e)? Pourquoi or pourquoi pas? 6. Où passais-tu tes vacances? 7. Faisais-tu du sport? 8. ?

Maintenant décrivez au reste de la classe ce que votre camarade faisait en 1980.

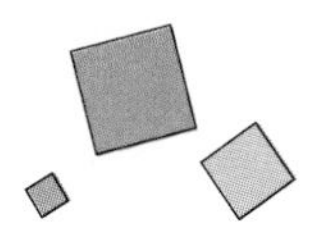

33. Speaking Succinctly: Direct Object Pronouns

Annick au téléphone

«Décrochez le combiné.» Voilà, je **le** décroche.
«Mettez une pièce d'un franc.» Je **la** mets... bon.
«Composez votre numéro.» Qu'est-ce que c'est, déjà? Ah! **Le** voilà.
Allô? allô? allô? Zut. Ça ne marche pas.
Bon, eh bien, ma bonne nouvelle, je vais l'envoyer par télégramme.

Trouvez la réponse correcte et complétez la phrase.

1. Qu'est-ce qu'Annick fait avec le combiné?
2. Qu'est-ce qu'elle fait avec la pièce d'un franc?
3. Qu'est-ce qu'elle fait avec le numéro?
4. Qu'est-ce qu'Annick va faire avec sa bonne nouvelle?

a. Elle ____ met.
b. Elle va ____ envoyer par télégramme.
c. Elle ____ décroche.
d. Elle ____ compose.

*The French use **les gens** (*m.*) to refer to an indeterminate number of people (**Ces gens-là sont très polis**). If the number of people can be counted, the French use **les personnes** (**Il y avait dix personnes dans la salle**). One person is always **une personne**.

A. Direct Object Nouns and Pronouns

Direct objects are nouns that receive the action of a verb. They usually answer the question *what?* or *whom?* For example, in the sentence *Robert dials the number,* the word *number* is the direct object of the verb *dials.*

Direct object pronouns replace direct object nouns: Robert dials *it.* In general, direct object pronouns replace nouns that refer to specific persons, places, objects, or situations—that is, nouns that have a definite article, a possessive adjective, or a demonstrative adjective, as well as proper nouns with no article.

J'admire **la France.** Je l'admire.	*I admire France. I admire it.*
Je regarde **ma sœur.** Je **la** regarde.	*I look at my sister. I look at her.*

B. Forms and Position of Direct Object Pronouns

DIRECT OBJECT PRONOUNS			
me (m')	me	**nous**	us
te (t')	you	**vous**	you
le (l')	him, it	**les**	them
la (l')	her, it		

Robert compose **le numéro.** → Robert **le** compose.

Robert composait **le numéro.** → Robert **le** composait.

Robert a composé **le numéro.** → Robert **l'**a composé.

Usually, French direct object pronouns immediately precede the verb in the present and the imperfect tenses and the auxiliary verb in the **passé composé.** Third-person direct object pronouns agree in gender and in number with the nouns they replace: **le** replaces a masculine singular noun, **la** replaces a feminine singular noun, and **les** replaces plural nouns.

—Pierre lisait-il **le journal**?	—*Was Pierre reading the newspaper?*
—Oui, il **le** lisait.	—*Yes, he was reading it.*
—Veux-tu **ma revue**?	—*Do you want my magazine?*
—Oui, je **la** veux.	—*Yes, I want it.*
—Est-ce que vous postez **ces lettres**?	—*Are you mailing these letters?*
—Oui, je **les** poste.	—*Yes, I'm mailing them.*
—Anne a-t-elle lu **le journal**?	—*Did Anne read the newspaper?*
—Oui, elle **l'**a lu.	—*Yes, she read it.*

If the verb following the direct object pronoun begins with a vowel sound, the direct object pronouns **me, te, le,** and **la** become **m', t',** and **l'.**

J'achète la carte postale. Je **l'**achète.	*I'm buying the postcard. I'm buying it.*
Monique **t'**admirait. Elle ne **m'**admirait pas.	*Monique used to admire you. She didn't admire me.*
Nous avons lu le journal. Nous **l'**avons lu.	*We read the newspaper. We read it.*

If the direct object pronoun is the object of an infinitive, it is placed immediately before the infinitive.

Annick va **chercher l'adresse.** Annick va **la chercher.**	*Annick is going to get the address. Annick is going to get it.*
Elle allait **la chercher.**	*She was going to get it.*
Elle est allée **la chercher.**	*She went to get it.*

In a negative sentence, the direct object pronoun always immediately precedes the verb of which it is the object.

Nous ne regardons pas **la télé.** Nous ne **la** regardons pas.	*We don't watch TV. We don't watch it.*
Je ne vais pas acheter **les billets.** Je ne vais pas **les** acheter.	*I'm not going to buy the tickets. I'm not going to buy them.*
Elle n'est pas allée chercher **le journal.** Elle n'est pas allée **le** chercher.	*She did not go to get the newspaper. She did not go to get it.*

The direct object pronouns also precede **voici** and **voilà.**

Le voici!	*Here he (it) is!*
Me voilà!	*Here I am!*

MAINTENANT A VOUS

A. De quoi parlent-ils? Vous êtes dans un café parisien et vous entendez les phrases suivantes. Trouvez dans la colonne de droite l'information qui correspond à chaque pronom.

1. Je vais les poster cet après-midi.	l'adresse
2. Elle le consulte.	la télé
3. Les étudiants l'écoutent.	les lettres
4. Je l'écris sur l'enveloppe.	le numéro
5. Nous venons de la lire.	l'annuaire
6. Je les achète à la poste.	la revue
7. Ma grand-mère la regarde souvent.	les timbres
8. Je l'ai déjà composé.	le professeur

B. Projets de voyage. Christian et Christiane font toujours la même chose. Avec un(e) camarade, parlez de leurs projets selon le modèle.

MODÈLE: étudier le français cette année →
—Est-ce qu'elle va étudier le français cette année?
—Oui, et il va l'étudier aussi.

1. apprendre le français très vite 2. prendre l'avion pour Paris en juin 3. visiter la Tour Eiffel 4. admirer la vue du haut de la Tour Eiffel 5. prendre ses repas dans de bons restaurants 6. regarder les gens sur les Champs-Élysées 7. essayer de lire les romans de Flaubert 8. inviter ses amis français à venir passer Noël aux États-Unis

Maintenant imaginez que Christian est l'opposé de Christiane.

MODÈLE: —Est-ce qu'elle va étudier le français cette année?
—Oui, mais lui, il ne va pas l'étudier.

C. Mini-test. Posez les questions suivantes à un(e) camarade. Il (elle) répond par **oui** ou **non** le plus vite possible.

MODÈLE: —Tu m'admires?
—Oui, je t'admire. (Non, je ne t'admire pas.)

1. Tu m'écoutes?
2. Tu m'entends?
3. Tu me regardes?
4. Tu me comprends?
5. Tu m'invites à dîner?
6. Tu m'appelles dimanche?
7. ?

Ensuite inversez les rôles selon le modèle.

MODÈLE: —Vous m'écoutez?
—Oui, je vous écoute. (Non, je ne vous écoute pas.)

Maintenant comparez les résultats. Qui a été le (la) plus rapide? Qui a répondu **oui** à la question 5? Quel restaurant va-t-il (elle) choisir?

D. Interview. Interviewez un(e) camarade de classe sur ses préférences. Votre camarade doit utiliser un pronom complément d'objet direct dans sa réponse.

1. Utilises-tu souvent le téléphone?
2. Appelles-tu souvent tes camarades de classe? tes professeurs? tes parents?
3. Est-ce que tes parents t'appellent souvent? et tes amis?
4. Regardes-tu souvent la télé?
5. Aimes-tu regarder la publicité?
6. Préfères-tu apprendre les nouvelles dans le journal ou à la radio? à la radio ou à la télé?
7. Essaies-tu de comprendre la politique internationale? la philosophie de Jacques Derrida?
8. Achètes-tu le journal tous les jours?
9. Lis-tu les romans de Michener? d'autres romans?

Commentaire culturel

Le Minitel. Depuis quelques années, il y a en France un nouveau moyen de communication: le Minitel. C'est un écran, un clavier et un modem qu'on loue à la compagnie de téléphone. Il permet de consulter un annuaire électronique et de chercher des numéros de téléphone et des adresses dans toute la France. Le Minitel donne aussi l'accès à plusieurs milliers de banques de données. On peut ainsi consulter les petites annonces locales, les horaires des trains ou des spectacles, avoir les dernières nouvelles ou la météo. Mais le Minitel, c'est plus qu'une source d'information. Grâce au Minitel, les Français peuvent aussi faire du shopping, payer des factures, acheter des billets d'avion, réserver une chambre d'hôtel, vérifier combien d'argent ils ont à la banque ou tout simplement communiquer avec d'autres abonnés, et tout cela, sans quitter leur maison.

TOUTE L'ESPAGNE AU BOUT DES DOIGTS.

36.15 DIALOGO

LE PREMIER MAGAZINE MINITEL FRANCO-ESPAGNOL

34. Talking About the Past: Agreement of the Past Participle

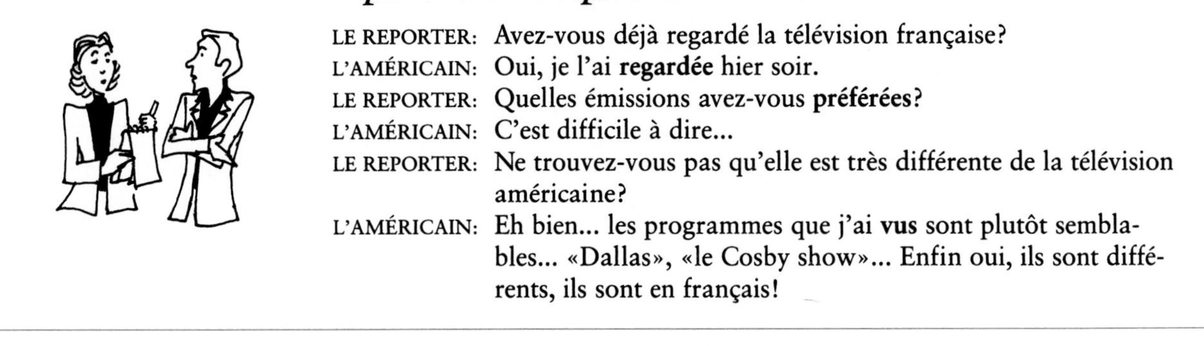

L'opinion d'un téléspectateur américain en France

LE REPORTER: Avez-vous déjà regardé la télévision française?
L'AMÉRICAIN: Oui, je l'ai **regardée** hier soir.
LE REPORTER: Quelles émissions avez-vous **préférées**?
L'AMÉRICAIN: C'est difficile à dire...
LE REPORTER: Ne trouvez-vous pas qu'elle est très différente de la télévision américaine?
L'AMÉRICAIN: Eh bien... les programmes que j'ai **vus** sont plutôt semblables... «Dallas», «le Cosby show»... Enfin oui, ils sont différents, ils sont en français!

In the **passé composé,** the past participle is generally used in its basic form. However, when a direct object—noun or pronoun—precedes the auxiliary verb **avoir** plus the past participle, the participle agrees with the preceding direct object in gender and number.

J'ai lu le **journal.**	J'ai lu les **journaux.**
Je **l'**ai **lu.**	Je **les** ai **lus.**
J'ai lu **la revue.**	J'ai lu les **revues.**
Je **l'**ai **lue.**	Je **les** ai **lues.**

Quels amis avez-vous **appelés**? — *Which friends did you call?*

Quelles **émissions** avez-vous **regardées**? — *Which programs did you watch?*

A. Au téléphone. Votre camarade est au téléphone. Vous entendez seulement ses questions. Que répond la personne au bout du fil? Attention à l'accord du participe passé.

MODÈLE: —As-tu cherché sa lettre?
—Oui, je l'ai cherchée.

1. As-tu trouvé sa lettre? 2. As-tu lu sa lettre? 3. As-tu mis sa lettre dans ton bureau? 4. As-tu écrit ta réponse? 5. As-tu écrit la bonne adresse sur l'enveloppe? 6. As-tu mis le timbre sur l'enveloppe? 7. As-tu envoyé ta lettre?

Maintenant imaginez que la personne répond toujours **non** aux questions de votre camarade.

MODÉLE: —As-tu cherché sa lettre?
—Non, je ne l'ai pas cherchée.

B. Préparatifs difficiles. Sylvie, Jean et Pauline ne sont pas très organisés. Voici l'histoire de leurs préparatifs de vacances. Finissez les phrases et mettez les verbes au passé composé. Faites attention à l'accord des participes.

1. Sylvie devait faire les réservations, mais elle *ne... pas / les / faire*. 2. Jean cherche ses chaussures de tennis; il *les / mettre* dans le grand sac. 3. Pauline avait les passeports, mais elle *les / perdre*. 4. Jean devait écrire l'adresse de l'hôtel à ses parents mais il *ne... pas / la / écrire*. 5. Sylvie et Pauline ont demandé l'heure du départ, mais elles *la / oublier*. 6. Et les billets d'avion? Jean et Pauline *les / laisser* à la maison!

35. Speaking Succinctly: Indirect Object Pronouns

Journalistes pour le Canard?

RÉGIS: Tu as écrit aux journalistes du *Canard Enchaîné*?*
NICOLE: Oui, je **leur** ai écrit.
RÉGIS: Ils **t'**ont répondu?
NICOLE: Oui, ils **nous** ont donné rendez-vous demain.
RÉGIS: Ils ont aimé nos caricatures politiques?
NICOLE: Ils ne **m'**ont encore rien dit: on va voir demain!

Retrouvez la phrase correcte dans le dialogue.

1. J'ai écrit aux journalistes.
2. Les journalistes ont donné rendez-vous à Nicole et à Régis.
3. Les journalistes n'ont encore rien dit à Nicole.

A. Indirect Objects

As you know, direct object nouns and pronouns answer the questions *what?* or *whom?* Indirect object nouns and pronouns usually answer the questions *to whom?* or *for whom?* In English, the word *to* is frequently omitted: I gave the book *to Paul*. → I gave *Paul* the book. In French, the preposition **à** is *always* used before an indirect object noun.

J'ai donné le cadeau **à** Paul.	*I gave the gift to Paul.*
Elle a écrit une lettre **à** son ami.	*She wrote a letter to her friend.*
Nous montrons le château **aux** touristes.	*We show the chateau to the tourists.*
Elle prête de l'argent **à** sa famille.	*She lends money to her family.*

*The *Canard Enchaîné* is a satirical weekly newspaper published in Paris.

—Allô. Oui je te vois et je t'entends très bien.

If a sentence has an indirect object, it usually has a direct object also. Some French verbs, however, can take only an indirect object. These include **téléphoner à, parler à,** and **répondre à.**

Je téléphone (*parle*) **à** mes amis.	*I telephone (speak) (to) my friends.*
Elle a répondu **à** ma lettre.	*She has answered my letter.*

B. Indirect Object Pronouns

1. Indirect object pronouns replace indirect object nouns. They are identical in form to direct object pronouns, except for the third-person forms, **lui** and **leur.**

INDIRECT OBJECT PRONOUNS			
me, m'	(*to/for*) *me*	nous	(*to/for*) *us*
te, t'	(*to/for*) *you*	vous	(*to/for*) *you*
lui	(*to/for*) *him, her*	**leur**	(*to/for*) *them*

2. The placement of indirect object pronouns is identical to that of direct object pronouns. However, the past participle does not agree with a preceding indirect object.

Je **lui** ai montré la réception.	*I showed him (her) the (front) desk.*
On **m'**a demandé l'adresse de l'auberge de jeunesse.	*They asked me for the address of the youth hostel.*
Marcel **nous** a envoyé une carte postale.	*Marcel sent us a postcard.*

Nous n'allons pas **leur** téléphoner maintenant.	*We're not going to telephone them now.*
Je **leur** ai emprunté la voiture.	*I borrowed the car from them.*
Ils **m'**ont prêté de l'argent.	*They loaned me some money.*

3. In negative sentences, the object pronoun immediately precedes the conjugated verb.

Je **ne** t'ai **pas** donné les billets.	*I didn't give you the tickets.*
Elle **ne** lui a **pas** téléphoné.	*She hasn't telephoned him.*

MAINTENANT A VOUS

A. L'après-midi de Blondine. Blondine va tous les vendredis après-midi chez sa grand-mère. Elle nous raconte ce qu'elle a fait vendredi dernier. Complétez son histoire avec les pronoms qui correspondent: **me, te, lui, nous, vous, leur.**

Après les cours, j'ai pris un café avec des amies. Je ______[1] ai montré mon nouveau baladeur (*Walkman*). Un peu plus tard, j'ai rendu visite à ma grand-mère. Je ______[2] ai apporté ses magazines préférés. Elle était très contente et elle ______[3] a dit: «Je vais ______[4] préparer un bon goûter». En fin d'après-midi, mon frère est arrivé. Il ______[5] a raconté ses aventures avec sa nouvelle moto. Nous avons beaucoup ri. Au moment de partir, ma grand-mère ______[6] a demandé (à mon frère et à moi): «Je vous revois la semaine prochaine, les enfants?» «Bien sûr», nous ______[7] avons répondu, «à vendredi prochain!»

B. Quelle honte! (*For shame!*)

MODÈLE: Est-ce que tu as envoyé des cartes postales à ta mère? →
Non, je ne lui ai pas envoyé de cartes postales.

1. As-tu téléphoné à ton grand-père? 2. Tu as écrit à ton vieil oncle? 3. Tu as donné des timbres à ta nièce pour sa collection? 4. As-tu répondu à ton amie en France? 5. Est-ce que tu as dit bonjour à ton prof de français? 6. Est-ce que tu as rendu à ton amie le livre que tu lui as emprunté*?

C. Des prêts. (*Loans.*) Qu'est-ce que vous allez prêter aux personnes suivantes?

MODÈLE: Jean est à la montagne. Il fait très froid. →
Je vais lui prêter mon chapeau et aussi mon manteau...

1. Marie est en ville. Il fait du vent, et elle a perdu son chapeau. Il pleut aussi. 2. Pierre et Marie sont au bord d'un lac. Il fait très chaud. 3. Vos parents font une promenade à la campagne. Ils sont fatigués (*tired*). 4. Marc et Christine font du camping. Ils ont oublié plusieurs choses essentielles. 5. Claudine va dîner dans un grand restaurant avec son fiancé et ses parents. Elle veut faire une très bonne impression. 6. Jacques va faire un long voyage. Il ne veut mettre que les choses les plus importantes dans sa valise.

***Emprunter** (*to borrow*) may take both a direct object (the thing borrowed) and an indirect object (the person from [à] whom it is borrowed).

© ANDREW BRILLIANT

Chère Aline,
J'ai bien reçu ta lettre...

D. Êtes-vous communicatif (*communicative*)? Posez les questions suivantes à un(e) camarade et créez de nouvelles questions sur le même sujet.

1. A qui as-tu écrit la semaine dernière? Qu'est-ce que tu lui as écrit? Pourquoi? En général, écris-tu souvent?
2. A qui as-tu téléphoné la semaine dernière? Qu'est-ce que tu lui as dit?
3. As-tu jamais envoyé un télégramme? A quelle occasion? A qui?

Ensuite, dites à la classe si votre camarade est très ou peu communicatif (communicative). Pouvez-vous déterminer la personne la plus (*the most*) communicative de la classe?

Coup de fil*

Contexte *Caroline Périllat rêve d'être hôtesse. Elle a terminé ses études à l'École Internationale d'Hôtesses de Paris et elle vient de trouver son premier job. Elle téléphone à sa sœur, Stéphanie, qui habite encore au Sénégal, pour lui annoncer la bonne nouvelle. Stéphanie est étudiante à l'Institut Supérieur de Tourisme de Dakar.*

Objectif *Caroline parle au téléphone.*

*Telephone call

CAROLINE:	Allô? Bonjour Madame, c'est bien l'Institut de Tourisme?	
LA STANDARDISTE:°	Oui, à qui voulez-vous parler?	*operator, receptionist*
CAROLINE:	A Stéphanie Périllat, s'il vous plaît.	
LA STANDARDISTE:	C'est de la part de qui°?	C'est... *Who may I say is calling?*
CAROLINE:	C'est de la part de Caroline Périllat, sa sœur.	
LA STANDARDISTE:	Ne quittez pas, je vous la passe.°	Ne... *Please hold, I'll transfer you to her*
CAROLINE:	Merci bien.	
CAROLINE	Allô, Stéphanie? Devine! Je viens de décrocher° mon premier job.	*to land (literally, to take down, detach, unhook)*
STÉPHANIE:	Mais c'est formidable, ça! Qu'est-ce que c'est?	
CAROLINE:	Je suis chargée de l'accueil° des vedettes° au Palais des Festivals de Cannes!	chargée... *responsible for welcoming / stars*
STÉPHANIE:	Pour le Festival du Film? Félicitations!	
CAROLINE:	Merci. Je regrette seulement de ne pas pouvoir célébrer tout ça avec toi...	
STÉPHANIE:	Écoute, je te quitte: tu vas avoir une facture° énorme. Mais je te rappelle demain soir, d'accord?	*(phone) bill*
CAROLINE:	A demain. Dis bonjour aux parents de ma part.	

VARIATIONS

1. Rejouez le dialogue avec la variation suivante: Vous avez obtenu le mauvais numéro. («C'est une erreur.») Puis, la ligne est occupée (*busy*), et vous ne voulez pas attendre: vous laissez un message.
2. Imaginez les conversations téléphoniques suivantes:

A propos

Comment réagir à une nouvelle (*react to news*)

Une bonne nouvelle: C'est sensationnel!
C'est formidable!
C'est super!
J'en suis très heureux (heureuse). (*I'm very happy about this.*)

Une mauvaise nouvelle: C'est triste.
C'est horrible.
C'est dégoûtant (*disgusting*).
C'est un scandale!
Ça me rend malade. (*That makes me sick.*)

Une nouvelle qui vous laisse indifférent(e): Ah bon!
Oh, ça m'est égal. (*That's all the same to me.*)
Ça n'a pas d'importance.
Je m'en fiche. (*I don't care.*)

LA PREMIÈRE TÉLÉVISION INTERNATIONALE FRANCOPHONE

LA CHAÎNE DE RÉFÉRENCE... "TYPICALLY BRITISH"!

LA GRANDE CHAÎNE DE L'EUROPE

A. **Jeu de rôles.** Rejouez le dialogue de la *Situation*. Changez l'identité des personnages (c'est peut-être vous et votre frère ou votre sœur qui parlez au téléphone). Imaginez d'abord une autre bonne nouvelle, puis une mauvaise nouvelle et enfin une nouvelle qui vous laisse indifférent(e). Utilisez le vocabulaire de l'*A propos*.

B. **Enquête (*Survey*) sur la télévision.** Faites une enquête parmi vos camarades sur le nombre d'heures qu'ils passent devant la télé chaque semaine. Qui sont les cinq téléspectateurs les plus fervents (*most enthusiastic*)?

Maintenant, interviewez ces cinq personnes sur leurs opinions de téléspectateur. Utilisez comme guide les questions suivantes.

1. Qu'est-ce que vous pensez de la télévision américaine en général? 2. Selon vous, quelle est la meilleure (*best*) chaîne pour les informations? pour les films? pour les programmes sportifs? 3. Êtes-vous pour ou contre la publicité destinée aux enfants? Donnez vos raisons. Pour ou contre la publicité pour l'alcool (*alcohol*)? Pour ou contre la publicité au milieu des (*in the middle of the*) programmes? 4. Qu'est-ce que vous pensez de la télévision publique américaine?

Qui dans la classe ne regarde jamais la télévision? Pourquoi?

Commentaire culturel

La télévision en France. La télévision française est un peu différente de la télévision américaine. Il existe en France six chaînes. Trois de ces chaînes sont privées: TF1, la 5 et M6. Elles retransmettent des programmes très variés mais sont obligées de diffuser un minimum de programmes, soit d'origine française, soit d'origine européenne. Certaines chaînes privées émettent jour et nuit et sont financées entièrement par la publicité. Antenne 2 et FR3, sont sous le contrôle du gouvernement et ne retransmettent que pendant la journée. Elles sont financées en partie par la publicité et en partie par une taxe que doivent payer toutes les personnes possédant un poste de télévision. Antenne 2 et FR3 font des efforts pour faire des programmes culturels. De plus, FR3 retransmet chaque après-midi des programmes locaux à travers ses divers émetteurs régionaux.

La sixième chaîne, Canal Plus, est une chaîne privée et codée et ne peut être vue qu'avec un appareil spécial, un décodeur, qu'il faut louer. Elle retransmet 24 heures sur 24 le vendredi et le samedi et passe surtout des films dont la plupart sont très récents. Dans les principales villes françaises il existe aussi des chaînes par câble auxquelles on peut s'abonner.

Maintenant avec l'emploi des satellites, un certain nombre de téléspectateurs peuvent voir les programmes des chaînes des autres pays européens, et prochainement des programmes des États-Unis et du monde entier. Beaucoup de Français attendent avec impatience de pouvoir profiter de ces programmes.

Actuellement, les pays de la communauté européenne préparent une chaîne commune qui retransmettra des programmes culturels européens.

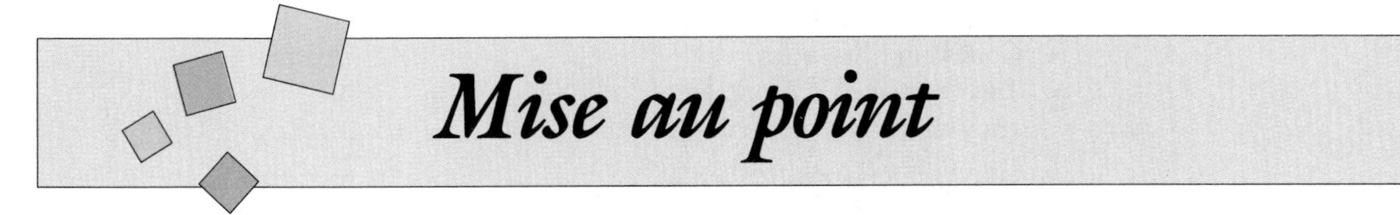

Mise au point

A. Tourisme au Canada. Eloic vient de rentrer du Canada et parle de son voyage avec son ami Vincent. Complétez le dialogue avec des pronoms d'objet direct ou indirect, selon le cas.

VINCENT: Quand tu étais à Montréal, est-ce que tu écoutais la radio?
ELOIC: Oui, je ______[1] écoutais souvent.
VINCENT: Tu comprenais l'accent québécois?

ELOIC: Oui, je ______[2] comprenais, mais avec difficulté. Une fois, j'ai téléphoné à tes amis Jacques et Marie, et j'ai eu beaucoup de mal à ______[3] comprendre.
VINCENT: De quoi ______[4] as-tu parlé?
ELOIC: D'une excursion que je voulais faire au lac Saint-Jean.
VINCENT: Est-ce que tu as pu ______[5] faire?
ELOIC: Oui, finalement nous ______[6] avons faite tous les trois. C'était formidable!
VINCENT: Est-ce que tu as envoyé beaucoup de cartes postales à Babette?
ELOIC: Oui, je ______[7] ai envoyé une carte postale tous les jours!
VINCENT: Et tu as pris beaucoup de photos?
ELOIC: Oh, oui. Tu veux ______[8] voir?
VINCENT: Avec plaisir. Tes photos sont toujours superbes!
ELOIC: Oh, j'oubliais, je ______[9] ai rapporté un petit souvenir. C'est un livre d'Antonine Maillet, un écrivain québécois.
VINCENT: Merci beaucoup, ça ______[10] fait très plaisir!

B. Mon enfance. D'abord, posez les questions suivantes (et encore d'autres) à un(e) camarade. Ensuite, trouvez quelque chose que vous avez en commun avec ce (cette) camarade et une chose que vous n'avez pas en commun.

- Quand tu étais petit(e), voyais-tu beaucoup de films? Quels films est-ce que tu aimais surtout (*especially*)? Avec qui allais-tu au cinéma?
- Qu'est-ce que tu regardais à la télé? Quels étaient tes programmes préférés? Jusqu'à quelle heure pouvais-tu regarder la télé?
- Lisais-tu beaucoup? Quels livres est-ce que tu aimais? quelles bandes dessinées (*comic strips*)? Quand est-ce que tu lisais?

C. Conversation au téléphone. Vous visitez la France, et un ami français (une amie française) de vos parents vous appelle. Complétez la conversation.

L'AMI(E)	VOUS
1. Allô, ______. Ici ______. Je vous dérange (*disturb*)?	2. ______
3. Comment allez-vous?	4. ______
5. Très bien, merci. Alors, êtes-vous content(e) d'être en France?	6. ______
7. Quand est-ce que vous partez pour les États-Unis?	8. ______
9. Ah, c'est trop tôt. Avez-vous écrit à vos parents?	10. ______
11. Qu'est-ce que vous faites ce soir? Vous sortez?	12. ______
13. Très bien. Je peux vous montrer Paris demain?	14. ______
15. D'accord. Je vous rappelle demain. Passez une bonne soirée.	16. ______

Interactions

In this chapter, you practiced describing past events and indicating specific people or things. Act out the following situations, using the vocabulary and structures from the chapter.

1. **Au téléphone.** A friend (your partner) will soon be going to France. Describe how to use the phone and what expressions to use. She or he will ask questions for clarification.
2. **La soirée.** Call a friend (your partner) to find out why she or he did not come to your party. Tell her or him who was there, what you talked about, and what you did. Describe how the party was. She or he will ask you questions to get a good description.

Vocabulaire

Verbes

appeler to call
chanter to sing
composer un numéro to dial a number
créer to create
décrire to describe
deviner to guess
dire to say, tell
écrire (à) to write (to)
emprunter (à) to borrow (from)
envoyer to send
essayer to try
lire to read
mettre to put, place
pleuvoir to rain
prêter (à) to lend (to)
raconter to tell, relate
rappeler to call back
sonner to ring

Substantifs

l'adresse (*f.*) address
l'anniversaire (*m.*) birthday
l'annuaire (*m.*) telephone book
la boîte aux lettres mailbox
le bureau de poste (la poste) post office
la cabine téléphonique telephone booth
le cadeau gift
la carte postale postcard
la chaîne television channel
le courrier mail
l'école (*f.*) school
l'enveloppe (*f.*) envelope
le (la) facteur (-trice) mail carrier
la fin end
les gens (*m.*) people
les informations (*f.*) (TV) news
le jeu game
le journal (les journaux) newspaper
le kiosque kiosk; newsstand
le magazine (illustrated) magazine
le numéro (de téléphone) (telephone) number
les petites annonces classified ads
la publicité commercial; advertisement; advertising
le roman novel
le télégramme telegram
le timbre stamp
la vérité truth

Adjectifs

content(e) happy, pleased
heureux (-euse) happy, fortunate
seul(e) only; alone
triste sad, unhappy

Au téléphone

Allô. Hello.
C'est de la part de qui? Who may I say is calling?
Ne quittez pas. Please hold.
Qui est à l'appareil? Who's calling?

L'ordinateur

le clavier keyboard
la disquette diskette
l'écran (*m.*) screen
l'imprimante (*f.*) printer
le logiciel software
le moniteur monitor

Mots divers

tous les jours (matins, etc.) every day (morning, etc.)
toutes les semaines every week
d'habitude habitually
en général generally
surtout especially

Expressions utiles

Ça m'est égal.	*It's all the same to me; it doesn't matter.*
Je m'en fiche.	*I don't care.*

Des timbres du monde francophone

INTERMÈDE 9

Lecture

AVANT DE LIRE

Recognizing less obvious cognates: An awareness of patterns of spelling variations will help you recognize less obvious cognates and guess the meanings of new words. Read the following hints and guess the meanings of the words you have not yet learned.

English words with the prefixes *dis-* and *un-* are often related in meaning to similar French words with the prefixes **dé-** or **dés-**.

désordre	**désastreux** (**-euse**)	**désagréable**
défaire	**dénouer** (**nouer** = *to tie*)	**découvrir**

French words beginning with **es-** or **é-** often correspond to English words spelled with an initial *s-*.

espace **estomac** **état** **étrange** **étudier**

The circumflex accent in French frequently corresponds to an *s* that has not disappeared from the English cognate.

honnête **hôpital** **île** **tempête**

Many English nouns ending in *-or* or *-er* correspond to the masculine noun-ending in French of **-eur.**

campeur **serveur** **collaborateur** **professeur** **réacteur**

Notice these patterns in the highlighted words in the following summaries from the film review *Première,* and watch for them in general as you read.

COMPRÉHENSION

Regardez bien le programme à la page suivante, puis répondez aux questions.

1. Est-ce que parmi les films recommandés il y a des films d'amour, d'aventure, de science fiction, de suspense? Nommez-les.
2. Quels acteurs connaissez-vous? Avez-vous déjà vu un de ces films? Si oui, l'avez-vous aimé? Expliquez votre réponse.
3. Choisissez maintenant le film que vous voulez voir. Faites un court résumé de l'histoire devant la classe en employant vos propres mots. Puis expliquez les raisons de votre choix.
4. Y a-t-il un film que vous ne voulez pas du tout voir? Lequel? Pourquoi?
5. Quel film avez-vous vu dernièrement? L'avez-vous aimé? Quels acteurs y jouaient? Racontez l'intrigue du film.

PROGRAMME

LES POINTS DE MIRE DE MAI

MERCREDI 6

Fatherland

de Ken Loach. Avec Gerulf Pannach, Fabienne Babe... L'odyssée d'un transfuge de l'Est et d'une journaliste, de Berlin à Cambridge. Le déracinement et la quête du père sont au cœur du nouveau film du réalisateur de "Family life".

La pelicula del rey

de Carlos Sorin. Avec Julio Chaves, Ulises Dumont, Villanueva Cosse... La folle aventure d'un tournage. Un film primé à Venise.

JEUDI 7

Un homme amoureux

de Diane Kurys Avec Peter Coyote, Greta Scacchi, Jamie Lee Curtis... Une star américaine venue tourner à Rome, tombe amoureux de sa partenaire. Une histoire d'amour, avec le cinéma pour cadre. Ce nouveau film de Diane Kurys fait l'ouverture du Festival de Cannes.

VENDREDI 8

Chronique d'une mort annoncée

de Francesco Rosi. Avec Rupert Everett, Ornella Muti, Gian Maria Volonte, Anthony Delon... Le célèbre livre du prix Nobel Gabriel Garcia Marquez enfin porté à l'écran. L'histoire de deux frères qui tuent pour venger l'honneur de leur sœur. Tout le village sait que ce crime va être commis, mais personne ne tente de l'empêcher.[a] Les traditions, le code de l'honneur, la loi du silence, ainsi qu'une étonnante histoire d'amour. Le film sera, lui aussi, à Cannes.

MERCREDI 13

Good morning, Babylonia

de Paolo et Vittorio Taviani. Avec Joaquim de Almeida, Vincent Spano, Greta Scacchi, Désiree Becker, Charles Dance... Deux frères quittent leur village italien, et partent en Amérique où ils participent à la naissance de Hollywood. Un rêve de pionnier.

Mannequin

de Michael Gottlieb. Avec Andrew McCarthy, Kim Cattrall... Un mannequin prend forme humaine pour séduire son créateur.

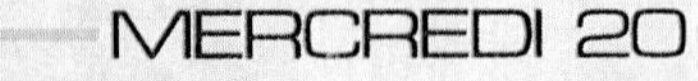

MERCREDI 20

Radio days

de Woody Allen. Avec Mia Farrow, Dianne Wiest, Diane Keaton, Seth Green, Michael Tucker, Josh Mostel... Les années quarante, un petit garçon rêve de ressembler au héros d'un feuilleton radiophonique. Autour de lui, une famille à la banalité irrésistible. Parallèlement, on suit l'ascension sociale d'une vendeuse de cigarettes qui deviendra chanteuse. Nostalgies.

La ménagerie de verre

de Paul Newman. Avec Joanne Woodward, John Malkovich, Karen Allen... L'adaptation de la pièce de Tennessee Williams.

Hôtel de France

de Patrice Chéreau. Avec Laurent Grevill, Valeria Bruni-Tedeschi, Vincent Perez... Une relecture de Tchekhov. Violence et passion.

MERCREDI 27

Pierre et Djemila

de Gérard Blain. Avec Jean-Pierre André, Nadja Reski, Séverine Debaisieux... Un "Roméo et Juliette" qui se déroule de nos jours, dans la banlieue de Roubaix. Roméo est français, Juliette est maghrébine.[b] Des deux côtés, les parents s'opposeront à ce premier et violent amour... Blain est un des Français sélectionné à Cannes.

Arizona Junior

de Joel et Ethan Coen. Avec Nicolas Cage, Holly Hunter... Une comédie délirante signée par les auteurs de "Sang pour sang".

a. *to prevent*
b. d'origine nord-africaine

Par écrit

A. La télévision américaine. Vous écrivez une critique de la télévision américaine. Utilisez les phrases suivantes comme guide, et ajoutez d'autres détails.

Le téléspectateur américain a le choix entre ______ chaînes. La publicité est ______ et les nouvelles sont ______. Les émissions les plus regardées par les Américains sont ______. Je regarde ______. Je préfère les émissions sportives de ______, les informations de ______ et les émissions culturelles de ______. Je trouve que la télévision américaine est ______.

B. Un télégramme. Vous êtes en France et vous allez à la poste pour envoyer un télégramme. Choisissez une des situations suivantes et écrivez votre message.

1. Vous voulez rendre visite à des amis en Belgique mais vous n'avez plus assez d'argent pour acheter votre billet de train. Alors vous envoyez un télégramme à vos parents pour leur demander de vous envoyer de l'argent.
2. Vous envoyez un télégramme à vos amis en Belgique pour leur annoncer votre arrivée. Vous pensez rester une semaine et aimeriez loger chez eux.

N° 698 TÉLÉGRAMME

Étiquettes

N° d'appel :

INDICATIONS DE TRANSMISSION

Ligne de numérotation

ZCZC

N° télégraphique

Taxe principale.

Timbre à date

Taxes accessoires

N° de la ligne du P.V. :

Ligne pilote

Bureau de destination Code Postal ou Pays

Total . .

Bureau d'origine | Mots | Date | Heure | Mentions de service

Services spéciaux demandés : (voir au verso)

Inscrire en **CAPITALES** l'adresse complète (rue, n° bloc, bâtiment, escalier, etc...), le texte et la signature (une lettre par case ; **laisser une case blanche entre les mots**).

Pour accélérer la remise des télégrammes indiquer le numéro de téléphone (1) ou de télex (3) du destinataire

TF ______ TLX ______

Nom et adresse

TEXTE et éventuellement signature très lisible

Pour avis en cas de non-remise, indiquer le nom et l'adresse de l'expéditeur (2) :

728678 Y

Communication et vie pratique 3

ACTIVITÉ

Souvenirs de vacances. Dominique Klein raconte les vacances de sa famille à sa meilleure amie. Imaginez ce qu'elle dit et ajoutez autant de détails que possible.

Scène 1 Nous sommes partis... Nous avons pris... Wolfgang était méchant (*naughty*); il voulait... Tout le monde était... Mais Béatrice et Jacques... Il faisait... Moi je portais... et les autres portaient... Maman et Papa ont chargé (*loaded*)... Mémé...

Scène 2 Pendant les deux semaines sur la côte, nous avons fait la même chose tous les jours. Papa et Maman... Il n'y a que Béatrice et Jacques qui ont trouvé ça formidable, parce que... Daniel... Jojo et Marie... Et moi, je voulais...

EXPRESSION ÉCRITE

Situation. The owner of a French restaurant, Madame Dupuy, has advertised in your campus newspaper. She would like to hire an American student waiter (waitress) because many of her clients are English-speaking tourists. Of course, the other staff members speak French. She is looking for someone with at least a few months of experience in restaurant work, who would benefit from the opportunity to work in France. Apply for the job. Say why you are interested, why you are qualified, and when you are available (**du 6 juin au 15 septembre**, for example). Mention your long-term goals (**le but à long terme**). Ask for more information. Useful opening line for job application: **J'aimerais me présenter pour le poste de serveur** (serveuse) **annoncé dans le** [*nom du journal*].

Avant d'écrire

Writing business letters. In French, a business letter begins with **Monsieur, Madame,** or **Mademoiselle.** If you do not know the gender of the recipient (**le destinataire**), use **Madame, Monsieur** together. There is a conventional closing sentence for the final paragraph of the letter; this sentence is loosely the equivalent of *Please accept my best wishes.* French business letters use the following format:

New York, le 6 mai, 1990
votre nom
votre adresse

nom du destinataire
adresse du destinataire

Madame, (Monsieur,)

J'ai l'intention de passer six mois en France pour perfectionner mon français. Pourriez-vous m'envoyer des renseignements sur vos cours de langues pour étudiants étrangers?

Je suis étudiant(e) en Sciences économiques à Columbia University; j'étudie le français depuis huit mois.

Je voudrais donc recevoir tous les renseignements nécessaires sur votre programme: description des cours, conditions d'admission, frais d'inscription, possibilités de logement, etc.

Veuillez agréer, Monsieur, Madame, l'expression de mes sentiments les meilleurs.

CHAPITRE DIX

La vie urbaine

—Est-ce que tu habites en ville?
—Non, j'habite en banlieue.
—Tu dois passer beaucoup de temps dans les transports en commun chaque jour!
—Oui, mais j'ai une jolie maison avec un jardin, alors ça vaut la peine.

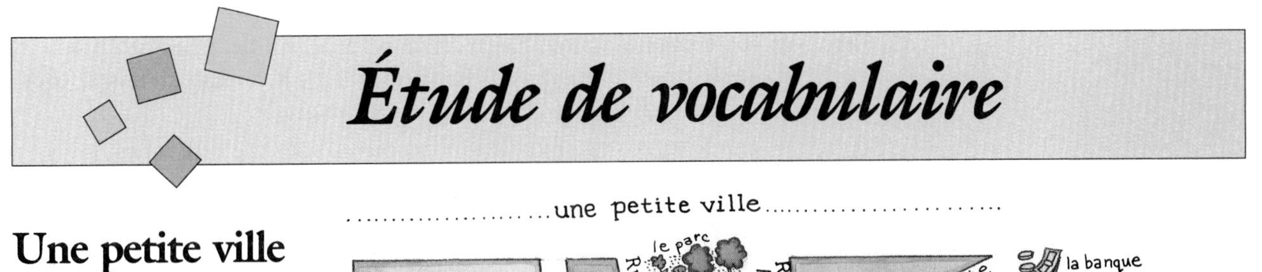

Étude de vocabulaire

Une petite ville

........................une petite ville........................

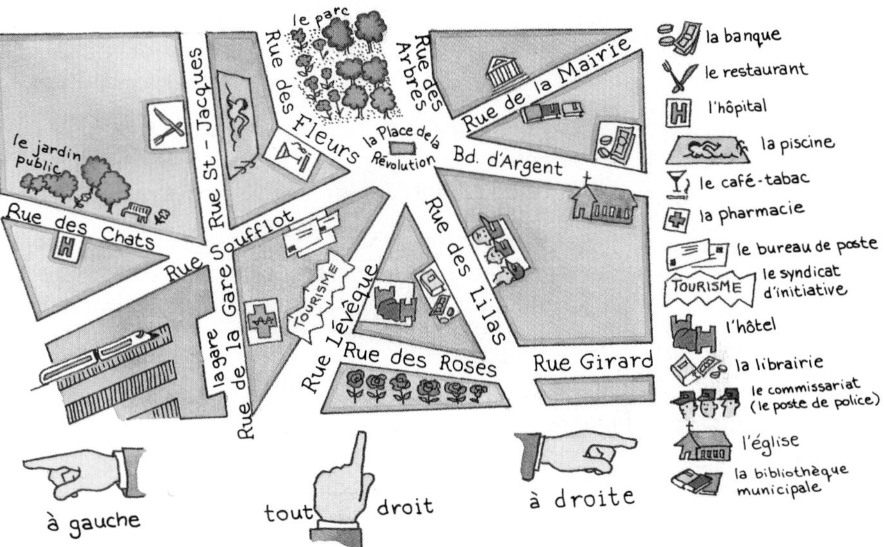

Comment va-t-on de la banque à la pharmacie? On **prend** le boulevard d'Argent à droite et on va **jusqu'à** la place de la Révolution. On **traverse** la rue des Lilas et on **prend la rue** Lévêque à gauche. On **continue tout droit jusqu'au coin** et on **prend** la rue de la Gare à droite. La pharmacie est **en face de** la gare.

A. Les endroits importants. Où va-t-on...

1. pour toucher (*to cash*) un chèque de voyage? 2. pour acheter de l'aspirine? 3. pour parler avec le maire de la ville? 4. pour obtenir des brochures touristiques? 5. pour nager? 6. pour admirer les plantes et les fleurs? 7. pour assister aux (*to attend*) services religieux? 8. pour acheter des timbres? 9. pour boire une bière?

B. Où est-ce? Précisez l'emplacement des endroits suivants.

MODÈLE: Où est l'hôtel? →
L'hôtel est en face du syndicat d'initiative dans la rue Lévêque.*

1. Où est le jardin public?
2. Où est le restaurant?
3. Où est la bibliothèque?
4. Où est l'église?
5. Où est la librairie?
6. Où est le syndicat d'initiative?

*The French say **dans la rue,** but **sur le boulevard** and **sur l'avenue.**

C. **Trouvez votre chemin** (*way*). Regardez le plan de la ville. Imaginez que vous êtes à la gare. Un(e) touriste vous demande où est le bureau de poste; vous lui indiquez le chemin. Jouez les rôles avec un(e) camarade.

MODÈLE: LE/LA TOURISTE: Excusez-moi, pouvez-vous me dire où est le bureau de poste?
VOUS: Tournez à gauche. Prenez la rue Soufflot à droite et vous y êtes (*you're there*).
LE/LA TOURISTE: Je tourne à gauche, je prends la rue Soufflot à droite et j'y suis.

1. le café-tabac 2. le restaurant 3. l'hôtel 4. la banque 5. le poste de police 6. le parc 7. la mairie 8. la pharmacie 9. le jardin public 10. la Place de la Révolution 11. la piscine 12. le syndicat d'initiative

Maintenant, avec un(e) autre camarade de classe, faites une liste de cinq ou six endroits sur votre campus ou dans votre ville. A tour de rôle (*Taking turns*), indiquez le chemin pour aller à ces endroits. Votre salle de classe est votre point de départ.

Paris et sa banlieue

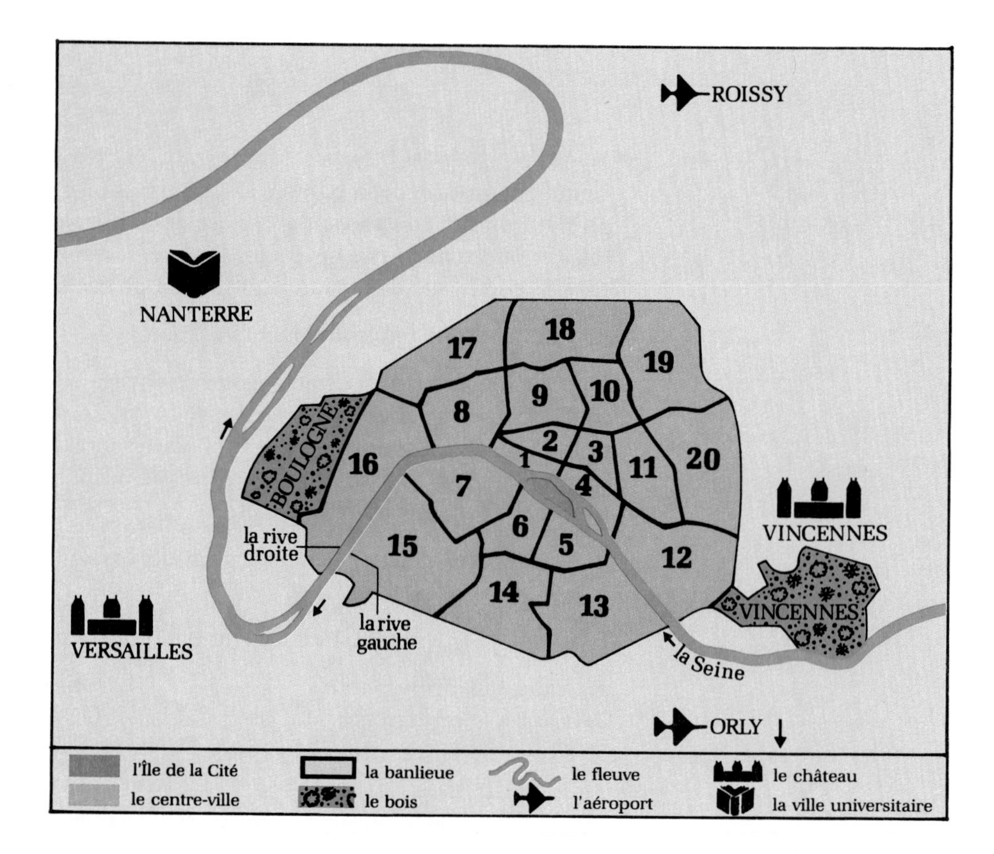

Les vingt arrondissements (*wards*) de Paris:

1er	le premier	11^{e}	le onzième
2^{e}	le deuxième	12^{e}	le douzième
3^{e}	le troisième	13^{e}	le treizième
4^{e}	le quatrième	14^{e}	le quatorzième
5^{e}	le cinquième	15^{e}	le quinzième
6^{e}	le sixième	16^{e}	le seizième
7^{e}	le septième	17^{e}	le dix-septième
8^{e}	le huitième	18^{e}	le dix-huitième
9^{e}	le neuvième	19^{e}	le dix-neuvième
10^{e}	le dixième	20^{e}	le vingtième

Ordinal numbers (*first, second,* and so on) are formed by adding **-ième** to cardinal numbers. Note the irregular form **premier** (**première**), and the spelling of **cinquième** and **neuvième. Le** and **la** do not elide before **huitième** and **onzième: le huitième.** The superscript abbreviation ^{e} indicates that a number should be read as an ordinal: 7 / **sept;** 7e / **le/la septième.**

A. Les arrondissements de Paris. Quels arrondissements trouve-t-on sur la Rive (*bank*) gauche de la Seine? sur la Rive droite? Quel arrondissement est situé au bord du Bois de Boulogne? du Bois de Vincennes? Où est l'île de la Cité?

B. La carte (*map*) de Paris. Qu'est-ce que c'est?

MODÈLE: Versailles →
C'est un château. Il est dans la banlieue ouest de Paris.

1. Roissy 2. la Seine 3. Boulogne 4. Vincennes 5. Nanterre 6. l'Île de la Cité* 7. Orly

C. Visites indispensables. Consultez de nouveau (*again*) le plan de Paris. Imaginez que vous parlez avec un Parisien ou une Parisienne. Jouez les rôles avec un(e) camarade.

MODÈLE:
VOUS: Moi, je suis étudiant(e) en art moderne.
LE/LA PARISIEN(NE): Alors, vous devez visiter le Centre Pompidou.
VOUS: C'est dans quel arrondissement?
LE/LA PARISIEN(NE): C'est dans le troisième.

1. spécialiste en architecture médiévale 2. étudiant(e) en histoire militaire 3. étudiant(e) en sciences naturelles 4. étudiant(e) en histoire de l'art 5. amateur de musique (*music lover*) 6. amateur de danse

*The **Île de la Cité** is the historical center of Paris; it is one of the two islands on the Seine in Paris. The other is the **Île St-Louis.**

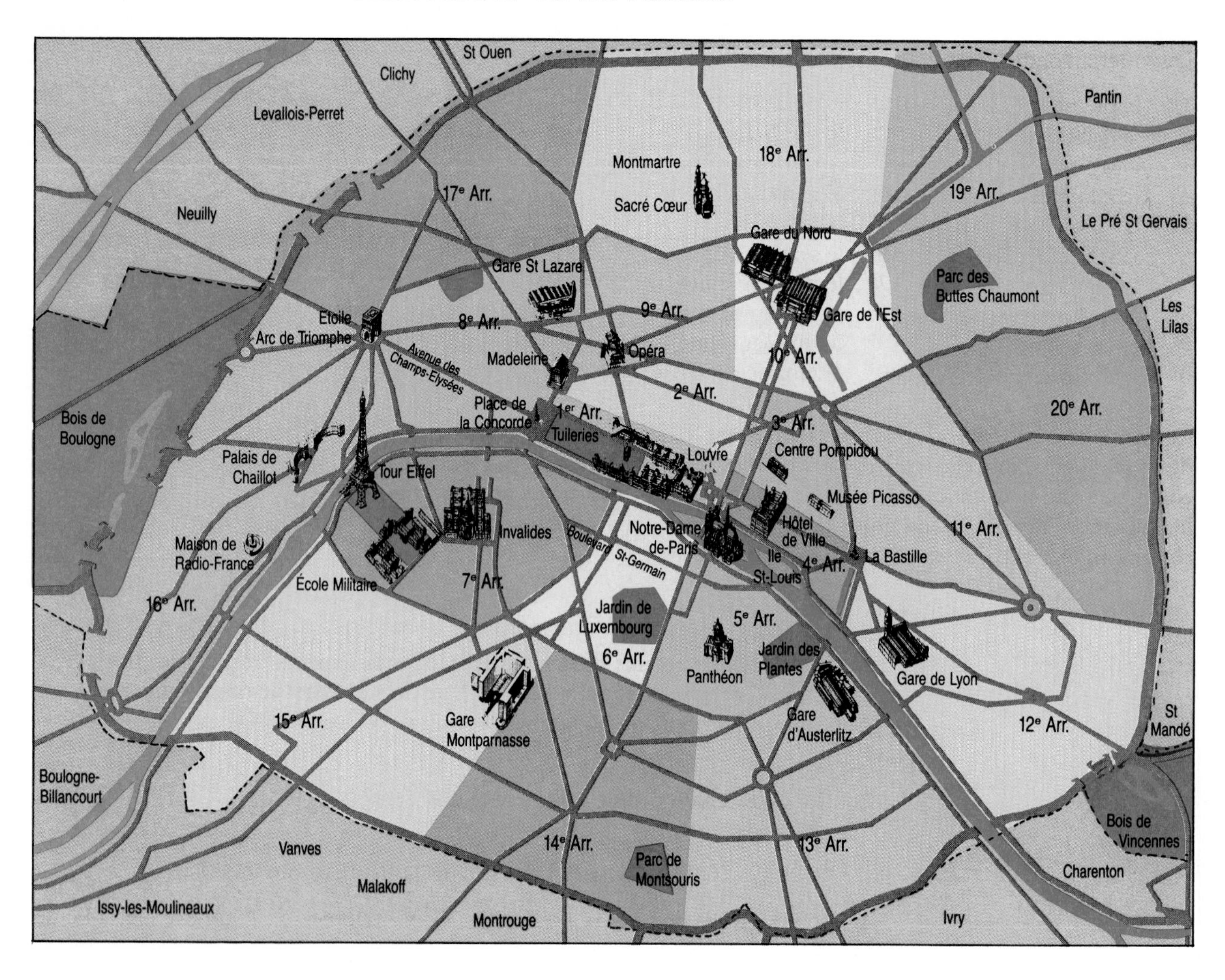

D. Les endroits intéressants de Paris. Avec deux autres camarades, regardez ce plan simplifié de Paris et répondez aux questions suivantes: **Il** (**Elle**) **se trouve...** (*It is situated . . .*)

1. Sur quelle rive se trouve la Tour Eiffel? l'Opéra? l'Arc de Triomphe? le Panthéon?
2. Sur quelle île se trouve Notre-Dame?
3. Dans quel arrondissement se trouve le musée du Louvre? le Sacré-Cœur? les Invalides? la Maison de Radio-France?
4. Combien de gares y a-t-il sur ce plan? Donnez leurs noms.
5. Donnez le nom de trois parcs et dites dans quels arrondissements ils se trouvent.

6. Où se trouve la Bastille?
7. Donnez le nom de quelques villes de la banlieue parisienne et dites où elles se trouvent. (nord, sud... de Paris)
8. Imaginez que vous restez à Paris pendant trois jours et que vous visitez la ville à pied. Où allez-vous? Choisissez votre itinéraire et dites dans quels arrondissements vous allez. Commentez votre réponse.

VISITES DE PARIS **1/2 JOURNÉE**

C 4 TOUR CITYRAMA 100 F

Circuit d'orientation de Paris.
Durée : 2 h environ
Tous les jours.
DÉPARTS : 9 h 30, 11 h, 13 h 30, 14 h.
Départs supplémentaires le samedi et le dimanche à 10 h.

Autocar à double-étage avec commentaire enregistré. Choix de 8 langues : français, anglais, espagnol, italien, allemand, japonais, portugais, hollandais. Ecouteurs individuels sous emballage scellé offerts à chaque client.

Circuit accompagné par une hôtesse. Pas de visite intérieure.

Itinéraire : Rue de Rivoli/Tuileries - Concorde - Louvre - Pont Neuf -Ile de la Cité - Notre-Dame - Hôtel de Ville - Place des Vosges - Bastille - Ile St Louis - Quartier Latin - Luxembourg St-Germain-des-Prés -Assemblée Nationale - Invalides - Tour Eiffel - Palais de Chaillot - Arc de Triomphe - Champs-Elysées Concorde - Madeleine - Opéra - Place Vendôme - Rue de Rivoli/ Place des Pyramides.

PA 1 PARIS ARTISTIQUE 195 F
Notre-Dame et Musée du Louvre

Tous les jours. DÉPART : à 9 h 30, sauf le mardi.
Durée : 3 h 30 environ.

Circuit accompagné par un guide-interprète officiel.

Circuit au coeur de Paris avec visite intérieure de la cathédrale Notre-Dame et visite d'orientation du Musée du Louvre. Vous y verrez des chefs d'oeuvre mondialement connus tels que la Joconde de Léonard de Vinci, la Victoire de Samothrace... Possibilité de rester sur place.

PP 1 PARIS PANORAMIQUE 195 F
Croisière sur la Seine et Tour Eiffel

Tous les jours. DÉPART : 14 h.
Durée : 3 h 30 environ.

Circuit accompagné par un guide-interprète officiel.

Les quartiers ouest de Paris, les Champs-Elysées, l'Arc de Triomphe, le Trocadéro, croisière sur la Seine , montée au 1er étage de la Tour Eiffel (vue panoramique de la ville). Possibilité de rester sur place.

E. **Visite de Paris.** Maintenant que vous connaissez un peu la ville de Paris, choisissez parmi ces trois circuits touristiques celui que vous préférez. Dites à un(e) camarade pourquoi ce circuit vous intéresse, pour le/la persuader de vous accompagner.

Commentaire culturel

Paris. Vieille de plus de 2000 ans, Paris est une ville où le présent et le passé cohabitent en harmonie. C'est aussi une ville de contrastes: il y a le Paris des cartes postales avec ses monuments et ses vues qui séduisent toujours le visiteur: Notre-Dame, le Sacré-Coeur, les quais de la Seine et la Tour Eiffel, symbole même de la ville. Il y a le Paris culturel avec ses galeries d'art, ses antiquaires, ses librairies et ses riches musées: le Centre Pompidou, le musée d'Orsay et bien sûr le Louvre, pour ne nommer que les plus connus. Il y a aussi le Paris des vingt arrondissements où vivent et où se retrouvent les dix millions d'habitants de la capitale et sa banlieue. Il y a encore le Paris élégant de la mode et des grands couturiers avec ses grands magasins (comme le Printemps et les Galeries Lafayette), ses rues aux boutiques de luxe et ses zones piétonnes aux petites boutiques pittoresques. Et puis il y a le Paris des lumières avec ses cabarets, ses théâtres, ses spectacles et ses restaurants. Mais il ne faut pas oublier le Paris travailleur des bureaux, des embouteillages, la vie toujours pressée que résume si bien la formule «métro-boulot-dodo».* Et enfin, il y a le Paris des affaires et son aspect traditionnel dans le quartier de la Bourse. Il est très difficile de séparer ces différents Paris; c'est l'ensemble de ces nombreuses facettes qui font la richesse de cette grande ville.

La Pyramide du Louvre

La gare de l'est à Paris

Une boutique chic rue du Faubourg Saint-Honoré à Paris

*Boulot is colloquial for **travail; dodo** is children's language for **sommeil** (*sleep*).

36. Describing Past Events: The *passé composé* versus the *imparfait*

Retour de France

ALAIN: Dites-moi, en France, **avez**-vous **trouvé** une différence entre le Nord et le Midi?

FRANÇOISE: Ah oui. A Roubaix, les rues **étaient** très propres et très animées, mais les gens ne **faisaient** que passer dans la rue.

JEAN-PIERRE: Quand nous **sommes arrivés** à Marseille, il nous **a semblé** que les gens **passaient** leur vie dans la rue!

FRANÇOISE: Alors, nous **avons fait** comme les autres... et nous **avons passé** des heures à boire du pastis* à la terrasse des cafés et à flâner sur la Canebière.†

Complétez les phrases pour le sens du dialogue.

1. En France, ____.
   - a. Jean-Pierre et Françoise ont trouvé une différence entre le Nord et le Midi
2. A Roubaix, ____.
3. A Marseille, ____.
   - b. les rues n'étaient pas propres
   - c. les rues étaient très propres
   - d. les gens ne faisaient que passer
   - e. les gens vivaient dans la rue
   - f. Jean-Pierre et Françoise ont passé des heures dans la rue

When speaking about the past in English, you choose which past tense forms to use in a given context: *I wrote letters, I did write letters, I was writing letters, I used to write letters,* and so on. Usually only one of these options will convey exactly the meaning you want to express. Similarly in French, the choice between the **passé composé** and the **imparfait** depends on the speaker's perspective: how does the speaker view the action or state of being?

The **passé composé** is used to indicate a single completed action, something that began and ended in the past, or a sequence of such actions.

*__Pastis__ is a licorice-flavored alcoholic beverage that is very popular in the south of France.
†__La Canebière__ is the most famous avenue in Marseilles.

The **imparfait** usually indicates an ongoing or habitual action in the past. It does not emphasize the end of that action.

J'**écrivais** des lettres.	*I was writing letters. (ongoing action)*
J'**ai écrit** des lettres.	*I wrote (have written) letters. (completed action)*
Je **commençais** mes devoirs.	*I was starting on my homework. (ongoing)*
J'**ai commencé** mes devoirs.	*I started (have started) my homework. (completed)*
Elle **allait** au parc le dimanche.*	*She went (used to go) to the park on Sundays. (habitual)*
Elle **est allée** au parc dimanche.	*She went to the park on Sunday. (completed)*

Contrast the two tenses by translating the sentences in this chart.

IMPARFAIT	PASSÉ COMPOSÉ
1. *Ongoing action with no emphasis on the completion or end of the action*	*Completed action*
J'**allais** en France. Je **visitais** des monuments.	Je **suis allé** en France. J'**ai visité** des monuments.
2. *Habitual or repeated action*	*A single event*
Je **voyageais** en France tous les ans. Je **visitais** souvent le Centre Beaubourg.	J'**ai voyagé** en France l'année dernière. Un jour j'**ai visité** Beaubourg.
3. *Description or "background" information; how things were or what was happening when . . .*	*. . . an event or events occurred. ("foreground" information)*
Je **visitais** Beaubourg...	...quand on **a annoncé** la projection d'un vieux film de Chaplin.
J'**étais** à Paris...	...quand une lettre **est arrivée.**

*Remember the role of the definite article with days of the week: **le dimanche** (*on Sundays*); **dimanche** (*on Sunday*).

4. *Physical or mental states of being*	*Changes or interruptions in an existing physical or mental state*
Ma nièce **avait** peur des chiens.	Ma nièce **a eu** peur quand le chien a aboyé (*barked*).

In summary, the **imparfait** is generally used for *descriptions* in the past, and the **passé composé** is generally used for the *narration* of specific events in the past. The **imparfait** also often sets the stage for an event expressed with the **passé composé.** The following passage, broken into two parts (**imparfait** and **passé composé**), illustrates how these two tenses are used together.

IMPARFAIT	PASSÉ COMPOSÉ
Il **faisait** beau; le ciel (*sky*) **était** clair; les terrasses des cafés **étaient** pleines (*filled*) de gens; c'**était** un beau jour de printemps à Paris.	J'**ai continué** tout droit dans la rue Mouffetard, j'**ai traversé** le boulevard de Port-Royal et j'**ai descendu** l'avenue des Gobelins jusqu'à la place d'Italie.

Mots-clés

Indicators of tense: Here are some time expressions that often accompany the **imparfait** and the **passé composé.**

IMPARFAIT	PASSÉ COMPOSÉ
d'habitude (*usually*)	une fois (*once*), deux fois...
autrefois (*formerly*)	plusieurs fois
le week-end	un week-end
le lundi (le mardi...)	un jour
	lundi (mardi...)
	soudain, tout d'un coup (*suddenly*)
D'habitude, nous étudiions à la bibliothèque.	**Un jour,** nous **avons étudié** au café.
Quand j'étais jeune, nous **allions** à la plage **le week-end.**	**Un week-end,** nous **sommes allés** à la montagne.

MAINTENANT A VOUS

A. Un dimanche pas comme les autres. Votre voisin Marc Dufour était une personne routinière, mais un dimanche il a changé ses habitudes. Voici son histoire.

MODÈLE: le dimanche matin / dormir en général jusqu'à huit heures
mais ce dimanche-là / dormir jusqu'à midi →
Le dimanche matin, il dormait en général jusqu'à huit heures, mais ce dimanche-là, il a dormi jusqu'à midi.

1. normalement au petit déjeuner / prendre des céréales et une tasse de café
mais ce matin-là / manger un petit déjeuner copieux
2. après le petit déjeuner / faire toujours du jogging dans le parc
mais ce jour-là / rester longtemps au téléphone
3. souvent l'après-midi / regarder le match de football à la télé
mais cet après-midi-là / lire des poèmes dans le jardin
4. d'habitude le soir / sortir avec ses copains
mais ce soir-là / sortir avec une jolie fille
5. parfois / aller au cinéma ou / jouer aux cartes
mais ce soir-là / inviter son amie dans un restaurant élégant
6. normalement / rentrer chez lui assez tôt
mais ce dimanche-là / danser jusqu'au petit matin

A votre avis, Marc est-il malade? amoureux? déprimé? ___?___ Justifiez votre réponse. Et vous, est-ce qu'il y a des choses que vous faisiez l'année dernière que vous ne faites plus maintenant? Expliquez.

B. Une année à l'université de Caen. Marc a passé un an à Caen, une des grandes villes de Normandie. Il raconte son histoire. Donnez le temps correct du verbe, **l'imparfait** ou **le passé composé.**

Je (*avoir*) cours le matin de 8 heures à 11 heures. L'après-midi, je (*étudier*), en général, à la bibliothèque. Le week-end, avec des amis, nous (*faire*) du tourisme. Le samedi, nous (*rester*) en ville et le dimanche, nous (*aller*) à la campagne. En octobre nous (*faire*) une excursion à Rouen. Ce (*être*) très intéressant. Pour Noël je (*rentrer*) chez mes parents. En février je (*faire*) du ski dans les Alpes. Nous (*avoir*) de la chance car il (*faire*) très beau et je (*rentrer*) bien bronzé. De temps en temps je (*manger*) chez les Levergeois, des amis français très sympathiques. Pendant ces dîners entre amis, je (*perfectionner*) mon français. Finalement, au début du mois de mai je (*devoir*) quitter Caen. Je (*être*) triste de partir.

C. Interruptions. Annie était à la maison hier soir. Elle voulait faire plusieurs choses, mais il y a eu toutes sortes d'interruptions. Décrivez-les.

MODÈLE: étudier... téléphone / sonner →
Annie étudiait quand le téléphone a sonné.

1. parler au téléphone / un ami... l'employé / couper la ligne (*to cut the line*)
2. écouter / disques... son voisin / commencer à faire / bruit (*noise*)
3. lire / journal... la propriétaire / venir demander / argent
4. faire / devoirs... un ami / arriver
5. regarder / informations... son frère / changer / chaîne
6. dormir... téléphone / sonner de nouveau

Mots-clés

Putting events in chronological order:

		DÉPANNAGE
d'abord	*first of all*	*D'abord,* j'ai garé la voiture.
puis	*next*	*Puis,* j'ai cherché une cabine téléphonique.
ensuite	*and then . . .*	*Ensuite,* j'ai tout expliqué au mécanicien.
après	*after that . . .*	*Après,* j'ai attendu dans la voiture.
enfin	*finally*	*Enfin,* il est arrivé. Maintenant, le carburateur fonctionne à merveille.

Puis and **ensuite** can be used interchangeably.

© GAMMA-LIAISON

D. Biographie de Marguerite Yourcenar. Voici quelques faits importants de la vie de cette romancière et historienne de langue française. Mettez-les dans l'ordre chronologique et utilisez des adverbes de temps.

1. Elle est allée aux États-Unis en 1958.
2. Elle a écrit son fameux livre *l'Œuvre au noir* en 1968.
3. Elle est née à Bruxelles en 1903.
4. Elle est morte en 1987 à l'âge de 84 ans dans l'état de Maine.
5. Elle a été la première femme élue à l'Académie Française, en 1979.

Maintenant, racontez brièvement (*briefly*) votre propre autobiographie. Utilisez des adverbes de temps.

E. Conversation. L'année dernière,...

1. Où étiez-vous? Où avez-vous étudié? Qu'est-ce que vous avez étudié?
2. Qu'est-ce que vous avez fait pendant vos vacances? Avez-vous fait un voyage intéressant? Êtes-vous allé(e) à l'étranger? en France? Comment était le voyage?
3. Et vos amis? Où étaient-ils l'année dernière? Qu'est-ce qu'ils ont fait?

F. Il était une fois... Racontez une histoire fantastique que vous avez vécue, ou inventez-la. Utilisez les éléments suggérés pour organiser votre histoire et choisissez le temps convenable (**passé composé** ou **imparfait**). **Suggestions:** l'heure, le temps, la description de la scène, la description des personnages, la description des sentiments...

Expressions utiles: soudain, tout à coup, d'habitude, en général, puis, ensuite, enfin, alors, autrefois, quand, souvent, parfois, toujours...

37. Speaking Succinctly: The Pronouns *y* and *en*

*Les trésors du bouquiniste**

© 1988 ULRIKE WELSCH

JEAN-MARC: Tu as de vieux timbres? J'**en** fais collection.
VÉRONIQUE: J'**en** ai trouvé de très beaux chez un bouquiniste du quai du Louvre.
JEAN-MARC: Fantastique! Dis... comment fait-on pour **y** aller?
VÉRONIQUE: Vas-**y** en métro: tu prends la ligne Vincennes-Neuilly en direction Château de Vincennes et tu descends à la station du Louvre. Tu traverses la rue de Rivoli, tu passes devant le musée et tu **y** es.
JEAN-MARC: Ça ne va pas prendre longtemps. J'espère seulement que ton bouquiniste a encore de vieux timbres.
VÉRONIQUE: Oh, je pense que oui. Il n'**en** avait pas beaucoup, mais... ils étaient hors de prix!

Retrouvez la phrase correcte dans le dialogue.

1. Je fais collection de vieux timbres.
2. J'ai trouvé de très beaux timbres chez un bouquiniste du quai du Louvre.
3. Comment fait-on pour aller au quai du Louvre?
4. Va au quai du Louvre en métro.
5. ...tu passes devant le musée et tu es au quai du Louvre.
6. Il n'avait pas beaucoup de vieux timbres, mais ils étaient hors de prix.

A. The Pronoun *y*

The pronoun y can refer to a place that has already been mentioned. It replaces a prepositional phrase, and its English equivalent is *there*.

*__Un bouquin__ is a colloquial term that means **un livre. Les bouquinistes** are booksellers who set up their stalls along the Seine and often sell stamps, engravings, postcards, and posters, as well as used and rare books.

—Jean est-il né **en France**?	*—Was Jean born in France?*
—Oui, il y est né.	*—Yes, he was born there.*
—Martine est-elle allée **à l'aéroport**?	*—Did Martine go to the airport?*
—Non, elle n'y est pas allée.	*—No, she didn't (go there).*
—On va **chez les Martin**?	*—Are we going to the Martins' house?*
—Oui, on y va.	*—Yes, we are (going there).*

After some verbs that take the preposition à before a noun (**répondre à, réfléchir à, réussir à, penser à, jouer à**), the word **y** can replace the à plus the noun, when the noun refers to a place or to a thing. **Y** cannot replace à plus a noun that refers to a person; a direct or indirect object pronoun is used instead.

—As-tu répondu **à la lettre**?	*—Did you answer the letter?*
—Oui, j'y ai répondu.	*—Yes, I answered it.*
—Vous pensez **au voyage**?	*—Are you thinking about the trip?*
—Non, je n'y pense pas.	*—No, I'm not thinking about it.*

but

—As-tu déjà répondu **à ta mère**?	*—Have you already answered your mother?*
—Oui, je **lui** ai répondu.	*—Yes, I answered her.*

The placement of **y** is identical to that of object pronouns; it precedes a conjugated verb, an infinitive, or an auxiliary verb in the **passé composé.**

La ville de Nice? Nous **y cherchons** une maison.	*The city of Nice? We're looking for a house there.*
Le bateau va **y arriver** jeudi.	*The boat will arrive there on Thursday.*
Y es-tu allé en train ou en avion?	*Did you go there by train or by plane?*

B. The Pronoun *en*

The pronoun **en** can replace a noun preceded by a partitive article (**du, de la, de l', des**) or by an indefinite article (**un, une, des**). **En** is then equivalent to English *some* or *any*. Like other object pronouns, **en** is placed directly before the verb of which it is the object and, in the case of the **passé composé,** directly before the auxiliary verb.

—Y a-t-il **des musées intéressants** à Avignon?	—*Are there any interesting museums in Avignon?*
—Oui, il y **en** a.	—*Yes, there are* (*some*).
—Avez-vous **des tickets de métro**?	—*Have you any subway tickets?*
—Non, je n'**en** ai pas.	—*No, I don't have any.*
—A-t-il acheté **des souvenirs**?	—*Did he buy any souvenirs?*
—Non, il n'**en** a pas acheté.	—*No, he didn't buy any.*
—Voici **du vin. En** veux-tu?	—*Here's some wine. Do you want some?*
—Non, merci. Je n'**en** veux pas.	—*No, thank you. I don't want any.*

En can also replace a noun modified by a number or by an expression of quantity, such as **beaucoup de, un kilo de, trop de, deux,** and so on. The noun is dropped, but the number or expression of quantity (minus **de**) remains. The English equivalent of **en** in this case is *of it, of them,* or *any*. While these phrases are often omitted in English, **en** cannot be omitted in French.

—Avez-vous **une chambre**?	—*Do you have a room?*
—Oui, j'**en** ai **une.***	—*Yes, I have one.*
—Y a-t-il **beaucoup de parcs**?	—*Are there many parks?*
—Oui, il y **en** a **beaucoup.**	—*Yes, there are many* (*of them*)
—**Combien de places** voulez-vous?	—*How many seats would you like?*
—J'**en** voudrais **cinq.**	—*I would like five* (*of them*).

En is also used to replace **de** plus a noun and its modifiers (unless the noun refers to people) in sentences with verbs or expressions that use **de: parler de, avoir envie de,** and so on.

—Avez-vous besoin **de ce guide?**	—*Do you need this guide?*
—Oui, j'**en** ai besoin.	—*Yes, I need it.*
—Parliez-vous **des ruines romaines**?	—*Were you talking about the Roman ruins?*
—Non, nous n'**en** parlions pas.	—*No, we weren't talking about them.*

*In a negative answer to a question containing **un**(e), the word un(e) is not repeated: **Je n'en ai pas.**

C. *Y* and *en* Together

Y precedes **en** when they are the objects of the same verb.

—Est-ce qu'on trouve des ruines romaines dans le sud?	—*Can you find Roman ruins in the south?*
—Oui, on **y en** trouve.	—*Yes, you can find some (there).*

The combination of **y en** is very common with the expression **il y a.**

—Combien de livres y a-t-il?	—*How many books are there?*
—Il **y en** a sept.	—*There are seven (of them).*
—Combien de magazines y avait-il sur la table?	—*How many magazines were there on the table?*
—Il **y en** avait quatre.	—*There were four (of them there).*

MAINTENANT A VOUS

A. Distractions parisiennes. Vous êtes à Paris depuis une semaine et vous ne savez pas quoi faire ce week-end. Un ami (une amie) vous donne des suggestions, mais vous avez déjà fait ce qu'il (elle) vous propose.

MODÈLE: Passe l'après-midi aux Galeries Lafayette! (lundi) →
J'y suis allé(e) lundi matin.

1. Monte à la Tour Eiffel! (hier après-midi)
2. Dîne chez Maxim! (mardi soir)
3. Fais une promenade au Bois de Boulogne! (mercredi)
4. Va au musée d'Orsay! (jeudi matin)
5. Reste à l'hôtel pour te reposer (*rest*)! (ce matin)
6. Alors pense à ce que tu veux faire la semaine prochaine! (cet après-midi)

B. Roman policier. Paul Marteau est détective. Il file (*trails*) une suspecte, Pauline Dutour. Doit-il aller partout (*everywhere*) où elle va?

MODÈLE: Pauline Dutour va à Paris → Marteau y va aussi.
(*ou*) Marteau n'y va pas.

1. La suspecte entre dans un magasin de vêtements. 2. Elle va au cinéma. 3. Elle entre dans une cabine téléphonique. 4. Pauline reste longtemps dans un bistro. 5. La suspecte monte dans un taxi. 6. Elle retourne au magasin. 7. Elle va chez le coiffeur (*hairdresser*). 8. Elle entre dans un hôtel. 9. La suspecte va au bar de l'hôtel. 10. Maintenant elle va en prison.

Maintenant, racontez les aventures de Marteau au passé composé.

C. Votre ville. Imaginez qu'un touriste vous pose des questions sur votre ville. Jouez les rôles avec un(e) camarade. Utilisez dans vos réponses le pronom **en** et un nombre ou une expression de quantité. Donnez aussi le plus de détails possible.

MODÈLE: —Y a-t-il de grands magasins dans votre ville?
—Oui, il y en a beaucoup—Saks, Macy's, Nordstrom...
(Non, il y en a seulement deux, Macy's et Saks.)

1. Avez-vous une université dans votre ville?
2. Y a-t-il des musées intéressants à visiter?
3. Y a-t-il beaucoup d'embouteillages aux heures de pointe (*rush hour*)?
4. Combien de cinémas et de théâtres avez-vous?
5. Est-ce qu'on peut faire beaucoup de sport?
6. Peut-on admirer des monuments historiques?
7. Combien d'habitants y a-t-il dans votre ville?
8. Rencontre-t-on beaucoup d'étrangers?

Maintenant, votre camarade décrit votre ville à la classe. Il (Elle) commence par «Mon (ma) camarade est de _____. Il y a beaucoup de grands magasins à _____... » Est-ce que tout le monde est d'accord avec cette description? Comparez les descriptions d'une même ville. Qui a donné le plus de détails? Qui a été le plus précis (la plus précise)?

D. **Correspondance.** Debbie va visiter la France. Elle pose des questions aux amis qui l'ont invitée. Donnez une réponse en utilisant **y** et **en.**

MODÈLE: Est-ce qu'on vend de la bonne moutarde à Dijon? →
Oui, on y en vend.

1. Est-ce qu'à Marseille on boit du pastis? 2. Est-ce qu'il y a beaucoup de fleurs à Nice? 3. Est-ce qu'on trouve des ruines romaines à Arles? 4. Est-ce qu'on trouve des châteaux dans la vallée de la Loire? 5. Est-ce que nous pouvons faire du bateau en Bretagne? 6. Est-ce qu'on fait du vin à Bordeaux?

Mots-clés

Asking someone's opinion:

Que pensez-vous de...	*What do you think of . . .*
Qu'en penses-tu?	*What do you think about that?*
Est-ce que tu crois que...	*Do you think that . . .*
A votre (ton) avis,...	*In your opinion, . . .*

E. **Échange d'opinions.** Avec un(e) camarade, donnez des opinions sur des sujets divers. **Suggestions:** les musées, les touristes, les chauffeurs de taxi, les monuments, les grandes villes américaines, la télévision, les transports publics...

MODÈLE:
VOUS: Que penses-tu des voitures japonaises?
VOTRE CAMARADE: Elles sont jolies (trop petites, bon marché) ... Et toi, qu'en penses-tu?
VOUS: Je (ne) les aime (pas). Elles (ne) sont (pas)...

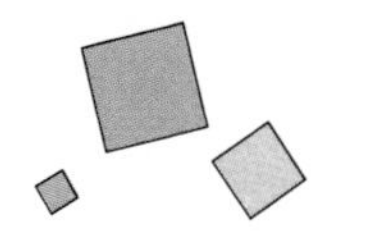

38. Saying What You Know: *savoir* and *connaître*

Labyrinthe

MARCEL: Taxi! Vous **connaissez** la rue Vaucouleurs?

LE CHAUFFEUR: Mais bien sûr, je **sais** où elle est! Je **connais** Paris comme le fond de ma poche!

MARCEL: Je ne **sais** pas comment vous faites. Je me suis perdu hier dans l'Île de la Cité.

LE CHAUFFEUR: Je **connais** mon métier et puis, vous **savez,** avec un plan de Paris, ce n'est pas si difficile!

Faites des phrases complètes pour décrire ce qui se passe (*what happens*) dans le dialogue.

Marcel	sait	la rue Vaucouleurs
le chauffeur	ne sait pas	où est la rue Vaucouleurs
	connaît	Paris
	ne connaît pas	comment le chauffeur fait son métier

The verbs **savoir** and **connaître** both correspond to the English verb *to know,* but they are used differently.

savoir			
je	sais	nous	savons
tu	sais	vous	savez
il, elle, on	sait	ils, elles	savent
Past participle: su			

connaître			
je	connais	nous	connaissons
tu	connais	vous	connaissez
il, elle, on	connaît	ils, elles	connaissent
Past participle: connu			

Savoir means *to know* or *to have knowledge of* a fact, *to know by heart,* or *to know how to* do something. It is frequently followed by an infinitive or by a subordinate clause introduced by **que, quand, pourquoi,** and so on.

Sais-tu l'heure qu'il est?	*Do you know what time it is?*
Sait-elle parler français?	*Does she know how to speak French?*
Je **sais** qu'il va en France cet été.	*I know that he's going to France this summer.*

In the **passé composé, savoir** means *to learn* or *to find out.*

J'**ai su** hier qu'il allait à Paris.	*I found out yesterday that he was going to Paris.*

Connaître means *to know* or *to be familiar* (*acquainted*) *with* someone or something. **Connaître**—never **savoir**—means *to know a person.* **Connaître** is always used with a direct object; it cannot be followed directly by an infinitive or by a subordinate clause.

Connais-tu Marie-Françoise?	*Do you know Marie-Françoise?*
Non, je ne la **connais** pas.	*No, I don't know her.*
Ils **connaissent** très bien Dijon.	*They know Dijon very well.*

In the **passé composé, connaître** means *to meet for the first time.* It is the equivalent of **faire la connaissance de.**

J'ai connu Jean à l'université.	*I met Jean at the university.*

MAINTENANT A VOUS

A. **Dialogue.** Complétez les phrases avec **connaître** ou **savoir.**

—_______[1]-vous Paris, Monsieur?
—Je _______[2] seulement que c'est la capitale.
—_______[3]-vous quelle est la distance entre Paris et Marseille?
—Non, mais je _______[4] une agence de voyages où on doit le _______[5]. Ils _______[6] très bien le pays.
—_______[7]-vous s'il y a d'autres villes intéressantes à visiter?
—Comme je l'ai dit, je ne _______[8] pas bien ce pays, mais hier j'ai fait la connaissance d'un homme qui _______[9] où aller pour passer de bonnes vacances. Je voudrais bien _______[10] cet homme.
—_______[11]-vous où il travaille?

B. **Vos connaissances.** Utilisez ces phrases pour interviewer un ami (une amie). Dans les réponses, utilisez les verbes **savoir** ou **connaître.**

1. Nomme deux choses que tu sais faire. 2. Nomme deux choses que tu veux savoir faire un jour. 3. Nomme deux domaines (*fields*) où tu es plus ou moins incompétent(e). (Je ne sais pas...) 4. Nomme deux domaines où tu es particulièrement fort(e) (*strong*). (Je sais très bien...) 5. Nomme un fait (*fact*) que tu as appris récemment.

La Tour Eiffel et les fontaines du Trocadéro illuminées

C. Et vous? Connaissez-vous Paris? Avec un(e) camarade, posez des questions et répondez-y.

MODÈLE: l'Opéra →

VOUS: Connaissez-vous l'Opéra?
UN(E) AMI(E): Non, je ne le connais pas, mais je sais qu'on y va pour écouter de la musique.

ENDROITS	DÉFINITIONS
l'Opéra	C'est le quartier des étudiants à Paris.
les Invalides	Le Président y habite.
le Panthéon	On y va pour écouter de la musique.
le Palais de l'Élysée	On y trouve une vaste collection de livres.
la Bourse	Napoléon y est enterré (*buried*).
la Bibliothèque nationale	C'est la structure en verre (*glass*) devant le Louvre.
le Quartier latin	D'autres grands hommes de France y sont enterrés.
la Pyramide	C'est le centre des affaires (*business*).

D. Une ville. Donnez le nom d'une ville que vous connaissez bien. Ensuite racontez ce que (*what*) vous savez sur cette ville.

MODÈLE: Je connais New York. Je sais qu'il y a d'immenses gratte-ciel (*skyscrapers*).

Situation

Aventure en métro

Contexte *Charles, un étudiant canadien, veut aller à l'École de Médecine, dans le Quartier latin, à Paris. Ses amis, Francis et Geneviève, lui expliquent comment y aller en métro.*

Objectif *Charles utilise le métro.*

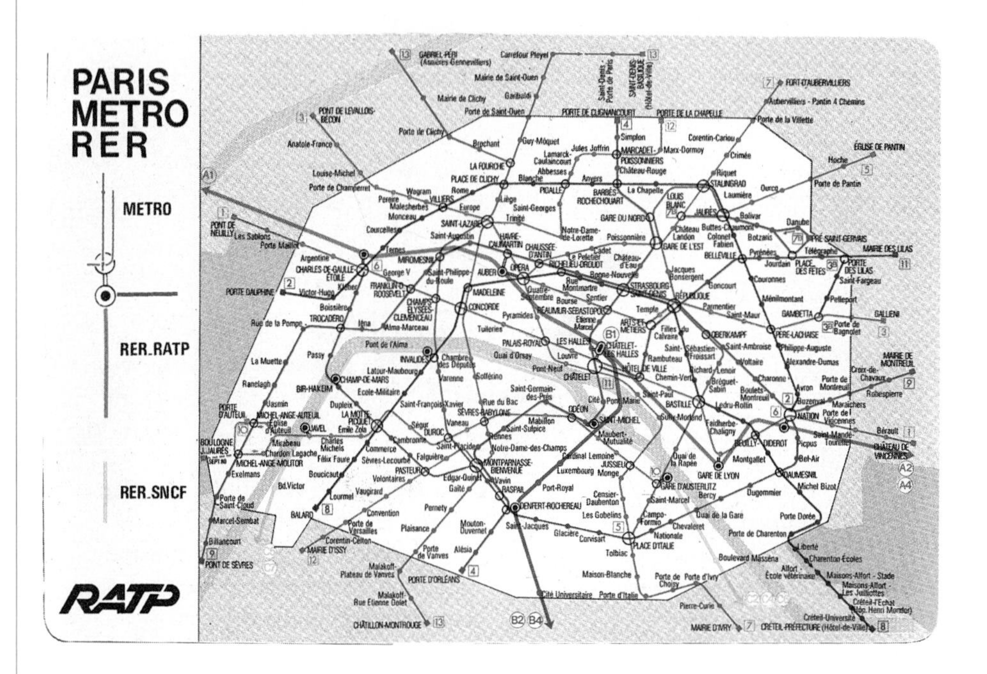

GENEVIÈVE: Charles, tu peux y aller en métro, à l'École de Médecine.
CHARLES: Oui, mais comment fait-on pour y aller?
GENEVIÈVE: Viens, on va regarder la carte: quelle est la station près de l'École?
CHARLES: Odéon.
FRANCIS: Bon, nous, nous sommes près de Oberkampf.
GENEVIÈVE: Cherchons la route entre Oberkampf et Odéon.
CHARLES: C'est Oberkampf, Strasbourg Saint-Denis, Odéon.

FRANCIS: Parfait. Ta correspondance° est Strasbourg Saint-Denis: c'est là que tu changes de ligne. *transfer*
CHARLES C'est simple.
FRANCIS: Mais oui, l'essentiel, c'est de vérifier la direction de ta ligne.
GENEVIÈVE: Quand tu vas de Oberkampf à Strasbourg Saint-Denis, c'est la direction Pont de Sèvres.
CHARLES: Et quand je vais de Strasbourg Saint-Denis à Odéon, c'est la direction Porte d'Orléans. Maintenant, je comprends. Vous connaissez bien Paris maintenant.
GENEVIÈVE: Pas vraiment. Mais nous apprenons vite!

VARIATIONS

1. Rejouez la scène avec cette différence: Charles veut prendre le métro pour retrouver (*to meet*) un ami qui arrive à la Gare du Nord.
2. Imaginez que vous habitez à Montreuil. Une amie américaine vous rend visite et veut visiter le musée du Louvre. Vous ne pouvez pas l'accompagner, mais vous lui expliquez comment y aller en métro. Pour vérifier qu'elle a bien compris, demandez-lui de vous expliquer comment elle va revenir chez vous après sa visite au musée. Jouez les rôles avec un(e) camarade.

A propos

Comment demander son chemin

Pouvez-vous (Peux-tu) me dire...
- où est... ?
- dans quelle direction est... ?
- par où je dois passer pour... ?
- si... est loin d'ici / près d'ici?

Comment indiquer le chemin

C'est...
- là-bas (*there*)
- derrière...
- devant...
- à côté de...
- de l'autre côté de...
- en face de...

Vous allez tout droit
Vous tournez { à droite... / à gauche...

A. Jeu de rôles. Un nouvel étudiant (Une nouvelle étudiante) vous demande le chemin pour aller dans divers endroits de votre campus. Jouez la scène avec un(e) camarade. Soyez précis(e) dans vos directions. Le nouvel étudiant (La nouvelle étudiante) doit répéter les directions pour vérifier qu'il (elle) les a bien comprises. Utilisez les expressions de l'*A propos*.

B. Les problèmes urbains de l'Amérique. Choisissez les quatre problèmes urbains les plus graves (*most serious*) de cette liste. Mettez ces problèmes dans l'ordre de vos priorités.

1. _____ la pollution de l'air
2. _____ le bruit
3. _____ les taudis (*slums*)
4. _____ la criminalité (les hold-ups, par exemple)
5. _____ le chômage (*unemployment*)
6. _____ le gaspillage (*waste*) d'énergie
7. _____ les embouteillages (*traffic jams*)
8. ?

Expliquez pourquoi vous avez choisi ces problèmes. Ensuite, répondez aux questions suivantes.

1. Quels problèmes urbains touchent l'individu? Quels problèmes concernent toute la société? 2. Quels problèmes concernent l'avenir (*future*) de nos enfants? 3. Quels problèmes concernent notre santé (*health*)? 4. Quels problèmes représentent une question de vie ou de mort? 5. Quels problèmes concernent la tranquillité de notre vie quotidienne? 6. Quelles solutions ont déjà été apportées à ces problèmes? Quelles autres sont à l'étude? Quelles sont vos suggestions personnelles?

Commentaire culturel

Les villes françaises. Les trois-quarts des Français habitent dans des villes. Il y a Paris, bien sûr, et puis Lyon, Marseille, Toulouse, Bordeaux, Lille, Strasbourg, parmi les capitales régionales les plus importantes. Mais surtout, la France compte de très nombreuses petites villes qui sont, en général, très anciennes et très différentes d'une région à l'autre.

© ULRIKE WELSCH

Vue d'ensemble du village de Montigny

© HUGH ROGERS / MONKMEYER

Une rue étroite au cœur de St. Paul de Vence

© GORDON E. SMITH / PHOTO RESEARCHERS, INC.

Hazebrouck, une petite ville du nord de la France

Mise au point

A. Voyage imaginaire. Pensez à une ville que vous aimez tout spécialement (aux États-Unis ou à l'étranger). Décrivez-la au reste de la classe. Utilisez des pronoms d'objet direct ou indirect, **y** ou **en** dans votre description. Vos camarades doivent deviner le nom de la ville.

MODÈLE: VOUS: On y trouve des collines. On la voit souvent dans des films. Beaucoup de touristes y vont pour admirer son célèbre pont. On lui donne parfois le nom de Frisco.
VOS CAMARADES: C'est San Francisco!

B. Le bonheur vu par les Français. Voici une partie d'un article tiré du magazine français *Le Point.* Il constate que la plupart des Français n'aiment plus vivre en ville; ils aspirent de plus en plus au silence et à la paix. Lisez-le, puis répondez aux questions suivantes. Utilisez des pronoms d'objet direct, indirect, **y** ou **en** dans vos réponses, si possible.

Le bonheur vu par les Français

Le refus de la ville va dans ce sens. Réaction stupéfiante quand on songe que 80 % des Français sont désormais des citadins. La condamnation vise[a] surtout les grandes villes. Les agglomérations moyennes[b] bénéficient d'une certaine indulgence. Un tiers[c] considère qu'il n'est pas désagréable d'y vivre. Denise Pumain, professeur de géographie à Paris-XIII, constate d'ailleurs qu'*« elles ont, en général, un taux de croissance[d] plus élevé que les grandes villes »*.

a. *is aimed at*
b. agglomérations... *middle-sized cities*
c. *third*
d. taux... *growth rate*

1. Quel pourcentage des Français habite en ville?
2. Est-ce que d'après ce sondage les Français rejettent toutes les villes?
3. «Un tiers considère qu'il n'est pas désagréable d'y vivre.» A quoi se réfère le pronom **y**?
4. Et vous, préférez-vous la grande ville, les villes moyennes ou la campagne? Quels sont à votre avis les avantages et les inconvénients de chacune (*each one*)? Y a-t-il une grosse différence entre une petite ville et une grande ville? Justifiez vos réponses.

C. Les grandes villes. Formez des phrases complètes et mettez les verbes de cette narration au passé composé ou à l'imparfait.

1. je / aimer / les grandes villes / quand / je / être / jeune
2. il y a / toujours / beaucoup / choses / à voir
3. les gens / être / intéressant / et / les bâtiments / être / beau
4. un jour / je / être / la banque / et je / voir / un hold-up
5. le voleur (*robber*) / avoir / un revolver / et il / le / montrer (*to show*) / gens
6. nous / avoir / peur
7. le voleur / prendre / l'argent / et il / partir
8. quelqu'un / téléphoner / la police
9. la police / le / trouver / en dix minutes / parce qu'il / avoir / difficultés / avec / voiture
10. voilà pourquoi / je / acheter / une maison / campagne

D. Interview. Interviewez un(e) camarade au sujet de sa première visite à une grande ville loin de chez lui (de chez elle). **Suggestions:** Où es-tu allé(e)? Quand? Combien de temps y es-tu resté(e)? Avec qui étais-tu? Qu'est-ce que tu y as fait? Qu'est-ce que tu y as vu? Étais-tu content(e) de ta visite? Pourquoi ou pourquoi pas?

Maintenant, résumez (*summarize*) pour la classe la visite de votre camarade. Utilisez les expressions **d'abord, puis, ensuite, après** et **enfin** pour décrire ce que votre camarade a vu et a fait.

Interactions

In this chapter, you learned how to tell stories in the past and to express the time of events. Act out the following situations, using the vocabulary and structures from this chapter.

1. **Journaliste.** You are interviewing a famous, rich person (your classmate) about his or her travels to France. Find out if she or he prefers the country or the cities. Ask what French city she or he prefers and why. Have him or her describe the city and a recent visit.
2. **Je suis perdu**(e)**!** Imagine that you are lost. Ask a stranger (your partner) the way to go downtown from where you are. She or he will give you directions, mentioning some landmarks. Ask questions if you are not sure where to go.

Vocabulaire

Verbes

connaître to know; to be familiar with
savoir to know (how)
toucher to cash (a check); to touch; to concern

Substantifs

l'arrondissement (*m.*) ward, section (*of Paris*)
la banlieue suburbs
le bois forest, woods
le bruit noise
le café-tabac bar-tobacconist
la carte map
le centre-ville downtown
le château castle, château
le chemin way (road)
le coin corner
le commissariat (**le poste de police**) police station
l'église (*f.*) church
l'île (*f.*) island
la mairie town hall
la piscine swimming pool
la place square
le poste de police police station
la Rive droite the Right Bank (*in Paris*)
la Rive gauche the Left Bank (*in Paris*)
le syndicat d'initiative tourist information bureau
la tour tower

Les nombres ordinaux

le premier (**la première**), **le** (**la**) **deuxième,...** , **le** (**la**) **cinquième,...** , **le** (**la**) **huitième, le** (**la**) **neuvième,...** , **le** (**la**) **onzième,** etc.

Les expressions temporelles

autrefois formerly
d'abord first, first of all, at first
de temps en temps from time to time
d'habitude usually
enfin finally
soudain suddenly
tout d'un coup suddenly

Mots divers

à droite (*prep.*) on (to) the right
à gauche (*prep.*) on (to) the left
de nouveau (*adv.*) again
en (*pron.*) of them; of it; some
en face de (*prep.*) across from
jusqu'à until
là (*adv.*) there
partout (*adv.*) everywhere
propre (*adj.*) clean
tout droit (*adv.*) straight ahead
y (*pron.*) there

Mots apparentés

Verbes: **continuer, tourner, commencer**
Substantifs: **la banque, l'hôpital** (*m.*), **l'hôtel** (*m.*), **la ligne, le monument, le musée, le parc, la pharmacie, la plante, la station** (**de métro**), **le week-end**
Adjectifs: **municipal**(**e**), **public** (**publique**)

Expressions utiles

A votre (ton) avis,... ?	*In your opinion, . . . ?*
Qu'en penses-tu?	*What do you think of that?*

INTERMÈDE 10

Lecture

Le Petit Prince est un conte (*tale*) très populaire en France. Il a été écrit par Antoine de Saint-Exupéry en 1943. Dans l'histoire, le Petit Prince habite sur une petite planète avec une rose pour seule compagnie. Un jour, il décide d'explorer d'autres planètes. Il arrive alors sur la terre où il découvre les hommes. Il trouve étrange leur façon de voir les choses. Après de nombreuses aventures, il devient l'ami d'un aviateur à qui il fait ses confidences. Dans l'extrait suivant, l'aviateur nous parle de la planète d'où vient le Petit Prince et donne son opinion sur les hommes.

AVANT DE LIRE

Awareness of audience: One of the ways we decide what a text means is by inferring for whom it was written. Obviously, an article about rock music written for the PTA bulletin will make different points from an article written for the campus newspaper, since one is meant for parents and the other for students. Inferring the intended audience is more difficult when you read fiction, yet it is crucial to understanding what the writer means. Look for subtle signs that suggest whom the writer is addressing. One common sign is a suggested complicity with the intended reader—the writer assumes that he or she has something in common with the reader. You can also deduce the assumed audience from the levels of ideas or language used. Are the ideas simple or sophisticated? Is the language straightforward and simple, or is it complex?

After you understand the general story line in this excerpt from *Le Petit Prince,* think about for whom the story was written. Look for clues in the text, and discuss your conclusions with your classmates.

Note that a few of the verbs in *Le Petit Prince* are conjugated in tenses that you do not yet know: the **passé simple** (a literary tense) and the **plus-que-parfait** (similar to the past perfect in English). Both are past tenses, as the context makes clear. You do not need to learn them; you need merely recognize their meaning to understand the story. Verbs whose meaning cannot be guessed have been glossed.

Le Petit Prince (extrait)*

J'ai de sérieuses raisons de croire que la planète d'où venait le petit prince est l'astéroïde B 612. Cet astéroïde n'a été aperçu° qu'une fois au télescope, en 1909, par un astronome turc.

découvert

Il avait fait alors une grande démonstration de sa découverte à un Congrès International d'Astronomie.

Mais personne ne l'avait cru à cause de son costume. Les grandes personnes° sont comme ça.

adultes

Heureusement pour la réputation de l'astéroïde B 612 un dictateur turc imposa° à son peuple, sous peine de mort,° s'habiller° à l'Européenne. L'astronome refit° sa démonstration en 1920, dans un habit très élégant. Et cette fois-ci tout le monde fut° de son avis.

a imposé / peine... *penalty of death* / *to dress*
a refait
a été

Si je vous ai raconté ces détails sur l'astéroïde B 612 et si je vous ai confié son numéro, c'est à cause des grandes personnes. Les grandes personnes aiment les chiffres.° Quand vous leur parlez d'un nouvel ami, elles ne vous questionnent jamais sur l'essentiel. Elles ne vous disent jamais: «Quel est le son de sa voix°? Quels sont les jeux qu'il préfère? Est-ce qu'il collectionne les papillons°?» Elles vous demandent: «Quel âge a-t-il? Combien a-t-il de

numbers
voice
butterflies

*Dessins réalisés par l'auteur, Antoine de Saint-Exupéry

frères? Combien pèse°-t-il? Combien gagne° son père?» Alors seulement elles croient le connaître. Si vous dites aux grandes personnes: «J'ai vu une belle maison en briques roses, avec des géraniums aux fenêtres et des colombes° sur le toit... » elles ne parviennent° pas à s'imaginer cette maison. Il faut leur dire: «J'ai vu une maison de cent mille francs.» Alors elles s'écrient: «Comme c'est joli!»

weighs / earns
doves
réussissent

COMPRÉHENSION

1. Comment s'appelle la planète d'où vient le Petit Prince?
2. C'est un astronome *français / turc / américain* qui a aperçu pour la première fois cet astéroïde au télescope en 1909.
3. Pourquoi est-ce que tout le monde a écouté cet astronome en 1920 et non en 1909? Qu'est-ce que l'astronome a changé?
4. Selon l'aviateur, qu'est-ce qui intéresse le plus les adultes? Qu'est-ce que les adultes ne voient pas quand ils font la connaissance de quelqu'un?
5. A votre avis, lesquelles des affirmations suivantes traduisent le mieux la pensée de l'auteur?
   a. Les hommes jugent les personnes et les choses d'après leur apparence, et non leur fond.
   b. Les hommes sont curieux de détails.
   c. Les hommes sont obsédés par les chiffres.

   Êtes-vous d'accord avec l'opinion de l'auteur? Justifiez votre réponse avec des exemples de la vie réelle.
6. Trouvez dans le texte les phrases qui indiquent l'ironie de l'auteur.

Par écrit

A. **Changements.** Écrivez une petite histoire de trois paragraphes pour décrire un changement qui a eu lieu (*has taken place*) dans votre ville ou dans votre région et qui vous intéresse personnellement. Voici des suggestions.

Paragraphe 1: *Une description du temps passé*
Quand j'étais jeune, j'aimais beaucoup...
Paragraphe 2: *Une description de la transformation*
Un jour, on a détruit (remplacé, enlevé, bâti, peint)...
Paragraphe 3: *Une description de votre attitude envers ce changement*
Cet événement m'a plu (*pleased*)/m'a déplu (*displeased*) parce que...

B. **Une lettre.** Vous écrivez à votre correspondant(e) français(e). Parlez-lui de votre dernier week-end. Dites ce que vous avez fait et donnez une courte description de chaque événement. Commencez par «**Cher (Chère)...** » Terminez par «**Amitiés**».

CHAPITRE ONZE

Les études en France

—Est-ce que tu viens au stade avec nous samedi?

—Non, je ne peux pas. J'ai une dissertation sur la valeur humaine pour mon cours de philo. Je crois que je vais passer mon week-end à faire de la recherche à la bibliothèque.

—Ça a l'air sérieux, ça! Bon, alors, à lundi et bon courage!

Étude de vocabulaire

L'enseignement en France

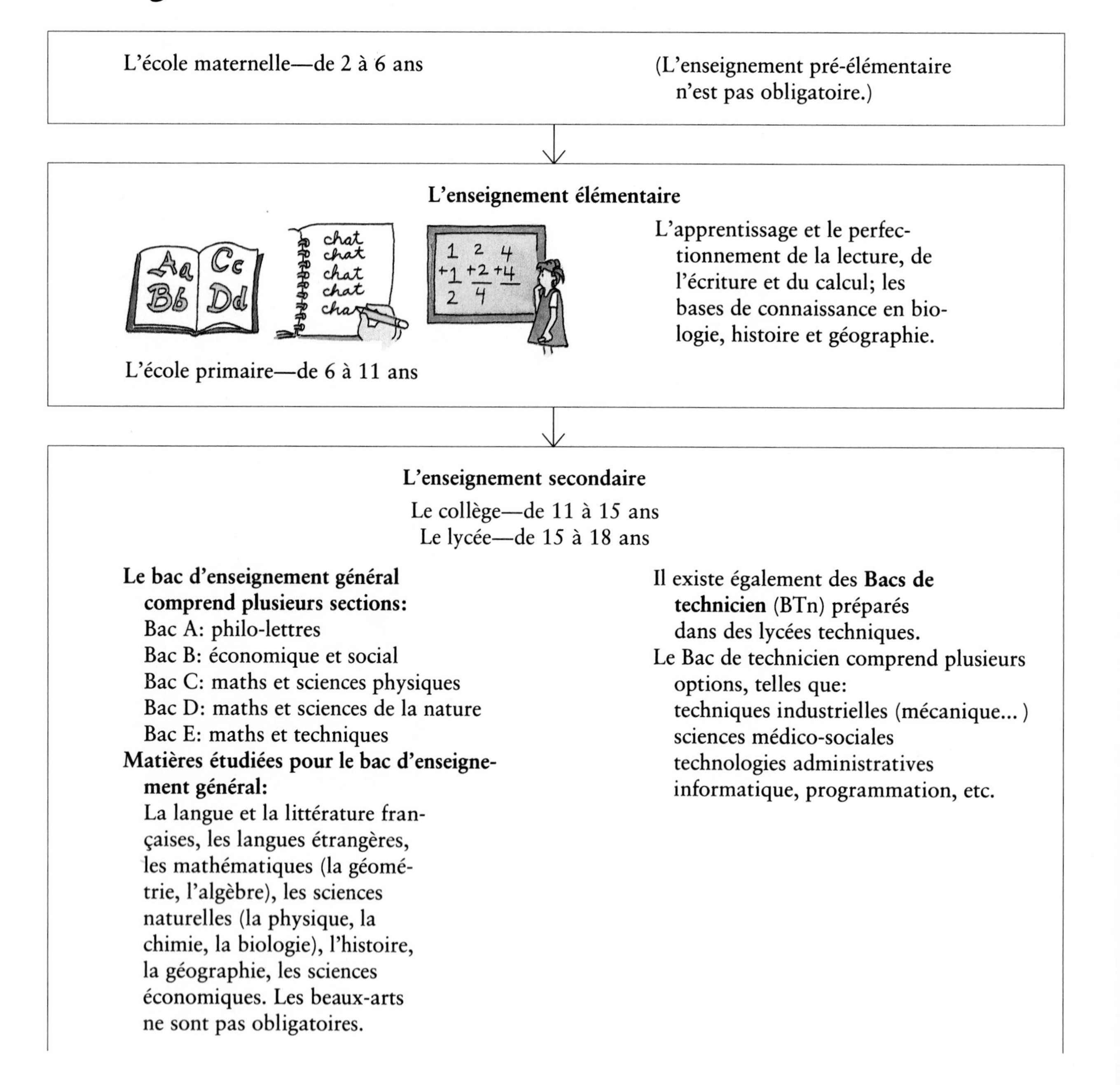

L'école maternelle—de 2 à 6 ans

(L'enseignement pré-élémentaire n'est pas obligatoire.)

L'enseignement élémentaire

L'école primaire—de 6 à 11 ans

L'apprentissage et le perfectionnement de la lecture, de l'écriture et du calcul; les bases de connaissance en biologie, histoire et géographie.

L'enseignement secondaire

Le collège—de 11 à 15 ans
Le lycée—de 15 à 18 ans

Le bac d'enseignement général comprend plusieurs sections:
- Bac A: philo-lettres
- Bac B: économique et social
- Bac C: maths et sciences physiques
- Bac D: maths et sciences de la nature
- Bac E: maths et techniques

Matières étudiées pour le bac d'enseignement général:
La langue et la littérature françaises, les langues étrangères, les mathématiques (la géométrie, l'algèbre), les sciences naturelles (la physique, la chimie, la biologie), l'histoire, la géographie, les sciences économiques. Les beaux-arts ne sont pas obligatoires.

Il existe également des **Bacs de technicien** (BTn) préparés dans des lycées techniques.

Le Bac de technicien comprend plusieurs options, telles que:
- techniques industrielles (mécanique...)
- sciences médico-sociales
- technologies administratives
- informatique, programmation, etc.

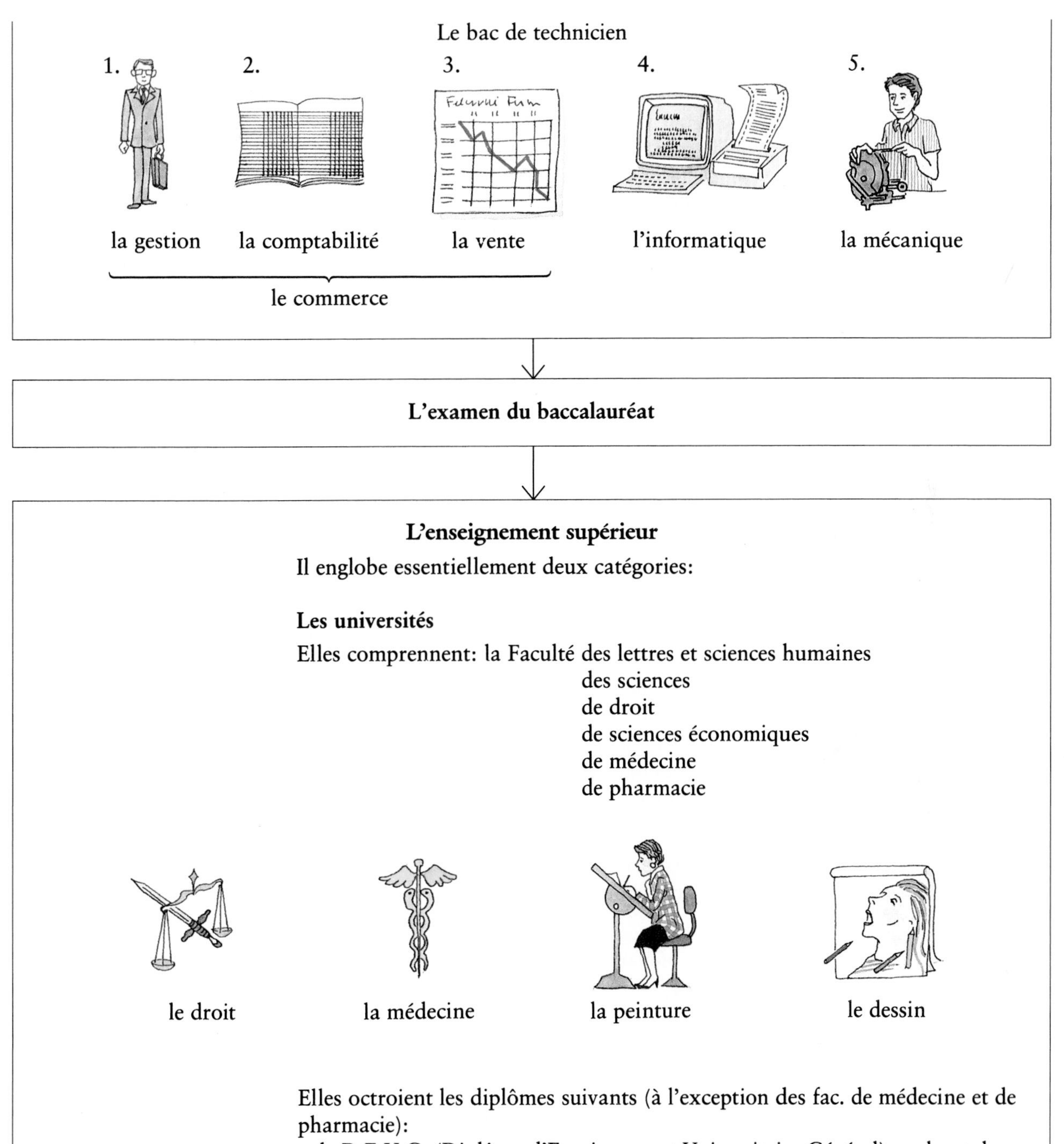

L'enseignement supérieur

Il englobe essentiellement deux catégories:

Les universités

Elles comprennent: la Faculté des lettres et sciences humaines
des sciences
de droit
de sciences économiques
de médecine
de pharmacie

Elles octroient les diplômes suivants (à l'exception des fac. de médecine et de pharmacie):

le D.E.U.G. (Diplôme d'Enseignement Universitaire Général), au bout de deux ans d'études
la Licence, au bout de trois ans d'études
la Maîtrise, au bout de quatre ou cinq ans d'études
le Doctorat

Les grandes écoles

Elles tiennent une place privilégiée dans l'enseignement supérieur. On y accède par concours (compétition), après le Bac. On peut y étudier:

le commerce
l'administration
le génie civil et militaire
les beaux-arts
la peinture
la sculpture
le dessin
la musique
l'art dramatique

A. Vive les études! Regardez bien le schéma et répondez aux questions suivantes.

1. A partir de quel âge peut-on envoyer les enfants à l'école en France? Est-ce que l'enseignement pré-élémentaire est obligatoire en France? Et aux États-Unis?
2. Quel âge ont les enfants à l'école primaire? Quelles matières étudient-ils?
3. Combien de cycles y a-t-il dans l'enseignement secondaire? Nommez-les. Quelles matières étudie-t-on? Lesquelles ne sont pas obligatoires?
4. Nommez deux catégories du baccalauréat. Quelles spécialités peut-on préparer dans chaque catégorie?
5. Quels sont les diplômes universitaires en France? Y a-t-il aussi trois diplômes dans les universités américaines?
6. Quels sont les choix des étudiants dans l'enseignement supérieur en France? Et aux États-Unis?

B. A l'École Victor Hugo. Lisez les paragraphes suivants et remplacez les tirets par les mots appropriés.

1. M. Sellier est instituteur (*teacher*) à l'École Victor Hugo. Les élèves de son cours préparatoire ont déjà appris l'alphabet. Aujourd'hui ils vont essayer d'identifier les lettres dans des mots très simples. C'est leur première leçon de _____.
2. Mme Dupont est institutrice à l'École Victor Hugo. Les élèves de son cours élémentaire 2e année écrivent des lettres au Père Noël. C'est une leçon d' _____.
3. Mlle Beaulieu enseigne (*teaches*) aussi à l'École Victor Hugo. Ses élèves font des opérations arithmétiques. Jean-Paul ne fait jamais d'erreurs. Il est très bon en _____.
4. Les élèves de l'école apprennent aussi des bases de _____ en biologie, histoire et géographie.

C. Identification. A partir des éléments donnés, nommez la discipline.

MODÈLE: la botanique, la zoologie, la génétique, l'embryologie,... → C'est la biologie.

1. l'étude des éléments, des composés, des catalyseurs
2. l'algèbre, la géométrie, le calcul infinitésimal
3. la littérature, l'histoire, la philosophie
4. l'art dramatique, la musique, le dessin, la sculpture, la peinture
5. les prix, les facteurs de production, le capitalisme, les besoins
6. la mémoire, l'utilisateur, le programmeur, le logiciel

D. Les universités à la loupe. Le magazine *Vos études* a réalisé une enquête sur les universités françaises pour la rentrée (le recommencement des cours). Par exemple, la ville de Grenoble a trois universités. Voici ce que le magazine dit de l'une d'elles: l'université de Grenoble 2.

1. Combien d'étudiants y a-t-il à l'université de Grenoble 2? de professeurs?
2. Quelles matières peut-on y étudier? Lesquelles ne peut-on pas étudier?
3. Avec quelles universités étrangères l'université de Grenoble 2 fait-elle des échanges? Où se trouvent-elles?
4. Que veut faire l'université pour aider les étudiants à réussir?
5. En quoi l'université de Grenoble 2 diffère-t-elle d'une université américaine?

UNIVERSITE DE GRENOBLE 2

47X - 38040 Grenoble cedex. Tél. : 76 82 55 65. Président : Bernard POUYET

L'UNIVERSITE EN CHIFFRES

12 982 étudiants dont 8 134 en premier cycle. 494 enseignants et 2 500 intervenants extérieurs. 125 chercheurs, 12 laboratoires dépendants des grands organismes et 3 recommandés par la Direction de la recherche du Ministère de l'Education Nationale. 14 400 M2 de superficie. Budget = 162 millions de francs. Disciplines : droit, économie, gestion, comptabilité, marketing, mathématiques appliquées et sciences sociales, psychologie, sciences de l'éducation, sociologie, philosophie, histoire, histoire de l'art, musique, urbanisme aménagement, études politiques, IUT.

L'OUVERTURE INTERNATIONALE

La liste des accords de Grenoble II avec les universités étrangères serait trop longue à donner tant ils sont variés. Retenons pour l'essentiel des échanges avec Fribourg (FRA), Martin Luther de Hall (RDA), Constantine (Algérie), Kingston Polytechnic et Sussex (GB), Rabat (Maroc), Madrid (Espagne), etc. Signalons un cursus intégré avec l'université de Sussex, des cours d'été en réciprocité avec Fribourg, sans oublier la vingtaine de projets ERASMUS déposés par Grenoble II... Nous reviendrons sur ces accords.

LES RELATIONS AVEC L'INDUSTRIE

Depuis cette année, l'université a mis en place une cellule « Université-entreprises » qui souhaite faire connaître, aux entreprises, à travers une plaquette, les apports des sciences sociales et le potentiel de l'université.

LES INNOVATIONS

Dans le 1er cycle, un seul Deug[a] rénové : AES. L'université a mis en place un observatoire des 1ers cycles qui ambitionne d'améliorer l'accueil, l'information, l'orientation et la réorientation des étudiants. Le Président Pouget souhaite développer l'évaluation précoce des étudiants dès[b] décembre. Enfin, la lutte contre l'échec passe par le renforcement des enseignements de base et la méthodologie (Travaux dirigés[c] et conférences de méthodes).

a. Diplôme d'Études Universitaires Générales
b. à partir de
c. Travaux... *Discussion sections*

E. Diplômés des Universités et des Grandes Écoles. Lisez les courtes autobiographies scolaires suivantes et remplacez les tirets par les mots appropriés. (Il y a des mots-clé dans les phrases.)

1. Je suis avocat (*lawyer*) parce que la science juridique m'intéresse beaucoup. Comment une société détermine-t-elle les règles (*rules*) de son organisation et de son fonctionnement? Comment trouve-t-on l'équilibre entre les droits de l'individu et les droits de la collectivité? C'est une question difficile, mais décisive. J'ai passé un bac en sciences économiques et j'ai fait mes études supérieures à la Faculté de ____ à Paris.
2. Je suis illustrateur de livres. J'ai passé mon bac en lettres et en arts et puis j'ai fait des études à l'École Normale Supérieure des Beaux-Arts où j'ai fait un peu de tout. J'aime bien sculpter des figurines et des statuettes, alors j'ai étudié la ____. J'aime bien peindre (*paint*) des portraits, alors j'ai fait de la ____. Mais dessiner au crayon, c'est ma passion. En fait (*In fact*), je crois que le ____ est la base de tous les arts.
3. Je fais à présent du marketing pour une grande compagnie aérienne. Au lycée, j'ai étudié la gestion et la vente. J'ai passé un bac en techniques commerciales et puis, après deux ans de préparation, j'ai commencé des études supérieures à H.E.C. (l'École des Hautes Études Commerciales) où j'ai continué à étudier le ____.

Maintenant, inventez une description de quelqu'un qui a déjà une profession. Vos camarades vont deviner ce qu'il (elle) a étudié.

Deux verbes pour parler de la vie universitaire

suivre (*to follow*)				**vivre** (*to live*)			
je	suis	nous	suivons	je	vis	nous	vivons
tu	suis	vous	suivez	tu	vis	vous	vivez
il, elle, on	suit	ils, elles	suivent	il, elle, on	vit	ils, elles	vivent
Past participle: suivi				*Past participle:* vécu			

Suivre and **vivre** are irregular verbs, and they have similar conjugations in the present tense. **Suivre un cours** means *to take a course.* **Poursuivre** (*to pursue*) is conjugated like **suivre.**

Combien de cours **suis-tu**?	*How many courses are you taking?*
Suivez mes conseils!	*Follow my advice!*
A-t-il **poursuivi** ses études de médecine?	*Did he pursue his medical studies?*

Mots-clés

Expressing to live: **vivre** *or* **habiter**

Use **vivre** to express *to be alive, to exist.* It also is used to express how one lives.

> Il **a vécu** jusqu'à 90 ans.
> Cette famille **vit** dans le luxe (la misère).

In general, use **habiter** to express *to reside.*

> Ses parents **habitent** Montpellier depuis dix ans.
> Nous **habitons** Rue de Rivoli.

Vivre is also used in certain idiomatic expressions.

Elle est **difficile** (**facile**) **à vivre.**	*She's hard (easy) to live with.*
Il est parti sans raison apparente, «pour **vivre ma vie**», a-t-il dit.	*He left without apparent reason, to "live my own life," as he put it.*

A. Vivez votre formation. Voici une publicité pour l'Institut des Petites et Moyennes Entreprises (P.M.E.) parue dans la revue *l'Étudiant.* Lisez-la et répondez aux questions suivantes.

1. Qu'est-ce que l'Institut des P.M.E.? Où se trouvent ses établissements? Qu'est-ce que les P.M.E.? Donnez un exemple de P.M.E. aux États-Unis.
2. A votre avis, que veut dire «vivre votre formation»? Avez-vous déjà vécu des expériences en entreprise?
3. Quelles sont les spécialités de l'Institut des P.M.E.? D'après vous, quels cours suivent les étudiants de l'Institut?
4. Quels sont les avantages et les inconvénients de voyager comme étudiant? Avez-vous envie de le faire? Pourquoi ou pourquoi pas? Où voulez-vous aller?

VIVEZ VOTRE FORMATION

La formation "Institut des Petites et Moyennes Entreprises", c'est çà : un enseignement souple, vivant, en plein dans la réalité du monde économique.

La Petite ou Moyenne Entreprise, c'est pour vous le moyen d'obtenir rapidement des responsabilités dans une équipe chaleureuse et dynamique.

Vivre votre formation, c'est libérer vos initiatives et votre créativité, vous exprimer, vous impliquer, voyager en étudiant : le marketing, la communication, la finance, le commerce international...

L'Institut des PME, c'est une École Supérieure de Commerce en 3 ans, 5 établissements en France, 1 à San Francisco, 750 étudiants...

INSTITUT DES PETITES ET MOYENNES ENTREPRISES

3, rue de Logelbach 75017 PARIS (1) 47.63.92.57 24, rue Léon-Frot 75011 PARIS (1) 43.79.45.29

B. Conversation

1. Quels cours suivez-vous ce semestre? Avez-vous suivi d'autres cours de langue avant ce cours-ci? Lesquels?
2. Avez-vous toujours vécu dans cette ville ou dans cette région? dans ce pays? Où viviez-vous avant de venir à l'université?
3. Allez-vous poursuivre des études pour votre maîtrise? pour votre doctorat? Si oui, dans quelle matière?

Le calendrier universitaire

OCTOBRE A MAI: On **suit les cours.** On **assiste aux conférences.** On **prépare les examens.** On **révise.** On **passe les examens.***

JUIN: On **réussit.** On obtient un diplôme.
(*ou*)
On **échoue.** On n'obtient pas de diplôme.

JUILLET: On part en vacances.
(*ou*)
On **prépare un deuxième examen.**

OCTOBRE: C'est **la rentrée** des classes. On **reprend** les études.
(*ou*)
On passe le deuxième examen et si on réussit, on continue ses études.

—Qu'est-ce que tu penses de mon CV?

© HENEBRY PHOTOGRAPHY

*Note that **passer un examen** means *to take an exam,* not *to pass an exam.* With exams, **réussir (à)** means *to pass.*

A. Conversation. Discutez des questions suivantes avec des camarades. Ensuite, déterminez qui dans la classe révise le plus; qui n'a jamais échoué à un examen; qui préfère les travaux pratiques* aux conférences.

1. Quel diplôme avez-vous déjà obtenu? 2. Révisez-vous beaucoup avant de passer un examen? Pourquoi? 3. A quelle occasion échouez-vous à un examen? 4. Réussissez-vous toujours aux examens finals? Pourquoi ou pourquoi pas? 5. Aimez-vous assister aux conférences? Lesquelles? 6. Préférez-vous les travaux pratiques?

B. Les études aux États-Unis. Imaginez qu'un étudiant français (une étudiante française) vient d'arriver dans votre université. En vous servant de (*Using*) l'information qui se trouve ici, présentez-lui le calendrier universitaire américain. Expliquez aussi en quoi il est différent du calendrier français.

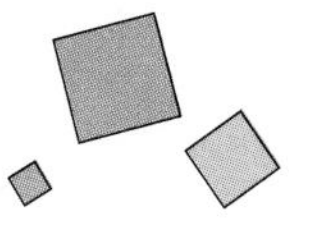

Étude de grammaire

39. Emphasizing and Clarifying: Stressed Pronouns

© BERYL GOLDBERG

L'après-bac

JEAN-PIERRE: Et **toi,** Françoise, qu'est-ce que tu vas faire après le bac?
FRANÇOISE: Je ne sais pas, j'y pense beaucoup, mais ça semble si compliqué!
JEAN-PIERRE: **Moi,** mon conseiller d'orientation m'a donné une tonne de brochures... c'est décourageant!
FRANÇOISE: Mon frère, **lui,** me dit que l'essentiel, c'est d'agir, de prendre des risques, de faire ce qu'on veut...
JEAN-PIERRE: Oui, mais le problème c'est que **moi,** je ne sais pas encore ce que je veux faire!

Les phrases suivantes sont des variantes des phrases dans le dialogue. Complétez ces phrases avec **moi, toi** ou **lui.**

Qu'est-ce que tu vas faire, _____?
Je ne sais pas, _____.
Mon frère, _____, me dit de prendre des risques.

***Les travaux pratiques** include work in the language lab or science lab, interaction with other students in small groups, and other similar individualized educational experiences.

A. Forms of Stressed Pronouns

These are the forms of the stressed pronouns. Stressed pronouns are used as objects of prepositions or for clarity or emphasis.

moi	*I, me*	**nous**	*we, us*
toi	*you*	**vous**	*you*
lui	*he, him, it*	**eux**	*they, them (m.)*
elle	*she, her, it*	**elles**	*they, them (f.)*
soi*	*oneself*		

Note that several of the stressed pronouns (**elle, nous, vous, elles**) are identical in form to subject pronouns.

B. Uses of Stressed Pronouns

Stressed pronouns are used in the following ways.

1. As objects of prepositions

Nous allons étudier chez **toi** ce soir.	*We're going to study at your house tonight.*
Après **vous**!	*After you!*
Après le match de football, tout le monde rentre chez **soi.***	*After the game, everybody goes back to his (her) (own) house.*

2. As part of compound subjects

Martine et elle† ont eu une bonne note à l'interrogation écrite.	*Martine and she got good grades on the written test.*
Claude et moi avons vécu un an en France.	*Claude and I spent a year living in France.*

3. With subject pronouns, to emphasize the subject

Et **lui,** a-t-il un doctorat?	He *has a doctorate?*
Eux, ils ont de la chance.	They *are lucky.*
Tu es brillant, **toi.**	You *are brilliant.*

When stressed pronouns emphasize the subject, they can be placed at the beginning or the end of the sentence.

---

*__Soi__ corresponds to the subjects **on, tout le monde,** and **chacun** (each one).

†In conversation, the plural subject is sometimes expressed in addition to the compound subject: **Martine et elle, elles ont eu une bonne note.**

4. After **ce** + **être**

—C'est **vous,** M. Lemaître?	—*Is it you, M. Lemaître?*
—Oui, c'est **moi.**	—*Yes, it's me (it is I).*
C'est **lui** qui faisait le cours de philosophie.	*It's he who was teaching the philosophy course.*

5. In sentences without verbs, such as one-word answers to questions and tag questions

—Qui a échoué à l'examen?	—*Who failed the exam?*
—Toi!	—*You!*
—As-tu pris mon livre?	—*Did you take my book?*
—Moi?	—*Me?*
—Nous allons au théâtre. **Et lui?**	—*We're going to the theatre. What about him?*

6. In combination with **même**(s) for emphasis

Préparent-ils la conférence **eux-mêmes**?	*Are they preparing the lecture by themselves?*
Allez-vous donner les résultats **vous-même**?	*Are you going to give the results yourself?*

MAINTENANT A VOUS

A. Bachotage. (*Cramming.*) Il neigeait hier soir et la bibliothèque était pleine de monde (*filled with people*). On préparait l'examen. Décrivez les étudiants.

MODÈLE: nous / occupé → Nous, nous étions occupés.

1. je / fatigué
2. tu / attentif
3. Robert et Jacques / bavard (*talkative*)
4. vous / sérieux
5. Mireille / travailleur
6. Chantal et Marie / paresseux
7. Marc / calme
8. Camille et Robert / content

B. Une dissertation* sur l'existentialisme. Le jour de l'examen est arrivé. Remplacez les mots en italique par des pronoms qui correspondent aux mots entre parenthèses.

1. Qui doit écrire une dissertation sur l'existentialisme? C'est *moi* qui dois le faire. (Jacques, Mireille et Chantal, Marc et son ami)
2. Vous faites la dissertation vous-même? Oui, *je* la fais moi-même. (elle, Marie, nous, tu, ton ami et toi)

***Dissertation** is the equivalent of a term paper. (A doctoral dissertation in France is **une thèse.**)

C. **Après l'interrogation** (***exam***). Les étudiants parlent entre eux. Complétez le dialogue avec les pronoms corrects.

CAMILLE: Claude et _____ avons choisi le sujet sur Jean-Paul Sartre. Et _____?
ROBERT: _____, j'ai fait comme _____.
CAMILLE: Et Jacques?
ROBERT: _____! Il a rendu feuille blanche (*blank page*).
CAMILLE: C'est _____ qui a rendu cette feuille blanche? Mais c'est _____ qui révise depuis dix jours!

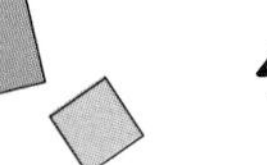

40. Expressing Actions: Pronominal Verbs

Une rencontre

DENIS: Madeleine! Comment vas-tu?
VÉRONIQUE: Vous **vous trompez,** je ne **m'appelle** pas Madeleine.
DENIS: Je **m'excuse,** je **me demande** si je ne vous ai pas déjà rencontrée...
VÉRONIQUE: Je ne **me souviens** pas de vous avoir rencontré. Mais ça ne fait rien... je **m'appelle** Véronique. Comment **vous appelez**-vous?

Retrouvez la phrase correcte dans le dialogue.

1. Vous avez tort, mon nom n'est pas Madeleine.
2. Pardon, je pense que je vous ai déjà rencontrée.
3. Mon nom est Véronique. Quel est votre nom?

Certain French verbs are always conjugated with two pronouns. Consequently, they are called pronominal verbs. The pronouns agree with the subject of the verb. **Se reposer** (*to rest*) and **s'amuser** (*to have fun*), for example, are pronominal verbs.

se reposer				s'amuser			
je	**me** repose	nous	**nous** reposons	je	**m'**amuse	nous	**nous** amusons
tu	**te** reposes	vous	**vous** reposez	tu	**t'**amuses	vous	**vous** amusez
il, elle, on	**se** repose	ils, elles	**se** reposent	il, elle, on	**s'**amuse	ils, elles	**s'**amusent

Est-ce que **tu t'amuses** en général chez tes grands-parents? — *Do you usually have fun at your grandparents' house?*
Oui, on **s'amuse** bien ensemble. — *Yes, we have a good time together.*

Nous **nous entendons** bien. — *We get along well.*

Note that the reflexive pronouns **me, te,** and **se** become **m', t',** and **s'** before a vowel or a nonaspirate **h.**

Common reflexive pronominal verbs include the following.

s'appeler	*to be named*
s'arrêter	*to stop*
se demander	*to wonder*
se détendre	*to relax*
se dépêcher	*to hurry*
s'excuser	*to excuse oneself*
s'entendre (avec)	*to get along (with)*
s'installer	*to settle down, settle in*
se rappeler	*to remember*
se souvenir (de)	*to remember*
se tromper	*to be wrong*
se trouver	*to be located*

L'autobus **s'arrête** devant l'université.	*The bus stops in front of the university.*
Où **se trouve** l'arrêt?	*Where is the bus stop?*
Jean-Luc ne **se souvient** pas de l'heure du départ.	*Jean-Luc doesn't remember what time it stops.*
Je vais **me dépêcher** pour arriver à l'heure.	*I'm going to hurry to arrive on time.*

Note that word order in the negative and infinitive form follows the usual word order for pronouns: the reflexive pronoun precedes the verb.

Commentaire culturel

L'enseignement hors de l'université. Le système d'enseignement français offre une grande variété de carrières pour les étudiants qui ne veulent pas suivre des études universitaires. Ainsi les élèves qui ne veulent pas préparer le baccalauréat peuvent suivre un programme d'apprentissage dans des lycées d'Enseignement professionnel et ils peuvent y obtenir un Certificat d'Aptitude Professionnelle (C.A.P.) en trois ans ou un Brevet d'Études Professionnelles (B.E.P.) en deux ans. Ces programmes permettent aux jeunes de commencer à travailler très vite dans des domaines tels que la mécanique, l'agriculture, le transport ou l'industrie en général.

Il existe aussi des études courtes pour ceux qui ont le baccalauréat et qui souhaitent obtenir un diplôme en deux ans. L'enseignement technique court est très populaire parmi les jeunes bacheliers, car ils y voient une solution pratique contre le chômage (*unemployment*). Il y a actuellement deux types de formation courte: les brevets de techniciens supérieurs (B.T.S.) obtenus dans un lycée technique et les diplômes universitaires de technologie (D.U.T.). Dans les deux cas, la sélection des candidats est sévère et les stages en entreprise font partie du programme. De plus, l'enseignement suit de très près l'évolution technologique et les besoins des entreprises. Les jeunes qui ont un B.T.S. ou un D.U.T. sont en général très appréciés des employeurs qui les jugent très qualifiés. Les étudiants ont aussi la possibilité de poursuivre leurs études après avoir obtenu leur diplôme, et les spécialisations post-B.T.S. ou D.U.T. se multiplient rapidement.

MAINTENANT A VOUS

A. Question de logique. Trouvez dans la colonne de droite la réponse logique aux phrases de la colonne de gauche.

1. Je dis que 37 et 21 font 68.
2. Vous êtes en retard!
3. Oh! J'ai oublié de frapper (*to knock*) avant d'entrer.
4. Francine et moi, nous ne nous disputons jamais.
5. Quelle est la date de la bataille de Waterloo?

a. Je ne me souviens pas de la date.
b. Tu te trompes!
c. Nous nous entendons bien.
d. Je m'excuse.
e. Il faut vous dépêcher.

B. Départ à la hâte. Il est l'heure de partir pour l'université mais vous avez un petit problème. Remplacez l'expression en italique par un des verbes pronominaux suivants: **se demander, se rappeler, se tromper, se trouver, se dépêcher.**

Où *est* mon sac à dos? Je ne *me souviens* plus où je l'ai mis. En plus, je dois *partir tout de suite,* je suis en retard. Mais je ne peux pas aller au cours sans cahier ni stylo. Je *veux savoir* si Jean-François l'a pris avec lui ce matin. Il peut facilement *faire une erreur* quand il est en retard.

C. Situations. Complétez les situations suivantes en vous servant d'un verbe pronominal.

1. Sylvie vient de trouver un endroit parfait pour passer l'après-midi. Que fait-elle? Elle ______ sous un arbre avec un bon livre. Elle a travaillé tout le week-end et aujourd'hui elle décide de ______.
2. Ma cousine Gertrude n'a pas changé son nom quand elle s'est mariée. Elle ______ toujours Martin.
3. Mon frère et moi, nous nous disputons tout le temps. Nous ne ______ pas du tout. Mes parents ______ parfois si nous appartenons (*belong*) à la même famille.

D. Réflexions sur la personnalité. Complétez les phrases suivantes. Puis comparez vos phrases avec celles de deux camarades de classe. Est-ce que vous vous ressemblez?

1. Je me dépêche quand...
2. Je ne m'entends pas du tout avec... parce que...
3. Quand je pense à mon enfance, je me rappelle surtout (*nom*).
4. Je me demande souvent si...
5. Quand je me trompe, je...
6. Pour me détendre, j'aime...

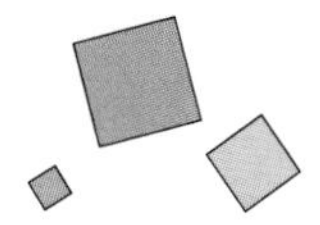

41. Giving Commands: Object Pronouns with the Imperative

© HENEBRY PHOTOGRAPHY

On conteste les examens!

MARYSE: La nécessité des examens...
JACQUES: N'**en parle** pas! C'est un mythe.
MARYSE: Qu'est-ce que tu suggères, à la place, **dis-moi.**
GILBERT: Oui, c'est ça, des suggestions: si tu en as, **parlons-en!**
JACQUES: Alors, **écoutez-les...** Vous n'avez jamais entendu parler du dossier de l'étudiant? Moi, je crois aux diplômes par examen de dossier!

Trouvez la phrase correcte dans le dialogue.

Ne parle pas de la nécessité des examens!
Dis-moi ce que tu suggères à la place des examens.
Alors, écoutez mes suggestions.

A. Negative Commands with Object Pronouns

The order of object pronouns in a negative command is the same as the order in declarative sentences. The pronouns precede the verb.

N'en parlons pas!	*Let's not talk about it!*
N'y pense pas!	*Don't think about it!*
Ne me donnez pas de cadeau!	*Don't give me a present!*
Ne leur dites pas que vous êtes venus!	*Don't tell them you came!*

B. Affirmative Commands with One Object Pronoun

In affirmative commands, object pronouns follow the verb and are attached with a hyphen. When **me** and **te** come at the end of the expression, they become **moi** and **toi.**

La lettre? **Écrivez-la!**	*The letter? Write it!*
Tes amis? **Écris-leur!**	*Your friends? Write to them!*
Voici du papier. **Prends-en!**	*Here's some paper. Take some!*
Parlez-moi des examens!	*Tell me about the exams!*

As you know, the final **-s** is dropped from the **tu** form of regular **-er** verbs and of **aller** to form the **tu** imperative: **Parle! Va, tout de suite!** However, to avoid pronunciation of two vowels together, the **-s** is *not* dropped before **y** or **en** in the affirmative imperative: **Parles‿*en*!** [parl zɑ̃], **Vas‿-*y*** [va zi]!

MAINTENANT A VOUS

A. Situations. Vous entendez des fragments de conversation. Imaginez la situation.

MODÈLE: N'y touche pas! → La mère de Jean vient de faire un gâteau. Jean essaie d'en manger un morceau.

1. Vas-y! 2. N'y touche pas! 3. Ne m'en donne pas! 4. Ne les regardez pas! 5. Donne-la-lui! 6. Ne lui parle pas si fort! 7. Montre-les-moi! 8. Ne le lui dis pas!

Mots-clés

Using pause fillers:

Eh bien,...	*Well . . .*
Voyons,...	*Let's see, . . .*
C'est-à-dire que...	*That is/I mean . . .*
Euh...	*Uhmm . . .*
Oui, mais...	*Yes, but . . .*
Alors,...	*So, then . . .*

B. Une carrière. Un ami (Une amie) vient de terminer ses études secondaires. Il (Elle) ne sait pas encore ce qu'il (elle) va faire l'année prochaine. Donnez-lui des conseils et justifiez vos réponses. Puis inversez les rôles.

MODÈLE: —Est-ce que je dois continuer mes études de langue?
—Eh bien, oui, continue-les. Alors tu peux beaucoup voyager. (Non, ne les continue pas. Tu veux faire médecine.)

1. Est-ce que je dois entrer à l'université?
2. Et si (*What if*) je faisais un long voyage en Amérique du Sud?
3. Est-ce que tu penses que je peux aller étudier dans une université française?
4. Est-ce que je dois étudier le droit?
5. Est-ce que je dois prendre des vacances?
6. Et si je suivais des cours du soir?
7. Est-ce que je dois préparer ma licence de français?

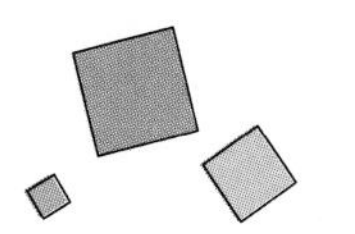

42. Saying *How* to Do Something: Adverbs

© FOURNIER

En cours de sociologie

SABINE: Je pense qu'en France, l'idéal du succès c'est **toujours** la «performance culturelle».

LE PROFESSEUR: Analysez **rapidement** pour nous les rapports entre cet idéal de la réussite et le système scolaire français.

SABINE: On peut dire que c'est à cause de cet idéal que l'enseignement français est **principalement** centré sur le diplôme.

JÉRÔME: Le diplôme, en France, est un moyen d'ascension sociale; les Français croient **beaucoup** à une élite diplômée.

LE PROFESSEUR: Dites-moi **maintenant** si vous pensez que cette attitude diffère **sensiblement** dans les autres pays. Aux États-Unis, par exemple...

1. Pour Sabine, est-ce que l'idéal du succès en France est parfois la «performance culturelle»?
2. Le professeur demande-t-il à Sabine d'analyser en détail les rapports entre cet idéal et le système scolaire?
3. Est-ce que Jérôme pense que les Français croient peu à une élite diplômée?

A. The Function and Formation of Adverbs

Adverbs (**les adverbes,** *m.*) modify a verb, an adjective, another adverb, or even a whole sentence: She learns *quickly*. He is *extremely* hardworking. They see each other *quite often. Afterward,* we'll go downtown. You have already learned a number of adverbs, such as **souvent, parfois, bien, mal, beaucoup, trop, peu, très, vite, d'abord, puis, ensuite, après,** and **enfin.** Many adverbs are formed from adjectives by adding the ending **-ment,** which often corresponds to *-ly* in English.

1. If the masculine form of the adjective ends in a vowel, **-ment** is usually added directly to the masculine adjective.

MASCULINE ADJECTIVE	ADVERB	
admirable (*m.* or *f.*)	**admirablement**	*admirably*
absolu	**absolument**	*absolutely*
poli	**poliment**	*politely*
vrai	**vraiment**	*truly, really*

2. If the masculine form of the adjective ends in a consonant, **-ment** is usually added to the feminine form of the adjective.

MASCULINE ADJECTIVE	FEMININE ADJECTIVE	ADVERB	
actif	active	**activement**	*actively*
franc	franche	**franchement**	*frankly*
heureux	heureuse	**heureusement**	*happily, fortunately*
lent	lente	**lentement**	*slowly*

3. If the masculine form of the adjective ends in **-ent** or **-ant,** the corresponding adverbs have the endings **-emment** and **-amment,** respectively. Note the identical pronunciation of the two endings: [a-mɑ̃].

MASCULINE ADJECTIVE	ADVERB	
différent	**différemment**	*differently*
évident	**évidemment**	*evidently, obviously*
constant	**constamment**	*constantly*
courant	**couramment**	*fluently*

4. **Brièvement** (*briefly*) and **gentiment** (*nicely*) are two irregular adverbs.

B. Position of Adverbs

When adverbs qualify adjectives or other adverbs, they usually precede them.

Elle est **très** intelligente.	*She is very intelligent.*
Il va **assez** souvent à la bibliothèque.	*He goes rather often to the library.*

When a verb is in the present or imperfect tense, the qualifying adverb usually follows it. In negative constructions, the adverb comes after **pas.**

Je travaille **lentement.**	*I work slowly.*
Elle voulait **absolument** devenir médecin.	*She wanted without question (absolutely) to become a doctor.*
Vous ne l'expliquez pas **bien.**	*You aren't explaining it well.*

Adverbs of time and place usually come at the beginning or end of a sentence.

Je vais à Lyon **demain.** (**Demain,** je vais à Lyon.)	*I'm going to Lyon tomorrow.*
Ici, on dîne tard. (On dîne tard **ici.**)	*Here we eat late.*
Êtes-vous allé voir Marie **hier**?	*Did you visit Marie yesterday?*

However, **bien, souvent, toujours,** and **déjà** are generally placed before the past participle in the **passé composé.**

Je n'ai pas **souvent** échoué aux examens.	*I have not often failed exams.*
Mon frère y a **toujours** réussi.	*My brother always passed them.*
Mon petit-fils a **déjà** commencé ses cours primaires.	*My grandson has already started elementary school.*

Other short adverbs also usually precede the past participle when the verb is in a compound form, coming after **pas** in a negative construction.

J'ai **trop** étudié ce semestre.	*I've studied too much this semester.*
Jean a **vite** répondu.	*Jean answered quickly.*
Elle ne m'a pas **beaucoup** parlé de cette conférence.	*She didn't say much to me about that lecture.*

Adverbs ending in **-ment** follow a verb in the present or imperfect tense, and usually follow the past participle when the verb is in the **passé composé.**

Tu parles **couramment** le français.	*You speak French fluently.*
Il était **vraiment** travailleur.	*He was really hardworking.*
Paul a répondu **intelligemment.**	*Paul responded intelligently.*

MAINTENANT A VOUS

A. Ressemblances. Donnez l'équivalent adverbial de chacun des adjectifs suivants.

1. heureux
2. actif
3. long
4. vrai
5. différent
6. rapide
7. certain
8. constant
9. absolu
10. admirable
11. poli
12. gentil
13. bref
14. intelligent

© THEODORE VOGEL / RAPHO

Un cours d'arabe pour des enfants d'immigrés en France

B. Carrières. Complétez les paragraphes suivants avec un adverbe logique.

1. Le linguiste. **Adverbes:** bien, ensuite, couramment, vite, bientôt, naturellement, évidemment, probablement.

Jean-Luc parle ____ l'anglais. Il a vécu aux États-Unis. Il est allé au lycée aux États-Unis et il a très ____ appris la langue pendant son séjour. ____, à l'université il a choisi la section langues étrangères. Il va ____ passer sa licence d'anglais. ____, il doit ____ choisir entre la recherche (*research*) et l'enseignement. Ses parents sont professeurs et je pense qu'il va ____ choisir de devenir professeur.

2. Le médecin. **Adverbes:** exactement, beaucoup, absolument, fréquemment, seulement, constamment, souvent, bien, très.

Marie-Hélène veut ____ devenir médecin. Elle travaille ____ pour y arriver: en général, le matin, elle arrive à l'hôpital à six heures ____ et elle y reste ____ jusqu'à neuf heures du soir. Dans la journée, elle travaille ____ et prend ____ quinze minutes pour déjeuner. ____, elle est fatiguée le soir. Mais je pense qu'elle va réussir parce qu'elle est ____ travailleuse et ambitieuse.

C. Opinions et habitudes. Posez les questions à un(e) camarade. Dans sa réponse il (elle) doit employer des adverbes.

1. A ton avis, doit-on beaucoup travailler pour réussir?
2. Comment doit-on parler à un professeur en classe?
3. Est-ce que l'argent fait le bonheur (*happiness*)?
4. Est-ce que l'amitié est plus importante que la réussite (*success*)?
5. Aimes-tu faire de longs voyages?

Situation

Dédale* administratif

Contexte *Martin est un étudiant californien qui arrive à Nice pour y étudier. Il doit faire beaucoup de démarches° pour s'inscrire à la Faculté des lettres. Didier, son voisin à la résidence universitaire, l'aide dans ses démarches.*

Objectif *Martin fait une démarche administrative.*

(démarches°: (*necessary*) *steps*)

MARTIN: Écoute, ça te gêne de° me donner un coup de main° avec ma fiche° d'inscription?
DIDIER: Pas du tout.
MARTIN: Eh bien, est-ce que je dois cotiser° à la Sécurité Sociale?
DIDIER: Oui, mais comme° tu es étranger, tu vas d'abord avoir besoin d'une attestation du Ministère des Affaires étrangères.
MARTIN: D'accord. Et à la mutuelle?†
DIDIER: Oh oui, la mutuelle complète ton assurance° avec la Sécurité Sociale. Avec les deux, tu es couvert° à 100 pour cent.
MARTIN: Est-ce que tu me recommandes de cotiser à une association sportive?
DIDIER: Absolument! Ça te permet de faire du basket, du volley, du tennis, du ski, du judo et de la danse pour presque° rien.
MARTIN: Voilà, alors, j'ai tout rempli.° Je dois payer 1 250 francs pour le semestre.
DIDIER: Oui, mais tu n'as pas encore fini. Maintenant, tu dois aller au secrétariat pour choisir tes heures de cours. On va aussi te donner un bulletin de vote° pour le conseil des étudiants° et une carte d'étudiant.
MARTIN: Tu sais, j'ai l'impression d'être en train de° passer un examen...

ça... *is it a bother for you* / me... m'aider / *form*
subscribe
since
insurance
covered
almost
filled out
bulletin... *voting paper* / conseil... *student council*
en... *in the process of*

VARIATIONS

1. **Improvisez!** Expliquez à un étudiant français (une étudiante française) comment obtenir son inscription dans votre université. Jouez la scène.

*Maze

†**La Mutuelle Nationale des Étudiants de France** is a health and hospitalization insurance program available to all students in France eighteen or older.

2. Rejouez le dialogue avec ces variations.

- Vous choisissez les cours que vous préférez.
- Il est aussi nécessaire de passer une visite médicale.
- Vous avez une assurance internationale; vous n'avez besoin de cotiser ni à la Sécurité Sociale ni à la mutuelle.

A propos

Comment féliciter quelqu'un

Félicitations! (*Congratulations!*)
Formidable!
Extra!
Super!
Bravo!
Génial!

Je suis content(e) pour vous (toi).
Je suis fier (fière) de vous (toi).
On doit fêter (*to celebrate*) cette bonne nouvelle!

Comment consoler quelqu'un

Quel dommage! (*Too bad!*)
Quelle mauvaise nouvelle!
Je suis désolé(e) pour vous (toi).
Ne vous en faites pas./Ne t'en fais pas. (*Don't worry.*)
Ça ne fait rien! (*That doesn't matter.*)

Jeu de rôles. Avec un(e) camarade, jouez les scènes suivantes. Utilisez les expressions de l'*A propos* et créez des conversations.

1. Une amie vous appelle pour vous dire qu'elle a réussi à son examen de chimie, un examen très difficile. Vous décidez ensemble comment vous allez fêter ce succès.
2. Un ami avec qui vous suivez un cours vous téléphone pour vous dire qu'il est allé voir le professeur et qu'il a vu votre examen. Vous avez reçu (*received*) une très mauvaise note.

Suggestions: C'était sûrement un examen très difficile.
Tu peux le repasser plus tard.
Je vais t'aider à le préparer.
Tu vas contester les résultats? C'était sûrement une erreur!

C'est génial!

Commentaire culturel

Les professeurs en France. En France, les professeurs sont des fonctionnaires nommés et payés par le Ministère de l'Éducation. Ils doivent leurs promotions à des inspecteurs généraux du gouvernement, eux aussi nommés par le Ministère. Ces inspecteurs visitent périodiquement les salles de classe et donnent aux professeurs une note pédagogique.

Quels sont les avantages d'être professeur? Tout d'abord, le fait d'être fonctionnaire, employé(e) du gouvernement, donne aux professeurs la sécurité de l'emploi. Leur salaire, modeste au début, va doubler en fin de carrière, plus ou moins rapidement, selon leurs notes et leurs promotions. Ensuite, les professeurs ne travaillent que trente-cinq semaines par an et ils ont la possibilité de faire une partie de leur travail chez eux. Enfin, ils bénéficient d'une assurance automobile et médicale et peuvent faire leurs achats dans des coopératives qui leur sont exclusivement réservées.

Mais, bien sûr, tout n'est pas rose dans la vie des professeurs. Souvent leur formation est mal adaptée à l'enseignement actuel. Les classes sont souvent surchargées. De plus, ils sont fréquemment nommés loin de leur lieu d'habitation et sont obligés de passer beaucoup de temps dans les transports en commun. Enfin, les professeurs sont souvent au centre des problèmes sociaux. Tout cela contribue à une tension permanente, qui est, de nos jours, la maladie des professeurs par excellence.

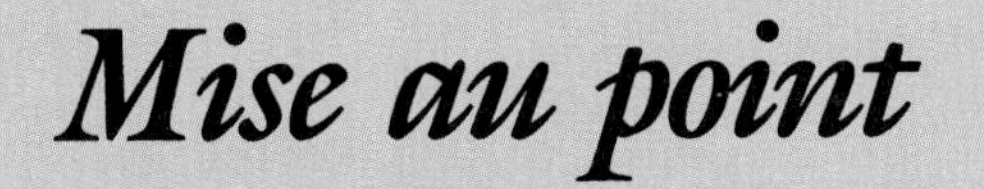

Mise au point

A. Le rôle de l'université. Quel est le rôle de l'université? Choisissez les quatre rôles les plus importants. Classez-les dans l'ordre de vos préférences.

L'université est ____.

1. ____ un centre de promotion sociale
2. ____ un centre de recherche scientifique
3. ____ un centre de formation professionnelle
4. ____ un centre de développement personnel
5. ____ une institution qui va permettre de gagner de l'argent

Qui n'est pas d'accord avec vous? Discutez des différents rôles et essayez de définir la fonction principale d'une université aux États-Unis.

B. Tête-à-tête. Posez les questions suivantes à un(e) camarade. Ensuite, faites une observation intéressante sur votre camarade.

1. T'entends-tu bien avec tes amis? avec tes professeurs? avec tes parents? (Si votre camarade ne s'entend pas bien avec eux, demandez-lui pourquoi.)
2. Est-ce que tu te rappelles pourquoi tu as décidé d'aller à l'université? d'étudier le français? Est-ce que tes premières raisons sont toujours valables?
3. Viens-tu de rencontrer une personne qui t'a beaucoup impressionné(e)? Comment s'appelle cette personne? De quels traits physiques (yeux, visage, cheveux, taille, etc.) te souviens-tu?
4. Veux-tu te marier (*to get married*) un jour? à quel âge? Où veux-tu t'installer avec ton mari (ta femme)?

C. Qu'en pensez-vous? Posez les questions suivantes à des camarades. Ils vont répondre en utilisant des adverbes. **Suggestions:** vite, tranquillement, admirablement, diligemment, heureusement, malheureusement, constamment, couramment, évidemment, franchement, poliment, absolument, lentement, souvent, intelligemment, brièvement, gentiment...

MODÈLE: Qu'est-ce qu'on doit faire pour avoir de bonnes notes? →
On doit étudier constamment.
On doit travailler intelligemment.

1. Qu'est-ce qu'on doit faire pour être bon professeur? 2. Qu'est-ce qu'on doit faire pour devenir président(e) des États-Unis? 3. Qu'est-ce qu'on doit faire pour courir dans un marathon? 4. Qu'est-ce qu'on doit faire pour devenir riche? 5. Qu'est-ce qu'on doit faire pour avoir de bons rapports (*a good relationship*) avec une autre personne?

Interactions

In this chapter, you practiced how to specify the people and objects you are discussing and how to qualify actions. Act out the following situations, using the vocabulary and structures from this chapter.

1. **Les études en Amérique.** Explain the American educational system to a French exchange student (your partner). Talk about the ages when one begins school and goes to high school, and about the possibilities after high school. She or he will ask you questions. You may wish to ask the exchange student some questions, too, about the French system.
2. **Sois sérieux (sérieuse).** A younger brother or sister (your partner) is talking about finding a job. Give him or her advice on preparing at the university and getting ready for interviews. She or he will ask you questions to get more information.

Vocabulaire

Verbes

aider (quelqu'un à faire quelque chose) to help (someone do something)
assister à to attend (*a class, a lecture, etc.*)
échouer (**à**) to fail
enseigner to teach
montrer to show
passer to take (*an exam*)
poursuivre to pursue
remplir to fill (in, up, out)
reprendre to take again; to continue; to start again
réviser to review (*for a test*)
suivre to follow; to take (*a course*)
vivre to live

Verbes pronominaux

s'amuser (**à**) to have fun
s'appeler to be named
s'arrêter to stop
se demander to wonder
se détendre to relax
se dépêcher to hurry
s'excuser to excuse oneself
s'entendre (**avec**) to get along (with)
s'installer to settle down, settle in
se rappeler to remember
se reposer to rest
se souvenir (**de**) to remember
se tromper to be wrong
se trouver to be situated, found

Substantifs

l'apprentissage (*m.*) apprenticeship, learning
le baccalauréat (**le bac**) French secondary school program and diploma
les beaux-arts (*m.*) fine arts
le calcul arithmetic; computation
le collège first cycle of secondary school in France
la comptabilité accounting
la conférence lecture; conference
la connaissance knowledge
le dessin drawing
le droit law
l'école maternelle (*f.*) preschool, kindergarten
l'école primaire (*f.*) elementary school
l'écriture (*f.*) writing; handwriting
l'élève (*m., f.*) pupil
l'enseignement (*m.*) teaching (*profession*)
le génie civil engineering
la gestion business management
l'informatique (*f.*) computer science; data processing
l'instituteur (**-trice**) teacher (*preschool and elementary levels*)
la lecture reading; reading material
la licence bachelor's degree (*in France*)
le lycée second cycle of French secondary school
la maîtrise master's degree

la mécanique mechanical engineering
la note grade
la peinture painting
la rentrée return to school/work in September
les sciences (*f.*) **économiques** economics
le secrétariat administrative center; office
la vente sales

Substantifs apparentés

l'administration (*f.*), **l'algèbre** (*f.*), **l'art dramatique** (*m.*), **le commerce, le cycle, le diplôme, le doctorat, la géométrie, la médecine, le perfectionnement, la sculpture**

Adjectifs

absolu(**e**) absolute
bref (**brève**) brief, short
certain(**e**) certain
constant(**e**) constant
lent(**e**) slow
malheureux (**-euse**) unhappy
obligatoire required
poli(**e**) polite
rapide rapid, fast
secondaire secondary
supérieur(**e**) graduate (*studies*); superior

Adverbes

brièvement briefly
couramment fluently
gentiment kindly

Pronoms disjoints

moi, toi, lui, elle, soi, nous, vous, eux, elles

Mots divers

avant de (+ *inf.*) before (*doing something*)
comme since

Expressions utiles

Ça ne fait rien.	*That doesn't matter.*
Je suis content(e)/désolé(e) pour vous.	*I'm happy / sorry for you.*
Quel dommage!	*That's too bad!*
Quelle mauvaise nouvelle!	*What bad news!*

INTERMÈDE 11

Lecture

AVANT DE LIRE

Review of general reading strategies: The following tasks give you the opportunity to review and put into practice the most important general reading strategies you have learned in Chapters 1–10.

- Anticipating content: Before you read, look at the title, photographs, photo caption, and lead lines. What do you expect the reading to deal with? As you read, confirm or modify your assumptions.
- Skimming for the gist: Skim the article, taking just a few minutes, then try to sum up the main points in a general way. What is it about? At this stage, do not focus on details.
- Scanning for specific information: Who is Lionel Dubreuil (age, nationality, background, current occupation)? Briefly sum up what Lionel Dubreuil says about himself and about the topic of the article.

Use these three strategies whenever you approach a passage in a foreign language, and you will probably find that your first reading will be much clearer and easier.

IAC-IEMI: LES CLEFS DE LA REUSSITE

SEQUOIA PRESSE

Lionel Dubreuil, Alain Hermelin et Laurent Daudenthun.

Une réussite «tranquille» fondée sur de solides connaissances, une recette IPSA.

Pour réussir, pas de recette miracle,
plutôt un état d'esprit.
Et si la chance ne s'apprend pas dans une école,
la motivation et le réalisme si.
Lionel Dubreuil et Laurent Daudenthun,
deux anciens élèves du groupe IPSA
en sont la preuve.

« J'avais une envie, apprendre les rouages[a] du commerce et fonder une entreprise ». A 24 ans, Lionel Dubreuil, jeune chef d'entreprise récemment diplômé de l'IAC (Institut européen de formation aux affaires et à la conduite des entreprises) sait où il va. Pour lui, l'entreprise n'est pas le fruit d'un hasard[b] ou d'un heureux concours[c] de circonstances mais le résultat d'un savoir[d] parvenu à maturité. « La grande différence entre les études et la vie d'une entreprise, explique-t-il, c'est que l'on n'a plus le droit[e] à l'erreur. Lorsqu'on rate une affaire, c'est fini. »

Pour Lionel Dubreuil, tout commence en 1984. Il entre à l'IAC, après concours, sur recommandation d'une entreprise où il avait effectué un stage[f] « une école sérieuse, garantie de résultats ». Et en choisissant la section commerce international, il avait déjà une idée derrière la tête : « Créer une entreprise avec comme fondement un management réellement international ». Durant la première année d'études, Lionel Dubreuil se renseigne, « galère » à la recherche d'un « bon plan ». Il visite les foires et expositions internationales au Portugal, en France... C'est de là qu'il tirera une certitude : utiliser la synergie que peut apporter la coopération avec l'étranger. C'est désormais[g] chose faite.

Aujourd'hui, son entreprise BDP (alias « Bébé, Dodo, Poussette » pour les intimes) diffuse trois types de produits et va tranquillement sur ses 5 millions de francs de chiffre d'affaires pour 1988. Au catalogue : des poussettes[h] ergonomiques, importées de Corée et conçues sur les spécifications de Lionel Dubreuil, des produits de parapuériculture[i] (lit, drap, couette... pour enfant) et le prêt-à-porter.

Stratégie de base : « Ne rien avoir, une stratégie que j'ai apprise à l'IPSA », confie Lionel Dubreuil. « Si vous n'avez rien, vous n'avez également rien à perdre. Vous pouvez prendre davantage[j] de risques sur le produit lui-même. » Exemples : pas de voiture de société[k] ni d'investissements lourds pour l'entreprise. « Avec 50 000 francs, poursuit Lionel Dubreuil, je peux importer 100 poussettes supplémentaires. Je préfère investir dans l'innovation. »

Second principe : « De l'ambition sans prétention », comme il aime à le souligner[l] lui-même. « Pas de bluff, pas de superflu. L'important, c'est le travail, sur le terrain. Ca aussi, c'est une grande leçon que je tiens d'Alain Hermelin, le président du groupe IPSA. »

D.H.

a. *workings*
b. *chance*
c. *contest*
d. *knowledge*
e. *right*
f. effectué... *finished a program*
g. *henceforth*
h. *baby carriages*
i. *baby care*
j. *more*
k. *company*
l. *emphasize*

COMPRÉHENSION

1. Que fait Lionel Dubreuil? Dans quel domaine se spécialise-t-il? Où a-t-il appris sa spécialisation? Que pense-t-il de cette école?
2. D'après lui, quel est le secret de son succès?
3. Quels adjectifs, à votre avis, décrivent le mieux la personnalité de Dubreuil?
4. D'après vous, qu'est-ce qu'il faut faire (ou ne pas faire) pour réussir dans la carrière que vous avez choisie?

Par écrit

A. Diplômes et débouchés. (*job openings*) Vous allez consulter un conseiller (une conseillère) pour discuter des carrières possibles. Pour être bien préparé(e), écrivez quelques paragraphes sur le rapport entre les études que vous faites maintenant et la profession que vous espérez exercer après vos études à l'université. Utilisez les questions suivantes comme guide.

Étudiez-vous une matière qui va vous permettre de trouver du travail? L'avez-vous choisie pour cette raison? Pourquoi l'avez-vous choisie? Êtes-vous content(e) de votre choix? Connaissez-vous quelqu'un qui a un diplôme dans une certaine discipline mais qui travaille dans un domaine très différent (par exemple, quelqu'un qui a un M.A. en beaux-arts mais qui enseigne le français)? Quelle est la meilleure (*best*) discipline quand on veut pouvoir trouver du travail?

B. Voici quelques petites annonces pour jeunes diplômés, publiées dans la revue *l'Etudiant*. Imaginez que vous êtes un étudiant français (une étudiante française) qui vient de finir ses études. Choisissez un des postes, ou inventez un autre poste, puis préparez une lettre à envoyer à l'Agence Nationale pour l'emploi. Expliquez quelles études vous avez faites, où vous avez étudié et quels diplômes vous avez obtenus. Dans votre lettre, vous parlez aussi de vos qualités. Donnez-en trois et utilisez des adverbes pour les décrire. (Voir *Avant d'écrire* à la page 299.)

Suggestions: Monsieur, Madame,
Je vous écris pour le poste de...
J'ai étudié...
J'ai un diplôme de...
Je suis une personne...
Dans l'attente d'une réponse, veuillez accepter, Monsieur, Madame, l'expression de mes sentiments distingués.

1 poste

SCULPTEUR OU PLASTICIEN VOLUME CADRE

Lieu de travail : Paris 9e.
Fonction : sculpture minutieuse sur figurines en cire. Formation : diplôme des Beaux-Arts ou BTS plasticien volume. Rémunération : 8 000 F.
Réf. 101 976 T

40 postes

ANALYSTES-PROGRAMMEURS CADRES

Activité entreprise : constructeur de système navigation (dimension européenne). Lieu de travail : France, Eragny-Pontoise. Fonction : services centraux, étude de produits nouveaux et technologie nouvelle. Formation : maîtrise informatique. Débutants ou expérimentés (1re expérience). Rémunération : 130 000 F/an et plus.
Réf. 39 724 D

1 poste

DIRECTEUR COMMERCIAL FREINAGE CADRE

Activité entreprise : équipementier automobile, dimension internationale. Lieu de travail : Saint-Ouen. Fonction : direction commerciale, pénétration RFA-GB. Anglais courant. Allemand si possible. Formation : ingénieur diplôme grande école. 1re expérience. Rémunération : 500 000 F/an.
Réf. 98 189 C

Adresser curriculum vitae et lettre manuscrite à :

ANPE

AGENCE NATIONALE POUR L'EMPLOI PARIS
CADRES 1
12, rue Blanche, 75436 Paris cedex 09,
tél. 42.85.44.40 poste 72

CHAPITRE DOUZE

La vie de tous les jours

—Alexandre et toi, vous pensez vous marier bientôt?
—Oui, l'été prochain.
—Ça fait longtemps que vous vous connaissez?
—Bientôt deux ans. Nous nous sommes rencontrés chez des amis et nous ne nous sommes plus quittés. Le vrai coup de foudre, quoi!

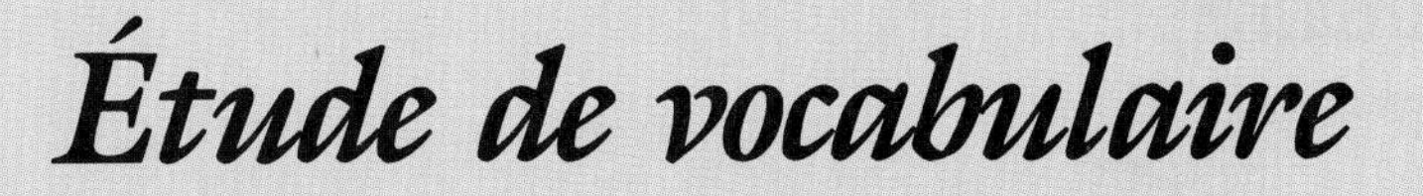

Étude de vocabulaire

L'amour et le mariage

Ils se rencontrent.

Les amoureux: le coup de foudre*

Ils se marient.

Le couple: le voyage de noces

Mais ils ne s'entendent pas toujours.

Les nouveaux mariés: parfois, ils se disputent.

A. Ressemblances. Quels verbes de la colonne de droite correspondent aux différentes étapes (*stages*) d'un mariage?

1. la rencontre	a. Ils vont en voyage de noces.
2. le coup de foudre	b. Ils se marient.
3. les rendez-vous	c. Ils sortent ensemble.
4. les fiançailles (*engagement*)	d. Ils tombent amoureux. (*They fall in love.*)
5. la cérémonie	e. Ils se rencontrent.
6. le premier voyage	f. Ils s'installent.
7. l'installation (*setting up house*)	g. Ils se fiancent.

B. Seul ou ensemble? D'après vous, quels sont les avantages et les inconvénients ____? **Mots utiles:** être indépendant, solitaire, en sécurité, responsable, irresponsable, bourgeois, ennuyeux (*boring*), patient, libre...

1. des fiançailles 2. du mariage 3. du célibat (*single life*) 4. du divorce

C. Conversation. Posez les questions suivantes à un(e) camarade.

1. Sors-tu souvent seul(e)? avec un(e) ami(e)? avec d'autres couples?
2. Es-tu déjà tombé(e) amoureux (amoureuse)? Tombes-tu souvent amoureux (amoureuse)?
3. Est-ce que le coup de foudre est une réalité? En as-tu fait l'expérience?
4. Est-ce que tout le monde doit se marier? Pourquoi? Pourquoi pas? A quel âge?

---

*Literally, *flash of lightning* = *love at first sight.*

Le corps humain

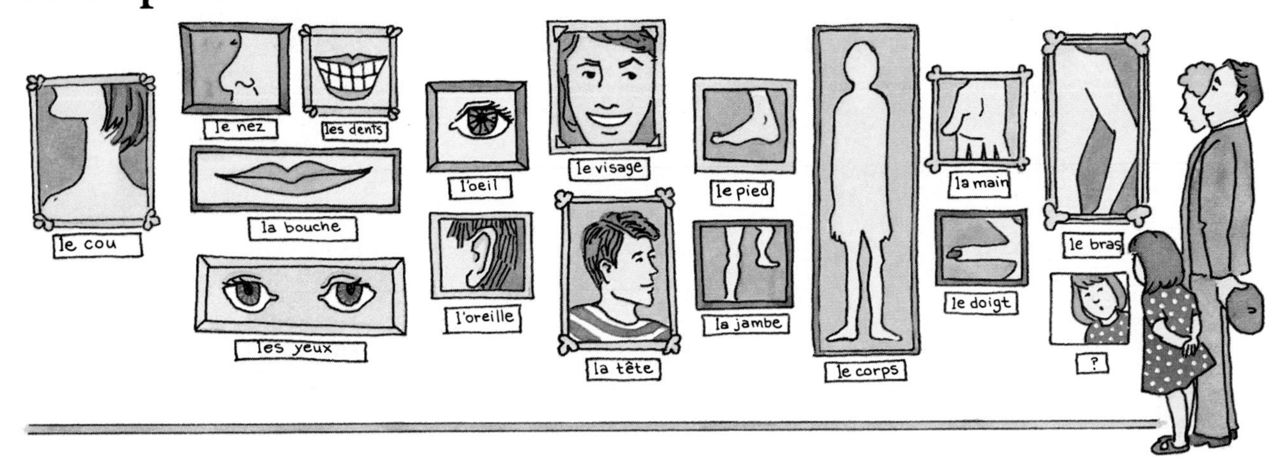

A. Exercice d'imagination. Où ont-ils mal? (*Where do they hurt?*) Discutez-en avec un(e) camarade.

MODÈLE: Il y a beaucoup de bruit chez Martine. → Elle a mal à la tête.

1. Vous portez des paquets très lourds (*heavy*). 2. Les nouvelles chaussures d'Henri-Pierre sont trop petites. 3. J'ai mangé trop de chocolat. 4. Vous apprenez à jouer de la guitare. 5. Patricia a marché très longtemps. 6. La cravate de Patrice est trop serrée (*tight*). 7. Ils font du ski et il y a beaucoup de soleil. 8. Il fait extrêmement froid dehors (*outside*) et vous n'avez pas de gants. 9. Claudine va chez le dentiste.

B. Devinettes. Pensez à une partie du corps et donnez-en une définition au reste de la classe. Vos camarades vont deviner de quelle partie il s'agit.

MODÈLE: Vous en avez deux. C'est la partie du corps qui porte un pantalon. → les jambes

La vie quotidienne*

Ils se réveillent et ils se lèvent.

Ils se brossent les dents.

Elle se maquille.

Ils se peignent.

*Everyday life

Ils s'habillent.

Ils s'en vont.

Ils se couchent.

Ils s'endorment.

A. Et votre journée? Décrivez-la. Employez le vocabulaire du dessin.

MODÈLE: A _____ heures, je me _____. → A sept heures, je me réveille.

B. Habitudes quotidiennes. Dites dans quelles circonstances on utilise les objets suivants.

1. un réveil 2. une brosse à dents 3. des vêtements 4. un fauteuil confortable 5. un lit 6. un peigne 7. du rouge à lèvres 8. du dentifrice

Étude de grammaire

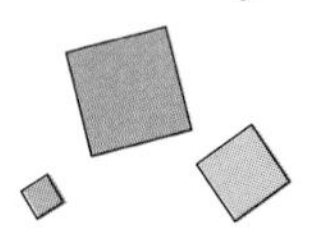

43. Reporting Everyday Events: Pronominal Verbs (continued)

Une rencontre

LAURENT: Tu **t'en vas**?
PAULINE: Oui, il fait beau et je **m'ennuie** ici. Je vais **me promener** au bord du lac. Tu viens?
LAURENT: Non, je ne peux pas, j'ai beaucoup de travail.
PAULINE: Oh, tu exagères, allez, on va **s'amuser** un peu!
LAURENT: Une autre fois. Si je **m'arrête** maintenant, je ne vais pas avoir le courage de finir plus tard.

1. Qui sort?
2. Est-ce que Pauline s'amuse?
3. Que va-t-elle faire?
4. Est-ce que Laurent se repose?
5. Est-ce qu'il veut s'arrêter de travailler?

A. Reflexive Pronominal Verbs

In reflexive constructions, the action of the verb "reflects back" to the subject: *The child dressed* ***himself.*** *Did you hurt* ***yourself?*** *She talks to* ***herself.*** In these examples, the subject and the object are the same person. The reflexive pronouns in boldface can be either direct object pronouns (as in the first two example sentences) or indirect object pronouns (as in the last sentence). Common reflexive pronominal verbs include the following.

se baigner *to bathe; to swim*
se brosser *to brush*
se coucher *to go to bed*
s'habiller *to get dressed*
se laver *to wash oneself*
se lever *to get up*
se maquiller *to put on makeup*
se peigner *to comb one's hair*
se raser *to shave*
se regarder *to look at oneself*
se réveiller *to wake up*

Toute la famille **se réveille** à six heures.	*The whole family wakes up at six o'clock.*
Pierre **se douche** et **se rase** pendant que Jacqueline **se maquille** et **se peigne.**	*Pierre showers and shaves while Jacqueline combs her hair and puts on makeup.*

Most reflexive pronominal verbs can also be used nonreflexively.

Le bruit **réveille** tout le monde.	*The noise wakes up everyone.*
Pierre **lave** la voiture.	*Pierre is washing his car.*

B. Reflexive Pronominal Verbs with Two Objects

Some reflexive pronominal verbs can have two objects, one direct and one indirect. This frequently occurs with the verbs **se brosser** and **se laver** plus a part of the body. The definite article—not the possessive article, as in English—is used with the part of the body.

Chantal se brosse **les** dents.	*Chantal is brushing her teeth.*
Je me lave **les** mains.	*I'm washing my hands.*

C. Idiomatic Pronominal Verbs

When certain verbs are used with reflexive pronouns, their meaning changes.

aller *to go*	**s'en aller** *to go away*
appeler *to call*	**s'appeler** *to be named*
demander *to ask*	**se demander** *to wonder*
endormir *to put to sleep**	**s'endormir** *to fall asleep*

*Ce livre **endort** Paul.

entendre *to hear*	**s'entendre** *to get along*
ennuyer *to bother*	**s'ennuyer** *to be bored*
fâcher *to make angry*	**se fâcher** *to get angry*
marier *to marry**	**se marier** *to marry, get married*
mettre *to place, to put*	**se mettre à** *to begin*
promener *to (take for a) walk*†	**se promener** *to take a walk*
tromper *to deceive*	**se tromper** *to be mistaken*
trouver *to find*	**se trouver** *to be located*

Les jeunes mariés **s'en vont** en voyage de noces.	*The newlyweds are going away on their honeymoon trip.*
Véronique va bientôt **se mettre à** chercher un appartement.	*Véronique is going to start looking for an apartment soon.*
Tu **te trompes**! Elle en a déjà trouvé un.	*You're wrong! She's already found one.*
Où **se trouve**-t-il?	*Where is it?*

MAINTENANT A VOUS

A. Habitudes matinales. Qui dans votre famille a les habitudes suivantes? Faites des phrases complètes. Puis comparez leurs habitudes aux vôtres. Commencez par «Moi aussi, je... » or «Mais moi, je... »

mon père	se regarder longtemps dans le miroir
ma mère	se lever souvent du pied gauche‡
ma sœur	se réveiller toujours très tôt
mon frère	s'habiller rapidement / lentement
mes parents	se maquiller / se raser très vite
?	se préparer à la dernière minute
	se brosser les cheveux pendant une heure
	s'en aller sans prendre de petit déjeuner
	se laver les cheveux tous les jours
	ne jamais se dépêcher
	se fâcher quand il (elle) n'a pas de café

Puis comparez vos habitudes avec celles de vos camarades. Trouvez quelqu'un qui...

- se lève dix minutes avant de partir
- s'en va sans prendre de petit déjeuner
- se réveille avant six heures
- se lève souvent du pied gauche

---

*M. et Mme Auban veulent **marier** leur fille à un médecin (*doctor*). C'est triste!

†Jacques **promène** son chien tous les matins à six heures.

‡**Se lever du pied gauche** is the equivalent of *to get up on the wrong side of the bed.*

B. La routine. Que font les membres de la famille Duteil?

MODÈLE: Annick se lave les mains.

Le matin...

Et vous, laquelle de ces activités faites-vous régulièrement?

C. Synonymes. Racontez l'histoire suivante. Remplacez l'expression en italique par un verbe pronominal.

A sept heures du matin, Sylvie *ouvre les yeux,* elle *sort de son lit, fait sa toilette* et *met ses vêtements*. A huit heures, elle *quitte la maison*. Au travail, elle *commence à* parler au téléphone. Sylvie *finit de* travailler vers six heures; elle *fait une promenade* et parfois ses amies et elle vont *nager* à la piscine. Le soir, elle *va au lit* et elle *trouve le sommeil* très vite!

D. Interview. Interrogez un(e) camarade sur une journée typique de sa vie à l'université. Posez-lui des questions avec les verbes **se réveiller, s'habiller, se dépêcher, s'en aller** (**en cours**), **s'amuser, s'ennuyer, se reposer, se promener** et **se coucher.** Ensuite, expliquez à la classe les différences et les ressemblances entre votre journée et celle de votre camarade.

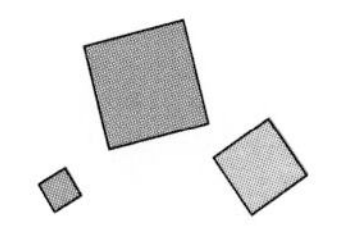

44. Expressing Reciprocal Actions: Pronominal Verbs

Le coup de foudre

Ils s'aiment!

1. Est-ce qu'ils s'embrassent (*kiss*)?
2. Est-ce qu'ils se détestent?
3. Est-ce qu'ils se regardent?
4. Est-ce qu'ils s'adorent?
5. Est-ce qu'ils se disputent?

The plural reflexive pronouns **nous, vous,** and **se** can be used to show that an action is reciprocal or mutual. Almost any verb that can take a direct or indirect object can be used reciprocally with **nous, vous,** and **se.**

Ils s'aiment.	*They love each other.*
Allons-nous **nous** téléphoner demain?	*Are we going to phone each other tomorrow?*
Vous ne **vous** quittez jamais.	*You are inseparable* (*never leave each other*).

MAINTENANT A VOUS

A. Une amitié sincère. Madame Chabot raconte l'amitié qui unit sa famille à la famille Marnier. Complétez son histoire au présent.

Gisèle Marnier et moi, nous _____[1] depuis plus de quinze ans. Nous _____[2] tous les jours et nous parlons longtemps. Nous _____[3] souvent en ville. Quand nous partons en voyage, nous _____[4] des cartes postales.

Nos maris _____[5] aussi très bien. Nos enfants _____[6] surtout pendant les vacances quand ils jouent ensemble. Parfois ils _____[7], mais comme ils _____[8] bien, ils oublient vite leurs différends (*disagreements*).

s'écrire
se rencontrer
se téléphoner
se connaître
se disputer
se voir
s'entendre
s'aimer

B. Scènes de la vie quotidienne. Regardez bien les photos suivantes. Par petits groupes, racontez (au présent) l'histoire suggérée sur chaque photo. Dites quand et où chaque action a lieu.

Maintenant, imaginez ce que les personnes peuvent dire. Avec vos camarades, jouez les différentes scènes à tour de rôle. Est-ce que chaque groupe a interprété les scènes suggérées sur les photos de la même façon? Quelle interprétation est la plus originale? la plus triste? la plus amusante?

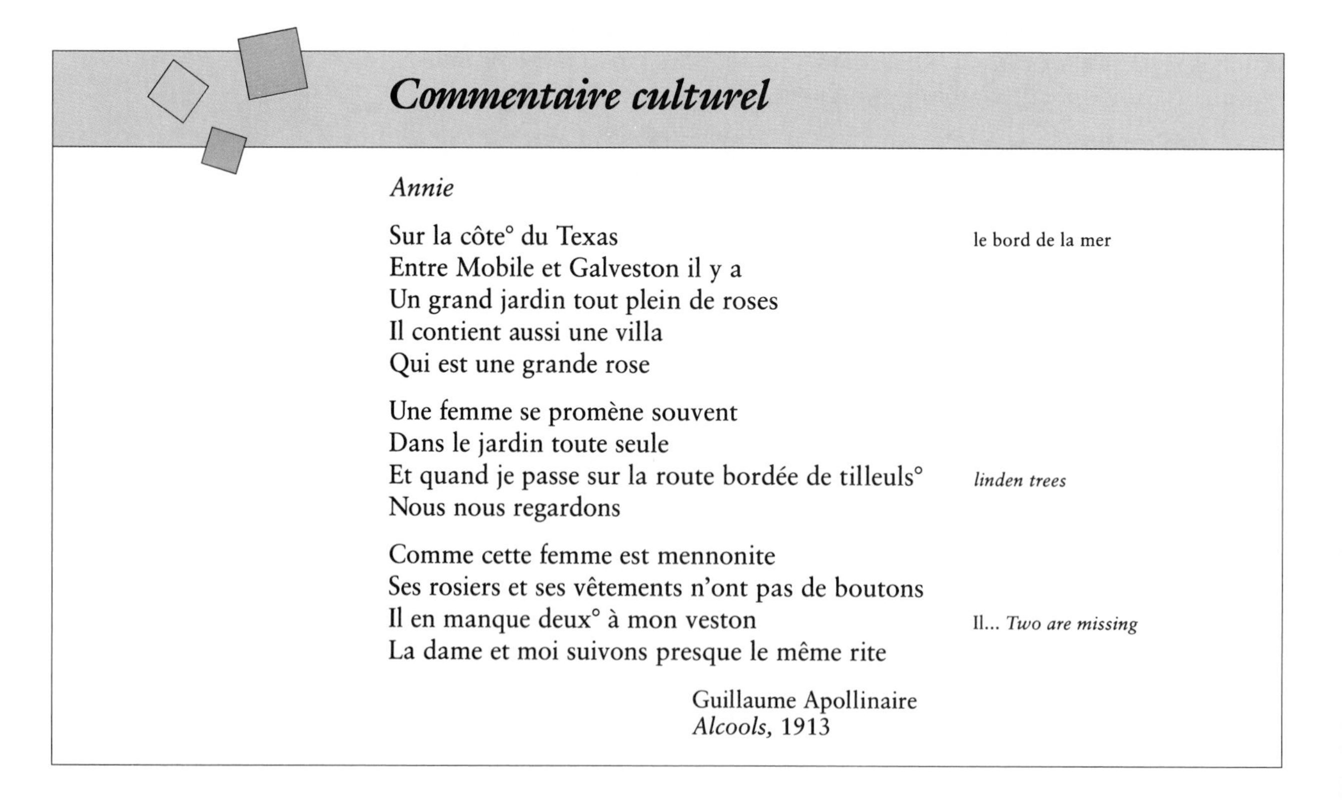

Commentaire culturel

Annie

Sur la côte° du Texas — *le bord de la mer*
Entre Mobile et Galveston il y a
Un grand jardin tout plein de roses
Il contient aussi une villa
Qui est une grande rose

Une femme se promène souvent
Dans le jardin toute seule
Et quand je passe sur la route bordée de tilleuls° — *linden trees*
Nous nous regardons

Comme cette femme est mennonite
Ses rosiers et ses vêtements n'ont pas de boutons
Il en manque deux° à mon veston — Il... *Two are missing*
La dame et moi suivons presque le même rite

Guillaume Apollinaire
Alcools, 1913

C. Amis et adversaires. Complétez les phrases suivantes pour décrire vos amis et les gens que vous n'aimez pas beaucoup.

1. _____ et moi nous nous téléphonons souvent.
2. _____ et moi nous nous aimons bien.
3. _____ et moi nous nous voyons souvent.
4. _____ et moi nous ne nous entendons pas!
5. _____ et moi nous nous _____.
6. Mon meilleur ami (Ma meilleure amie) et moi nous _____.
7. Mes parents et moi nous _____.

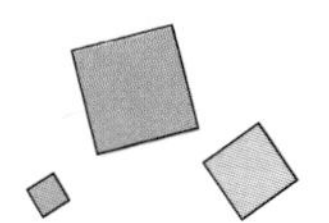

45. Talking About the Past and Giving Commands: Pronominal Verbs

Un mariage d'amour

MARTINE: Comment **vous êtes-vous rencontrés?**
DENIS: **Nous nous sommes vus** pour la première fois à Concarneau.
VÉRONIQUE: **Souviens-toi!** Il pleuvait, tu es entré dans la boutique où je travaillais et...
DENIS: Et ça a été le coup de foudre! **Nous nous sommes mariés** cette année-là.

1. Véronique et Denis se sont-ils rencontrés par hasard?
2. Où se sont vus Véronique et Denis pour la première fois?
3. Quand se sont-ils mariés?

A. *Passé composé* of Pronominal Verbs

All pronominal verbs are conjugated with **être** in the **passé composé.** The past participle agrees with the reflexive pronoun in number and gender when the pronoun is the *direct* object of the verb, but not when it is the *indirect* object.

PASSÉ COMPOSÉ OF **se baigner** (*to bathe; to swim*)			
je	me suis baigné(e)	nous	nous sommes baigné(e)s
tu	t'es baigné(e)	vous	vous êtes baigné(e)(s)
il	s'est baigné	ils	se sont baignés
elle	s'est baignée	elles	se sont baignées
on	s'est baigné(e)(s)		

Nous **nous sommes mariés** en octobre.	*We got married in October.*
Se sont-ils **fâchés**?	*Did they get angry?*
Vous ne vous **êtes** pas **vus** depuis Noël?	*You haven't seen each other since Christmas?*

Here are some of the more common pronominal verbs whose past participles do not agree with the pronoun: **se demander, se dire, s'écrire, s'envoyer, se parler, se téléphoner.** The reflexive pronoun of these verbs is indirect (**demander à, parler à,** etc.).

Elles se sont **écrit** des cartes postales.	*They wrote postcards to each other.*
Ne se sont-ils pas **téléphoné** hier soir?	*Didn't they phone each other last night?*
Vous êtes-vous **dit** bonjour?	*Did you say hello to each other?*

B. Imperative of Pronominal Verbs

Reflexive pronouns follow the rules for the placement of object pronouns. In the affirmative imperative, they follow and are attached to the verb with a hyphen; **toi** is used instead of **te.** In the negative imperative, reflexive pronouns precede the verb.

Habillez-**vous.** Ne **vous** habillez pas.	*Get dressed. Don't get dressed.*
Lève-**toi.** Ne **te** lève pas.	*Get up. Don't get up.*

a. Radio Télévision Luxembourg

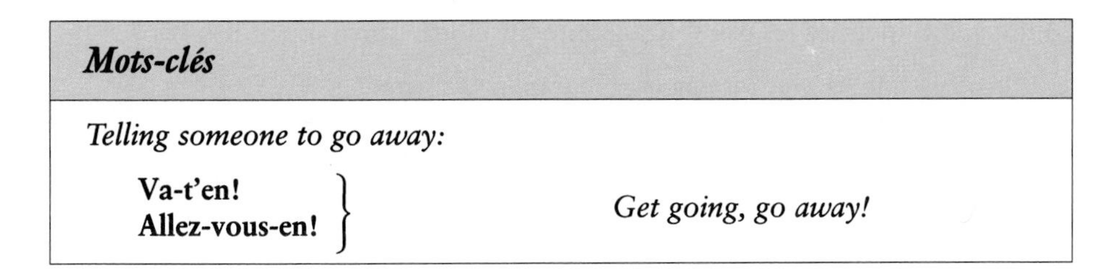

Mots-clés

Telling someone to go away:

Va-t'en!
Allez-vous-en! } *Get going, go away!*

MAINTENANT A VOUS

A. Le coup de foudre. Voici l'histoire d'amour de Pierre et de Sophie. Complétez les phrases suivantes avec un des verbes suggérés au passé composé. Ensuite, créez d'autres conclusions possibles.

Pierre et Sophie _____[1] chez des amis l'année dernière. Le lendemain matin ils _____[2] très tôt. Ils _____[3] longtemps. L'après-midi ils _____[4] dans le parc.	se promener se lever se rencontrer se parler
D'abord ils _____[5] du coin de l'œil, puis ils _____[6] par la main. Ils _____[7] des mots d'amour et ils _____[8] timidement.	se dire se prendre se regarder s'embrasser
Après, ils (ne... plus) _____.[9] Ils _____[10] deux mois plus tard. Ils forment le couple parfait. Ils _____[11] (*présent*) très bien et depuis qu'ils sont mariés, ils (ne... jamais) _____.[12]	se marier se quitter se disputer s'entendre

B. Souvenirs. Aline retrouve un vieil album de photos. Racontez son histoire au passé composé.

1. Elle s'installe pour regarder son album de photos. 2. Elle s'arrête à la première page. 3. Elle se souvient de son premier amour. 4. Elle ne se souvient pas de son nom. 5. Elle se trompe de personne. 6. Elle se demande où il est aujourd'hui. 7. Elle s'endort sur la page ouverte.

C. Un rendez-vous difficile. Un ami (Une amie) a rendez-vous avec quelqu'un qu'il (elle) ne connaît pas. Il (Elle) est très énervé(e). Réagissez (*React*)! Utilisez l'impératif.

MODÈLE: Je ne *me suis* pas encore *préparé*. (vite) → Prépare-toi vite!

1. A quelle heure est-ce que je dois *me rendre* chez elle? (à 5 h)
2. Je n'ai pas envie de *m'habiller*. (tout de suite [*immediately*])
3. Je ne *me souviens* pas de la rue. (rue Mirabeau)
4. J'ai peur de *me tromper*. (ne... pas)
5. Je dois *m'en aller* à 6 h. (maintenant)

On se téléphone demain, d'accord?

Maintenant, inversez les rôles. Mais cette fois votre camarade utilise *vous*.

MODÈLE: Je ne *me suis* pas encore *préparé*. (vite) →
Préparez-vous vite!

D. Rapports. Utilisez des verbes pronominaux au passé composé pour décrire les rapports entre les personnages historiques et fictifs suivants.

MODÈLE: Roosevelt, Churchill, de Gaulle →
Ils se sont vus, ils se sont parlé, ils se sont écrit des lettres et parfois ils se sont disputés.

1. Roméo et Juliette
2. Laurel et Hardy
3. Charlie Brown et Lucy
4. Sherlock Holmes et le Dr Watson
5. Antoine et Cléopâtre
6. Socrate et ses disciples
7. Caïn et Abel
8. Pierre et Marie Curie
9. Tarzan et Jane

46. Making Comparisons: The Comparative and Superlative of Adjectives

Problèmes de fin de mois

VÉRONIQUE: Tu sais, Denis, **la plus grande** de nos dépenses en ce moment, c'est l'alimentation.
DENIS: Eh bien, achetons tout à Carrefour*—leurs prix sont **les meilleurs.**
VÉRONIQUE: Nous pouvons aussi manger dans des restaurants **moins chers.**
DENIS: D'accord. Quand on n'en a pas les moyens, on est obligé de mener une vie **plus simple.**

1. Quelle est la plus grande des dépenses de ce jeune ménage?
2. Où est-ce que les prix sont les meilleurs?
3. Comment peuvent-ils réduire (*to lower*) leurs dépenses?
4. Quand est-il bon de mener une vie plus simple?

A. Comparison of Adjectives

In French, the following constructions can be used with adjectives to express a comparison. It is not always necessary to state the second term of the comparison.

*Supermarché très populaire

1. **plus... que** (*more . . . than*)

   Marina est **plus** intelligente (**que** sa sœur). — *Marina is more intelligent (than her sister).*

2. **moins... que** (*less . . . than*)

   Gilles est **moins sérieux** (**que** Jérôme). — *Gilles is less serious (than Jérôme).*

3. **aussi... que** (*as . . . as*)

   Jean-Paul est **aussi** blond **que** sa sœur. — *Jean-Paul is as blond as his sister.*

Stressed pronouns are used after **que** when a pronoun is required.

Elle est plus amoureuse que **lui.** — *She is more in love than he is.*

B. Superlative Form of Adjectives

To form the superlative of an adjective, use the appropriate definite article with the comparative adjective.

Monique est frisée. → Solange est plus frisée que Monique. → Alice est **la** plus frisée des trois.

(*ou*)

Alice est frisée. → Solange est moins frisée qu'Alice. → Monique est **la** moins frisée des trois.

Superlative adjectives normally follow the nouns they modify, and the definite article is repeated.

Alice est la jeune fille **la plus frisée** des trois. — *Alice is the girl with the curliest hair of the three.*

Adjectives that usually precede the nouns they modify can either precede or follow the noun in the superlative construction. If the adjective follows the noun, the definite article must be repeated.

les plus longues jambes

(*ou*)

les jambes les plus longues

The preposition **de** expresses *in* or *of* in a superlative construction.

Voilà le plus jeune couple **du** groupe. — *There's the youngest couple in the group.*
C'est la nouvelle la plus intéressante **de** la semaine. — *That's the most interesting news of the week.*

C. Irregular Comparative and Superlative Forms

The adjectives **bon**(**ne**) (*good*) and **mauvais**(e) (*bad*) have irregular comparative and superlative forms. **Mauvais**(e) has a regular and an irregular form.

	COMPARATIVE	SUPERLATIVE
bon(**ne**)	**meilleur**(e)	**le/la meilleur**(e)
mauvais(e)	**plus mauvais**(e) **pire**	**le/la plus mauvais**(e) **le/la pire**

Ma santé est bonne, mais ta santé est **meilleure.** — *My health is good, but your health is better.*
Hélène a obtenu **la meilleure** note de la classe. — *Hélène received the best grade in the class.*
Ce livre-ci est **plus mauvais** (**pire**) que ce livre-là. — *This book is worse than that book.*
C'était **le plus mauvais** (**le pire**) des présidents. — *He was the worst of the presidents.*

Mots-clés

Being emphatic: Like **très,** the adverbs **bien** and **fort** are used to emphasize a point.

—Je crois que tout le monde est d'accord. Les langues étrangères sont **bien** plus intéressantes à apprendre que les sciences!
—Pas du tout! Je trouve la physique **fort** intéressante! Et mes notes en physique sont **bien** meilleures qu'en espagnol.

MAINTENANT A VOUS

A. Comparaisons. Regardez les deux dessins et répondez aux questions suivantes.

1. Qui est plus grand, le jeune homme ou la jeune fille? plus mince?
2. Est-ce que la jeune fille a l'air aussi dynamique que le jeune homme? aussi sympathique?
3. Qui est plus timide? plus bavard?
4. Est-ce que le jeune homme est aussi bon étudiant que la jeune fille?
5. Est-ce que la jeune fille est moins intellectuelle que le jeune homme? moins sérieuse?
6. Est-ce que le jeune homme est plus ou moins travailleur que la jeune fille?
7. Qui est le plus ambitieux des deux? le plus sportif des deux?
8. A votre avis, qui est le plus optimiste des deux? Justifiez votre réponse.

B. Opinions. Changez les phrases suivantes en indiquant votre opinion personnelle: **plus/moins/aussi... que; meilleur**(e) / **plus mauvais**(e) **que.** Justifiez vos opinions.

1. Les sports sont aussi importants que les études.
2. L'argent est aussi important que l'amitié.
3. Grâce à la technologie, la vie est meilleure qu'en 1945.
4. Les cours universitaires sont plus intéressants que les cours à l'école secondaire.
5. Les profs à l'université sont moins bons que mes profs à l'école secondaire.
6. Je suis plus heureux (heureuse) que la plupart de mes ami(e)s.

C. **Sondage.** Voici un sondage publié par le magazine *Le Point.* Il montre l'échelle des valeurs des Français et leurs peurs. Étudiez le tableau, puis comparez les réponses des différents secteurs professionnels. Utilisez les formes comparatives **aussi... que, moins... que, plus... que.**

MODÈLE: Pour les agriculteurs, la santé est aussi importante que pour les inactifs.

D. **Mais ce n'est pas possible!** Vous aimez exagérer. Donnez votre opinion sur les sujets suivants. Pour chaque catégorie, proposez aussi d'autres exemples si possible.

1. Le président _____ / bon ou mauvais / président / le XXe siècle
2. Les Américains / les gens / généreux / le monde
3. Le manque (*lack*) d'éducation / le problème / sérieux / le monde actuel
4. _____ / le problème / grand / ma vie
5. _____ / la nouvelle / intéressant / l'année
6. _____ / l'athlète / bon / l'année

E. **Sondage en cour de français.** En groupes de trois ou quatre, faites un sondage dans votre classe. Chaque groupe choisit une catégorie et prépare une liste de cinq ou six questions à poser aux autres membres de la classe et aussi au professeur. Ensuite, annoncez les résultats. **Catégories suggérées:** votre université (*les professeurs, les cours, les résidences, etc.*), les acteurs (actrices), la littérature (*les livres les plus intéressants ou les plus ennuyeux*), la politique (*les meilleurs et les plus mauvais présidents*), les produits (*le dentifrice, le maquillage, les vêtements*)...

MODÈLE: **Catégorie:** l'amour
Questions: 1. Qui forme le couple le plus amoureux de l'histoire?
2. Qui a été le mari (la femme) le (la) plus horrible?
3. Quel est le mariage le plus célèbre de notre temps?
4. Quelle est la chose la plus importante en amour?

Situation

Visite à domicile

Contexte *Madame Guirardi est un médecin généraliste.° Elle fait souvent ses visites à domicile le matin et voit ses autres patients dans son cabinet° l'après-midi.*

Objectif *Jérôme s'explique avec le médecin.*

JÉRÔME: Bonjour, Docteur.

DR GUIRARDI: Bonjour, Jérôme. Asseyez-vous.* Alors, qu'est-ce qui ne va pas?

JÉRÔME: Docteur, j'ai très mal à la gorge,° et j'ai un peu de fièvre.

DR GUIRARDI: Et cela dure° depuis combien de temps?

JÉRÔME: Ça fait quatre ou cinq jours, déjà.

DR GUIRARDI: Bon, eh bien, laissez-moi vous ausculter°... Un peu de congestion, mais rien de grave. Ouvrez la bouche et dites *Aaaah*...

JÉRÔME: Aaaah...

DR GUIRARDI: Très bien. Vous avez des points° blancs dans la gorge, jeune homme. Je crois que c'est une angine.°

JÉRÔME: Ça fait très mal quand j'avale.°

DR GUIRARDI: Nous allons vous prescrire un sirop qui va arranger ça. Êtes-vous allergique à certains médicaments?

médecin... *general practitioner*
bureau
throat
persiste
(avec un stéthoscope)
spots
inflammation de la gorge
swallow

---

* *Sit down.* Consult the verb charts in the back of the text for the conjugation of the irregular verb **s'asseoir** (*to be seated, to sit down*). The form most useful to you now is the imperative: **Asseyez-vous; assieds-toi.**

JÉRÔME: Non, pas à ma connaissance.
DR GUIRARDI: Alors, voici votre ordonnance.° Prenez ces comprimés° trois fois par jour pendant cinq jours. — *prescription / tablets*
JÉRÔME: Merci bien, Docteur.
DR GUIRARDI: Si votre fièvre monte, appelez-moi. Et je veux vous revoir si ça ne va pas mieux° dans quatre ou cinq jours. — *better*

VARIATIONS

1. Rejouez la scène avec une des variations suggérées.
   a. **Un accident sportif**
   Le (La) malade explique: se tordre (*p.p.*: tordu) la cheville (*to twist an ankle*); ne pas pouvoir marcher (*to walk*)...
   Le diagnostic: pas de fracture; une entorse (*sprain*)...
   Les soins: bander (*to bandage*); prendre des bains d'eau chaude salée (avec du sel); ne pas marcher; prendre un peu d'aspirine si c'est nécessaire...
   b. **Un accident de moto**(cyclette)
   Le (La) blessé(e) (***injured person***) **explique:** l'épaule (*shoulder*), le bras, la jambe, etc.
   Le diagnostic: (se) casser (*to break*)...
   Les soins: prendre rendez-vous à la clinique pour faire des radios (*X-rays*); porter un plâtre (*cast*) pendant __?__...
2. **Improvisez!** Vous avez très mal aux dents et vous allez voir un(e) dentiste. Prenez rendez-vous par téléphone et puis, jouez la visite. **Expressions utiles:** une dent de sagesse (*wisdom tooth*); arracher une dent (*to pull a tooth*); un mauvais plombage (*filling*); remplacer; l'anesthésie locale; **Aïe** [aj]! (*Ouch!*)...

A propos

Pour exprimer votre compassion à un(e) ami(e) malade

Oh, mon (ma) pauvre!
Je suis désolé(e). (*I'm very sorry.*)
Je peux faire quelque chose?
Je peux t'apporter quelque chose?
Guéris vite! (*Get well soon!*)

Pour exprimer votre manque (lack) *de compassion à un(e) ami(e) malade*

C'est de ta faute, tu sais!
(*It's your fault, you know!*)
Tu l'as cherché!
Tu as eu tort de... (te coucher si tard, manger tout cela, etc.)

Jeu de rôles. Jouez les scènes suivantes avec des camarades. Utilisez les expressions de l'*A propos.*

1. Vous voyagez en France avec un(e) ami(e). Il (Elle) tombe malade. Essayez de trouver pourquoi il (elle) est tombé(e) malade. Qu'est-ce qu'il (elle) a mangé? Quand s'est-il (elle) couché(e)? Depuis quand a-t-il (elle) mal au ventre, à la tête, etc.? Ayez de la compassion pour lui (elle).
2. La scène se passe (*takes place*) dans une résidence universitaire. Un(e) de vos ami(e)s est sorti(e) hier soir et il (elle) a trop mangé et trop bu dans un restaurant très cher. Aujourd'hui il y a un examen, et votre ami(e) vient vous demander de l'aider à s'y préparer. Vous n'avez pas de compassion pour lui (elle).

Commentaire culturel

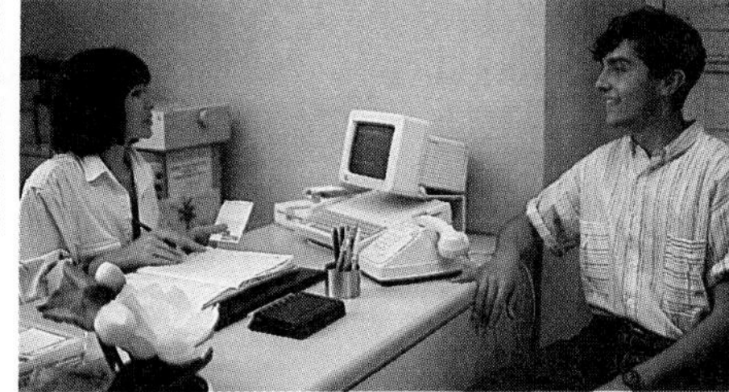

La médecine en France. Les Français font très attention à leur santé. C'est pour cela que le médecin de famille joue un rôle important dans leur vie. C'est lui que l'on appelle quand un membre de la famille tombe malade. En effet, en France les consultations à domicile font partie de la routine quotidienne des médecins. En général, le médecin de famille va voir ses patients tôt le matin, souvent avant d'aller à l'hôpital, ou le soir entre dix-huit et vingt heures, avant de rentrer chez lui. Les soins qu'il donne à domicile sont des soins de base, par exemple pour un rhume, une angine ou une autre maladie bénigne. L'après-midi, il donne des consultations dans son cabinet. Le prix de la consultation est fixé par la Sécurité Sociale, qui va rembourser le patient entre 80 et 100% des frais médicaux selon le cas.

Le pharmacien aussi joue un rôle important. Les Français demandent souvent conseil à leur pharmacien quand ils ont de petits problèmes de santé, comme par exemple un mal de gorge ou une indigestion. Le pharmacien leur recommande alors un médicament pour lequel on n'a pas besoin d'ordonnance. Les médicaments qui sont prescrits par un docteur sont aussi remboursés, complètement ou en partie selon le cas, par la Sécurité Sociale. Pour être remboursé, le malade doit remplir un formulaire sur lequel il colle la «vignette», un petit timbre qui se trouve sur la boîte de médicaments, et il envoie ensuite les papiers à la caisse de Sécurité Sociale de son quartier.

Cette protection médicale est un choix qu'a fait la société française. Son coût en est très élevé. Le gouvernement francais a dû augmenter les impôts (*taxes*) plusieurs fois pour la financer.

Mise au point

A. Vie quotidienne. Faites des phrases complètes. Utilisez les verbes indiqués au temps convenable.

1. Le dimanche, nous / se réveiller / tard. Mais le week-end passé, nous / se lever / assez tôt / et nous / se promener / le parc.
2. Autrefois (*Formerly*) ma sœur / se coucher / avant minuit. Maintenant elle / se préparer / à passer / examen. Elle / se mettre / travailler / semaine passée / et maintenant / elle / travailler / tout le temps.
3. Tu / se brosser / les cheveux / ce matin? Préparer / toi / plus vite. Tu / s'habiller / trop lentement. Rappeler / toi / l'entrevue (*job interview*) / 9 h.
4. Je / se demander / si les voisins / s'amuser / hier chez nous. Ils / partir / vers 10 h / soir. Ils / se regarder / plusieurs fois / avant de partir.

B. Le travail et la vie quotidienne. Voici une évaluation récente faite en France sur les professions suivantes (colonne de gauche). On a utilisé le système de notation suivant:

1 = une note supérieure à la moyenne (*average*)
2 = une note légèrement (*slightly*) supérieure à la moyenne
3 = une note légèrement inférieure à la moyenne
4 = une note très inférieure à la moyenne

	REVENUS ÉLEVÉS (*HIGH INCOME*)	TRAVAIL INTÉRESSANT	BONNES CONDITIONS DE TRAVAIL
un publicitaire (*publicity agent*)	2	2	2
un(e) psychologue	3	1	2
un chirurgien (*surgeon*)	1	2	2
un(e) secrétaire	4	4	4
un(e) dentiste	2	2	2
un(e) vétérinaire	2	2	3
un professeur de tennis	3	3	1

Comparez les différentes professions.

MODÈLE: publicitaire, psychologue →
Un publicitaire a des revenus plus élevés, un travail moins intéressant et des conditions de travail aussi bonnes qu'un psychologue.

(*ou*)

Un psychologue a des revenus moins élevés, un travail plus intéressant et des conditions de travail aussi bonnes qu'un publicitaire.

1. publicitaire, chirurgien
2. chirurgien, dentiste
3. secrétaire, vétérinaire
4. secrétaire, professeur de tennis
5. professeur de tennis, publicitaire
6. vétérinaire, psychologue
7. dentiste, vétérinaire
8. vétérinaire, publicitaire

Maintenant, faites deux phrases avec un superlatif pour chaque catégorie: **revenus élevés, travail intéressant, bonnes conditions de travail.**

MODÈLE: Les chirurgiens ont les revenus les plus élevés.

C. **Qui est-ce?** Regardez vos camarades de classe. Choisissez-en un(e) et décrivez-le (la). Aidez-vous des questions suivantes pour faire votre description. Vos camarades doivent deviner de qui il s'agit.

1. Qui a les cheveux les plus longs de la classe? Qui a les cheveux les plus roux? les plus noirs? le plus frisés?
2. Qui est la plus petite personne de la classe? la plus grande?
3. Qui a le nom le plus long? le plus court?
4. Qui est le plus jeune? le plus âgé?
5. Qui est la personne la plus bavarde? la plus animée?
6. Qui porte les vêtements les plus intéressants? les plus à la mode? les plus excentriques? Qui porte les chaussures les plus inhabituelles?
7. ?

Maintenant, trouvez d'autres camarades qui méritent une description au superlatif.

Interactions

In this chapter, you practiced talking about day-to-day activities and comparing people and things. Act out the following situations, using the vocabulary and structures from this chapter.

1. **Un cadeau.** You need to buy a gift for a relative. Tell the department store clerk (your partner) about this person. He (she) will make several

suggestions, describing and comparing the items. Choose the gift that you prefer, and thank the clerk.

2. **Un monstre.** Take a minute to draw an odd-looking monster that you saw roaming the streets near campus. Then, without showing your drawing to your partner, describe this strange being. Your partner will draw what you describe. Compare drawings to see how well your partner understood.

Vocabulaire

Verbes

avoir mal (**à**) to have pain; to hurt
se **baigner** to bathe; to swim
se **brosser** (**les cheveux, les dents**) to brush (one's hair, one's teeth)
se **coucher** to go to bed
se **disputer** to argue
s'en aller to go away, go off (to work)
s'endormir to fall asleep
s'ennuyer to be bored
se **fâcher** to get angry
s'habiller to get dressed
se **laver** to wash oneself
se **lever** to get up
se **maquiller** to put on makeup
se **marier** (**avec**) to marry (someone)
se **mettre à** (+ *inf.*) to begin to (*do something*)
se **peigner** to comb one's hair
se **préparer** to get ready
se **promener** to take a walk
se **rencontrer** to meet
se **réveiller** to awaken, wake up
se **sécher** to dry oneself
tomber amoureux (**-euse**) to fall in love

Substantifs

l'amour (*m.*) love
l'amoureux (**-euse**) lover, sweetheart
la bouche mouth
le bras arm
le célibat single life
le corps body
le cou neck
le coup de foudre flash of lightning; love at first sight
la dent tooth
le doigt finger
les fiançailles (*f.*) engagement
la gorge throat
la jambe leg
la main hand
le mariage marriage
le nez nose
l'œil (*m.*) (**les yeux**) eye
l'oreille (*f.*) ear
le pied foot
la rencontre meeting, encounter
la santé health
la tête head
le ventre abdomen
le visage face

Adjectifs

amoureux (**-euse**) loving, in love
élevé(**e**) high
ennuyeux (**-euse**) boring
frisé(**e**) curly
lourd(**e**) heavy
meilleur(**e**) better
pire worse
quotidien(**ne**) daily, everyday

Mots divers

asseyez-vous (**assieds-toi**) sit down
aussi... que as . . . as
bien (*adv.*) much
dehors outside
fort (*adv.*) very
moins... que less . . . than
plus... que more . . . than

Expressions utiles

Guéris vite! *Get well soon!*
C'est de ta faute, tu sais! *It's your fault, you know.*

INTERMÈDE 12

Lecture

Astroforme

Augmentez votre énergie pour mieux faire face aux jours stressants: mangez selon votre signe astrologique! Une astrologue et une diététicienne vous donnent leurs conseils pour une meilleure vie quotidienne.

BELIER
21 mars-19 avril

Quand vous vous mettez en colère,° vous êtes facilement fiévreux. Vous avez besoin de vous laisser aller! Consommez des aliments à base de fer.°

vous... *you get angry*
un métal (Fe)

Vous êtes gourmand; vous aimez une nourriture riche. Pour vous, des aliments sains° et frais, comme les céréales et les fruits. Abstenez-vous de manger de la charcuterie et du sucre.

healthy

GEMEAUX
21 mai-21 juin

Vous êtes nerveux et vous vous dépêchez toujours. Vous avez besoin de sommeil pour récupérer votre forme. Préparez des aliments phosphorés: poissons, œufs, fruits secs.°

sans liquide

Votre forme est très changeante: elle nécessite un repos régulier. Vous avez besoin d'iode, qui active la thyroïde. Mangez des fruits de mer,° tous les poissons de mer et des fromages frais.

fruits... *seafood*

Vous réagissez aux chocs émotionnels et votre santé dépend vraiment de votre état émotif. Votre organisme a besoin de magnésium. Pour vous, tous les agrumes,° et aussi les abricots, les figues et les dattes.

les oranges, les mandarines, les citrons (*lemons*), etc.

Vous avez tendance à vous croire souvent malade. Vous adorez essayer de nouvelles recettes, de nouveaux régimes. Vous avez besoin de calcium: fromages, céréales, œufs, légumes verts, laitages.°

produits de lait

Vous êtes plus gourmet que gourmand et vous supportez° mal les excès alimentaires. Conseil: les aliments à base de soufre et de phosphore: œufs, poissons, huîtres et légumes secs.

tolérez

Vous n'aimez pas vous préoccuper de votre santé. Vous avez le tempérament très robuste, mais vous avez besoin de fer et de magnésium pour vous aider à le préserver.

Vous avez besoin d'une nourriture plus saine. Mangez beaucoup d'aliments à base de fer et de sodium: les légumes à feuilles° vertes, le riz et les fruits bien mûrs.°

leaves

ripe

Vous êtes plus préoccupé par votre travail que par la bonne nourriture et vous avez la digestion difficile. Vous avez besoin de calcium et de magnésium.

Vous êtes très capricieux. Vous mangez ou vous ne mangez pas, selon vos humeurs.° Mangez plus régulièrement. Votre organisme a besoin de riz complet et de poisson.

° *moods*

Vous avez un tempérament très «psychique» et vous vous laissez trop influencer par les autres. Vous avez besoin d'un climat d'harmonie. Mangez en général plus de poisson que de viande.

COMPRÉHENSION

A. Lisez les petits dialogues suivants et corrigez les mauvais conseils selon la lecture. (Attention! Tous les conseils ne sont pas nécessairement inexacts.)

1. UN CLIENT: Je suis né le 10 octobre.
   L'ASTROLOGUE: Vous êtes moins gourmand que gourmet.
2. UNE CLIENTE: Je suis née le 28 décembre.
   L'ASTROLOGUE: Vous adorez essayer de nouvelles recettes.
3. UNE CLIENTE: Je suis née le 17 mai.
   L'ASTROLOGUE: Abstenez-vous de manger des céréales et des fruits.
4. UN CLIENT: Je suis né le 1er novembre.
   L'ASTROLOGUE: Pour vous, les agrumes.
5. UN CLIENT: Je suis né le 30 mars.
   L'ASTROLOGUE: Soyez moins impulsif.
6. UN CLIENT: Je suis né le 25 août.
   L'ASTROLOGUE: Surtout, ne mangez pas de yaourt.
7. UNE CLIENTE: Je suis née le 12 décembre.
   L'ASTROLOGUE: Vous avez de très bonnes habitudes gastronomiques.
8. UNE CLIENTE: Je suis née le 21 juin.
   L'ASTROLOGUE: Vous devez moins dormir.
9. UN CLIENT: Je suis né le 30 juillet.
   L'ASTROLOGUE: Vous avez une vie très tranquille en ce moment.
10. UN CLIENT: Je suis né le 15 février.
    L'ASTROLOGUE: Vous êtes raisonnable et persévérant.
11. UNE CLIENTE: Je suis née le 2 juin.
    L'ASTROLOGUE: Mangez des fruits secs.

B. Et vous?

- Maintenant, dites si la description de votre signe dans *Astroforme* correspond à votre tempérament. Justifiez votre réponse.
- Ensuite, discutez du rôle de l'astrologie dans la vie moderne. Croyez-vous à l'astrologie? Connaissez-vous des gens qui y croient? Consultez-vous votre horoscope dans le journal tous les jours? Expliquez votre réponse.

Par écrit

1. **Une lettre.** Un ami parisien (Une amie parisienne) va bientôt visiter une grande ville américaine que vous connaissez bien. Écrivez-lui une lettre pour expliquer comment la vie aux États-Unis est différente de la vie en France. Parlez surtout des gens et de leurs habitudes quotidiennes.
2. **Le courrier du cœur.** Inventez un problème d'amour que vous (ou quelqu'un d'autre) éprouvez en ce moment. Écrivez une lettre au courrier du cœur (l'équivalent de «Dear Abby») pour demander des conseils. Commencez par «**Chère Sylvie**» et terminez par «**J'attends ta réponse avec impatience.**»

Communication et vie pratique 4

ACTIVITÉ

La vie du quartier. Samedi matin, Rue Anatole France: le quartier se réveille. Décrivez la scène et les habitants. Qu'est-ce qu'ils sont en train de faire? Décrivez leur apparence et imaginez leur personnalité. Comparez-les les uns aux autres. Ensuite, choisissez deux personnes qui se parlent et inventez un dialogue entre eux.

EXPRESSION ÉCRITE

Situations

1. Write a description of an especially memorable day from your childhood. If your memory is deficient, call on your imagination. This may be a unique opportunity to reinvent the past.
2. Write a description of something memorable that happened to you recently.

In both essays, you will use the **passé composé** primarily, because you are writing about a unique event that occurred once. Occasionally, however, you may want to use the **imparfait** to describe the background (weather, scenery, what people were doing when an event occurred).

Avant d'écrire

Brainstorming and defining a topic. Probably the most difficult part of writing in any language is finding something interesting to say. One trick that experienced writers sometimes use is free association, or brainstorming. Devote fifteen or twenty minutes to jotting down everything that comes to mind about a given topic. Don't criticize your ideas at this stage; put them aside for a while when you have finished.

Later, go back and organize your notes. Look for the dominant ideas. The most interesting points will probably be obvious to you; these become the main points of your essay. Then look for supporting ideas—details that make the main points clear and vivid. Try to be as specific and detailed as possible. Many of your notes will seem irrelevant. Be sure to eliminate weak, uninteresting, or unrelated ideas before you begin writing.

When you start your essay, envision a potential reader (a classmate or friend, for example). If you can imagine yourself in the reader's position, you will be able to see ways to make your writing easier to understand.

CHAPITRE TREIZE

Cherchons une profession

—Est-ce que tu as trouvé un job pour cet été?
—Oui, je vais travailler pour une petite société près de Nice.
—Je croyais que tu voulais faire un stage dans une société multinationale.
—Oui, mais j'ai changé d'avis. Tu comprends, travailler à dix minutes de la plage, c'est beaucoup plus agréable!

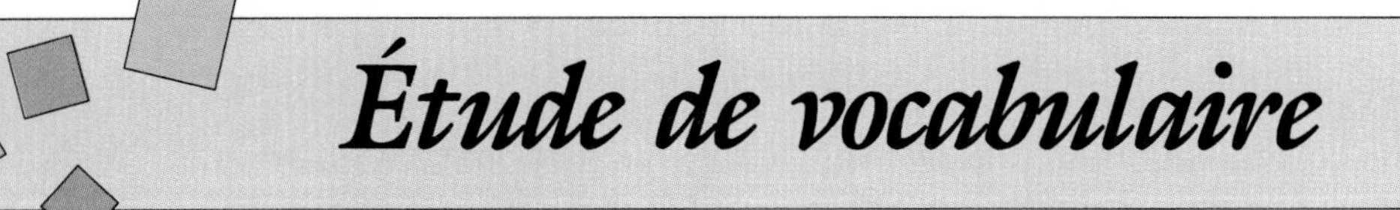

Étude de vocabulaire

Les Français au travail

1. **La profession agricole**

un agriculteur

un ouvrier agricole (une ouvrière agricole)

2. **Les fonctionnaires**

un facteur

une institutrice (un instituteur)

un agent de police

un banquier (une banquière)

une douanière (un douanier)

un magistrat

3. **Les travailleurs indépendants**

   Autres: les architectes,
   les chanteurs, les chanteuses,
   les danseurs, les danseuses,
   les artistes-peintres

un artisan (une artisane)

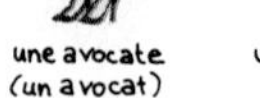
une avocate (un avocat)

un médecin

4. **Les travailleurs salariés**

   Autres: les ingénieurs,
   les interprètes, les comptables,
   les infirmiers, les infirmières,
   les vétérinaires, les publicitaires,
   les assureurs

un cadre

une employée (un employé)

un ouvrier (une ouvrière)

A. Définitions. Quelle est la profession des personnes suivantes?

MODÈLE: Elle enseigne à l'école primaire. → C'est une institutrice.

1. Elle vend des objets qu'elle a faits elle-même. 2. Il travaille à la campagne. 3. Il règle la circulation automobile. 4. Elle vérifie les valises à la douane. 5. Il s'occupe de la santé de ses patients. 6. Il distribue les lettres. 7. Il vend des assurances-vie. 8. Elle s'occupe de la santé des animaux. 9. Il préside au tribunal. 10. Il fait des portraits, des paysages (*landscapes*) ou des natures mortes (*still lifes*).

B. Stéréotypes. Voici quelques dessins du caricaturiste français Jean-Pierre Adelbert. Choisissez la profession qui correspond le mieux à chaque dessin. **Professions:** rédacteur en chef (*editor in chief*), reporter pour un journal de bricolage (*do-it-yourself projects*), journaliste de mode, caricaturiste, critique de cinéma, critique de cuisine, journaliste sportif, auteur de bandes dessinées (*comic strips*).

IMPORTANTE SOCIÉTÉ
SIÈGE PARIS

recherche

CHEF DES SERVICES COMPTABLES

— Gestion financière et gestion personnelle.

— Plusieurs années d'expérience nécessaires.

— D.E.C.S. indispensable ou équivalent.

— Poste d'avenir et évolutif pour candidat (e) motivé (e) et dynamique dans société en pleine expansion.

Adresser C.V., photo, au journal petites annonces, en précisant bien la réf. 2199 sur l'enveloppe, 25, avenue Matignon, 75008 Paris, qui transmettra.

C. Embauche. (*Hiring.*) Vous travaillez pour un cabinet de recrutement qui aide des employeurs à recruter leur personnel. Vous vous spécialisez dans la création d'entreprises. Vos clients vous demandent conseil. Jouez les deux rôles. **Les professionnels:** reporter, directeur (directrice), cadres moyens, employé(e), ingénieur, journaliste, architecte, maître d'hôtel, musicien, ouvrier (ouvrière), cuisinier (cuisinière), professeur, secrétaire, serveur (serveuse), instituteur (institutrice)...

MODÈLE: ouvrir une banque →
—Je veux ouvrir une banque. Quel genre de personnel est-ce que je dois embaucher?
—Vous avez besoin d'un directeur, de secrétaires, de comptables...

1. créer une entreprise de bâtiment
2. publier un journal
3. ouvrir un restaurant
4. ouvrir une école

Préparez maintenant une petite annonce pour un des postes. Décrivez le travail à faire, le profil de la personne recherchée (études, expérience). Puis, présentez l'annonce à la classe. Ensuite, déterminez, parmi les petites annonces, laquelle semble décrire le travail le plus intéressant. Expliquez pourquoi.

D. **Curriculum vitae.** Interrogez votre professeur sur son expérience professionnelle. Demandez-lui...

1. quels emplois il (elle) a eus dans le passé 2. quels jobs il (elle) a aimés ou détestés 3. s'il (elle) a travaillé à l'étranger (si oui, demandez-lui ce qu'il (elle) y a fait, pendant combien de temps, etc.) 4. quand et pourquoi il (elle) a décidé de devenir professeur 5. depuis quand il (elle) est professeur et depuis quand il (elle) enseigne dans votre université

Qu'est-ce que vous avez appris sur la vie de votre professeur que vous ne saviez pas?

E. **Projets d'avenir.** Découvrez les futures professions de vos camarades de classe. Interviewez cinq étudiant(e)s pour découvrir quel job ils aimeraient avoir après avoir terminé leurs études. Ensuite analysez les résultats. En général, avez-vous des ambitions différentes ou semblables?

MODÈLE: —Qu'aimerais-tu faire après tes études?
—J'aimerais devenir hôtelier (hôtelière) dans une station de ski.

A la banque

un compte courant (pour pouvoir **faire des chèques**)

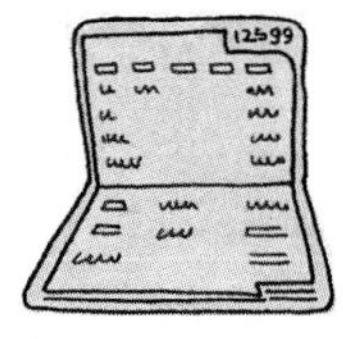

un compte d'épargne (pour pouvoir **faire des économies**)

CHANGES	Monnaies	Cours du jour
Etats Unis......	1 USD	6,3529

Il faut connaître **le cours du jour** pour changer des dollars en francs.

On peut déposer ou **retirer** (*to withdraw*) de l'argent au **distributeur automatique.** N'oubliez pas de prendre **le reçu** et votre **carte bancaire.**

Quand vous faites un chèque, n'oubliez pas de le **signer**!

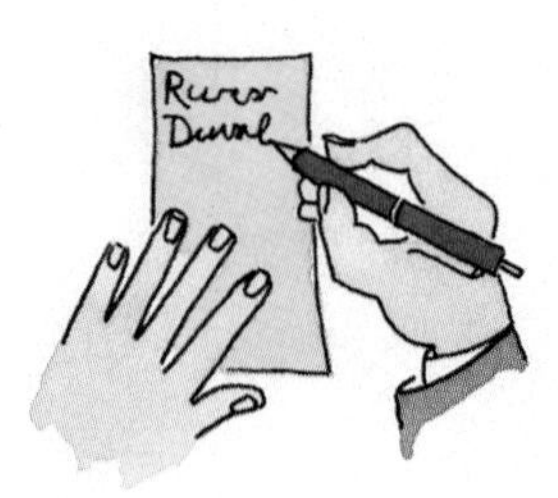

Pour **toucher** (*to cash*) ce chèque, vous devez d'abord **l'endosser.**

A. Un compte en banque en France. D'après cette brochure, indiquez si les déclarations suivantes sont vraies ou fausses. Si elles sont fausses, corrigez-les.

Comment utiliser un Compte-Chèques. En deux mots.

Votre Compte-Chèques vous sert à régler[a] vos dépenses (ou à les faire régler directement par le Crédit Lyonnais), à recevoir votre argent et à mieux gérer[b] votre budget.

Réglez vos dépenses courantes en toute sécurité.

Faites un chèque barré : sans avoir d'argent liquide, vous payez vos achats dans les magasins, vos factures, vos frais de voyage...

Et si vous avez besoin d'argent liquide, vous pouvez en retirer facilement dans votre agence, comme dans toutes les agences du Crédit Lyonnais (jusqu'à 2.000 F par période de 7 jours).

Cependant, n'oubliez pas qu'avant d'émettre un chèque, vous devez disposer sur votre compte d'une provision au moins égale au montant du chèque.

Comment verser de l'argent à votre compte.

Pour alimenter votre compte, vous pouvez déposer des sommes en espèces[c] ou sous forme de chèques bancaires ou postaux. Selon le cas, vous remplissez un formulaire de versement ou de remise de chèques. Vous endossez (c'est-à-dire que vous signez au dos) les chèques que vous remettez. Vous pouvez aussi envoyer les chèques endossés à votre agence, en précisant votre numéro de compte.

a. payer
b. contrôler
c. *cash*

1. Il s'agit d'un compte d'épargne.
2. Vous pouvez vous servir de ce compte pour payer vos achats quand vous n'avez pas d'argent liquide sur vous.
3. Il n'y a aucune limite à la somme d'argent qu'on peut retirer.
4. Avant de déposer un chèque sur votre compte, vous devez signer à côté de votre nom.
5. Vous êtes obligé d'aller à la banque pour déposer de l'argent sur votre compte.
6. Ce compte-chèques ressemble à un compte courant typique aux États-Unis.

B. Une globe-trotter. Audrey vient d'arriver à Paris et veut changer de l'argent. Expliquez-lui les démarches à suivre en mettant les conseils suivants en ordre chronologique.

1. demander le cours du jour 2. prendre des chèques de voyage avec soi 3. prendre le reçu 4. compter l'argent 5. se présenter à un bureau de change ou à une banque 6. vérifier le montant sur le reçu 7. montrer son passeport 8. dire combien d'argent on veut changer

CHANGES	Monnaies	Cours centraux	Cours préc.	Cours du jour
Etats-Unis	1 USD		6,3200	6,3235
Ecu	1 ECU	6,96280	7,0530	7,0520
Allemagne	100 DEM	335,386	338,8600	338,8800
Belgique	100 BEF	16,2608	16,1860	16,1935
Pays-Bas	100 NLG	297,661	300,3300	300,4000
Italie	1000 ITL	4,65362	4,6190	4,6200
Danemark	100 DKK	87,92570	86,9300	86,9600
Irlande	1 IEP	8,98480	9,0600	9,0525
Gde-Bretagne	1 GBP		10,8520	10,8375
Grece	100 GRD		4,0330	4,0260
Espagne	100 ESP		5,4515	5,4480
Portugal	100 PTE		4,1140	4,1155
Suisse	100 CHS		396,8000	396,1200
Suede	100 SEK		99,1200	99,0600
Norvege	100 NOK		93,1200	93,1200
Autriche	100 ATS		48,1600	48,1800
Canada	1 CAD		5,2735	5,2825
Japon	100 JPY		4,8650	4,8650

Audrey suit vos conseils et entre dans un bureau de change Avenue des Champs-Élysées. Elle veut changer des chèques de voyage en dollars, mais aussi, comme c'est une véritable globe-trotter, de l'argent liquide des pays qu'elle a visités. A l'aide des cours publiés dans le journal, calculez approximativement combien de francs français elle va obtenir. Jouez la scène dans le bureau de change avec un(e) camarade.

Audrey a dans son porte-monnaie 350 dollars en chèques de voyage, 180 livres, 120 dollars canadiens, 30 deutschmarks, 155 francs suisses et 75 yens.

Le budget de Marc Convert

Marc travaille dans une petite **société** (enterprise) près de Marseille où il est responsable commercial.

Il **gagne** 9 500 francs par mois.

Il **dépense** presque tout ce qu'il gagne pour vivre; le **coût de la vie** est très élevé dans les villes françaises. Mais il espère avoir une **augmentation de salaire** dans six mois. En ce moment, il **fait des économies** pour acheter son première voiture.

A. Le budget d'un étudiant. Un de vos amis a besoin de faire un emprunt à la banque pour continuer ses études. La banque lui demande de préparer un budget approximatif. Aidez-le à remplir le formulaire, en vous basant sur les dépenses d'un étudiant typique de votre université.

DÉPENSES (PAR MOIS)

Loyer (frais de logement) ____________

Nourriture ____________

Vêtements ____________

Transports ____________

Sorties/Loisirs ____________

Fournitures scolaires ____________

Frais de scolarité ____________

Autres ____________

____

Maintenant, comparez vos calculs avec ceux de vos camarades de classe. Essayez de vous mettre d'accord sur le budget d'un étudiant moyen (*average*) de votre université, puis répondez aux questions suivantes.

1. Combien doit gagner votre ami par mois?
2. S'il travaille quinze heures par semaine dans un restaurant près du campus, combien peut-il gagner?
3. Quelles autres sources de revenu lui sont disponibles?
4. Combien doit-il emprunter alors pour continuer ses études ce semestre? (Il reste encore deux mois de classe.)

B. Les économies. Presque tout le monde gaspille (*wastes*) de l'argent de temps en temps. Interviewez un(e) camarade pour savoir comment il (elle) dépense son argent, et notez ses réponses. Ensuite, quelqu'un dans la classe va tabuler les réponses au tableau. Y a-t-il des réponses très variées? Quelles conclusions en tirez-vous?

1. Est-ce qu'il t'arrive de gaspiller ton argent? Cite un ou deux exemples.
2. Que fais-tu habituellement pour économiser de l'argent?
3. Est-ce que tu as un budget, ou vis-tu au jour le jour sans faire attention aux dépenses?
4. Que fais-tu si tu n'as plus d'argent avant la fin du mois?

Pour parler de l'argent: le verbe ouvrir (*to open*)

ouvrir			
j'	ouvre	nous	ouvrons
tu	ouvres	vous	ouvrez
il, elle, on	ouvre	ils, elles	ouvrent
Past participle: ouvert			

The verb **ouvrir** (*to open*) is irregular. Verbs conjugated like **ouvrir** are **couvrir** (*to cover*), **découvrir** (*to discover*), **offrir** (*to offer*), and **souffrir** (*to suffer*). Note that these verbs are conjugated like **-er** verbs.

A. Finances. Ce mois-ci Jean-Paul a des problèmes d'argent. Racontez la même histoire en remplaçant le sujet par **nous, les Mercier** et **vous,** et faites les changements nécessaires. Changez aussi les mots en italique, en faisant preuve d'imagination.

Le mois dernier Jean-Paul a ouvert un compte courant et aussi un compte d'épargne avec l'argent que lui a offert *sa grand-mère* pour son anniversaire. Jean-Paul est très économe et s'arrange toujours pour couvrir ses dépenses. Mais ce mois-ci, il a acheté *une nouvelle moto* et il souffre de ne pas pouvoir *sortir* aussi souvent. Alors il découvre les plaisirs de *la lecture!*

B. Profil psychologique. Demandez à un(e) camarade...

1. s'il (elle) a un compte bancaire (Si oui, quelle sorte de compte a-t-il/elle?) (Si c'est un compte d'épargne, quel est le taux [*rate*] d'intérêt?); s'il (elle) a une carte de crédit (Si oui, laquelle)
2. dans quelle banque il (elle) a ouvert son compte et pourquoi
3. s'il (elle) a jamais souffert des pertes (*losses*) d'argent et dans quelles circonstances
4. s'il (elle) couvre toujours ses dépenses
5. s'il (elle) a jamais perdu son carnet de chèques ou son portefeuille (*wallet*)
6. combien de fois par semaine, ou par mois, il (elle) retire de l'argent de son compte et combien de fois il (elle) dépose de l'argent sur son compte
7. si quelqu'un lui a offert de l'argent à Noël et ce qu'il (elle) en a fait
8. s'il (elle) fait des économies (*saves money*) et pourquoi

Maintenant, dites ce que vous avez appris et faites un petit portrait psychologique de votre camarade. **Mots utiles:** avare (*stingy*), économe, impulsif (impulsive), généreux (généreuse), (im)prudent(e), négligent(e), un magnat d'affaires (*business magnate*)

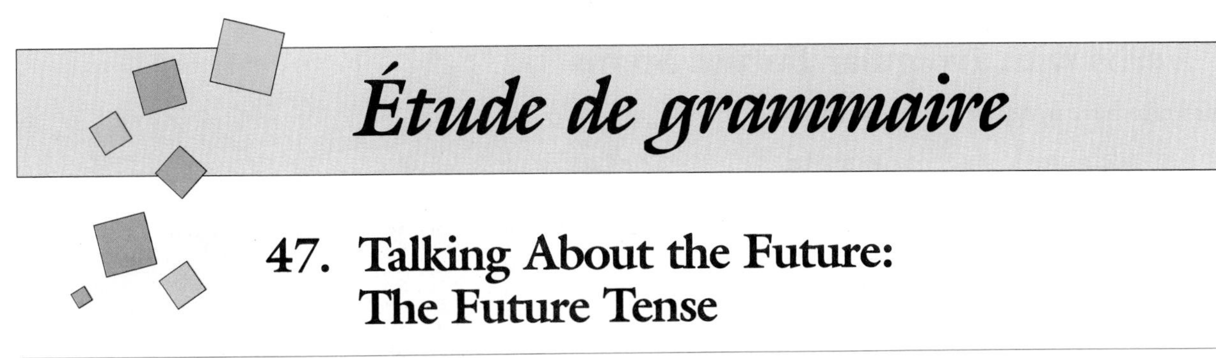

Étude de grammaire

47. Talking About the Future: The Future Tense

Son avenir

LE PÈRE: Il **sera** écrivain, il **écrira** des romans et nous **serons** célèbres.
LA MÈRE: Il **sera** homme d'affaires, il **dirigera** une société et nous **serons** riches.
L'ENFANT: On **verra...** je **ferai** mon possible.

1. D'après son père, quelle sera la profession de l'enfant? Que fera-t-il?
2. D'après sa mère, quelle sera la profession de l'enfant? Que fera-t-il?
3. D'après l'enfant, que fera-t-il?

A. The Future Tense

In French, the future is a simple tense, formed with the infinitive as the stem plus the endings **-ai, -as, -a, -ons, -ez, -ont.** The final -e of the infinitive of **-re** verbs is dropped.

	parler (*to speak*)	**finir** (*to finish, to end*)	**vendre** (*to sell*)
je	parler**ai**	finir**ai**	vendr**ai**
tu	parler**as**	finir**as**	vendr**as**
il, elle, on	parler**a**	finir**a**	vendr**a**
nous	parler**ons**	finir**ons**	vendr**ons**
vous	parler**ez**	finir**ez**	vendr**ez**
ils, elles	parler**ont**	finir**ont**	vendr**ont**

Demain nous **parlerons** avec le conseiller d'orientation. — *Tomorrow we will talk with the job counselor.*
Il te **donnera** des conseils. — *He will give you some advice.*
Ces conseils t'**aideront** peut-être à trouver du travail. — *Maybe this advice will help you to find a job.*

B. Verbs with Irregular Future Stems

Some verbs have irregular future stems.

aller: **ir-**	faire: **fer-**	venir: **viendr-**
avoir: **aur-**	pleuvoir: **pleuvr-**	voir: **verr-**
devoir: **devr-**	pouvoir: **pourr-**	vouloir: **voudr-**
envoyer: **enverr-**	savoir: **saur-**	
être: **ser-**		

J'**aurai** bientôt un poste. — *I will soon have a position.*
Demain, on **devra** partir tôt. — *Tomorrow, we will have to leave early.*

Quand **enverras**-tu ta demande d'emploi? — *When will you send your job application?*
Je crois qu'il **pleuvra.** — *I think it will rain.*

Verbs with spelling irregularities in the present tense also have irregularities in the future tense. These include such verbs as **acheter, appeler,** and **payer.** See the *Appendix: -er Verbs with Spelling Changes* at the end of the book.

Mots-clés

Saying when you will do something in the future:

demain
après-demain
ce week-end
dans trois jours (une demi-heure / un mois / deux semaines, etc.)
lundi (mardi, etc.) prochain
la semaine prochaine / le mois prochain / l'année prochaine
un jour (*someday*)
à l'avenir (*from now on*)

La maison sera prête **lundi prochain.**
Nous partirons pour Paris **dans dix jours** (**la semaine prochaine**).
Un jour, vous aurez peut-être votre propre entreprise.
A l'avenir, tu feras plus attention, n'est-ce pas?

C. Uses of the Future Tense

As you can see from the preceding examples, the use of the future tense parallels that of English. This is also true of the tense of verbs after an *if* clause in the present tense.

Si je **réussis** à cet examen, **je poserai** ma candidature à l'École Polytechnique. — *If I pass this test, I will apply to the École Polytechnique.*

However, in time clauses (dependent clauses following words like **quand, lorsque,** [*when*], **dès que** [*as soon as*], or **aussitôt que** [*as soon as*]), the future tense is used in French if the action is expected to occur at a future time. English uses the present tense in this case.

Je te **téléphonerai** *dès que* **j'arriverai.**	*I'll phone you as soon as I arrive.*
Nous **pourrons** en discuter *lorsque* l'avocat **sera** là.	*We'll be able to discuss it when the lawyer arrives.*
La construction **commencera** *dès que* les ingénieurs **seront** prêts.	*Construction will begin as soon as the engineers are ready.*

MAINTENANT A VOUS

A. **Cherchons un emploi.** Voici une des petites annonces publiées par le magazine *L'Express* dans la section «Les entreprises proposent». Parcourez-la et cherchez l'information demandée.

Créer un nouveau marché

MATTEL

Attaquer le marché de la bagagerie et de la papeterie fantaisie, c'est l'objectif de WONDERLAND, filiale de MATTEL, leader du jouet[a] en France. Pour y parvenir, elle recherche son

Chef de produits sénior

Après avoir acquis sur le terrain une bonne connaissance de ce marché et grâce à un travail d'équipe[b] il :
- développera et lancera de nouveaux produits
- sera le support de la force de vente
- établira un plan de communication
- imaginera et mettra en œuvre des opérations promotionnelles.

Agé de 25 ans environ, diplômé d'une école supérieure de commerce, il a une première expérience réussie de 2 à 3 ans dans les produits cosmétiques ou de grande distribution.
Sensibilisé par les produits de mode et de diffusion grand public, il est créatif, ouvert, a de la personnalité et aime les contacts.
De nombreux déplacements sont à prévoir essentiellement en France.
Anglais indispensable.

Ecrivez sous référence 801653/EX

BERNARD KRIEF CONSULTANTS
115, rue du Bac - 75007 Paris
PARIS LYON STRASBOURG LILLE

a. *toy*
b. *team*

1. Cherchez dans cette annonce les verbes qui sont au futur et donnez leur infinitif.
2. Quels produits fabrique la société Wonderland? Donnez-en des exemples.
3. Nommez trois responsabilités du candidat qui sera choisi. Utilisez vos propres mots.
4. Quel diplôme devra avoir le candidat? Combien d'années d'expérience? Dans quel domaine?
5. Donnez trois traits de personnalité importants pour ce poste.
6. Le candidat aura-t-il besoin de voyager? Aura-t-il besoin d'une autre langue dans son travail?

B. Stratégies. Votre meilleur ami (meilleure amie) cherche un travail pour cet été. Il (Elle) doit se présenter demain à une interview. Comme vous l'avez aidé(e) à la préparer, vous savez d'avance ce qu'il (elle) fera demain.

MODÈLE: se lever très tôt → Il (Elle) se lèvera très tôt.

1. faire un peu de gymnastique pour se relaxer 2. s'habiller avec soin 3. prendre un petit déjeuner léger 4. mettre son curriculum vitae dans sa serviette 5. aller au rendez-vous en métro pour éviter les embouteillages 6. y arriver un peu en avance 7. se présenter brièvement 8. parler calmement 9. répondre aux questions de l'employeur avec précision 10. remercier l'employeur en partant (*when leaving*)

A votre avis, que devra-t-il (elle) aussi faire pour être sûr(e) de réussir son interview?

C. Chez la voyante (*fortune-teller*). Vous allez voir une voyante avec des amis. Jouez la scène avec un(e) camarade. Puis décidez entre tous quelles prédictions pourront peut-être se réaliser un jour. Lesquelles sont complètement invraisemblables (*unlikely*)? Expliquez pourquoi.

MODÈLE: LA VOYANTE: Vous ferez le portrait des meilleurs acteurs d'Hollywood.
SON (SA) CLIENT(E): Vous voulez dire que je serai artiste en Californie?

1. Vous deviendrez cosmonaute. 2. Vous vendrez des bijoux à Alger. 3. Vous jouerez le rôle de Hamlet à Londres. 4. Vous participerez à la construction d'un stade à Mexico. 5. Vous écrirez des articles pour le *New York Times*. 6. Vous vendrez des assurances-automobile à Québec. 7. Vous ferez de la publicité pour Toyota. 8. Vous vous occuperez des malades à Dakar. 9. Vous enseignerez dans une école primaire à Seattle. 10. ?

D. Interview. Vous voulez savoir ce que votre camarade pense de l'avenir et vous lui posez les questions suivantes. Mais malheureusement il (elle) ne vous prend pas au sérieux! L'interviewé(e) utilise toute son imagination et son humour pour répondre. A la fin, inversez les rôles.

MODÈLE: dès que tu auras ton diplôme →
—Que feras-tu dès que tu auras ton diplôme?
—Moi, à l'avenir, je vendrai des légumes organiques à Athènes.

1. quand tu seras vieux (vieille) 2. si un jour tu es milliardaire 3. dans dix ans 4. lorsque tu te marieras 5. dès que tu pourras réaliser un de tes rêves 6. si tu n'obtiens pas tout ce que tu veux 7. lorsque tu auras des enfants 8. si ton entreprise t'envoie travailler dans un autre pays 9. ?

A votre avis, parmi toutes les réponses, laquelle est la plus originale? la plus amusante? la plus bizarre?

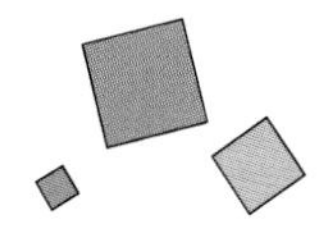

48. Linking Ideas: Relative Pronouns

Interview d'un chef d'entreprise

LE JOURNALISTE: Et pourquoi dites-vous que vous avez fait trois ans d'études inutiles?

GENEVIÈVE: Eh bien, parce que pendant tout ce temps-là, c'était la création de bijoux **qui** m'intéressait.

LE JOURNALISTE: Les bijoux **que** vous créez sont fabriqués avec des matériaux naturels?

GENEVIÈVE: Oui. Je dessine aussi pour les magazines des bijoux fantaisie **qu'**on peut réaliser à la maison.

LE JOURNALISTE: Maintenant, votre entreprise fabrique des milliers de bijoux **dont** les trois-quarts partent au Japon?

GENEVIÈVE: Oui, et j'ai des tas de nouveaux projets!

1. Qu'est-ce qui intéressait Geneviève pendant ses études?
2. Qu'est-ce qu'on peut réaliser à la maison?
3. Les trois-quarts de quoi partent au Japon?

A relative pronoun (*who, that, which, whom, whose*) links a dependent (relative) clause to a main clause. A dependent clause is one that cannot stand by itself—for example, the italicized parts of the following sentences: The suitcase *that he is carrying* is mine; there is the store *in which we met.* In French, there are two sets of relative pronouns: those used as the subject or direct object of a dependent clause and those used after a preposition.

A. Relative Pronouns Used as Subject or Direct Object of a Dependent Clause

The relative pronoun used as the *subject* of a dependent clause is **qui** (*who, that, which*). The relative pronoun used as the *direct object* of a dependent clause is **que** (*whom, that, which*). Both can refer to people and to things.

Subject: Je cherche l'artisane. **Elle** fabrique des bijoux.

Je cherche l'artisane **qui** fabrique des bijoux.

Object: J'ai acheté des bijoux. Geneviève a fabriqué **ces bijoux.**

J'ai acheté les bijoux **que** Geneviève a fabriqués.

Qui replaces the subject (**elle**) in the dependent clause in the first sentence. Since it is the subject of the clause, **qui** will always be followed by a conjugated verb (**qui fabrique**).

Que replaces the direct object (**ces bijoux**) in the second sentence. **Que** is followed by a subject plus a conjugated verb (**...que Geneviève a fabriqués**).

QUI + CONJUGATED VERB	QUE + SUBJECT + VERB
Les architectes **qui sont arrivés** à huit heures viennent des États-Unis.	Les architectes **que j'ai vus** à la conférence viennent des États-Unis.

Note the agreement of the past participle in dependent clauses containing the **passé composé:** in the sentence with **arriver,** it agrees with the plural subject **qui,** and in the sentence with **voir,** the past participle agrees with the preceding plural direct object **que.**

Qui never elides with a following vowel sound: L'architecte **qui est** arrivé à huit heures vient des États-Unis. **Que** does elide: L'architecte **qu'elle** a rencontré vient des États-Unis.

B. Relative Pronouns Used as Objects of Prepositions

The relative pronoun **qui** can be used as the object of a preposition to refer to people.

Le comptable **avec qui** je travaille est agréable.	*The accountant with whom I work is pleasant.*
L'ouvrier **à qui** M. Mesnard a donné du travail est travailleur.	*The worker to whom M. Mesnard gave some work is industrious.*

C. The pronoun *dont* is used to replace *de* (*du, de la, de l', des*) plus an object.

Où est le reçu? J'ai besoin du reçu.	*Where is the receipt? I need the receipt.*
↓	↓
Où est le reçu **dont** j'ai besoin?	*Where is the receipt that I need?*

The pronoun **dont** is also used to express possession.

C'est la passagère. Ses valises sont à la douane.	*That's the passenger. Her suitcases are at the customs office.*
↓	↓
C'est la passagère **dont** les valises sont à la douane.	*That's the passenger whose suitcases are at the customs office.*

D. *Où* is the relative pronoun of time and place. It can mean *where, when,** or *which*.

Le guichet **où** vous changez votre argent est là-bas.	*The window where you change your money is over there.*
Le 1er janvier, c'est le jour **où** je commence mon nouveau travail.	*The first of January, that's the day (when) I begin my new job.*
L'aéroport d'**où** vous êtes partis est maintenant fermé.	*The airport from which you departed is closed now.*

MAINTENANT A VOUS

A. A la recherche d'un emploi. Jean-Claude raconte comment il a passé sa semaine à chercher du travail. Reliez les phrases suivantes avec le pronom relatif **qui.**

1. Lundi, j'ai déjeuné avec un ami. Il connaît beaucoup de comptables.
2. Mardi, j'ai eu une interview à la Banque Nationale de Paris. Elle est près de la place de la Concorde.
3. Mercredi, j'ai parlé à un employé du Crédit Lyonnais. Il m'a beaucoup encouragé.
4. Jeudi, j'ai pris rendez-vous avec un membre de la Chambre de Commerce. Il est expert-comptable.
5. Vendredi, j'ai lu le livre de Bernard Croquette. Il est professeur à l'École Supérieure de Commerce.
6. Enfin samedi, j'ai reçu une lettre d'une société belge. Elle m'offre un poste de comptable à Bruxelles.
7. Et aujourd'hui je prends l'avion. Il me conduit à ma nouvelle vie.

***Quand** is never used as a relative pronoun.

B. A la gare de Lyon. Pendant les vacances d'hiver vous travaillez au Bureau des objets perdus (*lost and found*) à la gare de Lyon. Avec des camarades, jouez les situations suivantes. Soyez imaginatif (imaginative) et donnez beaucoup de détails.

MODÈLE: chercher / une valise / oublier sur le quai

LE/LA PASSAGER (-ÈRE): Je cherche une valise que j'ai oubliée sur le quai hier matin.
VOUS: Comment est la valise que vous avez oubliée?
LE/LA PASSAGER (-ÈRE): Elle est petite, en cuir rouge.
VOUS: Est-ce que c'est la valise que vous cherchez?
LE/LA PASSAGER (-ÈRE): Oui, merci beaucoup.

1. chercher / un parapluie / laisser au restaurant
2. chercher / des clés / perdre dans le hall
3. chercher / un livre / oublier dans le train
4. chercher / un billet de train / venir d'acheter

C. Promenade sur la Seine. Cet été, Marie-Claude travaille comme guide sur un bateau-mouche* à Paris. Complétez ses explications avec les pronoms relatifs **qui, que** ou **où.**

Ce bâtiment _____[1] vous voyez à présent dans l'Île de la Cité, c'est la Conciergerie. Autrefois une prison, c'est l'endroit _____[2] Marie-Antoinette a passé ses derniers jours. Et cette église _____[3] se trouve en face de nous, c'est Notre-Dame. Est-ce que vous voyez cette statue _____[4] ressemble à la Statue de la Liberté? Eh bien, c'est l'original de la statue _____[5] la France a donnée aux Américains. Voici le musée d'Orsay _____[6] vous pourrez admirer les peintres impressionnistes et _____[7] je vous recommande de visiter. Et un peu plus loin, le musée du Louvre _____[8] vous trouverez la Joconde et la Vénus de Milo. Et enfin, voici la Tour Eiffel, _____[9] est le symbole de notre ville.

D. Photos de vacances. Jeannine a passé un mois dans un village d'artistes dans le Midi. Elle y a rencontré beaucoup de gens intéressants. Elle commente maintenant ses photos de vacances à ses amis.

MODÈLE: Voici un artisan. Ses poteries sont très chères. →
Voici l'artisan dont **les** poteries sont très chères.

1. Michel est un jeune artiste. On peut admirer ses tableaux au musée de Marseille.
2. Voici Yan. Ses sculptures sont déjà célèbres dans le milieu artistique.
3. Et voilà Claire. On vend ses écharpes peintes à la main à Saint-Tropez.
4. Laurent est un jeune écrivain. Son premier roman vient d'être publié.

---

*The **bateaux-mouche** are well-known tourist boats that travel up and down the Seine.

Voici une autre photo. Imaginez que vous êtes Jeannine. Expliquez qui est la personne sur la photo et ce qu'elle fait.

MODÈLE: Voici ______, dont...

E. Énigme. Décrivez un objet, une personne ou un endroit à vos camarades. Utilisez des pronoms relatifs. Vos camarades vont essayer de trouver la chose dont vous parlez. **Catégories suggérées:** une ville, un pays, un plat, une personne, une classe, un moyen de transport, une profession...

MODÈLE: VOUS: Je pense à un gâteau qui est français et dont le nom commence par un *e*.
UN(E) AMI(E): Est-ce que c'est un éclair?

Maintenant, continuez ce jeu avec une différence. Vous ne donnez que le nom d'un object ou d'une personne. Vos camarades vous demandent des précisions. Répondez-leur par **oui** ou **non. Autres catégories suggérées:** un film, un programme de télévision, une pièce de théâtre, un acteur (une actrice), un chanteur (une chanteuse), un homme (une femme) politique (*politician*), un(e) athlète...

MODÈLE: VOUS: Je pense à un film.
VOS CAMARADES: C'est un film que tu as vu il y a longtemps?
C'est un film dont l'action se passe (*happens*) aux États-Unis?
C'est un film qui a gagné un «Oscar»?
C'est un film où Dustin Hoffman a joué le rôle principal?
C'est *Rain Man*.

Commentaire culturel

La femme française. Le rôle traditionnel de la femme au foyer a beaucoup évolué depuis les années soixante. Actuellement les femmes françaises sont de plus en plus nombreuses sur le marché du travail. Elles arrivent à concilier travail et vie de famille avec l'aide de leur mari ou d'un parent et de la multiplication de crèches et de garderies. Pour un grand nombre d'entre elles, le travail est synonyme d'épanouissement (*growth*) et d'autonomie. Elles occupent progressivement des postes jusqu'ici réservés aux hommes. Si on trouve encore relativement peu de femmes parmi les cadres supérieurs, elles sont proportionnellement plus nombreuses dans les professions libérales (dentistes, docteurs, avocates, pharmaciennes). La loi sur l'égalité professionnelle entre les hommes et les femmes a été votée en 1983, mais les femmes ont encore à vaincre beaucoup d'obstacles au niveau des salaires et des promotions internes.

Situation

Un travail temporaire

Contexte *Chaque année à la fin de l'été, les vendanges° sont un rendez-vous traditionnel des étudiants français et étrangers. Ils savent qu'ils gagneront peu d'argent, mais qu'ils auront vécu une expérience enrichissante: l'accueil° chez les viticulteurs° est chaleureux° et l'ambiance des vendanges toujours joyeuse.*

grape harvests

welcome / winegrowers / warm

Objectif *Jean-Marc cherche du travail.*

JEAN-MARC: Bonjour, Monsieur, j'ai entendu dire que vous embauchez pour les vendanges.
M. MICHAUD: Oui, c'est exact. Vous avez déjà vendangé? C'est pas toujours drôle, on travaille sous le soleil, sous la pluie...
JEAN-MARC: Oui, je sais, mais je travaille bien. Vous payez à l'heure?
M. MICHAUD: Oui, nous payons 15 francs de l'heure.
JEAN-MARC: Et vous demandez des journées longues?
M. MICHAUD: Je demande des journées de huit à dix heures.
JEAN-MARC: Et pour le logement et les repas?
M. MICHAUD: Je retiens° deux heures de travail par jour seulement.
JEAN-MARC: Je suppose que ça va durer° deux ou trois semaines au maximum?
M. MICHAUD: Oh oui, sans doute, s'il ne fait pas trop mauvais temps.
JEAN-MARC: Eh bien, si vous voulez bien me prendre, ça m'intéresse.
M. MICHAUD: C'est d'accord. Mais n'oubliez pas: ici, on s'amuse bien, mais on travaille dur°!

withhold, charge
last
hard

VARIATIONS

1. Rejouez la scène en utilisant les variations suivantes.

- M. Michaud paie 150 francs par jour.
- Les journées sont de neuf heures maximum.
- Le logement et les repas sont gratuits.

2. **Improvisez!** Vous cherchez un job de serveur (serveuse) dans un café. Un(e) camarade joue le rôle de M. Marius, le cafetier. Voici le scénario:

- On gagne 17 francs de l'heure, plus les pourboires.
- Vous êtes embauché à mi-temps (*part-time*).
- Vous allez servir des consommations et des sandwichs.
- Vous devez être rapide, adroit et aimable.

A propos

Comment parler au téléphone

Allô, j'écoute.
A qui voulez-vous parler?
Je voudrais parler (avec, à)...
Qui est à l'appareil? (C'est Vincent qui parle.)
C'est bien le 376-89-21?
Ne quittez pas! (*Just a moment!* Literally, *Don't hang up!*)
Rappelez plus tard, s'il vous plaît.
Je vous passe (la personne à qui vous voulez parler).
C'est de la part de qui?
C'est de la part de (Jacques).
Au revoir, monsieur (madame, mademoiselle).

Jeu de rôles. Jouez la scène suivante avec un ou plusieurs camarades.

Vous téléphonez à une personne qui cherche un tuteur (une tutrice) pour donner des leçons particulières (*tutorial lessons*) à ses enfants. Vous avez vu son annonce dans le journal et vous avez besoin d'un job à mi-temps. Utilisez les expressions de l'*A propos* et n'oubliez pas de vous renseigner (*to get information*) sur les horaires, le salaire, le nombre d'enfants, leur âge, les matières étudiées, etc. Rappelez plus tard pour dire si vous acceptez ou refusez le poste en question et expliquez pourquoi. Si l'employeur vous refuse le poste, il (elle) vous expliquera pourquoi.

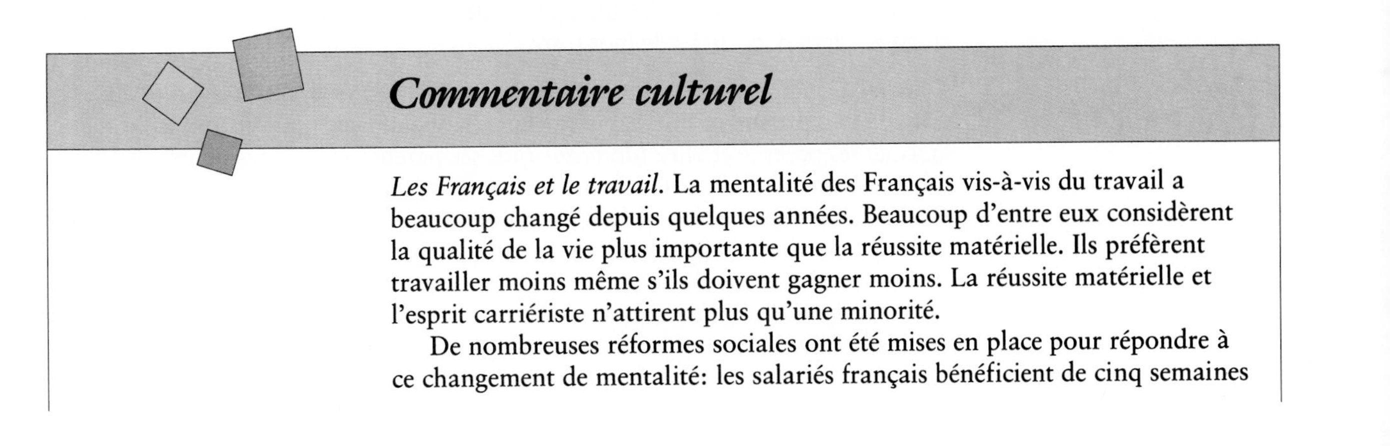

Commentaire culturel

Les Français et le travail. La mentalité des Français vis-à-vis du travail a beaucoup changé depuis quelques années. Beaucoup d'entre eux considèrent la qualité de la vie plus importante que la réussite matérielle. Ils préfèrent travailler moins même s'ils doivent gagner moins. La réussite matérielle et l'esprit carriériste n'attirent plus qu'une minorité.

De nombreuses réformes sociales ont été mises en place pour répondre à ce changement de mentalité: les salariés français bénéficient de cinq semaines de vacances par an, et beaucoup ne travaillent que trente-cinq heures par semaine. De plus, le travail à mi-temps et les horaires flexibles sont très populaires, surtout parmi les femmes qui peuvent ainsi consacrer plus de temps à leur famille. C'est le cas de cette jeune mère qui préfère renoncer à une partie de son salaire pour passer les mercredis, jour de congé scolaire, avec son enfant.

© STUART COHEN / COMSTOCK, INC.

Ce refus de l'aspect aliénant du travail révèle l'importance qu'on donne, en France, à la qualité de la vie. Le bonheur pour beaucoup de Français, c'est la réalisation de soi. On aime prendre le temps de vivre. Mais cette nouvelle conception du travail n'est pas obligatoirement synonyme d'improductivité. Éliminer le stress, c'est améliorer la qualité du travail. On retrouve alors un rythme plus naturel et efficace qui permet d'avoir un meilleur équilibre personnel dans son travail. C'est le rejet de la routine. Ainsi le Français part à la reconquête du temps!

Mise au point

A. Un poste au Canada. Claudette rêve déjà de son voyage au Canada. Voici ce qu'elle fera. Choisissez le mot juste.

Claudette, (*qui/que/qu'*) est une jeune Parisienne, (*ira/sera/aura*) travailler au Canada l'an prochain. Elle habitera chez les Regimbault (*qui/que/qu'*) sont des amis de ses parents et chez (*dont/que/qui*) ses parents sont restés quand ils (*seront/ont/sont*) passés par Québec il y a assez longtemps. Le jour (*que/qui/où*) Claudette (*arrivera/arrive/arrivée*), la famille Regimbault (*viendront/viendra/verra*) la chercher à l'aéroport. Son avion, (*que/qui/où*) partira de l'aéroport Roissy-Charles de Gaulle, passera par New York. Ses bagages (*arriveraient/arriveront/arrivent*) plus tard. M. et Mme Regimbault, (*qui/que/dont*) le père de Claudette lui a beaucoup parlé, sont très gentils. Le bureau (*où/que/qui*) Claudette travaillera n'est pas loin de chez eux. Ce (*sera/aura été/a été*) un séjour (= une visite) très agréable.

B. Travail et vacances. Racontez les projets de Sabine. Reliez les deux phrases avec un pronom relatif. Le symbol ▲ indique le début (*beginning*) d'une proposition relative.

MODÈLE: Je travaille au tribunal (*court*). ▲ Je suis avocate au tribunal. →
Je travaille au tribunal où je suis avocate.

1. Je prendrai bientôt des vacances. ▲ J'ai vraiment besoin de ces vacances.
2. Ma camarade de chambre ▲ viendra avec moi. Elle s'appelle Élise.
3. Elle travaille avec des comptables. ▲ Ces comptables sont très exigeants (*demanding*).
4. Nous irons à Neufchâtel. ▲ Les parents d'Élise ont une maison à Neufchâtel.
5. Le père d'Élise ▲ nous a invitées. Élise a téléphoné à son père la semaine passée.
6. Élise a envie de voir sa mère. ▲ Elle pense souvent à sa mère.
7. J'ai acheté une nouvelle valise. ▲ Je mettrai tous mes vêtements de ski dans cette valise.
8. Nous resterons deux jours à Strasbourg. ▲ Nous visiterons le Parlement Européen à Strasbourg.
9. Nous rentrerons trois semaines plus tard, prêtes à reprendre le travail. ▲ Ce travail se sera accumulé.

Cherchez l'information demandée ci-dessous dans le récit de Sabine.

1. saison 2. durée des vacances 3. nationalité probable d'Élise 4. état d'esprit (= mental) de Sabine

C. La poste. En France, la poste joue aussi le rôle de banque. On peut y ouvrir un compte d'épargne, obtenir une carte de crédit ou des chèques de voyage. Regardez ces deux publicités.

LA CARTE BLEUE VISA DE LA POSTE : LE PAIEMENT PRATIQUE ET SÛR

Voyagez en toute liberté grâce à la carte bleue Visa de la Poste :

- des retraits d'espèces auprès de 15 000 distributeurs automatiques de billets et des 400 000 agences bancaires des réseaux Visa et Eurochèque,
- des paiements auprès de 6 000 000 de commerçants dans 160 pays.

La sécurité de disposer de votre argent et de pouvoir payer partout, à tout moment, chez les commerçants du réseau Visa.

Un moyen de paiement très simple : pas besoin de présenter votre carte d'identité, votre signature suffit.

LE CHÈQUE DE VOYAGE : LA SÉCURITÉ

La Poste vous propose des chèques de voyage émis en francs français ou en dollars U.S. par Visa et American Express.

Sécurité : En cas de perte ou de vol, les chèques de voyage vous seront immédiatement remplacés ; vous pourrez ainsi terminer tranquillement votre voyage. Vous pouvez obtenir vos chèques de voyage très rapidement auprès d'un bureau de poste offrant le service de change, ou les commander par correspondance auprès de votre centre de chèques postaux. (La commission de vente n'est que de 1 % du montant total).

- Mentionnez deux choses qu'on peut faire avec la carte bleue Visa.
- A quoi correspond le chiffre 160 sur cette publicité?
- Doit-on présenter une carte d'identité quand on paye avec une carte bleue Visa?
- Quel genre de chèques de voyage propose la poste?
- Que se passe-t-il si on perd ses chèques de voyage ou si quelqu'un les vole?
- En cas de perte ou de vol, où peut-on obtenir de nouveaux chèques?
- Quand vous voyagez, que faites-vous de votre argent? Emportez-vous du liquide ou des chèques de voyage? Payez-vous avec une carte de crédit? Discutez des avantages et des inconvénients de chaque mode de paiement.

Interactions

In this chapter, you practiced talking about the future, and you learned to link sentences. Act out the following situations, using the vocabulary and grammar from this chapter.

1. **A la banque.** You need to cash some traveler's checks. Go to the teller (your partner) at the window. Tell him or her how much money you want to change. Unfortunately, you have forgotten your passport. Ask whether you can change the money anyway and whether you can establish a checking account, because you will be in France for a while. Thank the teller for the information.
2. **Un job.** You are being interviewed for a job as a bilingual teller in a bank. Greet the interviewer (your partner). Answer any questions the interviewer may have. Ask about salary (**le salaire**), advancement (**les possibilités d'avancement**), job security (**la sécurité de l'emploi**), and working with people (**les conditions de travail**). Tell the interviewer why you would particularly like the job, and explain why you are qualified.

Vocabulaire

Verbes

couvrir to cover
dépenser to spend (*money*)
déposer to deposit
endosser to endorse (*a check*)
faire des économies to save (up) money
gagner to earn; to win
intéresser to interest
  s'intéresser à (quelque chose) to be interested in (*something*)
offrir to offer
ouvrir to open
retirer to withdraw
signer to sign
souffrir to suffer
toucher to cash (*a check*)

Substantifs

l'argent liquide cash
l'augmentation (*f.*) increase
l'avenir (*m.*) future
le budget budget
la caisse cash register
le carnet de chèques checkbook
le chèque check

le compte account
  le compte courant checking account
  le compte d'épargne savings account
le conseil advice
le cours exchange rate
le coût de la vie cost of living
la dépense expense
le distributeur automatique automatic teller
l'horaire (*m.*) schedule (*working hours*)
le montant sum; amount
le passeport passport
le portefeuille wallet
le reçu receipt
le salaire salary
la société company

Les professions

l'agent (*m.*) **de police** policeman
l'agriculteur (*m.*) farmer
l'architecte (*m., f.*)
l'artisan(e) artisan, craftsperson
l'artiste-peintre (*m., f.*) artist (painter)
l'assureur (*m.*) insurance agent
l'avocat(e) lawyer
le (la) **banquier** (-**ière**) banker
le **cadre** manager
le (la) **caissier** (-**ière**) cashier
le (la) **chanteur** (-**euse**) singer
le (la) **commerçant**(e) storekeeper, merchant
le (la) **comptable** accountant
le (la) **danseur** (-**euse**) dancer
le (la) **douanier** (-**ière**) customs officer
l'employé(e) employee
le (la) **fonctionnaire** civil servant
l'infirmier (-**ière**) nurse
l'ingénieur (*m.*) engineer
l'interprète (*m., f.*) interpreter
le (la) **journaliste** reporter
le **magistrat** judge
le **médecin** doctor
l'ouvrier (-**ière**) worker
le **publicitaire** advertising agent
le (la) **travailleur** (-**euse**) worker
  le travailleur indépendant self-employed worker
  le travailleur salarié salaried worker
le (la) **vétérinaire** veterinarian

Mots divers

agricole agricultural
aussitôt que as soon as
dès que as soon as
dont whose, of whom, of which
dur(e) hard, difficult
lorsque when
que whom, that, which
qui who, that, which
prochain(e) next

Expressions utiles

à l'avenir	*from now on*
un jour	*someday*

INTERMÈDE 13

Lecture

AVANT DE LIRE

(Review) *Skimming for the gist:* The following article is excerpted from *L'Étudiant,* a French magazine. It may seem difficult at first because of the many unfamiliar words. Use your skills at contextual guessing, and make use of all available clues. Before you begin, answer the following questions to get the gist of the article. Base your answers on the titles, introduction, photo, accompanying chart (below), and the first paragraph, if necessary. You do not need to know the meaning of every word to understand the main points.

- For whom is the article written?
- About what topic does it give advice?
- What season(s) does it refer to?
- What regions and/or countries does it refer to?

When you are skimming a complicated article for the general meaning, it is sometimes helpful to find the main sections first. Find the four parts of this article. What does each one deal with? Now read through the entire excerpt and answer the questions that follow.

CAMPAGNE DES TRAVAUX SAISONNIERS AGRICOLES
(France métropolitaine)

PERIODE approximative	REGIONS	TRAVAUX	REMUNERATION	NOURRITURE LOGEMENT	EMPLOIS	TRANSPORT
Mi-mai-juin	Vallée du Rhône Périgord - Centre	Cerises Fraises		Camping	Très peu	A la charge du candidat
Juin-juillet-août	Toutes régions	Manutention (foin, paille), conduite de tracteurs (garçons)		Oui	Peu	
Mi-juillet-mi-août	Sud-Ouest Auvergne	Ecimage du maïs		Camping obligatoire	Nombreux	
Août-septembre	Sud-Ouest Est	Tabac (garçons)		Oui	Très peu	
Mi-sept.-31 oct.	Val de Loire Vallée du Rhône	Pommes		Camping obligatoire	Peu	
Mi-sept.-15 oct. (environ)	Beaujolais Midi-Pyrénées	Vendanges	Tarif départemental fondé sur le SMIC[a]	Oui ou camping obligatoire	Peu	Indemnité si toute la campagne
début oct.-20 oct. (environ)	Pays de Loire Centre			Oui	Nombreux	
début oct.-20 oct. (environ)	Bourgogne			Oui		
début oct.-30 oct. (environ)	Aquitaine Champagne			Oui		

a. *minimum wage*

PISTES

RATS DES VILLES AUX CHAMPS

CRAMPON / JERRICAN

Décidément, la terre est basse. Cueillette des fraises ou des myrtilles[a], écimage du maïs[b], moisson, récolte du tabac, vendanges, débroussaillage des bois[c]... Les possibilités sont nombreuses, mais les travaux durs et souvent mal payés.

Curieusement, les jobs ou stages à l'étranger sont plus faciles à obtenir en agriculture que dans d'autres domaines. Différents organismes peuvent vous aider.

L'Association France-Québec (24, rue Modigliani, 75015 Paris, tél. 45.54.35.37) organise plusieurs programmes d'échange :

– pour tout public, la cueillette des pommes, de mi-septembre à fin octobre (de deux à trois semaines) ;

– pour les jeunes qui se destinent à la production maraîchère, la récolte du céleri et de la salade, de fin juillet à fin septembre ;

– en priorité pour les garçons expérimentés, le reboisement des forêts. Stages d'un mois ou deux à partir de la mi-mai. *« Allergiques aux moustiques s'abstenir »*, précise la brochure ;

– assez difficile aussi, la récolte du tabac. Stages de six à huit semaines, échelonnés de fin juillet à fin septembre.

Dans tous les cas, le transport est à la charge des participants, ainsi que les frais de nourriture. Le logement en revanche est assuré sur place. La rémunération est d'environ 150 F par jour, un peu plus pour le reboisement.

Le Canadian National (1, rue Scribe, 75009 Paris, tél. 47.42.76.50) gère la récolte du tabac en Ontario. Pour un peu plus de 4 000 F, cet organisme vous trouvera un emploi de deux mois en août-septembre. Tous les frais, y compris le transport, seront pris en charge. Sur place, vous gagnerez à peu près 250 F par jour. Attention, ces stages sont réservés aux seuls garçons, élèves ou étudiants en agriculture. Le travail est très dur et intense.

Objectif kibboutz (15, rue Béranger, 75003 Paris, tél. 42.77.96.11) envoie les volontaires qui le souhaitent dans des kibboutzim en Israël. Ils y sont nourris, logés et reçoivent un minimum d'argent de poche. Ils effectuent en échange toute sorte de travaux, principalement agricoles : récolte d'oranges, de pamplemousses... La durée minimum d'un séjour individuel est de cinq semaines. Ces kibboutzim ne sont pas religieux.

Jeunesse et Reconstruction (10, rue de Trévise, 75009 Paris, tél. 47.70.15.88) peut vous envoyer dans une famille norvégienne. Vous participerez aux travaux de l'exploitation contre logement, nourriture et 1 000 F d'argent de poche mensuel. L'association organise aussi des camps de jeunes internationaux, qui peuvent vous accueillir de trois semaines à un mois en Angleterre ou en Ecosse. Vous serez logé et nourri, mais payé à la tâche.

Les deux programmes sont destinés aux plus de 18 ans. Les frais d'inscription sont de 470 F. Le transport reste à la charge des participants.

a. *bilberries* b. *corn* c. *forests*

COMPRÉHENSION

1. En France, si on veut travailler à l'étranger, quels organismes peut-on contacter?
2. Dans quels pays peut-on aller? Quelle est la durée approximative des différents stages?
3. Quels adjectifs associez-vous aux travaux agricoles?
4. Nommez les travaux que peut faire un étudiant (une étudiante) au Québec. Essayez d'expliquer de quoi il s'agit dans chacun des cas.
5. Quelle récolte (*harvest*) est-ce que Le Canadian National dirige?
6. Si vous décidez de travailler en Israël, qu'y ferez-vous? Et en Norvège?
7. En France métropolitaine, quels travaux offrent beaucoup d'emplois? peu d'emplois?
8. Maintenant, imaginez que vous cherchez un travail saisonnier. Choisissez le lieu où vous voulez aller et ce que vous voulez y faire et expliquez pourquoi.

Par écrit

A. L'Amérique et le travail. Vous écrivez pour un journal français trois courts paragraphes sur l'attitude des Américains dans leur vie professionnelle. Utilisez les questions suivantes comme guide. Ajoutez aussi vos propres idées.

1. Quelles professions les Américains admirent-ils le plus? Pourquoi? Quelles professions admirent-ils le moins? Pourquoi?
2. Est-ce que les Américains admirent certaines professions où on gagne peu d'argent? Lesquelles? Pourquoi les admirent-ils?
3. Les Américains prennent-ils leur travail au sérieux? Pour la plupart d'entre eux, le travail est-il plus important que la vie de famille? que la réalisation de soi?

B. Après l'interview. Vous venez d'avoir une interview pour un poste d'employé bilingue dans une banque. Vous écrivez une lettre à la personne qui vous a interviewé(e) pour la remercier (M. ou Mme Dupont, Société Générale, 29, boulevard Haussmann, 75009 Paris). Expliquez-lui pourquoi vous pensez que vous êtes qualifié(e) pour le poste. Dites-lui quels sont vos projets futurs et pourquoi ce job est important pour votre avenir. Expliquez aussi quelles contributions vous pouvez apporter à la société. Finissez votre lettre par «Je vous prie d'accepter, Monsieur (Madame), mes sentiments les plus distingués.»

CHAPITRE QUATORZE

Vive les loisirs!

—Qu'est-ce que tu fais le week-end?
—Je fais beaucoup de sport.
—Moi, je préfère rester à la maison et bricoler ou jardiner. Nous venons d'acheter une très vieille maison que nous sommes en train de remettre en état. Alors, tu sais, il y a toujours quelque chose à faire!

Étude de vocabulaire

Les loisirs préférés des Français

Les spectacles
La chanson de variété*
Le cinéma

Les activités de plein air
La pêche
La pétanque
Le pique-nique

Les sports
Le cyclisme
Le football

Les jeux
Les jeux de hasard
Les jeux de société

Le bricolage†
Le jardinage

Les passe-temps
Les collections
La lecture
La peinture

*__Une chanson de variété__ is a popular song, frequently associated with a particular singer—in the past, Édith Piaf, Jacques Brel—and sung in a music hall, such as **l'Olympia,** or in a small nightclub.
†**Le bricolage** is puttering around, doing odd jobs around the house, building and repairing things oneself.

A. Catégories. La chanson de variété est un spectacle. Dans quelle(s) catégorie(s) de distractions classez-vous _____?

1. un match de boxe
2. une collection de papillons (*butterflies*)
3. la fabrication de nouvelles étagères
4. la pêche
5. la roulette
6. la lecture
7. une partie (*game*) de frisbee
8. la réparation de votre bicyclette
9. un pique-nique
10. la loterie nationale
11. un concert de jazz
12. la pétanque
13. le cyclisme

Le jardinage et la construction d'un barbecue sont deux formes de bricolage. Nommez deux formes de loisirs pour chaque catégorie.

1. manifestations sportives 2. jeux de société 3. bricolage 4. spectacles 5. activités de plein air 6. passe-temps

Sélection spectacles

THÉÂTRE

Fièvre romaine, d'Edith Wharton. Mise en scène : Jean-Claude Buchard. Avec Suzanne Flon et Judith Magre. Théâtre du Rond-Point.
21 h du mardi au samedi ; 15 h le dimanche.
128 F (au lieu de 140 F). Code FIEVR.

Good, de C.P. Taylor.
Adaptation : Sam Karmann. Mise en scène : Jean-Pierre Bouvier. Avec Jean-Pierre Bouvier, Sam Karmann, Hélène Arie, Anne Jacquemin...
Théâtre de la Renaissance.
20 h 45 du mardi au samedi ; 15 h 30 le dimanche.
163, 123 F (au lieu de 180, 140 F). Code GOOD1.

Père, de Strindberg.
Mise en scène : Claude Yersin.
Théâtre de l'Est parisien.
Du 16 avril au 7 mai.
20 h 30 les mardi, mercredi, vendredi, samedi ; 19 h le jeudi ; 15 h le dimanche.
88 F (au lieu de 110 F). Code PERE1.

Hors limite, de Philippe Malignon. Mise en scène : Raymond Acquaviva. Avec Philippe Lelièvre et Jean-Pierre Malignon.
Théâtre Fontaine.
21 h du mardi au jeudi ; 18 h le samedi. 139 F (au lieu de 150 F). Code HLIMI.

MUSIQUE-OPÉRA

Ensemble orchestral de Paris. Christian Ivaldi (piano), Christian Crenne (violon) : Brahms, Schubert. Salle Gaveau.
20 h 30 le 17 mai.
140, 115, 70, 36 F (au lieu de 160, 125, 75, 40 F). Code EOP34.

L'enfant et les sortilèges. Opéra en deux parties. Musique de Maurice Ravel. Livret de Colette. Direction musicale : Marc Soustrot.
Orchestre philharmonique des Pays de la Loire.
Théâtre des Champs-Elysées.
20 h 30 le mercredi 18 mai.
192 et 142 F (au lieu de 200 et 150 F). Code TCE27.

DANSE

Nous, les Tziganes. Spectacle du Théâtre tzigane Romen de Moscou. Théâtre Mogador.
21 h les 5, 7, 10, 12 mai ; 16 h le 15 mai. 130, 98 F (au lieu de 150, 115 F). Code TZIGA.

ROCK

Pink Floyd. Château de Versailles.
21 h 30 le 22 juin. 195 F. Code PINKF.

SPORT

Masters d'escrime. Palais des Sports.
20 h 15 le 5 mai. 73 F (au lieu de 80 F). Code ESCRI.

Prière de réserver vos spectacles 15 jours avant la date que vous avez choisie.

B. Vive les loisirs! Imaginez que vous êtes en vacances et que vous ne savez pas quoi faire. Voici quelques suggestions.

D'après ces publicités...

1. Quelles sont les différentes activités proposées?
2. Dans quelles catégories les classez-vous?
3. Quelle activité vous semble la plus amusante? la moins intéressante? Expliquez pourquoi.
4. Imaginez que ni l'argent ni la distance ne sont un obstacle. Quel genre d'activité allez-vous choisir? Expliquez les raisons de votre choix.

C. Interview. Posez les questions suivantes à un(e) camarade. Si vous apprenez quelque chose sur lui (elle) que vous ne saviez pas avant, dites-le à la classe. Parlez brièvement du caractère ou de la personnalité de votre camarade.

Expressions utiles: sentimental(e), terre à terre (= pratique), actif (active), passif (passive), paresseux (paresseuse), sportif (sportive), énergique, (peu) doué(e) (*gifted*) pour les sports, audacieux (audacieuse), (im)prudent(e), adroit(e), être un homme (une femme) à tout faire (*handy*), (n')avoir (pas) le goût du risque

Demandez-lui...

1. quelles sortes de chansons il (elle) aime (les chansons d'amour? les chansons folkloriques? politiques?)
2. qui est son chanteur favori et sa chanteuse favorite, et pourquoi
3. à quelles sortes de spectacles il (elle) assiste souvent et à quel spectacle il (elle) a assisté récemment
4. s'il (si elle) préfère faire du sport ou s'il (si elle) préfère assister à des manifestations sportives; à quelle manifestation sportive il (elle) a assisté récemment
5. quel jeu de société il (elle) préfère (le bridge? le poker? le Monopoly?)
6. à quels jeux de hasard il (elle) a joué, où il (elle) y a joué et combien il (elle) a gagné ou perdu
7. s'il (si elle) aime bricoler et quels objets il (elle) a réparés ou fabriqués (= construits)
8. s'il (si elle) collectionne quelque chose

Pour parler des loisirs: *courir* (to run) et *rire* (to laugh)

	courir	rire
je	cours	ris
tu	cours	ris
il, elle, on	court	rit
nous	courons	rions
vous	courez	riez
ils, elles	courent	rient
Past participle:	couru	ri
Future stem:	courr-	rir-

A. Sondage sur le jogging. Interviewez un(e) camarade pour savoir s'il (si elle) fait du jogging. Demandez-lui...

1. Combien de fois court-il (elle) par semaine?
2. Pendant combien de temps court-il (elle)?
3. Combien de kilomètres fait-il (elle)? (1 mile = 1,6 kilomètres)
4. Depuis quand fait-il (elle) du jogging?

S'il (elle) a répondu non...

1. Pourquoi ne court-il (elle) pas?
2. Pratique-t-il (elle) un autre sport?
3. Qu'a-t-il (elle) contre le jogging?
4. Que pense-t-il (elle) des gens qui courent souvent?

Puis comparez les résultats des différents sondages.

1. Dans votre classe y a-t-il plus d'étudiants qui courent ou plus d'étudiants qui ne courent pas?
2. Parmi les coureurs, qui court le plus par semaine? le moins? Qui a déjà couru dans un marathon ou une autre course importante?
3. Parmi les non-coureurs, qui a donné la raison la plus comique? la plus bizarre? Quels sont les sports les plus populaires?
4. Est-ce que dans votre classe les sportifs sont les plus nombreux ou les moins nombreux? Qu'aiment faire les étudiants qui font peu ou pas du tout de sport?

B. Le rire. Le rire est le passe-temps préféré de beaucoup de gens. Pourquoi les gens aiment-ils rire? Comment le sens de l'humour nous aide-t-il à vivre? Avec un(e) camarade, choisissez trois situations où le sens de l'humour nous aide, et expliquez pourquoi.

Le sens de l'humour nous aide dans les occasions où ______.

1. on a peur
2. on est embarrassé
3. on veut critiquer quelqu'un
4. il y a de la tension
5. on cache (*is hiding, concealing*) quelque chose
6. ?

Et vous? Aimez-vous rire? Avec un(e) autre camarade, répondez aux questions suivantes. Chaque fois que vous répondez **oui,** donnez un exemple.

1. Racontez-vous des blagues (*jokes*)? 2. Faites-vous souvent des jeux de mots? 3. Aimez-vous jouer des tours (*tricks*)? 4. Inventez-vous des anecdotes? 5. Avez-vous un(e) comique préféré(e)? 6. Aimez-vous particulièrement un film amusant ou une pièce amusante? 7. Aimez-vous lire des revues satiriques?

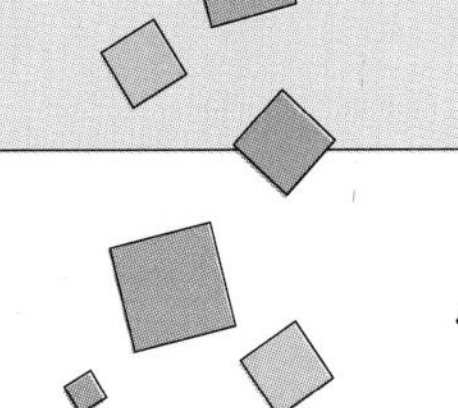

Étude de grammaire

49. Getting Information: Interrogative Pronouns

© JEAN-MARC LOUBAT / AGENCE VANDYSTADT

Au match de rugby

BILL: **Qu'est-ce qu'**ils essaient de faire?
JEAN-PAUL: Eh bien, ils essaient de poser le ballon derrière la ligne de but de l'équipe adverse.
BILL: Oui, je sais, mais **que** font-ils en ce moment?
JEAN-PAUL: Ça s'appelle une mêlée.
BILL: Et c'est **quoi,** une mêlée?
JEAN-PAUL: C'est quand plusieurs joueurs de chaque équipe sont regroupés autour du ballon. Tu vois, un des joueurs l'a récupéré.
BILL: **Lequel?**
JEAN-PAUL: Philippot.
BILL: **Qu'est-ce qui** l'empêche de le passer vers le but?
JEAN-PAUL: Les règles du jeu, mon vieux! C'est du rugby, ce n'est pas du football américain.

Voici des réponses. Quelles en sont les questions?

1. Ils essaient de plaquer (*tackle*) le joueur qui court avec le ballon.
2. C'est Duval qui passe le ballon à Philippot.
3. Un essai, c'est l'avantage obtenu quand un joueur réussit à poser le ballon derrière la ligne de but.

A. Forms of Interrogative Pronouns

Interrogative pronouns—in English, *who? whom? which? what?*—can be used as the subject in a question, as the object of the verb, or as the object of a preposition. You have been using some of the French interrogative pronouns: **qui, qu'est-ce que,** and **quoi.** On the next page is a list of French interrogative pronouns. Note that several have both a short form and a long form that is based on **est-ce que.**

USE	PEOPLE	THINGS
Subject of a question	qui qui est-ce qui	(*no short form*) qu'est-ce qui
Object of a question	qui qui est-ce que	que qu'est-ce que
Object of a preposition	à qui	à quoi

B. Interrogative Pronouns as the Subject of a Question

As the *subject* of a question, the interrogative pronoun that refers to people has both a short and a long form. The pronoun that refers to things has only one form. Note that **qui** is always followed by a singular verb.

PEOPLE	THINGS
Qui fait du jogging ce matin? **Qui est-ce qui** fait du jogging ce matin?	**Qu'est-ce qui** se passe? (*What's happening?*)

C. Interrogative Pronouns as the Object of a Question

As the *object* of a question, the interrogative pronouns referring to people, as well as those referring to things, have both a short and a long form.

1. *Long forms*

People: **Qui est-ce que**
Things: **Qu'est-ce que** + *subject* + *verb* + (*other elements*)?

Qui est-ce que tu as vu sur le court de tennis ce matin? — *Whom did you see on the tennis court this morning?*

Qu'est-ce que Marie veut faire ce soir? — *What does Marie want to do this evening?*

Remember that **qu'est-ce que** (**Qu'est-ce que c'est que**) is a set phrase used to ask for a definition: *What is ____?* **Qu'est-ce que la pétanque?**

2. *The short form* **qui** is followed by an inverted subject and verb.

Qui (+ *noun subject*) + *verb-pronoun* + (*other elements*)?

Qui as-tu vu à la salle de sports?	*Whom did you see at the gym?*
Qui Marie a-t-elle vu sur le court de tennis?	*Whom did Marie see on the tennis court?*

3. *The short form* **que** is followed by an inverted subject and verb. This is true for both noun and pronoun subjects.

Que + *verb* + *subject* (*noun or pronoun*) + (*other elements*)?

Que cherches-tu?	*What are you looking for?*
Que cherche Jacqueline?	*What is Jacqueline looking for?*

D. Use of *qui* and *quoi* After Prepositions

After a preposition or as a one-word question, **qui** is used to refer to people, and **quoi** is used to refer to things (including things that are indefinite or unknown).

De qui parles-tu?	*Whom are you talking about?*
As-tu vu mon ami?	*Have you seen my friend?*
Qui?	*Who?*
De quoi parlez-vous?	*What are you talking about?*

E. The Interrogative Pronoun *lequel*

Lequel, laquelle, lesquels, and **lesquelles** (*which one*[*s*]*?*) are used to ask about a person or thing that has already been specified. These pronouns agree in gender and number with the nouns to which they refer.

—Avez-vous vu cet opéra?	—*Have you seen this* (*that*) *opera?*
—**Lequel**?	—*Which one?*
—Vous rappelez-vous cette pièce de théâtre?	—*Do you remember this* (*that*) *play?*
—**Laquelle**?	—*Which one?*

The forms **lequel, lesquels,** and **lesquelles** must combine with **à** and **de.**

—Tu penses à un roman de Sartre.	—*You're thinking of a novel by Sartre.*
—**Auquel**?	—*Which one?*

—Vous avez besoin de livres d'anglais.	—*You need some English books.*
—**Desquels** avez-vous besoin?	—*Which ones do you need?*
but	
—Tu penses à une pièce de théâtre de Ionesco.	—*You're thinking of an Ionesco play.*
—**A laquelle**?	—*Which one?*

MAINTENANT A VOUS

Le paysage montagneux, à la fois harmonieux et varié du Nord des Ardennes Luxembourgeoises, offre au visiteur le calme, le repos et la détente. De vastes hauts-plateaux ondulés où se développe une agriculture poussée, sont creusés par d'innombrables vallées étroites parfois aux rochers abrupts dont les flancs sont couverts de sapins et de chênes. La suite des saisons fait changer sans cesse le décor de ce paysage ardennais. Des sentiers

bien signalés parcourant les hauteurs et les pentes et permettant des vues magnifiques, invitent à de longues promenades bienfaisantes. Au terme de ces randonnées – l'appétit étant stimulé par l'air pur des hauteurs – le touriste saura apprécier les spécialités gastronomiques qu'une hostellerie traditionnaliste lui offre. En parcourant cette région, on découvre ses beautés.

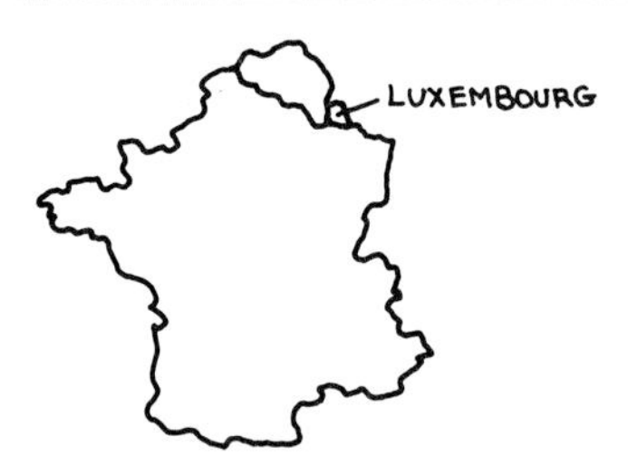

A. Le Grand-Duché du Luxembourg. Ce petit pays est un endroit idéal pour les amoureux de la nature. Voici une description des montagnes dans le sud du pays et du paysage (*landscape*) de la région. Lisez-la rapidement, puis posez les questions suivantes à un(e) camarade de classe. Inversez les rôles au milieu de l'exercice.

1. Où se trouve le Luxembourg?
2. Comment s'appelle la chaîne de montagnes dans le sud du pays?
3. Qu'est-ce que ce paysage offre au visiteur?
4. De quoi sont couverts les flancs de la montagne?
5. Qu'est-ce qui fait changer sans cesse le paysage?
6. A quoi nous invitent les sentiers?
7. Qu'est-ce que le touriste appréciera après les randonnées (*walks in the country*)?
8. Selon la brochure, que découvre-t-on quand on se promène dans la région?

Maintenant, décrivez un endroit de votre région ou un endroit que vous avez visité récemment (un parc national, une vallée, une ville, une forêt...) à vos camarades. Puis ils vous posent des questions pour avoir plus de détails sur ce qu'on peut y voir et y faire.

B. A la Maison des jeunes et de la culture.* Un(e) camarade vous raconte ce que les jeunes font à la MJC. Mais comme il y a beaucoup de bruit à la cafétéria, vous n'entendez pas ce qu'il (elle) vous dit. Posez-lui des questions avec **que** ou **qu'est-ce que.**

MODÈLE: —Sylvie regarde un film de François Truffaut au ciné-club.
—Que regarde Sylvie au ciné-club? (Qu'est-ce que Sylvie regarde au ciné-club?)

1. Les jeunes font des vases dans le cours de poterie.
2. On joue un air de Jacques Brel dans le cours de guitare.
3. Jean a fabriqué des étagères dans l'atelier de bricolage.
4. Marie a travaillé sur son service pendant son cours de tennis.

Maintenant, posez-lui des questions avec **qui** or **qui est-ce qui.**

MODÈLE: —Pierrot apprend à jouer du piano.
—Qui (Qui est-ce qui) apprend à jouer du piano?

5. Astrid va suivre un cours de poésie.
6. Paul apprend à faire un portrait dans le cours de peinture.
7. Jean-Loup écoute un concert de Debussy.
8. Le professeur choisit les meilleures œuvres à exposer.

C. Exposition à la MJC. Vous êtes responsable d'organiser l'exposition annuelle des ateliers de votre MJC. Un des professeurs a laissé un petit mot sur votre bureau. Malheureusement, vous avez posé votre tasse de café dessus et une partie du mot est illisible. Vous téléphonez au professeur. Quelles questions allez-vous lui poser?

MODÈLE: (que / qui) ... va exposer un dessin de Notre-Dame. →
Qui va exposer un dessin de Notre-Dame?

1. (qui / qu'est-ce qui) Le directeur a invité...
2. (que / qu'est-ce que) Mariona va nous apporter une...
3. (qui / qui est-ce qui) Vous devez téléphoner à...
4. (à quoi / de quoi) Demain, je veux vous parler de...
5. (qui est-ce que / qui) Nadine viendra avec son...
6. (que / qu'est-ce que) William nous prêtera une...
7. (quoi / que) Je pense beaucoup à la...
8. (qu'est-ce qui / qui est-ce qui) La... me préoccupe beaucoup.

---

*The **MJC** (**Maison des jeunes et de la culture**) are recreational centers created by the French government in 1961 at the request of André Malraux, then the minister of culture. There are now **MJCs** all over France. They offer work areas (**ateliers**) and courses in many hobbies and sports, and they sponsor cultural events, such as concerts, plays, art exhibits, and movies.

Maintenant, jouez la conversation téléphonique avec un(e) camarade. L'étudiant(e) qui joue le rôle du professeur improvise les réponses. Inversez les rôles au milieu de l'exercice.

D. Interview. Avec un(e) camarade de classe, posez des questions et répondez-y à tour de rôle.

MODÈLE: acteurs comiques: Danny Devito, Eddie Murphy →

VOUS: Lequel de ces acteurs comiques préfères-tu, Danny Devito ou Eddie Murphy?
UN(E) AMI(E): Je préfère Eddie Murphy. Et toi, lequel préfères-tu?
VOUS: Je préfère ____.

1. actrices: Sigourney Weaver, Candice Bergen
2. peintres: les Français Monet et Degas, les Espagnols Picasso et Dali
3. chanteuses: Madonna, Tina Turner
4. loisirs: le bricolage, le jardinage
5. spectacles: les manifestations sportives, les chansons de variété
6. cours: les cours de langues, les cours de sciences
7. restaurants: McDonald's, Burger King
8. chansons: les chansons romantiques de Barry Manilow, les chansons rock de Bruce Springsteen
9. ?

Que pouvez-vous dire des goûts de votre camarade?

E. Un jeu. Pensez à un sport. Un(e) camarade vous pose des questions pour deviner le sport auquel vous pensez.

Mots utiles: ***une balle:*** le Ping-Pong, le tennis, le hockey sur gazon (*field hockey*), le base-ball; ***un ballon:*** le football, le football américain, le rugby, le volley-ball, le basket-ball; ***un palet*** (*puck*): le hockey sur glace; ***les buts*** (*goal; goalposts*): le hockey, le football américain, le rugby, le water-polo; ***un coup de pied*** (*kick*): le football; ***dribbler:*** le basket-ball; ***frapper*** (*to hit, to strike*); ***le terrain de jeu*** (*playing area*): le basket-ball, le football; ***le court:*** le tennis, le squash, le badminton; ***le filet*** (*net*): le tennis, le volley-ball

MODÈLE: VOTRE CAMARADE: Avec quoi est-ce qu'on joue à ce sport?
VOUS: On y joue avec un ballon.
VOTRE CAMARADE: Qu'est-ce qu'on fait avec le ballon?
VOUS: On le lance et on le passe.
VOTRE CAMARADE: Chaque équipe a combien de joueurs?
VOUS: Cinq.
VOTRE CAMARADE: Penses-tu au basket-ball?
VOUS: Oui, c'est ça. Je pense au basket-ball.

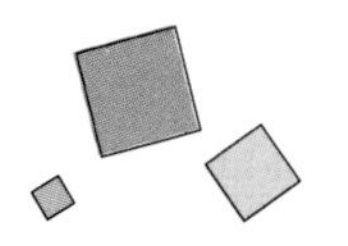

50. Being Polite; Speculating: The Present Conditional

Les loisirs sont parfois fatigants

FRANÇOIS: Qu'est-ce que tu **aimerais** faire aujourd'hui?

VINCENT: S'il faisait beau, nous **pourrions** aller au match de football.

FRANCINE: Si nous étions libres ce soir, Paul et Yvette **aimeraient** nous emmener dîner Chez Marcel.

VINCENT: Si vous aviez le temps, on **pourrait** aller au cinéma pour voir un western.

FRANÇOIS: Vous ne trouvez pas que ça **serait** formidable si nous ne faisions rien pendant tout un week-end?

Racontez les suggestions de Vincent, de Francine et de François pour passer leur week-end.

A. Forms of the Conditional

In English, the conditional is a compound verb form consisting of *would* plus the infinitive: *he would travel, we would go*. In French, the **conditionnel** is a simple verb form. The imperfect tense endings **-ais, -ais, -ait, -ions, -iez, -aient** are added to the infinitive. The final -e of -re verbs is dropped before the endings are added.

	parler (*to speak*)	**finir** (*to finish, to end*)	**vendre** (*to sell*)
je	parlerais	finirais	vendrais
tu	parlerais	finirais	vendrais
il, elle, on	parlerait	finirait	vendrait
nous	parlerions	finirions	vendrions
vous	parleriez	finiriez	vendriez
ils, elles	parleraient	finiraient	vendraient

J'**aimerais** vous accompagner au match de football.	*I'd like to go with you to the soccer game.*
Nous, entre un match de boxe et une soirée à l'opéra, nous **choisirions** le match de boxe.	*For us, between a boxing match and an evening at the opera, we would choose the boxing match.*

Verbs that have irregular stems in the future tense (Section 47) have the same irregular stems in the conditional.

S'il ne pleuvait pas, nous **irions** tous à la pêche.	*If it weren't raining, we would all go fishing.*
Elle **voudrait** aller les chercher.	*She would like to pick them up.*
Est-ce que tu **aurais** le temps de m'aider?	*Would you have time to help me?*

B. Uses of the Conditional

1. The conditional is used to express wishes or requests. It lends a tone of deference or politeness that makes a request seem less abrupt. Compare these sentences.

Je **veux** un billet.	*I want a ticket.*
Je **voudrais** un billet.	*I would like a ticket.*
Pouvez-vous m'indiquer ma place?	*Can you show me my seat?*
Pourriez-vous m'indiquer ma place?	*Could you show me my seat?*

2. The conditional is used in the main clause of some sentences containing **si** (*if*) clauses. When the verb of an *if* clause is in the imperfect, it expresses a condition, a conjecture, or a hypothetical situation that may or may not come true. The conditional is used in the main clause to express what would happen if the hypothesis of the *if* clause were true.

Si j'**avais** le temps, je **jouerais** au tennis.	*If I had time, I would play tennis.*
Si je **pouvais** pique-niquer tous les jours, je **serais** content.	*If I could go on a picnic every day, I would be happy.*
J'**irais** avec vous au bord de la mer si je **savais** nager.	*I would go to the seashore with you if I knew how to swim.*
Ils **joueraient** à la pétanque s'ils **avaient** des boules.	*They would play bocce ball if they had some bowling balls.*

The **si** clause containing the condition is sometimes understood but not directly expressed.

Je **viendrais** avec grand plaisir... (si tu m'invitais, si j'avais le temps, etc.).	*I would like to come . . . (if you invited me, if I had the time, etc.).*

Remember that an *if* clause in the present expresses a condition that, if fulfilled, will result in a certain action (stated in the future).

Si j'**ai** le temps, je **jouerai** au tennis cet après-midi.	*If I have the time, I'll play tennis this afternoon.*

Note that the future and the conditional are *never* used in the dependent clause (after **si**) of an *if*-clause sentence.

3. The present conditional of the verb **devoir** is used to give advice and corresponds to the English *should.*

—J'aime bien les jeux de hasard.	—*I like games of chance.*
—Vous **devriez** aller à Monte Carlo.	—*You should go to Monte Carlo.*
—Elle a besoin d'exercice.	—*She needs some exercise.*
—Elle **devrait** faire du jogging.	—*She should go jogging.*
—Mon ami s'intéresse aux livres sur les sports.	—*My friend is interested in books about sports.*
—Il **devrait** visiter le Métropolivre à Paris.	—*He should visit the Métropolivre in Paris.*

Mots-clés

How to make requests and say thank you: As you know, the conditional mode can be used to make requests politely. You might want to begin your request with a general question.

Est-ce que je peux vous demander un petit service? *May I ask you a favor?*

Don't forget to add **s'il vous plaît** (**s'il te plaît**) to the request and to say thank you.

Merci, Monsieur.
Je ne sais pas comment vous remercier, Madame.

Appropriate answers:

Je vous en prie. (*formal*)
De rien.
Il n'y a pas de quoi. (*more familiar*)

In polite conversation, the French use **Monsieur, Madame,** or **Mademoiselle** much more often than Americans use *ma'am* or *sir.*

MAINTENANT A VOUS

A. Après-midi de loisir. Imaginez que cet après-midi vous n'avez pas cours. Si vous pouviez choisir, laquelle de ces activités feriez-vous? Jouez la scène avec un(e) camarade.

MODÈLE: faire une promenade en ville ou à la campagne →

—Est-ce que tu ferais une promenade en ville ou à la campagne?
—Je ferais une promenade à la campagne.

1. jouer au tennis ou au squash 2. aller au cinéma ou au café 3. visiter un musée ou un parc 4. manger une pizza ou un sandwich 5. boire un café ou un Coca-Cola 6. parler anglais ou français 7. faire des courses ou la sieste 8. écouter de la musique classique ou du rock 9. acheter des vêtements ou des livres 10. lire des bandes dessinées ou un roman 11. rendre visite à un(e) ami(e) ou à la famille 12. ?

B. **Soyons diplomates.** Vous avez un(e) ami(e) qui a toujours l'habitude de donner des ordres. Donnez-lui deux façons de dire la même chose, mais poliment. Commencez avec **pourriez-vous...** et **je voudrais...** Jouez les rôles avec deux camarades.

MODÈLE: UN(E) AMI(E): Dites-moi à quelle heure le spectacle commence.
VOUS: Non! Pourriez-vous me dire à quelle heure le spectacle commence?
UN(E) AUTRE AMI(E): Tu peux dire aussi: Je voudrais savoir à quelle heure le spectacle commence.

1. Donnez-moi un billet pour l'opéra jeudi soir! 2. Indiquez-moi quand commence le premier acte! 3. Dites-moi où sont les places! 4. Dites-moi qui joue le rôle principal! 5. Expliquez-moi pourquoi les places sont si chères! 6. Donnez-moi des places moins chères! 7. Dites-moi à quelle heure le spectacle se termine! 8. Vendez-moi quatre billets!

C. **Problèmes de loisir.** Un(e) ami(e) vous confie qu'il (elle) a des difficultés à organiser son temps libre. Donnez-lui des conseils. Commencez par «A ta place, je ______.»

MODÈLE: UN(E) AMI(E): J'ai envie de danser!
VOUS: A ta place, j'irais dans une boîte de nuit (*nightclub*).

1. J'aime les sports. 2. J'aime les timbres rares. 3. J'ai envie de lire quelque chose d'intéressant. 4. J'aime fabriquer des meubles. 5. J'ai besoin de tranquillité. 6. J'admire les tableaux des impressionnistes français.

D. **Suppositions.** De temps en temps, ça fait du bien de rêver un peu. Imaginez ce que vous feriez dans les situations suivantes. Justifiez vos choix.

MODÈLE: si vous gagniez un voyage →
Si je gagnais un voyage, j'irais à Tahiti.

1. si vous receviez un chèque de 100 000 dollars
2. si vous deviez vivre dans une autre ville
3. si vous pouviez avoir la maison de vos rêves
4. si vous preniez de longues vacances
5. si vous étiez quelqu'un d'autre

E. Tête-à-tête. Avec un(e) camarade de classe, jouez les rôles d'un(e) étudiant(e) qui décrit un problème et de son ami(e) qui lui donne conseil. N'oubliez pas de remercier votre camarade.

MODÈLE: SERGE: Le cours d'algèbre est peut-être trop difficile pour moi.
SON AMI(E): Tu devrais en parler avec M. Pascal, le prof de maths.

1. JEAN-PIERRE: J'ai besoin de lire des articles sur les tropiques.
2. PATRICIA: Je cherche des articles de revue sur la profession de programmeur.
3. VINCENT: Je me demande s'il y a des programmes d'été dans les universités francophones d'Afrique.
4. HÉLÈNE: J'ai grand besoin d'un job à mi-temps.

Maintenant, expliquez à votre camarade un de vos problèmes actuels.

F. L'été aux Arcs. En France, beaucoup de stations de ski sont ouvertes l'été et offrent aux vacanciers de nombreux sports et loisirs. Voici ce qu'on peut faire aux Arcs, dans les Alpes.

D'après cette brochure, si vous alliez aux Arcs cet été...

1. Pourriez-vous faire du sport? Quel(s) sport(s) aimeriez-vous pratiquer?
2. Prendriez-vous beaucoup de photos? Pourquoi?
3. Auriez-vous le temps de prendre le soleil? de vous reposer?
4. Danseriez-vous tous les soirs?
5. Quelles autres activités aimeriez-vous faire?

Les Arcs, la station sports.

L'été aux Arcs, c'est la grande fête du sport. Golf, tennis, équitation, tir à l'arc, ski sur herbe, mountain-bike, rafting, canoë, delta-plane, alpinisme, escalade, randonnée, jogging, gymnastique, natation, arts martiaux... En tout, plus de 30 activités pour tous les goûts et tous les niveaux. Aux Arcs, on peut vraiment tout faire et toujours dans le cadre extraordinaire de l'un des plus beaux domaines de montagne d'Europe.
Mais aux Arcs, il n'y a pas que le sport et le soleil. Les Arcs, c'est autre chose. Aux Arcs, tout est conçu pour rendre la vie plus agréable et plus riche, qu'il s'agisse de l'agencement des résidences, du confort des appartements, des animations de la station ou de l'accueil des hôtels. Aux Arcs, les responsables forment une véritable équipe et travaillent tous en harmonie pour que chacun puisse vivre ses vacances comme il l'entend. Aux Arcs, on est plus libre. Libre de vivre à 100 à l'heure ou de se faire simplement bronzer au soleil, libre de se dépenser toute la journée ou de danser toutes les nuits, libre de s'éclater entre copains ou de profiter de sa famille...

G. Si je pouvais... Par petits groupes, posez à tour de rôle les questions qui correspondent aux conditions suivantes, et répondez-y avec imagination. N'hésitez pas à rêver!

MODÈLE: changer de spécialisation →
—Qu'est-ce que tu ferais si tu pouvais changer de spécialisation?
—Si je pouvais changer de spécialisation, j'étudierais la philosophie.

1. être riche 2. avoir un emploi idéal 3. parler parfaitement français 4. être libre de voyager 5. être recteur (*president*) de l'université 6. changer le monde

Maintenant, inventez trois ou quatre nouvelles conditions. Vos camarades vont y répondre. Puis décidez qui dans votre groupe est le plus ambitieux (la plus ambitieuse).

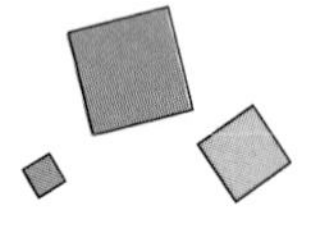

51. Expressing Actions: Prepositions After Verbs

Sortie au cabaret

CORINNE: Ce soir, nous avons **décidé de** t'emmener au cabaret de la Contrescarpe, à Montmartre.
CHUCK: Qu'est-ce que c'est qu'un cabaret?
JACQUES: Un cabaret, c'est une sorte de café où on **peut écouter** des chansons poétiques, ou satiriques...
CORINNE: Tu connais Georges Brassens, Jacques Brel, Barbara?
JACQUES: C'est grâce aux cabarets qu'ils **ont réussi à** percer.

1. Qu'est-ce que Corinne et Jacques ont décidé de faire?
2. Qu'est-ce qu'on peut faire dans un cabaret?
3. Qu'est-ce que Georges Brassens, Jacques Brel et Barbara ont réussi à faire grâce aux cabarets?

A. Verbs Directly Followed by an Infinitive

Some verbs can be directly followed by an infinitive, without an intervening preposition. Among the most frequently used are the following.

aimer	**détester**	**laisser**	**savoir**
aller	**devoir**	**pouvoir**	**venir**
désirer	**espérer**	**préférer**	**vouloir**

J'espère **devenir** chanteur un de ces jours; j'**aimerais transformer** mon passe-temps en profession.	*I hope to become a singer one of these days; I would love to turn my hobby into a profession.*
Mes amis **viennent m'écouter** au cabaret ce soir.	*My friends are coming to listen to me tonight at the cabaret.*

B. Verbs Followed by *à* Before an Infinitive

Other verbs require the preposition **à** directly before the infinitive.

aider à	**commencer à**	**s'habituer à**	**se préparer à**
s'amuser à	**continuer à**	**inviter à**	**réussir à**
apprendre à	**enseigner à**	**se mettre à**	**tenir à**
chercher à			

Paul **apprend à faire** la cuisine, et il **s'est habitué à utiliser** les expressions gastronomiques françaises.	*Paul is learning how to cook, and he has gotten used to using French cooking expressions.*
Corinne et Jacques **ont invité** Chuck **à passer** la soirée avec eux à la Contrescarpe.	*Corinne and Jacques invited Chuck to spend the evening with them at the Contrescarpe.*

C. Verbs Followed by *de* Before an Infinitive

Other verbs require the preposition **de** directly before the infinitive.

accepter de	**décider de**	**oublier de**	**rêver de**
s'arrêter de	**demander de**	**permettre de**	**venir de**
choisir de	**empêcher de**	**refuser de**	
conseiller de	**essayer de**		

Mireille **a accepté de travailler** comme interprète à l'ONU; cela ne l'**empêchera** pas **de continuer** ses études.	*Mireille has accepted a job as an interpreter at the UN; it won't keep her from continuing her studies.*
Mon médecin m'**a conseillé de faire** du sport; alors, j'**ai décidé de prendre** des leçons de judo.	*My doctor advised me to be active in sports, so I chose to take judo lessons.*

D. *Commencer à* and *finir de*

These two verbs are regularly followed by **à** or **de** plus an infinitive. When they are followed by **par**, their meaning changes.

Il y a deux mois **nous avons commencé à aller** aux boîtes le samedi soir. Une fois là, **nous commençons** toujours **par danser.** Quand **on a fini de danser, on commence à parler** de choses et d'autres. **On finit** toujours **par être fatigué,** mais heureux.	*Two months ago we started to go to nightclubs every Saturday night. Once there, we always start by dancing. When we've finished dancing, we begin to talk about one thing or another. We always end up (being) tired, but happy.*

E. *Penser* + Infinitive

When **penser** is followed by an infinitive, it means to count or plan on doing something.

Je pense rester chez moi ce week-end.	*I'm planning on staying home this weekend.*

F. *Venir*

Note the change in meaning that occurs when the verb **venir** is directly followed by an infinitive and when it is followed by **de.**

Ils **viennent dîner.**	*They are coming to dinner (to dine).*
Ils **viennent de dîner.**	*They've just had dinner (dined).*

G. Verbs + *à* + Indirect Object + *de* + Infinitive

Several verbs require a construction with two prepositions.

Chantal **a demandé à** Vincent **de** l'accompagner au match de rugby.	*Chantal asked Vincent to accompany her to the rugby match.*
La concierge **a dit aux** enfants **de** ne pas jouer au frisbee dans la cour.	*The concierge told the children not to play frisbee in the courtyard.*

Other such verbs include **commander, conseiller, permettre** (*to permit*), and **offrir.**

MAINTENANT A VOUS

A. Au cabaret de la Contrescarpe. Corinne, Chuck et Jacques arrivent à la Contrescarpe. Classez leurs activités par ordre chronologique.

1. Ils décident de partir vers deux heures du matin.
2. Ils se mettent à parler de poésie.
3. Le serveur leur conseille de goûter le cocktail maison.
4. Ils demandent au serveur de leur apporter l'addition.
5. Ils acceptent de s'asseoir à une table loin de la scène.
6. Ils continuent à chanter en rentrant chez eux.
7. Ils s'arrêtent de parler quand le spectacle commence.
8. Ils n'oublient pas de laisser un pourboire au serveur.

B. Projets et activités. Posez des questions à vos camarades pour vous informer de leurs projets et de leurs activités.

MODÈLE: aller / ce soir →

VOUS: Qu'est-ce que tu vas faire ce soir?
VOTRE CAMARADE: Je vais...

1. vouloir / ce week-end
2. rêver / l'été prochain
3. devoir / demain
4. tenir / bientôt
5. penser / la semaine prochaine
6. désirer / avant la fin du semestre
7. espérer / de ta vie

C. Résolutions de Nouvel An. Racontez vos bonnes résolutions à vos camarades. Complétez les phrases suivantes avec un infinitif.

1. Cette année, je voudrais apprendre...
2. Je me prépare...
3. J'ai aussi décidé...
4. Je vais essayer...
5. En plus, je tiens...
6. Mais je refuse...
7. Je vais continuer...
8. Enfin, je rêve...

D. Interview. Posez les questions suivantes—en français, s'il vous plaît—à un(e) camarade de classe. Puis faites un résumé de ses réponses. Demandez à votre camarade...

1. what he (she) likes to do in the evening 2. what he (she) hates to do in the house 3. if he (she) is learning to do something interesting, and what it is 4. what he (she) is eager to do soon 5. if he (she) has decided to continue to study French 6. what he (she) has to do after class 7. if he (she) has fun (**s'amuser à**) going to museums 8. if he (she) prefers going to a play or to a movie 9. if he (she) has just read a good book, and what it was 10. what he (she) knows how to do well 11. what he (she) doesn't do well but likes to do 12. if he (she) forgot to do something this morning, and what it was 13. if he (she) has stopped doing something recently, and what it was. 14. ?

Commentaire culturel

Distractions. Paris offre au visiteur une grande variété de spectacles, de restaurants, d'expositions. Il existe de nombreux guides, comme *l'officiel des spectacles, Pariscope, Parispoche* ou *La semaine de Paris*, que l'on peut acheter chaque semaine dans les kiosques, et qui donnent une liste détaillée de toutes les activités culturelles de la capitale, ainsi que des restaurants.

- Qu'est-ce qu'il y a sur la couverture de ce guide?
- Y a-t-il des guides semblables aux États-Unis? Lesquels?
- Que consultez-vous pour savoir quels spectacles il y a dans votre ville?

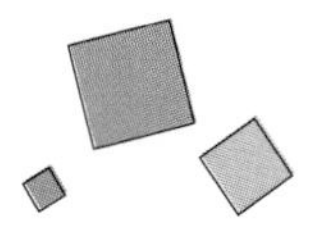

52. Making Comparisons: Adverbs and Nouns

Danse, disco et vidéoclips

DANNY: Qu'est-ce que vous faites, en général, le week-end?
MARTINE: **Le plus souvent,** nous allons danser en boîte.
HENRI: Tu aimes le disco?
DANNY: J'avoue que j'ai **plus de disques** de country **que de disco...**
MARTINE: Moi, j'adore les vidéoclips qu'on y projette **autant que** la musique.
HENRI: C'est vrai, il y avait **moins d'ambiance,** avant le vidéoclip!

Corrigez les phrases erronées.

1. Henri et Martine dansent rarement en boîte.
2. Danny a autant de disques de country que de disco.
3. Martine adore l'ambiance des boîtes autant que la musique.
4. Henri croit qu'il y avait plus d'ambiance dans les boîtes avant le disco.

A. Comparative Forms of Adverbs

The same constructions you learned in Chapter 12 for the comparative forms of adjectives are used for the comparative forms of adverbs.

1. **plus... que** (*more . . . than*)

   Jeannine assiste aux manifestations sportives **plus** volontiers (**que** moi). — *Jeannine attends sports events more willingly (than I).*

2. **moins... que** (*less . . . than*)

   Jackie Joyner court **plus** vite **que** Mary Decker. — *Jackie Joyner runs faster than Mary Decker.*

3. **aussi... que** (*as . . . as*)

   Nous nous promenons à la montagne **aussi** souvent **que** possible. — *We take walks in the mountains as often as possible.*

Canadi▸n *va plus loin*

B. Superlative Forms of Adverbs

To form the superlative of an adverb, place **le** in front of the comparative form (**le plus...** or **le moins...**). Since there is no direct comparison, **que** is not used.

Pierre s'en va tard. Louis s'en va plus tard. Michel s'en va **le plus tard.**

C. The Irregular and Superlative Forms of *bien* and *mal*

Note the irregular comparative and superlative forms of **bien.** The comparative and superlative forms of **mal** are regular.*

	COMPARATIVE	SUPERLATIVE
bien	mieux	le mieux
mal	plus mal	le plus mal

Tu parles français **mieux** que moi.	*You speak French better than I.*
Mais c'est Jean-Claude qui le parle **le mieux.**	*But Jean-Claude speaks it best.*
Roland joue **plus mal** au tennis que moi.	*Roland plays tennis worse than I.*
Mais c'est Marc qui y joue **le plus mal.**	*But Marc plays the worst.*

D. Comparisons with Nouns

Plus de... (**que**), **moins de...** (**que**), and **autant de...** (**que**) express quantitative comparisons with nouns.

*Irregular comparative and superlative forms of **mal** (**pis, le pis**) exist, but the regular forms are much more commonly used.

Ils ont **plus d'argent** (**que** nous), mais nous avons **moins de** problèmes (**qu'**eux).	*They have more money (than we), but we have fewer problems (than they).*
Je suis **autant de** cours **que** toi ce semestre.	*I'm taking as many courses as you this semester.*

MAINTENANT A VOUS

A. Rivalités. Voici deux familles, les Bayard et les Pascal. Comparez-les et imaginez leur vie d'après le dessin. Utilisez **plus de, moins de** et **autant de.**

Mots utiles: argent, maisons, voitures, domestiques, vêtements, enfants, problèmes, moments heureux, moments amoureux, dépenses, scènes de ménage, vacances, temps libre...

B. Travail et loisirs. Dans un sondage récent, les Français ont évalué certaines professions selon le temps que chaque profession laisse pour les loisirs. Dans le système de notation utilisé, le nombre **1** indique que la profession demande peu de travail et le nombre **5** indique que la profession demande beaucoup de travail. Faites au moins trois comparaisons pour chaque profession selon le modèle.

MODÈLE: Le chirurgien a plus de travail que le professeur d'université, il a autant de travail que l'avocat et il a moins de travail que le comptable.

Chirurgien	4	Assureur	3
Professeur d'université	2	Footballeur	2
Avocat	4	Cadre	4
Magistrat	3	Musicien	1
Comptable	5	Vétérinaire	3

Quelles observations peut-on faire sur les professions de comptable et de musicien (qu'on ne peut pas faire sur les autres) selon ce sondage?

C. **Opinions.** Avec un(e) camarade, imaginez que vous entendez les affirmations suivantes. Êtes-vous d'accord ou non? Réagissez et donnez votre propre opinion en utilisant une forme comparative.

1. Les hommes conduisent mieux que les femmes. 2. Les étudiants travaillent moins que les professeurs. 3. Madonna chante aussi bien que Whitney Houston. 4. Dans notre ville, il pleut plus en été qu'en hiver. 5. On apprend plus vite les verbes français que les verbes anglais. 6. Les joueurs de football gagnent autant d'argent que les joueurs de tennis.

Maintenant, inventez d'autres affirmations et votre camarade réagira d'après ses opinions. Puis inversez les rôles.

D. **Habitudes.** (*Habits.*) Demandez à un(e) camarade combien de fois par semaine, par jour, par mois, ou par an il (elle) fait quelque chose, et puis comparez sa réponse avec vos propres habitudes. **Autres possibilités:** lire le journal, faire du sport, regarder la télévision...

MODÈLE: VOUS: Combien de fois par semaine vas-tu au cinéma?
UN(E) CAMARADE: Une ou deux fois par semaine.
VOUS: J'y vais plus (moins, aussi) souvent que toi.

Situation

Séance de cinéma

Contexte *Maureen, une Américaine, travaille au pair dans une famille française à Toulouse. Aujourd'hui elle va au cinéma avec une amie française, Gisèle.*
Objectif *Gisèle explique certaines différences culturelles.*

GISÈLE: Bonjour, je voudrais deux billets pour la séance° de deux heures, s'il vous plaît. Tiens, Maureen, tu peux donner les tickets à l'ouvreuse°?
MAUREEN: Oui, mais qu'est-ce que tu fais?
GISÈLE: Je cherche un peu de monnaie pour lui donner un pourboire.
MAUREEN: Ah, d'accord... C'est curieux, il n'y a pas de queue.°

show *usherette* *line*

GISÈLE:	Oui, ici les cinémas ouvrent un peu avant la séance et on attend dans la salle.	
MAUREEN:	Et il n'y a rien à boire ou à manger?	
GISÈLE:	Si, une ouvreuse va passer pendant l'entracte.°	*intermission*
	Maureen et Gisèle regardent l'annonce d'un film de Stephen Frears, Les liaisons dangereuses, *un vidéoclip de Prince comme court-métrage et les publicités. Puis, c'est l'entracte.*	
MAUREEN:	J'aimerais bien grignoter quelque chose.° Il y a du popcorn?	grignoter... *nibble, have a snack*
GISÈLE:	Pas de popcorn, désolée°! Appelle l'ouvreuse!	*sorry*
MAUREEN:	Écoute, Gisèle, c'est vraiment trop drôle.	
GISÈLE:	Qu'est-ce qui est drôle?	
MAUREEN:	C'est d'entendre Glenn Close parler français, avec cette drôle de voix.°	*voice*
GISÈLE:	C'est vrai, j'ai oublié. Les films étrangers sont généralement doublés° ici. Ça surprend°!	*dubbed / surprises (people)*

VARIATIONS

1. Rejouez la scène avec cette différence: elle se passe maintenant en Amérique et c'est Maureen qui explique les différences culturelles à Gisèle.
2. Improvisez! Imaginez qu'un ami français (une amie française) vous rend visite en Amérique et que vous assistez ensemble à un spectacle ou à une manifestation sportive (un match de base-ball ou un match de football américain, par exemple). Votre ami(e) vous pose beaucoup de questions sur les coutumes (*customs*) américaines. Jouez les rôles avec un(e) camarade.

A propos

Comment critiquer un film

Pour exprimer une opinion favorable:

Quel chef d'œuvre!
Je l'ai trouvé extraordinaire.
C'est un film remarquable.
Il est formidable.
Il est super.

Pour exprimer une opinion défavorable:

Je ne le recommande à personne.
C'est un film vraiment minable (*shabby*),
très décevant (*disappointing*),
banal,
ennuyeux.
Quel désastre!
Quel navet (*flop*)!

Expressions utiles:

le metteur en scène } (*director*)
le cinéaste }
tourner un film (*to make a film*)
les personnages (*m.*) (*characters*)
jouer le rôle principal
la séquence (*scene*)
l'intrigue (*f.*) (*plot*)
vraisemblable (*believable, realistic*)
invraisemblable (*unbelievable, unrealistic*)
l'action
lente, rapide, ennuyeuse, sensationnelle/passionnante (*exciting*), mouvementée (*action-packed*), inexistante

A. Les distractions. Regardez cette comparaison entre les distractions préférées des habitants de différents pays européens. (1) Faites maintenant une enquête sur les distractions préférées de vos camarades de classe. Que font-ils au moins trois fois par semaine? une fois par semaine? une fois par mois? une fois par an? Utilisez comme guide les phrases de *Façons de se distraire.* (2) Faites une synthèse des réponses de vos camarades et comparez-les avec celles des Français. Est-ce que les Américains et les Français sont vraiment différents?

FAÇONS DE SE DISTRAIRE	MARCHÉ COMMUN	ALLEMAGNE	BELGIQUE	FRANCE	HOLLANDE	ITALIE	LUXEMBOURG	GRANDE-BRETAGNE
AU MOINS 3 FOIS PAR SEMAINE	%	%	%	%	%	%	%	%
S'asseoir devant la porte et regarder passer les gens	19	26	11	13	9	21	13	4
Lire des livres (autres que livres de classe)	33	34	20	42	45	21	41	45
Regarder la télévision	43	45	44	33	51	49	25	85
Lire un journal	72	83	71	76	89	48	89	93
AU MOINS UNE FOIS PAR SEMAINE								
Faire du jardinage	30	34	33	42	34	11	60	45
Faire des mots croisés	12	17	7	9	18	8	12	24
Aller à un club	6	10	3	3	11	2	17	21
Aller au café	17	13	18	14	7	27	35	26
Jouer aux cartes	20	17	23	18	29	23	21	22
Jouer aux échecs ou aux dames	5	5	2	5	7	4	5	11
Ecouter de la musique chez soi	50	54	47	59	69	34	80	76
Jouer d'un instrument de musique chez soi	4	6	3	3	9	2	6	5
Pratiquer un sport	7	8	5	7	13	3	10	13
Pour les femmes: tricoter, broder, coudre	66	68	71	84	85	42	89	82
Pour les hommes: bricoler	25	20	34	21	37	29	57	41
Discuter avec des amis	39	33	23	49	37	40	43	67
Lire une revue	42	47	36	47	72	25	51	63
AU MOINS UNE FOIS PAR MOIS								
Assister à une manifestation sportive	16	16	19	16	23	14	28	20
Aller au cinéma	30	23	27	30	15	44	51	20
Lire des poésies	6	6	4	7	7	5	7	8
Se promener à pied ou à bicyclette	33	45	26	38	42	12	64	35
Aller danser	8	9	7	7	9	8	19	14
Inviter des gens ou être invité	27	28	7	55	20	5	32	20
Faire de la gymnastique, du judo, du yoga	4	5	2	3	9	2	7	3
AU MOINS UNE FOIS PAR AN								
Aller au théâtre, music-hall, concert, opéra	17	22	15	14	18	13	45	27
Visiter des musées, expositions, monuments	10	9	10	15	11	7	29	22
Assister à une réunion politique	4	6	3	3	5	4	15	5

B. Jeu de rôles. Les expressions de l'*A propos* vous seront utiles dans les activités suivantes.

1. En groupe de trois ou quatre, créez des scènes où des amis sortent du cinéma en parlant (*while speaking*) du film qu'ils viennent de voir. Ils ne font pas mention du titre. Les autres étudiants essaient de deviner quel est le film en question. **Suggestions:** *Le Magicien d'Oz, Autant en emporte le vent, L'Empire contre-attaque, Le dernier Empereur, Rain Man, Aliens: le Retour, Un poisson nommé Wanda...*
2. Chaque membre de la classe nomme le dernier film qu'il (elle) a vu et explique aux autres pourquoi ils devraient ou ne devraient pas aller le voir.
3. Chaque membre de la classe nomme son film, son acteur (actrice) ou son cinéaste favori et explique brièvement pourquoi.

Les loisirs des Français. Les loisirs occupent une place importante dans la vie des Français. Il existe actuellement un Ministère du Temps Libre pour les aider à organiser leurs activités. Mais que font-ils donc de leur temps libre?

L'un des passe-temps favoris du Français est le bricolage: dans sa maison ou dans son jardin, il trouve toujours quelque chose à réparer, à embellir ou à remplacer. Cet amour du travail manuel montre l'importance que le Français accorde à son foyer (*household*). Les Français sont aussi de grands collectionneurs: par exemple, de timbres, d'objets rares ou de bandes dessinées. Ils passent souvent leurs week-ends à la recherche d'objets rares, même si parfois ils doivent conduire très loin.

Les Français aiment aussi beaucoup les sports, et ils sont de plus en plus

Greg Lemond, vainqueur du Tour de France, 1989

nombreux à en faire régulièrement. Leur sport favori est le football, avec plus de vingt mille clubs et près de deux millions de membres dans tout le pays. Le ski aussi est très populaire et beaucoup de familles profitent des vacances de Noël pour partir à la montagne, les Alpes ou les Pyrénées entre autres. Les stations sont nombreuses et très bien équipées, et comptent parmi les plus grandes surfaces skiables du monde. Les prochains Jeux olympiques d'hiver auront lieu à Albertville, dans les Alpes françaises, en 1992.

Le cyclisme connaît aussi un grand succès. Le Tour de France est peut-être l'événement sportif français le plus connu aux États-Unis. Cette course cycliste professionnelle effectue un parcours de plus de 5 000 kilomètres en trois semaines à travers la France.

D'autres sports très pratiqués par les Français sont le tennis, la planche à voile, le jogging et, de plus en plus, la gymnastique aérobique.

Parmi les loisirs il faut aussi nommer la musique, la lecture, le cinéma, le théâtre, la télévision ou les sorties entre amis, et bien sûr la conversation qui, pour certains, reste encore le sport préféré!

Mise au point

A. Loisirs et vacances. Les Français peuvent voyager sans passeport et sans visa dans les départements et les territoires français d'outre-mer (*overseas*). Faites des phrases complètes pour décrire ces vacances, en employant l'imparfait ou le conditionnel.

1. si / on / avoir (*imparfait*) / temps / argent / on / pouvoir / aller en Guyane, aux Antilles, en Polynésie ou à la Réunion
2. on / pouvoir / fréquenter / petits restaurants / à la Réunion
3. on / nous / inviter / survoler (*fly over*) / île / en avion
4. les plages / nous / permettre / goûter (à) / plaisirs des tropiques
5. on / pouvoir / apprendre / faire de la pêche sous-marine (*underwater*)
6. à Tahiti / on / nous / conseiller / visiter / parcs / où / on / cultiver / perles (*pearls*) noires
7. aux Antilles / nous / (ne... pas) pouvoir / s'empêcher / gouter / fruits exotiques
8. (ne... pas) oublier / manger / plats créoles
9. en Guyane / nous / s'amuser / descendre / grands fleuves
10. si / on / choisir (*imparfait*) / voyage organisé / on / trouver / meilleur prix / mais / on / (ne... pas) s'amuser / autant

B. Nommez trois choses... Donnez par écrit votre réaction spontanée aux questions suivantes. Écrivez des phrases complètes. Puis, comparez vos réponses avec celles d'un(e) camarade de classe. Lesquelles sont identiques?

1. Nommez trois choses que vous feriez si vous étiez riche. 2. Donnez trois raisons pour lesquelles vous vous battriez (*you would fight*) si c'était nécessaire. 3. Nommez trois instruments de musique dont vous aimeriez jouer. 4. Nommez trois sports auxquels vous aimeriez bien jouer. 5. Nommez trois personnes qui vous font souvent rire. 6. Nommez trois chanteurs (ou chanteuses) que vous admirez. 7. Nommez trois choses que vous feriez ce week-end si vous en aviez le temps.

C. Interview. Posez les questions suivantes en français à un(e) camarade. Ensuite, résumez ses réponses.

1. Who in class has more leisure time than you? Why? 2. What sport would you like to be able to play better? 3. Which American plays tennis best? 4. What athlete (**athlète,** *m. et f.*) would you like to speak to the most? 5. With whom in the French class have you played a sport or a game? Who won? 6. Who in the class runs faster than you? How do you know? 7. Who in the class goes to the library as often as you? 8. Who in the class needs to study the least in order to (**pour**) have good grades (**notes,** *f.*)?

Interactions

In this chapter, you practiced getting information, comparing and contrasting, and expressing wishes, requests, and conditions. Using the chapter vocabulary and structures, act out the following situations.

1. **Des conseils.** One of your children (your partner) needs to work harder in school. Compare your life with his (hers). You think that she (he) has too many distractions. Find out more thoroughly what she (he) does and with whom. Express your wishes and give advice on what to give up and how to get down to work.
2. **Un ancien ami (Une ancienne amie).** You run into an old friend (your partner) whom you have not seen for five years. Stop and chat. Find out how she (he) is getting along. Ask how her (his) life has changed, whom she (he) has seen lately, what her (his) leisure activities are, what work she (he) does. She (he) will get the same information from you.

Vocabulaire

Verbes

collectionner to collect, make a collection of
conseiller (à, de) to advise
courir to run
emmener to take (someone)
empêcher (de) to prevent
fabriquer to make
fumer to smoke
s'habituer (à) to become accustomed to
indiquer to show, point out
lancer to throw
se passer to happen, take place
permettre (de) to permit
promettre (de) to promise
refuser (de) to refuse
remercier to thank
rire to laugh

Substantifs

l'atelier (*m.*) workshop, studio, work area
le bricolage do-it-yourself work, puttering
la chanson de variété popular song
la collection collection
le cyclisme cycling
la détente relaxation
l'équipe (*f.*) team
le jardinage gardening
les jeux de hasard (*m.*) games of chance
les jeux de société (*m.*) social games, group games
les loisirs (*m.*) leisure activities
la manifestation sportive sporting event
le match game (*sports*)
l'oiseau (*m.*) bird
le passe-temps hobby
la pêche fishing
la pétanque bocce ball, lawn bowling
la pièce de théâtre play (*theater*)
la règle rule
la séance show (*movies*)
le service favor
le spectacle show, performance
le vidéoclip music video

Adjectifs

désolé(e) sorry
doué(e) (pour) talented, gifted (*in*)
fatigué(e) tired
formidable wonderful
plein(e) full, filled
  de plein air outdoors (*activities*)
  en plein air outdoors
ravi(e) delighted

Expressions interrogatives

qui est-ce que, qu'est-ce qui, lequel, laquelle, lesquels, lesquelles

Mots divers

autant (de)... que as much (*many*) . . . as
autour de around (*something*)
avant before
bien, mieux, le mieux well, better, best
être en train de to be in the process of; to be in the middle of
qu'est-ce qui se passe? what's happening? what's going on?

Expressions utiles

Je ne sais pas comment vous (te) remercier.	*I don't know how to thank you.*
Je vous en prie. **Il n'y a pas de quoi.**	*You're welcome.*

INTERMÈDE 14

Lecture

Appétit des loisirs

Moins de temps de travail, davantage° de temps libre: le Français a l'appétit des loisirs. Pour occuper ce temps personnel, il choisit souvent des activités qui révèlent un double intérêt pour son enrichissement personnel et pour la communication avec les autres.

Le stage° est symptomatique de ce besoin de réalisation personnelle. Le concept de stage est né dans les années 65–70 avec le sentiment° écologique: on redécouvrait° poterie, tissage,° agriculture biologique. Mais aujourd'hui, les stagiaires° ne sont plus des marginaux:° ils sont cadres supérieurs, fonctionnaires, enseignants, membres de professions libérales ou paramédicales. La passion des stages est aussi récupérée par° les professionnels du tourisme et par les associations. Par exemple, on voit un restaurateur° de la Creuse° proposer une «initiation à la pêche à la mouche°» ou une association sportive offrir un stage «ski et tennis». Le Club Méditerranée, qui se spécialise depuis longtemps dans les vacances organisées, a ouvert depuis 1970 de nombreux ateliers, y compris° le cinéma, la magie,° la vie pratique ou «comment ne pas passer pour un(e) idiot(e) aux yeux de son conjoint°» avec au programme: électricité, plomberie, maçonnerie, jardinage et mécanique!

Cet engouement° pour le stage se double d'une passion pour la vie associative. La France est un pays d'adhérents:° ils seraient vingt millions selon certains sondages, des plus sérieux aux plus farfelus.° Il existe, par exemple, une association «pour le droit à la paresse°», et d'autres pour les «descendants des corsaires°», pour les «parents bébés-nageurs» ou encore pour les «astronomes amateurs de Toulouse». Il existe ainsi entre trois cent et cinq cent mille associations. Avec les années, de nouveaux thèmes apparaissent:° l'informatique, par exemple. La politique, pourtant,° en est presque° exclue: il existe beaucoup plus de pêcheurs à la ligne et de boulistes que de militants anti-nucléaires. De même, chez les jeunes, 35 pour cent seraient membres d'associations sportives, et seulement 14 pour cent feraient partie d'un syndicat.°

Beaucoup de jeunes sont membres d'une MJC, c'est-à-dire d'une Maison des jeunes et de la culture. Ces centres de loisirs pour jeunes, situés dans de nombreuses villes de France, sont subventionnés° par l'État, par la ville et par les cotisations° de leurs adhérents. Ils comprennent° en général un théâtre, une discothèque, une bibliothèque, des salles de réunion et parfois un

plus

période d'études
le... la conscience
rediscovered / *weaving*
personnes qui font un stage / minoritaires
récupérée... utilisée pour le profit de
personne qui tient un restaurant / département au centre de la France
la pêche... *fly-fishing*
y... *including* / *magic*
son... son mari ou sa femme

admiration
membres d'une association
≠ sérieux
substantif de **paresseux**
pirates
appear
however / *almost*
labor union

subsidized
l'argent qu'on paie pour être membre / *include*

bar-restaurant. De nombreux «ateliers», clubs, conférences et manifestations culturelles s'y tiennent tous les jours. La MJC est un lieu de rencontre et aussi un lieu d'apprentissage.

S'associer en petits groupes d'intérêts communs, pour les Français, c'est retrouver une vie plus locale et plus sociable. Cette nouvelle mode des loisirs refuse aussi le plus souvent la facilité.° L'ère de la sieste et du farniente° est-elle terminée?

loisir / (mot italien) ne rien faire

COMPRÉHENSION

A. Vrai ou faux? Corrigez les phrases inexactes selon la lecture.

1. Plus de travail, moins de temps libre: le Français perd l'appétit des loisirs.
2. Les stages sont un bon exemple du besoin de réalisation personnelle.
3. Aujourd'hui, les stagiaires sont encore des marginaux.
4. Le Club Méditerranée, qui se spécialise depuis peu dans les vacances organisées, a lancé depuis 1980 de nombreux ateliers.
5. Il y a entre 300 000 et 500 000 associations.
6. Avec les années, de nouveaux thèmes disparaissent: l'informatique, par exemple.
7. Les MJC ne sont subventionnées que par les cotisations de leurs adhérents.

B. Commentaire. En Amérique, existe-t-il des associations et des stages comparables à ceux (*those*) que vous venez de découvrir? Êtes-vous membre d'une association? Laquelle? Avez-vous fait des stages? Décrivez-les.

Par écrit

A. Les vacances. Imaginez que vous voulez passer des vacances au Club Méditerranée de la Guadeloupe. Écrivez une lettre pour avoir des renseignements sur le village et le type de logement. Décrivez ce que vous aimeriez y faire et demandez si le village a les structures d'accueil nécessaires. Expliquez que vous souhaitez recevoir une réponse avant une date précise et donnez vos raisons. Terminez votre lettre par «En vous remerciant à l'avance de votre aide, je vous prie d'accepter mes salutations les plus distinguées.»

B. Une association. Imaginez que vous allez fonder une société qui se spécialise dans les loisirs telle que le Club Med. Donnez-lui un nom et décrivez ses activités. En quoi se différencie-t-elle d'autres sociétés qui offrent les mêmes services? Expliquez pourquoi des personnes choisiraient votre société plutôt qu'une autre.

CHAPITRE QUINZE

Opinions et points de vue

—A mon avis, il faut que le gouvernement prenne des mesures sévères contre les sociétés qui polluent l'environnement.

—Oui, mais ce n'est pas toujours facile.

—Tu sais, la pluie acide détruit nos forêts et les déchets industriels empoisonnent nos rivières. On finira par détruire la vie sur notre planète!

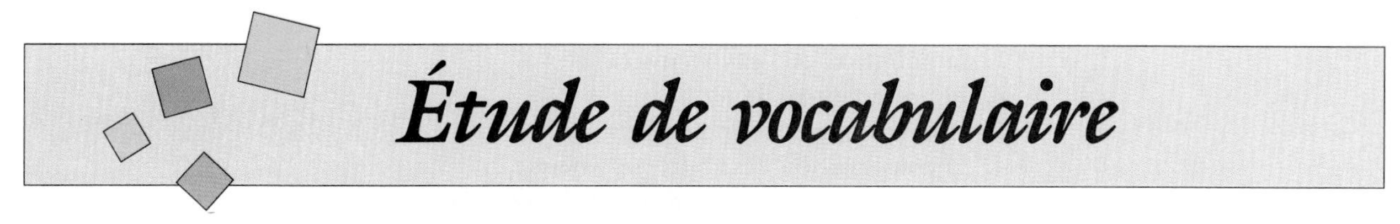

Étude de vocabulaire

Les problèmes de l'environnement

A. Association de mots. Quels problèmes écologiques associez-vous avec les verbes suivants?

MODÈLE: gaspiller → le gaspillage des sources d'énergie

1. conserver 2. protéger 3. polluer 4. recycler 5. développer

B. Remèdes. Expliquez quelles sont les actions nécessaires pour sauver (*to save*) notre planète. Utilisez **Il faut** ou **Il ne faut pas** suivi d'un infinitif.

MODÈLES: le contrôle des déchets industriels →
Il faut contrôler les déchets industriels.

le gaspillage de l'énergie → Il ne faut pas gaspiller l'énergie.

1. la pollution de l'environnement
2. la protection de la nature
3. le développement de l'énergie solaire
4. la conservation des sources d'énergie
5. le gaspillage des ressources naturelles
6. le développement des transports publics

C. **L'actualité.** Voici les résultats d'une enquête faite pendant la dernière campagne présidentielle en France. Lisez-les, puis répondez aux questions suivantes.

Pour chacun des thèmes suivants, estimez-vous qu'au cours de cette campagne électorale : on leur accorde trop d'importance, pas assez d'importance ou comme il faut ?

	Trop d'importance	Pas assez d'importance	Comme il faut
	%	%	%
- La pauvreté	3	**83**	11
- L'emploi	6	**76**	17
- L'éducation nationale	6	**64**	22
- Le rôle de la France dans le monde	7	**61**	25
- L'insécurité	14	50	32
- La construction* de l'Europe	12	46	32
- Les impôts	19	45	28
- L'immigration	29	34	29

*Voir le *Commentaire culturel,* p. 469.

- Lesquels de ces thèmes sont discutés pendant les campagnes électorales aux États-Unis?
- Parmi ceux-là, lequel considérez-vous comme le plus important? le moins important? Comparez vos conclusions avec celles de vos camarades.
- Selon vous, que peut-on faire pour résoudre ces problèmes?
- Quels autres thèmes ajouteriez-vous à ce sondage? Choisissez deux thèmes qui vous intéressent particulièrement et commentez-les en commençant par **Il faut.**

Mots-clés

How to carry on a discussion:

To express a personal point of view:

A mon avis,...	**Je crois que...**
Personnellement,...	**J'estime que...**
Pour ma part,...	**Je trouve que...**

Your point will often seem more convincing if you give examples or refer to other people's opinions. You can use the following expressions:

Par exemple,...
On dit que...
J'ai entendu dire que...

D. A mon avis. Choisissez une des expressions ci-dessus pour exprimer votre point de vue.

MODÈLE: possible / contrôler le problème des déchets nucléaires →

A mon avis (Personnellement, Pour ma part), je crois (estime, trouve) qu'il est (qu'il n'est pas) possible de contrôler le problème des déchets nucléaires, parce que...

1. essentiel / développer de nouvelles sources d'énergie
2. impossible / empêcher les accidents nucléaires
3. important / respecter la femme dans les publicités
4. indispensable / accorder aux médias la liberté d'expression
5. inutile / donner aux étudiants beaucoup d'examens
6. ennuyeux / lire des romans d'amour

E. Réagissez! Donnez votre opinion personnelle sur les idées suivantes.

1. envoyer des cartes de Noël 2. obtenir toujours de bonnes notes 3. avoir un job d'été 4. apprendre une langue étrangère 5. voter dans les élections 6. avoir un diplôme universitaire 7. savoir utiliser un ordinateur 8. être sociable avec tout le monde

Étude de grammaire

53. Expressing Attitudes: Regular Subjunctive Verbs

Votez pour Françoise!

FRANÇOISE: Alors, vous voulez que je **pose** ma candidature au Conseil de l'université!
SIMON: Oui, nous souhaitons que le Conseil **sorte** de son inertie et que ses délégués **prennent** conscience de leurs responsabilités politiques.
FRANÇOISE: Mais je me suis déjà présentée sans succès l'an dernier.
LUC: Cette année, Françoise, nous voulons que tu **réussisses.** Et nous te soutiendrons jusqu'au bout.

Retrouvez la phrase correcte dans le dialogue.

1. Est-ce que je dois poser ma candidature au Conseil de l'université?
2. Nous espérons que le Conseil sortira de son inertie.
3. Nous espérons que ses délégués prendront conscience de leurs responsabilités.
4. Nous espérons que tu réussiras cette année.

A. The Subjunctive Mood

All the verb tenses you have learned so far have been in the *indicative* mood (past, present, and future), in the *imperative* mood, which is used for direct commands or requests, or in the *conditional* mood, which is used to express hypothetical situations. In this chapter, you will begin to learn about the *subjunctive* mood.

The indicative is used to state facts. The subjunctive is used to express the opinions or attitudes of the speaker. It expresses such personal feelings as uncertainty, doubt, emotion, possibility, and desire, rather than fact.

The subjunctive is used infrequently in English. Compare the use of the indicative and the subjunctive in the following examples.

INDICATIVE	SUBJUNCTIVE
He *goes* to Paris.	I insist that he *go* to Paris.
We *are* on time.	They ask that we *be* on time.
She *is* the president.	She wishes that she *were* the president.

Une manifestation à Paris contre le racisme

In French, the subjunctive is used more frequently than in English. It almost always occurs in a dependent clause beginning with **que** (*that*). The main clause contains a verb that expresses desire, emotion, uncertainty, or some other subjective view of the action to be performed. Here and in Grammar Section 54, where the forms of the subjunctive are presented, the examples and the exercises will illustrate the use of the subjunctive in dependent clauses introduced by **que** after verbs of volition, such as **désirer, souhaiter** (*to want, to wish*), **vouloir, aimer bien** (*to like*), and **préférer.**

Usually, the subjects of the main and dependent clauses are different.

MAIN CLAUSE *Indicative*	DEPENDENT CLAUSE *Subjunctive*
Je veux	**que** vous **partiez.**

B. The Meaning of the Subjunctive

The French subjunctive has many possible English equivalents.

que je parle → *that I speak, that I'm speaking, that I do speak, that I may speak, that I will speak, me to speak*

De quoi veux-tu **que je parle**?	*What do you want me to talk about?*
Il veut **que je** lui **parle.**	*He wants me to speak to him.*

C. Forms of the Present Subjunctive

For most verbs, the stem for the forms **je, tu, il, elle, on, ils, elles** of the subjunctive is found by dropping the **-ent** of the third-person plural (**ils/elles**) form of the present indicative. The endings are **-e, -es,** and **-ent.**

INFINITIVE	**parler**	**vendre**	**finir**	**voir**
STEM	(ils) **parl**/ent	(ils) **vend**/ent	(ils) **finiss**/ent	(ils) **voi**/ent
... que je	parle	vende	finisse	voie
... que tu	parles	vendes	finisses	voies
... qu'il, elle, on	parle	vende	finisse	voie
... qu'ils, elles	parlent	vendent	finissent	voient

The stem for the **nous** and **vous** forms of the subjunctive is found by dropping the **-ons** from the first-person indicative plural (**nous**). The endings are **-ions** and **-iez.**

INFINITIVE	**parler**	**vendre**	**finir**	**voir**
STEM	(nous) **parl**/ons	(nous) **vend**/ons	(nous) **finiss**/ons	(nous) **voy**/ons
... que nous	parlions	vendions	finissions	voyions
... que vous	parliez	vendiez	finissiez	voyiez

Verbs that are regular in the indicative have the same stem for all persons in the subjunctive. Irregular verbs and verbs with spelling changes have two stems in the subjunctive.

Marc veut que je **parl**e maintenant avec la journaliste.
Mais elle préfère que nous nous **parl**ions plus tard.

J'aimerais bien qu'on **prenn**e le métro.
Mais Jacqueline préfère que vous **pren**iez l'autobus.

Voulez-vous que je lui **rappell**e l'heure du rendez-vous?
Je veux bien que vous la lui **rappel**iez.

MAINTENANT A VOUS

A. Stratégie électorale. Françoise accepte de poser sa candidature au Conseil universitaire. Avec un groupe d'étudiants, elle prépare soigneusement sa campagne. Que veut Françoise?

MODÈLE: Elle veut que les étudiants / choisir / des délégués responsables. → Elle veut que les étudiants choisissent des délégués responsables.

1. Elle veut que les étudiants / réfléchir / aux problèmes de l'université.
2. Elle aimerait que nous / préparer / une stratégie électorale tout de suite.
3. Elle préfère que vous / finir / les affiches aujourd'hui.
4. Elle veut que Luc et Simon / organiser / un débat.
5. Elle souhaite que la trésorière / établir / un budget.
6. Elle insiste pour que je / convoquer / tous les volontaires ce soir.

B. Discours politique. Ce soir, Françoise fait son premier discours de la campagne électorale. Voici ce qu'elle dit aux étudiants.

1. Je veux que le Conseil universitaire / agir / en faveur des étudiants.
2. Je souhaite que vous / participer / aux décisions du Conseil.
3. Je préfère que nous / discuter / librement des mesures à prendre.
4. Je voudrais que nous / trouver / tous ensemble des solutions à vos problèmes.
5. Je désire que l'université / prendre / en considération nos inquiétudes.
6. Je voudrais que les professeurs / comprendre / nos positions.
7. Je souhaite enfin que tous les candidats / se réunir / bientôt pour mieux exposer leurs idées.
8. ?

C. Opinions. Complétez les phrases suivantes et donnez vos opinions personnelles. Commencez avec **Je voudrais que...**

1. notre gouvernement (choisir de) ____
2. notre Président (essayer de) ____
3. les étudiants (manifester plus/moins/pour) ____
4. nous (apprendre à) ____
5. nous (ne pas oublier que) ____
6. ?

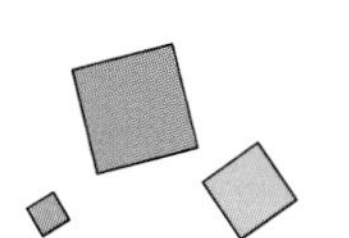

54. Expressing Attitudes: Irregular Subjunctive Verbs

Ancien ministre des droits de la femme

LA JOURNALISTE: On vous appelle «le ministre qui a fait des remous (*waves*)». Pourquoi?

YVETTE ROUDY: C'est parce que quand j'étais ministre j'ai lancé beaucoup de campagnes pour les droits de la femme.

- pour la contraception: Je voulais que les femmes **soient** convenablement informées.
- contre le sexisme: Nous ne voulions pas qu'on **puisse** exploiter le corps féminin dans les publicités.

- pour la féminisation des noms de profession: Nous ne voulions pas qu'il y **ait** des métiers féminins et des métiers masculins, mais des métiers pour tous!
- pour l'orientation et la formation professionnelle des femmes: Nous souhaitions que les femmes **sachent** s'engager vers des métiers d'avenir.

1. On est souvent mal informé sur la contraception. Mme Roudy voulait que les femmes _____ (être) convenablement informées.
2. De nos jours, les publicitaires exploitent souvent les femmes. Mme Roudy ne voulait pas qu'on _____ (pouvoir) exploiter le corps féminin.
3. Il y a des métiers masculins (*e.g.*, **le magistrat**) et des métiers féminins (*e.g.*, **l'ouvreuse**). Mme Roudy ne voulait pas qu'il y _____ (avoir) des métiers féminins et des métiers masculins, mais des métiers pour tous.
4. Souvent, les filles ne savent pas s'engager vers des métiers d'avenir. Mme Roudy voulait qu'elles le _____ (savoir).

Some verbs have irregular subjunctive stems. Except for those of **avoir** and **être,** the endings themselves are all regular.

	aller: ***aill-/all-***	**faire:** ***fass-***	**pouvoir:** ***puiss-***	**savoir:** ***sach-***	**vouloir:** ***veuill-/voul-***	**avoir:** ***ai-/-ay***	**être:** ***soi-/-soy***
... que je/j'	aille	fasse	puisse	sache	veuille	aie	sois
que tu	ailles	fasses	puisses	saches	veuilles	aies	sois
qu'il, elle, on	aille	fasse	puisse	sache	veuille	ait	soit
que nous	allions	fassions	puissions	sachions	voulions	**ayons**	soy**ons**
que vous	alliez	fassiez	puissiez	sachiez	vouliez	**ayez**	soy**ez**
qu'ils, elles	aillent	fassent	puissent	sachent	veuillent	aient	soient

Le prof veut que nous **allions** au laboratoire. — *The professor wants us to go to the laboratory.*

Son parti veut que le gouvernement **fasse** des réformes. — *His (Her) party wants the government to make reforms.*

Le Président préfère que les sénateurs **soient** présents. — *The President prefers the senators to be there.*

MAINTENANT A VOUS

A. Revendications. Les délégués du Conseil universitaire donnent leurs directives aux étudiants. Recommencez leurs notes en remplaçant les sujets en italique par **vous,** puis par **les étudiants.**

Nous ne voulons pas que *tu* ailles en cours aujourd'hui. Nous préférons que *tu* sois présent à la manifestation et que *tu* fasses grève. Nous désirons que *tu* aies une affiche lisible (*legible*). Naturellement, nous voudrions que *tu* puisses exprimer tes opinions librement.

B. Confrontation. Vous avez l'occasion de parler avec le sénateur de votre état. Complétez les phrases 1 et 2 afin de lui exprimer vos opinions. Puis complétez les phrases 3 et 4 pour exprimer les idées du sénateur.

VOUS:

1. D'une façon générale, nous voulons que nos représentants au congrès ____.
   avoir le sens des responsabilités
   savoir écouter les opinions des autres
   être honnête
   ?
2. En particulier, Monsieur (Madame) ____, nous voulons que vous ____.
   faire respecter nos traditions
   pouvoir souvent rencontrer vos électeurs
   aller à Washington défendre nos intérêts
   ?

LE SÉNATEUR:

3. Je voudrais que vous, les électeurs, ____.
   avoir confiance en moi
   connaître mieux mes idées sur les problèmes de notre société
4. Je voudrais aussi que nous ____.
   savoir travailler ensemble
   faire un effort pour garder (*to keep*) le contact
   ?

C. Slogans. Composez votre propre slogan politique selon les modèles des dessins. Utilisez **Vous voulez que ____?** et les verbes suivants: avoir, être, faire, pouvoir, savoir, choisir, réformer, réussir à, servir à, vivre, perdre, comprendre, changer, préparer, s'unir, écouter, gagner, apporter, élire, voter.

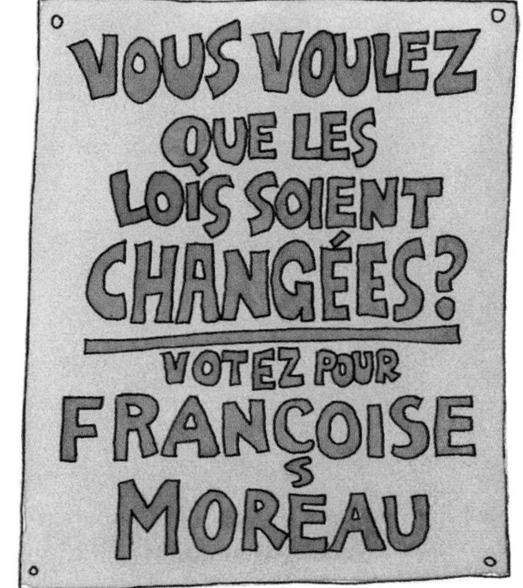

55. Expressing Wishes and Opinions: The Subjunctive

© C. STEELE-PERKINS / MAGNUM

Service militaire obligatoire ou volontaire?

PATRICK FAURE (22 ANS): A mon avis, le service obligatoire, c'est un anachronisme à l'âge nucléaire.

GÉRARD BOURRELLY (36 ANS): *Il* **est possible** que les jeunes s'intéressent plus au service si on leur donne une formation professionnelle.

FRANCIS CRÉPIN (25 ANS): *Il* **faut** qu'on abolisse le service obligatoire et qu'on établisse une armée de métier.

CHARLES PALLANCA (18 ANS): Mais si j'étais volontaire, **j'exigerais** que la solde soit au moins de 5 000 francs par mois!

Retrouvez la phrase correcte selon le dialogue.

1. Il se peut que les jeunes s'intéressent plus à un service comprenant une formation professionnelle complémentaire.
2. Il faut abolir le service obligatoire et établir une armée de métier.
3. J'insisterais pour que la solde soit au moins de 5 000 francs par mois!

A. Subjunctive with Verbs of Volition

When someone expresses a desire for someone else (or something) to behave in a certain way, the verb in the subordinate clause is usually in the subjunctive. The following construction is used.

Mes parents **veulent que je fasse** mon service militaire.	*My parents want me to do my military service.*
Je **voudrais que le service militaire soit** aboli.	*I'd like compulsory military service to be abolished.*

Note that an infinitive construction is used in English to express such a desire. The infinitive construction is impossible in French, unless the speaker is talking about a wish for him- or herself.

Je veux faire le tour du monde.	*I want to travel around the world.*
Et **j'aimerais que** tu m'**accompagnes**.	*And I'd like you to come with me.*

Verbs expressing desires (volition) include **aimer bien, désirer, exiger** (*to demand*), **préférer, souhaiter, vouloir,** and **vouloir bien.**

B. The Subjunctive with Impersonal Expressions

An impersonal expression is one in which the subject does not refer to any particular person or thing. In English, the subject of an impersonal expression is usually *it*: ***It*** *is important that I go to class*. In French, many impersonal expressions—especially those that express will, necessity, emotion, judgment, possibility, or doubt—are followed by the subjunctive in the dependent clause.

IMPERSONAL EXPRESSIONS USED WITH THE SUBJUNCTIVE		
Will or necessity	*Emotion*	*Possibility, judgment, or doubt*
il est essentiel que il est important que il est indispensable que il est nécessaire que il faut que* (*it's necessary that*)	il est stupide que il est bizarre que il est bon que il est dommage que (*it's too bad that*) il est étrange que il est juste/injuste que il est préférable que il est utile/inutile que il vaut mieux que* (*it's better that*)	il est normal que il est peu probable que il est possible/impossible que il se peut que (*it's possible that*) il semble que (*it seems that*)

Il est peu probable que le sexisme **soit** tout à fait éliminé. — *It's not likely that sexism will be totally eliminated.*

Il se peut que d'autres pays **possèdent** des armes nucléaires. — *It's possible that other countries possess nuclear weapons.*

Il est dommage que l'Union Soviétique et les États-Unis ne **s'entendent** pas mieux. — *It's too bad the Soviet Union and the United States don't get along better.*

Il est important que tu **voyages** à l'étranger. — *It's important that you travel abroad.*

Est-il bon que nous **exprimions** toujours nos opinions? — *Is it good that we always express our opinions?*

Il faut que vous **soyez** au courant de la politique internationale. — *You must (it's necessary that you) keep up with international politics.*

*The infinitive of the verb conjugated in the expression **il faut que** is **falloir** (*to be necessary*). The infinitive of the verb in **il vaut mieux que** is **valoir** (*to be worth*).

C. The Infinitive with Impersonal Expressions

As you know, when no specific subject is mentioned, impersonal expressions are followed by the infinitive instead of the subjunctive. Compare the following sentences.

Il vaut mieux **attendre.**	*It's better to wait.*
Il vaut mieux **que nous attendions.**	*It's better that we wait.*
Il est important **de voter.**	*It's important to vote.*
Il est important **que vous votiez.**	*It's important that you vote.*

Remember that the preposition **de** is used before the infinitive after impersonal expressions that contain **être.**

D. The Indicative with Expressions of Certainty or Probability

The following impersonal expressions are followed by the *indicative* because they imply certainty or probability.

IMPERSONAL EXPRESSIONS USED WITH THE INDICATIVE	
il est certain que	il est probable que
il est clair que	il est sûr que
il est évident que	il est vrai que

Il est probable qu'il va pleuvoir demain.	*It's probable that it will rain tomorrow.*
Il est clair que l'influence américaine **restera** importante en Europe.	*It's clear that American influence will remain important in Europe.*
Il est vrai que les Européens **veulent** préserver leur propre identité.	*It's true that Europeans want to preserve their own identity.*

MAINTENANT A VOUS

A. Longévité. Quel est le secret des centenaires (*one hundred-year-old persons*)? Jouez le rôle de Jean Laviolette, un centenaire, et donnez des conseils aux gens qui veulent vivre longtemps.

MODÈLE: Il est important de bien manger. →
Il est important que vous mangiez bien!

1. Il faut prendre un peu de vin à chaque repas. 2. Il est essentiel de ne pas fumer. 3. Il est nécessaire de rester calme en toutes circonstances. 4. Il est bon de faire de la gymnastique régulièrement. 5. Il faut s'intéresser aux autres. 6. Il est indispensable d'avoir envie de vivre. 7. ?

B. Catastrophes: Qui est coupable (*guilty*)? Les accidents d'avion ont fait la une (*were on page one*) des journaux à plusieurs reprises en 1988. Voici un tableau des catastrophes aériennes de ces dernières années.

Lisez-le, puis répondez aux questions. Utilisez les expressions suivantes si possible: il semble que, il est normal que, il est dommage que, il est vrai que, il n'est pas vrai que, il est (in)juste que, il est clair que, il est étrange que.

1. En quelle année y a-t-il eu le plus d'accidents? le moins d'accidents? le plus de morts? le moins de morts?
2. Que pensez-vous de ces chiffres? Est-ce que les experts en sont inquiets?
3. Quelle est votre réaction à la conclusion des experts?
4. En général, que pensez-vous de l'opinion des experts en ce qui concerne les problèmes de la technologie moderne et leurs effets sur la vie de tous les jours? Justifiez votre réponse.

Catastrophes : air plus

Du simple au double. Qui est coupable ?

En une seule année, les accidents aériens ont doublé, d'après le pointage du magazine britannique *Flight*. Un retour en arrière de quinze ans ! Et encore ce chiffre n'inclut-il pas les six accidents dus aux détournements, sabotages et « erreurs » militaires (674 tués supplémentaires).
L'essor du trafic aérien (+ 10 % par an environ) est loin de tout expliquer. Alors, à qui la faute ? Aux pilotes, responsables de trois fois plus de catastrophes (30 en 1988, contre 10 en 1987)... A la météo (19, contre 9)... Mais, en tout cas, pas à l'avion (6 défaillances mécaniques, contre 7). Faut-il s'inquiéter ? Les experts se veulent rassurants : rapporté aux 22 millions d'heures de vol annuelles, le taux d'accidents, quoique double, reste négligeable. C'est eux qui le disent !

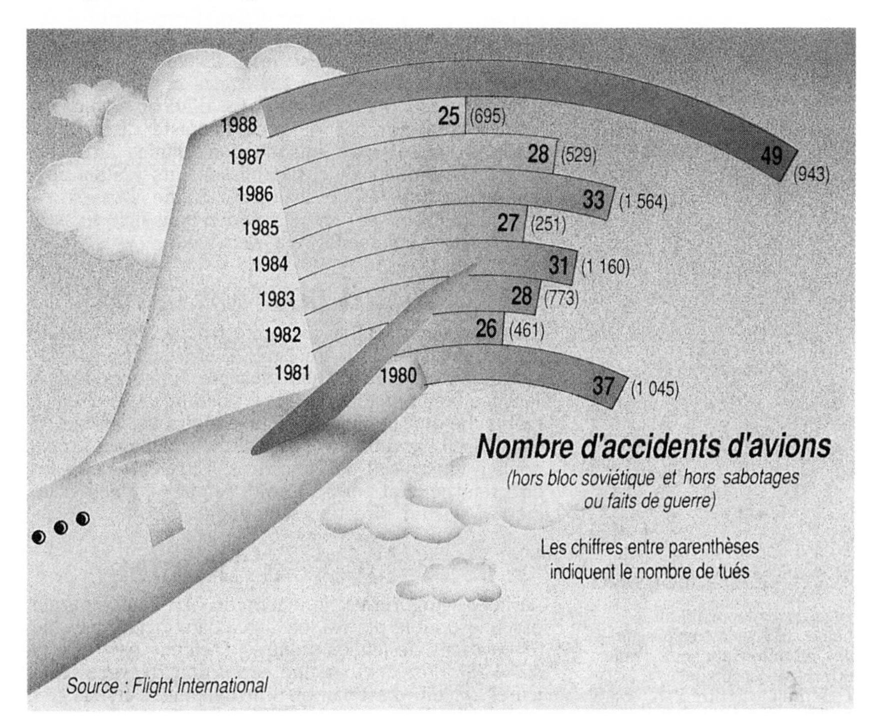

C. Possibilités et probabilités. Quelle sera votre vie? Répondez aux questions suivantes. Dans chaque réponse, utilisez une de ces expressions: il est certain que, il se peut que, il est peu probable que, il est impossible que.

MODÈLE: Ferez-vous une découverte (*discovery*) importante? →
Il est peu probable que je fasse une découverte importante.
(Il est certain que je ferai une découverte importante.)

1. Vous marierez-vous? 2. Apprendrez-vous une langue étrangère? 3. Voyagerez-vous beaucoup? 4. Deviendrez-vous célèbre? 5. Serez-vous riche? 6. Saurez-vous jouer du piano? 7. Écrirez-vous un roman? 8. Ferez-vous la connaissance d'un Président des États-Unis? 9. Irez-vous en Chine? 10. Vivrez-vous jusqu'à l'âge de cent ans?

Maintenant, utilisez ces questions pour interviewer un(e) camarade de classe.

MODÈLE: VOUS: Feras-tu une découverte importante?
UN(E) AMI(E): Oui, il est probable que je ferai une découverte importante. (Non, il est peu probable que je fasse une découverte importante.)

D. Problèmes contemporains. Discutez des problèmes suivants avec un(e) camarade. Offrez des solutions. Utilisez une des expressions suivantes: il est important que, il faut que, il est nécessaire que, il est indispensable que, il est essentiel que, il est préférable que.

1. l'immigration clandestine aux États-Unis
2. le stress chez les jeunes
3. la pollution
4. le chômage (*unemployment*)
5. le gaspillage des sources d'énergie
6. la violence dans les villes
7. l'effet de serre (*greenhouse*)

E. Et vous? Y a-t-il quelqu'un qui essaie d'influencer vos choix?

MODÈLE: Oui. Mes amis veulent que j'arrête de fumer.
(*ou*) Oui. Mon ami Philippe me dit qu'il est essentiel que j'arrête de fumer.

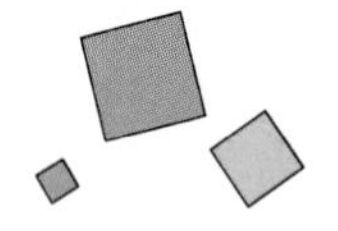

56. Expressing Emotion: The Subjunctive

La majorité à 18 ans

Depuis plus de dix ans, les Français atteignent leur majorité légale à 18 ans. Qu'en pensent les personnes suivantes?

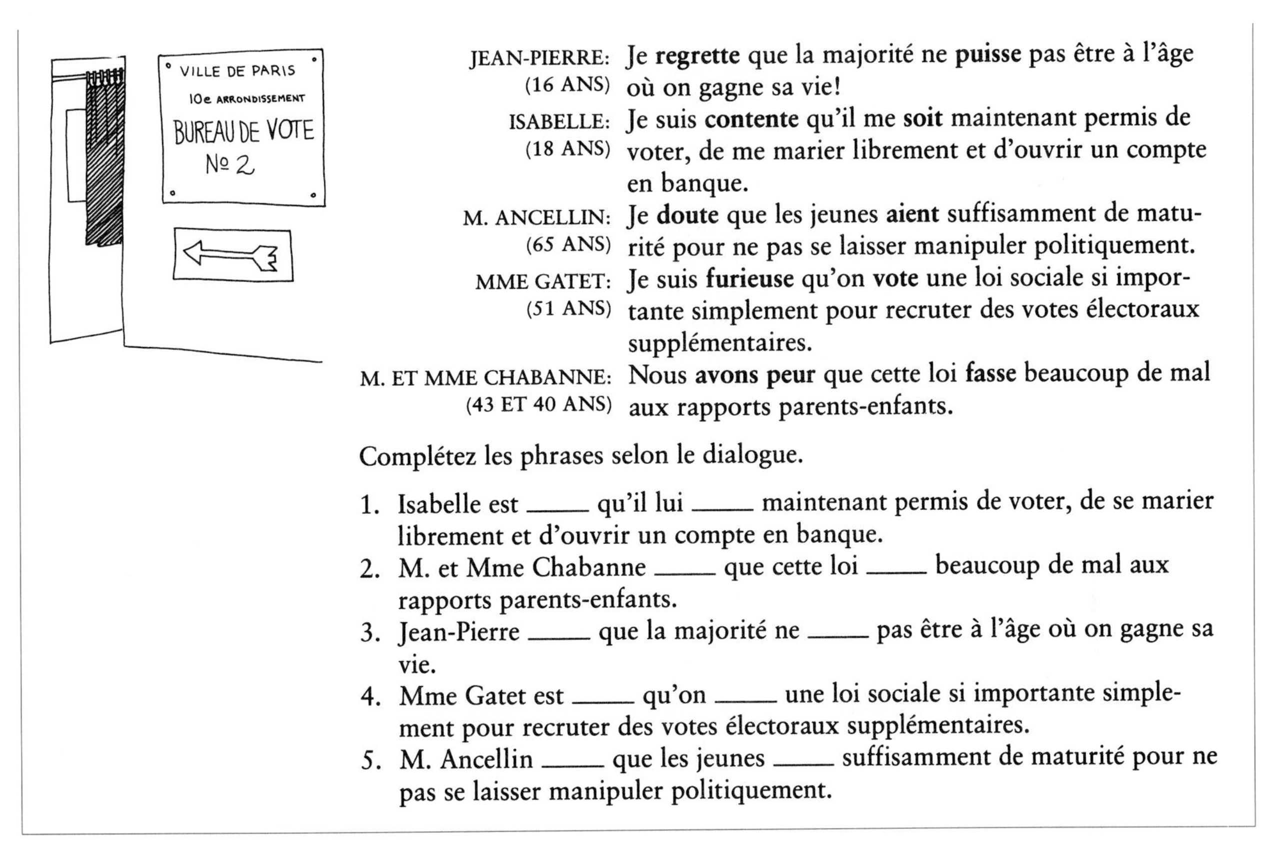

JEAN-PIERRE: (16 ANS) Je **regrette** que la majorité ne **puisse** pas être à l'âge où on gagne sa vie!

ISABELLE: (18 ANS) Je suis **contente** qu'il me **soit** maintenant permis de voter, de me marier librement et d'ouvrir un compte en banque.

M. ANCELLIN: (65 ANS) Je **doute** que les jeunes **aient** suffisamment de maturité pour ne pas se laisser manipuler politiquement.

MME GATET: (51 ANS) Je suis **furieuse** qu'on **vote** une loi sociale si importante simplement pour recruter des votes électoraux supplémentaires.

M. ET MME CHABANNE: (43 ET 40 ANS) Nous **avons peur** que cette loi **fasse** beaucoup de mal aux rapports parents-enfants.

Complétez les phrases selon le dialogue.

1. Isabelle est _____ qu'il lui _____ maintenant permis de voter, de se marier librement et d'ouvrir un compte en banque.
2. M. et Mme Chabanne _____ que cette loi _____ beaucoup de mal aux rapports parents-enfants.
3. Jean-Pierre _____ que la majorité ne _____ pas être à l'âge où on gagne sa vie.
4. Mme Gatet est _____ qu'on _____ une loi sociale si importante simplement pour recruter des votes électoraux supplémentaires.
5. M. Ancellin _____ que les jeunes _____ suffisamment de maturité pour ne pas se laisser manipuler politiquement.

A. Expressions of Emotion

The subjunctive is frequently used after expressions of emotion, such as **avoir peur, être content/désolé/furieux/heureux/surpris,** and **regretter** (*to be sorry*). As with verbs of volition, there must be a different subject in the dependent clause.

Le Président **est content** que les électeurs **aient** confiance en lui.	*The President is pleased that the voters have confidence in him.*
Les électeurs **ont peur** que l'inflation **soit** un problème insoluble.	*The voters are afraid that inflation is an insurmountable problem.*
Les écologistes **sont furieux** que les forêts et les rivières **soient** polluées.	*The ecologists are angry that the forests and rivers are polluted.*

Note that **espérer** (*to hope*) is followed by the indicative.

B. Expressions of Doubt and Uncertainty

The subjunctive is also used—with a change of subject—after expressions of doubt and uncertainty, such as **je doute, je ne suis pas sûr,** and **je ne suis pas certain.**

Beaucoup de femmes **ne sont pas sûres** que leur statut **soit** égal au statut des hommes.	*Many women aren't sure that their status is equal to the status of men.*
Les jeunes **doutent** souvent que les hommes et les femmes politiques **soient** honnêtes.	*Young people often doubt that politicians are honest.*

C. *Penser* and *croire*

In the affirmative, such verbs as **penser** and **croire** are followed by the indicative. In the negative and interrogative, they express a degree of doubt and uncertainty and can then be followed by the subjunctive. In spoken French, however, the indicative is more commonly used.

	Je **pense** que la presse **est** libre.	*I think the press is free.*
	Pensez-vous que la presse **soit** libre?	*Do you think the press is free?*
(*ou*)	**Pensez-vous** que la presse **est** libre?	
	Je **ne crois pas** que la démocratie **soit** en danger.	*I don't think that democracy is in danger.*
(*ou*)	Je **ne crois pas** que la démocratie **est** en danger.	

MAINTENANT A VOUS

A. Discussion politique. Avec un(e) camarade, discutez des idées ci-dessous. Choisissez une phrase et posez une question. Votre camarade répond selon sa conviction.

MODÈLE: Le Président est honnête. →

VOUS: Crois-tu que le Président soit honnête?
UN(E) AMI(E): Oui, je crois qu'il est honnête. (Non, je ne crois pas qu'il soit honnête.)

Les idées à discuter

1. Le président des États-Unis est compétent (honnête).
2. Les sénateurs veulent représenter les intérêts des citoyens de leurs états (leurs propres intérêts).
3. Les lois sont toujours justes (injustes).

4. Il y a beaucoup d'espionnage politique dans le gouvernement (corruption dans le gouvernement).
5. Nous avons besoin d'une armée plus moderne (de plus de programmes sociaux).
6. Le public américain sait voter intelligemment.
7. Les Américains veulent aider les pays pauvres (les pauvres aux États-Unis).
8. Le gouverneur de votre état a de bonnes idées (des idées progressistes).
9. Le pouvoir (*power*) doit être dans les mains du peuple* (dans les mains d'un dictateur).
10. Les législateurs font de bonnes choses la plupart du temps (*most of the time*).

Réponses possibles: Je crois _____. Je ne crois pas _____. Je pense _____. Je ne pense pas _____. Je suis sûr(e) _____. Je doute _____. Je suis certain(e) _____. Je ne suis pas certain(e) _____. J'espère _____.

B. Êtes-vous sceptique? Vos camarades et vous allez faire des observations douteuses (*doubtful*). Réagissez!

MODÈLE: UN(E) ÉTUDIANT(E): Bruce Springsteen a quarante-trois ans.
UN(E) AUTRE ÉTUDIANT(E): Je doute (je ne suis pas sûr[e], je ne suis pas certain[e]) qu'il ait quarante-trois ans.

Idées: Perth est la capitale d'Australie; L'Asie est le plus grand continent; ...

C. Réactions aux nouvelles. Vos amis et vous parlez des nouvelles. Chacun raconte un événement (*event*) qui s'est passé récemment et un autre exprime l'émotion qu'il en a ressenti (*felt*).

MODÈLE: UN(E) ÉTUDIANT(E): En 1988, les footballeurs de San Francisco ont gagné la coupe (*championship*).
UN(E) AUTRE ÉTUDIANT(E): J'étais furieux (furieuse)/content(e) qu'ils gagnent parce que...

Commentaire culturel

Le gouvernement en France. Depuis la révolution de 1789, la France a connu divers régimes politiques, dont cinq Républiques, et seize constitutions avant de retrouver son équilibre dans la démocratie parlementaire. La cinquième République est née de la constitution de 1958, créée par le Général de

*__Le peuple__ is generally used to refer to the population of a nation: **Le peuple français a perdu un grand chef quand de Gaulle est mort.** Use **les gens** to express *people* in the sense of "many persons."

© VIP PARIS / GAMMA-LIAISON

Charles de Gaulle (1890–1970), homme d'état et général français

Gaulle. Elle en est à son quatrième président: le Général de Gaulle (1958–1969), Georges Pompidou (1969–1974), Valéry Giscard d'Estaing (1974–1981) et François Mitterrand qui est président depuis 1981.

La constitution de 1958 se caractérise par un pouvoir exécutif très fort. Le Président de la République est élu au suffrage universel direct pour une durée de sept ans. Le Président a pour fonction, entre autres, de choisir son premier ministre et les membres de son cabinet, de promulguer les lois et de signer les décrets, de négocier et de ratifier les traités. Il est aussi le chef de l'armée et dispose de pouvoirs exceptionnels en cas de menace grave.

Le Parlement se compose de deux assemblées: l'Assemblée nationale, dont les 490 députés sont élus pour cinq ans, et le Sénat, composé de 306 sénateurs élus pour neuf ans.

Comme les députés sont élus pour cinq ans et le Président de la République pour sept, il est possible pour un Président d'une tendance politique donnée (socialiste, par exemple) de faire face à une Assemblée de majorité d'opposition. C'est ce qui s'est produit entre 1986 et 1988 pendant la période dite de «cohabitation» où François Mitterrand, socialiste, a été obligé de gouverner avec un premier ministre de la droite, Jacques Chirac. La possibilité d'élire le Président de la République pour cinq ans a été proposée, afin de (= pour) réduire les chances qu'une telle situation se reproduise.

Situation

L'Amérique en question

Contexte *Linda est une étudiante américaine en première année de faculté à Montpellier. Ses amis, tous étudiants français ou francophones, aiment discuter avec elle des États-Unis.*

Objectif *Linda participe à un échange d'opinions.*

LINDA: Il y a des stéréotypes sur les Américains ici?
NADINE: Oui, on dit souvent que les Américains sont naïfs, qu'ils ne pensent qu'à l'argent...
LOUIS: Mais on est aussi fasciné par certains aspects des États-Unis: Hollywood, les hippies, la conquête de l'espace, la Silicon Valley...
LINDA: C'est un sentiment un peu ambivalent, quand même,° non?

quand... *all the same*

VIVIANE: Oui. Et en politique, par exemple, ça a été très difficile pour les Français de voir des présidents américains qui n'étaient pas des «spécialistes», tu sais... des membres d'une élite intellectuelle.

LINDA: Je crois que c'est particulièrement vrai des Parisiens. En province, on admire l'Amérique, non?

NADINE: Oui, mais il y a aussi des cycles d'opinion en France. En 68, l'Amérique, c'était l'impérialisme. Avec Carter, c'était l'idéalisme un peu puéril.° Avec Reagan, c'était la réussite économique. — *childish*

LOUIS: Je crois que l'Amérique a connu avant nous des problèmes sociaux très graves: racisme, drogue, violence...

DANIEL: Maintenant que nous nous débattons° aussi avec ces problèmes, il est difficile d'être aussi critique envers les U.S.A. — nous... *we're struggling*

LINDA: Mais est-ce que vous connaissez l'Amérique seulement par les films et les journaux?

LOUIS: Eh bien moi, j'ai vécu aux États-Unis, et j'ai trouvé qu'il faut beaucoup se battre° pour y survivre.° On n'est pas protégé contre la maladie ou le chômage. Finalement, j'ai trouvé que l'individu est très isolé. — se... *fight, struggle* / *survive*

VIVIANE: Oui, mais malgré tout, beaucoup de jeunes voudraient partir vivre aux États-Unis. Ils veulent tenter° l'aventure américaine. — essayer

DANIEL: En ce moment, les Français envient le dynamisme de la société américaine.

NADINE: Mais, dis-nous, Linda, qu'est-ce que les Américains pensent de la France?

VARIATIONS

1. Recréez la scène. Jouez le rôle de Linda et donnez vos opinions personnelles sur les observations suivantes:
   - Les Américains sont naïfs.
   - L'argent est la préoccupation essentielle aux États-Unis.
   - Les présidents américains n'appartiennent (*belong*) pas à une élite intellectuelle.
   - L'individu est isolé et mal protégé.
2. Improvisez! Avec des camarades, continuez le dialogue. Linda parle des stéréotypes américains sur les Français. Les étudiants français y réagissent.
3. Une nouvelle patrie (*nation, homeland*). Imaginez que vous travaillez pour une grande société internationale qui veut vous envoyer à l'étranger pour quatre ans. On vous donne le choix du pays. Discutez avec vos camarades des avantages et des inconvénients des pays qui vous attirent (*attract*). Ensuite, prenez une décision commune. (Votez, si c'est nécessaire!)

A propos

Comment donner des conseils

Je vous (te) conseille de (+ *infinitif*)...
A votre (ta) place, je (+ *verbe au conditionnel*)...
Je suis convaincu(e)/persuadé(e) que (+ *sujet* + *verbe à l'indicatif*)...
Savez-vous (Sais-tu) que (+ *sujet* + *verbe à l'indicatif*)...
Je recommande que vous (tu) (+ *verbe au subjonctif*)...
Vous devriez (Tu devrais) (+ *infinitif*)...
N'oubliez pas (Oublie) que (+ *sujet* + *verbe à l'indicatif*)...

A. **Jeu de rôles.** Avec plusieurs camarades, jouez une scène dans laquelle une personne doit prendre une décision de grande importance. Les autres étudiants donnent des conseils à cette personne et discutent avec elle de son problème. Utilisez les expressions de l'*A propos*. **Suggestions:** Quelqu'un va...

- refuser de s'inscrire (*register*) au service militaire
- manifester contre les centrales nucléaires
- poser sa candidature au Conseil de l'université
- se marier avec quelqu'un dont il vient de faire la connaissance
- quitter l'université sans obtenir son diplôme

B. **Vous intéressez-vous à la politique?** Avec un(e) camarade de classe ou seul(e), répondez aux questions suivantes pour déterminer si vous vous intéressez à la politique ou non.

1. Avez-vous voté aux dernières élections? Pourquoi ou pourquoi pas? 2. Appartenez-vous à un parti politique? Quel parti? 3. Avez-vous déjà manifesté (*demonstrated*)? Quand et pourquoi? 4. Avez-vous déjà fait campagne pour un(e) candidat(e)? Pour qui? 5. Avez-vous déjà donné de l'argent pour une cause politique? Pour quelle cause? 6. Êtes-vous abonné(e) (*subscriber*) à une revue politique? A laquelle? 7. Assistez-vous à des réunions politiques? Auxquelles? 8. Avez-vous jamais fait un discours politique? Quand? 9. Avez-vous jamais distribué des tracts? Où?

Comptez combien de fois vous avez répondu oui.

8–9: Vous serez un jour candidat(e) à une fonction politique.
4–7: Vous vous intéressez à la politique et vous êtes bon(ne) citoyen(ne).
0–3: Vous n'êtes pas très actif (active) politiquement. Expliquez à la classe pourquoi la politique ne vous intéresse pas.

Commentaire culturel

1992: Le défi européen. Les pays européens rêvent de construire un marché européen depuis bientôt quarante ans. Pensez donc: avec plus de 250 millions de consommateurs, il serait plus grand que le marché américain; en fait, ce serait le premier marché du monde! Aujourd'hui, l'Europe est plus près que jamais de réaliser ce rêve.

Pour comprendre les énormes progrès accomplis dans l'unité de l'Europe, il faut remonter à 1950. C'est à cette date que s'est créée la Communauté Européenne du Charbon et de l'Acier (CECA), qui marquait un accord de coopération entre les industries sidérurgiques (*iron and steel*) de six nations: l'Allemagne, la Belgique, la France, la Hollande, l'Italie et le Luxembourg.

Ce sont encore ces six pays qui, en 1958, ont formé la Communauté Économique Européenne (CEE), que l'on appelle aussi le Marché Commun. Son objectif principal était la libre circulation des biens (*goods*) et des personnes. Depuis 1958, la CEE a accueilli six autres pays membres: le Danemark, l'Espagne, la Grande-Bretagne, la Grèce, l'Irlande et le Portugal. C'est donc aujourd'hui «l'Europe des Douze».

Plusieurs institutions européennes ont été créées pour diriger cette grande communauté économique, dont la gestion est très compliquée. Tout d'abord, la **Commission européenne,** située à Bruxelles: elle administre en particulier les budgets de chaque état membre. Ensuite, la **Cour de Justice européenne:** installée au Luxembourg, elle veille à l'application équitable des lois européennes dans toute la Communauté. Enfin, un **Parlement européen:** il siège à Strasbourg et son rôle est de veiller à l'application des lois européennes.

On estime généralement que la CEE compte ses plus grands succès dans le domaine agricole, avec la création de ce que l'on appelle l'«Europe verte». Mais le nouvel objectif de la CEE est encore plus ambitieux: c'est la construction d'un véritable marché européen avec l'abolition, dès 1992, de toutes les frontières douanières (*customs*) entre les pays membres. Sa conséquence logique serait l'utilisation d'une monnaie européenne unique, une révolution dans les coutumes de chaque pays!

Ce projet a été salué avec enthousiasme par les douze pays partenaires. Mais il présente aussi de nombreux défis. Tout d'abord, plusieurs industries européennes—aujourd'hui protégées par un système de quotas et de taxes d'importation—vont être obligées de s'adapter aux règles de la concurrence (= compétition) ouverte. Cela concerne l'industrie automobile, en particulier. Ensuite, les taxes indirectes imposées par chaque pays vont devoir être harmonisées: elles varient aujourd'hui de 0 pour cent à plus de 30 pour cent. Mais la question fondamentale qui se pose est le choix entre une **Europe fédérale,** à l'image des États-Unis d'Amérique, ou une **Europe fédérée,** où chaque pays membre conserverait sa souveraineté nationale dans les domaines économiques et fiscaux.

Cette évolution, qui passionne les Européens, inquiète aussi de nombreuses entreprises étrangères, américaines en particulier, qui désirent renforcer leur présence en Europe. Beaucoup ont peur que la CEE érige des barrières protectionnistes pour les non-membres. Alors, pour éviter le risque d'être exclues du marché européen, un grand nombre de ces sociétés établissent aujourd'hui des usines de production en Europe. Comme les européens, ils pourront ainsi bénéficier, dans l'avenir, du label «*Made in Europe*».

Mise au point

A. Émotions. Complétez les phrases qui se trouvent à côté de chaque dessin. Puis, un(e) étudiant(e) fait sa propre phrase pour expliquer cette émotion. Enfin, les autres étudiants choisissent la phrase qu'ils préfèrent comme légende (*caption*).

1. Pierre est content que ____.
   a. sa sœur / s'en aller / bientôt / université
   b. son père / venir de / lui / acheter / voiture
   c. ?

2. Chantal est triste que ____.
   a. Jean-Pierre / (ne... pas) vouloir / sortir / soir
   b. personne / (ne...) comprendre / son / idées
   c. ?

3. Jacques est furieux que ____.
   a. tu / (ne... pas) / le prendre / au sérieux
   b. Chantal / lui / (ne... pas) téléphoner / plus souvent
   c. ?

4. Mme Hugo doute que ____.
   a. son mari / être / à l'heure / soir
   b. ses enfants / comprendre / son / problèmes
   c. ?

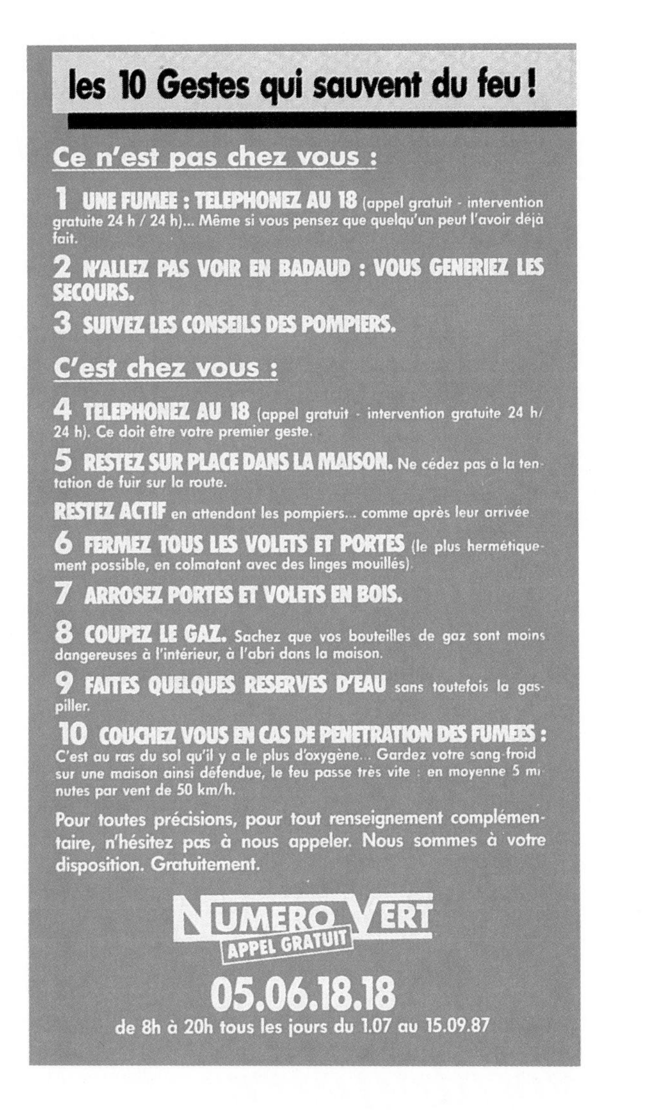

B. Contre le feu, je sais quoi faire! Voici quelques conseils pour vous protéger du feu (*fire*), publiés par le Conservatoire de la forêt méditerranéenne.

Imaginez que vous expliquez à un(e) camarade ce qu'il (elle) doit faire en cas de feu chez lui (elle). Reprenez les conseils donnés et faites des phrases avec des expressions impersonnelles.

MODÈLE: Il faut (il est indispensable, essentiel) que tu téléphones au 18 immédiatement:

Puis, par petits groupes, imaginez quels conseils on pourrait donner dans les situations suivantes:

1. En cas d'inondation
2. En cas de tremblement de terre

C. L'avenir. Comment sera la société de l'avenir? Exprimez vos opinions. Commencez chaque phrase par une des expressions de la colonne de droite.

1. Il y aura des colons (*settlers*) sur la lune (*moon*).
2. Il n'y aura qu'une seule nation.
3. L'anglais sera la langue universelle.
4. Les robots auront remplacé les gens dans beaucoup de domaines.
5. Tous les robots parleront anglais.
6. Les fleurs auront disparu (*will have disappeared*).
7. On fera tout par ordinateur.
8. Les villes seront sous terre (*underground*).
9. ?

Il est possible que
Il se peut que
Il est peu probable que
Il est sûr que
J'espère que
Il est préférable que
Il est probable que

Interactions

In this chapter, you practiced expressing opinions, attitudes, and judgments in French. Use the vocabulary and structures from the chapter to act out the following situations.

1. **Une journée horrible.** You have had a terrible day. You lost your wallet (**le portefeuille**), you failed an exam, your dog (or cat) is sick, you were late for French class, etc. A good friend (your partner) will react sympathetically and give you advice.
2. **A mon avis.** Working with four classmates, pick one of the following topics and give your opinions. Be sure that everyone has a chance to talk.

la pollution
les cartes de crédit
le mariage
la mode

Vocabulaire

Verbes

abolir to abolish
conserver to conserve
contrôler to inspect, monitor
développer to develop
douter to doubt
élire to elect
estimer to consider; to believe; to estimate
exiger to require; to demand
falloir to be necessary
manifester to demonstrate
polluer to pollute
protéger to protect
reconnaître to recognize
recycler to recycle
regretter to regret, be sorry
sauver to save, rescue
souhaiter to wish, desire
valoir to be worth

Substantifs

le chômage unemployment
le (la) citoyen(ne) citizen
le contrôle control, overseeing
le déchet waste (material)
l'électeur (-trice) voter
le gaspillage waste
la guerre war
le problème problem
la réussite success, accomplishment

Termes apparentés

l'accident (*m.*), **l'atmosphère** (*f.*), **le budget** (**militaire**), **le conflit**, **la conservation**, **le développement**, **l'énergie** (*f.*) **nucléaire/solaire**, **l'environnement** (*m.*), **le gouvernement**, **l'inflation** (*f.*), **la légalisation**, **la liberté d'expression**, **les médias** (*m.*), **la nature**, **l'opinion publique** (*f.*), **la pollution**, **la prolifération**, **la protection**, **le recyclage**, **la réforme**, **les ressources naturelles**, **le sexisme**, **la source**

Adjectifs

écologiste ecological
furieux (**-euse**) furious
industriel(**le**) industrial
sûr(e) sure, certain
surpris(e) surprised

Les expressions impersonnelles

il est... it is . . .
dommage too bad
étrange strange
fâcheux unfortunate
(**in**)**utile** useless/useful
il se peut que... it is possible that . . .
il semble que... it seems that . . .
il vaut mieux (**que**)... it is better (that . . .)

Expressions apparentées

il est... clair, **essentiel**, **évident**, **important**, (**im**)**possible**, **indispensable**, (**in**)**juste**, **nécessaire**, **normal**, **peu probable**, **préférable**, **probable**, **stupide**, **urgent**

Mots divers

par exemple for example
personnellement personally
la plupart (**de**) most (of)
pour ma part in my opinion, as for me

Expressions utiles

A votre (**ta**) **place, je...** (+ conditionnel)	*In your place, I . . .*
Je vous (**te**) **conseille de...** (+ infinitif)	*I advise you to . . .*

INTERMÈDE 15

Lecture

AVANT DE LIRE

Anticipating content. In the spring of 1989, *L'Express* magazine published an article surveying the environmental problems threatening the planet. Similar articles appeared in the American press at that time. As you read the introduction to this feature article and the accompanying summaries, recall what you already know about these topics, to help you guess what is being said.

You may find it useful to skim rather than read the summaries of particular environmental problems. These summaries contain a certain amount of scientific detail; you do not need to understand every idea, however, to grasp the essential points.

Before you begin reading:

- Look at the title. What is the writer's aim in this article?
- Glance at the titles of the five boxed paragraphs. What specific problems are summarized? Are any of them unfamiliar to you? If so, look for visual clues to their meaning.
- Now read the first paragraph of the introduction (in italics). Underline the topic sentence.
- Name the six environmental problems mentioned in the third paragraph.

Menaces sur la Terre : le vrai, le faux

Apocalypse now. Cette fois, ce n'est plus du cinéma. Depuis six mois, une rumeur s'étend sur toute la planète : l'humanité ne survivra pas aux dégâts[a] qu'elle fait subir à la Terre. Elle est l'artisan de sa propre destruction. A court terme. Résultat : l'écologie, hier affaire de militants, devient l'affaire de tous. Les hommes politiques s'en emparent[b], réunissent colloques et conférences. Cette mobilisation générale, sur fond de catastrophisme, pose plus de questions qu'elle n'offre de réponses. Marée[c] noire ici, déchirure d'ozone là. On se demande si la fin du monde est pour demain ou pour plus tard. A force de mettre tous les sujets au même niveau[d] — le pire — on finit par tout mélanger[e].

Depuis cinquante ans, le développement technologique a amélioré le confort des hommes. Mais il a aussi bouleversé[f] les grands équilibres planétaires. Et perturbé cet organisme géant — la Terre — où chaque être vivant jouait son rôle — prédateur et proie à la fois[g] — depuis des millénaires.

Les mers, où naquit[h] la vie, océans immenses qui nourrissent les hommes et absorbent leurs déchets, sont malades, c'est sûr. Mais jusqu'à quel point et où ? Le climat, qui a façonné l'agriculture et le mode de vie de milliards d'êtres humains, est-il en train de se modifier ? Quelles certitudes a-t-on au sujet de ce trou dans l'ozone qui déchire le dôme protecteur de l'atmosphère ? Sait-on combien d'espèces animales ou végétales disparaissent ? combien d'êtres humains la Terre peut supporter ? L'Express a enquêté. Quelles sont les vraies conséquences de la destruction des forêts qu'on défriche tout autour du monde ? Principal point noir : l'Amazonie. C'est pourquoi L'Express se joint à TF 1, qui organise, du 7 au 16 avril, une vaste opération autour de la planète Amazone.

Sylvie O'Dy ■

a. *damage*
b. s'en... *seize upon it.*
c. *tide*
d. *level*
e. *confuse*
f. *upset*
g. à... en même temps
h. est née

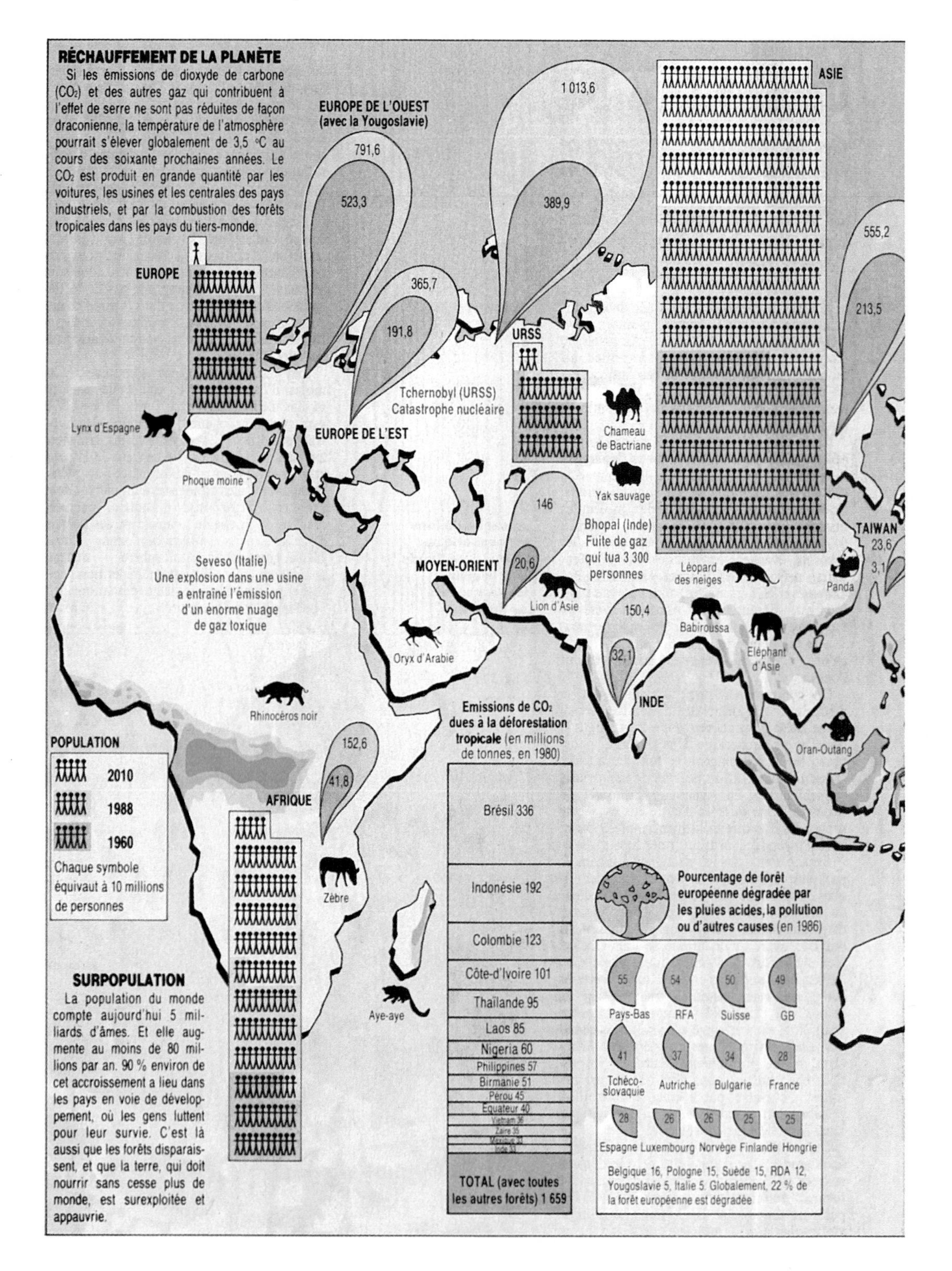
RÉCHAUFFEMENT DE LA PLANÈTE
Si les émissions de dioxyde de carbone (CO_2) et des autres gaz qui contribuent à l'effet de serre ne sont pas réduites de façon draconienne, la température de l'atmosphère pourrait s'élever globalement de 3,5 °C au cours des soixante prochaines années. Le CO_2 est produit en grande quantité par les voitures, les usines et les centrales des pays industriels, et par la combustion des forêts tropicales dans les pays du tiers-monde.
EUROPE DE L'OUEST (avec la Yougoslavie)
791,6
523,3
1 013,6
389,9
ASIE
555,2
213,5
EUROPE
365,7
191,8
URSS
Tchernobyl (URSS) Catastrophe nucléaire
EUROPE DE L'EST
Lynx d'Espagne
Phoque moine
Chameau de Bactriane
Yak sauvage
146
Bhopal (Inde) Fuite de gaz qui tua 3 300 personnes
TAIWAN
23,6
3,1
Seveso (Italie) Une explosion dans une usine a entraîné l'émission d'un énorme nuage de gaz toxique
MOYEN-ORIENT
20,6
Lion d'Asie
Léopard des neiges
Panda
150,4
32,1
Babiroussa
Eléphant d'Asie
Oryx d'Arabie
INDE
Rhinocéros noir
Emissions de CO_2 dues à la déforestation tropicale (en millions de tonnes, en 1980)
Oran-Outang
POPULATION
2010
1988
1960
Chaque symbole équivaut à 10 millions de personnes
152,6
41,8
AFRIQUE
Brésil 336
Indonésie 192
Colombie 123
Côte-d'Ivoire 101
Thaïlande 95
Laos 85
Nigeria 60
Philippines 57
Birmanie 51
Pérou 45
Equateur 40
Vietnam 36
Zaïre 35
Mexique 33
Inde 33
TOTAL (avec toutes les autres forêts) 1 659
Zèbre
Aye-aye
Pourcentage de forêt européenne dégradée par les pluies acides, la pollution ou d'autres causes (en 1986)
55 Pays-Bas
54 RFA
50 Suisse
49 GB
41 Tchécoslovaquie
37 Autriche
34 Bulgarie
28 France
28 Espagne
26 Luxembourg
26 Norvège
25 Finlande
25 Hongrie
Belgique 16, Pologne 15, Suède 15, RDA 12, Yougoslavie 5, Italie 5. Globalement, 22 % de la forêt européenne est dégradée
SURPOPULATION
La population du monde compte aujourd'hui 5 milliards d'âmes. Et elle augmente au moins de 80 millions par an. 90 % environ de cet accroissement a lieu dans les pays en voie de développement, où les gens luttent pour leur survie. C'est là aussi que les forêts disparaissent, et que la terre, qui doit nourrir sans cesse plus de monde, est surexploitée et appauvrie.

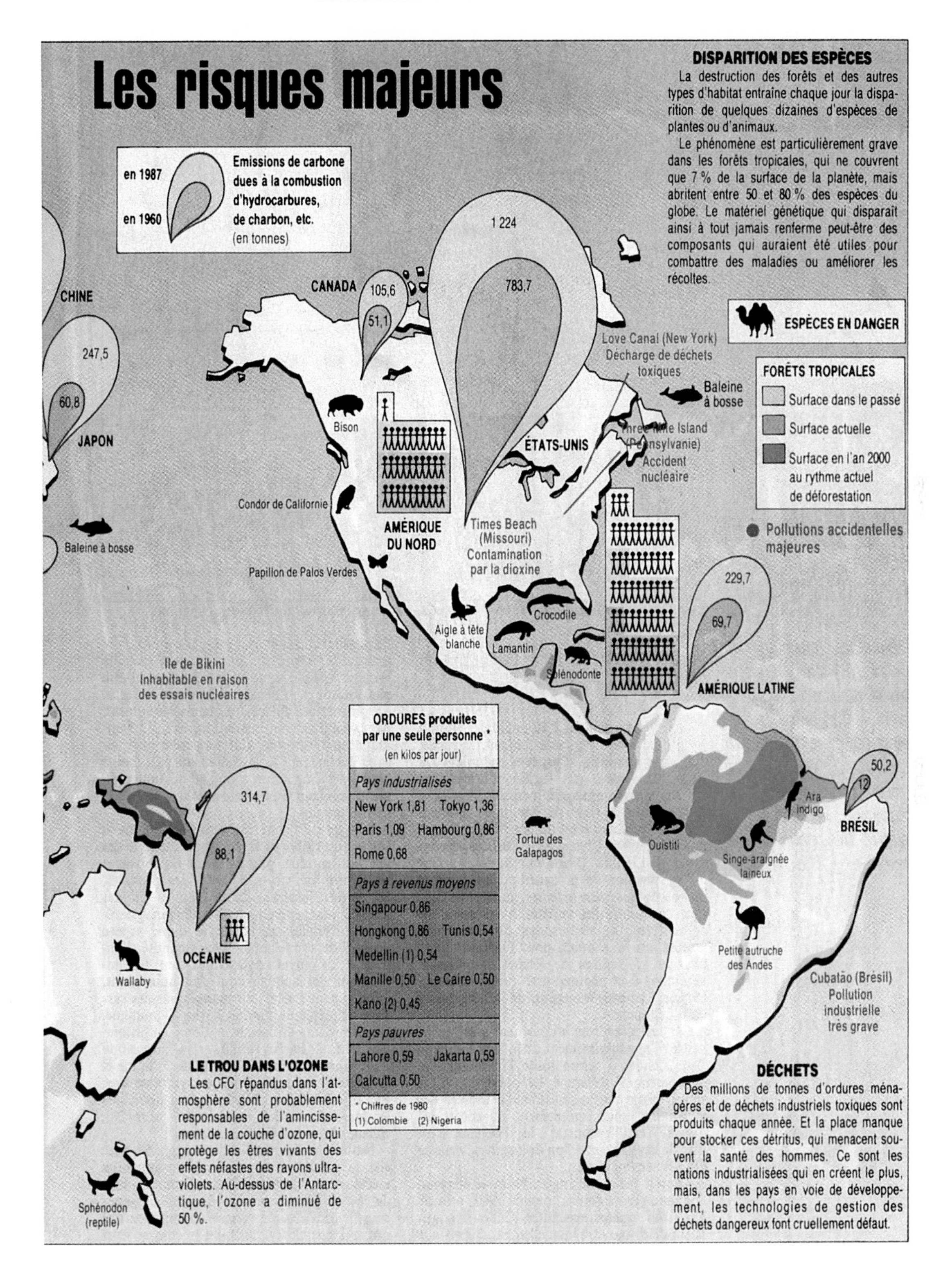
Les risques majeurs
en 1987
en 1960
Emissions de carbone dues à la combustion d'hydrocarbures, de charbon, etc. (en tonnes)
CHINE
247,5
60,8
JAPON
Baleine à bosse
CANADA
105,6
51,1
1 224
783,7
ÉTATS-UNIS
AMÉRIQUE DU NORD
Bison
Condor de Californie
Papillon de Palos Verdes
Aigle à tête blanche
Lamantin
Crocodile
Solénodonte
Times Beach (Missouri) Contamination par la dioxine
Love Canal (New York) Décharge de déchets toxiques
Baleine à bosse
Accident nucléaire
229,7
69,7
AMÉRIQUE LATINE
50,2
12
BRÉSIL
Ara indigo
Ouistiti
Singe-araignée laineux
Tortue des Galapagos
Petite autruche des Andes
Cubatão (Brésil) Pollution industrielle très grave
Ile de Bikini Inhabitable en raison des essais nucléaires
314,7
88,1
OCÉANIE
Wallaby
Sphénodon (reptile)
DISPARITION DES ESPÈCES
La destruction des forêts et des autres types d'habitat entraîne chaque jour la disparition de quelques dizaines d'espèces de plantes ou d'animaux.
Le phénomène est particulièrement grave dans les forêts tropicales, qui ne couvrent que 7 % de la surface de la planète, mais abritent entre 50 et 80 % des espèces du globe. Le matériel génétique qui disparaît ainsi à tout jamais renferme peut-être des composants qui auraient été utiles pour combattre des maladies ou améliorer les récoltes.
ESPÈCES EN DANGER
FORÊTS TROPICALES
Surface dans le passé
Surface actuelle
Surface en l'an 2000 au rythme actuel de déforestation
Pollutions accidentelles majeures
ORDURES produites par une seule personne * (en kilos par jour)
Pays industrialisés
New York 1,81 Tokyo 1,36
Paris 1,09 Hambourg 0,86
Rome 0,68
Pays à revenus moyens
Singapour 0,86
Hongkong 0,86 Tunis 0,54
Medellin (1) 0,54
Manille 0,50 Le Caire 0,50
Kano (2) 0,45
Pays pauvres
Lahore 0,59 Jakarta 0,59
Calcutta 0,50
* Chiffres de 1980
(1) Colombie (2) Nigeria
LE TROU DANS L'OZONE
Les CFC répandus dans l'atmosphère sont probablement responsables de l'amincissement de la couche d'ozone, qui protège les êtres vivants des effets néfastes des rayons ultraviolets. Au-dessus de l'Antarctique, l'ozone a diminué de 50 %.
DÉCHETS
Des millions de tonnes d'ordures ménagères et de déchets industriels toxiques sont produits chaque année. Et la place manque pour stocker ces détritus, qui menacent souvent la santé des hommes. Ce sont les nations industrialisées qui en créent le plus, mais, dans les pays en voie de développement, les technologies de gestion des déchets dangereux font cruellement défaut.

COMPRÉHENSION

1. Selon l'auteur, les problèmes écologiques sont exagérés par ____.
2. Ce qui a perturbé l'équilibre de la planète, c'est ____.
3. Deux fonctions écologiques des océans sont ____.
4. Ce qui déchire (*tears*) le dôme protecteur de l'atmosphère, c'est ____.
5. Cinq espèces animales en danger de disparition sont ____.
6. La raison de leur disparition est principalement ____.
7. Le réchauffement de la planète est la conséquence de ____.
8. La population augmente le plus vite dans les pays ____ tels que (*such as*) ____.
9. La couche d'ozone est importante pour les êtres humains parce que ____.
10. Les pays qui créent le plus de déchets toxiques et polluants sont les pays ____ tels que ____.

Par écrit

A. Une lettre de recommandation. Un de vos amis (Une de vos amies) a de fortes chances d'être nommé(e) secrétaire adjoint au Ministère de l'environnement. Il (Elle) tient beaucoup à ce poste et a donné votre nom comme référence. Écrivez une lettre dans laquelle vous parlerez de votre ami(e) et expliquerez pourquoi il (elle) est le candidat idéal (la candidate idéale) pour ce poste.

B. Lettre au rédacteur. Écrivez votre opinion sur un des sujets traités dans ce chapitre ou sur un événement ou une catastrophe qui a eu lieu récemment. Commencez votre lettre par «Monsieur (Madame)», et concluez par «Je vous prie, Monsieur (Madame), de croire à mes sentiments les plus distingués». Utilisez les phrases suivantes comme guide.

A mon avis, ____ est un des problèmes les plus graves de notre société. L'origine de ce problème est ____. Il en résulte que (*As a result,*) ____. Il me semble qu'il y a une solution assez simple. Il faudrait que ____.

Communication et vie pratique 5

ACTIVITÉ

La vie de M. Toutlemonde. M. Toutlemonde a une vie plutôt monotome. Il rêve souvent d'une vie meilleure. Commentez chacune des scènes de son rêve.

- Sur le premier dessin, que fait-il? Pourquoi? Jouez le rôle de M. Toutlemonde et dites comment vous imaginez son avenir. Donnez beaucoup de détails.
- Sur le deuxième dessin, comment la vie de M. Toutlemonde a-t-elle changé? Que fait-il maintenant? Quelle est son attitude envers la vie? S'il pouvait changer sa vie, que ferait-il? Que feriez-vous à sa place?
- Sur le troisième dessin, M. Toutlemonde a réalisé certains de ses rêves. Décrivez ce qu'il est devenu. Mettez-vous à sa place et dites ce que vous espérez pour l'avenir.
- Dessin 4: Où est M. Toutlemonde maintenant? Commentez sa vie. Avec un(e) camarade, inventez la fin de son histoire. De quoi rêve-t-il maintenant?
- D'après vous, quelle est la moralité de cette histoire? Si M. Toutlemonde vous demandait conseil, que lui diriez-vous?

EXPRESSION ÉCRITE

Sujet de composition. The following brief passage is excerpted from the autobiography of Françoise Giroud (1920–), *Si je mens.* After you read it and finish the task in *Avant d'écrire,* write your own paragraph, answering the question **Quel genre d'enfance avez-vous eu?**

Avant d'écrire

Linking sentences. Now that you can write more complex sentences in French, you will be able to show the relationships among ideas more clearly. Four of the many ways to make transitions between sentences are listed here.

- Repeat a word or phrase from the preceding sentence.
- Use relative pronouns, such as **qui, que, où,** and **lequel.**
- Use adverbs, such as **d'abord, et puis, enfin,** etc., to show the chronological relationship among ideas.
- Raise a question—genuine or rhetorical—then answer it.

Now look for examples of all four of these devices in the following excerpt.

> —Quel genre d'enfance avez-vous eu?
> —Le genre bizarre.
> —Bizarre? Pourquoi?
> —Ce n'est pas facile à expliquer... Mon père a été essentiellement une absence, une légende. Une absence d'abord à cause de la guerre, puis d'une mission aux États-Unis dont il a été chargé par le gouvernement français, ensuite d'une maladie que l'on ne savait pas soigner à l'époque et dont il est mort. Cette maladie a duré des années pendant lesquelles je ne l'ai jamais vu. J'ai eu pour lui un amour fou. On parlait de lui, à la maison, comme d'un héros qui avait tout sacrifié à la France, ...

CHAPITRE SEIZE

La France et son patrimoine

—Nous arrivons à Chartres. Oh, regarde la cathédrale, là-bas!
—Allons la visiter tout de suite.
—Tu as vu ces vitraux? Quelles couleurs!
—Oui. Le guide dit que sa collection de vitraux qui date du XIIIe siècle est la plus riche de France.

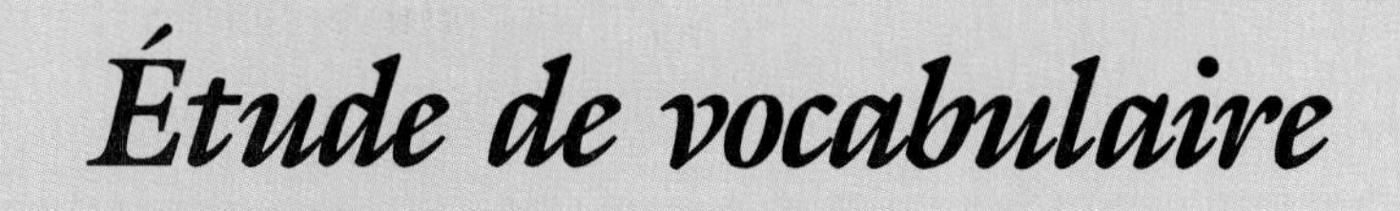

Étude de vocabulaire

Le patrimoine historique

La cathédrale d'Amiens, chef-d'œuvre (*masterpiece*) du moyen âge (l'époque médiévale: V^e^–XIVe siècle)

Les arènes d'Arles, monument de l'époque romaine (59 av. J.C.*–Ve siècle)

Chenonceaux, château de la Renaissance (XVe–XVIe siècle)

*avant Jésus Christ

Versailles, château de l'époque classique (XVIIe siècle)

A. Définitions. Regardez les photos et complétez les phrases suivantes.

1. Une période historique, c'est une _____.
2. Une durée de cent ans, c'est un _____.
3. On a bâti (*built*) la cathédrale d'Amiens à l'époque _____.
4. L'époque historique qui se situe entre le Ve et le XIVe siècles s'appelle le _____.
5. Le château de Chenonceaux a été bâti au _____.
6. Le château de Versailles date de l'époque _____.
7. Les arènes d'Arles datent de l'époque _____.

B. Leçon d'histoire. Faites une phrase complète pour nommer le siècle et l'époque où les événements (*events*) suivants se sont passés. Remplacez les éléments en italique par des pronoms.

MODÈLE: *Christophe Colomb* est arrivé *au Nouveau Monde* en 1492. →
Il y est arrivé au XVe siècle, à l'époque de la Renaissance.

1. *Blaise Pascal* a inventé *la première machine à calculer* en 1642.
2. On a bâti *les arènes de Nîmes* au premier siècle.
3. *Guillaume, Duc de Normandie,* a conquis (*conquered*) *l'Angleterre* en 1066.
4. *La ville de Paris* s'est appelée Lutèce du IIe siècle av. J.C. jusqu'au IVe siècle après J.C.
5. *Jacques Cartier* a pris possession *du Canada* au nom de la France en 1534.
6. *Jeanne d'Arc* a essayé de prendre *la ville de Paris* en 1429.
7. *René Descartes* a écrit *sa «Géométrie»* en 1637.
8. *Charlemagne* est devenu roi (*king*) en *768*.

C. A vous. Imaginez que votre classe de français est en visite à Paris. Votre guide vous propose le choix de trois sites à visiter cet après-midi. Divisez-vous en groupes de trois ou quatre pour décider du site. Chaque groupe doit justifier son choix. Les autres peuvent poser des questions et faire des objections. Enfin, on vote.

Voir, à la page suivante, les sites et les endroits à considérer:

© MARK ANTMAN / THE IMAGE WORKS

Les arènes de Lutèce

Histoire: des arènes romaines de 15 000 places avec une arène séparée pour les combats des gladiateurs

Aujourd'hui: un jardin public très agréable où on peut flâner (*stroll*), pique-niquer ou rêver

A proximité: le Quartier latin

© COMSTOCK, INC.

Le Palais du Louvre

Histoire: ancienne résidence royale commencée au XIIIe siècle

Aujourd'hui: un des plus célèbres et des plus riches musées au monde

A proximité: le quartier élégant de l'Opéra où se trouvent les plus beaux magasins de mode de Paris

© ALAN PADLEY

La Cathédrale de Notre-Dame

Histoire: Le grand chef-d'œuvre du moyen âge. Commencée en 1163 et finie en 1330. Son architecture de style gothique crée une atmosphère de mystère et de beauté.

Aujourd'hui: Toujours une église catholique. Il faut du courage pour monter les 387 marches (*steps*) qui conduisent jusqu'au sommet de sa tour où on peut prendre les photos de Paris les plus romantiques

A proximité: le Quartier latin, l'Île Saint-Louis, l'Hôtel de Ville (*City Hall*) de Paris

Le patrimoine naturel

La terre

A. Définitions. Complétez les phrases suivantes.

1. Une exploitation agricole, c'est une ____.
2. Un espace (*space*) ouvert où on cultive la terre, c'est un ____.
3. Le fruit qui donne le vin est le ____. On le cultive sur la ____, qui se trouve dans le ____. La personne qui fait le vin s'appelle un ____.
4. Les ____ sont des régions où la flore et la faune sont protégées et où seule la chasse (*hunting*) photographique est autorisée.

B. Les parcs nationaux. Imaginez que vous êtes employé au Ministère de l'environnement. A l'aide des descriptions ci-dessous, conseillez les personnes suivantes.

> **Le Parc national du Mercantour:** gorges rouges et arides; forêts, lacs et cascades impressionnantes
> **Le Parc national de l'Île de Port-Cros:** sur la côte méditerranéenne; îles; réserve naturelle; oiseaux migrateurs
> **Le Parc national du Vercors:** falaises (*cliffs*) vertigineuses; sites grandioses

MODÈLE: Je vais passer trois semaines de vacances dans le sud de la France et je voudrais savoir s'il y a des sites maritimes protégés. →
Vous devriez visiter le Parc national de l'Île de Port-Cros, où il y a une réserve naturelle.

1. Je suis zoologiste et je voudrais savoir où on peut observer des animaux migrateurs en France. 2. Je suis photographe et je travaille pour la revue *National Geographic*. On m'a demandé de prendre des photos originales. 3. Je suis cinéaste et je vais tourner un film d'aventures en France. Il y a une scène où notre héros doit descendre une chute d'eau (*waterfall*). Où peut-on faire cela?

C. **Et en Amérique?** Y a-t-il des parcs nationaux aux États-Unis où on peut trouver des sites semblables aux (*similar to*) parcs du Mercantour, de l'Île de Port-Cros ou du Vercors? Quels parcs nationaux américains avez-vous visités ou aimeriez-vous visiter? Pourquoi? Qu'est-ce qu'on peut y trouver?

Quelques verbes de perception et d'action: *recevoir, (s')apercevoir*

PRESENT TENSE OF **recevoir** (*to receive; to welcome*)	
je reçois	nous recevons
tu reçois	vous recevez
il, elle, on reçoit	ils, elles reçoivent
Past participle: reçu	
Future stem: recevr-	

Other verbs conjugated like **recevoir** include **apercevoir** (*to perceive; to see*) and **s'apercevoir (de)** (*to notice*).

TOUR EIFFEL

La super-star du tourisme français, elle attire chaque année plus de trois millions de visiteurs; fascinante, incongrue, majestueuse, laide... aucun qualificatif n'a été omis pour la décrire; elle reste malgré cela un symbole: celui du triomphe de l'industrie du début du XXe siécle.

A. **A la campagne.** Mireille passe le week-end chez des amis en Normandie. Complétez son récit avec les verbes **apercevoir, recevoir** et **s'apercevoir.**

Ce week-end, les Joubert me ____[1] dans leur maison de campagne en Normandie. J'ai une jolie chambre au premier étage et de la fenêtre j'____[2] les champs fleuris. Très vite je ____[3] que l'air de la campagne me fait beaucoup de bien. Que c'est agréable, je ne ____[4] pas du tout du bruit des voitures.

Ensuite, mettez le récit au passé. Commencez par «Le week-end dernier... » Enfin, mettez-le au futur. Commencez par «Le week-end prochain... » Faites tous les changements nécessaires.

B. **Patrimoine et tourisme.** Voici une brève description d'un des monuments parisiens les plus visités.

1. Combien de visiteurs reçoit la Tour Eiffel chaque année?
2. Quels qualificatifs a-t-elle reçus au cours des années? Qu'est-ce qu'elle symbolise?
3. A votre avis, qu'aperçoit-on du sommet de la tour?
4. Quel monument ou site historique est le plus visité dans votre région? Combien de personnes reçoit-il approximativement chaque année?
5. Y a-t-il un endroit dans votre région d'où on aperçoit une jolie vue? Expliquez.

C. Chez vous. Avec un(e) camarade de classe, répondez aux questions suivantes.

1. Qu'est-ce que vous avez reçu récemment dans le courrier? 2. Que feriez-vous si vous receviez un cadeau de cinq mille dollars? 3. Chez vous, qu'est-ce qu'on aperçoit de la fenêtre de la cuisine? de la salle de séjour? 4. Chez vous, vous êtes-vous aperçu de quelque chose de bizarre récemment? Expliquez.

Mots-clés

Circumlocution: To circumlocute is to communicate an idea without the exact terms. Circumlocution is obviously an essential strategy for foreign-language students. Here are some useful expressions for getting "around" a word you don't know or can't remember.

- **C'est l'endroit où...**
  C'est l'endroit où on cultive le raisin. (le vignoble)
- **C'est quelque chose qu'on utilise pour...**
  C'est quelque chose qu'on utilise pour calculer. (une calculatrice)
- **une chose, un truc** (*familier*)
  Passe-moi le truc pour ouvrir la bouteille de vin. (un tire-bouchon)
- **C'est ce qu'on fait** (**ce qui arrive**) **quand...**
  C'est ce qu'on fait quand on déjeune en plein air. (pique-niquer)

Practice using circumlocution whenever you can, and your French vocabulary should increase substantially.

D. Un jeu. Faites une liste de dix mots français que vous avez appris le mois dernier. (Voir les sections de vocabulaire si nécessaire.) Ensuite, choisissez un(e) partenaire et faites-lui deviner chacun de vos mots. Vos explications, ou circonlocutions, doivent être en français et doivent être faciles à comprendre.

MODÈLE: VOUS: C'est la partie de la ferme où on cultive les produits agricoles.
VOTRE PARTENAIRE: C'est le champ.

Étude de grammaire

57. Talking About the Past: The Pluperfect

Le Mont-Saint-Michel est en danger.

Sandrine, Marc et Raymond, touristes canadiens, viennent de visiter le Mont-Saint-Michel.

SANDRINE: Nous n'**avions** jamais **vu** le Mont-Saint-Michel avant. C'est vraiment splendide!

MARC: Mais n'a-t-on pas découvert récemment qu'on **avait détruit** son équilibre écologique?

RAYMOND: C'est exact. Si on ne fait rien, le Mont-Saint-Michel ne sera plus une île en 1991.

SANDRINE: Il y a quelques années, les experts **avaient** déjà **estimé** le budget pour sauver le site à cent millions de francs, je crois.

RAYMOND: C'est un budget énorme, mais c'est aussi un des sites les plus visités en province.

Trouvez une phrase synonyme dans le dialogue.

1. Nous n'avions jamais visité le Mont-Saint-Michel avant cette visite.
2. On a découvert qu'on avait ruiné son équilibre écologique.
3. En 1983, les experts avaient déjà calculé le budget pour restaurer le site à 100 millions de francs.

The pluperfect tense (also called the past perfect) is used to indicate an action or event that occurred before another past action or event, either stated or implied: ***I had already left** for the country (when my friends arrived in Paris)*. It is formed with the imperfect of the auxiliary (**avoir** or **être**) plus the past participle of the main verb.

Un paysage bourguignon

	parler	sortir	se réveiller
je/j'	avais parlé	étais sorti(e)	m'étais réveillé(e)
tu	avais parlé	étais sorti(e)	t'étais réveillé(e)
il, elle, on	avait parlé	était sorti(e)	s'était réveillé(e)
nous	avions parlé	étions sorti(e)s	nous étions réveillé(e)s
vous	aviez parlé	étiez sorti(e)(s)	vous étiez réveillé(e)(s)
ils, elles	avaient parlé	étaient sorti(e)s	s'étaient réveillé(e)s

Quand j'ai téléphoné aux Dupont, ils **avaient** déjà **décidé** d'acheter la ferme. — *When I phoned the Duponts, they had already decided to buy the farm.*

Nous étions pressés parce que les autres **étaient** déjà **partis** à la campagne. — *We were in a hurry because the others had already left for the countryside.*

Marie **s'était réveillée** avant moi. Elle **était** déjà **sortie** à sept heures. — *Marie had awakened before me. She had already left by seven o'clock.*

MAINTENANT A VOUS

A. Voyage en Alsace. Jean-Pierre, Marion et Julie ont passé une semaine en Alsace. Complétez leur récit avec les verbes suggérés au plus-que-parfait. **Verbes suggérés:** acheter, arriver, conduire, envoyer, étudier, imaginer, manger...

Nous sommes arrivés en Alsace sans problèmes parce que Jean-Pierre _____[1] la carte avant de partir. Nous _____[2] à Strasbourg depuis quelques minutes quand nous sommes allés visiter le Parlement européen. Avant de reprendre la route nous avons dormi un peu, car à midi nous _____[3] trop de choucroute. Comme Julie _____[4] tout l'après-midi, elle était très fatiguée quand nous sommes arrivés à Colmar. Marion et Jean-Pierre _____[5] dix cartes postales chacun le premier jour de notre voyage. Nous _____[6] beaucoup de souvenirs bien avant la fin de notre séjour. Notre voyage en Alsace s'est passé encore mieux que ce que nous l'_____[7]!

B. Bordeaux et ses vignobles. Marc et Marie-Claire ont passé le week-end dernier dans la région de Bordeaux. Ils y étaient déjà allés, mais séparément. Quels endroits connaissaient-ils déjà?

MODÈLE: Ce week-end ils ont fait une excursion. (Marc) →
Ce week-end ils ont fait une excursion que Marc avait déjà faite.

1. A Bordeaux ils ont visité la cathédrale Saint-André. (Marie-Claire)
2. Ils ont visité un vignoble. (Marc)
3. Ils se sont promenés dans des champs. (Marie-Claire)
4. Ils ont acheté des vins. (Marc)
5. Ils ont dîné dans un excellent restaurant. (tous les deux)

C. **Aujourd'hui.** Qu'est-ce que vous aviez déjà fait ou pas encore fait aux moments suivants? **Suggestions:** se réveiller, se brosser les dents, s'habiller, se coucher, préparer la leçon de français...

58. Speculating: The Past Conditional

Une aventure en pleine nature

MARC: Si tu n'**avais** pas **oublié** la boussole (*compass*), nous ne **nous serions** jamais **perdus.**

YVETTE: Mais si je ne l'**avais** pas **oubliée,** notre randonnée* n'**aurait** pas **été** si palpitante...

MARC: Tu veux dire que je n'**aurais** pas **attrapé** un rhume, sans doute!

YVETTE: Voyons, Marc, pense à ce que nous **aurions manqué:** une journée de marche en pleine nature, le plaisir d'exercer notre sens pratique. C'est mieux que la télé, tu ne trouves pas?

Que serait-il arrivé (*would have happened*) si Yvette n'avait pas oublié la boussole? Complétez les phrases selon le dialogue.

1. Ils ne se ____.
2. Leur randonnée ne ____.
3. Marc ____.
4. Ils auraient manqué ____.

A. Forms of the Past Conditional

The past conditional (or conditional perfect) is used to express an action or event that would have occurred if some set of conditions (stated or implied) had been present: *We **would have worried** (if we had known)*. The French past conditional, **le conditionnel passé,** is formed with the conditional of the auxiliary (**avoir** or **être**) plus the past participle of the main verb.

	parler	**sortir**	**se réveiller**
je/j'	aurais parlé	serais sorti(e)	me serais réveillé(e)
tu	aurais parlé	serais sorti(e)	te serais réveillé(e)
il, elle, on	aurait parlé	serait sorti(e)	se serait réveillé(e)
nous	aurions parlé	serions sorti(e)s	nous serions réveillé(e)s
vous	auriez parlé	seriez sorti(e)(s)	vous seriez réveillé(e)(s)
ils, elles	auraient parlé	seraient sorti(e)s	se seraient réveillé(e)s

*__La randonnée,__ a form of hiking, is a popular outdoor activity in France.

B. Uses of the Past Conditional

The past conditional is used in the main clause of an *if*-clause sentence when the verb of the *if* clause is in the pluperfect.

Si j'**avais eu** le temps, j'**aurais visité** Nîmes.	*If I had had the time, I would have visited Nîmes.*
Si j'**avais grandi** dans une ferme, j'**aurais eu** un cheval.	*If I had grown up on a farm, I would have had a horse.*
Si les Normands n'**avaient** pas **conquis** l'Angleterre en 1066, l'anglais **aurait été** une langue très différente.	*If the Normans had not conquered England in 1066, English would have been a very different language.*

The underlying set of conditions (the *if* clause) is sometimes not stated.

A ta place, j'**aurais parlé** au guide.	*In your place, I would have spoken to the guide.*
Nous **serions allés** au lac.	*We would have gone to the lake.*
Aurais-tu fait une randonnée à bicyclette avec nous?	*Would you have taken a bike trip with us?*

C. The Past Conditional of *devoir*

The past conditional of **devoir** means *should have* or *ought to have*. It expresses regret about something that did not take place in the past.

J'**aurais dû prendre** l'autre chemin.	*I should have taken the other road.*
Nous **aurions dû acheter** un plan.	*We should have bought a map.*

D. Time Sequence in *if*-clause Sentences

In French, there are three tense sequences most often used in *if*-clause sentences.

CONTEXT	*IF* CLAUSE		MAIN CLAUSE (RESULT)
Plans for the future	**si** + *present*	→	future (indicative)
Present situation	**si** + *imperfect*	→	conditional
Past situation	**si** + *pluperfect*	→	past conditional

S'il ne **pleut** pas, nous **irons** à la montagne demain.	*If it doesn't rain, we'll go to the mountains tomorrow.*
S'il ne **pleuvait** pas, nous **irions** à la montagne.	*If it weren't raining, we'd go to the mountains.*
S'il n'**avait** pas **plu,** nous **serions allés** à la montagne.	*If it hadn't rained, we would have gone to the mountains.*

Note that the future and the conditional never follow **si** in an *if*-clause sentence.

MAINTENANT A VOUS

A. Un voyage trop court. Les Wilson, des touristes américains, visitent Paris en voyage organisé. Malheureusement, ils ne peuvent pas tout voir. Voici une partie de leur conversation avec leur guide à la fin du voyage. Dans chaque phrase, cherchez les verbes au plus-que-parfait ou au conditionnel passé, puis dites si les Wilson ont visité ou non les endroits mentionnés.

1. C'est dommage, on aurait tellement aimé visiter le zoo de Vincennes.
2. Heureusement, on avait visité les jardins du Château de Versailles avant la pluie.
3. On aurait dû descendre la Seine en bateau mouche; j'ai entendu dire que c'est formidable.
4. Hier après-midi il faisait très beau. On aurait dû monter à la Tour Eiffel.
5. On était déjà allé au musée d'Orsay; c'est pour ça que nous étions si fatigués quand nous avons visité le Louvre.
6. On aurait dû aussi visiter le musée Rodin. J'aurais aimé voir «le Penseur».

B. A leur place. Qu'est-ce que vous auriez fait si vous aviez été à la place des personnes suivantes? (**J'aurais... , je serais... , je me serais...**) **Verbes suggérés:** crier (*to shout*), avoir peur, partir en courant, se retourner, parler, plonger (*to dive*)...

1. Maurice faisait du camping dans la forêt quand il a entendu un bruit mystérieux et terrifiant. 2. Hélène se promenait en famille au bois de Vincennes quand sa nièce est tombée dans le lac. 3. Marylou et Amy-Jo flânaient dans le quartier élégant de l'Opéra quand elles ont vu Pierre Cardin. 4. Mme Gaudin faisait une randonnée dans le Parc national des Pyrénées quand elle a rencontré un ours (*bear*).

C. Conditions et conséquences. Nous sommes obligés quotidiennement de nous excuser ou de demander des renseignements avec diplomatie. Choisissez les propositions de la colonne de droite qui complètent logiquement les débuts de phrase de la colonne de gauche.

1. Si j'avais su que c'était ton anniversaire,...
2. Je viendrais avec plaisir à ta soirée,...
3. Si tu me dis la date de la réunion,...
4. Nous nous serions dépêchés un peu plus,...
5. S'il n'était pas si tard,...
6. J'aimerais bien t'accompagner en ville,...

a. si tu pouvais attendre encore une demi-heure.
b. Michel et moi viendrons sans faute.
c. je prendrais volontiers un café avec toi.
d. si nous avions su que tu attendais.
e. je t'aurais invité à dîner Chez Antoine.
f. si je n'avais pas cours ce soir-là.

D. Conseils. Utilisez le verbe **devoir** pour conseiller les personnes suivantes. Qu'est-ce qu'elles auraient dû faire pour éviter (*avoid*) ces situations?

1. Pierre est arrivé à l'hôtel, mais il n'y avait plus de chambres. 2. Marguerite a écrit une lettre à ses amis parisiens pour leur dire qu'elle allait arriver, mais ils avaient quitté Paris avant de recevoir sa lettre. 3. Isabelle et moi, nous voulions vous envoyer une carte postale, mais nous n'avions pas de timbres. 4. Françoise a fait la connaissance d'un jeune homme admirable, mais elle ne sait pas où il habite. 5. David a passé toute une journée à la plage sur la Côte d'Azur. Il a fini par avoir très mal aux yeux.

59. Talking About Quantity: Indefinite Adjectives and Pronouns

Un petit village renaît

BENOÎT: Voilà **plusieurs** mois que je n'ai pas vu Marion et Clément. **Tout** va bien chez eux?

VINCENT: Oui, ils font **quelque chose** de passionnant, avec **quelques** amis.

BENOÎT: Tu parles de ce petit village abandonné qu'ils sont **tous** en train de reconstruire?

VINCENT: Oui, chacun y a acheté une maison en ruine. **Quelques-uns** travaillent à la construction, **d'autres** au jardinage...

BENOÎT: **Chaque** fois que j'entends parler d'eux, j'ai envie de **tout** laisser tomber ici et de les rejoindre!

VINCENT: Tu devrais d'abord terminer **quelques-uns** des projets de bricolage que tu as commencés l'année dernière!

1. Depuis combien de temps Benoît n'a-t-il pas vu Marion et Clément?
2. Est-ce que tout va bien chez eux?
3. Qu'est-ce qu'ils sont en train de faire?
4. Est-ce que d'autres amis travaillent avec eux?
5. Que devrait faire Benoît, selon Vincent?

A. Forms and Uses of *tout*

1. The adjective **tout** (**toute, tous, toutes**)

As an adjective, **tout** can be followed by an article, a possessive adjective, or a demonstrative adjective.

Nous avons marché **toute la journée** pour arriver au sommet.	*We hiked all day to reach the summit.*

Voici **tous mes amis.**	*Here are all of my friends.*
Veux-tu apporter **toutes ces provisions?**	*Do you want to bring all those supplies?*

2. The pronoun **tout**

As a pronoun (masculine singular), the form **tout** means *all, everything.*

Tout va bien!	*Everything is fine!*
Tout est possible dans ce monde.	*Everything is possible in this world.*

Tous and **toutes** mean *everyone, every one* (*of them*), *all of them.* When **tous** is used as a pronoun, the final **s** is pronounced: **tous** [tus].

Tu vois ces jeunes gens? Ils veulent **tous** faire du camping.	*Do you see those young people? All of them want to go camping.*
Ces lettres sont arrivées hier. Dans **toutes,** il est question d'écologie.	*These letters arrived yesterday. All of them deal with ecology.*

B. Other Indefinite Adjectives and Pronouns

Indefinite adjectives and pronouns refer to unspecified things, persons, or qualities. They are also used to express sameness (the same one) and difference (another). Here is a list of the most frequently used indefinite adjectives and pronouns in French.

ADJECTIVES	PRONOUNS
quelques } + *noun*	**quelqu'un**, **quelque chose** } + **de** + *masculine adjective*
chaque } + *noun*	**quelques-uns/unes**, **chacun/chacune** } + **de** + *noun*
EXPRESSIONS USED AS ADJECTIVES AND PRONOUNS	
un(e) autre	**certain(e)s**
d'autres*	**le/la même; les mêmes**
l'autre/les autres	**plusieurs (de)**

*Note that **de** is used without an article before **autres** whether **autres** modifies a noun or stands alone as a pronoun.

ADJECTIVES		PRONOUNS
J'ai **quelques** amis à la campagne.	→	**Quelques-uns** (de mes amis) sont vignerons.
		Quelqu'un m'a envoyé un livre sur l'écologie.
		Lui as-tu envoyé **quelque chose**?
Nous avons **plusieurs** choix.	→	**Plusieurs** de ces choix sont extrêmement difficiles.
Chaque étudiante suit le cours de gymnastique.	→	**Chacune** des étudiantes recevra une note de gymnastique au Bac.
Veux-tu **une autre** tasse de thé?	→	Non, si j'en prenais **une autre,** je ne pourrais pas dormir.
Où est **l'autre** avion du club?	→	**L'autre** est parti.
Les autres passagers sont partis.	→	**Les autres** sont partis.
J'ai **d'autres** problèmes.	→	J'en ai **d'autres.**
Ce sont **les mêmes** étudiants.	→	**Les mêmes** sont absents.

The indefinite pronouns **quelqu'un** and **quelque chose** are singular and masculine. Remember that adjectives that modify these pronouns follow them and are introduced by **de.**

Je connais **quelqu'un d'intéressant.**	*I know someone interesting.*
Je veux **quelque chose de bon** à manger.	*I want something good to eat.*

MAINTENANT A VOUS

A. Excursion à Versailles. Jean-Paul a passé sa journée au Château de Versailles. Il a tout vu en détail. Posez les questions suivantes à un(e) camarade. Il (elle) répond en utilisant une forme de **tout.**

MODÈLE: —Est-ce qu'il a vu les chambres du roi?
—Oui, il a vu **toutes** les chambres du roi.

1. visiter le château	a. tout
2. photographier les fontaines	b. tous
3. voir les meubles	c. toutes
4. lire l'histoire du château	d. toute
5. admirer les peintures du plafond de la Galerie des Glaces	
6. se promener dans les jardins	

B. Le patrimoine naturel est en danger. Un accident en mer a provoqué une grave marée noire (*oil spill*) en Bretagne. A la suite de cette catastrophe, il y a eu une conférence sur la protection des océans. Complétez les notes d'un journaliste avec des adjectifs et des pronoms indéfinis. Plusieurs solutions sont possibles. **Suggestions:** plusieurs, quelques, même(s), (d')autre(s), chaque, quelqu'un, chacun(e), quelques-un(e)s...

_____[1] pays étaient représentés à la conférence. _____[2] défendait ses intérêts. _____[3] des victimes de la marée noire ont accepté la tragédie; d'_____[4] ont manifesté dans les rues de Brest. _____[5] a parlé d'une autre marée noire en Alaska. Heureusement, _____[6] plages ont échappé à la marée noire, mais pas toutes. Tous les pays connaissent les _____[7] problèmes. _____[8] ont téléphoné au ministre de l'environnement. _____[9] conférence aura lieu dans un mois pour discuter d'_____[10] problèmes écologiques graves.

C. La première chose qui vient à l'esprit (*mind*). Avec un(e) camarade de classe, posez des questions—en français, s'il vous plaît—à partir des indications suivantes. Votre camarade doit donner la première réponse qui lui vient à l'esprit.

MODÈLE: someone boring → Nomme quelqu'un d'ennuyeux. → ?

1. someone important 2. something important 3. something stupid 4. something red 5. someone funny 6. all the large cities in the state 7. a few of the French professors in the university 8. several French artists (authors, singers, _____) 9. other French artists (authors, singers, _____) 10. another French artist (author, singer, _____) 11. ?

Commentaire culturel

Le village de Salignac avec son château des XIII–XVIe siècles

La sauvegarde du passé. Les Français sont très fiers de leur passé et de leur patrimoine. Chaque été des groupes de volontaires aident à la restauration de châteaux, monuments ou sites historiques en ruine. Grâce aux efforts d'organisations telles que R.E.M.P.A.R.T.S. (Réhabilitation et Entretien des Monuments et du Patrimoine Artistique), ces groupes travaillent sous la direction d'un architecte, d'un ingénieur ou d'un archéologue. Ces stages sont très convoités (= désirés), surtout par les étudiants en architecture, car ils apprennent non seulement à retracer les plans d'un bâtiment historique à partir de vestiges (portes, fenêtres, poutres [*beams*]) mais aussi à le restaurer en utilisant des matériaux authentiques. Ainsi, par exemple, quand on a besoin de ciment pour refaire le mur d'un château, on utilisera les éléments naturels de la région (sable, pierres), comme on l'aurait fait à l'époque où le château a été construit. Le ministère de la culture joue aussi un rôle important dans la sauvegarde des bâtiments en ruine. C'est lui qui classe les monuments historiques et établit les sites archéologiques.

D. Sondage. Quelques étudiants préparent deux ou trois questions sur la vie à l'université. Les autres donnent leurs réponses par écrit. Les premiers examinent les réponses et annoncent les résultats en utilisant des adjectifs ou des pronoms indéfinis. Par exemple:

Certains étudiants disent que...
Quelqu'un a répondu que...
Plusieurs d'entre nous pensent que...
Quelqu'un estime que...
Le même étudiant ajoute (*adds*) que...
Les autres trouvent que...

Situation

Un village perché* en Provence

Contexte *Francine montre son pays natal à Karen, une jeune Américaine qui étudie avec elle à l'Université de Nice. Les deux étudiantes vont passer quelques jours dans la petite maison de campagne de la famille de Francine. Karen connaît les plages et les villes célèbres de la Côte d'Azur. Mais elle n'a jamais vu les collines° pittoresques de l'arrière-pays.° Le village perché de Saint-Paul-de-Vence est pour elle une véritable découverte.*

collines: *hills*
l'arrière... *inland*

Objectif *Karen exprime son admiration pour le paysage vençois.°*

vençois: *de Vence*

Vue d'ensemble de Saint-Paul-de-Vence. De nos jours ce petit village provençal est un centre artistique important.

**hillside (lit., perched)*

FRANCINE: Voilà, nous arrivons. Ce village fortifié, là-bas,° c'est Saint-Paul-de-Vence. *over there*

KAREN: Mais il est absolument spectaculaire, ce village: il est bâti sur un rocher°! *rock*

FRANCINE: C'est parce que les villageois° devaient se protéger contre les pirates maures,° au moyen âge. Tous les vieux villages par ici sont construits sur des hauteurs.° habitants d'un village / *Moorish* / *heights*

KAREN: Je n'ai jamais rien vu d'aussi beau!

FRANCINE: Maintenant, regarde la vue du côté de la Méditerranée.

KAREN: Quel panorama splendide! Les couleurs sont si brillantes.

FRANCINE: Oui, c'est pourquoi tant de° peintres sont venus vivre ici. tant... *so many*

KAREN: La plupart d'entre eux étaient des artistes du dix-neuvième et surtout du vingtième siècle, n'est-ce pas?

FRANCINE: Oui, demain nous pourrions aller voir la chapelle Matisse, ou le musée Picasso ou la maison de Renoir. Ils sont tous près d'ici. Viens, on va s'arrêter ici un moment et prendre quelque chose.

VARIATIONS

1. Recréez le dialogue. Changez la structure des exclamations de Karen. Par exemple, «il est absolument spectaculaire, ce village» devient «Quel village extraordinaire!»
2. Improvisez! Imaginez que vous montrez un site extraordinaire (New York? San Francisco? Yosemite? le Grand Canyon?) à un ami français (une amie française) qui visite l'Amérique pour la première fois. Créez un nouveau dialogue rempli d'expressions d'admiration.

A propos

Comment exprimer l'admiration ou l'indignation

Verbes:

J'aime (admire, adore)...	Je n'aime pas (déteste)...

Constructions verbales:

Ça me plaît.	Ça ne me plaît pas du tout.
Ça me séduit (*appeals to me*).	Ça me dépasse. (*That's beyond me.*)
Ce qui me plaît, c'est que...	Ce qui me déplaît, c'est que...

Constructions suivies d'adjectifs:

C'est agréable.	C'est désagréable.
... beau.	... moche.
... merveilleux.	... scandaleux.

Exclamations avec **quel:**

Quelle beauté!	Quelle horreur!
Quelle splendeur!	

Commentaire. Quelle est votre réaction devant les photos ci-dessous? Discutez-en avec des camarades. Utilisez les expressions de l'*A propos*.

Un ensemble d'immeubles modernes dans la banlieue nord parisienne

La fontaine Stravinsky à Paris

Commentaire culturel

Le patrimoine naturel. Quand on parle du patrimoine de la France, on pense généralement à ses monuments, ses châteaux et ses œuvres d'art. Mais une de ses plus grandes richesses est son patrimoine naturel. En effet, la France offre au visiteur une grande variété de paysages, les uns plus beaux que les autres. Chaque région a sa propre personnalité, résultat du climat et de siècles d'histoire. En voici quelques exemples.

Un paysage fleuri, en Provence

La Provence est le pays du soleil. Une lumière unique baigne le paysage. Le rose, l'ocre et le jaune des murs et le rouge des toits des petits villages se marient avec un paysage parfois désertique de maquis et de garrigues (*scrublands*). La Provence est aussi le royaume des fleurs et des parfums. La ville de Grasse est la capitale mondiale des parfums. On y traite les fleurs récoltées dans la région, surtout la rose et le jasmin, mais aussi des plantes sauvages comme la lavande ou le thym. Mais ce sont ses plages de sable, ses calanques (*rocky inlets*) profondes et sa mer d'un bleu intense, synonymes de vacances, qui attirent des millions de touristes chaque année.

Les falaises d'Étretat, en Normandie

La Normandie est la région la plus verte de France. Elle se caractérise par un paysage varié de vallées et de plateaux, de champs et de prairies. Ses fermes à l'architecture typique produisent des produits laitiers. Ses arbres fruitiers, et en particulier les pommiers, symbolisent le paysage normand, surtout au printemps quand ils sont en fleur. On y produit un cidre d'excellente qualité. La côte normande est très pittoresque avec ses falaises dont la plus connue est celle d'Étretat. Les plages de la Manche sont entrées dans l'histoire lors de la Deuxième Guerre mondiale avec le débarquement allié en juin 1944.

© IPAI / THE IMAGE WORKS

Un alignement de menhirs, en Bretagne

La Bretagne est séparée de la Normandie par un îlot rocheux où a été construite il y a plus de mille ans une magnifique abbaye: le Mont-Saint-Michel. C'est une région qui garde un caractère mystérieux et mystique à la fois, avec ses menhirs de l'époque celtique et ses chapelles très anciennes. Sa côte est assez sauvage et découpée avec des plages et de petits ports de pêche. L'intérieur du pays se caractérise par des prés verdoyants et des forêts ténébreuses qui rappellent toujours les vieilles légendes bretonnes.

Mise au point

A. Si on pouvait choisir? Dans un cours d'histoire, le professeur demande aux étudiants de décrire une période historique qu'ils aimeraient observer s'ils le pouvaient. Lisez leurs réponses et dites à quelle époque ou à quel siècle ils auraient aimé vivre.

VINCENT: Je m'intéresse beaucoup à la vie de Jules César. Je trouve qu'il serait fascinant de connaître la vie de la Rome antique.

CHRISTINE: Moi, j'admire le courage des individus qui s'opposent à un gouvernement qu'ils n'ont pas choisi. L'époque des révolutions américaine et française a dû être extraordinaire.

Maintenant, dites à quelle époque vous auriez aimé vivre et pourquoi.

MODÈLE: J'aurais aimé vivre à l'époque médiévale parce que...

B. Projets du soir. Complétez le dialogue suivant avec une forme des verbes entre parenthèses, ou un adjectif ou un pronom indéfini.

BÉNÉDICTE: Qu'allons-nous faire ce soir? Si nous avions de l'argent, nous ____ (pouvoir) descendre à Monte Carlo.
JULIEN: Moi, je tiens à faire ____ d'intéressant.
BÉNÉDICTE: D'accord. Qui pouvons-nous inviter? ____ tes amis sont ennuyeux.
JULIEN: Ce n'est pas vrai. Nous n'avons pas vu Benoît et Laurence depuis trois mois. Invitons-les.
BÉNÉDICTE: Oh, ils n'arrêtent pas de parler. J'____ (aimer) plutôt aller voir un film. Il y a un film américain au Bijou.
JULIEN: Auquel penses-tu?
BÉNÉDICTE: Je pensais à celui de Woody Allen, *Radio Days*.
JULIEN: Très bien. Si tu n'a pas ____ idées, je ____ (téléphoner) pour demander à quelle heure est la séance.
BÉNÉDICTE: Si j'____ (avoir) le temps hier, j' ____ (pouvoir) acheter l'*Officiel des spectacles*.
JULIEN: Tant pis (*Too bad*). C'est le meilleur guide des spectacles, mais c'est trop tard.

C. **Si j'avais pu...** Qu'est-ce que vous auriez fait pour améliorer (*to improve*) les conditions de vie dans votre université l'année passée ou dans votre ville d'origine quand vous étiez plus jeune? Faites au moins six phrases complètes. Utilisez chaque phrase de la colonne de gauche. Les phrases de la colonne de droite sont des suggestions.

Les occasions

1. si je / avoir / argent
2. si je / avoir / courage
3. si on / me / écouter
4. si je / avoir / temps
5. si je / être élu(e) au Congrès

Les actions suggérées

(ne pas) augmenter / prix / essence
(ne pas) protéger / la vie animale / l'environnement
(ne pas) organiser / manifestation / contre / centrales nucléaires (*nuclear power plants*)
(ne pas) interdire (*to forbid*) / voitures / dans le centre-ville

D. **Si tu étais... tu serais.** Voici le «portrait chinois» d'un homme politique français, publié dans *Le Point*. Lisez-le, puis posez des questions à un(e) camarade de classe pour faire son «portrait chinois». Ensuite, comparez les différents portraits obtenus. Lequel est le plus original? le plus insolite? Pourriez-vous faire votre propre «portrait chinois»? Que seriez-vous?

PORTRAIT CHINOIS

Si vous étiez	Vous seriez
une pierre	une topaze blanche
une voiture	une Porsche
une couleur	le vert
une boisson	du château margaux
un métier	celui que je fais
un animal	un tigre
un monument	le stade d'Olympie
un instrument de musique	un orgue

Interactions

In this chapter, you practiced using the pluperfect and the past conditional, and you learned about indefinite adjectives and pronouns. Use the vocabulary and structures from the chapter to act out the following situations.

1. **Si j'avais vécu il y a 100 ans...** With a partner, imagine how life would have been different one hundred years ago. Talk about education, family life, lifestyle, leisure activities, and employment opportunities.
2. **Un conseiller (Une conseillère).** Imagine that you are talking to a counselor (your partner) about what would have happened if you had made other choices in your life. She (He) will react and ask you questions. Talk about school, family, friends, sports, and so forth.

Vocabulaire

Verbes

apercevoir to perceive
 s'apercevoir de to become aware of
avoir lieu to take place
avoir l'occasion (de) to have the chance (opportunity) (*to do something*)
bâtir to build
diriger to direct, lead
 se diriger (vers) to make one's way (toward); to go
échapper à to escape
flâner to stroll
recevoir to receive

Substantifs

l'appareil-photo (*m.*) (still) camera
les arènes (*f.*) arena
la beauté beauty
la cathédrale cathedral
le champ field
la chasse hunt
le chef-d'œuvre masterpiece
l'époque (*f.*) period (*of history*)
l'espace (*m.*) space
l'événement (*m.*) event
la ferme farm
la feuille leaf; sheet (*of paper*)
l'horreur (*f.*) horror
le moyen âge Middle Ages
l'œuvre (d'art) (*f.*) work (of art)
l'or (*m.*) gold
le palais palace
le patrimoine legacy, patrimony
le paysage countryside, landscape
le raisin grape
la randonnée cross-country hike
le roi (la reine) king (queen)
le siècle century
le tableau painting
la vigne vine
le vigneron wine grower
le vignoble vineyard

Adjectifs

classique classical
gothique Gothic
incroyable unbelievable
médiéval(e) medieval
merveilleux (-euse) marvelous
moche ugly
pareil(le) (à) similar (to)
romain(e) Roman
semblable (à) similar (to)

Mots divers

à votre (ta) place in your place (if I were you, . . .)
c'est-à-dire that is to say (in other words, . . .)
le (la) même the same one
quelques (*adj.*) some, a few
quelques-uns, quelques-unes (*pron.*) some, a few
tant (de) so much, so many
un de ces jours one of these days (someday)
vers toward (*a place*)

INTERMÈDE 16

Lecture

La chasse aux trésors

Le sous-sol° français est une véritable caverne d'Ali Baba. Toutes les régions de France ont connu des invasions barbares ou romaines, d'incessantes migrations humaines et de longues périodes troublées. Un grand nombre de trésors est encore à découvrir.° Par exemple, le trésor de Louis XVI: lorsque le roi a décidé de fuir° le royaume,° en 1791, il a appris qu'une troupe de révolutionnaires l'attendait près de la frontière belge. On l'a arrêté avant le village de Montmédy, où l'attendait une fortune considérable destinée à préparer son retour. Les soldats royalistes ont caché les caisses° d'or et d'argent° dans un souterrain.° Et le trésor de Louis XVI dort toujours.

De nos jours, la vente de centaines de milliers de détecteurs de métaux apporte de grands changements dans le monde de la chasse au trésor. Les Français se transforment en «détectives du passé» et n'en finissent pas de sonder° le sous-sol à la recherche d'un trésor enterré.°

Jean, 35 ans, est un de ces prospecteurs passionnés. Il passe en moyenne quinze à vingt heures par semaine à prospecter. Son butin°? Mille deux cent cinquante pièces de monnaie d'argent de l'époque romaine, un calice° en argent, une magnifique bague° de 1925 et cent cinquante bagues et alliances° contemporaines! Où prospectent les chasseurs de trésors? Dans les mares,° les sources,° les fontaines; dans les rivières, près des piles de pont;° dans les caves,° dans les bois, et près des anciennes voies° romaines, souvent transformées en routes nationales. Pourtant, il est rare de trouver un véritable trésor par hasard. En général, ces trésors ne sont détectés qu'après de longues recherches en bibliothèque. Il faut explorer les archives et lire les anciennes cartes. Il faut connaître son histoire, et certains vétérans connaissent par cœur° les textes anciens, en particulier les *Commentaires sur la conquête des Gaules* de Jules César!

Ce nouveau loisir préoccupe très sérieusement le ministère de la culture. Le pillage d'un terrain qui contient des vestiges archéologiques est punissable d'un mois à deux ans de prison. En fait, seuls des prospecteurs surpris° sur l'un des vingt mille sites archéologiques connus ont été condamnés à ce jour. Des sites d'intérêt historique sont chaque jour saccagés° par les prospecteurs amateurs. Une pièce de monnaie trouvée dans une couche° de sol brûlé° peut aider à préciser la date où ce feu° s'est produit. On peut alors

subsoil
à... *to be discovered*
quitter brusquement à cause d'un danger / un roi règne sur son **royaume**
grandes boîtes
un métal (Ag) / passage sous le sol
examiner / déposé sous la terre
haul, plunder
cup, chalice
on la porte au doigt / la bague symbolisant le mariage
ponds
springs / piles... *bridge piers*
cellars (of houses) / routes
connaissent... ont mémorisé
trouvés
mis au pillage
layer
burned / *fire*

dater tout autre objet découvert dans cette même couche et reconstituer l'histoire du site. Le patrimoine français est en danger. La guerre est ouverte entre prospecteurs amateurs et archéologues. Certains archéologues voudraient faire interdire° la vente des détecteurs de métaux. D'autres réclament° l'institution d'un «permis de fouilles°». Dans plusieurs régions, des responsables des antiquités ont répandu° sur les sites des morceaux d'aluminium, qui trompent les détecteurs. Mais ce phénomène est difficile à arrêter: la tentation est bien grande. Récemment on vient de découvrir des trous° dans les jardins du Louvre. Les coupables°? Des prospecteurs, bien sûr. Il faut dire que peu avant son arrestation, Louis XVI (encore lui!) avait enterré mille louis d'or,° quelques bijoux° et une partie du trésor national sous les pelouses° du Louvre! Comment résister?

rendre illégal / demandent
excavation
distribué
holes
les personnes responsables du crime
louis... ancienne monnaie / les bagues, les bracelets, etc.
lawns

COMPRÉHENSION

A. Répondez aux questions suivantes.

1. Pourquoi y a-t-il tant de trésors cachés dans le sous-sol français?
2. Qu'est-ce qui a beaucoup changé la chasse aux trésors en France?
3. Pourquoi peut-on trouver des trésors près des routes nationales en France?
4. Quel est le rôle des bibliothèques dans la chasse aux trésors?
5. Pourquoi le ministère de la culture s'occupe-t-il des prospecteurs?
6. Pourquoi a-t-on percé des trous dans les jardins du Louvre?

B. La lecture fait allusion à plusieurs personnages historiques ou fabuleux. Pouvez-vous les identifier à partir des descriptions suivantes?

1. A l'époque romaine, ce peuple habitait dans la région qui s'appelle aujourd'hui la France. 2. Mari de Marie-Antoinette, il a été guillotiné par les révolutionnaires en 1793. 3. Général et homme d'état romain qui a conquis la Gaule.

Par écrit

A. L'Amérique. Écrivez un article sur le patrimoine américain pour un magazine québécois selon votre point de vue. Essayez de convaincre les Québécois de visiter les États-Unis. Utilisez les suggestions suivantes.

Paragraphe 1—le patrimoine naturel: Quelles sont les plus belles régions des États-Unis? Décrivez-les.

Paragraphe 2—le patrimoine culturel: Qui sont les meilleurs écrivains, peintres, architectes, etc.? Expliquez pourquoi leur œuvre est importante.

B. Qu'est-ce que vous auriez dit? Imaginez que vous avez l'occasion d'assister à une soirée lors du festival du cinéma à Cannes. Vous rencontrez des célébrités françaises et américaines, entre autres Catherine Deneuve, Gérard Depardieu, Tom Cruise et Sigourney Weaver. Vous avez beaucoup de choses à leur dire, mais quand on vous les présente, vous êtes tellement ému(e) que vous n'arrivez plus à dire un mot. Écrivez ce que vous auriez aimé leur dire et leur demander, et ce qui se serait passé si vous n'aviez pas été aussi timide.

C. Interprétez le dessin suivant.

CHAPITRE DIX-SEPT

Le monde francophone

—Je me crois au paradis.
—Moi aussi. Je n'ai jamais vu un coucher de soleil aussi beau.
—C'était une excellente idée de venir à Raiatea.
—C'est vrai, c'est moins connu que Tahiti ou Bora-Bora et beaucoup plus tranquille.

Étude de vocabulaire

Histoire de la francophonie

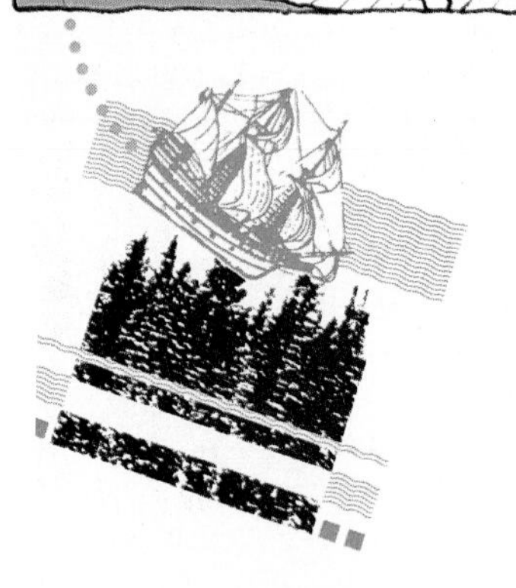

XVIe siècle: Arrivée de Jacques Cartier au Canada; expansion française dans la région des Alpes et de la Côte d'Azur.

XVIIe siècle: Champlain fonde Québec; établissements des Antilles (Haïti, Martinique, Guadeloupe). Fondation de Montréal; la Nouvelle-France s'étend vers l'Ouest jusqu'aux Rocheuses et le long du Mississippi jusqu'en Louisiane.
En Inde, établissements français de Chandernagor et de Pondichéry.

XIXe siècle: Implantation française en Algérie (1830), en Indochine (1859), au Sénégal (1854), en Tunisie (1881), à Madagascar (1883). Établissements de «l'Afrique équatoriale française» et de «l'Afrique occidentale française». Indépendance d'Haïti.

XXe siècle: De 1954 à 1962, indépendance de l'Indochine, du Maroc, de la Tunisie, de l'Algérie et de seize pays de l'Afrique noire.
1961 – Création de l'Association des universités partiellement ou entièrement de langue française (AUPELF)
1962 – Début de l'implantation d'ambassades canadiennes en Afrique francophone
1965 – Premiers accords de coopération entre la France et le Québec
1967 – Création de l'Association internationale des parlementaires de langue française (A.I.P.L.F.)
1970 – Création de l'Agence de coopération culturelle et technique (A.C.C.T.)
1986 – Premier Sommet de la francophonie à Paris
1987 – Deuxième Sommet de la francophonie à Québec

A. Un peu d'histoire et de géographie. D'après cet article:

1. En quel siècle Jacques Cartier est-il arrivé au Nouveau Monde?
2. Qui a fondé Québec?
3. Dans quelles régions d'Amérique s'étend la Nouvelle-France?
4. Nommez trois colonies françaises au XIXe siècle. Quel pays devient indépendant à cette époque?
5. Où et quand a eu lieu le premier Sommet de la francophonie?
6. Avez-vous déjà visité un pays francophone? Si oui, lequel? Sinon, lequel aimeriez-vous visiter? Expliquez votre réponse.
7. Maintenant, consultez la carte au début du livre et nommez cinq pays francophones d'Afrique occidentale. Où est-ce qu'on parle français en Afrique orientale? Nommez trois îles francophones. Que savez-vous de ces différents pays ou régions? Avec quels pays associez-vous les expressions suivantes: le tourisme? le Maghreb? la décolonisation? les territoires d'outre-mer? le bilinguisme? les Cajuns?

B. Le Nouveau Monde francophone. Voici des faits qui ont marqué l'histoire du Nouveau Monde. Trouvez dans la colonne de droite le nom qui correspond à chaque définition. Puis, avec un(e) camarade, essayez de mettre ces événements par ordre chronologique.

1. Il a vendu l'état de la Louisiane aux États-Unis en 1803.
2. Il a exploré le Canada au XVIème siècle et pris possession de ces territoires au nom de la France.
3. Il a descendu le Mississippi jusqu'au golfe du Mexique en 1682.
4. Il a exploré la mer des Caraïbes et a découvert l'île de Haïti en 1492.
5. Il a fondé la ville de Québec en 1608.
6. Un état américain doit son nom à ce roi de France.
7. Il était l'ami de Franklin et il a soutenu la guerre d'indépendance américaine.
8. Bienville a fondé cette ville en 1718 et l'a nommée en l'honneur du régent, le duc d'Orléans.

a. Louis XIV
b. Christophe Colomb
c. Napoléon
d. La Nouvelle-Orléans
e. Jacques Cartier
f. La Fayette
g. Cavalier de La Salle
h. Samuel de Champlain

C. La francophonie aux États-Unis. Avec un(e) camarade, regardez la carte des États-Unis à la page suivante. Qu'est-ce que ces villes ont de particulier? Savez-vous ce que ces noms veulent dire?

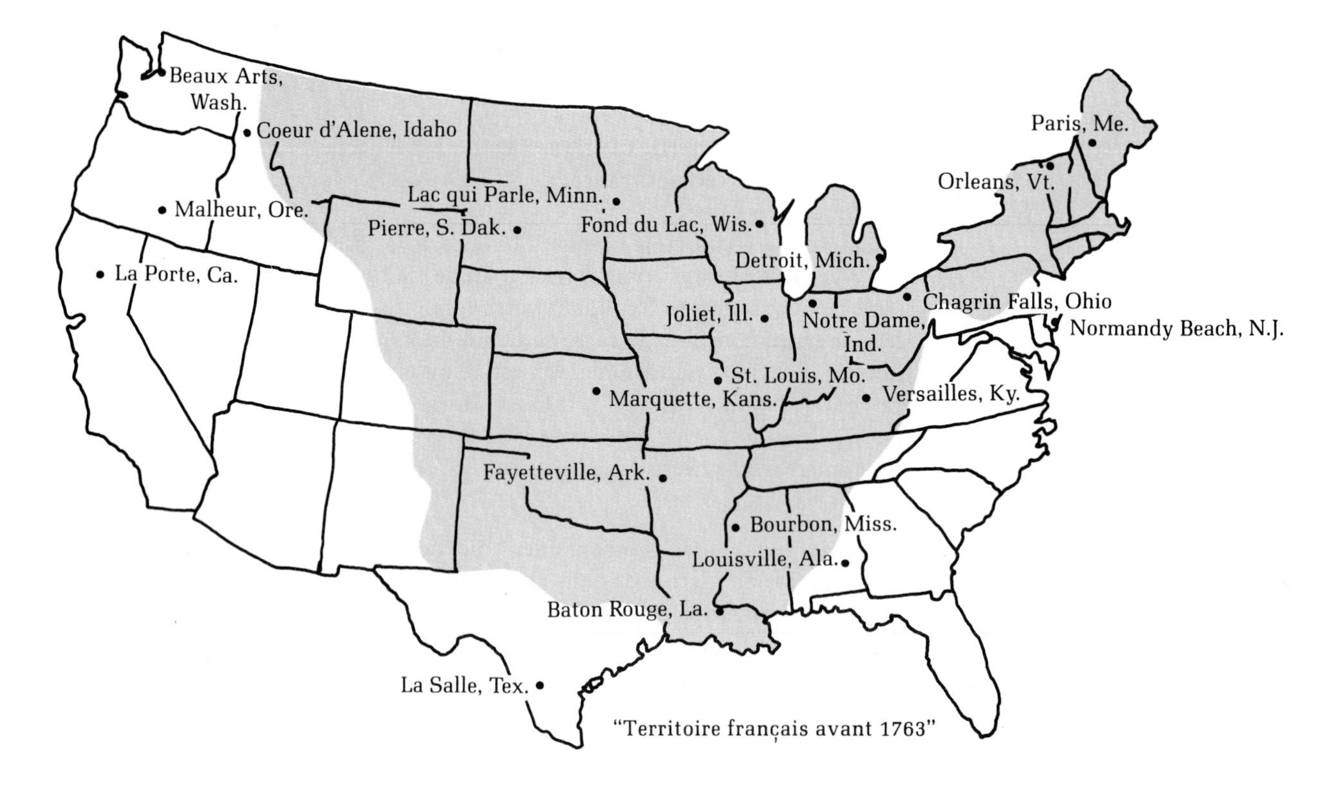

D. Interview. Bien sûr, il n'y a pas que des personnes d'origine française en Amérique! Interrogez votre camarade sur l'origine de sa famille et ensuite, présentez à la classe un résumé de ce que vous avez appris. Demandez à votre camarade...

1. de quelle nationalité il (elle) est
2. d'où viennent ses parents, ses grands-parents et ses arrière-grands-parents (*great-grandparents*)
3. quand ses ancêtres sont venus en Amérique
4. quelle a été, à son avis, la réaction de ses ancêtres quand ils sont arrivés aux États-Unis
5. s'il (si elle) a visité (ou visitera) le pays de ses ancêtres
6. s'il (si elle) parle la langue de ses ancêtres
7. si on conserve, chez lui (chez elle) certaines traditions ethniques
8. s'il (si elle) trouve qu'il est important de connaître ses origines

Le Carnaval

Un défilé de chars à Québec

A. Le Carnaval. Cette fête populaire est célébrée dans plusieurs pays francophones. Regardez le dessin et la photo ci-dessus et répondez aux questions suivantes.

1. Qui est le roi du carnaval au Québec?
2. Quel est l'événement de Mardi Gras le plus important à La Nouvelle-Orléans?
3. Quel est le dernier jour du Carnaval?
4. Que portent les gens à Haïti pour fêter le Mardi Gras?
5. Comment s'appelle une procession de gens déguisés et de musiciens?
6. Comment s'appelle le véhicule décoré qui fait partie d'un défilé?
7. Connaissez-vous d'autres pays, régions ou villes où on fête le Carnaval? Avez-vous déjà participé à un Carnaval? Où et quand?
8. A quelle occasion y a-t-il un grand défilé à New York? Y en a-t-il aussi un dans votre ville ou votre région? De quoi se compose généralement ce défilé?
9. Pour quelle fête américaine se déguise-t-on généralement? Quels costumes avez-vous portés dans le passé? Quel costume avez-vous l'intention de porter la prochaine fois? Avez-vous jamais eu de grandes aventures lorsque vous étiez déguisé(e)? Racontez-les à la classe.

La Guinée

Vue d'avion, la Guinée se présente sous la forme d'une banane, au sud du Sénégal et s'étend de l'océan à la forêt vierge.

Renseignements pratiques

- **Capitale :** Conakry.
- **Superficie :** 245 587 km^2.
- **Population :** 5,2 millions.
- **Langue officielle :** français.
- **Religions :** Islam 80 %, Animisme 15 %, Christianisme 1,5 %.
- **Economie :** agriculture, élevage, gisements de fer et de bauxite.
- **Monnaie :** franc guinéen ; 1 FF = 45 FG
- **Heure locale :** G.M.T. (France + 1 h en hiver, + 2 h en été).
- **Ambassade :** 24, rue Emile Menier, 75116 Paris. Tél. : 45.53.72.25.
- **Formalités :** passeport valide + visa.
- **Vaccinations :** fièvre jaune, choléra, traitement antipaludéen.
- **Climat :** le climat tropical du pays est caractérisé par l'alternance de deux saisons qui varient suivant les régions et l'altitude. En général : juillet à octobre saison des pluies, décembre à avril saison sèche.

Un village fortifié dans l'Atlas, au Maroc

© GRUYAERT/MAGNUM

Le Maroc

Un Royaume aux mille facettes : villes impériales, grands souks de Marrakech, étroite Médina de Fèz, route des Kasbahs du Sud, déserts, longues plages de sable blanc d'Agadir...

Le Maroc, c'est tout cela et bien plus... Un pays de soleil chaleureux et accueillant.

Renseignements pratiques

- **Formalités :** Carte d'identité valide si l'on voyage avec un groupe. Un passeport valide est plutôt conseillé.
- **Monnaie. Change :** L'unité monétaire est le Dirham qui vaut 0,75 FF environ.
- **Taxis :** Choisir les "petits taxis" en ville, les grands taxis pour courses hors ville et demander toujours le prix de la course avant. Ne pas oublier les calèches à Marrakech.
- **Climat :** A Marrakech, les températures varient de 5° le soir à 20° en janvier jusqu'à 37/38° en août et même plus lorsque souffle l'hamattan.

  A Agadir, il ne fait jamais moins de 7° le soir et 20/21° à midi jusqu'à 27° en été, mais temps couvert le matin et toujours du vent pour rafraîchir.

  Attention ! Dans le grand Sud, l'hiver, les nuits sont très froides.

B. Splendeurs africaines. La beauté et les variétés culturelles des pays africains attirent (*attract*) des visiteurs du monde entier. Voici quelques brochures pour vous faire rêver. Lisez-les, puis répondez aux questions suivantes.

- Où se trouve chaque pays? Consultez la carte au début de votre livre.
- Quelles langues y parle-t-on?
- Quelles religions sont pratiquées en Guinée? au Maroc?
- Décrivez le climat des deux pays.
- Quels paysages sont typiques de chaque pays?
- Quels attraits culturels trouve-t-on au Maroc?
- Si vous pouviez visiter un de ces deux pays, lequel choisiriez-vous? Justifiez votre choix.
- Que savez-vous sur d'autres pays africains? Comment est-ce que vous les avez connus? d'après des lectures? des cours?

Commentaire culturel

Une rue du Vieux Carré à La Nouvelle-Orléans

Le français en Amérique du Nord. On retrouve les traces de l'influence française un peu partout aux États-Unis et au Canada. De nombreuses villes américaines portent des noms d'origine française, tels que Baton Rouge, Des Moines, Montpelier ou Detroit. D'autres portent le nom d'explorateurs français comme Marquette, Joliet, La Salle ou Champlain.

C'est en Louisiane que cette influence est la plus visible. En 1682 l'explorateur français Cavelier de La Salle a pris possession d'un immense territoire de chaque côté du Mississippi au nom de Louis XIV. Il l'a baptisé, en son honneur, Louisiane. En 1718 Bienville a fondé la ville de La Nouvelle-Orléans. Le nombre des colons français a rapidement augmenté avec l'arrivée des Acadiens. Les Acadiens étaient les Canadiens français qui vivaient en Acadie (Nouvelle-Écosse) et qui ont été chassés par les Anglais quand la France leur a cédé le territoire en 1713. C'est alors que beaucoup d'entre eux ont fui ou ont été déportés et sont venus s'installer aux États-Unis, en Nouvelle-Angleterre et surtout dans les bayous en Louisiane. Avec le temps la prononciation du mot «Acadien» a changé et est devenue «Cajun», nom que l'on utilise toujours pour nommer leurs descendants. Les Cajuns ont préservé leur langue et leurs coutumes. Et depuis la fondation de CODOFIL (Conseil pour le développement du français en Louisiane) en 1969, le français est enseigné comme deuxième langue dans de nombreuses écoles élémentaires de Louisiane.

Au Canada, 28 pour cent de la population parle français. La majorité des Francophones vivent dans la province de Québec. Montréal est la deuxième ville francophone du monde après Paris, et son université est la plus importante université de langue française en dehors du territoire français. De nos jours, l'anglais et le français sont les deux langues officielles du pays.

Le français parlé dans la province de Québec, le québécois, est sensiblement différent du français parlé en France. Isolé, le québécois n'a pas suivi la même évolution linguistique que le français d'Europe, de plus il a subi l'influence de la langue anglaise. Le québécois est donc un français ancien teinté d'anglicismes. Voici quelques exemples d'expressions québécoises.

MOTS QUÉBÉCOIS	FORME ANGLAISE	FORME FRANÇAISE
une station-wagon	*station wagon*	une familiale/un break
un locker	*locker*	une armoire/un casier
les annonces classées	*classified ads*	les petites annonces
un tapis mur à mur	*wall-to-wall carpet*	une moquette
lousse	*loose*	relâché(e)
un tinque	*tank*	un réservoir

Les écrivains francophones

Les auteurs

© GEORGES PIERRE / SYGMA

Simone de Beauvoir.
Une romancière écrit des romans.

© AP / WIDE WORLD PHOTOS

Eugène Ionesco.
Un dramaturge écrit des pièces de théâtre.

© MARK ANTMAN / THE IMAGE WORKS

Les personnes fictives d'une pièce de théâtre, d'un roman ou d'un poème sont des personnages (*m.*).

(detail from painting) © MUSÉE D'ORSAY, PARIS / ART RESOURCE

Arthur Rimbaud.
Un poete écrit des poèmes.

A. Qui sont-ils? Lisez chaque définition et dites de qui il s'agit. Si vous ne savez pas, devinez!

1. Romancière franco-canadienne qui a reçu le prix Goncourt en 1979 pour son roman *Pélagie-la-charrette*
2. Poète et homme d'état sénégalais, membre de l'Académie française depuis 1983
3. Romancière française née à Bruxelles, elle a été la première femme à être élue à l'Académie française
4. Poète et homme d'état antillais, né en Martinique en 1912
5. Écrivain belge qui a surtout écrit des romans policiers autour du personnage du commissaire de police Maigret
6. Écrivain français né en Algérie, auteur de *l'Étranger*
7. Écrivain et philosophe né à Genève en 1712, qui a célébré les vertus de la nature et dont l'œuvre a influencé les révolutionnaires français
8. Romancier et dramaturge né à Dublin en 1906, maître incontesté du théâtre de l'Absurde, qui a écrit en français et en anglais

a. Jean-Jacques Rousseau
b. Samuel Beckett
c. Antonine Maillet
d. Albert Camus
e. Marguerite Yourcenar
f. Georges Simenon
g. Aimé Césaire
h. Léopold Senghor

B. Expatriés. De nombreux écrivains étrangers ont vécu et travaillé en France. Faites des phrases complètes à partir des éléments suivants. Notez qu'ils ne sont pas dans le bon ordre.

MODÈLE: Gertrude Stein était une femme poète américaine qui a écrit «Une rose est une rose est une rose».

F. Scott Fitzgerald		*De l'importance d'être constant*
James Joyce		*Tropique du cancer*
Henry James	roumain	*La cantatrice chauve*
Oscar Wilde	irlandais	*Les Européens*
Henry Miller	américain	*L'adieu aux armes*
Eugène Ionesco		*Gatsby le magnifique*
Ernest Hemingway		*Ulysse*

C. **Anthologie.** Nommez en anglais ou en français une des œuvres suivantes: un roman de Jean-Paul Sartre, une pièce de théâtre d'Oscar Wilde, un poème d'Edgar Allan Poe et un personnage d'une des pièces de Shakespeare.

Maintenant, nommez trois ou quatre romans ou pièces de théâtre que vous avez lus ou que vous avez vu jouer récemment. Ensuite, dites quel ouvrage (*work*) vous avez aimé le plus et lequel vous avez aimé le moins. Expliquez pourquoi.

Mots-clés

How to refer to something vague: In conversation, it is sometimes appropriate to be vague about what you are referring to. The relative pronouns **ce qui** and **ce que** enable you to talk about something unspecified or unclear; they express *what* in English.

Qu'est-ce qui est arrivé à ton frère?
Je ne sais pas **ce qui** lui est arrivé. (*I don't know* **what** *happened to him.*)
Qu'est-ce que tu as fait en ville hier?
Je ne me rappelle même plus **ce que** j'ai fait. (*I don't even remember* **what** *I did.*)

D. **Interview.** Posez des questions à votre professeur ou à un(e) camarade de classe pour mieux le (la) connaître. Puis, faites un résumé de ses réponses.

MODÈLE: les choses qu'il (elle) aime faire →
Dites-nous **ce que** vous aimez faire.
(*ou*) Dis-moi **ce que** tu aimes faire.

1. les choses qui l'amusent 2. les choses qui l'ennuient 3. les choses qu'il (elle) admire 4. les choses qu'il (elle) déteste 5. les choses qu'il (elle) veut voir 6. les choses qu'il (elle) trouve intéressantes 7. les choses qu'il (elle) trouve choquantes 8. ?

Mandela l'Indomptable
Par F SOUDAN
Un livre qu'il faut avoir lu si l'on est contre l'apartheid.

Le Football Africain, Trente Ans de Coupe d'Afrique des Nations
Par F MAHJOUB
Un document de référence indispensable à tous les vrais amateurs de football.

Étude de grammaire

60. Linking Ideas: Conjunctions Used with the Subjunctive

Des îles françaises près du Canada

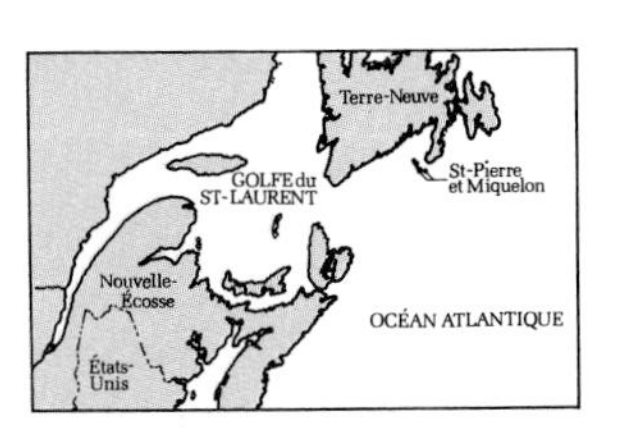

MONIQUE: Je vais rendre visite à mes cousins français à St-Pierre-et-Miquelon **avant que** mes vacances **se terminent.**

GÉRARD: Je ne sais pas où c'est... **à moins que** ce **soient** ces îles au sud de Terre-Neuve?

MONIQUE: C'est ça! **Quoique** ces îles **soient** très petites, on y trouve plus de cinq mille Français.

BERNARD: Et **bien que** Cartier les **ait** découvertes il y a plus de quatre cent quarante ans, elles sont restées territoire français jusqu'à nos jours. Des îles françaises à la porte des États-Unis!

1. Quand est-ce que Monique va à St-Pierre-et-Miquelon?
2. Est-ce que Gérard sait où ces îles se trouvent?
3. Combien de Français y vivent?
4. En dépit de (*In spite of*) quelles circonstances ces îles sont-elles restées territoire français?

In French, certain conjunctions are always followed by the subjunctive.

1. conjunctions of purpose:

afin que, pour que — *in order that, so that*

Nous lirons des pièces québécoises **afin que tu connaisses** un peu la langue avant ton voyage. — *We will read some Quebecois plays so that you will be somewhat familiar with the language before your trip.*

2. conjunctions of concession:

bien que, quoique — *although, even though*

Bien que 28 pour cent des Canadiens **soient** francophones, il y a seulement douze quotidiens français au Canada. — *Although 28 percent of Canadians are French-speaking, there are only twelve daily French newspapers in Canada.*

3. conjunctions of limitation or time restriction:

LIMITATION	TIME RESTRICTION
à condition que *on the condition that*	**sans que** *without*
à moins que *unless*	**avant que** *before*
pourvu que *provided that*	**jusqu'à ce que** *until*

Nous irons au défilé de Mardi gras **pourvu qu'il fasse** beau.	*We'll go to the Mardi Gras parade provided that the weather is nice.*
Nous allons partir **sans qu'elle** le **sache.**	*We're going to leave without her knowing it.*
Je vais rester ici **jusqu'à ce que tu** me **téléphones.**	*I'll stay here until you call me.*

MAINTENANT A VOUS

A. Changements en Afrique. Voici quelques solutions à certains problèmes africains. Combinez les éléments des deux colonnes afin de faire des phrases logiques.

1. Les enfants africains auront un meilleur avenir...
2. Beaucoup de jeunes reviendront travailler dans leur pays...
3. Il n'y aura pas assez à manger pour tout le monde...
4. La mortalité infantile restera élevée...
5. Il sera difficile d'améliorer la situation politique de certains pays africains...

a. à condition qu'on augmente le nombre d'emplois professionnels
b. à moins qu'on ne modernise l'agriculture
c. jusqu'à ce que les soins prénatals soient accessibles à toutes les femmes
d. pourvu qu'on ouvre des écoles dans les régions les plus isolées
e. sans qu'on prenne des mesures contre la corruption gouvernementale

Êtes-vous d'accord avec les solutions proposées? Quelles autres mesures proposeriez-vous?

A votre avis, est-ce que certains de ces problèmes existent toujours aux États-Unis? Lesquels? Où? Que faudrait-il faire pour les résoudre?

B. A la découverte du Québec. Vous voulez utiliser le français pendant vos vacances. Votre professeur de français vous a conseillé d'aller au Québec.

MODÈLE: Mon professeur m'a conseillé d'aller au Québec afin que...
je / pouvoir découvrir / autre / culture →
Mon professeur m'a conseillé d'aller au Québec afin que je puisse découvrir une autre culture.

Mon professeur m'a conseillé d'aller au Québec afin que...

1. je / avoir l'occasion de / rencontrer / des Québécois
2. je / perfectionner / mon français
3. je / apprendre / l'histoire du Canada
4. je / voir / pays francophone

J'irai, bien que...

5. voyage / être / cher
6. je / ne... personne connaître / là-bas
7. je / avoir / peu de / vacances
8. mon meilleur ami / ne pas pouvoir / venir avec moi

Je visiterai Montréal pourvu que...

9. il / me / rester / encore / argent
10. je / trouver / hôtel bon marché
11. il / faire / beau
12. je / avoir / assez / temps

C. Une journée à La Nouvelle-Orléans. Vous allez visiter La Nouvelle-Orléans avec des amis. Voici vos projets. Reliez les deux phrases avec la conjonction entre parenthèses.

MODÈLE: Je viendrai. Tu es là. (à condition que) →
Je viendrai à condition que tu sois là.

1. Je conduirai la voiture. Mon ami(e) peut lire le guide de la ville. (afin que) 2. Nous quitterons l'hôtel. Les magasins ferment. (avant que) 3. Nous mangerons un gumbo. Tu es d'accord. (pourvu que) 4. Nous irons au Preservation Hall. Tu peux écouter du jazz. (pour que) 5. Nous parlerons avec des Cajuns. Nous aurons du mal à les comprendre. (quoique) 6. Nous resterons ici. Nous finissons de visiter le Vieux Carré. (jusqu'à ce que) 7. Nous prendrons beaucoup de photos. On oublie l'appareil-photo. (à moins que)

D. De bonnes intentions. Complétez avec imagination les phrases suivantes.

1. J'étudie le français afin que mes amis français ____.
2. Je continuerai mes études à l'université à condition que mes parents ____.
3. J'obtiendrai un diplôme bien que les études ____.
4. Je terminerai mes cours avant que les vacances ____.
5. J'étudierai beaucoup ce soir à moins qu'il y ____.
6. Je suivrai un cours de français le trimestre prochain pourvu que l'examen de français de ce trimestre ne ____.

E. Souvenirs de vacances. Après vos dernières vacances, quelles étaient vos impressions? Complétez les phrases suivantes et racontez vos souvenirs.

1. J'ai été content(e) que ____. 2. J'ai été malheureux (malheureuse) que ____. 3. J'ai été surpris(e) que ____. 4. J'ai été content(e), bien que ____.

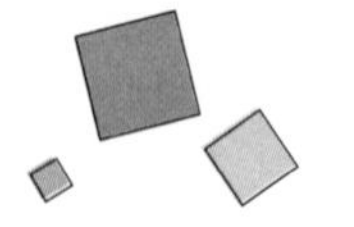

61. Expressing Subjective Viewpoints: Alternatives to the Subjunctive

Les Antilles, mythe et réalité

FRANCINE: Les Antilles, pour moi, ce sont les récifs coraliens, les sites archéologiques précolombiens, les plages de sable blanc...

SYLVAIN: **Il faut** tout de même **savoir** que nous n'avons pas que du soleil à vendre!

VINCENT: **Avant de partir,** tu devrais visiter une bananeraie, une distillerie de rhum et notre port très moderne.

SYLVAIN: **J'espère** que **tu sais** que notre niveau de vie, ici en Martinique,* est le plus élevé des Caraïbes...

FRANCINE: C'est vrai, **il est important** de **se moderniser.** Mais **j'espère,** moi, que **vous saurez** protéger la beauté de votre pays.

Trouvez la phrase équivalente selon le dialogue.

1. Il faut qu'on sache que nous n'avons pas que du soleil à vendre.
2. Avant que tu partes, tu devrais visiter une bananeraie, une distillerie de rhum et notre port très moderne.
3. Je souhaite que tu saches que notre niveau de vie, ici en Martinique, est le plus élevé des Caraïbes.
4. C'est vrai, il est important que les pays se modernisent.
5. Mais je veux, moi, que vous sachiez protéger la beauté de votre pays!

*The French generally say **à la Martinique** and **à la Guadeloupe,** but the inhabitants of those islands tend to say **en Martinique** and **en Guadeloupe.**

A. Infinitive as Alternative to the Subjunctive

An infinitive is generally used instead of the subjunctive if the subject of the dependent clause is the same as that of the main clause, or if the subject is not specified.

1.

CONJUGATED VERB + INFINITIVE	CONJUGATED VERB + **que** + SUBJUNCTIVE
Je **veux** le **savoir.** (*I want to know it.*)	Je **veux que** tu le **saches.** (*I want you to know it.*)

2.

PREPOSITION + INFINITIVE	CONJUNCTION + SUBJUNCTIVE
Nous t'appellerons **avant de partir.** (*We'll call you before leaving. / We'll call you before we leave.*)	Nous t'appellerons **avant que tu partes.** (*We'll call you before you leave.*)
Prepositions with a corresponding conjunction include **à condition de, à moins de, afin de, avant de, pour,** and **sans.**	

3.

IMPERSONAL EXPRESSION + INFINITIVE	IMPERSONAL EXPRESSION + **que** + SUBJECT + CONJUNCTION
Il est bon de faire ce voyage. (*It's a good idea to take this trip.*)	Il est bon **que vous fassiez** ce voyage. (*It's good for you to take this trip. / It's good that you're taking this trip.*)

B. *Espérer* plus Indicative

The verb **espérer,** followed by the indicative, can be used instead of the verb **souhaiter** or other constructions that express a wish or desire. When **espérer** is in the main clause, the verb in the dependent clause is in the future tense if the action is expected to occur in the future.

Je **souhaite** que ton voyage **soit** intéressant.	*I hope that your trip is (will be) interesting.*
J'**espère** que ton voyage **sera** intéressant.	*I hope that your trip will be interesting.*

C. *Devoir* plus Infinitive

The verb **devoir,** followed by an infinitive, can sometimes be used instead of **il faut que** or **il est nécessaire que.** There is a slight difference in meaning, however, since **devoir** does not convey as strong a sense of obligation as **il faut que** and **il est nécessaire que.**

Je **dois aller** en classe.	*I must (should) go to class.*
Il **faut que** j'**aille** en classe.	*I have to go to class.*
Il **est nécessaire que** j'**aille** en classe.	*It's necessary for me to go to class.*

MAINTENANT A VOUS

A. Un étudiant modèle. Peter est un étudiant modèle. Jouez le rôle de Peter et complétez les phrases suivantes avec des infinitifs. **Mots utiles:** apprendre tout le vocabulaire, terminer mes devoirs, apprendre toute la leçon, bien étudier le Chapitre 17, perfectionner mon français...

1. Ce soir, je vais beaucoup étudier afin de _____.
2. Je ne vais pas regarder la télévision avant de _____.
3. Je ne vais pas me coucher sans _____.

B. Cours d'été à Montréal. La classe de Thierry va suivre des cours d'été dans une université canadienne. Exprimez leurs espoirs (*hopes*). Employez **espérer** au lieu de **souhaiter.**

MODÈLE: Je souhaite que mes amis puissent me rendre visite! →
J'espère que mes amis pourront me rendre visite!

1. Nous souhaitons que le campus soit agréable. 2. Je souhaite que les cours soient intéressants. 3. Mes camarades souhaitent qu'on aille danser tous les soirs. 4. Tu souhaites qu'il y ait un bon restaurant à la faculté. 5. Notre professeur souhaite que nous apprenions beaucoup.

C. Vie européenne. Il faut que les Canadiens francophones et anglophones apprennent à vivre ensemble. En Europe, la diversité linguistique et culturelle est encore plus prononcée. Qu'est-ce qui est important pour les Européens? Donnez l'équivalent de chacune des phrases suivantes. Utilisez **devoir** + *infinitif* au lieu de l'expression **il faut que.**

MODÈLE: Il faut que nous nous respections mutuellement. →
Nous devons nous respecter mutuellement.

1. Il faut que l'Europe soit unie (*unified*) politiquement. 2. Il faut que nous développions nos échanges culturels. 3. Il faut que les nations européennes travaillent ensemble. 4. Il faut que les Anglais achètent des Renault. 5. Il faut que les Français achètent des Rolls-Royce!

D. Des conseils. Donnez des conseils à vos amis qui vous expliquent leurs souhaits. Utilisez des expressions comme **il faut, il est nécessaire de, vous devez, j'espère que.**

1. Je veux vivre longtemps (*a long time*). Qu'est-ce que je dois faire?
2. Je veux perfectionner mon français. Qu'est-ce que je dois faire?
3. Je veux être riche un jour. Qu'est-ce que je dois étudier?
4. Je veux m'amuser beaucoup cet été. Où est-ce que je dois voyager?
5. Je veux rencontrer beaucoup de francophones. Qu'est-ce que je peux faire aux États-Unis pour en rencontrer? et à l'étranger?

Situation

Promenade à La Nouvelle-Orléans

Contexte *Corinne Legrand et ses cousins français, Thierry et Fabrice, font le tour de La Nouvelle-Orléans, où Corinne est née. Partout en ville, ses cousins retrouvent les traces de l'héritage français, mais ils découvrent aussi une culture locale, résultat d'une histoire mouvementée° qui a rassemblé° avec les Créoles,* des populations d'origines et de cultures très diverses.*

Objectif *Corinne raconte à ses cousins l'origine du vaudou à La Nouvelle-Orléans.*

mouvementée: avec beaucoup d'événements différents / a rassemblé: a... a groupé

THIERRY: Dis-moi ce que ça représente, ce culte vaudou de La Nouvelle-Orléans.

CORINNE: C'est un mélange° de croyances° locales et de catholicisme dont le but° est de libérer l'homme du démon.°

FABRICE: Mais quelle est l'origine du vaudou?

CORINNE: Eh bien, son développement est lié° à l'histoire des Antilles françaises.

THIERRY: Raconte... C'est Christophe Colomb qui a découvert les Antilles, n'est-ce pas?

CORINNE: Oui, mais bien que ce soit lui qui ait découvert les Antilles, ce sont les Français qui les ont colonisées.

FABRICE: Et alors, qu'est-ce qui s'est passé?

un... une fusion, une combinaison / *beliefs*
objectif / *Satan*
attaché

*Here, **Créoles** refers to the descendants of French settlers in Louisiana and the Antilles.

CORINNE: Alors, ces colons° ont créé d'immenses plantations de canne à sucre, de café et de coton pour lesquelles il fallait° trouver une main-d'œuvre° très abondante. C'est comme ça que les esclaves africains ont introduit leurs croyances dans les Caraïbes.

THIERRY: Mais, quel rapport avec la Louisiane?

CORINNE: Eh bien, voilà: d'abord, beaucoup d'esclaves antillais sont venus en Louisiane lorsque la Révolution française a aboli l'esclavage en 1794. Ensuite, un très grand nombre de planteurs blancs ont abandonné Haïti quand ce pays est devenu une république indépendante en 1804.

FABRICE: Et ils ont emmené leurs esclaves avec eux?

CORINNE: C'est exact. Et c'est comme ça que La Nouvelle-Orléans est devenue une capitale du vaudou.

FABRICE: Et ce culte, est-ce qu'il existe toujours?

CORINNE: Ça, c'est une autre histoire...

colons: les pionniers qui colonisent
fallait: imparfait de **falloir**
main-d'œuvre: une... des groupes de travailleurs

VARIATIONS

1. Voici une série de phrases qui raconte très brièvement l'histoire d'une autre partie de la population francophone de Louisiane. Avec des camarades, transformez cette narration en un dialogue entre une personne qui raconte l'histoire et une ou plusieurs autres personnes qui posent de temps en temps des questions.

- Jacques Cartier a exploré le Canada au XVIe siècle.
- En 1608, des colons ont fondé la Nouvelle-France.
- La Nouvelle-France comprenait (*included*) l'Acadie.
- En 1763, le traité de Paris a donné les provinces canadiennes aux Anglais.
- C'est d'abord les gens francophones qu'ils ont voulu asservir (*subjugate*).
- Il les ont déportés.
- Les Anglais ont déporté des milliers (*thousands*) d'Acadiens qui sont partis à travers (*across*) le continent américain.
- Beaucoup d'entre eux sont allés dans l'état où il y avait déjà beaucoup de francophones.
- C'était la Louisiane.
- C'est là l'origine de la population cajun des bayous louisianais.
- Le mot **cajun** vient du mot **acadien.**
- Il y avait d'autres Acadiens qui se sont installés en Nouvelle-Angleterre ou qui sont retournés en Acadie.
- Aujourd'hui, l'Acadie, c'est la Nouvelle-Écosse.
- Il y existe une communauté acadienne avec sa propre culture et sa propre langue.

2. Improvisez! Racontez l'aventure des pèlerins (*pilgrims*) du *Mayflower,* ou bien d'un autre peuple immigré dont vous connaissez l'histoire.

Commentaire culturel

L'histoire de la langue française. Toutes les langues ont une histoire. Elles naissent, se développent et se transforment constamment. Voici une liste de mots que le français a empruntés à d'autres langues. Regardez-la, puis, avec un(e) camarade de classe, répondez aux questions ci-dessous.

- Y a-t-il des langues dans cette liste que vous ne reconnaissez pas? Essayez de deviner le nom du pays correspondant.
- Pouvez-vous nommer d'autres mots français empruntés à l'anglais?
- Quels mots anglais d'origine française pouvez-vous citer? Maintenant, comparez votre liste avec celles des autres étudiants afin de découvrir quels mots vous avez oubliés.

QUELQUES MOTS ASSIMILÉS PAR LE FRANÇAIS

de l'italien: canon, bravo, banque, balcon, opéra.
de l'anglais: budget, boxe, record, tourisme, parlement, redingote (de **riding coat**).
de l'espagnol et des **langues latino-américaines:** tomate, cigare, compliment, chocolat.
de l'allemand: accordéon, bretelle, anglais.
de l'arabe et **du persan**: alcool, algèbre, zéro, matelas, orange, guitare, cerise, divan, magasin, matraque.
du russe et **du slave**: cravate, vampire, yogourt.
du hollandais: crabe, vacarme, choquer, drogue, bière, chaloupe, dame, bosse.
du malais: thé, rotin.
du turc: gilet, tulipe.
du cinghalais: pyjama, bungalow.
du norvégien: anorak.
des langues amérindiennes et de l'inuktitut: totem, caribou, kayak, igloo.
du breton: bijou, goéland, cohue.

A propos

Comment hésiter en français

L'hésitation, dans la conversation, joue un rôle important dans toutes les langues. Voici des expressions qui marquent l'hésitation en français.

Euh,... ou Heu (*alternate spelling*) [ø]	... vous savez...
Voyons,...	... tu sais...
Écoutez...	... comment dirais-je...
Eh bien...	

6

7

Commentaire d'un dessin. La bande dessinée de la page précédente raconte une histoire. Avec des camarades, décrivez chacune des actions ou chaque incident au passé. Quand vous devez hésiter, utilisez les expressions de l'*A propos.*

1. un jour
2. tout d'un coup
3. alors
4. ensuite
5. un peu plus tard
6. enfin
7. à ce moment-là
8. et alors
9. depuis (ce jour)

MODÈLE: Un jour, M. et Mme Dupont sont allés faire une promenade dans leur Deux Chevaux.

Commentaire culturel

© P. JORDAN / GAMMA LIAISON

Léopold Senghor, homme d'état et poète sénégalais, a été président de la République du Sénégal de 1963 à 1980.

Le français en Afrique. L'héritage français le plus frappant, en Afrique, est peut-être tout simplement le français. En effet, le français est la langue officielle de dix-huit pays d'Afrique noire et il est aussi parlé couramment dans bien d'autres, comme ceux du Maghreb. Mais pourquoi parle-t-on français en Afrique?

On le parle pour des raisons historiques. Déjà au XVIIe siècle, les Français faisaient du commerce avec certains pays africains, tels que le Sénégal, où ils ont fondé le port de Saint-Louis en 1659. Mais l'histoire de la francophonie commence avec la colonisation de l'Afrique par les Français et les Belges au XIXe siècle.

A la veille de la Deuxième Guerre mondiale la France était la seconde puissance coloniale du monde. Cet empire colonial se composait de presque toute l'Afrique du Nord, de l'Afrique occidentale et équatoriale, ainsi que de l'île de Madagascar. Les Français ont imposé leur langue dans tous ces pays. Ils ont fait venir de France des instituteurs qui l'ont enseignée dans les écoles. Beaucoup d'Africains sont aussi allés faire leurs études en France.

Après la guerre, les pays africains ont l'un après l'autre proclamé leur indépendance. Ils ont dû alors faire face à de nombreuses difficultés politiques et économiques. Ils ont aussi essayé de retrouver leur propre identité. Alors pourquoi ont-ils gardé la langue de leurs colonisateurs?

Le plus souvent par nécessité. Tout d'abord, le découpage artificiel des frontières par les colons a souvent rassemblé des populations d'origines ethniques différentes; ensuite, à cause de la diversité des langues locales, le français s'est trouvé être la seule langue commune; enfin le besoin de maintenir une ouverture avec le reste du monde a poussé de nombreux pays africains à conserver le français, langue internationale, comme langue officielle ou comme seconde langue. De nos jours, le français est aussi la langue littéraire des pays africains. Le nombre d'écrivains et de poètes francophones y augmente de jour en jour. Léopold Senghor, élu à l'Académie française en 1983, reste le symbole de la littérature africaine en France.

Mise au point

A. Les Francophones d'Amérique. Reliez les deux phrases avec la conjonction entre parenthèses.

1. Certaines familles acadiennes ont émigré. On les laisse tranquille. (pour que)
2. D'autres familles se sont installées dans le Maine. Le climat y est très rude (*harsh*). (bien que)
3. Certains Acadiens sont restés au Canada. La coexistence avec les Anglais n'a pas été facile. (quoique)
4. Au Canada, on a voté une loi sur les langues officielles en 1975. Les Québécois francophones peuvent travailler sans devoir connaître l'anglais. (afin que)
5. Au Québec, on emploie beaucoup de mots anglais. Plus de 80 pour cent des Québécois parlent français. (bien que)

B. Voyage au Québec. En français, s'il vous plaît.

1. It is essential that we try to learn French.
2. I want to learn it before going to Montreal.
3. It is better to speak French to each other when we go to Quebec.
4. It is unlikely that we'll take the train to Quebec.
5. We're happy that we're taking the plane.
6. Is it true that the trip is expensive?
7. I don't know how much the trip costs.
8. I'll go there, provided that it's not too expensive.
9. I'm glad that my friends have already gone to Quebec.
10. I'm sure that the stay (**le séjour**) will be interesting.

C. Interview. Interrogez un(e) camarade sur l'importance de l'étude des langues étrangères. Vous allez utiliser des constructions subjonctives dans vos questions, mais votre camarade va éviter (*avoid*) l'emploi du subjonctif dans ses réponses.

MODÈLE:

VOUS: Est-il important qu'on connaisse d'autres cultures?

VOTRE CAMARADE: Oui, il est très important de connaître d'autres cultures parce que...

Suggestions: Demandez à votre camarade...

- s'il est préférable que les gens parlent deux langues (et pourquoi ou pourquoi pas)
- s'il est essentiel qu'il (elle) parle français dans un ou deux ans (et pourquoi ou pourquoi pas)
- s'il est nécessaire qu'il (elle) étudie le français tous les jours (et pourquoi ou pourquoi pas)
- s'il est important qu'il (elle) aille souvent au laboratoire de langues (et pourquoi ou pourquoi pas)
- s'il est possible qu'il (elle) visite un pays francophone un jour (et pourquoi ou pourquoi pas)
- ?

Interactions

A. Les émotions. Working in groups of three, each of you will choose one of the following emotions: You are happy. You are sad. You are very angry. Explain to your partners why you are feeling this way. Try to convince them to share your mood. They will express their opinions about your feelings and make conjectures about how events could have been different.

B. Mon avenir. You have been a very successful student. Everyone agrees that you will be famous in your field. You are being interviewed by the student newspaper about what you will be doing in ten years. Describe what you will be famous for and what your life will be like then, if all goes as planned.

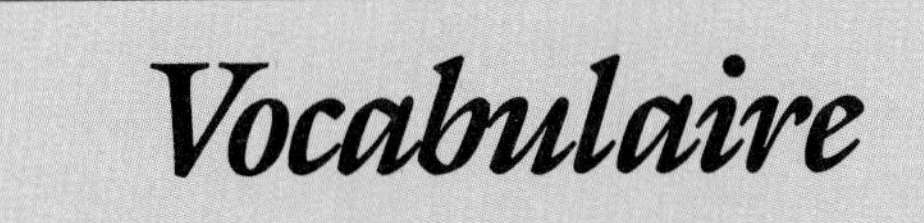

Vocabulaire

Verbes

amener to bring (*a person somewhere*)
coloniser to colonize
découvrir to discover
se déguiser to disguise oneself (to dress up in disguise)
fêter to celebrate
perfectionner to perfect

Noms géographiques

l'Acadie (*f.*) Acadia
les Antilles (*f.*) Antilles (Islands) (Caribbean Islands)
la mer des Caraïbes (**la mer des Antilles**) Caribbean Sea
la Guadeloupe Guadeloupe
Haïti (*m.*) Haiti
la Martinique Martinique
Montréal Montreal
la Nouvelle-Écosse Nova Scotia
La Nouvelle-Orléans New Orleans
le Québec Quebec (province)
Québec Quebec (city)
Terre-Neuve (*f.*) Newfoundland

Substantifs

l'ancêtre (*m.*) ancestor
le bal masqué masked ball

le bonhomme de neige snowman
le Carnaval Carnival
le char float (*parade*)
le colon colonist, settler
le costume costume
le culte cult
le défilé parade
le/la dramaturge playwright
l'écrevisse (*f.*) crayfish
l'esclave (*m.*) slave
le Mardi Gras Mardi Gras, Shrove Tuesday
le mélange mixture
le personnage character (*in fiction*)
le poème poem
le poète poet
le québécois Quebecois (*language*)
le/la romancier (**-ière**) novelist
le vaudou voodoo

Conjonctions et prépositions

à condition que (**à condition de**) on the condition that
à moins que (**à moins de**) unless
afin que (**afin de**) in order that, so that
avant que (**avant de**) before
bien que although, even though
jusqu'à ce que until
pour que (**pour**) in order that, so that
pourvu que provided that
quoique although, even though
sans que (**sans**) without

Adjectifs

acadien(ne) Acadian, Cajun
anglophone English-speaking
francophone French-speaking
québécois(e) of Quebec

Pronoms relatifs

ce que what, that which (*object of a verb*)
ce qui what, that which (*subject of a verb*)

Mots divers

longtemps a long time

INTERMÈDE 17

Lecture

Yves Duteil est un chanteur-poète contemporain, très populaire en France. Comme beaucoup de chanteurs français, il écrit lui-même la musique et les paroles (les mots) de ses chansons. Il a dédié «La langue de chez nous» à Félix Leclerc, le «père de la chanson québécoise». Félix Leclerc a été pendant toute sa vie le défenseur des droits des francophones dans un pays à large majorité anglophone. Ce n'est que pendant les années soixante-dix que le français a été reconnu comme langue officielle du Québec.

AVANT DE LIRE

Understanding poetry and songs. In poetry and songs, sentence structure may be more complicated than in prose texts, in order to create aural effects such as rhythm and rhyme. On your first reading of «*La langue de chez nous*», look for the core of each sentence. Find the main clause of each stanza, in particular the subject and the verb, and underline it.

It is also helpful to pay attention to the structure of the poem or song as a whole. Look for repeating sections; repetition suggests that these stanzas are particularly important to the meaning of the piece. Is there a repeating stanza in «*La langue de chez nous*»? What is the main image in the stanza—that is, to what does the songwriter compare the French language?

Poetry and songs often have meaning partly because of what they suggest or evoke. That is why they are often built around comparisons. In reading «*La langue de chez nous*», you may find it helpful to jot down some of the things the writer compares the French language to. First, make a list of the nouns he uses in place of the word **langue.** Next, list four or five images or ideas he associates with French. (Key words: **ressembler à, comme, on dirait que...**)

Note: «*La langue de chez nous*» contains a verb form that you have not yet studied—the present participle. You will encounter it from time to time in written French, but you only need to learn to recognize it when you read. The sign of the present participle is the **-ant** ending, which corresponds to the *-ing* ending in English.

> **en parlant** → *while speaking*
> **en polissant** → *while polishing*

Once you learn to recognize the meaning of the **-ant** ending, you should be able to guess the meaning of most present participles you encounter.

J'ai voulu offrir une chanson d'amour à la langue française, ma langue maternelle, pour dire sa beauté et sa richesse, et la fierté qu'elle m'inspire.

Je l'ai dédiée à Félix Leclerc qui s'est battu pour la défendre au Québec.

La langue de chez nous

1 C'est une langue belle avec des mots superbes	
Qui porte son histoire à travers ses accents°	(*here*) *sounds*
Où l'on sent la musique et le parfum des herbes	
Le fromage de chèvre° et le pain de froment°	*goat* / *wheat*
2 Et du Mont-Saint-Michel jusqu'à la Contrescarpe°	une place à Paris
En écoutant parler les gens de ce pays	
On dirait que le vent s'est pris dans° une harpe	vent... *wind got caught in*
Et qu'il a en gardé° toutes les harmonies	*kept*
3 Dans cette langue belle aux couleurs de Provence°	région dans le sud-est de la France
Où la saveur des choses est déjà dans les mots	
C'est d'abord en parlant que la fête commence	
Et l'on boit des paroles aussi bien que de l'eau	
4 Les voix° ressemblent aux cours des fleuves et des rivières	*voices*
Elles répondent aux méandres,° au vent dans les roseaux°	*windings* / *reeds*
Parfois même aux torrents qui charrient° du tonnerre°	*carry* / *thunder*
En polissant les pierres° sur le bord des ruisseaux°	*stones* / *creeks*
5 C'est une langue belle à l'autre bout du monde	
Une bulle° de France au nord d'un continent	*bubble*
Sertie° dans un étau° mais pourtant si féconde°	*held* / *vise* / *fertile*
Enfermée dans les glaces au sommet d'un volcan	
6 Elle a jeté des ponts par-dessus l'Atlantique	
Elle a quitté son nid° pour un autre terroir°	*nest* / *land*
Et comme une hirondelle° au printemps des musiques	*swallow* (*bird*)
Elle revient nous chanter ses peines et ses espoirs	

7 Nous dire que là-bas dans ce pays de neige
Elle a fait face° aux vents qui soufflent de partout — a... a confronté
Pour imposer ses mots jusque dans les collèges
Et qu'on y parle encore la langue de chez nous

8 C'est une langue belle à qui sait la défendre
Elle offre les trésors de richesses infinies
Les mots qui nous manquaient° pour pouvoir nous comprendre — qui... *that we lacked*
Et la force qu'il faut pour vivre en harmonie

9 Et de l'Île d'Orléans° jusqu'à la Contrescarpe — au nord de Québec
En écoutant chanter les gens de ce pays
On dirait que le vent s'est pris dans une harpe
Et qu'il a composé toute une symphonie

10 Et de l'Île d'Orléans jusqu'à la Contrescarpe
En écoutant chanter les gens de ce pays
On dirait que le vent s'est pris dans une harpe
Et qu'il a composé toute une symphonie.

Yves Duteil

COMPRÉHENSION

1. Pourquoi Yves Duteil a-t-il dédié cette chanson à Félix Leclerc, un Québécois?
2. A quoi Duteil compare-t-il le français dans la première strophe (*stanza*)?
3. Et dans le refrain?
4. Qu'est-ce que les mots français évoquent pour l'écrivain dans la troisième strophe?
5. Quelles images de la nature Duteil emploie-t-il dans la quatrième strophe?
6. Dans la cinquième strophe, de quel continent et de quel pays s'agit-il? Que veut suggérer l'auteur quand il dit «sertie dans un étau»? Pouvez-vous donner un exemple?
7. A quoi se réfère le pronom «elle» dans les sixième et septième strophes? En disant qu'«elle a fait face aux vents qui soufflent de partout», à quoi Duteil fait-il allusion?
8. Dans la huitième strophe, l'auteur suggère que la défense de la langue française mènera (*will lead*) à la compréhension et à l'harmonie. Pouvez-vous spécifier entre qui et qui?
9. A votre avis, qu'est-ce que Duteil a voulu indiquer en substituant «l'Île d'Orléans» au «Mont-Saint-Michel» dans le refrain à la fin de la chanson?

Maintenant, choisissez l'image qui vous plaît le plus dans cette chanson et expliquez pourquoi.

Par écrit

A. **La France chez vous.** Écrivez un article sur les aspects «français» de la vie américaine pour un journal français. Utilisez les mots suivants comme guide.

Paragraphe 1: la nourriture, les boissons, les restaurants
Paragraphe 2: les autres produits français (pneus, vêtements, parfums, voitures, magazines, etc.)
Paragraphe 3: vie culturelle (les films français, les livres, la philosophie)

B. **Ma vie dans 25 ans.** Essayez d'imaginer comment sera votre vie dans 25 ans. Écrivez un court passage au futur en donnant le plus de détails possible. Votre professeur ramassera les compositions et en lira quelques extraits à la classe. Vos camarades essaieront de deviner qui en est l'auteur.

CHAPITRE DIX-HUIT

La société contemporaine: lectures et activités

Le bicentenaire de la Révolution française, 1989

Les coopérants

La coopération avec les pays du Tiers Monde (les pays en voie de développement) est une des priorités de la politique extérieure de la France. Les coopérants français jouent un rôle majeur dans l'aide au développement de nombreuses nations francophones. L'article ci-dessous décrit leur mission et l'évolution de leur fonction.

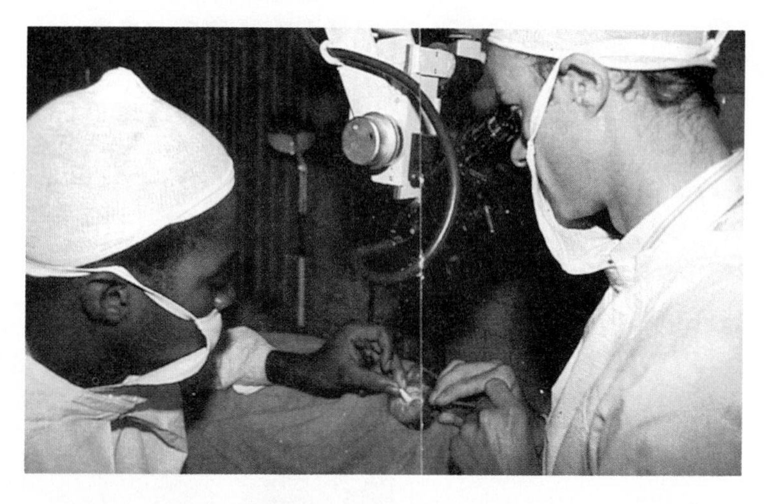

Les Coopérants

Un important réseau d'hommes et de femmes sur le terrain

Qui sont-ils ?

Ils sont 16 000 civils français à travers[a] le monde à coopérer, auxquels il convient d'ajouter les quelque 5 500 volontaires du Service National, techniciens et enseignants, partis pour 16 mois.

Où sont-ils ?

La France est ainsi le pays qui envoie proportionnellement à sa population le plus d'assistants techniques outre-mer. Les trois quarts d'entre eux assument des tâches d'enseignement. 85 % résident en Afrique, dont 55 % en Afrique subsaharienne et 30 % en Afrique septentrionale.

Que font-ils ?

Exerçant aussi dans des domaines aussi variés que la formation et la recherche agricoles, l'industrie et les travaux publics, les services culturels, les assistants techniques représentent la force humaine indispensable à la réussite de la coopération. L'aide au développement ne pourrait se faire sans leur capacité d'intégration, leur faculté d'apprécier sur place une situation donnée, leur habitude d'œuvrer avec les partenaires locaux à la réalisation d'objectifs arrêtés en commun.

a. á... *across*

COMPRÉHENSION

1. A votre avis, que veut dire le terme «coopérer»? 2. Quels sont les deux types de coopérants? Qu'est-ce que le Service National? 3. Où vont les coopérants, en général? 4. Dans quels domaines les coopérants travaillent-ils? Donnez un exemple de métier dans chaque domaine. 5. Pensez-vous que leur travail soit important? Justifiez votre réponse. 6. Aimeriez-vous être coopérant? Pourquoi ou pourquoi pas?

MAINTENANT A VOUS

A. Profil d'un coopérant. Connaissez-vous des Américain(e)s qui font de la «coopération», en travaillant, par exemple, pour le Peace Corps, Vista ou d'autres organisations semblables? Par petits groupes, essayez de définir ce qui pousse les coopérants à partir.

1. le goût de l'aventure
2. le sens civique
3. le non-conformisme
4. la générosité
5. l'esprit d'indépendance
6. l'expérience
7. l'argent
8. la tradition
9. l'ambition
10. ?

D'après les résultats obtenus, choisissez les trois adjectifs qui définissent le mieux la personnalité du coopérant. Puis faites son portrait psychologique: goûts, passe-temps, sports.

MODÈLE:

Fiche signalétique

Nom de famille __________

Prénom __________

Né(e) __________

Domicile __________

Nationalité __________

Profession __________

Diplômes __________

Personnalité __________

Préférences __________

Enfin, comparez vos résultats avec ceux des autres groupes et commentez-les. Y aurait-il un profil typique? Lequel?

Assistance technique civile
CHIFFRES 1985,
PRINCIPAUX PAYS

Pays	
Côte-d'Ivoire	2 781
Maroc	1 773
Algérie	1 248
Sénégal	1 111
Tunisie	674
Gabon	674
Cameroun	662
Madagascar	624
Djibouti	446
Niger	413
Congo	398
Centrafrique	378
Mauritanie	314
Mali	303
Burkina-Faso	299
Togo	210
Zaïre	170
Bénin	136
Burundi	113
Comores	108

B. Jeu géographique. Familiarisez-vous avec les pays francophones d'Afrique en étudiant la carte d'Afrique au début du livre. Notez aussi les villes principales. Ensuite, en utilisant le tableau ci-contre, faites deviner à un(e) partenaire l'emplacement géographique de dix pays sur le tableau. En prime: nommez une des villes principales. Celui (Celle) qui réussit à situer le plus de pays est le gagnant (la gagnante).

MODÈLE: —Où se trouve l'Algérie?
—L'Algérie se trouve en Afrique du nord, entre le Maroc et la Tunisie. Alger est une des villes principales.

C. Offre d'emploi. Vous travaillez pour une agence qui place des coopérants à l'étranger. Vous avez un poste d'enseignant à pourvoir.

1. Définissez le poste en donnant le plus de détails possible. Inventez les renseignements mais soyez logique.
   a. en quoi consiste le travail
   b. le lieu de travail
   c. le salaire
   d. la durée du travail
   e. les conditions de logement
   f. les conditions du voyage
   g. les loisirs sur place
   h. le genre de personne recherchée
2. Un(e) candidat(e) se présente pour le poste. Préparez une liste de questions, puis interviewez-le (la). Il (Elle) vous pose beaucoup de questions sur le travail, les conditions et le pays. A votre tour, vous lui posez des questions sur son éducation, ses goûts et les raisons qui le (la) poussent à partir à l'étranger. Jouez les rôles avec un(e) camarade.
3. Allez-vous l'embaucher? Va-t-il (elle) accepter l'offre? Justifiez vos réponses.

D. En route! Imaginez que vous avez la possibilité de partir à l'étranger pour travailler pendant un an grâce à un programme d'échange. Où iriez-vous? Qu'aimeriez-vous faire? Faites d'abord une liste détaillée de vos projets, du choix du pays, type de travail, de ce que vous vous attendez à trouver là-bas et de ce que vous pensez pouvoir y faire. A quels problèmes vous faudra-t-il sans doute faire face? Ensuite, faites une courte présentation à la classe en utilisant le futur et le conditionnel.

E. Par écrit. Vous aimeriez partir pour la coopération. Écrivez une demande d'emploi à Mme Péguy, responsable du recrutement. Dans votre lettre, définissez le poste que vous désirez. Puis expliquez en détail vos qualifications professionnelles et parlez aussi de vos goûts. Donnez votre adresse et votre numéro de téléphone. Soyez convaincant(e) pour persuader Mme Péguy de vous embaucher.
Expressions utiles: assistant(e) technique, médical(e); enseignant(e) (anglais, maths, sciences naturelles, informatique...); ingénieur agricole...

Le bicentenaire de la Révolution française

L'année 1989 était l'année du bicentenaire. Réfléchissez à ce que vous connaissez de la Révolution française.

En 1989, la France a organisé toutes sortes de cérémonies pour commémorer cet événement historique qui avait profondément marqué la société française et influencé un grand nombre de pays occidentaux. Que pensent les Français, de nos jours, de leur Révolution? Voici un extrait d'un sondage publié dans le *Figaro Magazine* qui essaie de répondre à cette question. A quoi est-ce que vous associez la Révolution? Quels personnages historiques de l'époque connaissez-vous?

1 Pour vous, quels sont les événements qui symbolisent le mieux la Révolution française ?

	ENSEMBLE DES FRANÇAIS	PRÉFÉRENCE PARTISANE	
		GAUCHE	DROITE
La Déclaration des droits de l'homme et du citoyen	**74**	**79**	**72**
La prise de la Bastille	55	58	56
La nuit du 4-Août (l'abolition des privilèges)	27	30	25
Les Etats Généraux	20	22	22
L'exécution de Louis XVI	13	12	16
La vente des biens du clergé	8	11	5
La Terreur et les massacres de septembre	6	5	8
Le soulèvement de la Vendée	5	5	7
La victoire de Valmy	4	3	6
La Fête de la Fédération en 1790	4	4	3
Sans opinion	8	6	5
	%	%	% (1)

(1) Le total des pourcentages est supérieur à 100, les personnes interrogées ayant pu donner trois réponses.

2 Avec le recul du temps, pensez-vous qu'il fallait...

		OUI	NON	SANS OPINION
... exécuter Louis XVI	100 %	14	61	**25**
... exécuter Marie-Antoinette	100 %	8	**68**	24
... abolir la monarchie	100 %	75	10	15
... abolir les privilèges	100 %	**81**	7	12

3 Pensez-vous que les exécutions pendant la Révolution française par la guillotine, les fusillades, etc. ont été une nécessité ou une abomination ?

	ENSEMBLE DES FRANÇAIS	PRÉFÉRENCE PARTISANE	
		GAUCHE	DROITE
Une nécessité	19	23	16
Une abomination	**68**	**64**	**73**
Sans opinion	13	13	11
	100 %	100 %	100 %

4 Des trois grandes révolutions — la Révolution américaine, la Révolution française et la Révolution soviétique —, quelle est celle qui au bout du compte, a eu les effets les plus positifs ?
Et quelle est celle qui a eu les effets les plus négatifs ?

	LA REVOLUTION QUI A EU LES EFFETS LES PLUS POSITIFS	LA REVOLUTION QUI A EU LES EFFETS LES PLUS NEGATIFS
- La Révolution américaine..	16	7
- La Révolution française.....	**52**	4
- La Révolution soviétique....	7	**46**
Sans opinion....................	25	43
	100 %	100 %

5 Diriez-vous que la Révolution de 1789 a eu une portée plutôt nationale, plutôt européenne ou plutôt mondiale ?

	ENSEMBLE DES FRANÇAIS	PRÉFÉRENCE PARTISANE	
		GAUCHE	DROITE
Plutôt nationale	31	29	33
Plutôt européenne.........	20	22	20
Plutôt mondiale	**35**	**36**	**36**
Sans opinion	14	13	11
	100 %	100 %	100 %

8 A vos yeux, dans l'héritage de la Révolution française, quels sont les trois points les plus importants ?

	ENSEMBLE DES FRANÇAIS	PRÉFÉRENCE PARTISANE	
		GAUCHE	DROITE
L'égalité des citoyens devant la loi..................	**69**	**72**	**71**
L'idéal de « Liberté-Egalité- Fraternité ».......	47	47	47
L'instruction publique....	42	46	35
La Constitution	25	25	30
Un Etat laïc, indépendant de la religion.........	24	32	19
« La Marseillaise » et le drapeau bleu-blanc-rouge............................	21	18	23
L'idée d'une mission de la France dans le monde...........................	11	9	13
L'appauvrissement de la France.......................	6	4	6
Les divisions entre les Français	5	4	5
Le recrutement des fonctionnaires sur concours	4	3	4
Sans opinion	4	4	4
	%	%	% (1)

(1) Le total des pourcentages est supérieur à 100, les personnes interrogées ayant pu donner trois réponses.

COMPRÉHENSION

1. Pour les Français, qu'est-ce qui symbolise le mieux la Révolution de 1789? Et pour vous?
2. Est-ce que dans l'ensemble les Français approuvent ou non les exécutions qui ont eu lieu pendant la Révolution? Qu'en pensez-vous?
3. Quelle Révolution a eu les effets les plus positifs? les plus négatifs? Êtes-vous d'accord avec les réponses du sondage?
4. Pouvez-vous expliquer l'expression «Liberté, Égalité, Fraternité»? Avant la Révolution, est-ce que tous les Français étaient égaux devant la loi? Expliquez.
5. Lequel des héritages de la Révolution française vous semble le plus important? le moins important? le plus bizarre?

MAINTENANT A VOUS

A. Sondage sur la Révolution américaine

1. Par petits groupes, préparez cinq questions sur la Révolution américaine. Prenez le sondage précédent comme modèle. Un membre du groupe est chargé de prendre des notes.
2. Ensuite, comparez les questions de tous les groupes et incorporez les meilleures dans le sondage.
3. Distribuez le sondage à tous les étudiants de la classe. A la fin, analysez les résultats.

Sujets possibles: personnages historiques, événements importants, influences, héritages, etc.

B. Devinette. Pensez à un personnage historique français ou américain mais ne dites pas son nom. Faites deviner son identité aux autres étudiants en racontant les événements importants de sa vie. Il est permis de mentionner l'époque où il (elle) a vécu, et même la première lettre de son nom de famille.

C. Refaisons l'histoire. Imaginez que vous êtes un personnage historique célèbre (George Washington, La Fayette, Abraham Lincoln, Napoléon...) et racontez un fait historique ou une aventure personnelle. Si vous ne connaissez pas tous les détails, inventez-les! Utilisez le passé composé et l'imparfait. Ensuite, racontez votre histoire à la classe.

D. La société en mouvement. Qu'est-ce qui caractérise le plus notre société? Qu'est-ce qui a le plus d'importance pour vous? Choisissez dans la liste ci-dessous les deux points qui influencent le plus votre vie et expliquez pourquoi.

1. le droit de vote
2. l'égalité devant la loi
3. la liberté de presse
4. le droit à l'éducation
5. la liberté
6. la propriété privée
7. les valeurs morales
8. la démocratie
9. la solidarité
10. le droit d'être élu

De quoi avez-vous peur? Choisissez dans la liste suivante les deux points qui menacent le plus votre vie et expliquez pourquoi. Quelles solutions proposeriez-vous pour les régler?

1. le chômage
2. la pauvreté
3. la maladie
4. la crise du logement
5. le terrorisme
6. la vieillesse
7. la drogue
8. l'analphabétisme
9. la faim
10. la violence

E. Par écrit. Imaginez comment sera votre vie en l'an 2050. Où serez-vous et que ferez-vous? Comment sera la vie de tous les jours? Comment la vie professionnelle évoluera-t-elle? Et les loisirs? A votre avis, la société sera-t-elle meilleure ou pire? Expliquez votre réponse.

Les lois de la nature

Jacques Prévert (1900-1977) est un poète français qui décrit dans ses poèmes les problèmes de la vie quotidienne. Dans «Soyez polis», il présente les difficultés de la vie en société, vis-a-vis des autres et de notre environnement. Avant de lire ce poème, parcourez-le et cherchez les verbes pour comprendre le sens général.

Soyez polis

Vue d'ensemble des Alpes françaises

Soyez polis
Crie l'homme
Soyez polis avec les aliments
Soyez polis
Avec les éléments avec les éléphants
Soyez polis avec les femmes
Et avec les enfants
Soyez polis
Avec les gars du bâtiment°
Soyez polis
Avec le monde vivant.

. . .

Il faut aussi être très poli avec la terre
Et avec le soleil
Il faut les remercier le matin en se réveillant
Il faut les remercier
Pour la chaleur
Pour les arbres
Pour les fruits
Pour tout ce qui est bon à manger
Pour tout ce qui est beau à regarder
A toucher
Il faut les remercier
Il ne faut pas les embêter°... les critiquer
Ils savent ce qu'ils ont à faire
Le soleil et la terre
Alors il faut les laisser faire°

gars... ouvriers

ennuyer

les... les laisser libres

Ou bien ils sont capables de se fâcher
Et puis après
On est changé
En courge°
gourde (légume)
En melon d'eau
Ou en pierre à briquet°
Et on est bien avancé°...

. . .

En somme pour résumer
Deux points° ouvrez les guillemets:°
«Il faut que tout le monde soit poli avec
le monde ou alors il y a des
guerres... des épidémies des tremblements
de terre des paquets de mer° des
coups de fusil°...
Et de grosses méchantes° fourmis° rouges
qui viennent vous dévorer les pieds
pendant qu'on dort la nuit.»

Jacques Prévert

gourde (légume)
pierre... pour faire du feu
on... on n'a pas fait de progrès
: (deux points) / « » (guillemets)
paquets... tempêtes en mer
coups... décharges d'une arme à feu
cruelles / insectes qui aiment les pique-niques

COMPRÉHENSION

1. D'après ce poème, avec qui et avec quoi faut-il être poli? De quelle façon doit-on manifester notre politesse?
2. Quelles sont les conséquences quand on n'est pas poli avec la terre?
3. D'après vous, quel message veut communiquer le poète?
4. En quoi est-ce poétique de parler de la politesse envers la nature?

MAINTENANT A VOUS

A. Opinions personnelles. Avec un(e) camarade, discutez des questions suivantes. Utilisez dans vos réponses «je pense, je ne pense pas, je crois, je ne crois pas, je doute, je suis certain(e), je ne suis pas certain(e), j'espère... »

1. Pensez-vous que Jacques Prévert utilise des images exagérées pour établir son point de vue? Quelles images considérez-vous les plus drôles? les plus bizarres? Pensez-vous qu'elles soient enfantines? A votre avis, quel adjectif décrirait le mieux ce poème?
2. Est-ce que les gens sont, en général, polis ou pas polis entre eux? avec la nature? Et vous, quel est votre comportement envers les autres? envers la nature?

3. Pensez-vous que l'indifférence envers les autres soit la cause de certains problèmes humains? Desquels? Comment pourrait-on éviter la violence dans notre société?

B. Débat sur l'environnement. Voici quelques problèmes qui menacent l'environnement. Par petits groupes, classez-les par ordre d'importance, *1* étant le plus urgent. Puis, décidez quelles sont les solutions possibles et quelles seront les conséquences si aucune mesure n'est prise assez rapidement. Utilisez des expressions impersonnelles («il est important que, il est indispensable que... ») dans vos suggestions. Enfin, comparez vos résultats avec ceux des autres groupes. Quel problème semble être le plus urgent? le moins urgent? Quelles solutions sont les plus réalistes? les plus utopiques?

1. la disparition des espèces animales 2. la surpopulation 3. la pollution des mers 4. la destruction des forêts 5. les accidents nucléaires 6. le bruit 7. ?

C. La politique écologiste. Voici un extrait d'un article sur le mouvement écologiste, paru en 1989 dans le magazine *Le Point*. Lisez-le, puis répondez aux questions.

ÉCOLOGIE

Le fond de l'air est vert

Depuis la catastrophe de Tchernobyl et le nuage itinérant qui a pollué l'Europe, la nature, contrariée par l'action de l'homme, n'a cessé de rappeler aux gouvernants qu'elle avait ses lois. Avec la déchirure de la couche d'ozone, les pollutions successives du Rhin et de la Loire, la tempête qui a ravagé la Bretagne fin 1987 et la marée noire qui défigure l'Alaska (*voir page 46*), les événements se sont précipités comme pour donner raison au discours vert.[a]

a. du mouvement écologiste

1. Connaissiez-vous quelques-unes des catastrophes mentionnées dans cet extrait? Lesquelles?
2. Où se trouvent le Rhin et la Loire?
3. Selon cet extrait, quel effet devraient avoir les catastrophes naturelles citées sur les gouvernements?
4. Imaginez ce que dirait un politicien écologiste lors d'une campagne électorale dans votre ville ou dans votre état.

Appendices

The International Phonetic Alphabet

The International Phonetic Alphabet (IPA) consists of the phonetic symbols used to represent the different sounds of a language. The sounds of the French language are listed below. The IPA symbol representing a sound appears in the column on the left. In the middle column is the normal spelling of a word or words containing that sound. On the right is the phonetic transcription of that word in the IPA.

ORAL VOWELS					
[a]	madame	[madam]	[o]	**au**	[o]
[i]	dix	[dis]	[ɔ]	porte	[pɔrt]
[e]	répétez	[repete]	[ø]	deux	[dø]
[ɛ]	merci	[mɛrsi]	[œ]	neuf	[nœf]
[u]	jour	[ʒur]	[ə]	de	[də]
[y]	salut	[saly]			

NASAL VOWELS		
[ɑ̃]	**en, comment**	[ɑ̃], [kɔmɑ̃]
[ɛ̃]	**bien, vingt**	[bjɛ̃], [vɛ̃]
[ɔ̃]	**bon, pardon**	[bɔ̃], [pardɔ̃]

SEMI-VOWELS		
[ɥ]	huit	[illegible]
[j]	rien	[illegible]
[w]	moi, oui	[illegible]

CONSONANTS					
[b]	bon	[bɔ̃]	[n]	non	[nɔ̃]
[ʃ]	chalet	[ʃalɛ]	[p]	plaît	[plɛ]
[d]	des	[de]	[r]	revoir	[rəvwar]
[f]	photo	[foto]	[k]	comme	[kɔm]
[g]	Guy	[gi]	[s]	ça, si	[sa], [si]
[ʒ]	je	[ʒ(ə)]	[z]	mademoiselle	[madmwazɛl]
[ɲ]	champagne	[ʃɑ̃paɲ]	[t]	Martin	[martɛ̃]
[l]	appelle	[apɛl]	[v]	va	[va]
[m]	mal	[mal]			

The *passé simple*

1. The **passé simple** is a past tense often used in printed narrative material. It is not a conversational tense. Verbs that would be used in the **passé composé** in informal speech or writing are in the **passé simple** in formal writing. You may want to learn to recognize the forms of the **passé simple** for reading purposes. The **passé simple** of regular **-er** verbs is formed by adding the endings **-ai, -as, -a, -âme, -âtes,** and **-èrent** to the verb stem. The endings for **-ir** and **-re** verbs are: **-is, -is, -it, -îmes, -îtes,** and **-irent.**

	parler	finir	perdre
je	parlai	finis	perdis
tu	parlas	finis	perdis
il, elle, on	parla	finit	perdit
nous	parlâmes	finîmes	perdîmes
vous	parlâtes	finîtes	perdîtes
ils, elles	parlèrent	finirent	perdirent

2. Here are the third person forms (**il, elle, on; ils, elles**) of some verbs that are irregular in the **passé simple.** The rest can be found in Appendix C.

INFINITIVE	passé simple
avoir	il eut, ils eurent
dire	il dit, ils dirent
être	il fut, ils furent
faire	il fit, ils firent

Conjugation of Verbs

A. Auxiliary verbs

VERB	INDICATIVE				CONDITIONAL	SUBJUNCTIVE	IMPERATIVE
	PRESENT	IMPERFECT	PASSÉ SIMPLE	FUTURE	CONDITIONAL	PRESENT	
avoir[1]	ai	avais	eus	aurai	aurais	aie	
(*to have*)	as	avais	eus	auras	aurais	aies	aie
ayant	a	avait	eut	aura	aurait	ait	
eu	avons	avions	eûmes	aurons	aurions	ayons	ayons
	avez	aviez	eûtes	aurez	auriez	ayez	ayez
	ont	avaient	eurent	auront	auraient	aient	
	PASSÉ COMPOSÉ	PLUPERFECT			PAST CONDITIONAL		
	ai eu	avais eu			aurais eu		
	as eu	avais eu			aurais eu		
	a eu	avait eu			aurait eu		
	avons eu	avions eu			aurions eu		
	avez eu	aviez eu			auriez eu		
	ont eu	avaient eu			auraient eu		
	PRESENT	IMPERFECT	PASSÉ SIMPLE	FUTURE	CONDITIONAL	PRESENT	
être	suis	étais	fus	serai	serais	sois	
(*to be*)	es	étais	fus	seras	serais	sois	sois
étant	est	était	fut	sera	serait	soit	
été	sommes	étions	fûmes	serons	serions	soyons	soyons
	êtes	étiez	fûtes	serez	seriez	soyez	soyez
	sont	étaient	furent	seront	seraient	soient	
	PASSÉ COMPOSÉ	PLUPERFECT			PAST CONDITIONAL		
	ai été	avais été			aurais été		
	as été	avais été			aurais été		
	a été	avait été			aurait été		
	avons été	avions été			aurions été		
	avez été	aviez été			auriez été		
	ont été	avaient été			auraient été		

[1]The left-hand column of each chart contains the infinitive, the present participle, and the past participle of each verb. Conjugated verbs are shown without subject pronouns.

B. Regular verbs

VERB	INDICATIVE				CONDITIONAL	SUBJUNCTIVE	IMPERATIVE
-er verbs	PRESENT	IMPERFECT	PASSÉ SIMPLE	FUTURE	CONDITIONAL	PRESENT	
parler	parle	parlais	parlai	parlerai	parlerais	parle	
(*to speak*)	parles	parlais	parlas	parleras	parlerais	parles	parle
parlant	parle	parlait	parla	parlera	parlerait	parle	
parlé	parlons	parlions	parlâmes	parlerons	parlerions	parlions	parlons
	parlez	parliez	parlâtes	parlerez	parleriez	parliez	parlez
	parlent	parlaient	parlèrent	parleront	parleraient	parlent	
	PASSÉ COMPOSÉ	PLUPERFECT			PAST CONDITIONAL		
	ai parlé	avais parlé			aurais parlé		
	as parlé	avais parlé			aurais parlé		
	a parlé	avait parlé			aurait parlé		
	avons parlé	avions parlé			aurions parlé		
	avez parlé	aviez parlé			auriez parlé		
	ont parlé	avaient parlé			auraient parlé		
-ir verbs	PRESENT	IMPERFECT	PASSÉ SIMPLE	FUTURE	CONDITIONAL	PRESENT	
finir	finis	finissais	finis	finirai	finirais	finisse	
(*to finish*)	finis	finissais	finis	finiras	finirais	finisses	finis
finissant	finit	finissait	finit	finira	finirait	finisse	
fini	finissons	finissions	finîmes	finirons	finirions	finissions	finissons
	finissez	finissiez	finîtes	finirez	finiriez	finissiez	finissez
	finissent	finissaient	finirent	finiront	finiraient	finissent	
	PASSÉ COMPOSÉ	PLUPERFECT			PAST CONDITIONAL		
	ai fini	avais fini			aurais fini		
	as fini	avais fini			aurais fini		
	a fini	avait fini			aurait fini		
	avons fini	avions fini			aurions fini		
	avez fini	aviez fini			auriez fini		
	ont fini	avaient fini			auraient fini		

VERB	INDICATIVE				CONDITIONAL	SUBJUNCTIVE	IMPERATIVE
-re verbs	PRESENT	IMPERFECT	PASSÉ SIMPLE	FUTURE	CONDITIONAL	PRESENT	
perdre	perds	perdais	perdis	perdrai	perdrais	perde	
(*to lose*)	perds	perdais	perdis	perdras	perdrais	perdes	perds
perdant	perd	perdait	perdit	perdra	perdrait	perde	
perdu	perdons	perdions	perdîmes	perdrons	perdrions	perdions	perdons
	perdez	perdiez	perdîtes	perdrez	perdriez	perdiez	perdez
	perdent	perdaient	perdirent	perdront	perdraient	perdent	
	PASSÉ COMPOSÉ	PLUPERFECT			PAST CONDITIONAL		
	ai perdu	avais perdu			aurais perdu		
	as perdu	avais perdu			aurais perdu		
	a perdu	avait perdu			aurait perdu		
	avons perdu	avions perdu			aurions perdu		
	avez perdu	aviez perdu			auriez perdu		
	ont perdu	avaient perdu			auraient perdu		

C. Intransitive verbs conjugated with *être*[1]

VERB	INDICATIVE				CONDITIONAL	SUBJUNCTIVE	IMPERATIVE
	PRESENT	IMPERFECT	PASSÉ SIMPLE	FUTURE	CONDITIONAL	PRESENT	
entrer	entre	entrais	entrai	entrerai	entrerais	entre	
(*to enter*)	entres	entrais	entras	entreras	entrerais	entres	entre
entrant	entre	entrait	entra	entrera	entrerait	entre	
entré	entrons	entrions	entrâmes	entrerons	entrerions	entrions	entrons
	entrez	entriez	entrâtes	entrerez	entreriez	entriez	entrez
	entrent	entraient	entrèrent	entreront	entreraient	entrent	
	PASSÉ COMPOSÉ	PLUPERFECT			PAST CONDITIONAL		
	suis entré(e)	étais entré(e)			serais entré(e)		
	es entré(e)	étais entré(e)			serais entré(e)		
	est entré(e)	était entré(e)			serait entré(e)		
	sommes entré(e)s	étions entré(e)s			serions entré(e)s		
	êtes entré(e)(s)	étiez entré(e)(s)			seriez entré(e)(s)		
	sont entré(e)s	étaient entré(e)s			seraient entré(e)s		

[1]Other intransitive verbs conjugated with **être** in compound tenses are **aller, arriver, descendre, devenir, monter, mourir, naître, partir (repartir), passer, rentrer, rester, retourner, revenir, sortir, tomber,** and **venir.** Note that **descendre, monter, passer, retourner,** and **sortir** may sometimes be used as transitive verbs (i.e., with a direct object), in which case they are conjugated with **avoir** in compound tenses.

D. Pronominal verbs

VERB	INDICATIVE: PRESENT	IMPERFECT	PASSÉ SIMPLE	FUTURE	CONDITIONAL: CONDITIONAL	SUBJUNCTIVE: PRESENT	IMPERATIVE
se laver	me lave	me lavais	me lavai	me laverai	me laverais	me lave	
(*to wash*	te laves	te lavais	te lavas	te laveras	te laverais	te laves	lave-toi
oneself)	se lave	se lavait	se lava	se lavera	se laverait	se lave	
se lavant	nous lavons	nous lavions	nous lavâmes	nous laverons	nous laverions	nous lavions	lavons-nous
lavé	vous lavez	vous laviez	vous lavâtes	vous laverez	vous laveriez	vous laviez	lavez-vous
	se lavent	se lavaient	se lavèrent	se laveront	se laveraient	se lavent	

INDICATIVE: PASSÉ COMPOSÉ	PLUPERFECT	CONDITIONAL: PAST CONDITIONAL
me suis lavé(e)	m'étais lavé(e)	me serais lavé(e)
t'es lavé(e)	t'étais lavé(e)	te serais lavé(e)
s'est lavé(e)	s'était lavé(e)	se serait lavé(e)
nous sommes lavé(e)s	nous étions lavé(e)s	nous serions lavé(e)s
vous êtes lavé(e)(s)	vous étiez lavé(e)(s)	vous seriez lavé(e)(s)
se sont lavé(e)s	s'étaient lavé(e)s	se seraient lavé(e)s

E. Irregular verbs

VERB	PRESENT	IMPERFECT	PASSÉ COMPOSÉ	PASSÉ SIMPLE	FUTURE	CONDITIONAL	PRESENT SUBJUNCTIVE	IMPERATIVE
aller	vais	allais	suis allé(e)	allai	irai	irais	aille	
(*to go*)	vas	allais	es allé(e)	allas	iras	irais	ailles	va
allant	va	allait	est allé(e)	alla	ira	irait	aille	
allé	allons	allions	sommes allé(e)s	allâmes	irons	irions	allions	allons
	allez	alliez	êtes allé(e)(s)	allâtes	irez	iriez	alliez	allez
	vont	allaient	sont allé(e)s	allèrent	iront	iraient	aillent	
asseoir[1]	assieds	asseyais	ai assis	assis	assiérai	assiérais	asseye	
(*to seat*)	assieds	asseyais	as assis	assis	assiéras	assiérais	asseyes	assieds
asseyant	assied	asseyait	a assis	assit	assiéra	assiérait	asseye	
assis	asseyons	asseyions	avons assis	assîmes	assiérons	assiérions	asseyions	asseyons
	asseyez	asseyiez	avez assis	assîtes	assiérez	assiériez	asseyiez	asseyez
	asseyent	asseyaient	ont assis	assirent	assiéront	assiéraient	asseyent	

[1] **S'asseoir** (pronominal form of **asseoir**) means *to be seated* or *to take a seat*. The imperative forms of **s'asseoir** are **assieds-toi, asseyons-nous,** and **asseyez-vous.**

VERB	PRESENT	IMPERFECT	PASSÉ COMPOSÉ	PASSÉ SIMPLE	FUTURE	CONDITIONAL	PRESENT SUBJUNCTIVE	IMPERATIVE
battre	bats	battais	ai battu	battis	battrai	battrais	batte	
(*to beat*)	bats	battais	as battu	battis	battras	battrais	battes	bats
battant	bat	battait	a battu	battit	battra	battrait	batte	
battu	battons	battions	avons battu	battîmes	battrons	battrions	battions	battons
	battez	battiez	avez battu	battîtes	battrez	battriez	battiez	battez
	battent	battaient	ont battu	battirent	battront	battraient	battent	
boire	bois	buvais	ai bu	bus	boirai	boirais	boive	
(*to drink*)	bois	buvais	as bu	bus	boiras	boirais	boives	bois
buvant	boit	buvait	a bu	but	boira	boirait	boive	
bu	buvons	buvions	avons bu	bûmes	boirons	boirions	buvions	buvons
	buvez	buviez	avez bu	bûtes	boirez	boiriez	buviez	buvez
	boivent	buvaient	ont bu	burent	boiront	boiraient	boivent	
conduire	conduis	conduisais	ai conduit	conduisis	conduirai	conduirais	conduise	
(*to lead,*	conduis	conduisais	as conduit	conduisis	conduiras	conduirais	conduises	conduis
to drive)	conduit	conduisait	a conduit	conduisit	conduira	conduirait	conduise	
conduisant	conduisons	conduisions	avons conduit	conduisîmes	conduirons	conduirions	conduisions	conduisons
conduit	conduisez	conduisiez	avez conduit	conduisîtes	conduirez	conduiriez	conduisiez	conduisez
	conduisent	conduisaient	ont conduit	conduisirent	conduiront	conduiraient	conduisent	
connaître	connais	connaissais	ai connu	connus	connaîtrai	connaîtrais	connaisse	
(*to be*	connais	connaissais	as connu	connus	connaîtras	connaîtrais	connaisses	connais
acquainted)	connaît	connaissait	a connu	connut	connaîtra	connaîtrait	connaisse	
connaissant	connaissons	connaissions	avons connu	connûmes	connaîtrons	connaîtrions	connaissions	connaissons
connu	connaissez	connaissiez	avez connu	connûtes	connaîtrez	connaîtriez	connaissiez	connaissez
	connaissent	connaissaient	ont connu	connurent	connaîtront	connaîtraient	connaissent	
courir	cours	courais	ai couru	courus	courrai	courrais	coure	
(*to run*)	cours	courais	as couru	courus	courras	courrais	coures	cours
courant	court	courait	a couru	courut	courra	courrait	coure	
couru	courons	courions	avons couru	courûmes	courrons	courrions	courions	courons
	courez	couriez	avez couru	courûtes	courrez	courriez	couriez	courez
	courent	couraient	ont couru	coururent	courront	courraient	courent	
craindre	crains	craignais	ai craint	craignis	craindrai	craindrais	craigne	
(*to fear*)	crains	craignais	as craint	craignis	craindras	craindrais	craignes	crains
craignant	craint	craignait	a craint	craignit	craindra	craindrait	craigne	
craint	craignons	craignions	avons craint	craignîmes	craindrons	craindrions	craignions	craignons
	craignez	craigniez	avez craint	craignîtes	craindrez	craindriez	craigniez	craignez
	craignent	craignaient	ont craint	craignirent	craindront	craindraient	craignent	

VERB	PRESENT	IMPERFECT	PASSÉ COMPOSÉ	PASSÉ SIMPLE	FUTURE	CONDITIONAL	PRESENT SUBJUNCTIVE	IMPERATIVE
croire	crois	croyais	ai cru	crus	croirai	croirais	croie	
(*to believe*)	crois	croyais	as cru	crus	croiras	croirais	croies	crois
croyant	croit	croyait	a cru	crut	croira	croirait	croie	
cru	croyons	croyions	avons cru	crûmes	croirons	croirions	croyions	croyons
	croyez	croyiez	avez cru	crûtes	croirez	croiriez	croyiez	croyez
	croient	croyaient	ont cru	crurent	croiront	croiraient	croient	
devoir	dois	devais	ai dû	dus	devrai	devrais	doive	
(*to have to,*	dois	devais	as dû	dus	devras	devrais	doives	dois
to owe)	doit	devait	a dû	dut	devra	devrait	doive	
devant	devons	devions	avons dû	dûmes	devrons	devrions	devions	devons
dû	devez	deviez	avez dû	dûtes	devrez	devriez	deviez	devez
	doivent	devaient	ont dû	durent	devront	devraient	doivent	
dire[2]	dis	disais	ai dit	dis	dirai	dirais	dise	
(*to say,*	dis	disais	as dit	dis	diras	dirais	dises	dis
to tell)	dit	disait	a dit	dit	dira	dirait	dise	
disant	disons	disions	avons dit	dîmes	dirons	dirions	disions	disons
dit	dites	disiez	avez dit	dîtes	direz	diriez	disiez	dites
	disent	disaient	ont dit	dirent	diront	diraient	disent	
dormir[3]	dors	dormais	ai dormi	dormis	dormirai	dormirais	dorme	
(*to sleep*)	dors	dormais	as dormi	dormis	dormiras	dormirais	dormes	dors
dormant	dort	dormait	a dormi	dormit	dormira	dormirait	dorme	
dormi	dormons	dormions	avons dormi	dormîmes	dormirons	dormirions	dormions	dormons
	dormez	dormiez	avez dormi	dormîtes	dormirez	dormiriez	dormiez	dormez
	dorment	dormaient	ont dormi	dormirent	dormiront	dormiraient	dorment	
écrire[4]	écris	écrivais	ai écrit	écrivis	écrirai	écrirais	écrive	
(*to write*)	écris	écrivais	as écrit	écrivis	écriras	écrirais	écrives	écris
écrivant	écrit	écrivait	a écrit	écrivit	écrira	écrirait	écrive	
écrit	écrivons	écrivions	avons écrit	écrivîmes	écrirons	écririons	écrivions	écrivons
	écrivez	écriviez	avez écrit	écrivîtes	écrirez	écririez	écriviez	écrivez
	écrivent	écrivaient	ont écrit	écrivirent	écriront	écriraient	écrivent	
envoyer	envoie	envoyais	ai envoyé	envoyai	enverrai	enverrais	envoie	
(*to send*)	envoies	envoyais	as envoyé	envoyas	enverras	enverrais	envoies	envoie
envoyant	envoie	envoyait	a envoyé	envoya	enverra	enverrait	envoie	
envoyé	envoyons	envoyions	avons envoyé	envoyâmes	enverrons	enverrions	envoyions	envoyons
	envoyez	envoyiez	avez envoyé	envoyâtes	enverrez	enverriez	envoyiez	envoyez
	envoient	envoyaient	ont envoyé	envoyèrent	enverront	enverraient	envoient	

[2]**Verbs like dire: contredire (vous contredisez), interdire (vous interdisez), prédire (vous prédisez)**

[3]Verbs like **dormir: mentir, partir, repartir, sentir, servir, sortir. (Partir, repartir,** and **sortir** are conjugated with **être.)**

[4]Verbs like **écrire: décrire**

VERB	PRESENT	IMPERFECT	PASSÉ COMPOSÉ	PASSÉ SIMPLE	FUTURE	CONDITIONAL	PRESENT SUBJUNCTIVE	IMPERATIVE
faire	fais	faisais	ai fait	fis	ferai	ferais	fasse	
(*to do,*	fais	faisais	as fait	fis	feras	ferais	fasses	fais
to make)	fait	faisait	a fait	fit	fera	ferait	fasse	
faisant	faisons	faisions	avons fait	fîmes	ferons	ferions	fassions	faisons
fait	faites	faisiez	avez fait	fîtes	ferez	feriez	fassiez	faites
	font	faisaient	ont fait	firent	feront	feraient	fassent	
falloir	il faut	il fallait	il a fallu	il fallut	il faudra	il faudrait	il faille	
(*to be*								
necessary)								
fallu								
lire[5]	lis	lisais	ai lu	lus	lirai	lirais	lise	
(*to read*)	lis	lisais	as lu	lus	liras	lirais	lises	lis
lisant	lit	lisait	a lu	lut	lira	lirait	lise	
lu	lisons	lisions	avons lu	lûmes	lirons	lirions	lisions	lisons
	lisez	lisiez	avez lu	lûtes	lirez	liriez	lisiez	lisez
	lisent	lisaient	ont lu	lurent	liront	liraient	lisent	
mettre[6]	mets	mettais	ai mis	mis	mettrai	mettrais	mette	
(*to put*)	mets	mettais	as mis	mis	mettras	mettrais	mettes	mets
mettant	met	mettait	a mis	mit	mettra	mettrait	mette	
mis	mettons	mettions	avons mis	mîmes	mettrons	mettrions	mettions	mettons
	mettez	mettiez	avez mis	mîtes	mettrez	mettriez	mettiez	mettez
	mettent	mettaient	ont mis	mirent	mettront	mettraient	mettent	
mourir	meurs	mourais	suis mort(e)	mourus	mourrai	mourrais	meure	
(*to die*)	meurs	mourais	es mort(e)	mourus	mourras	mourrais	meures	meurs
mourant	meurt	mourait	est mort(e)	mourut	mourra	mourrait	meure	
mort	mourons	mourions	sommes mort(e)s	mourûmes	mourrons	mourrions	mourions	mourons
	mourez	mouriez	êtes mort(e)(s)	mourûtes	mourrez	mourriez	mouriez	mourez
	meurent	mouraient	sont mort(e)s	moururent	mourront	mourraient	meurent	
naître	nais	naissais	suis né(e)	naquis	naîtrai	naîtrais	naisse	
(*to be born*)	nais	naissais	es né(e)	naquis	naîtras	naîtrais	naisses	nais
naissant	naît	naissait	est né(e)	naquit	naîtra	naîtrait	naisse	
né	naissons	naissions	sommes né(e)s	naquîmes	naîtrons	naîtrions	naissions	naissons
	naissez	naissiez	êtes né(e)(s)	naquîtes	naîtrez	naîtriez	naissiez	naissez
	naissent	naissaient	sont né(e)s	naquirent	naîtront	naîtraient	naissent	

[5]Verbs like **lire: élire, relire**

[6]Verbs like **mettre: permettre, promettre, remettre**

VERB	PRESENT	IMPERFECT	PASSÉ COMPOSÉ	PASSÉ SIMPLE	FUTURE	CONDITIONAL	PRESENT SUBJUNCTIVE	IMPERATIVE
ouvrir[7]	ouvre	ouvrais	ai ouvert	ouvris	ouvrirai	ouvrirais	ouvre	
(*to open*)	ouvres	ouvrais	as ouvert	ouvris	ouvriras	ouvrirais	ouvres	ouvre
ouvrant	ouvre	ouvrait	a ouvert	ouvrit	ouvrira	ouvrirait	ouvre	
ouvert	ouvrons	ouvrions	avons ouvert	ouvrîmes	ouvrirons	ouvririons	ouvrions	ouvrons
	ouvrez	ouvriez	avez ouvert	ouvrîtes	ouvrirez	ouvririez	ouvriez	ouvrez
	ouvrent	ouvraient	ont ouvert	ouvrirent	ouvriront	ouvriraient	ouvrent	
plaire	plais	plaisais	ai plu	plus	plairai	plairais	plaise	
(*to please*)	plais	plaisais	as plu	plus	plairas	plairais	plaises	plais
plaisant	plaît	plaisait	a plu	plut	plaira	plairait	plaise	
plu	plaisons	plaisions	avons plu	plûmes	plairons	plairions	plaisions	plaisons
	plaisez	plaisiez	avez plu	plûtes	plairez	plairiez	plaisiez	plaisez
	plaisent	plaisaient	ont plu	plurent	plairont	plairaient	plaisent	
pleuvoir	il pleut	il pleuvait	il a plu	il plut	il pleuvra	il pleuvrait	il pleuve	
(*to rain*)								
pleuvant								
plu								
pouvoir	peux, puis	pouvais	ai pu	pus	pourrai	pourrais	puisse	
(*to be able*)	peux	pouvais	as pu	pus	pourras	pourrais	puisses	
pouvant	peut	pouvait	a pu	put	pourra	pourrait	puisse	
pu	pouvons	pouvions	avons pu	pûmes	pourrons	pourrions	puissions	
	pouvez	pouviez	avez pu	pûtes	pourrez	pourriez	puissiez	
	peuvent	pouvaient	ont pu	purent	pourront	pourraient	puissent	
prendre[8]	prends	prenais	ai pris	pris	prendrai	prendrais	prenne	
(*to take*)	prends	prenais	as pris	pris	prendras	prendrais	prennes	prends
prenant	prend	prenait	a pris	prit	prendra	prendrait	prenne	
pris	prenons	prenions	avons pris	prîmes	prendrons	prendrions	prenions	prenons
	prenez	preniez	avez pris	prîtes	prendrez	prendriez	preniez	prenez
	prennent	prenaient	ont pris	prirent	prendront	prendraient	prennent	
recevoir[9]	reçois	recevais	ai reçu	reçus	recevrai	recevrais	reçoive	
(*to receive*)	reçois	recevais	as reçu	reçus	recevras	recevrais	reçoives	reçois
recevant	reçoit	recevait	a reçu	reçut	recevra	recevrait	reçoive	
reçu	recevons	recevions	avons reçu	reçûmes	recevrons	recevrions	recevions	recevons
	recevez	receviez	avez reçu	reçûtes	recevrez	recevriez	receviez	recevez
	reçoivent	recevaient	ont reçu	reçurent	recevront	recevraient	reçoivent	

[7]Verbs like **ouvrir: couvrir, découvrir, offrir, souffrir**
[8]Verbs like **prendre: apprendre, comprendre, surprendre**
[9]Verbs like **recevoir: apercevoir, s'apercevoir de, décevoir**

VERB	PRESENT	IMPERFECT	PASSÉ COMPOSÉ	PASSÉ SIMPLE	FUTURE	CONDITIONAL	PRESENT SUBJUNCTIVE	IMPERATIVE
rire	ris	riais	ai ri	ris	rirai	rirais	rie	
(*to laugh*)	ris	riais	as ri	ris	riras	rirais	ries	ris
riant	rit	riait	a ri	rit	rira	rirait	rie	
ri	rions	riions	avons ri	rîmes	rirons	ririons	riions	rions
	riez	riiez	avez ri	rîtes	rirez	ririez	riiez	riez
	rient	riaient	ont ri	rirent	riront	riraient	rient	
savoir	sais	savais	ai su	sus	saurai	saurais	sache	
(*to know*)	sais	savais	as su	sus	sauras	saurais	saches	sache
sachant	sait	savait	a su	sut	saura	saurait	sache	
su	savons	savions	avons su	sûmes	saurons	saurions	sachions	sachons
	savez	saviez	avez su	sûtes	saurez	sauriez	sachiez	sachez
	savent	savaient	ont su	surent	sauront	sauraient	sachent	
suivre	suis	suivais	ai suivi	suivis	suivrai	suivrais	suive	
(*to follow*)	suis	suivais	as suivi	suivis	suivras	suivrais	suives	suis
suivant	suit	suivait	a suivi	suivit	suivra	suivrait	suive	
suivi	suivons	suivions	avons suivi	suivîmes	suivrons	suivrions	suivions	suivons
	suivez	suiviez	avez suivi	suivîtes	suivrez	suivriez	suiviez	suivez
	suivent	suivaient	ont suivi	suivirent	suivront	suivraient	suivent	
tenir	tiens	tenais	ai tenu	tins	tiendrai	tiendrais	tienne	
(*to hold,*	tiens	tenais	as tenu	tins	tiendras	tiendrais	tiennes	tiens
to keep)	tient	tenait	a tenu	tint	tiendra	tiendrait	tienne	
tenant	tenons	tenions	avons tenu	tînmes	tiendrons	tiendrions	tenions	tenons
tenu	tenez	teniez	avez tenu	tîntes	tiendrez	tiendriez	teniez	tenez
	tiennent	tenaient	ont tenu	tinrent	tiendront	tiendraient	tiennent	
valoir	vaux	valais	ai valu	valus	vaudrai	vaudrais	vaille	
(*to be*	vaux	valais	as valu	valus	vaudras	vaudrais	vailles	vaux
worth)	vaut	valait	a valu	valut	vaudra	vaudrait	vaille	
valant	valons	valions	avons valu	valûmes	vaudrons	vaudrions	valions	valons
valu	valez	valiez	avez valu	valûtes	vaudrez	vaudriez	valiez	valez
	valent	valaient	ont valu	valurent	vaudront	vaudraient	vaillent	
venir[10]	viens	venais	suis venu(e)	vins	viendrai	viendrais	vienne	
(*to come*)	viens	venais	es venu(e)	vins	viendras	viendrais	viennes	viens
venant	vient	venait	est venu(e)	vint	viendra	viendrait	vienne	
venu	venons	venions	sommes venu(e)s	vînmes	viendrons	viendrions	venions	venons
	venez	veniez	êtes venu(e)(s)	vîntes	viendrez	viendriez	veniez	venez
	viennent	venaient	sont venu(e)s	vinrent	viendront	viendraient	viennent	

[10]Verbs like **venir: devenir (elle est devenue), revenir (elle est revenue), maintenir (elle a maintenu), obtenir (elle a obtenu), se souvenir de (elle s'est souvenue de...)**

VERB	PRESENT	IMPERFECT	PASSÉ COMPOSÉ	PASSÉ SIMPLE	FUTURE	CONDITIONAL	PRESENT SUBJUNCTIVE	IMPERATIVE
vivre	vis	vivais	ai vécu	vécus	vivrai	vivrais	vive	
(*to live*)	vis	vivais	as vécu	vécus	vivras	vivrais	vives	vis
vivant	vit	vivait	a vécu	vécut	vivra	vivrait	vive	
vécu	vivons	vivions	avons vécu	vécûmes	vivrons	vivrions	vivions	vivons
	vivez	viviez	avez vécu	vécûtes	vivrez	vivriez	viviez	vivez
	vivent	vivaient	ont vécu	vécurent	vivront	vivraient	vivent	
voir	vois	voyais	ai vu	vis	verrai	verrais	voie	
(*to see*)	vois	voyais	as vu	vis	verras	verrais	voies	vois
voyant	voit	voyait	a vu	vit	verra	verrait	voie	
vu	voyons	voyions	avons vu	vîmes	verrons	verrions	voyions	voyons
	voyez	voyiez	avez vu	vîtes	verrez	verriez	voyiez	voyez
	voient	voyaient	ont vu	virent	verront	verraient	voient	
vouloir	veux	voulais	ai voulu	voulus	voudrai	voudrais	veuille	
(*to wish,*	veux	voulais	as voulu	voulus	voudras	voudrais	veuilles	veuille
to want)	veut	voulait	a voulu	voulut	voudra	voudrait	veuille	
voulant	voulons	voulions	avons voulu	voulûmes	voudrons	voudrions	voulions	veuillons
voulu	voulez	vouliez	avez voulu	voulûtes	voudrez	voudriez	vouliez	veuillez
	veulent	voulaient	ont voulu	voulurent	voudront	voudraient	veuillent	

-er Verbs with Spelling Changes

Certain verbs ending in **-er** require spelling changes. Models for each kind of change are listed here. Stem changes are in boldface type.

F. Stem-changing verbs

VERB	PRESENT	IMPERFECT	PASSÉ COMPOSÉ	PASSÉ SIMPLE	FUTURE	CONDITIONAL	PRESENT SUBJUNCTIVE	IMPERATIVE
commencer[1]	commence	**commençais**	ai commencé	**commençai**	commencerai	commencerais	commence	commence
(*to begin*)	commences	**commençais**	as commencé	**commenças**	commenceras	commencerais	commences	
commençant	commence	**commençait**	a commencé	**commença**	commencera	commencerait	commence	**commençons**
commencé	**commençons**	commencions	avons commencé	**commençâmes**	commencerons	commencerions	commencions	commencez
	commencez	commenciez	avez commencé	**commençâtes**	commencerez	commenceriez	commenciez	
	commencent	**commençaient**	ont commencé	commencèrent	commenceront	commenceraient	commencent	

[1]Verbs like **commencer: dénoncer, divorcer, menacer, placer, prononcer, remplacer, tracer**

VERB	PRESENT	IMPERFECT	PASSÉ COMPOSÉ	PASSÉ SIMPLE	FUTURE	CONDITIONAL	PRESENT SUBJUNCTIVE	IMPERATIVE
manger[2]	mange	**mangeais**	ai mangé	**mangeai**	mangerai	mangerais	mange	mange
(*to eat*)	manges	**mangeais**	as mangé	**mangeas**	mangeras	mangerais	manges	
mangeant	mange	**mangeait**	a mangé	**mangea**	mangera	mangerait	mange	**mangeons**
mangé	**mangeons**	mangions	avons mangé	**mangeâmes**	mangerons	mangerions	mangions	mangez
	mangez	mangiez	avez mangé	**mangeâtes**	mangerez	mangeriez	mangiez	
	mangent	**mangeaient**	ont mangé	mangèrent	mangeront	mangeraient	mangent	
appeler[3]	**appelle**	appelais	ai appelé	appelai	**appellerai**	**appellerais**	**appelle**	
(*to call*)	**appelles**	appelais	as appelé	appelas	**appelleras**	**appellerais**	**appelles**	**appelle**
appelant	**appelle**	appelait	a appelé	appela	**appellera**	**appellerait**	**appelle**	
appelé	appelons	appelions	avons appelé	appelâmes	**appellerons**	**appellerions**	appelions	appelons
	appelez	appeliez	avez appelé	appelâtes	**appellerez**	**appelleriez**	appeliez	appelez
	appellent	appelaient	ont appelé	appelèrent	**appelleront**	**appelleraient**	**appellent**	
essayer[4]	**essaie**	essayais	ai essayé	essayai	**essaierai**	**essaierais**	**essaie**	
(*to try*)	**essaies**	essayais	as essayé	essayas	**essaieras**	**essaierais**	**essaies**	**essaie**
essayant	**essaie**	essayait	a essayé	essaya	**essaiera**	**essaierait**	**essaie**	
essayé	essayons	essayions	avons essayé	essayâmes	**essaierons**	**essaierions**	essayions	essayons
	essayez	essayiez	avez essayé	essayâtes	**essaierez**	**essaieriez**	essayiez	essayez
	essaient	essayaient	ont essayé	essayèrent	**essaieront**	**essaieraient**	**essaient**	
acheter[5]	**achète**	achetais	ai acheté	achetai	**achèterai**	**achèterais**	**achète**	
(*to buy*)	**achètes**	achetais	as acheté	achetas	**achèteras**	**achèterais**	**achètes**	**achète**
achetant	**achète**	achetait	a acheté	acheta	**achètera**	**achèterait**	**achète**	
acheté	achetons	achetions	avons acheté	achetâmes	**achèterons**	**achèterions**	achetions	achetons
	achetez	achetiez	avez acheté	achetâtes	**achèterez**	**achèteriez**	achetiez	achetez
	achètent	achetaient	ont acheté	achetèrent	**achèteront**	**achèteraient**	**achètent**	
préférer[6]	**préfère**	préférais	ai préféré	préférai	préférerai	préférerais	**préfère**	
(*to prefer*)	**préfères**	préférais	as préféré	préféras	préféreras	préférerais	**préfères**	**préfère**
préférant	**préfère**	préférait	a préféré	préféra	préférera	préférerait	**préfère**	
préféré	préférons	préférions	avons préféré	préférâmes	préférerons	préférerions	préférions	préférons
	préférez	préfériez	avez préféré	préférâtes	préférerez	préféreriez	préfériez	préférez
	préfèrent	préféraient	ont préféré	préférèrent	préféreront	préféreraient	**préfèrent**	

[2]Verbs like **manger: bouger, changer, dégager, engager, exiger, juger, loger, mélanger, nager, obliger, partager, voyager**

[3]Verbs like **appeler: épeler, jeter, projeter, (se) rappeler**

[4]Verbs like **essayer: employer, (s')ennuyer, nettoyer, payer**

[5]Verbs like **acheter: achever, amener, emmener, (se) lever, (se) promener**

[6]Verbs like **préférer: célébrer, considérer, espérer, (s')inquiéter, pénétrer, posséder, répéter, révéler, suggérer**

The Future Perfect *(Le futur antérieur)*

The future perfect can be used to express a future action that will already have taken place when another future action occurs. The subsequent action is always expressed by the simple future.

The future perfect is formed with the auxiliary verbs **avoir** or **être** + *the past participle of the main verb.*

Je publierai mes résultats quand **j'aurai terminé** cette expérience. — *I'll publish the results when I've finished this experiment.*

Aussitôt que mes collègues **seront revenus,** ils liront mon rapport. — *As soon as my colleagues have returned, they'll read my report.*

Demonstrative Pronouns

Demonstrative pronouns such as *this one, that one,* refer to a person, thing, or idea that has been mentioned previously. In French, they agree in gender and number with the nouns they replace.

	SINGULAR	PLURAL
Masculine	**celui** *this one, that one, the one*	**ceux** *these, those, the ones*
Feminine	**celle** *this one, that one, the one*	**celles** *these, those, the ones*

French demonstrative pronouns cannot stand alone. They must be used in one of the following ways:

1. with the suffix **-ci** (to indicate someone or something located close to the speaker) or **-là** (for someone or something more distant from the speaker)

   Voici deux affiches. Préférez-vous **celle-ci** ou **celle-là**? — *Here are two posters. Do you prefer this one or that one?*

2. followed by a prepositional phrase (often a construction with **de**)

   Quelle époque t'intéresse? **Celle** du moyen âge ou **celle** de la Renaissance? — *Which period interests you? That of the Middle Ages or that of the Renaissance?*

3. followed by a dependent clause introduced by a relative pronoun

   On trouve des villages anciens dans plusieurs parcs: **ceux** qui sont dans le Parc de la Brière sont en ruine; **ceux** qui sont dans les parcs de la Lorraine et du Morvan ont été restaurés. — *One finds very old villages in several parks: those that are in Brière Park are in ruins; those that are in the Lorraine and Morvan parks have been restored.*

Indefinite demonstrative pronouns. **Ceci** *(this),* **cela** *(that),* and **ça** (*that,* informal) are indefinite demonstrative pronouns; they refer to an idea or thing with no definite antecedent. They do not show gender or number.

Cela (**Ça**) n'est pas important. — *That's not important.*
Regarde **ceci** de près. — *Look at this closely.*
Qu'est-ce que c'est que **ça**? — *What's that?*

Relative Pronouns

A. *Ce qui* and *ce que*

Ce qui and **ce que** are indefinite relative pronouns similar in meaning to **la chose qui** (**que**) or **les choses qui** (**que**). They refer to an idea or a subject that is unspecified and has neither gender nor number, often expressed as *what*.

—Dites-moi **ce qui** est arrivé au touriste américain. *—Tell me what happened to the American tourist.*
—Je ne sais pas **ce qui** lui est arrivé. *—I don't know what happened to him.*

—Dites-moi **ce que** vous avez fait à Pointe-à-Pitre. *—Tell me what you did in Point-à-Pitre.*
—Je n'ai pas le temps de vous dire tout **ce qu'**on a fait. *—I don't have time to tell you everything we did.*

B. Lequel

Lequel (**laquelle, lesquels, lesquelles**) is the relative pronoun used as an object of a preposition to refer to things and people. **Lequel** and its forms contract with **à** and **de.**

Où est l'agence de voyage **devant laquelle** il attend? *Where is the travel agency in front of which he's waiting?*

L'hôtel **auquel** j'écris est à la Guadeloupe. *The hotel to which I am writing is in Guadeloupe.*
Ce sont des gens parmis **lesquels** je me sens bien. *They're people among whom I feel comfortable.*

The Past Subjunctive

The past subjunctive is formed with the present subjunctive of **avoir** or **être** plus a past participle.

	PAST SUBJUNCTIVE OF **parler**	PAST SUBJUNCTIVE OF **venir**
que je/j'	**aie parlé**	**sois venu(e)**
que tu	**aies parlé**	**sois venu(e)**
qu'il, elle, on	**ait parlé**	**soit venu(e)**
que nous	**ayons parlé**	**soyons venu(e)s**
que vous	**ayez parlé**	**soyez venu(e)(s)**
qu'ils, elles	**aient parlé**	**soient venu(e)s**

Je suis content que tu **aies parlé** avec Claudette. *I'm glad you've spoken with Claudette.*
Il est dommage qu'elle ne **soit** pas encore **venue.** *It's too bad that she hasn't come yet.*

Use of the past subjunctive. The past subjunctive is used under the same circumstances as the present subjunctive except that it indicates that the action or situation described in the dependent clause occurred *before* the action or situation described in the main clause. Compare these sentences:

Je suis content que tu **viennes.** *I'm happy that you are coming.*
Je suis content que tu **sois venu**(e). *I'm happy that you came.*

Je doute qu'ils le **comprennent.** *I doubt that they understand it.*
Je doute qu'ils **l'aient compris.** *I doubt that they have understood it.*

The Present Participle

In English, the present participle ends in *-ing*. It is used to describe an action that takes place simultaneously with the action of the main verb: *While reading a book about the Congo, John began to understand the problems of colonialism.*

The French present participle is formed by dropping the **-ons** ending from the **nous** form of the present indicative and adding **-ant.**

donner: nous donn~~ons~~ → donn- → **donnant**
finir: nous finiss~~ons~~ → finiss- → **finissant**
perdre: nous perd~~ons~~ → perd- → **perdant**

Three French verbs have irregular present participles:

avoir: **ayant** être: **étant** savoir: **sachant**

Possessive Pronouns

Possessive pronouns replace nouns that are modified by a possessive adjective or other possessive construction. In English, the possessive pronouns are *mine, yours, his, hers, its, ours,* and *theirs.* In French, the definite article is always used with the appropriate forms of the possessive pronoun.

	SINGULAR		PLURAL	
	Masculine	*Feminine*	*Masculine*	*Feminine*
mine	le mien	la mienne	les miens	les miennes
yours	le tien	la tienne	les tiens	les tiennes
his/hers/its	le sien	la sienne	les siens	les siennes
ours	le nôtre	la nôtre	les nôtres	
yours	le vôtre	la vôtre	les vôtres	
theirs	le leur	la leur	les leurs	

POSSESSIVE CONSTRUCTION + *NOUN*		POSSESSIVE PRONOUN
Où sont **leurs bagages**?	→	**Les leurs** sont ici.
C'est **mon frère** là-bas.	→	Ah oui? C'est **le mien** à côté de lui.
La **voiture de Frédérique** est plus rapide que **ma voiture.**		**Ah oui? La sienne** est aussi plus rapide que **la mienne.**

Causative *faire*

When a form of the verb **faire** is directly followed by an infinitive, it indicates that the subject of the sentence is causing something to be done to something or someone, or making someone do something. The word order is:

SUBJECT + **FAIRE** + *INFINITIVE* + *NOUN OBJECT*

Je **fais laver** ma voiture. *I'm having my car washed.*

If the object is replaced by a pronoun, the word order is:

SUBJECT + *PRONOUN OBJECT* + **FAIRE** + *INFINITIVE*

Je le **fais laver.** *I'm having it washed.*

The Passive Voice

In passive voice constructions, the subject receives the action of the verb instead of performing it. Compare these sentences. The subjects are in italics.

ACTIVE VOICE	PASSIVE VOICE
Les Arqué vendent la maison.	*La maison* est vendue par les Arqué.
Un ami algérien a acheté leur voiture.	*Leur voiture* a été achetée par un ami algérien.
Leurs amis français les ont invités à venir à Toulouse.	*Ils* ont été invités à venir à Toulouse par leurs amis français.

The passive voice consists of a form of **être** plus a past participle, which agrees in number and gender with the subject. If the person or thing that causes the action is expressed, it is introduced by the word **par.** The tense of **être** is the same as the tense of the verb in the corresponding active voice sentence.

ACTIVE VOICE	PASSIVE VOICE
Jean-Paul **apporte** les provisions.	Les provisions **sont apportées par** Jean-Paul.
Jean-Paul **a apporté** les provisions.	Les provisions **ont été apportées par** Jean-Paul.
Jean-Paul **apportera** les provisions.	Les provisions **seront apportées par** Jean-Paul.
Jean-Paul **aurait apporté** les provisions.	Les provisions **auraient été apportées par** Jean-Paul.

Translations of Functional Minidialogues

1. Identifying People and Things: Articles and Nouns

In the University District

Alex, an American student, is visiting the university with Mireille, a French student. MIREILLE: There's the library, the university bookstore, and the student cafeteria. And here's the café. ALEX: There's one student in the library and twenty students in the café . . . MIREILLE: Oh yes, the café is the center of university life!

2. Expressing Quantity: Plural Articles and Nouns

An Eccentric Professor

THE PROFESSOR: Here is the grading system: zero [points] for imbeciles, four for mediocre students, eight for geniuses, and ten for the professor. Are there any questions?

3. Expressing Actions: *-er* Verbs

Meeting of Friends at the Sorbonne
XAVIER: Hi, Françoise! Are you visiting the university? FRANÇOISE: Yes, we're admiring the library right now. This is Paul, from New York, and Mireille, a friend [of mine]. XAVIER: Hello, Paul. Do you speak French? PAUL: Yes, a little bit. XAVIER: Hello, Mireille. Are you a student here? MIREILLE: Oh, no. I work here.

4. Expressing Disagreement: Negation Using *ne... pas*

The End of a Friendship?
BERNARD: Things aren't great with Martine [and me]. She likes to dance, I don't like dancing. I like to go skiing, and she doesn't like sports. She's studying biology, and I don't like science . . . MARTINE: Things aren't great with Bernard [and me]. He doesn't like to dance, I like dancing. I don't like skiing, and he likes sports. He's a humanities student, and I don't like literature . . .

5. Identifying People and Things: *être*

Roger's Ingenuity
ROGER: Well, I'm ready to work! MARTINE: Me too, but where are the books and the dictionary? ROGER: Um . . . oh yeah, look, there they are. The dictionary is under the hat and the notebooks are on top of the jacket. Now we're ready. MARTINE: You know, Roger, you do very well in literature, but as far as organization is concerned, you're a zero! ROGER: Maybe, but chaos is a sign of genius!

6. Describing People and Things: Descriptive Adjectives

Computerized Dating Services
He is [should be] sociable, charming, serious, good-looking, idealistic, athletic . . . She is [should be] sociable, charming, serious, good-looking, idealistic, athletic . . . [COMPUTER]: They're hard to please!

7. Getting Information: Yes/No Questions

A Discussion Between Friends
TOURIST: Is this an accident? POLICE OFFICER: No, it's not an accident. TOURIST: Is it a demonstration? POLICE OFFICER: Of course not! TOURIST: So it's a fight? POLICE OFFICER: Not really. It's an animated discussion between friends.

8. Mentioning a Specific Place or Person: The Prepositions *à* and *de*

Pierre and Francine. Two Typical French Students
They live in the dormitory. They eat in the cafeteria. They play volleyball in the gym. On the weekend, they play cards with friends. They like talking about professors, the English exam, French literature class and university life.

9. Expressing Actions: *-ir* Verbs

Down with Chatter
FLORENCE: You know, Pierre is getting on my nerves. ARMAND: Why? FLORENCE: Well, because he always manages to monopolize the conversation, and besides, he doesn't think about what he's saying!

10. Expressing Possession and Sensations: *avoir*

Roommates
JEAN-PIERRE: You have a very pleasant room, and it seems quiet . . . MARIE-CLAUDE: Yes. I need lots of quiet in order to work. JEAN-PIERRE: Do you have a nice roommate? MARIE-CLAUDE: Yes, we're lucky: we both like tennis, quiet . . . and messiness!

11. Expressing the Absence of Something: Indefinite Articles in Negative Sentences

An Interesting Room
There's a lamp . . . but no lightbulb. There's a sink . . . but no mirror. There's a racket . . . but no ball. Patrick doesn't have any luck.

12. Getting Information: *où, quand, comment, pourquoi,* etc.

Yvette Is Looking for a Room to Rent
MME GÉRARD: What's your name? YVETTE: My name is Yvette Delorme. MME GÉRARD: Where are you from? YVETTE: I'm from Normandy. MME GÉRARD: Where are you studying? YVETTE: I'm studying at the Sorbonne. MME GÉRARD: What are you studying? YVETTE: I'm studying French literature. MME GÉRARD: Do you like music, shows, animals? YVETTE: Yes, but I don't have a radio, a television, or any animals. MME GÉRARD: How many friends do you have? YVETTE: A lot, but no visitors. MME GÉRARD: Young lady, you're perfect. When will you start renting the room? YVETTE: Right away, because I have to find a room today!

13. Expressing Possession: *mon, ton,* etc.

One's House as a Reflection of One's Personality
1. The house that looks strange and rich is called ____. 2. The house that looks agreeable is called ____. 3. The house that looks disorderly is called ____.

14. Talking About Your Plans and Destinations: *aller*

A Model Father

SIMON: Are we playing tennis this afternoon? STÉPHANE: No, I'm going to the zoo with Céline. SIMON: So [how about] tomorrow? STÉPHANE: I'm sorry, but tomorrow I'm going to take Sébastien to the dentist. SIMON: What a model father [you are]!

15. Expressing What You Are Doing or Making: *faire*

A Question of Organization

SANDRINE: Do you eat in the cafeteria, you and your roommate? MARION: No, Candice and I are very organized. She does the shopping and I cook. SANDRINE: And who does the dishes? MARION: The dishwasher, of course!

16. Expressing Actions: *-re* Verbs

Beauregard at the Restaurant

JILL: Do you hear that? GÉRARD: No. What is it? JILL: I hear a noise under the table. GENEVIÈVE: Oh, that! That's Beauregard . . . He's waiting for the chicken . . . and he doesn't like waiting . . .

17. Talking About Food and Drink: *-re* Verbs

At the restaurant

WAITER: What will you have, sir? Ma'am? JEAN-MICHEL: We'll have the veal with cream and the vegetables. WAITER: And what will you have to drink? JEAN-MICHEL: I'll have a beer, and for the lady, a bottle of mineral water, please.

18. Expressing Quantity: Partitive Articles

To Your Health!

Here is Vittel mineral water. Here is a French mineral water and [this is] an American mineral water. Here is [some] mineral water.

19. Giving Commands: The Imperative

The Enemy of a Good Meal

FRANÇOIS: Martine, pass me the salt, please . . . *[Martine passes the salad to François.]* FRANÇOIS: No, come on! Use your ears a little . . . I asked for the salt! MARTINE: François, be a dear—don't talk so loud. I can't hear the television . . .

20. Pointing Out People and Things: Demonstrative Adjectives

A Hard Choice

FERNAND: Good morning, ma'am. May I taste these cheeses? GROCERY CLERK: But of course, take your pick. FERNAND: Thank you very much. I'd like to taste a little of this Emmenthal and some of that cheese over there. That's Brie, isn't it? GROCERY CLERK: Yes, but it's not very ripe. Taste this Roquefort instead. It's excellent. So, are you ready to make a choice? FERNAND: Yes, give me some Emmenthal . . . there, that piece over there, and a little of this Roquefort, please.

21. Expressing Desire, Ability, and Obligation: *vouloir, pouvoir,* and *devoir*

Le Procope

MARIE-FRANCE: Would you like some coffee? CAROLE: No, thanks, I can't drink coffee. I have to be careful. I have an exam today. If I drink coffee, I'll be too nervous. PATRICK: I only drink coffee on the days when I have exams. It inspires me, the way it inspired Voltaire!

22. Asking About Choices: *quel...* ?

What Will You Have?

Which wine will you have? What kind of meat will you have? What vegetables will you have? What pastries will you have?

23. Describing People and Things: The Placement of Adjectives

La Tour d'Argent (The Silver Tower)

MARGUÉRITE: What a lovely restaurant! Look at the pretty tables and the big windows looking out on Notre-Dame. VINCENT: You know, we're in a great Parisian restaurant. Every dish is delicious here. MARGUÉRITE: Yes, but there's a little something missing. VINCENT: What's that? MARGUÉRITE: There aren't any prices on the menu!

24. Expressing Actions: *dormir* and Similar Verbs; *venir* and *tenir*

The Joys of Nature

JEAN-PIERRE: Where are you going to go on vacation this summer? MICHÈLE: This year we're set on going down to Spain. We want to camp out on the beach. The sea, the pines, the flowers smell so good in the summer! Come with us, it'll be fabulous! We're leaving August 2nd. JEAN-PIERRE: Um . . . sleeping under a tent . . . I don't like that [kind of thing] very much . . . ÉDOUARD: A tent? Out of the question! We sleep in the camper, it's much more comfortable that way.

25. Talking About the Past: The *passé composé* with *avoir*

At the Hotel

GUEST: Good morning, ma'am. I made a reservation for a room for two people. EMPLOYEE: Your name, please? GUEST: Bernard Meunier. EMPLOYEE: Hmm . . . yes, here you are. You asked for a room with a view of the sea, is that right? GUEST: Yes, that's right. EMPLOYEE: All right, then, please fill out this card.

26. Expressing How Long: *depuis, pendant*

A Question of Practice

MONIQUE: How long have you been entering competitions? FRANÇOISE: Since 1985. How about you: how long have you been windsurfing? MONIQUE: Only for the last two weeks! FRANÇOISE: I started eight years ago. Ever since I started windsurfing, I've been spending my vacations at the beach. MONIQUE: It's hard, but it's fabulous. Yesterday I was able to stay on the board for four minutes.

27. Expressing Observations and Beliefs: *voir* and *croire*

A Boat Ride

GISÈLE: You're not taking a sweater! RAOUL: I don't see why [I should]. It's such nice weather. GISÈLE: Didn't you see the fog come in yesterday afternoon? And according to Mr. Weather, on television . . . RAOUL: OK, fine. I believe Mr. Weather. But don't forget your compass. If it gets foggy . . .

28. Talking About the Past: The *passé composé* with *être*

A Car Accident

JEAN-FRANÇOIS:. . . well, just now, I got to the Magnan crossroads, and a truck ran the red light right in front of me. I couldn't get out of the way: I drove right into it. So the other driver and I got out of our cars and we . . . um . . . discussed the right of way . . . MICHÈLE: But, Jean-François, why haven't you left yet? JEAN-FRANÇOIS: Because the drivers behind us stayed to put their two cents in and then . . . there's a little traffic jam here now.

29. Expressing Location: Using Prepositions with Geographical Names

At the Charles de Gaulle–Roissy Airport

"Your attention, please! Immediate boarding for passengers in transit from Algiers, final destination Washington, Air France flight no. 82, with a stopover in Ottawa." MARYVONNE: There, that's for us. JEAN-LUC: Are you sure? MARYVONNE: Of course, she was just talking about us: we're en route from Africa, from Algeria; we've been in transit in France for a few hours and now we're leaving for North America; first Canada and then the United States!

30. Expressing Negation: Affirmative and Negative Adverbs

The High-speed Train

PATRICIA: I haven't ridden a high-speed train yet . . . Did you like it? FRÉDÉRIC: Yes, it's fabulous! It's very fast and comfortable. PATRICIA: You have to reserve a seat in advance, don't you? FRÉDÉRIC: Yes, because there are only seats [and no standing room] on the high-speed train, you can never get on without a reservation. But the reservation system is super-quick. You can reserve your seat [up to] three minutes before the train leaves!

31. Expressing Negation: Affirmative and Negative Pronouns

Coin-operated Luggage Lockers

SERGE: Is there something wrong? JEAN-PIERRE: Yes, I'm having trouble with the locker. SERGE: Oh, that! There's nothing more annoying [than that]! JEAN-PIERRE: Everyone always seems to find a locker that works, except me. SERGE: Look, someone is taking their luggage out of one of the lockers. There, you can be sure that one works. JEAN-PIERRE: Excellent idea!

32. Describing the Past: The *imparfait*

Poor Grandmother!

MME CHABOT: You see, when I was little, television didn't exist. CLÉMENT: So what did you do in the evenings? MME CHABOT: Well, we read, we chatted; our parents told us stories . . . CLÉMENT: Poor Grandma, it must have been sad not to be able to watch *Miami Vice* at night . . .

33. Speaking Succinctly: Direct Object Pronouns

Annick on the Telephone

"Pick up the receiver." There, I'm picking it up. "Insert a one-franc coin." I'm inserting it . . . fine. "Dial your number." What is it again? Oh. There it is. Hello? Hello? Hello? Darn. It doesn't work. Well, all right, I'll take my good news and send it by telegram.

34. Talking About the Past: Agreement of the Past Participle

Opinion of an American TV Watcher in France

REPORTER: Have you watched French television yet? AMERICAN: Yes, I watched it last night. REPORTER: Which shows did you like best? AMERICAN: That's hard to say . . . REPORTER: Don't you think it's very different from American TV? AMERICAN: Well . . . the programs I watched are rather similar . . . *Dallas, The Cosby Show* . . . That is, sure, they're different: they're in French!

35. Speaking Succinctly: Indirect Object Pronouns

Journalists for the Canard?

RÉGIS: Did you write to the journalists at the *Canard Enchaîné*? NICOLE: Yes, I wrote to them. RÉGIS: Have they answered you? NICOLE: Yes, they made an appointment with us for tomorrow. RÉGIS: Did they like our political cartoons? NICOLE: They haven't said anything to me [about that] yet: we'll see tomorrow!

36. Describing Past Events: The *passé composé* versus the *imparfait*

Back from France

ALAIN: Tell me, did you see a difference between the North and the South in France? FRANÇOISE: Oh, yes. In Roubaix [in northern France], the streets were very clean and busy, but people were only passing through them. JEAN-PIERRE: When we got to Marseille [in southern France], it seemed to us that people spent their lives in the street! FRANÇOISE: So we did what everyone else was doing . . . and we spent hours drinking pastis on café terraces and strolling along Canebière Avenue!

37. Speaking Succinctly: The Pronouns *y* and *en*

The Bookseller's Treasures

JEAN-MARC: Do you have any old stamps? I collect them. VÉRONIQUE: I found some very beautiful ones at a bookseller's stall on the Quai du Louvre. JEAN-MARC: Fantastic! Say . . . how do you get there? VÉRONIQUE: Take the metro. You take the Vincennes-Neuilly line toward Château de Vincennes and get off at the Louvre station. Cross Rivoli Street, go past the museum, and there you are. JEAN-MARC: That won't take long. I only hope your bookseller still has some old stamps. VÉRONIQUE: Oh, I think he will. He didn't have many, but . . . they were very, very expensive!

38. Saying What You Know: *savoir* and *connaître*

Labyrinth

MARCEL: Taxi! Are you familiar with Vaucouleurs Street? TAXI DRIVER: Of course I know where it is! I know Paris like the back of my hand [literally, pocket]! MARCEL: I don't know how you do it. I got lost yesterday in the Île de la Cité. TAXI DRIVER: I know my job; and besides, you know, with a map of Paris it's not that hard!

39. Emphasizing and Clarifying: Stressed Pronouns

After the Baccalaureate Exam

JEAN-PIERRE: How about you, Françoise, what are you going to do after the baccalaureate exam? FRANÇOISE: I don't know. I think about it a lot, but it seems so complicated! JEAN-PIERRE: My guidance counselor gave me a ton of brochures . . . it's discouraging! FRANÇOISE: My brother says that the important thing is to do something, to take risks, to do what you want . . . JEAN-PIERRE: Yes, but the problem is that I don't know yet what I want to do.

40. Expressing Actions: Pronominal Verbs

A Meeting

DENIS: Madeleine! How are you? VÉRONIQUE: You're making a mistake. My name is not Madeleine. DENIS: I'm sorry. I wonder . . . haven't I met you before . . . ? VÉRONIQUE: I don't remember having met you. But that doesn't matter . . . my name is Véronique. What's your name?

41. Giving Commands: Object Pronouns with the Imperative

Questioning Exams!

MARYSE: The necessity of exams . . . JACQUES: Don't [even] mention it! It's a myth. MARYSE: Tell me, what do you suggest instead? GILBERT: Yes, that's it, some suggestions: if you have any, let's talk about them! JACQUES: All right, listen to them . . . Haven't you ever heard of a student's record? I believe in [granting] degrees based on an examination of the records!

42. Saying *How* to Do Something: Adverbs

In Sociology Class

SABINE: I think that in France, the ideal of success is always "social achievement." PROFESSOR: Briefly analyze for us the relationship between this ideal of success and the French educational system. SABINE: One could say that it is due to this ideal that French education focuses primarily on the degree [obtained]. JÉRÔME: A degree, in France, is a way to move up the social ladder; the French believe deeply in an educated elite. PROFESSOR: Now tell me whether you think that this attitude is appreciably different in other countries. In the United States, for example . . .

43. Reporting Everyday Events: Pronominal Verbs (*continued*)

An Encounter

LAURENT: Are you leaving? PAULINE: Yes, it's nice out and I'm bored here. I'm going to take a walk along the lake. Will you come along? LAURENT: No, I can't, I have a lot of work. PAULINE: Oh, you're making too much of it. Come on, we'll go have some fun! LAURENT: Some other time. If I stop now, I won't have the courage to finish up later.

44. Expressing Reciprocal Actions: Pronominal Verbs

Love at First Sight [Lightning Bolt] They love each other!

45. Talking About the Past and Giving Commands: Pronominal Verbs

A Love Match

MARTINE: How did you meet each other? DENIS: We saw each other for the first time in Concarneau. VÉRONIQUE: Remember? It was raining, you came into the boutique where I worked and . . . DENIS: And it was love at first sight! We got married that same year.

46. Making Comparisons: The Comparative and Superlative of Adjectives

End-of-Month Problems

VÉRONIQUE: You know, Denis, our biggest expense right now is food. DENIS: Well then, let's buy everything at Carrefour—their prices are the best. VÉRONIQUE: We could also eat in less expensive restaurants. DENIS: All right. When you don't have enough money, you have no choice but to lead a simpler life.

47. Talking About the Future: The Future Tense

His Future

FATHER: He'll be a writer, he'll write novels, and we'll be famous. MOTHER: He'll be a businessman, he'll be the head of a company, and we'll be rich. CHILD: We'll see . . . I'll do what I can.

48. Linking Ideas: Relative Pronouns

Interviewing the Head of a Business

JOURNALIST: And why do you say that you studied for three years in vain? GENEVIÈVE: Well, because all that time, it was making jewelry that interested me. JOURNALIST: The jewelry you create is made out of natural materials? GENEVIÈVE: Yes. I also design costume jewelry for magazines, that people can make at home. JOURNALIST: Now, your business makes thousands of pieces of jewelry, three quarters of which go to Japan? GENEVIÈVE: Yes, and I have loads of new projects!

49. Getting Information: Interrogative Pronouns

At the Rugby Game

BILL: What are they trying to do? JEAN-PAUL: Well, they're trying to get the ball behind the goal line of the other team. BILL: Yes, I know, but what are they doing right now? JEAN-PAUL: This is called a scrummage. BILL: And what's a scrummage? JEAN-PAUL: That's when several players from each team are clustered around the ball. You see, one of the players got it. BILL: Which one? JEAN-PAUL: Philippot. BILL: What's keeping him from throwing it toward the goal? JEAN-PAUL: The rules of the game, buster! This is rugby! This is rugby; it's not American football.

50. Being Polite; Speculating: The Present Conditional

Fun Is Sometimes Exhausting

FRANÇOIS: What would you like to do today? VINCENT: If the weather was nice, we could go to the soccer game. FRANCINE: If we were free tonight, Paul and Yvette would like to take us out to dinner at Chez Marcel. VINCENT: If you had time, we could go to the movies and see a Western. FRANÇOIS: Don't you think it would be fabulous if we didn't do anything for a whole weekend?

51. Expressing Actions: Prepositions After Verbs

Going out to the Cabaret

CORINNE: Tonight we've decided to take you to the Contrescarpe cabaret in Montmartre. CHUCK: What is a cabaret? JACQUES: A cabaret is a kind of café where you can listen to ballads and satirical songs . . . CORINNE: Do you know Georges Brassens, Jacques Brel, and Barbara? JACQUES: It's because of the cabarets that they were able to make a name for themselves.

52. Making Comparisons: Adverbs and Nouns

Dancing, Disco, and Music Videos

DANNY: What do you usually do on the weekend? MARTINE: Most of the time, we go dancing in nightclubs. HENRI: Do you like disco? DANNY: I must admit that I have more records of country music than of disco . . . MARTINE: I just love the videos that they show there, as much as the music . . . HENRI: It's true, there was less atmosphere before music videos.

53. Expressing Attitudes: Regular Subjunctive Verbs

Vote for Françoise!

FRANÇOISE: So, you want me to run for the university council! SIMON: Yes, we wish the council would get over its inertia and that the delegates would realize what their political responsibilities are. FRANÇOISE: But I already ran without any luck last year. LUC: This year, Françoise, we want you to win. And we'll support you to the end.

54. Expressing Attitudes: Irregular Subjunctive Verbs

Former Minister of Women's Rights

JOURNALIST: They call you "the minister who made waves." Why is that? YVETTE ROUDY: That's because, when I was minister, I initiated a lot of campaigns for women's rights: ■ for birth control; I wanted women to be properly informed ■ against sexism: We didn't want advertising to be able to exploit the female body ■ for the feminization of professional titles: We didn't want there to be female careers and male careers, but careers for everyone! ■ for career counseling and training for women: We wanted women to know how to prepare for the careers of the future.

55. Expressing Wishes and Opinions: The Subjunctive

The Draft or Voluntary Military Service?

PATRICK FAURE (22): In my opinion, the draft is an anachronism in the nuclear age. GÉRARD BOURRELLY (36): It's possible that young people will become more interested in military service if it gives them professional training. FRANCIS CRÉPIN (25): We have to do away with obligatory military service and set up a career army. CHARLES PALLANCA (18): But if I was a volunteer, I would insist that the salary be at least 5,000 francs a month!

56. Expressing Emotion: The Subjunctive

Coming of Age at 18

For more than ten years, the French have legally come of age at 18. What do the following people think of this? JEAN-PIERRE (16): I'm sorry that legal age is not the age at which a person earns a living! ISABELLE (18): I'm happy that now I can vote, marry whom I please, and open a bank account. M. ANCELLIN (65): I doubt whether young people are mature enough not to let themselves be politically manipulated. MME GATET (51): I'm furious that they would pass such important legislation just to get some extra votes. M. ET MME CHABANNE (43 AND 40): We're afraid that this law will do a lot of harm to parent–child relations.

57. Talking About the Past: The Pluperfect

Mont-Saint-Michel Is Threatened

Sandrine, Marc, and Raymond, Canadian tourists, have just visited Mont-Saint-Michel. SANDRINE: We had never seen Mont-Saint Michel before. It's really splendid! MARC: But haven't they recently discovered that its ecological balance has been destroyed? RAYMOND: That's right. If nothing is done, Mont-Saint-Michel will no longer be an island by 1991. SANDRINE: A few years ago, the experts had already estimated the budget [needed] to save the site at a hundred million francs, I think. RAYMOND: That's a huge budget, but it is also one of the most often visited sites in the provinces.

58. Speculating: The Past Conditional

An Adventure in the Wilderness

MARC: If you hadn't forgotten the compass, we would never have gotten lost. YVETTE: But if I hadn't forgotten it, our hike would not have been so thrilling . . . MARC: You must mean that I wouldn't have caught a cold! YVETTE: Come on, Marc, think of what we would have missed: a day of hiking in the wilderness, the pleasure of using our common sense. That's better than TV, don't you think?

59. Talking About Quantity: Indefinite Adjectives and Pronouns

A Village Is Revived

BENOÎT: I haven't seen Marion and Clément for several months. Is everything all right with them? VINCENT: Yes, they're doing something fascinating with a few friends. BENOÎT: Do you mean that little abandoned village that they're all rebuilding? VINCENT: Yes, they've each bought a ruin in the village. Some of them are doing construction, others are doing gardening . . . BENOÎT: Every time I hear about them, I feel like dropping everything here and going to join them! VINCENT: First you should finish some of the handyman projects you started last year!

60. Linking Ideas: Conjunctions Used with the Subjunctive

French Islands Near Canada

MONIQUE: I'm going to visit my French cousins on St. Pierre and Miquelon before my vacation is over. GÉRARD: I don't know where that is . . . unless it's those islands south of Newfoundland. MONIQUE: That's it. Even though the islands are very small, there are more than five thousand French people there. BERNARD: And even though Cartier discovered them more than four hundred and forty years ago, they have stayed French territory up to now. French islands in the U.S.'s backyard [on the U.S.'s doorstep]!

61. Expressing Subjective Viewpoints: Alternatives to the Subjunctive

The Antilles, Myth and Reality

FRANCINE: For me, the Antilles are coral reefs, pre-Columbian archaeological sites, beaches of white sand . . . SYLVAIN: Still, you have to know that we don't just have sun to offer! VINCENT: Before you leave, you should visit a banana plantation, a rum distillery, and our very modern port. SYLVAIN: I hope you know that our standard of living here in Martinique is the highest in the Caribbean . . . FRANCINE: It's true, it's important to modernize. But I hope you'll be able to safeguard the beauty of your country.

Lexique français-anglais

This end vocabulary provides contexual meanings of French words used in this text. It does not include exact cognates or regular past participles if the infinitive is listed. Adjectives are listed in the masculine singular form, with irregular feminine endings or forms included in parentheses. An asterisk (*) indicates words beginning with an aspirate *h*. Active vocabulary is indicated by the number of the chapter in which it is first listed. The active vocabulary of the *Premier rendez-vous* is indicated by (0).

Abbreviations

ab. abbreviation
adj. adjective
adv. adverb
art. article
conj. conjunction
contr. contraction
excl. exclamation
fam. familiar or colloquial
f. feminine noun
gram. grammatical
inf. infinitive
int. interjection
inv. invariable
m. masculine noun
n. noun
inv. invariable
pl. plural
p.p. past participle
prep. preposition
pron. pronoun
Q. Quebec usage

à *prep.* to, at, in, with (1)
abandonné *adj.* abandoned
abandonner to leave; to abandon
abbaye *f.* abbey
Abidjan *m.* capital of the Ivory Coast
aboli *adj.* abolished
abolir to abolish (15)
abondance *f.* abundance
abondant *adj.* abundant
abonné: être abonné à to subscribe to
s'abonner à to take out a subscription to
abord: d'abord *adv.* first, at first (10); **tout d'abord** initially, in the first place
aboyer to bark
abri *m.* shelter, protection
abricot *m.* apricot
abrupt *adj.* steep, sheer; abrupt
absolument *adv.* absolutely; completely
absorber to absorb
s'abstenir de to refrain from
absurde *m.* the absurd; nonsense
académie *f.* academy; society of learned people
Acadie *f.* Acadia (17)
acadien(ne) *adj.* Acadian, Cajun (17)
accéder to reach, to attain
accélérer to speed up, to accelerate
accepter to accept; to agree to (4)
accès *m.* access; **donner accès à** to give access to
accessoire *adj.* secondary, incidental
accidentel(le) *adj.* accidental
accompagner to accompany
accomplir to accomplish
accord *m.* agreement; **d'accord** okay (1); **être d'accord** to agree; **se mettre d'accord** to come to an agreement
accorder to grant; to award
accroissement *m.* increase
ACCT *ab* of **Agence de coopération culturelle et technique**
accueil *m.* reception; welcome
accueillant *adj.* welcoming, friendly
accueillir to greet, to welcome; to accommodate
accumuler to accumulate
achat *m.* purchase (7)
acheminement *m.* transporting, conveying
acheter to buy (5)
acide *adj.* acid
acier *m.* steel
acquérir to acquire
acquis *p.p. of* **acquérir**
acrylique *adj.* acrylic
acte *m.* act; action
acteur (-trice) *m., f.* actor, actress
actif (-ive) *adj.* active; energetic
activer to activate
activité *f.* activity
actualité *f.* actuality; current event or situation
actuel(le) *adj.* present, contemporary
actuellement *adv.* at present
adapter to adapt; **s'adapter (à)** to adapt (to)
addition *f.* bill, check (6)
adhérent *m.* member
adieu *int.* good-bye
adjectif *m.* adjective
administratif (-ive) *adj.* administrative
administration *f.* government, management (11)
administrer to manage, govern
admirer to admire; to wonder at
adorer to adore, love (1)
adresse *f.* address (9)
adresser to address
adroit *adj.* skilled
adulte *m., f.* adult
adverbe *m.* adverb
adversaire *m.* adversary, opponent
adverse *adj.* contrary, opposite
aéré *adj.* airy, well-ventilated
aérien(ne) *adj.* aerial; **catastrophe** (*f.*) **aérienne** air disaster; **compagnie** (*f.*) **aérienne** airline company; **ligne** (*f.*) **aérienne** airline
aérobique *f.* aerobics
aéroport *m.* airport (8)
affaire *f.* business; affair; bargain; *pl.* personal effects; business; **chiffre** (*m.*) **d'affaires** turnover; **homme (femme) d'affaires** *m., f.* businessman (woman)
s'affamer to starve (oneself)
affichage *m.* posting up; billposting

affiche *f.* poster, placard (3)
affirmatif(-ive) *adj.* affirmative
affirmation *f.* assertion
affreux (-euse) *adj.* terrible (4)
afin *prep.*: **afin de** (+ *inf.*) in order to (17); **afin que** (+ *subject*) *conj.* so that (17)
africain *adj.* African
Afrique *f.* Africa
age *m.* age; **le moyen âge** the Middle Ages
âgé *adj.* old
agence *f.* agency; bureau; **agence de voyages** travel agency
agent(e) *m., f.* agent; **agent de police** policeman (13)
agglomération *f.* town, built-up area
agir to act (3); **s'agir de** to be a question of
agité *adj.* restless; troubled
agneau *m.* lamb; **navarin** (*m.*) **d'agneau** lamb stew
agréable *adj.* agreeable, pleasant (2)
agréer to accept; **veuillez agréer l'expression de mes sentiments distingués...** yours truly (*formal*)
agricole *adj.* agricultural (13)
agriculteur *m.* farmer, farm worker (13)
agronomique *adj.* agronomical
agrumes *m. pl.* citrus fruits
aide *f.* support, relief
aide-comptable *m.* accountant's assistant
aider to help (11)
aigle *m.* eagle
aigu *adj.* acute
ail *m.* garlic
aile *f.* wing
ailleurs: d'ailleurs *adv.* besides
ailloli *m.* garlic sauce
aimable *adj.* kind, amiable
aimer to like, love (1); **aimer bien** to be fond of; **aimer mieux** to prefer (1)
ainsi *adv.* thus, so; **ainsi que** *conj.* as well as
AIPLF *ab.* of **Association internationale des parlementaires de langue française**
air *m.* air, atmosphere; tune; **avoir l'air** to look, seem (3); **de plein air** *adj.* outdoors; **en plein air** in the open air; **l'hôtesse** (*f.*) **de l'air** flight attendant
ajouter to add
alcool *m.* alcohol
algèbre *f.* algebra (11)
Algérie *f.* Algeria (8)
algérien(ne) *adj.* Algerian
aliénant *adj.* alienating
aliment *m.* food
alimentaire *adj.* related to food
alimentation *f.* nourishment
alimenter to feed, sustain
Allemagne (de l'Est/Ouest) *f.* (East/West) Germany (8)
allemand *adj.* German (1)
aller to go (4); **aller** (+ *inf.*) to be going (*to do something*); **aller mal** to feel ill (4); **aller en cours** to go to class; **aller mieux** to feel better; **comment allez-vous?** how are you? **s'en aller** to go away (12); **aller-retour** *m.* round-trip
allergique *adj.* allergic
alliance *f.* wedding ring
allié *adj.* allied; *m., f.* ally
allô *int.* hello (*telephone*) (9)
allocation *f.* allowance
allumette *f.* match(stick)
alors *adj.* then; in that case (4)
Alpes *f. pl.* the Alps
alpinisme *m.* mountaineering (7)
alsacien(ne) *adj.* Alsatian
alternance *f.* alternation
altruiste *adj.* altruistic
aluminium *m.* aluminum
Amazone *f.* Amazon
ambassade *f.* embassy
ambiance *f.* atmosphere
ambitieux (-ieuse) *adj.* ambitious
ambitionner to strive after
âme *f.* soul
améliorer to improve
aménagé *adj.* fitted out; laid out
aménagement *m.* fitting-out; fixing-up
amener to lead, bring (a person) (17)
Amérique *f.* America; **Amérique latine/du Nord/du Sud** Latin/North/South America
ami(e) *m., f,* friend (1); **petit(e) ami(e)** *m., f.* boyfriend (girlfriend)
amical *adj.* friendly
amicalement: bien amicalement truly yours (*informal*)
amincir to thin (down)
amincissement *m.* thinning (down)
amitié *f.* friendship, affection
amour *m.* love (12); **amour fou** wild passion
amoureux (-euse) *adj.* in love, amorous (12); **tomber amoureux** to fall in love
amphithéâtre *m.* lecture hall, amphitheatre (1)
ampoule *f.* light bulb
amusant *adj.* entertaining, amusing (2)
amuser to entertain; **s'amuser** to have a good time (11)
an *m.* year (7); **le nouvel an** New Year's Day
anachronisme *m.* anachronism
analphabétisme *m.* illiteracy
analyste-programmeur (-euse) *m., f.* systems analyst
ancêtre *m., f.* ancestor (17)
ancien(ne) *adj.* former; old, ancient (6)
anesthésie *f.* anesthesia
angine *f.* tonsillitis
anglais *adj.* English, British
Angleterre *f.* England (8)
anglicisme *m.* Anglicism
anglophone *adj.* English-speaking (17)
animal *m.* (*pl.* **animaux**) animal, beast
animation *f.* (hustle and) bustle
animé *adj.* animated
animisme *m.* animism
année *f.* year (7)
anniversaire *m.* birthday; anniversary (9)
annonce *f.* advertisement, sign; **petites annonces** classified ads (9); **annonces classées** Q. want-ads
annoncer to announce
annuaire *m.* telephone directory (9)
annuel(le) *adj.* yearly, annual
anorak *m.* windbreaker, ski jacket (7)
Antarctique *m.* the Antarctic
antenne *f.* antenna, aerial
anthologie *f.* anthology
anti-âge *adj.* anti-aging
antillais *adj.* West Indian
Antilles *f. pl.* Antilles, West Indies (17); **la mer des Antilles** *f.* the Caribbean Sea (17); **les Petites Antilles** the Lesser Antilles
antinucléaire *adj.* antinuclear
antipathique *adj.* unpleasant
antipaludéen(ne) *adj.* anti-malarial (treatment)
antiquaire *m., f.* antique dealer
antique *adj.* ancient
antiquité *f.* antiquity
août *m.* August (3)
apaiser to pacify; to appease
apercevoir to perceive (16); **s'apercevoir de** to become aware of (16)
aperçu *p.p.* of **apercevoir**
apéritif *m.* aperitif (*before-dinner drink*)
apparaître to appear
appareil *m.* telephone; **qui est à l'appareil?** who is on the line? (9)
appareil-photo *m.* camera (16)
apparence *f.* appearance, aspect
apparenté *adj.* similar; **mot apparenté** cognate
appartement *m.* apartment (4)
appartenir (à) to belong (to)
appauvri *adj.* impoverished
appauvrissement *m.* impoverishment
appel *m.* (telephone) call
appeler to call; to name (9); **s'appeler** to be called, named (11); **comment vous appelez-vous?** what is your name? (0) **je m'appelle...** my name is . . . (0)
appétit *m.* appetite; **bon appétit!** have a good meal!; **couper l'appétit** to spoil one's appetite
appliqué: mathématiques (*f. pl.*) **appliquées** applied mathematics
apporter to bring; to supply (6)
apprécier to appreciate
apprendre to learn; to teach (5)
apprentissage *m.* apprenticeship (11)
appris *p.p.* of **apprendre**
approprié *adj.* appropriate

approuver to sanction, approve of
approximatif (-ive) *adj.* approximate
approximativement *adv.* approximately
après *prep.* after (4); **d'après** according to; **de l'après-midi** P.M., in the afternoon (5)
après-demain *adv.* the day after tomorrow
après-midi *m., f.* afternoon (4)
à-propos *m.* aptness
aquariophile *adj.* relating to aquariums
arabe *adj.* Arabic
Arabie *f.* Arabia; **Arabie Saoudite** Saudi Arabia
arbre *m.* tree (4); **arbre fruitier** fruit tree; **arbre généalogique** family tree
arc *m.* arch; bow; **tir** (*m.*) **à l'arc** archery
archéologique *adj.* archaeological
archéologue *m., f.* archaeologist
architecte *m., f.* architect (13)
ardennais *adj.* from Ardennes
arène *f.* arena (16)
argent *m.* money; silver (6); **argent de poche** pocket money; **argent liquide** cash (13)
Argentine *f.* Argentina
aride *adj.* dry, arid
arme *f.* arm, weapon
armé *adj.* armed; **les forces** (*f.*) **armées** the armed forces
armée *f.* army
armoire *f.* armoire, wardrobe
arracher to tear out
arranger to fix, put right; to sort out
arrestation *f.* arrest
arrêt *m.* stop, pause
arrêter to stop (*someone, something*); **s'arrêter** to stop (oneself) (11)
arrière *m.* rear, back; **en arrière de** *prep.* behind
arrière-grand-parent *m.* great grandparent
arrière-pays *m.* hinterland
arrivée *f.* arrival, landing (8)
arriver to arrive, reach (2); **arriver (à)** to manage; to succeed (in); **qu'est-ce qui est arrivé (à)** what happened (to)
arrondissement *m.* district, ward (in Paris) (10)
arroser to soak, water, spray
art: art dramatique *m.* dramatic arts (11); **arts martiaux** martial arts: **les beaux-arts** fine arts; **œuvre d'art** *f.* work of art (16)
artichaut *m.* artichoke
article *m. gram.*: **article défini** definite article; **article indéfini** indefinite article
artificiel(le) *adj.* artificial
artisan(e) *m., f.* craftsperson (13)
artiste *m., f.* artist; **artiste peintre** painter (13)
artistique *adj.* artistic
ascenseur *m.* elevator
ascension *f.* ascent
Asie *f.* Asia
aspect *m.* look, appearance; aspect
aspirer to aspire to; to desire
aspirine *f.* aspirin
assassinat *m.* murder, assassination
assemblée *f.* assembly, meeting; **l'Assemblée nationale** one of the two houses of the French parliament
assembler to gather
asseoir to seat; **s'asseoir** to sit down; **asseyez-vous (assieds-toi)** sit down (12)
asservir to enslave
assez *adv.* rather (2); **assez (de)** enough (of) (5); **assez peu** not very much
assiette *f.* plate (5)
assis *adj.* seated
assister à to attend (11)
associatif: la vie associative community life
associer to associate; **s'associer** to join together
assumer to assume
assurance *f.* insurance; **assurance-automobile** *f.* car insurance; **assurance-vie** *f.* life insurance
assurer to assure; to guarantee; to insure
assureur *m.* insurance agent (13)
astéroïde *m.* asteroid
astrologie *f.* astrology
astrologique *adj.* astrological
astrologue *m., f.* astrologer
astronome *m.* astronomer
astronomie *f.* astronomy
atelier *m.* studio, workshop (14)
Athènes Athens
athlète *m., f.* athlete
Atlantique *m.* Atlantic Ocean
atmosphère *f.* atmosphere (15)
attacher to bind; to attach
attaque *f.* attack; **contre-attaque** *f.* counter-attack
attaquer to attack
atteindre to attain; to reach
attendre to wait (for) (4)
attente: salle (*f.*) **d'attente** waiting room
attentif (-ive) *adj.* attentive, considerate
attention *f.* attention; *int.* look out!
attentivement *adv.* attentively, carefully
attirer to attract
attrait *m.* appeal, attraction
attraper to catch
attribuer to award, grant, assign
au *contr.* of **à le**
auberge *f.* inn; **auberge de jeunesse** youth hostel
aucun: ne... aucun *adj., pron.* no, no one, not any
audacieux (-ieuse) *adj.* audacious, daring
augmentation *f.* increase
augmenter to raise, augment
aujourd'hui *adv.* today (0)
AUPELF *ab.* of **Association des universités partiellement ou entièrement de langue française**
auprès de *adv.* near; close to, by
auquel *contr.* of **à lequel**
au revoir good-bye
ausculter to examine with a stethoscope
aussi *adv.* also (2); **aussi... que** as . . . as (12)
aussitôt: aussitôt que as soon as (13)
autant *adv.* much, many; **autant de** as much (many) (14); **autant que** as much (many) as (14)
auteur *m.* author, creator
authenticité *f.* authenticity
authentique *adj.* authentic, genuine
autobiographie *f.* autobiography
autobus *m.* bus (4)
autocar *m.* coach, bus
autographe *m.* autograph
automatique *adj.* automatic; **distributeur** (*m.*) **automatique** automatic teller; **distributeur** (*m.*) **automatique de billets** cash dispenser, ATM
automne *m.* autumn (5)
automobiliste *m., f.* motorist, driver
autonomie *f.* autonomy
autorisé *adj.* authorized
autoroute *f.* highway, freeway (8)
auto-stop *m.* hitchhiking
autour (de) *prep.* around (14)
autre *adj.* other (3); **autre chose** something else, anything else
autrefois *adv.* formerly, in the past (10)
Autriche *f.* Austria
aux *contr.* of **à les**
auxiliaire *adj.* auxiliary, secondary
avaler to swallow
avance *f.* advance; **à l'avance** in advance; **en avance** early, beforehand
avant (de) *prep.* before (14); **avant que** *conj.* before (17); **avant-hier** *adv.* the day before yesterday (7)
avantage *m.* advantage
avare *adj.* stingy
avec *prep.* with (1)
avenir *m.* the future (13); **à l'avenir** in the future, from now on (13)
aventure *f.* adventure
aventureux (-euse) *m., f.* adventurous
aviateur(-trice) *m., f.* pilot
avion *m.* airplane (8)
avis *m.* opinion; **à mon avis** in my opinion (8); **changer d'avis** to change one's mind
avocat(e) *m., f.* lawyer, counsel (13)
avoir to have (3); **avoir besoin de** to need (3); **avoir chaud** to be hot (3); **avoir confiance en** to have confidence in; **avoir de bonnes (mauvaises) manières** to have good (bad) manners; **avoir de la chance** to be lucky (3); **avoir des ennuis** to have problems; **avoir... ans**

to be . . . years old (3); **avoir envie (de)** to want (to) (3); **avoir faim** to be hungry (3); **avoir froid** to be cold (3); **avoir honte** to be ashamed; **avoir l'air de** to look, appear (3); **avoir lieu** to take place (16); **avoir mal** to have (a) pain (12); **avoir l'occasion** to have the chance, opportunity (16); **avoir peur** to be afraid (3); **avoir raison** to be right (3); **avoir soif** to be thirsty (3); **avoir sommeil** to be sleepy (3); **avoir tort** to be wrong (3)
avouer to confess, admit
avril *m.* April (3)
azur *adj.* azure; **Côte** (*f.*) **d'Azur** French Riviera (7)

bac(calauréat) *m.* French secondary school program of study; examination for university admission; diploma required for university admission (11)
bacchante *f.* bacchante
bachelier (-ière) *m., f.* person who has passed the *baccalauréat*
bachotage *m.* cramming
bactriane: chameau (*m.*) **bactriane** bactrian camel
badaud: en badaud as an onlooker; gawking
bagage(s) *m. pl.* baggage
bagagerie *f.* bags, luggage
bague *f.* ring
baguette (de pain) *f.* loaf of French bread (6)
baignade *f.* bathing, swimming
baigner to bathe; **se baigner** to go swimming (12)
bain *m.* bath; **maillot** (*m.*) **de bain** (*woman's*) swimsuit (7); **salle** (*f.*) **de bains** bathroom (4); **slip** (*m.*) **de bain** (*man's*) swimsuit (7)
bal: bal masqué masked ball (17)
baladeur *m.* walkman
Balance *f.* Libra
balcon *m.* balcony
baleine *f.* whale; **baleine à bosse** humpback whale
balle *f.* ball
ballon *m.* balloon, ball (*football, soccer*)
balnéaire *adj.* related to bathing, swimming
banal *adj.* ordinary, common
banalité *f.* banality
banane *f.* banana
bananeraie *f.* banana plantation
bancaire *adj.* banking; **carte bancaire** bank (ATM) card
bande: bande dessinée *f.* comic strip
bander to bandage
banlieue *f.* suburb (10)
banque *f.* bank (10)
banquier (-ière) *m., f.* banker (13)
bantou *m.* Bantu (language family)
baptiser to baptize
barbare *adj.* barbarian
barré: chèque (*m.*) **barré** crossed check (*British*)
barrière *f.* barrier
bas (basse) *adj.* low; **à bas** down with; **là-bas** over there; **les Pays-Bas** the Netherlands
bassin *m.* pond
bateau (à voile) *m.* (sail)boat (7); **bateau-mouche** passenger riverboat; **faire du bateau** to go boating
bâtiment *m.* building
bâtir to build (16)
bâton: bâton (*m.*) **de craie** stick of chalk
battre to beat; **se battre** to fight
battu *p.p.* of **battre**
bavard *adj.* talkative
bavardage *m.* chatter; gossip
bavarder to chat; to gossip
bavarois *adj.* Bavarian
bavette *f.* bib; cut of sirloin
Bd. *ab.* of **boulevard**
beau (bel, belle) *adj.* beautiful (3); **beaux-arts** (*m. pl.*) fine arts (11); **il fait beau** it's nice out
beaucoup *adv.* very much, a lot (0); many
beauté *f.* beauty (16)
bébé *m.* baby
belge *adj.* Belgian
Belgique *f.* Belgium (8)
bélier *m.* ram; **Bélier** Aries
bénéficier to profit, benefit
bénin (-igne) *adj.* mild; minor
berger (-ère) *m., f.* shepherd
Berne Bern
besoin *m.* need; **avoir besoin de** to need; to want (3)
beurre *m.* butter (5)
bibliothèque *f.* library (1)
bicentenaire *m.* bicentennial
bicyclette *f.* bicycle (7); **faire de la bicyclette** to go bicycling
bien *m.* property; *adv.* well, very (14); completely; **aimer bien** to be fond of; **bien que** *conj.* although (17); **bien sûr** of course (5); **eh bien!** well! now then! (17); **ou bien** or, or else; **vouloir bien** to be willing
bien-être *m.* well-being, comfort
bienfaisant *adj.* beneficial
biens *m. pl.* property, possessions
bientôt *adv.* soon; **à bientôt** see you soon (4)
bienvenue *f.* welcome
bière *f.* beer
bifteck *m.* steak (5)
bijou *m.* jewel
bilan *m.* assessment; **bilan de santé** checkup; **faire le bilan de** to take stock of
bilingue *adj.* bilingual
bilinguisme *m.* bilingualism
billet *m.* ticket (8); bill (*currency*) (6); **distributeur** (*m.*) **automatique de billets** cash dispenser, ATM
biographie *f.* biography
biologie *f.* biology (1)
biologique *adj.* biological
bise *f. fam.* kiss
bistro(t) *m.* café; bar
bitume *m.* asphalt
blague *f.* joke; trick
blanc (blanche) *adj.* white (2)
blasé *adj.* indifferent
blé *m.* corn, wheat
blesser to wound; to hurt
bleu *adj.* blue (2); (*meat*) underdone, rare; **Carte Bleue** Visa card
bloc *m.* block
blouson *m.* windbreaker (*jacket*) (2)
bœuf *m.* beef; **bœuf bourguignon** beef stewed in red wine
boire to drink (5)
bois *m.* forest, woods (10)
boisson *f.* drink (5)
boîte *f.* box, can (6); **boîte aux lettres** mailbox (9); **boîte de nuit** nightclub; **boîte de conserve** can (of food) (6); **boîte postale** post office box
bol *m.* bowl (5)
bon(ne) *adj.* good (6); **bon appétit!** have a good meal!; **bon courage** keep your chin up; **bon marché** *inv.* cheap, inexpensive (6); **bonne chance!** good luck!; **bonne route!** have a safe journey!
bonheur *m.* happiness; prosperity
bonhomme: bonhomme de neige *m.* snowman (17)
bonjour *int.* hello, good day (0)
bonsoir *int.* good night, good evening
bord *m.* edge, shore; **au bord de la mer** at the seaside
bordé *adj.* bordered, lined, edged
bordure *f.* border, edge
bosse: baleine (*f.*) **à bosse** humpback whale
botanique *f.* botany
botte *f.* boot (2)
boucanier *m.* buccaneer
bouche *f.* mouth (12)
boucherie *f.* butcher shop (6)
bouger to stir, budge
bouillabaisse *f.* fish soup
bouillir to boil
boulangerie *f.* bakery (6)
boule *f.* ball, bowl, bead; *pl.* bocce ball
bouleverser to turn upside down, disrupt
bouliste *m.* bocce ball player
boulot *m. fam.* job, work
bouquiniste *m.* used-book dealer
bourgeois *m.* middle-class person
Bourgogne *f.* Burgundy region (of France)

bourguignon(ne) *adj.* Burgundian; **bœuf bourguignon** beef stewed in red wine
bourse *f.* scholarship; stock exchange
boussole *f.* compass
bout *m.* end
bouteille *f.* bottle (5)
boutique *f.* shop
bouton m. button
boxe *f.* boxing
BP *ab.* of **boîte postale** post office box
braise *f.* live charcoal
brandade: brandade (*f.*) **de morue** dish made with cod
bras *m.* arm (12)
break *m.* station wagon
bref (brève) *adj.* brief, short (11); *adv.* in a word
Brésil *m.* Brazil (8)
Bretagne *f.* Brittany; **Grande-Bretagne** Great Britain
breton(ne) *adj.* from Brittany
brevet *m.* diploma, certificate
bricolage *m.* do-it-yourself work, puttering around (14)
bricoler to do odd jobs, tinker
brie *m.* Brie cheese
brièvement *adv.* briefly (11)
brillant *adj.* brilliant, bright
brique: en briques made out of bricks
britannique *adj.* British
brochette *f.* skewer; kabab
broder to embroider; to embellish
bronzer to tan
brosse *f.* brush; **brosse à dents** toothbrush
brosser to brush; **se brosser les...** to brush (*one's hair, teeth, etc.*) (12)
brouillard *m.* fog, mist
brousse: en brousse in the bush; in the middle of nowhere
bruit *m.* noise (10)
brûlé *adj.* burned
brun *adj.* brown
brut *adj.* rough, crude; gross; **produit** (*m.*) **intérieur brut** gross national product
Bruxelles Brussels
bruyant *adj.* noisy, boisterous
BTS *ab.* of **brevet de technicien supérieur**
bu *p.p.* of **boire**
bûcheron *m.* woodcutter, lumberjack
Bulgarie *f.* Bulgaria
bulle *f.* bubble; blister; balloon
bulletin *m.* registration form; voting paper
bureau *m.* office; desk (0); **bureau de change** (foreign) exchange office
but *m.* mark, objective, goal
butin *m.* plunder, loot

ça *pron.* it; that (6); **ça va?** (*informal*) how are you? (0); **ça va bien** (*informal*) fine (0); **comme ci, comme ça** so-so
cabaret *m.* public house, nightclub
cabillaud *m.* (fresh) cod
cabine *f.* cabin; **cabine téléphonique** telephone booth (9)
cabinet *m.* office; (doctor's) consulting room
câble *m.* cable
cacao *m.* cocoa
cacher to hide
cadeau *m.* gift (9)
cadre *m.* manager (13); context, scope; *pl.* management; **cadre moyen** middle manager; **cadre supérieur** executive
café *m.* coffee; café (1); **café en mazagran** Arabic coffee; **café liégeois** coffee ice cream with whipped cream; **café-tabac** (*m.*) bar–tobacco shop (10)
cafétéria *f.* cafeteria
cafetier *m.* café owner
cahier *m.* notebook (0)
caille *f.* quail
caisse *f.* cash register (13)
caissier (-ière) *m., f.* cashier (13)
calanque *f.* rocky inlet
calcaire *adj.* chalky
calcul *m.* arithmetic (11); **calcul infinitésimal** calculus
calculatrice *f.* calculator
calculer to calculate; **machine à calculer** adding machine
calèche *f.* barouche, four-wheeled carriage
calendrier *m.* calendar
calice *m.* chalice
Californie *f.* California
californien(ne) *adj.* Californian
calme *m.* calm, stillness (2)
calmement *adv.* calmly
camarade *m., f.* friend; companion; **camarade de chambre** roommate (3); **camarade de classe** classmate
camembert *m.* Camembert cheese
caméra *f.* camera
Cameroun *m.* Cameroon
camion *m.* truck (8)
campagne *f.* countryside, the country (7)
campement *m.* encampment
camper to camp (7)
campeur (-euse) *m., f.* camper
camping: faire du camping to go camping (7)
canadien(ne) *adj.* Canadian (2)
canal *m.* canal; channel
canapé *m.* sofa (3)
canard *m.* duck
candidat(e) *m., f.* candidate; applicant
candidature *f.* candidacy; application
canne à sucre *f.* sugarcane
cantatrice *f.* (professional) singer
capacité *f.* capacity
capitalisme *m.* capitalism
capricieux (-ieuse) *adj.* capricious
car *conj.* for, because
caractère *m.* character
caractériser to characterize; to distinguish; **se caractériser par** to be distinguished by
caractéristique *f.* characteristic
carafe *f.* decanter (5)
Caraïbes: les Caraïbes the Caribbean; **mer des Caraïbes** *f.* Caribbean Sea (17)
caravane *f.* trailer
carbone *m.* carbon
carburateur *m.* carburator
Carcassone capital of Aude in S. France
caricaturiste *m., f.* caricaturist, cartoonist
Carnaval *m.* Carnival, Mardi Gras (17)
carnet *m.* notebook; book of *métro* tickets; **carnet de chèques** checkbook (13)
carotte *f.* carrot (5)
carré *adj.* square
carrefour *m.* crossroads
carrière *f.* career
carriériste *adj.* careerist
carte *f.* menu (6); map (10); **carte bancaire** bank (ATM) card; **Carte Bleue** Visa card; **carte de crédit** credit card (7); **carte d'embarquement** boarding pass (8); **carte de Noël** Christmas card; **carte d'étudiant** student ID card; **carte d'identité** ID card; **carte postale** postcard (9); **jouer aux cartes** to play cards
cartouche *f.* cartouche; cartridge; cigarette carton
cas *m.* case, instance; **en cas de** in case of, in the event of; **en tout cas** in any case, however; **selon le cas** as the case may be
cascade *f.* waterfall
case *f.* space; compartment
casier *m.* compartment, drawer, locker
cassé *adj.* broken
casse-croûte *m.* snack
casse-tête *m.* puzzle
cassoulet *m.* casserole dish of S.W. France
catalyseur *m.* catalyst
catastrophe *f.* catastrophe; **catastrophe aérienne** air disaster
catégorie *f.* category
cathédrale *f.* cathedral (16)
catholicisme *m.* (Roman) Catholicism
catholique *adj.* (Roman) Catholic
cause *f.* cause; **à cause de** because of
cavalier *m.* horseman
caverne *f.* cave
ce (cet, cette, ces) *adj.* this; **ce** *pron.* it; **ce que** what (17); **ce qui** what, that (17); **c'est** it (that) is (0); **c'est-à-dire** that is to say (16)
CECA *ab.* of **Communauté européenne de charbon et de l'acier**
ceci *pron.* this (16)
céder to give up, give away; to give in
cédille *f.* cedilla

CEE *ab.* of **Communauté économique européenne**
cela *pron.* that (6)
célèbre *adj.* famous
célébrer to celebrate
célébrité *f.* celebrity
céleri *m.* celery
célibat *m.* single life; celibacy
célibataire *adj.* unmarried
celui (celle) *pron.* the one; **celui-ci** this one; **celui-là** that one
cellule *f.* cell; unit
celtique *adj.* Celtic
cent *m.* one hundred; **pour cent** percent
centaine *f.* about a hundred
centenaire *m., f.* centenarian
centime *m.* one hundredth of a franc (*coin*) (6)
centrafricain *adj.* of the Central African Republic
centrale nucléaire *f.* nuclear power plant
centre *m.* center; **centre-ville** *m.* downtown (10)
cercle *m.* circle
cercler to circle
céréale *f.* cereal
cérémonie *f.* ceremony
cerise *f.* cherry
certain *adj.* positive, certain (11)
certificat *m.* certificate, diploma
certitude *f.* certainty
cerveau *m.* brain; **lavage** (*m.*) **de cerveau** brainwashing
ces *adj.* these, those
cesse: sans cesse unceasingly
cesser to cease, stop
ceux (celles) *pron.* those, these; **ceux-ci** the latter; **ceux-là** the former
CFA *ab.* of **Communauté financière africaine**
chacun(e) *pron.* each one (8)
chaîne *f.* channel (*TV*) (9); **chaîne stéréo** stereo system (3)
chaise *f.* chair (0)
chalet *m.* chalet, summer cottage
chaleureux (-euse) *adj.* warm, cordial
chambre *f.* room, bedroom (3); **camarade** (*m., f.*) **de chambre** roommate; **chambre à deux lits** room with two beds (7); **Chambre de commerce** Chamber of Commerce; **chambre meublée** furnished room; **chambre pour deux personnes** double room (7); **musique de chambre** chamber music
chameau *m.* camel; **chameau de bactriane** bactrian camel
champ *m.* field (16)
champignon *m.* mushroom
chance *f.* luck, fortune; **avoir de la chance** to be lucky (3); **bonne chance!** good luck!
chandail *m.* sweater
change: bureau (*m.*) **de change** (foreign) exchange office
changement *m.* variation, change
changer (de) to change (4); to exchange; **changer d'avis** to change one's mind
chanson *f.* song; **chanson de variété** popular song (14)
chanter to sing (9)
chanteur (-euse) *m., f.* singer (13)
chapeau *m.* hat (2)
chapelle *f.* chapel
chaque *adj.* each, every (3)
char *m.* wagon, cart, tank (17)
charbon *m.* coal
charcuterie *f.* pork butcher's shop, delicatessen (6)
charge: à la charge de chargeable to, supported by; **prendre en charge** to take care of
chargé de *adj.* charged with
chargement *m.* loading
charmant *adj.* charming, delightful
charme *m.* charm
charrette *f.* cart, barrow
charrier to carry; to cart (along)
chasse *f.* hunting (16)
chasser to hunt; to chase
chasseur (-euse) *m., f.* hunter
chat *m.* cat (3)
châtain *adj.* chestnut brown *(hair)* (3)
château *m.* castle, mansion, palace (10)
châtelain(e) *m., f.* owner of an estate
chaud *adj.* hot, warm; **il fait chaud** it's hot (weather) (5)
chauffeur *m.* driver
chaumine *f.* little cottage
chaussée: rez-de-chaussée *m.* ground floor
chaussette *f.* sock (2)
chaussure *f.* shoe (2)
chauve *adv.* bald
chef *m.* leader, head; chef; **chef d'entreprise** company manager; **chef de l'État** head of state; **rédacteur (-trice)** (*m., f.*) **en chef** editor in chief; **terrine** (*f.*) **du chef** chef's special pâté
chef-d'œuvre *m.* masterpiece (16)
chemin *m.* road, way (10); **chemin de fer** railroad
chemise *f.* shirt (2)
chemisier *m.* blouse (2)
chêne *m.* oak
chèque *m.* check (13); **chèque bancaire** check; **chèque barré** crossed check (*British*); **chèque de voyage** traveler's check (7)
cher (chère) *adj.* expensive, dear (2)
chercher to look for (1); **chercher à** to try to
cheval *m.* (*pl.* **chevaux**) horse
chevalier *m.* knight
cheveux *m. pl.* hair (3)
cheville *f.* ankle
chèvre *f.* goat
chez *prep.* at the house of (4); **chez nous** in our country; **chez soi** at home; **chez vous** where you live
chien *m.* dog (3)
chiffre *m.* number, digit; **chiffre d'affaires** turnover
chimie *f.* chemistry (1)
chimique *adj.* chemistry
Chine *f.* China (8)
chinois *adj.* Chinese (1)
chirurgien(ne) *m., f.* surgeon
choc *m.* shock
chocolat *m.* chocolate (5); **chocolat liégeois** chocolate ice cream with whipped cream
choisir to choose (3)
choix *m.* choice (3)
choléra *m.* cholera
chômage *m.* unemployment (15)
choquant *adj.* offensive
chose *f.* thing (7); **c'est autre chose** that's another matter (altogether); **pas grand-chose** not much; **quelque chose** something
chou *m.* cabbage; **chou-fleur** (*m.*) cauliflower
choucroute *f.* sauerkraut
chouette *adj. fam.* neat, great
christianisme *m.* Christianity
chronique *f.* chronicle
chronologique *adj.* chronological
chute *f.* fall; waterfall
ci-dessous *adv.* below
ci-dessus *adv.* above
cidre *m.* cider
ciel *m.* sky, heavens; **gratte-ciel** (*m., inv.*) skyscraper
ciment *m.* cement
cinéaste *m., f.* film producer, filmmaker
ciné-club *m.* film club
cinéma *m.* cinema, movies (1)
cinq *adj.* five (0)
cinquante *adj. inv.* fifty (0)
cinquième *adj.* fifth (10)
circonflexe *m.* circumflex
circonlocution *f.* circumlocution
circonstance *f.* circumstance
circuit *m.* tour, (round) trip
circulation *f.* traffic
cire *f.* wax
citadin(e) *m., f.* citizen, city dweller
cité *f.* city; **la Cité** historical center of Paris; **cité universitaire** university living quarters, dormitory (1)
citer to cite, name; to quote
citoyen(ne) *m., f.* citizen (15)
citron *m.* lemon
civet *m.* stew
civil *m.* civilian; **génie** (*m.*) **civil** civil engineering
civique *adj.* civic
clair *adj.* clear, light
classe *f.* class; **camarade de classe** classmate; **classe d'affaires** business

class (8); **classe économique** tourist class (8); **en classe** at school
classer to classify, sort
classique *adj.* classical (16)
clavier *m.* keyboard (9)
clé: mot-clé *m.* key word
clef *f. adj., inv.* key
clergé *m.* clergy
climat *m.* climate
climatisation *f.* air conditioning
climatisé *adj.* air-conditioned
clin: clin (*m.*) **d'œil** wink
clinique *f.* clinic
club: ciné-club *m.* film club
coco: noix (*f.*) **de coco** coconut
cocoteraie *f.* coconut plantation
code *m.* code; **code postal** zip code
codé *adj.* coded; scrambled to non-subscribers (*cable TV channel*)
CODOFIL *ab.* of **Conseil pour le développement du français en Louisiane**
cœur *m.* heart; **courrier du cœur** lonely hearts column
coffre *m.* trunk, chest
cohabiter to live together
coiffeur (**-euse**) *m., f.* hairdresser
coin *m.* corner (10)
coincé *adj.* wedged, jammed, stuck
colère *f.* anger; **se mettre en colère** to get angry
collaborateur (**-trice**) *m., f.* colleague
collation *f.* light meal
collectionner to collect (14)
collectionneur (**-euse**) *m., f.* collector
collectivité *f.* group
collège *m.* first cycle of French secondary school (11)
coller to glue, paste
colline *f.* hill
colloque *m.* colloquium
colmater to seal off, plug
colombe *f.* dove
Colombie *f.* Columbia
colon *m.* colonist, settler (17)
colonie *f.* colony; **colonie de vacances** summer camp
colonisateur (**-trice**) *m., f.* colonizer
colonisation *f.* colonization
coloniser to colonize (17)
colonne *f.* column, row
combat *m.* fight, battle
combattre to combat, fight
combien *adv.* how much, how many (0)
combinaison *f.* combination
combiné *m.* telephone receiver
combiner to combine
comédie *f.* comedy, theater
comique *adj.* comical
commander to order (a meal) (5)
comme *adv.* as, like, how (7); *conj.* because, since (11); **comme ci, comme ça** so-so; **comme d'habitude** as usual
commémorer to commemorate
commencer to begin (10)
comment *adv.* how (0); **comment?** what? (3); **comment allez-vous?** how are you? (0); **comment vous appelez-vous?** what is your name? (0)
commentaire *m.* commentary
commenter to comment on
commerçant(e) *m., f.* merchant, storekeeper (13)
commerce *m.* business, trade (11); **Chambre de commerce** Chamber of Commerce; **faire du commerce (avec)** to trade (with)
commettre to commit
commissaire *m.* superintendent
commissariat *m.* police station (10)
commode *f.* chest of drawers (3)
commun *adj.* common; **en commun** in common; **Marché commun** Common Market
communauté *f.* community
communicatif (**-ive**) *adj.* communicative, talkative
communiquer to communicate
compagnie *f.* company; **compagnie aérienne** airline company
compagnon *m.* companion
comparaison *f.* comparison
comparer to compare
compartiment *m.* (train) compartment (8)
compétent *adj.* competent, qualified
compétition *f.* competition
complément *m.* complement; compliment; **complément d'objet** object (*of verb*)
complémentaire *adj.* complementary
complet *m.* suit; *adj.* (**complète** *f.*) full, complete; **riz** (*m.*) **complet** brown rice
complètement *adv.* completely
compléter to complete
complexe: complexe (*m.*) **d'infériorité** inferiority complex
compliquer to complicate
comportement *m.* behavior
composé *adj.* compound; **passé composé** present perfect tense
composer to compose, make up; **composer le numéro** to dial the number (9)
composter to date; to cancel
compote *f.* stewed fruit
compréhensif (**-ive**) *adj.* understanding
compréhension *f.* comprehension
comprendre to understand (5)
comprimé *m.* tablet (*pharmaceutical*)
compris *p.p.* of **comprendre;** *adj.* included
comptabilité *f.* bookkeeping (11)
comptable *m., f.* accountant (13); **aide-comptable** (*m.*) accountant's assistant; **expert-comptable** (*m.*) certified public accountant
compte *m.* account (13); **compte courant** checking account (13); **compte d'épargne** savings account (13); **prendre en compte** to take into account
compter to count
comptoir *m.* counter
concerner to concern, regard
concierge *m., f.* caretaker
Conciergerie *f.* chateau that houses the Palace of Justice in Paris
concilier to reconcile
conclure to conclude
conclu *p.p.* of **conclure**
concours *m.* competitive examination
conçu *adj.* conceived, designed, planned
concurrence *f.* competition
condamnation *f.* sentencing
condamné *adj.* sentenced, condemned
condition condition; **à condition que** *conj.* on condition that (17)
conditionnel *m.* conditional tense
conducteur (**-trice**) *m., f.* conductor, driver (8)
conduire to drive (8); **permis** (*m.*) **de conduire** driver's license
conduite *f.* running, management; driving
confectionné *adj.* prepared
conférence *f.* conference, lecture (11)
conférencier (**-ière**) *m., f.* speaker, lecturer
confiance *f.* confidence, trust; **avoir confiance en** to have confidence in; **faire confiance** (**à**) to trust (in)
confier to confide, entrust
confit: confit (*m.*) **de lapin** potted rabbit
confiture *f.* preserve, jam
conflit *m.* conflict (15)
conformisme *m.* conformity
conformiste *adj.* conformist (2)
confort *m.* comfort
confortable *adj.* comfortable
confronter to confront
congé *m.* leave, vacation; **congés scolaires** school vacation
congrès *m.* congress
conjoint(e) *m., f.* spouse
conjonction *f. gram.* conjunction
connaissance *f.* acquaintance; knowledge (11); **faire la connaissance de** to make the acquaintance of (4)
connaître to know, understand, be familiar with (10)
connu *p.p.* of **connaître**
conquérir to conquer
conquête *f.* conquest
conquis *p.p.* of **conquérir**
consacrer to devote to
conscience *f.* consciousness, awareness; **prendre conscience de** to become conscious of
consciencieux (**-euse**) *adj.* conscientious
conseil *m.* advice, counsel (13); **donner**

des conseils (à) to give advice (to)
conseiller to advise (14); *m.* (**conseillère** *f.*) counselor; **conseiller (-ère) d'orientation** career advisor
conséquence *f.* consequence, result
conservatoire *m.* academy, conservatory; protection, conservation
conserve *f.* preserve, canned food; **boîte** (*f.*) **de conserve** tin, can (*of food*)
conserver to preserve, retain (15)
considérer to consider
consigne *f.* cloak room, baggage room
consister (à) to consist (of)
consommateur *m.* consumer
consommation *f.* consumption
consommer to eat, consume
consonne *f.* consonant
constamment *adv.* constantly, steadily
constater to note, notice
constructeur (-trice) *m., f.* builder
construire to construct, build (8)
consulat *m.* consulate
consulter to consult
contacter to contact, get in touch with
conte *m.* story
contempler to contemplate
contemporain *adj.* contemporary
contenir to contain, consist of
content *adj.* content, pleased (9)
contenter to satisfy
contexte *m.* context
continuer to continue (10)
contradiction *f.* opposition
contrainte *f.* constraint, restraint
contraire *m.* opposite; **au contraire** on the contrary (5)
contrarié *adj.* frustrated, thwarted; annoyed
contraste *m.* contrast
contraster to contrast
contrat *m.* contract, agreement
contravention *f.* (parking) fine
contre *prep.* against (3)
contre-attaque *f.* counterattack
contrescarpe *f.* *(military)* counterscarp
contribuer to contribute
contrôle *m.* control (15)
contrôler to monitor, inspect (15)
contrôleur (-euse) *m. f.* superintendent, inspector
convaincre to convince, persuade
convaincu *p.p.* of **convaincre**
convenable *adj.* suitable
convenablement *ad.* suitably
convenir to suit, fit
convivialité *f.* social interaction
convoité *adj.* coveted
convoquer to call together, summon
coopérant *m.* member of the Peace Corps
coopération *f.* cooperation
coopérer to cooperate
copain *m.* (**copine** *f.*) pal, buddy
Copenhague Copenhagen
copieux (-ieuse) *m., f.* copious
coque: œuf (*m.*) **à la coque** soft-boiled egg
coquillage *m.* shellfish
corallien(ne) *adj.* coralline
Corée *f.* Korea
corporel(le) *adj.* corporal; bodily
corps *m.* body (12)
correct *adj.* correct, right
correctement *adv.* correctly
correspondance *f.* correspondence; transfer
correspondant *m.* correspondent
correspondre to correspond
corriger to correct
corsaire *m.* pirate
cosmétique *adj.* cosmetic
cosmonaute *m., f.* cosmonaut
costume *m.* outfit, suit (2); costume (17)
côte *f.* coast; rib; **la Côte d'Azur** the French Riviera; **la Côte d'Ivoire** the Ivory Coast
côté *m.* side; *prep.* **à côté de** next to (2)
côtelette *f.* cutlet
cotisation *f.* contribution
coton *m.* cotton
cou *m.* neck (12)
couchage: sac de couchage *m.* sleeping bag
couche *f.* layer
coucher: se coucher to go to bed (12)
couchette *f.* berth (8)
coudre to sew
couette *f.* quilt
couleur *f.* color (2)
couloir *m.* corridor, hallway (4)
coup *m.* blow, stroke; **coup de foudre** flash of lightning; love at first sight (12); **coup de téléphone (de fil)** telephone call (4); **coup d'œil** glance; **tout à coup** all of a sudden; **tout d'un coup** suddenly; **coup de pied** kick
coupable *adj.* guilty
coupe *f.* cup; gold or silver cup
couper to cut, cut off; **couper l'appétit** to spoil one's appetite
coupure *f.* split
cour *f.* courtyard
courage *m.* courage; **bon courage** keep your chin up
courageux (-euse) *adj.* courageous; spirited (2)
couramment *adv.* fluently (11)
courant *adj.* current, usual; **compte** (*m.*) **courant** checking account; **être au courant de** to be informed about
coureur (-euse) *m., f.* runner, competitor
courir to run (14)
couronne *f.* crown
couronné *adj.* crowned
courrier *m.* mail (9); (newspaper) column; **courrier du cœur** advice column; lonely hearts column
cours *m.* course (1); exchange rate (13); **aller en cours** to go to class; **au cours de** *prep.* during; **cours préparatoire** nursery school
course *f.* race; **faire les courses** to go grocery shopping (4); **faire des courses** to do errands
court *adj.* short (3); **court-métrage** *m.* short film; **court de tennis** *m.* tennis court
couru *p.p.* of **courir**
couscoussier *m.* cookware used to make couscous
cousin(e) *m., f.* cousin (4)
coût *m.* cost; **coût de la vie** cost of living (13)
couteau *m.* knife (5)
coûter to cost (8)
coutre *m.* colter (sharp blade attached to the beam of a plow)
coutume *f.* custom
couturier (-ière) *m., f.* fashion designer
couvent *m.* convent
couvert *adj.* covered; *m.* place setting; **mettre le couvert** to set the table
couverture *f.* blanket
couvrir to cover (13)
crabe *m.* crab (6)
craie: bâton (*m.*) **de craie** stick of chalk (0)
cravate *f.* tie (2)
crayon *m.* pencil
créateur (-trice) *m., f.* creator
créatif (-ive) *adj.* creative
création *f.* creation, establishment
créativité *f.* creativity
crèche *f.* crib; day-care center
crédit *m.* credit; **carte** (*f.*) **de crédit** credit card
créer to create (9)
crème *f.* cream (5); custard
créole *adj.* Creole
crêpe *f.* French pancake (6)
crêperie *f.* place where crepes are sold
creusé *adj.* hollowed; dug out
crevette *f.* prawn, shrimp
crier to shout
criminalité *f.* criminality; crime
crise *f.* crisis
critère *m.* criterion
critique *adj.* critical; *m.* critic; *f.* critique, evaluation
croire (à) to believe (in) (7)
croisé: mots (*m. pl.*) **croisés** crossword puzzle
croisière *f.* cruise
croissance *f.* growth
croissant *m.* crescent roll (5)
croissanterie *f.* place where croissants are sold
croque-monsieur *m. inv.* toasted cheese sandwich with ham
croûte *f.* crust of bread, pie; **casse-croûte** *m.* snack
croyance *f.* belief
cru *p.p.* of **croire**; *adj.* uncooked, raw

crudité *f.* crudity; *pl.* raw vegetables or fruit
cruellement *adv.* cruelly, ferociously
crustacé *m.* shellfish
cueillette *f.* picking, gathering; harvest
cuillère *f.* spoon (5); **cuillère à soupe** tablespoon, soupspoon
cuir *m.* leather
cuisine *f.* kitchen (4); cooking (5); **faire la cuisine** to cook (4); **livre de cuisine** cookbook
cuisiner to cook
cuisinier (-ière) *m., f.* cook
cuit *adj.* cooked
culinaire *adj.* culinary
culte *m.* cult (17)
cultivé *adj.* cultivated
cultiver to cultivate, grow
culture *f.* culture; **maison des jeunes et de la culture** youth club and arts center
culturel(le) *adj.* cultural; **manifestation culturelle** cultural event
cure *f.* course of treatment; **faire une cure** to go through treatment
curieusement *adv.* strangely, peculiarly
curieux (-ieuse) *adj.* curious; odd
curiosité *f.* curiosity
cursus *m.* (degree) course
cycle *m.* cycle, academic level (11); **premier cycle** middle school, first and second years of university study
cyclisme *m.* cycling (14)
cycliste *m., f.* cyclist

dame *f.* lady
Danemark *m.* Denmark
danger *m* danger; **en danger** endangered
dangereux (-euse) *adj.* dangerous
danois(e) *m., f.* Danish
dans *prep.* in (1)
danse *f.* dance
danser to dance (1)
danseur (-euse) *m., f.* (13) dancer
dater (de) to date (from)
datte *f.* date (*fruit*)
davantage *adv.* more
de *prep.* from, of, about (1)
débarquement *m.* landing, disembarkation
débat *m.* debate
débattre to debate
debroussaillage *m.* clearing
début *m.* beginning; **au début** at the beginning
débutant *adj.* novice
décembre *m.* December (3)
décentralisation *f.* decentralization
décevant *adj.* deceiving
décharge *f.* discharge
déchet *m.* waste, debris (15)
déchirer to tear
déchirure *f.* tear, rip, rent; gap
décidément *adv.* certainly
décider to decide, determine
décisif (-ive) *adj.* decisive
décision *f.* decision
déclaration *f.* proclamation
décodeur *m.* decoder
décolonisation *f.* decolonization
décontracté *adj.* relaxed, laid-back
décor *m.* decoration
décorer to decorate
découpage *m.* cutting up; apportionment
découpé *adj.* jagged; indented
décourageant *adj.* discouraging
découvert *p.p.* of **découvrir**
découverte *f.* discovery
découvrir to uncover; to discover (17)
décret *m.* decree
décrire to describe (9)
décrocher to unhook, lift (*receiver*)
dedans *adv.* within
dédier to dedicate
défaillance *f.* blackout; failure, breakdown
défaire to undo; to dismantle
défaut *m.* fault, flaw
défavorable *adj.* unfavorable
défendre to defend, protect
défense *f.* defense; **défense de doubler** no passing; **défense de stationner** no parking
défenseur *m.* defender, champion (of a cause)
défi *m.* challenge
défiguré *adj.* deformed
défilé *m.* parade (17)
défini *adj.* definite
définir to define, describe
définition *f.* definition
déforestation *f.* deforestation
défricher to clear; to bring land to cultivation
dégoûtant *adj.* disgusting
dégradé *adj.* degraded
déguiser to disguise; **se déguiser** to dress up in disguise, disguise oneself (17)
déguster to taste, sample; to enjoy
dehors *adv.* outside (12)
déjà *adv.* already, previously (8)
déjeuner to lunch; *m.* lunch (5); **petit déjeuner** breakfast
délégué(e) *m., f.* delegate
délicieux (-ieuse) *adj.* delicious
délirant *adj.* extraordinary, wild
deltaplane *m.* hang glider
déluge *m.* flood
demain *adv.* tomorrow (4); **après-demain** *adv.* the day after tomorrow
demande *f.* request, application
demander to ask, demand (3); **se demander** to wonder (11)
démaquillant *m.* make-up remover
démarche *f.* walk, step
démarrer to start up, move off
demi *adj.* half; **demi-heure** (*f.*) half an hour; **demi-pension** (*f.*) half-board (at a hotel); **et demie** and a half (hour) (5); **demi-saison** (*f.*) spring (*cool season*); **demi-tarif** (*m.*) half-price; **demi-tour** (*m.*) turnabout, U-turn
démocratie *f.* democracy
démon *m.* demon
démonstration *f.* demonstration
démordre to stick to, refuse to budge
dénouer to undo, untie
dent *f.* tooth (12); **brosse à dents** toothbrush; **mal** (*m.*) **aux dents** toothache
dentifrice *m.* toothpaste
dentiste *m., f.* dentist
dépannage *m.* repairing, fixing
départ *m.* departure (8)
département *m.* department, province
départmental *adj.* departmental, ministerial
dépasser to pass, go past; **ça me dépasse** it is beyond me
dépêcher to do quickly; **se dépêcher** to hurry up (11)
dépendant *adj.* answerable to; dependent upon
dépendre (de) to depend (on)
dépense *f.* expenditure, expense (13)
dépenser to spend (13)
dépit *m.* spite; **en dépit de** in spite of
déplacement *m.* travel, commuting
déplacer to move, shift, transfer
déplaire to displease
déplu *p.p.* of **déplaire**
déporter to deport
déposer to deposit (13)
déprimé *adj.* depressed
depuis *prep.* since, for (7); **depuis combien de temps...** ? for how long . . . ? (7); **depuis longtemps** for a long time; **depuis quand...** ? since when . . . ? (7); **depuis que** since
député *m.* member of Parliament, representative
déracinement *m.* uprooting, eradication
déranger to disturb
dériveur *m.* sailing dinghy
dernier (-ière) *adj.* last, past (7)
dernièrement *adv.* recently, of late
se dérouler to take place; to come unwound
derrière *prep.* behind (2)
des *contr.* of **de les**
désagréable *adj.* disagreeable, offensive (2)
désastre *m.* disaster
désastreux (-euse) *adj.* disastrous, unfortunate
descendre to descend, get off (4)
désert *m.* desert; *adj.* deserted
désertique *adj.* barren
désir *m.* wish, desire
désirer to want, desire
désolé *adj.* very sorry, grieved (14)
désordonné *adj.* disorderly

désordre *m.* disorder; **en désordre** disorderly, disheveled (3)
désormais *adv.* from now on
dès que *conj.* as soon as (13)
desquels *contr.* of **de lesquels**
dessin *m.* drawing (11)
dessiné: bande dessinée *f.* comic strip
dessiner to draw, sketch
dessous *adv.* under; **ci-dessous** below; **par-dessous** underneath
dessus *adv.* upon; **au-dessus, ci-dessus** above; **par-dessus** over
destinataire *m., f.* addressee
destiné (**à**) *adj.* intended (for)
se **destiner** to be marked for, set one's sights on
détail *m.* detail
détaillé *adj.* detailed
détecteur *m.* detector; **détecteur de métaux** metal detector
détective *m.* detective
se **détendre** to relax (11)
détendu *adj.* relaxed
détente *f.* relaxation (14)
déterminer to determine
détester to detest, hate (1)
détournement *m.* diversion, rerouting; hijacking
détritus *m. pl.* rubbish, garbage
détruire to destroy (8)
DEUG *ab.* of **diplôme d'études universitaires générales**
Deutschmark *m.* German mark
deux *adj.* (0): **tous les deux** both
deuxième *adj.* second (10); **Deuxième Guerre mondiale** World War II
devant *prep.* before, in front of (2)
développement *m.* development, growth (15)
développer to develop; to expand (15); se **développer** to grow, expand
devenir to become (7)
deviner to guess (9)
devinette *f.* riddle
devoir to have to, be obliged to (6); *m.* duty; homework (4); **faire ses devoirs** to do (one's) homework (4)
diagnostic *m.* diagnosis
diapositive *f.* slide, transparency
dictateur (**-trice**) *m., f.* dictator
dictature *f.* dictatorship
dictionnaire *m.* dictionary (1)
diététicien(ne) *m., f.* dietitian
dieu *m.* god
différemment *adv.* differently
différence *f.* difference
différencier to differentiate
différent *adj.* different (2)
difficile *adj.* difficult, hard (2)
difficulté *f.* difficulty
diffuser to diffuse
dimanche *m.* Sunday (0)
diminuer to reduce, diminish
dinde *f.* turkey; **dinde rôtie** roast turkey (5)
dindonneau *m.* turkey pheasant
dîner to dine (5); *m.* dinner (5)
dioxine *f.* dioxin
dioxyde *m.* dioxide
diplomate *m.* diplomat
diplomatie *f.* diplomacy
diplôme *m.* diploma (11), degree
diplômé(e) *m., f.* graduate
dire to say, tell (9); **c'est-à-dire** that is to say (16); **entendre dire** (**que**) to hear it said (that); **vouloir dire** to mean
directement *adv.* directly
directeur (**-trice**) *m., f.* director, manager
direction *f.* address; direction; management
directive *f.* instruction
dirigeant *m., f.* leader, director
diriger to direct, govern, control; se **diriger vers** to make one's way toward (16)
discernement *m.* discernment
discipline *f.* discipline, subject
discothèque *f.* discotheque
discours *m.* speech, discourse; **faire un discours** to deliver a speech
discrétion: à discrétion unlimited, as much as is desired
discuter to discuss
disparaître to disappear
disparition *f.* disappearance
disparu *p.p.* of **disparaître**
disponible *adj.* available
disposer de to have at one's disposal
disposition: à votre disposition at your disposal
dispute *f.* quarrel
disputer to argue; se **disputer** to quarrel, dispute (12)
disque *m.* record (3)
disquette *f.* diskette (9)
dissertation *f.* essay
distillerie *f.* distillery
distingué *adj.* distinguished; **veuillez agréer l'expression de mes sentiments distingués** yours truly
distraction *f.* recreation, diversion
distraire: se distraire to entertain oneself
distributeur *m.* dispenser; **distributeur** (*m.*) **automatique** automatic teller (13); **distributeur** (*m.*) **automatique de billets** cash dispenser, ATM
dit *p.p.* of **dire**
divers *adj.* diverse, miscellaneous
diversité *f.* variety
divisé *adj.* divided
diviser to divide
dix *adj.* ten (0); **dix-huit** eighteen (0); **dix-neuf** nineteen (0); **dix-sept** seventeen (0)
dixième *adj.* tenth
docteur *m.* doctor
doctorat *m.* Ph.D., doctorate (11)
documentation *f.* informational literature
dodo *m. fam.* sleep
doigt *m.* finger (12)
domaine *m.* area, domain
dôme *m.* dome; cathedral
domestique *m., f.* servant
domicile *m.* residence; **visite** (*f.*) **à domicile** house call
dommage *m.* harm, injury; **il est dommage** it is too bad (15); **quel dommage** that's too bad (11)
donc *conj.* therefore, there (2); **pensez donc!** just imagine! **quoi donc?** what did you say?
donner to give (1); **donner accès à** to give access to; **donner des conseils** (**à**) to give advice (to); **donner rendez-vous à** to arrange to meet
dont *pron.* whose, of which, of whom (13)
dormir to sleep (7)
dortoir *m.* dormitory
dos *m.* back; **sac à dos** backpack
douane *f.* customs
douanier (**-ière**) *m., f.* customs officer (13)
doubler to double; to pass; **défense de doubler** no passing
douceur *adj.* softness, gentleness
douche *f.* shower
doué *adj.* gifted (14)
doute *m.* doubt; **sans doute** doubtless
douter to doubt, question (15)
douteux (**-euse**) *adj.* doubtful
doux (**douce**) *adj.* smooth, soft
douze *adj.* twelve (0)
douzième *adj.* twelfth
draconien(ne) *adj.* drastic, excessively severe
dramatique *adj.* dramatic
dramaturge *m.* dramatist (17)
drame *m.* drama
drap *m.* sheet
drapeau *m.* flag
dribbler to dribble
drogue *f.* drug
droit *m.* right, law (11); *adj.* straight, right; **à droite** to the right (10); **tout droit** straight ahead (10)
drôle *adj.* funny (2)
du *contr.* of **de le**
dû *p.p.* of **devoir**
duc *m.* duke
duché: grand-duché *m.* grand duchy
duquel *contr.* of **de lequel**
dur *adj.* hard, difficult (13); **en dur** permanent; **œuf** (*m.*) **dur** hard-boiled egg
durant *prep.* during
durée *f.* duration
durer to last
dynamique *adj.* dynamic (2)
dynamisme *m.* dynamism

eau *f.* water; **eau minérale** mineral water (5); **salle** (*f.*) **d'eau** shower room
échange *m.* exchange
échanger to exchange
échapper (**à**) to escape (16)
écharpe *f.* scarf
échec *m.* failure; check (*in chess*)
échelle *f.* ladder, scale
échelon *m.* rung, step, grade
échouer (**à**) to fail (11)
écimage *m.* polling, pollarding
éclair *m.* chocolate pastry (6)
éclairci *adj.* thinning (hair)
éclat *m.* glamour, sparkle, brilliance, dazzle
s'éclater to have a ball, to get one's kicks
école *f.* school (9); **école maternelle** kindergarten, preschool (11); **école primaire** grade school (11); **école privé** private school
écologie *f.* ecology, environmentalism
écologique *adj.* ecological
écologiste *m., f.* ecologist, environmentalist (15)
économe *adj.* thrifty, economical
économie *f.* economy; *pl.* savings; **faire des économies** to save money
économique *adj.* economic; **sciences économiques** economics
économiser to economize
Écosse *f.* Scotland; **Nouvelle-Écosse** Nova Scotia
écouter to listen to, hear (1)
écouteur (**-euse**) *m., f.* listener; **écouteurs** earphones
écran *m.* screen (9)
écrémé: lait (*m.*) **écrémé** skimmed milk
écrevisse *f.* (fresh-water) crayfish (17)
écrire to write (9); **s'écrire** to write each other
écrit *p.p.* of **écrire**; *adj.* written; **par écrit** in writing
écriture *f.* writing (11)
écrivain *m.* writer
éducation *f.* education, training
effectuer to carry out, execute
effet *m.* effect; **en effet** indeed; **l'effet de serre** the greenhouse effect
efficace *adj.* effective; efficient (*person*)
égal *adj.* equal; **ça m'est égal** it's all the same to me; it doesn't matter (9)
également *adv.* equally
egalité *f.* equality
église *f.* church (10)
égotiste *adj.* egotistical
Égypte *f.* Egypt
eh bien well, now then (2)
électeur (**-trice**) *m., f.* elector, voter (15)
élection *f.* election
électoral *adj.* electoral
électricité *f.* electricity
électronique *adj.* electronic
élégant *adj.* elegant, fashionable
élément *m.* element
élémentaire *adj.* elementary
éléphant *m.* elephant
élève *m., f.* student, pupil (11)
élevé *adj.* high, raised (12)
s'élever to rise, go up
éliminer to eliminate
élire to elect (15)
élite *f.* elite
elle *pron.* she, her, it (11)
éloquent *adj.* eloquent
élu *p.p.* of **élire**
Élysée *m.* Elysium
émancipation *f.* emancipation
emballage *m.* packaging
embarquement *m.* embarkation; **carte** (*f.*) **d'embarquement** boarding pass
embarquer to embark
embarrassé *adj.* embarrassed, ill at ease
embaucher to hire
embellir to beautify, to embellish
embouteillage *m.* traffic jam
embrasser to kiss; to hug; **s'embrasser** to kiss (each other)
embryologie *f.* embryology
émettre to emit, to transmit
émetteur *m.* transmitter
émigrer to emigrate
émission *f.* broadcast, emission
emmagasiner to store up
emmener to take (someone somewhere) (14)
emmenthal *m.* Emmenthal cheese
émotif (**-ive**) *adj.* emotional
émotion *f.* emotion
émotionnel(le) *adj.* emotional
s'emparer de to take possession of
empêcher (**de**) to prevent (14); **s'empêcher de** to refrain from
empereur *m.* emperor
emplacement *m.* site
emploi *m.* job, employment, use
employé(e) *m., f.* employee (13)
employer to use; to employ (5)
employeur (**-euse**) *m., f.* employer
empoisonner to poison
emporter to take along, away
emprunt: faire un emprunt to take out a loan
emprunter to borrow (9)
ému *adj.* moved, touched
en *prep.* in, to (1); on, of, by; *pron.* of him, of her, of it, some (10)
enchaîner to chain up
enchaînement *m.* linking
enchanté *adj.* enchanted, delighted
encore *adv.* still (5); yet, again, more
encourager to encourage
s'endormir to go to sleep; fall asleep (12)
endosser to endorse (a check) (13)
endroit *m.* place, spot (8)
énergie *f.* energy; **énergie nucléaire** nuclear energy (15); **énergie solaire** solar energy (15)
énergique *adj.* energetic
énervant *adj.* irritating, annoying
énerver to irritate, annoy
enfance *f.* childhood
enfant *m., f.* child (4)
enfermé *adj.* imprisoned, shut up
enfin *adv.* finally, at last (10)
engagé *adj.* engaged; hired; committed
engagement *m.* commitment
engager to involve, engage; **s'engager** to get involved, join
engouement *m.* infatuation
engraisser to fatten up
énigme *f.* riddle, enigma
enlever to remove
ennemi(e) *m., f.* enemy
ennui *m.* boredom; **avoir des ennuis** to have problems
ennuyer to bore; **s'ennuyer** to have a bad time (12)
ennuyeux (**-euse**) *adj.* boring (12)
énorme *adj.* enormous
enquête *f.* inquiry, investigation
enregistré *adj.* recorded, taped
enrichissant *adj.* enriching
enrichissement *m.* enrichment
enseignant(e) *m., f.* teacher
enseignement *m.* teaching, education (11)
enseigner to teach (11)
ensemble *adv.* together; *m.* whole
ensuite *adv.* after, then, next (6)
entendre to hear (4); **entendre dire** (**que**) to hear it said (that); **s'entendre** to be heard; to get along (with each other) (11)
enterrer to bury
enthousiasme *m.* enthusiasm
enthousiaste *adj.* enthusiastic (2)
entier (**-ière**) *adj.* entire
entièrement *adv.* entirely
entorse *f.* sprain
entracte *m.* intermission
entraînement *m.* training
entraîner to bring about, lead to
entre *prep.* between, among (3)
entrecôte *f.* rib steak
entrée *f.* entry, first course (6)
entreprise *f.* enterprise, business; **chef** (*m.*) **d'entreprise** company manager
entrer to enter, step in (8)
entretien *m.* upkeep, maintenance
entrevue *f.* interview
envahir to invade
enveloppe *f.* envelope (9)
envers *prep.* toward, to
envie *f.* desire; **avoir envie** (**de**) to want (3)
envier to envy
environ *adv.* about, around
environnement *m.* environment (15)
envoyer to send (5)
épanouissement *m.* blossoming out, opening up
épargne: compte (*m.*) **d'épargne** savings account

épaule *f.* shoulder
épeler to spell
épicerie *f.* grocery store (6)
épinards *m. pl.* spinach
époque *f.* period, era (16)
épreuve *f.* test, contest
éprouver to experience, feel
Équateur *m.* Ecuador
équatorial *adj.* equatorial
équilibre *m.* balance, equilibrium
équipé *adj.* equipped
équipe *f.* team (14)
équipement *m.* equipment
équipementier *m.* automobile manufacturing
équitable *adj.* equitable, impartial
équitation *f.* horse-riding
équivalent *adj.* equivalent
équivaloir to be equivalent
érable: sirop (*m.*) **d'érable** maple syrup
ergonomique *adj.* ergonomical
ériger to erect, set up
erreur *f.* error
erroné *adj.* erroneous
éruption *f.* eruption
escalade *f.* climbing
escale *f.* port of call, stop
escalier *m.* stairs, staircase
escargot *m.* snail (6)
esclavage *m.* slavery
esclave *m., f.* slave (17)
escrime *f.* fencing
espace *m.* space (16)
Espagne *f.* Spain (8)
espagnol *adj.* Spanish (1)
espèce *f.* species, kind
espérer to hope
espionnage *m.* espionage
espoir *m.* hope
esprit *m.* spirit; mind
essai *m.* trial
essayer (de) to try, try out (9)
essence *f.* gasoline
essentiel(le) *adj.* essential (15)
essentiellement *adv.* essentially
essor *m.* rising
est *m.* east; **à l'est** in the east (8)
esthéticien(ne) *m., f.* beautician
esthétique *adj.* aesthetic
estimer to estimate; to consider (15)
estomac *m.* stomach
et *conj.* and (1)
établir to set, establish
établissement *m.* establishment
étage *m.* floor, stage, story; **premier étage** second story
étagère *f.* set of shelves (3)
étang *m.* pond
étape *f.* stage
état *m.* state, government (8); condition; **chef** (*m.*) **de l'État** Head of State; **état d'esprit** frame of mind
États-Unis *m. pl.* United States (8)
étau *m.* vice (*technical*)
été *p.p.* of **être**
été *m.* summer; **en été** in summer (5)
s'étendre to extend
Éthiopie *f.* Ethiopia
ethnique *adj.* ethnic
étiquette *f.* label; etiquette
étoile *f.* star
étonnant *adj.* surprising
étrange *adj.* strange (15)
étranger (-ère) *adj.* foreign; *m., f.* foreigner; **à l'étranger** abroad
être to be (2); **être abonné à** to subscribe to; **être d'accord** to agree; *m.* being
étroit *adj.* narrow
étude *f.* study; **études supérieures** higher education
étudiant(e) *m., f.* student (0); **carte** (*f.*) **d'étudiant** student ID card
étudier to study (1)
eu *p.p.* of **avoir**
Europe: l'Europe verte European agriculture
européen(ne) *adj.* European
eux *pron.* they, them (11); **eux-mêmes** themselves
évaluation *f.* evaluation
évaluer to evaluate
évasion *f.* escape
événement *m.* event, occurrence (16)
éventuellement *adv.* possibly
évident *adj.* obvious (15)
éviter to avoid
évolué *adj.* advanced, developed
évolutif (-ive) *adj.* evolutionary
évolution *f.* evolution
évoquer to evoke
exact *adj.* exact, correct
exagérer to exaggerate
examen *m.* examination (1)
examiner to examine
excentrique *adj.* eccentric (2)
exceptionnel(le) *adj.* exceptional
excès *m.* excess
exclu *adj.* excluded
exclusif (-ive) *adj.* exclusive
exclusivité *f.* something exclusive (to)
excuser to excuse; **s'excuser** to apologize (11)
exécutif: pouvoir (*m.*) **exécutif** executive power
exécution *f.* execution
exemplaire *adj.* model, exemplary
exemple *m.* example; **par exemple** for example
exercer to exercise; to practice
exercice *m.* exercise
exigeant *adj.* demanding
exiger to require (15)
existentialisme *m.* existentialism
existentialiste *adj.* existentialist
exister to exist
exotique *adj.* exotic, foreign
expatrié *m., f.* expatriate
expéditeur (-euse) *m., f.* sender
expédition *f.* expedition
expérience *f.* experience; experiment
expérimenté *adj.* experienced
expert *adj.* skilled, expert; *m.* expert; **expert-comptable** *m.* certified public accountant
explication *f.* explanation
expliquer to explain
exploiter to cultivate; to make the most of
explorateur (-trice) *m., f.* explorer
explorer to explore
exposer to expose
exposition *f.* exhibition, show
exprimer to express
extérieur *adj.* exterior, external; **intervenant** (*m., f.*) **extérieur** outside contributor
extra *adj.* first-rate
extrait *m.* extract
extraordinaire *adj.* extraordinary, unusual
extraterrestre *m.* extraterrestrial
extrêmement *adv.* extremely
exubérant *adj.* exuberant

fabrication *f.* manufacture
fabriquer to make, manufacture (14)
fabuleux (-euse) *adj.* fabulous, extraordinary
façade *f.* front
face *f.* front, face; **en face de** in front of, across from (10); **faire face à** to face, be opposite
facette *f.* facet
se fâcher to get angry (12)
fâcheux (-euse) *adj.* unfortunate, troublesome, annoying (15)
facile *adj.* easy (2)
facilement *adv.* easily
facilité *f.* ease, facility
façon *f.* manner, way
facteur (-trice) *m., f.* mail carrier (9)
facture *f.* bill
faculté *f.* division (*academic*) (1); **faculté des lettres** college of liberal arts
faim *f.* hunger; **avoir faim** to be hungry (3)
faire to make; to do (4); **faire attention** to look out; **faire beau** to be good (*weather*); **faire de la bicyclette** to go bicycling; **faire de la pêche sous-marine** to go underwater fishing; **faire de la planche à voile** to go windsurfing; **faire de la voile** to go sailing; **faire des économies** to save (up) money (13); **faire du bateau** to go boating; **faire du camping** to go camping; **faire du commerce (avec)** to trade (with); **faire du jardinage** to do gardening; **faire du jogging** to go jogging; **faire du shopping** to go shopping; **faire du ski nautique** to go water-skiing; **faire du sport** to

participate in sports; **faire du vélo** to go cycling; **faire face à** to face, to be opposite; **faire froid** to be cold; **faire la connaissance de** to make the acquaintance of (4); **faire la cuisine** to cook (4); **faire la grève** to go on strike; **faire la preuve de** to prove; **faire la sieste** to take a nap; **faire la vaisselle** to do the dishes (4); **faire le bilan de** to take stock of; **faire le marché** to go to the market (4); **faire le ménage** to clean the house (4); **faire le plein** to fill one's tank with gas (8); **faire les courses** to go grocery shopping (4); **faire mention de** to make mention of; **faire plaisir à** to please; **faire sa valise** to pack one's suitcase; **faire ses devoirs** to do (one's) homework (15); **faire un discours** to deliver a speech; **faire un emprunt** to take out a loan; **faire une cure** to go through treatment; **faire une promenade** to take a walk (4)
fait *p.p.* of **faire**; *m.* fact
falaise *f.* cliff
falloir to be necessary (15); **il faut** it is necessary (15)
fameux (-euse) *adj.* famous
familial *adj.* (*related to the*) family
familiale *f.* station wagon
se familiariser to familiarize oneself
famille *f.* family (4); **en famille** with the family; **famille proche** close family
fantaisie *f.* fantasy
fantastique *adj.* fantastic
farfelu *adj.* eccentric
farine *f.* flour
farniente *m.* (pleasant) idleness
fascinant *adj.* fascinating
fasciner to fascinate
fatigant *adj.* tiring, wearisome
fatigué *adj.* tired, fatigued (14)
faune *f.* fauna
faute *f.* mistake (12); **sans faute** without fail
fauteuil *m.* armchair
faux (fausse) *adj.* false (6)
faveur: en faveur (*f.*) **de** in favor of, on behalf of
favori (favorite) *adj.* favorite
fécond *adj.* fertile
fédéral *adj.* federal
fédération *f.* federation
fédéré *adj.* confederated
fée *f.* fairy
félicitations *f. pl.* congratulations
féminin *adj.* feminine
féminisation *f.* feminization
femme *f.* woman (1); wife (4); **femme d'affaires** businesswoman; **femme de ménage** cleaning woman; **femme politique** political figure
fenêtre *f.* window (0)
fenouil *m.* fennel
fer *m.* iron; **chemin** (*m.*) **de fer** railroad
ferme *f.* farm (16)
fermer to shut, close (7)
ferreux (-euse) *adj.* ferrous
fervent *adj.* enthusiastic
fête *f.* holiday, festival (3); **Fête du Travail** Labor Day; **Fête-Dieu** Corpus Christi; **fête légale** public holiday; **fête nationale** national holiday
fêter to celebrate (17)
fétiche *m.* fetish; mascot
feu *m.* fire; traffic light; **feu rouge** red light
feuille *f.* leaf; sheet of paper; form (16)
feuilleté *adj.* flaky pastry; **pâte** (*f.*) **feuilletée** puff pastry
feuilletine (de veau) *f.* manner of preparing veal
feuilleton *m.* serial, series
feutré *adj.* lined with felt
février *m.* February (3)
fiançailles *f. pl.* engagement (12)
fiancer: se fiancer to get engaged
fiche *f.* card, form; **fiche signalétique** (police) identification sheet
ficher: je m'en fiche I don't care (9)
fictif (-ive) *adj.* fictional
fidèle *adj.* faithful
fier (fière) *adj.* proud (2)
fierté *f.* pride
fièvre *f.* fever
fièvreux (-euse) *adj.* feverish
figue *f.* fig
filer to trail; to track
filet *m.* fillet (beef, fish, etc.) (6)
filiale *f.* subsidiary company
fille *f.* daughter (4); **jeune fille** young girl (2); **petite-fille** *f.* granddaughter (4)
fils *m.* son (4); **petit-fils** *m.* grandson (4)
filtre *m.* filter
fin *f.* end (9); **fin de semaine** weekend; **mettre fin à** to put an end to; *adj.* acute, sharp
finalement *adv.* finally
financer to finance
financier (-ière) *adj.* financial
finir to finish, end (3)
Finlande *f.* Finland
fixe *adj.* fixed, set
flamand *adj.* Flemish
flanc *m.* side, flank; slope
flâner to stroll (16)
fleur *f.* flower (3); **chou-fleur** (*m.*) cauliflower
fleuri *adj.* in bloom
fleuve *m.* river (7)
flore *f.* flora
flot: les flots (*m. pl.*) waves
flûte *f.* flute
flûté *adj.* flutelike (voice)
foie *m.* liver
foin *m.* hay
foire *f.* fair
fois *f.* time, occasion (8); **une fois** once; **deux fois** twice; **une fois par semaine** once a week (4); **une fois que vous...** once you have . . .
folklorique *adj.* folkloric, folk
folle *f.* (**fou** *m.*) *adj.* crazy
fonction *f.* post, office, function
fonctionnaire *m., f.* official, civil servant (13)
fonctionnement *m.* working, operation
fonctionner to work, to function
fond *m.* bottom; **au fond (de)** at the end (of)
fondamental *adj.* fundamental
fondation *f.* foundation
fondement *m.* foundation
fonder to found
fontaine *f.* fountain, spring
football *m.* soccer
footballeur *m.* football player
force *f.* strength; **les forces armées** the armed forces
forestier (-ière) *adj.* forest
forêt *f.* forest (7)
forfait; à forfait for a fixed sum
formalité *f.* formality
formation *f.* education, training
forme *f.* form; **en forme** in good shape; **mise** (*f.*) **en forme** fitness, working out; **sous forme de** in the form of
former to form
formidable *adj.* terrific (14)
formulaire *m.* formulary
formule *f.* formula
formuler to formulate
fort *adj.* strong; energetic; loud (12); *adv.* very
fortifier to fortify
fou (fol, folle) *adj.* mad, crazy; **amour** (*m.*) **fou** wild passion
foudre *f.* lightning; **coup** (*m.*) **de foudre** flash of lightning; love at first sight (12)
fouille *f.* excavation; **permis** (*m.*) **de fouille** search warrant
foule *f.* crowd
fourchette *f.* fork (5)
fournir to furnish, supply
fourniture: fournitures (*f. pl.*) **scolaires** school supplies
foyer *m.* hearth, home, dormitory
frais (fraîche) *adj.* fresh, cool (6); **il fait frais** it's cool (*weather*) (5); *m. pl.* expenses
fraise *f.* strawberry (5)
franc *m.* franc (French, Belgian, or Swiss monetary unit) (6)
français *adj.* French (1)
franchement *adv.* frankly, candidly
franchir to cover, get over
franco-canadien(ne) *adj.* French Canadian
francophone *adj.* French-speaking (17)

francophonie *f.* French-speaking communities
franglais *m.* French marked by borrowings from English
frappant *adj.* striking
frapper to strike, hit
fraternité *f.* fraternity, brotherhood
freinage *m.* braking
fréquent *adj.* frequent
fréquenter to frequent, visit frequently
frère *m.* brother (4)
frisé *adj.* curly (hair) (12)
frit *adj.* fried
frite: les frites (*f. pl.*) French fries
friture: les fritures (*f. pl.*) fried foods
frivole *adj.* frivolous, trivial
froid *adj.* cold; **avoir froid** to be cold (3); **il fait froid** it's cold (*weather*) (5)
fromage *m.* cheese (5)
froment *m.* wheat
frontière *f.* frontier, border
fruit *m.* fruit; **fruits de mer** seafood; **fruit sec** dried fruit
fruitier: arbre (*m.*) **fruitier** fruit tree
fuir to flee
fuite: fuite (*f.*) **de gaz** gas leak
fumée *f.* smoke
fumer to smoke (14)
fumeur: zone (non) fumeur (non) smoking area
furieux (-ieuse) *adj.* furious (15)
fusillade *f.* gunfire
futur *m.* future

gâcher to spoil
gagnant(e) *m., f.* winner
gagner to earn; to win (13); **gagner sa vie** to earn one's living
galère *f.* galley
galerie *f.* roof rack, gallery
gant (de ski) *m.* (ski) glove (7)
garanti *adj.* guaranteed; *f.* guarantee
garçon *m.* boy (2); waiter (*somewhat pejorative*)
garde *f.* guard, protection
garder to keep; **garder son sang-froid** to keep one's cool
garderie *f.* day-care center
gare *f.* (train) station (8)
garer to park
garni *adj.* garnished
garniture *f.* garnish
garrigue *f.* scrubland
gaspillage *m.* waste (15)
gaspiller to waste
gastronomique *adj.* gastronomical
gâteau *m.* cake (5)
gauche *adj.* left; *f.* the political left; **à gauche** to the left
Gaule *f.* Gaul
gaver to force-feed; to cram full
gaz *m.* gas; **fuite** (*f.*) **de gaz** gas leak
gazon *m.* lawn
GB *ab.* of **Grande-Bretagne**
géant(e) *m., f.* giant
Gémeaux *m. pl.* Gemini
généalogique: arbre (*m.*) **généalogique** family tree
gêner to inconvenience, brother
général *adj.* general, universal; *adv.* **en général** generally; *m.* general (9)
généralement *adv.* generally
généraliste: médecin (*m.*) **généraliste** general practitioner
génération *f.* generation
généreux (-euse) *adj.* generous, liberal
générosité *f.* generosity
genêt *m.* broom, shrub
génétique *f.* genetics
Genève Geneva
génie *m.* genius; **génie civil** civil engineering (11)
genre *m.* kind, sort; gender
gens *m. pl.* people (9); **jeunes gens** young people; young men
gentil(le) *adj.* nice, pleasant (2)
gentiment *adv.* kindly (11)
géographie *f.* geography (1)
géographique *adj.* geographical
géologie *f.* geology (1)
géométrie *f.* geometry (11)
géranium *m.* geranium
gérer to manage
geste *m.* gesture
gestion *f.* administration, management (11)
gisement *m.* (mineral) deposit
glace *f.* ice; ice cream (6)
glacé *adj.* frozen, iced
gladiateur *m.* gladiator
se glisser to slide; to glide along
globalement *adv.* globally
GMT *ab.* Greenwich Mean Time
golfe *m.* gulf, bay
gorge *f.* throat (12)
gothique *adj.* gothic (16)
gourmand *adj.* fond of sweet things; gluttonous (5)
gourmet *m.* epicure, gourmet
goût *m.* taste, flavor
goûter to taste (6); *m.* snack (5)
gouvernant: les gouvernants (*m. pl.*) the government
gouvernement *m.* government (15)
gouvernemental *adj.* governmental
gouverneur *m.* governor
grâce (à) *f.* thanks (to)
grammaire *f.* grammar
grand *adj.* great, tall, large (3); **la Grande-Bretagne** Great Britain; **grand-duché** (*m.*) grand duchy; **grande école** (*f.*) prestigious university; **grand magazin** (*m.*) department store; **grande personne** (*f.*) grownup; **grand public** (*m.*) general public; **pas grand-chose** *adv.* not much
grandir to grow (up)
grand-mère *f.* grandmother (4)
grand-père *m.* grandfather (4)
grand-parent *m.* grandparent (4)
gras(se) *adj.* fat; **Mardi Gras** Shrove Tuesday; **matière** (*f.*) **grasse** fat content
gratte-ciel *m.* skyscraper
gratuit *adj.* free
gratuitement *adv.* free (of charge)
grave *adj.* serious
grec (grecque) *adj.* Greek
Grèce *f.* Greece (8)
grève *f.* strike; **faire la grève** to go on strike
grignotage *m.* nibbling, snacking
grignoter to nibble
grillade *f.* grill
grillé *adj.* grilled
gris *adj.* gray (2)
gros(se) *adj.* fat, big, great
grossir to get fat; to swell
grotte *f.* grotto, cave
groupe *m.* group
guérir to cure, heal; **guéris vite!** get well soon! (12)
guerre *f.* war (15); **Deuxième Guerre mondiale** World War II
guichet *m.* box office (window) (8)
guide-interprète *m.* guide-interpreter
guider to guide
guillotiner to guillotine
Guinée *f.* Guinea
guinéen(ne) *adj.* Guinean
guitare *f.* guitar
Guyane *f.* Guyana
gymnastique *f.* gymnastics

s'habiller to dress (12)
habitant(e) *m., f.* inhabitant, owner
habitation *f.* housing
habiter to live in, inhabit (1)
habitude *f.* habit, custom; **comme d'habitude** as usual; **d'habitude** usually (9)
habituellement *adv.* usually
s'habituer à to get used to (14)
***haché** *adj.* minced
Haïti *f.* Haiti (17)
***hâlé** *adj.* (sun)tanned; (sun)burnt
hanter to haunt
***haricot** *m.* bean; **haricots verts** green beans (5)
harmonie *f.* harmony
harmonieux (-ieuse) *adj.* harmonious
harmonisé *adj.* harmonized
***harpe** *f.* harp
hasard *m.* chance; **jeu** (*m.*) **de hasard** game of chance (14); **par hasard** accidentally
***haut** *adj.* high, superior
***hauteur** *f.* height
hébergement *m.* accommodation
***hélas** *excl.* alas

hélicoptère *m.* helicopter
herbe *f.* grass
héritage *m.* heritage, inheritance
hermétiquement *adv.* tightly
***héros** *m.* hero
hésitation *f.* hesitation
hésiter to hesitate
heu *excl.* ahem! er . . .
heure *f.* hour; o'clock; **à l'heure** on time (8); **demi-heure** half an hour; **heure de pointe** rush hour; **quelle heure est-il?** what time is it? (5); **tout à l'heure** a little while ago; in a little while
heureusement *adv.* fortunately
heureux (-euse) *adj.* happy, fortunate (9)
hier *adj.* yesterday (7); **hier soir** last night
Himalaya: l'Himalaya *m.* Himalayas
hippodrome *m.* racecourse
hirondelle *f.* swallow (*bird*)
histoire *f.* history, story (1)
historien(ne) *m., f.* historian
historique *adj.* historic
hiver *m.* winter; **en hiver** in winter (5)
***hollandais** *adj.* Dutch
***Hollande** *f.* Holland
hommage *m.* tribute
homme *m.* man (1); **homme d'affaires** businessman; **homme politique** political figure; **jeune homme** young man
***Hongrie** *f.* Hungary
honnête *adj.* honest
honnêteté *f.* honesty
honneur *m.* honor
honte *f.* shame; **avoir honte** to be ashamed, embarrassed (3)
hôpital *m.* hospital (10)
hôpitalier (-ière) *m., f.* hotel keeper
horaire *m.* schedule (13)
horreur *f.* horror (16)
***hors** *prep.* out of; **hors-d'œuvre** *m.* appetizer (6); **hors de prix** outrageously expensive; **hors saison** out of season
hostellerie *f.* hostelry
hôte *m.* (**hôtesse** *f.*) host, hostess; **hôtesse de l'air** airline stewardess (8)
hôtel *m.* hotel (10)
hôtelier (-ière) *m., f.* hotelkeeper
huile *f.* oil; **huile solaire** suntan oil
huit *adj. inv.* eight (0)
huitième *adj.* eighth (10)
huître *f.* oyster (5)
humain *adj.* human; humane; **les sciences** (*f. pl.*) **humaines** social sciences
humanité *f.* humanity
humeur *f.* mood, humor
humoristique *adj.* humorous
humour *m.* humor
hydratant *adj.* moisturizing
hydrocarbure *m.* hydrocarbon
hygiène *f.* hygiene
hypocrite *adj.* hypocritical
ici *adv.* here (1)
idéal *adj.* ideal
idéalisme *m.* idealism
idéaliste *adj.* idealistic (2)
idée *f.* idea
identifier to identify
identique *adj.* identical
identité *f.* identity; **carte** (*f.*) **d'identité** ID card
il *pron.* he, it, there; **il y a** there is, there are (0); ago (7)
île *f.* island (10)
illisible *adj.* illegible
illustrateur (-trice) *m., f.* illustrator
îlot *m.* small island
ils *pron.* they
image *f.* picture, image
imaginaire *adj.* imaginary
imaginatif (-ive) *adj.* imaginary
imaginer to imagine, suppose
imbécile *m., f.* imbecile
imiter to imitate
immédiat *adj.* immediate
immédiatement *adv.* immediately
immeuble *m.* building (3)
immigré *adj.* immigrant
imparfait *m.* imperfect (*past*) tense
impératif *m.* imperative
impérial *adj.* imperial
impérialisme *m.* imperialism
imperméable *m.* raincoat (2)
impersonnel(le) *adj.* impersonal
implantation *f.* introduction; settling
impliquer to imply
important *adj.* important (2)
importe: n'importe quel(le) no matter which; **n'importe quoi** no matter what
importer to import
imposer to impose
impossibilité *f.* impossibility
impôt *m.* tax, duty
s'imprégner to become permeated with
impressionnant *adj.* impressive
impressionner to impress
impressionnisme *m.* impressionism
impressionniste *m., f.* impressionist
imprimante *f.* printer (9)
improductivité *f.* unproductiveness
improviser to improvise
impulsif (-ive) *adj.* impulsive
inactif (-ive) *adj.* inactive
incessant *adj.* unending, incessant
inclus *adj.* included
incompétent *adj.* incompetent
incongru *adj.* unseemly
incontesté adj. uncontested
inconvénient *m.* drawback, disadvantage
incroyable *adj.* incredible, unbelievable (16)
Inde *f.* India
indéfini *adj.* indefinite
indemnité *f.* allowance
indépendance *f.* independence
indépendant *adj.* independent; **travailleur (-euse) indépendant**(e) self-employed worker (13)
indicatif (-ive) *adj.* indicative
indication *f.* information; indication
indien(ne) *adj.* Indian
indifférement *adv.* indifferently, without preference
indifférence *f.* indifference
indifférent *adj.* indifferent
indiquer to indicate, show (14)
individu *m.* individual
individualiste *adj.* individualistic (2)
individuel(le) *adj.* individual
Indochine *f.* Indochina
Indonésie *f.* Indonesia
industrialisé *adj.* industrialized
industrie *f.* industry, business
industriel(le) *adj.* industrial (15)
inertie *f.* inertia
inexact *adj.* inaccurate, wrong
inexistant *adj.* nonexistent
inférieur *adj.* lower
infériorité *f.* inferiority; **complexe** (*m.*) **d'infériorité** inferiority complex
infini *adj.* infinite
infinitésimal *adj.* infinitesimal
infinitif *m.* infinitive
infirmier (-ière) *m., f.* nurse (13)
influencer to influence
informations *f. pl.* news (9)
informatique *f.* data processing (11)
informer to inform
ingénieur *m.* engineer (13)
ingrédient *m.* ingredient
inhabitable *adj.* uninhabitable
inhabituel(le) *adj.* unusual
initiative *f.* initiative; **syndicat** (*m.*) **d'initiative** tourist information bureau
injuste *adj.* unfair (15)
innombrable *adj.* innumerable
inondation *f.* flood
inoubliable *adj.* unforgettable
inquiet (-iète) *adj.* uneasy, worried
inquiéter: s'inquiéter de worry, be anxious
inquiétude *f.* anxiety
inscription *f.* registration, matriculation
inscrire to write down; **s'inscrire** to register
insécurité *f.* insecurity
insistant *adj.* insistent
insister to insist; to stress
insociable *adj.* unsociable (2)
insolite *adj.* unusual, strange
insoluble *adj.* unsolvable
inspirer to inspire
instable *adj.* unstable
installer to install; **s'installer** to settle (into); to move in (12)
institut *m.* institute
instituteur (-trice) *m., f.* (elementary school) teacher (11)
intégration *f.* integration
intégré *adj.* integrated

intellectuel(le) *adj.* intellectual (2)
intelligemment *adv.* intelligently
intensité *f.* intensity
interdire to forbid; **sens** (*m.*) **interdit** wrong way
intéressant *adj.* interesting, attractive (2)
intéresser to interest (13); **s'intéresser (à)** to take an interest in, be interested in (13)
intérêt *m.* interest
intérieur *m.* interior; **produit intérieur brut** gross national product
intermède *m.* interlude
interne *adj.* internal
interplanétaire *adj.* interplanetary
interprétation *f.* interpretation
interprète *m., f.* interpreter (13); **guide-interprète** *m.* guide-interpreter
interrogatif (-ive) *adj.* interrogative
interroger to question, interrogate
intervenant: intervenant (*m., f.*) **extérieur** outside contributor
interviewer to interview
intime *adj.* personal, intimate
intimité *f.* privacy
intrigue *f.* plot
introduire to introduce
introduit *p.p.* of **introduire**
intrus(e) *m., f.* intruder
inutile *adj.* useless (15)
invalide *m., f.* disabled person
inventer to invent
inverser to reverse
inversion *f.* reversal
investir to invest
investissement *m.* investment
invité *m., f.* guest
inviter to invite (4)
invraisemblable *adj.* unreasonable
iode *m.* iodine
irlandais *adj.* Irish
Irlande *f.* Ireland
ironie *f.* irony
irréconciliable *adj.* irreconcilable
irrésistible *adj.* irresistible
irresponsable *adj.* irresponsible
isolé *adj.* isolated, solitary
Israël *m.* Israel
Italie *f.* Italy (8)
italien(ne) *adj.* Italian (1)
italique *adj.* italic
itinéraire *m.* itinerary
itinérant *adj.* traveling
IUT *ab.* of **Institut universitaire de technologie**
Ivoire: Côte d'Ivoire *f.* Ivory Coast
ivoirien(ne) *adj.* from the Ivory Coast

jamais *adv.* ever, never; **ne... jamais** never, not ever (8)
jambe *f.* leg (12)
jambon *m.* ham (5)
janvier *m.* January (3)
Japon *m.* Japan (8)
japonais *adj.* Japanese (1)
jardin *m.* garden (4); **jardin zoologique** zoo
jardinage *m.* gardening (14); **faire du jardinage** to do gardening
jardinier (-ière) *m., f.* gardener
jaune *adj.* yellow (2)
je *pron.* I
jean *m.* jeans (2)
jeter to throw
jeu *m.* (*pl.* **jeux**) game, play (9); **jeu de hasard** game of chance (14); **jeu de mots** pun; **jeu de rôle** role-play; **jeu de société** parlor game, group game (14); **terrain** (*m.*) **de jeu** playing field or court
jeudi *m.* Thursday (0)
jeune *adj.* young (6); **jeune fille** *f.* girl, young woman (2); **jeunes gens** *m. pl.* young people, young men; **jeune homme** *m.* young man (2); **les jeunes** young people; **maison des jeunes et de la culture** youth club and arts center
jeunesse *f.* youth; **auberge de jeunesse** *f.* youth hostel
joconde: la Joconde the Mona Lisa
jogging: faire du jogging to go jogging
joie *f.* joy
se joindre to join
joli *adj.* pretty (6)
Jordanie *f.* Jordan
jouer to play; to perform (2); **jouer aux cartes** to play cards; **jouer un rôle** to play a role
jouet *m.* toy
joueur (-euse) *m., f.* player
jour *m.* day; **de nos jours** these days; **tous les jours** every day (4); **quel jour sommes-nous?** what day is it? (0); **un de ces jours** one of these days, someday (16)
journal *m.* newspaper, diary (9)
journaliste *m., f.* journalist (13)
journée *f.* day, daytime (5)
joyeux (-euse) *adj.* joyous; **Joyeux Noël** Merry Christmas
juger to judge
juillet *m.* July (3)
juin *m.* June (3)
Junon *f.* Juno
jupe *f.* skirt (2)
juridique *adj.* legal
jus (de fruit) *m.* fruit juice (6)
jusque *prep.* as far as, up to; **jusqu'à** until (10); **jusqu'à ce que** *conj.* until (17)
juste *adv.* just, right, fair (15); *adv.* exactly
justifier to justify

katangais *adj.* from Katanga
kibboutz *m. inv.* kibbutz
kilo *m.* kilogram
kilomètre *m.* kilometer
kiosque *m.* kiosk, newsstand (9)

la *f. art.* the; *f. pron.* it
là *adv.* there (10); **là-bas** over there
label *m.* stamp, seal
laboratoire *m.* laboratory
lac *m.* lake (7)
lâche *adj.* slack, loose
lagune *f.* lagoon
laid *adj.* ugly
laine *f.* wool
laisser to leave; to let (6)
lait *m.* milk (5)
laitage *m.* milk; milk product
laitier (-ière) *adj.* dairy; **produits** (*m. pl.*) **laitiers** dairy products
laitue *f.* lettuce
lampe *f.* lamp (3)
lancer to throw (14)
langage *m.* language; speech
langue *f.* language (1)
lapin *m.* rabbit; **confit** (*m.*) **de lapin** potted rabbit
laquelle *pron. f.* which, which one (14)
latte *f.* lath; board
lavabo *m.* wash basin (3)
lavage *m.* washing; **lavage de cerveau** brainwashing
lavande *f.* lavender
se laver to wash (12)
le *m. art.* the; *m. pron.* it
leçon *f.* lesson
lecture *f.* reading (11)
légal *adj.* legal; **fête** (*f.*) **légale** public holiday
légalisation *f.* legalization (15)
légaliser to legalize
légende *f.* legend
léger (légère) *adj.* light
légèrement *adv.* lightly, slightly
légion *f.* legion
législateur (-trice) *m., f.* legislator
législation *f.* legislation
légume *m.* vegetable (5)
lendemain *m.* the day after
lent *adj.* slow (11)
lentement *adv.* slowly
lequel (laquelle, lesquels, lesquelles) *pron.* which one (14); who, whom, that
les *pl. art.* the; *pl. pron.* them
lettre *f.* letter (4); *pl.* liberal arts, humanities
leur *pron.* to them; *adj.* their
lever: se lever to get up
lèvre *f.* lip
liaison *f.* liaison, link(ing)
libéral *adj.* liberal, generous
libérer to liberate, release
liberté *f.* liberty, freedom; **liberté d'expression** freedom of expression (15)

libraire *m., f.* bookseller
librairie *f.* bookstore (1)
libre *adj.* free (4)
librement *adv.* freely
licence *f.* bachelor's degree (*in France*) (11)
liégeois: café/chocolat liégeois coffee/ chocolate ice cream with whipped cream
lier to connect, link
lieu *m.* (*pl.* **lieux**) place (1); **au lieu de** instead of; **avoir lieu** to take place (16)
ligne *f.* line (10)
lilas *m.* lilac
limite *f.* limit, boundary
limité *adj.* bordered, limited
linge *m.* linen
linguistique *f.* linguistics (1)
liquide *m.* liquid; **argent** (*m.*) **liquide** cash
lire to read (9)
lis *m.* lily
Lisbonne Lisbon
lisible *adj.* legible
lisse *adj.* smooth
liste *f.* list
lit *m.* bed (3)
litre *m.* liter
littéraire *adj.* literary
littéralement *adv.* literally
littérature *f.* literature (1)
livre *m.* book (0); **livre de cuisine** cookbook
livret *m.* libretto
logement *m.* housing, dwelling (3)
loger to live, lodge
logiciel *m.* software (9)
logique *adj.* logical
logiquement *adv.* logically
loi *f.* law
loin (de) *adv.* far (from) (4)
lointain *adj.* remote, distant
loisir *m.* leisure; *pl.* spare-time activities (14)
Londres London
long (longue) *adj.* long (3)
longévité *f.* longevity
longtemps *adv.* long, a long while (17); **assez longtemps** quite a long time; **depuis longtemps** for a long time
lors (de) at the time (of)
lorsque *conj.* when (13)
loterie *f.* lottery
louer to rent (3)
louisianais(e) *m., f.* inhabitant of Louisiana
Louisiane *f.* Louisiana
loup *m.* wolf
loupe: étudier à la loupe to examine something as though under a microscope; to scrutinize
lourd *adj.* heavy (12)
loyaliste *m., f.* loyal supporter
loyer *m.* rent
lu *p.p.* of **lire**
lucidement *adv.* lucidly
lucidité *f.* lucidity
lui *pron.* he, it; to him, to her, to it (11); **lui-même** himself
lumière *f.* light, lamp
lumineux (-euse) *adj.* luminous
lundi *m.* Monday (0); **lundi de Pâques / de Pentecôte** Easter / Whit Monday
lune *f.* moon
lunettes *f. pl.* glasses (7); **lunettes de ski** ski goggles (7); **lunettes de soleil** sunglasses (7)
Lutèce *f.* Lutetia (*old name for Paris*)
lutte *f.* struggle, contest
luxe *m.* wealth, luxury; **de luxe** *adj.* luxury
luxembourgeois *adj.* from Luxembourg
luxueux (-euse) *adj.* luxurious
lycée *m.* second cycle of French secondary education (11)
Lyon Lyons
lyonnais(e) *m., f.* inhabitant of Lyons

ma *adj. f.* my
machine: machine; **machine à calculer** adding machine
maçonnerie *f.* masonry
madame (Mme) *f.* madam (0)
mademoiselle (Mlle) *f.* miss (0)
magasin *m.* store (6); **grand magasin** department store
maghrébin *adj.* from the Maghreb (N. Africa)
magicien(ne) *m., f.* magician; wizard
magie *f.* magic
magistrat *m.* magistrate, judge (13)
magnat *m.* tycoon, magnate
magnésium *m.* magnesium
magnétophone *m.* tape recorder
magnétoscope *m.* videotape recorder, VCR
magnifique *adj.* splendid, magnificent
mai *m.* May (3)
maigre *adj.* thin
maillot: maillot de bain *m.* (*woman's*) swimsuit (7)
main *f.* hand (12); **main-d'œuvre** (*f.*) labor, workforce
maintenant *adv.* now, at present (1)
maintenir to maintain, uphold
maire *m.* mayor
mairie *f.* town hall (10)
mais *conj.* but (2)
maison *f.* house; **à la maison** at home (2); **maison des jeunes et de la culture** youth club and arts center
maître *m.* master; **maître d'hôtel** butler, headwaiter
maîtrise *f.* master's degree (*in France*) (11)
majestueux (-euse) *adj.* majestic
majeur *adj.* major
majorité *f.* majority
mal *adv.* poorly, badly (4); *m.* evil; **avoir mal** to have (a) pain (12); **ça va mal** things are going badly (0); **mal** (*m.*) **aux dents** toothache; **pas mal** not bad (0)
malade *adj.* sick (4); **tomber malade** to fall ill
maladie *f.* illness
maladif (-ive) *adj.* sickly, weak
maladroit *adj.* clumsy, awkward
malgré *prep.* in spite of
malheureusement *adv.* unfortunately
malheureux (-euse) *adj.* unhappy, unfortunate (11)
maman *f.* mama
Manche: la Manche the English Channel
mangeoire *f.* trough, manger
manger to eat (2); **salle** (*f.*) **à manger** dining room
manière *f.* manner; way; **avoir de bonnes (mauvaises) manières** to have good (bad) manners
manifestation *f.* (political) demonstration; **manifestation culturelle** cultural event; **manifestation sportive** sporting event (14)
manifester to demonstrate (15)
manipuler to manipulate
manque *m.* lack
manquer to miss, lack
manteau *m.* overcoat (2)
manucurer to manicure
manuel(le) *adj.* manual
manufacture *f.* factory
manutention *f.* handling
maquillage *m.* makeup
maquiller: se maquiller to put on makeup (12)
maquis *m.* scrub, bush
maraîcher (-ère) *adj.* market gardening
marché *m.* market (5); **bon marché** *inv.* cheap, inexpensive; **faire le marché** to go shopping (4); **Marché Commun** Common Market
marcher to walk; to go (well) (7)
mardi *m.* Tuesday (0); **Mardi Gras** Shrove Tuesday (17)
marée: marée noire oil spill
mari *m.* husband (4)
mariage *m.* marriage (12)
marié(e) *m., f.* married person, bride, bridegroom
marier: se marier (à, avec) to get married (to) (12)
marin *adj.* marine
mariné *adj.* marinated
Maroc *m.* Morocco (8)
marocain(e) *m., f.* from Morocco
marque *f.* mark, brand
marquer to mark; to make a note of
marron *m.* chestnut; **marron glacé**

candied chestnut (5); *adj. inv.* (chestnut) brown (2)
mars *m.* March (3)
marseillais *adj.* from Marseilles; **La Marseillaise** French national anthem
Marseille Marseilles
martial: arts (*m. pl.*) **martiaux** martial arts
martiniquais *adj.* from Martinique (17)
masculin *adj. gram.* masculine; male
masque *m.* mask
masqué: bal (*m.*) **masqué** masked ball, costume ball (17)
masser to assemble
match *m.* match, game (14)
matérialiste *adj.* materialistic
matériaux *m. pl.* materials
matériel *m.* material
matériel(le) *adj.* material
maternel(le) *adj.* motherly; **école maternelle** kindergarten (11)
mathématicien(ne) *m., f.* mathematician
mathématiques (maths) *f. pl.* mathematics (1); **mathématiques appliquées** applied mathematics
matière *f.* subject, field; **matière grasse** fat content
matin *m.* morning; **du matin** A.M. (5)
matinal *adj.* morning
matinée *f.* morning (7)
maturité *f.* maturity
maure *adj.* Moorish
mauvais *adj.* bad, poor (6); **il fait mauvais** the weather is bad (5)
mazagran: café (*m.*) **en mazagran** Arabic coffee
me *pron.* me; to me
méandre *m.* meander; twists and turns
mécanicien(ne) *m., f.* mechanic
mécanique *f.* mechanics (11)
méchanceté *f.* nastiness, wickedness
méchant *adj.* nasty, wicked
médaille *f.* medal
médecin *m.* doctor (13); **médecin généraliste** *m.* general practitioner
médecine *f.* medicine (11)
média(s) *m. pl.* media (15)
médical *adj.* medical
médicament *m.* medicine
médiéval *adj.* medieval (16)
médiocre *adj.* mediocre
Méditerranée *f.* the Mediterranean
méditerranéen(ne) *adj.* Mediterranean
meilleur *adj.* better (12); **le meilleur** the best
mélange *m.* mixture (17)
mélanger to mix, blend
mêlée *f.* fray, scuffle
membre *m.* member
même *adj.* same (6); *adv.* even; **en même temps** at the same time; **moi-même** myself; **le (la) même** the same one (16); **quand même** even though; **tout de même** all the same
mémoire *f.* memory
menace *f.* threat
menacer to threaten
ménage *m.* household, housekeeping; **faire le ménage** to clean the house (4); **femme de ménage** (*f.*) housewife
ménager (-ère) *adj.* household, domestic
mener to lead
menhir *m.* (*archeological*) an upright monumental stone standing alone or with others, as in an alignment
mensuel(le) *adj.* monthly
mentalité *f.* mentality
mention: faire mention de to make mention of
mentionner to mention
mentir to lie
menu *m.* fixed-price menu (6)
mer *f.* sea (7); **au bord de la mer** seashore; **fruits** (*m. pl.*) **de mer** seafood; **outre-mer** overseas; **pleine mer** the open sea
merci *adv.* thanks, thank you (0)
mercredi *m.* Wednesday (0)
Mercure *m.* Mercury
mère *f.* mother (4); **grand-mère** grandmother
mériter to deserve
merveille *f.* wonder, marvel
merveilleux (-euse) *adj.* wonderful (16)
mes *adj. pl.* my
mesdames *f. pl.* of **madame**
mesdemoiselles *f. pl.* of **mademoiselle**
messieurs *m. pl.* of **monsieur**
mesure *f.* measure; **prendre des mesures** to take action
métal *m.* metal; **détecteur** (*m.*) **des métaux** metal detector
météo *f. ab.* of **météorologique** weather report
méthode *f.* method
méthodologie *f.* methodology
métier *m.* trade, profession, job
métrage: court métrage *m.* short film
métro (Métropolitain) *m.* Paris subway (8); **métro-boulot-dodo** *m.* subway-work-sleep (*daily grind*)
métropolitain *adj.* metropolitan
mettre to put (on), to place (9); **mettre en œuvre** to make use of; **mettre fin à** to put an end to; **mettre le couvert** to set the table; **se mettre à** to begin (12); **se mettre d'accord** to come to an agreement; **se mettre en colère** to get angry
meuble *m.* piece of furniture (4)
meublé *adj.* furnished; **chambre** (*f.*) **meublée** furnished room
meurtre *m.* murder
mexicain *adj.* Mexican
Mexico *m.* Mexico City
Mexique *m.* Mexico (8)
mi- *adv.* (*prefix*) half, mid-, semi-; **mi-temps** part-time
midi *m.* noon; **il est midi** it's noon (5); **après-midi** *m.* or *f.* afternoon; **de l'après-midi** P.M., in the afternoon; **le Midi** the South of France
miel *m.* honey
mien(ne) *pron.* mine
mieux *adv.* better (14); **le mieux** best (14); **aimer mieux** to prefer (1); **tant mieux** so much the better; **valoir mieux** to be better
migrateur (-trice) *adj.* migratory
milieu *m.* middle; environment; **au milieu** in the midst
mille *m., adj.* thousand
milliard *m.* billion
milliardaire *m., f.* billionaire
milliers *m. pl.* thousands
minable *adj.* pitiful
mince *adj.* thin, slight
minceur *f.* thinness
mincir to get slimmer
mine *f.* expression; appearance
minéral *adj.* mineral
minet(te) *m., f. fam.* trendy young man (woman)
mini-jupe *f.* miniskirt
ministère *m.* ministry
ministre *m.* minister, cabinet member; **premier ministre** prime minister
minitel *m.* home terminal of the French telecommunications system
minorité *f.* minority
minuit *m.* midnight; **il est minuit** it's midnight (5)
minutieux (-euse) *adj.* minutely detailed
mirabelle *f.* plum
mire: point (*m.*) **de mire** focal point
miroir *m.* mirror (3)
mis *p.p.* of **mettre**
mise *f.* putting, setting; **mise au point** focusing, tuning; **mise en forme** fitness, working out; **mise en scène** staging, production
misère *f.* misery, destitution
MJC *ab.* of **maison des jeunes et de la culture**
mobylette *f.* moped
moche *adj.* ugly (16)
mode *f.* fashion; **à la mode** fashionable
modèle *m.* model, pattern
modéré *adj.* moderate
moderne *adj.* modern
moderniser to modernize
modeste *adj.* modest, simple
modifier to modify
moi *pron.* I, me (11)
moine *m.* monk
moins (de) (que) *adv.* less, fewer (5, 12); **au moins** at least; **à moins que (de)** *conj.* unless (17); **le moins** the least;

moins le quart quarter to (the hour) (5)
mois *m.* month (7)
moisson *f.* harvest
moment *m.* moment, instant; **à tout moment** continually; **au moment de** just as; **en ce moment** at present
mon *m. adj.* my
monde *m.* world (8); **tout le monde** everyone (8); **Nouveau Monde** the New World; **Tiers Monde** the Third World
mondial *adj.* worldwide; **Deuxième Guerre mondiale** World War II
mondialement *adv.* the world over
monétaire *adj.* monetary
moniteur *m.* monitor (9)
monnaie *f.* change, coin (5); **pièce** (*f.*) **de monnaie** coin; **porte-monnaie** *m.* change purse
monopoliser to monopolize
monotone *adj.* monotonous
monotonie *f.* monotony
monsieur (M.) *m.* sir, mister (0)
monstre *m.* monster
mont *m.* mount, mountain
montagne *f.* mountain (7)
montagneux (-euse) *adj.* mountainous
montant *m.* sum, amount (13)
montée *f.* ascent, climbing
monter to climb (up); to get in (8)
montpellierain(e) *m., f.* person from Montpellier
montre *f.* watch
Montréal *m.* Montreal (17)
montrer to show (11)
moquette *f.* wall-to-wall carpet
morale *f.* ethic, moral
moralité *f.* morality
morceau *m.* piece (6)
mort *adj.* dead; *f.* death; *m., f.* dead person; **sous peine de mort** on pain of death
mortalité *f.* mortality, death rate
morue *f.* cod
Moscou Moscow
mot *m.* word (3); **mot-clé** *m.* key word; **mots croisés** crossword puzzle
motivé *adj.* motivated
moto *f. fam.* motorbike (8)
motocyclette *f.* motorcycle (8)
mouche *f.* fly
mouillé *adj.* wet
mourir to die (8)
mousquetaire *m.* musketeer
moustique *m.* mosquito
moutarde *f.* mustard
mouvement *m.* movement
mouvementé *adj.* animated, action-packed
moyen *m.* means, way; *adj.* **moyen(ne)** middle, average; **moyen âge** Middle Ages (16); **de taille moyenne** of average height (3); **en moyenne** on average
se multiplier to multiply
mur *m.* wall (3)
musculation *f.* muscle development
musée *m.* museum (10)
musicien(ne) *m., f.* musician
musique *f.* music (1); **musique de chambre** chamber music
mutuellement *adv.* mutually
myrtille *f.* blueberry
mystère *m.* mystery
mystérieux (-ieuse) *adj.* mysterious
mystique *adj.* mystic(al)
mythe *m.* myth

nager to swim (7)
nageur (-euse) *m., f.* swimmer
naïf (naïve) *adj.* naive, simple (2)
naissance *f.* birth
naître to be born (8)
natal *adj.* native
natation *f.* swimming
national *adj.* national; **l'Assemblée nationale** one of the two houses of the French parliament; **fête** (*f.*) **nationale** national holiday
nationalité *f.* nationality
naturel(le) *adj.* natural; **ressources** (*f.*) **naturelles** natural resources (15)
naturellement *adj.* naturally
nautique *adj.* nautical; **ski** (*m.*) **nautique** waterskiing
navarin: navarin (*m.*) **d'agneau** lamb stew
navet *m.* third-rate, rubbish
navette *f.* shuttle
navré *adj.* sorry
ne *adv.* no, not; **ne... jamais** never (8); **ne... pas du tout** not at all (8); **ne... pas encore** not yet (8); **ne... personne** no one, nobody (8); **ne... plus** no longer (8); no more (5); **ne... que** only (8); **ne... rien** nothing, not anything (8)
né *p.p.* of **naître**
nécessaire *adj.* necessary
nécessairement *adv.* necessarily
nécessité *f.* necessity
néfaste *adj.* harmful
négatif (-ive) *adj.* negative
négation *f.* negation
négligeable *adj.* negligible
négligent *adj.* negligent
négocier to negotiate
neige *f.* snow; **bonhomme** (*m.*) **de neige** snowman (17)
neiger to snow; **il neige** it's snowing (5)
nerveux (-euse) *adj.* nervous (2)
net: prix (*m.*) **net** net price
neuf (neuve) *adj.* nine (0); new; **quoi de neuf?** what's new? **Terre-Neuve** (*f.*) Newfoundland
neuvième *adj.* ninth (10)
neveu *m.* nephew (4)
nez *m.* nose (12)
ni *conj.* nor; **ni... ni** neither . . . nor
niçois *adj.* of Nice
nid *m.* nest
nièce *f.* niece (4)
Nil: le Nil the Nile river
niveau *m.* level
noces *f. pl.* wedding; **voyage** (*m.*) **de noces** honeymoon
Noé *m.* Noah
Noël *m.* Christmas; **carte** (*f.*) **de Noël** Christmas card; **Joyeux Noël** Merry Christmas
noir *adj.* black (2); **tableau noir** blackboard (0); **marée noire** oil spill; *m.* darkness
noisette *f.* hazelnut
noix *f.* walnut; **noix de coco** coconut
nom *m.* name; **au nom de** in the name of
nombre *m.* number
nombreux (-euse) *adj.* numerous
nommer to name
non *int.* no (0); not; non- (*prefix*)
nord *m.* north; **au nord** to the north (8)
normalement *adv.* normally
normand *adj.* Norman
Normandie *f.* Normandy
Norvège *f.* Norway
norvégien(ne) *adj.* Norwegian
nos *adj. pl.* our
nostalgie *f.* nostalgia
nostalgique *adj.* nostalgic
note *f.* grade (11); mark; bill
notre *adj.* our
nouer to tie, knot
nourrir to feed
nourriture *f.* food
nous *pron.* we, to us, ourselves (11)
nouveau (nouvel, nouvelle) *adj.* new (6); **Nouveau Monde** the New World; **le nouvel an** New Year's Day; *adv.* **à nouveau** freshly; **de nouveau** again (10)
nouvelle *f.* (often *pl.*) news (9)
Nouvelle-Écosse *f.* Nova Scotia (17)
La Nouvelle-Orléans *f.* New Orleans (17)
novembre *m.* November (3)
nu *adj.* nude, bare
nuage *m.* cloud
nucléaire *adj.* nuclear; **centrale** (*f.*) **nucléaire** nuclear power plant; **énergie nucléaire** nuclear energy (15)
nuit *f.* night (7); **boîte** (*f.*) **de nuit** nightclub
nul(le) *adj.* nul, nothing
numéro *m.* number; **composer le numéro** to dial the number; **numéro de téléphone** telephone number (9)
numérotation *f.* numeration
nymphéa *m.* white water lily

obéir to obey
obélisque *m.* obelisk
objectif *m.* objective; aim
objet *m.* object, thing
obligatoire *adj.* obligatory (11)
obligatoirement *adv.* inevitably
obligé *adj.* bound, compelled, obligated
obliger to require
obsédé *adj.* obsessed
observer to observe
obtenir to obtain, get (7)
occasion *f.* opportunity, occasion; **avoir l'occasion (de)** to have the chance (to) (16)
occident *m.* the West; **occidental(le)** *adj.* Western
occupé *adj.* busy
occuper to occupy; **s'occuper de** to look after; to occupy oneself with
océan *m.* ocean
Océanie *f.* Oceania (South Sea Islands)
ocre *f.* ochre
octobre *m.* October (3)
odeur *f.* odor
odyssée *f.* odyssey
œil *m.* (*pl.* **yeux**) eye (12); **clin** (*m.*) **d'œil** wink; **coup** (*m.*) **d'œil** glance
œuf *m.* egg (5); **œuf à la coque** soft-boiled egg; **œuf dur** hard-boiled egg
œuvre *f.* work, creation; **chef-d'œuvre** *m.* masterpiece; **œuvre d'art** work of art (16); **hors-d'œuvre** (*m.*) appetizer; **main-d'œuvre** (*f.*) labor, workforce
offert *p.p.* of **offrir**
officiel(le) *adj.* official
offrir to offer (13)
oie *f.* goose
oignon *m.* onion
oiseau *m.* bird (14)
olympique *adj.* Olympic
omis *adj.* omitted
on *pron.* one, they, we, I, you, people, someone
oncle *m.* uncle (4)
ondulé *adj.* undulating
ongle *m.* (finger)nail
ONU *ab.* of **Organization des Nations Unies** the United Nations
onze *adj.* eleven (0)
onzième *adj.* eleventh (10)
opéra *m.* opera
opération *f.* operation
opportunité *f.* opportunity; opportuneness
opposer to contrast; **s'opposer à** to rebel against
opter to opt for
optimiste *adj.* optimistic (2)
option: en option as an optional extra
optométrie *f.* optometry
or *m.* gold (16); *conj.* but, well
orchestre *m.* orchestra
ordinaire *adj.* ordinary
ordinateur *m.* computer (3)
ordre *m.* order, command; **en ordre** neat, orderly (3)
ordure *f.* rubbish, refuse
oreille *f.* ear (12)
oreiller *m.* pillow
organique *adj.* organic
organisation *f.* organization
organisé *adj.* organized, arranged
organiser to organize
organisme *m.* body, organism
orgue *m.* organ
orientation *f.* orientation, positioning; **conseiller (-ère) d'orientation** career advisor
origine *f.* origin: **à l'origine** originally
os *m.* bone
ou *conj.* or, either (1)
où *adv.* where (2)
oublier to forget (7)
ouest *m.* west; **à l'ouest** in the west (8)
Ouganda *m.* Uganda
oui *adv.* yes (0)
ours *m.* bear
outrage *m.* insult
outre-mer *adv.* overseas
ouvert *adj.* open; *p.p.* of **ouvrir**
ouverture *f.* opening; overture
ouvrage *m.* work
ouvreuse *f.* usherette
ouvrier (-ière) *m., f.* worker, laborer (13)
ouvrir to open (13)
oxygène *m.* oxygen

paiement *m.* payment
pain *m.* bread (5)
pair *m.* peer; **travailler au pair** to work in exchange for room and board
paisible *adj.* peaceful
paix *f.* peace.
palais *m.* palace (16)
palet *m.* hockey puck
palmarès *m.* prize list (*at school*)
palpitant *adj.* exciting
pamplemousse *m.* grapefruit
panaché *adj.* mixed (salad)
panne *f.* breakdown; **en panne** out of order; **tomber en panne** to break down (*vehicle*)
panneau *m.* panel, sign
panoramique *adj.* panoramic
pantalon *m.* trousers, pants (2)
panthéon *m.* pantheon
panure *f.* breadcrumb dressing
pape *m.* pope
papeterie *f.* stationer's shop
papier *m.* paper
papillon *m.* butterfly
papillote: en papillote (*f.*) cooked in a tinfoil wrapper
Pâques *m. pl.* Easter; **lundi** (*m.*) **de Pâques** Easter Monday
paquet *m.* package, bundle
par *prep* by, through, out of, from, for (3); **par écrit** in writing; **par exemple** for example (15); **par hasard** by chance; **par terre** on the ground (2)
paradis *m.* paradise
paragraphe *m.* paragraph
parallèlement *adv.* at the same time, in the same way
parapluie *m.* umbrella (7)
parc *m.* park (10)
parce que *conj.* because, as (3)
parcourir to travel; to skim through
pardon *int.* excuse me (0)
pareil(le) (à) *adj.* similar (to) (16)
parenthèse *f.* parenthesis
parent *m.* parent, relative (4); **grand-parent** grandparent
paresse *f.* laziness
paresseux (-euse) *adj.* lazy, idle (2)
parfait *adj.* perfect; perfect tense
parfaitement *adv.* perfectly
parfois *adv.* sometimes, occasionally (6)
parfum *m.* perfume
parisien(ne) *adj.* Parisian (2)
parking *m.* parking place, lot
parlement *m.* parliament
parlementaire *adj.* parliamentary
parler to speak (1)
parmi *prep.* among
parole *f.* word
part *f.* part, portion; **pour ma part** in my opinion (15); **c'est de la part de qui?** who's calling? (9); **quelque part** somewhere
partager to share; to divide
partenaire *m., f.* partner (1)
parti *m.* (political) party
participer to participate
particulier (-ière) *adj.* private, particular, exceptional
particulièrement *adv.* particularly
partie *f.* part, party; **faire partie (de)** to belong (to)
partiellement *adv.* partially
partir to leave, set out (7); **à partir de** from (7)
partitif (-ive) *adj.* partitive
partout *adv.* everywhere (10)
paru *adj.* appeared
parvenir to get to, reach, achieve
pas: ne... pas not, not any; **ne... pas encore** not yet (8); **pas encore** not yet (1); **pas mal** *int.* not bad (0)
passage *m.* passage, way
passager (-ère) *adj.* passing, short-lived; *m., f.* passenger (8)
passé *adj.* last, past (7)
passeport *m.* passport (13)
passer to spend (*time*) (5); to take (*a test*) (11); to pass; **passer par** pass through; **se passer** to happen (14); **qu'est-ce qui se passe?** what's going on? (14)
passe-temps *m.* pastime (14)

passif (-ive) *adj.* passive
passionnant *adj.* exciting, fascinating
passionné *m., f.* passionate, impassioned
pastis *m.* aniseed alcoholic drink
pâte *f.* pastry; **pâte feuilletée** puff pastry
pâté *f.* pâté, paste; **pâté de campagne** country-style pâté (6); **pâté de foie gras** goose liver pâté (5)
patin *m.* skate; **patins à glace** ice skates
pâtisserie *f.* pastry (shop) (6)
patrie *f.* country
patrimoine *m.* patrimony, legacy (16)
patron(ne) *m., f.* boss, patron, owner
paupiette: paupiette de dindonneau turkey pheasant
pauvre *adj.* poor, unfortunate (6)
pauvreté *f.* poverty
payer to pay (for) (5)
pays *m.* country (8); native land; **les Pays-Bas** the Netherlands
paysage *m.* countryside, landscape (16)
paysan(ne) *m., f.* peasant, country person
peau *f.* skin
pêche *f.* fishing (14); peach; **faire de la pêche sous-marine** to go underwater fishing
pêcher to fish
pêcheur (-euse) *m., f.* fisherman, fisherwoman
peigne *m.* comb
peigner: se peigner to comb one's hair (12)
peindre to paint
peine *f.* sorrow, sadness; **sous peine de mort** on pain of death; **valoir de la peine** to be worth the trouble
peint *p.p.* of **peindre**
peintre *m.* painter; **artiste peintre** painter (13)
peinture *f.* painting (11)
pèlerin *m.* pilgrim
pèlerinage *m.* pilgrimage
pelote *f.* ball
pelouse *f.* lawn
pendant *prep.* during, for
pénétration *f.* penetration
penser to think (3); to expect
pension *f.* pension, food and lodging; **demi-pension** *f.* half-board (at a hotel)
pente *f.* slope
Pentecôte: lundi (*m.*) **de Pentecôte** Whit Monday
percer to get a break (*as an actor, etc.*)
perche *f.* perch (*fish*)
perché *adj.* perched
perdre to lose (4)
père *m.* father (4); **grand-père** *m.* grandfather
perfectionnement *m.* perfection; improvement (11)
perfectionner to perfect; to improve (17)
performant *adj.* outstanding
période *f.* period
périple *m.* voyage, trip
perle *f.* pearl
permettre to permit, allow (14)
permis *m.* license; **permis de conduire** driver's license; **permis de fouille** search warrant
persévérant *adj.* persevering, persistent
personnage *m.* character (17); individual
personnalité *f.* personality
personne *f.* person (2); *indef. pron.* no one, anyone; **grande personne** grownup; **ne... personne** no one, nobody (8)
personnel(le) *adj.* personal
personnellement *adv.* personally (15)
persuader to convince, persuade
persuasif (-ive) *adj.* persuasive
perte *f.* loss
perturber to disrupt
pessimisme *m.* pessimism
pessimiste *adj.* pessimistic (2)
pétanque *f.* lawn bowling, bocce ball (14)
petit *adj.* small, little (3); **petit déjeuner** breakfast (5); **petites annonces** classified ads (9); **petite-fille** granddaughter (4); **petit-fils** grandson (4); **petit(e) ami(e)** boy/girlfriend; **les Petites Antilles** the Lesser Antilles; **petits pois** (*m. pl.*) green peas
peu *adv.* little, few, not very (2); **à peu près** about; **assez peu** not very much; **un peu de** a (little) bit of (5); **peu probable** not likely (15)
peuple *m.* people, nation
peur *f.* fear; **avoir peur** to be afraid (3)
peut-être *adv.* perhaps (4)
pharmacie *f.* drugstore (10)
pharmacien(ne) *m., f.* pharmacist
phénomène *m.* phenomenon
philharmonique *adj.* philharmonic
philo *fam. ab.* of **philosophie**
philosophe *m.* philosopher
philosophie *f.* philosophy (1)
phosphore *m.* phosphorus
photo *f.* picture; **appareil-photo** *m.* camera (16)
photocopieur *m.* photocopier
photographe *m., f.* photographer
photographier to photograph
photographique *adj.* photographic
phrase *f.* sentence
physicien(ne) *m., f.* physicist
physique *f.* physics (1); *adj.* physical
pianiste *m., f.* pianist
pic *m.* pick; summit
pichet *m.* pitcher, jug
pièce *f.* room (4); coin (6); **pièce** (*f.*) **de monnaie** coin (6); **pièce de théâtre** stage play (14)
pied *m.* foot (12); **à pied** on foot; **coup** (*m.*) **de pied** kick; **de plain-pied** on the same level, at street level
pierre *f.* stone
piéton(ne) *m., f.* pedestrian
pilote *m.* pilot (8)
pin *m.* pine
pionnier (-ière) *m., f.* pioneer
pique-nique *m.* picnic
pique-niquer to picnic
pire *adj.* worse, the worst (12)
pirogue *f.* dug-out canoe
pis *adv.* worse; **tant pis** too bad
piscine *f.* swimming pool (10)
piste *f.* track
pittoresque *adj.* picturesque
place *f.* place, position; seat; square (10); **à votre place** in your place, if I were you (16); **sur place** installed
placer to place
plafond *m.* ceiling
plage *f.* beach (7)
plain-pied: de plain-pied *adv.* on the same level; at street level
plaire to please; **s'il vous plaît** please (0)
plaisir *m.* pleasure (4); **faire plaisir** (**à**) to please
plan *m.* map; plane (*surface*); plan
planche *f.* board; **faire de la planche à voile** to go windsurfing; **planche à voile** windsurfer (7)
planétaire *adj.* planetary
planète *f.* planet
plante *f.* plant (10)
planteur *m.* planter, plantation owner
plaquer to tackle
plaquette *f.* plaque
plasticien *m.* plastic surgeon
plat *m.* dish (5); course (6); **plat du jour** (special) dish of the day
platane *m.* plane tree
plateau *m.* tray; plateau
plâtre *m.* plaster cast
plein *adj.* full (14); complete: **de plein air** *adj.* outdoor (14); **en plein air** in the open air (14); **faire le plein** to fill up (*gas tank*); **pleine mer** the open sea
pleuvoir to rain (9); **il pleut** it's raining (5)
plombage *m.* filling (*tooth*)
plomberie *f.* plumbing
plongée *f.* diving; **plongée sous-marine** scuba diving
plonger to dive
plu *p.p.* of **plaire**
pluie *f.* rain
plume *f.* pen; feather
plupart: la plupart (**de**) most (of), the majority (of) (15)
pluriel *m.* plural
plus *adv.* more (5); most; **de plus** besides; **de plus en plus** more and more; **ne... plus** no longer (8); no more (5); **plus... que** more . . . than (12)
plusieurs *adj.* several, some (8)
plutôt *adv.* rather, sooner (6)

pluvieux (-**ieuse**) *adj.* rainy
pneu *m.* tire
poche *f.* pocket; **argent** (*m.*) **de poche** pocket money
poème *m.* poem (17)
poésie *f.* poetry
poète *m.* poet (18); **femme-poète** *f.* female poet
poétique *adj.* poetic
poids *m.* weight
point *m.* point: **à point** medium (*meat*): **mise** (*f.*) **au point** focusing, tuning; **point de mire** focal point; **point de vue** viewpoint; **ne... point** *adv.* not at all
pointage *m.* checking
pointe *f.* point, tip; **heure** (*f.*) **de pointe** rush hour
poire *f.* pear (5)
pois *m.* pea; **petits pois** green peas
poisson *m.* fish (5)
poissonnerie *f.* fish market (6)
poivre *m.* pepper (5)
poivrière *f.* pepper shaker
poivron: poivron (*m.*) **vert** green pepper
poli *adj.* polite (11)
policier (-**ière**) *adj.* pertaining to the police; **roman policier** detective novel
poliment *adj.* politely
polir to polish
politesse *f.* politeness
politicien(ne) *m., f.* politician
politique *adj.* political; **homme/femme politique** *m., f.* politician; *f.* politics; policy
politiquement *adv.* politically
polluant *adj.* polluting
polluer to pollute (15)
Pologne *f.* Poland
polonais *adj.* Polish
Polynésie *f.* Polynesia
polytechnique *adj.* polytechnic
pomme *f.* apple (5); **pomme de terre** potato (5)
pommier *m.* apple tree
pompier (-**ière**) *m., f.* firefighter
poncer to pumice, sand down
ponctuel(le) *adj.* punctual
pont *m.* bridge
populaire *adj.* popular
popularité *f.* popularity
porc *m.* pork (6)
porte *f.* door (0)
porté *f.* impact
portefeuille *m.* pocketbook, wallet (13)
porte-monnaie *m.* change purse
porter to wear; to carry (2); **prêt-à-porter** ready-to-wear
portugais *adj.* Portuguese
poser to put, place; **poser une question** to ask a question (3); **se poser** to arise
positif (-**ive**) *adj.* positive
posséder to possess
possessif (-**ive**) *adj.* possessive
possibilité *f.* possibility
postal *adj.* postal; **boîte** (*f.*) **postale** post office box; **carte postale** postcard
poste *m.* position, station; *f.* post office; **bureau** (*m.*) **de poste** post office; **poste de police** police station (10); **poste de télévision** TV set (4)
potentiel(le) *adj.* potential
poterie *f.* pottery
pouce *m.* thumb
poule *f.* hen
poulet *m.* chicken (5)
pour *prep.* for, in order to (1); **pour cent** percent; **pour que** *conj.* in order that (17)
pourboire *m.* tip (6)
pourcentage *m.* percentage
pourquoi *adv., conj.* why (3)
poursuivre to pursue, carry through (11)
pourtant *adv.* yet, even so, nevertheless
pourvoir to provide
pourvu que *conj.* provided that (17)
pousser to push; to grow
poussette *f.* push chair, stroller
poutre *f.* beam, girder
pouvoir to be able to, can (6); **il se peut que** it's possible that (15); *m.* power, authority; **pouvoir exécutif** executive power
pratique *adj.* practical; **sens** (*m.*) **pratique** common sense; **travaux** (*m. pl.*) **pratiques** small group work or lab
pratiquer to practice
précédent *adj.* former, preceding
précieux (-**ieuse**) *adj.* precious, invaluable
précipité *adj.* precipitated
précis *adj.* precise
préciser to make clear; to classify
précision *f.* precision
précoce *adj.* early; precocious
prédateur *m.* predator
prédiction *f.* prediction, forecast
préférable *adj.* preferable
préférence *f.* preference
préférer to prefer (5)
premier (-**ière**) *adj.* first (10); **premier cycle** (*m.*) middle school, first and second years of university studies; **Première Guerre mondiale** World War I; **premier ministre** prime minister
prénatal *adj.* prenatal
prendre to take (5); **prendre conscience** (**de**) to become aware (of); **prendre des mesures** to take action; **prendre en charge** to take care of; **prendre le soleil** to sunbathe; **prendre un verre** to have a drink; **prendre une photo** to take a picture; **prendre rendez-vous** to make an appointment; **prendre un repas** to have (eat) a meal; **prendre au sérieux** to take seriously; **prendre une décision** to make a decision
prénom *m.* first name
préoccupation *f.* preoccupation
préparatifs *m. pl.* preparations
préparatoire *adj.* preparatory; **cours** (*m.*) **préparatoire** nursery school
préparer to prepare (for) (4); **se préparer** (**à**) to get ready (to) (12)
prépondérant *adj.* dominating
préposition *f.* preposition
près (**de**) *adv., prep.* near, by (3); **à peu près** about; **tout près** very near
prescrire to prescribe
présence *f.* presence
présent *adj.* present
présentation *f.* presentation, introduction
présenter to present, introduce; **se présenter** to present oneself; to run for office
préservation *f.* preservation
préserver to preserve; to defend
président(e) *m., f.* president
présidentiel(le) *adj.* presidential
présider to preside
presque *adv.* almost, nearly (5)
presse *f.* press
pressé *adj.* pressed, hurried
prestigieux (-**ieuse**) *adj.* prestigious
prêt (**à**) *adj.* ready; **prêt-à-porter** ready-to-wear (6)
prêter to lend (9)
preuve *f.* proof, evidence; **faire la preuve de** to prove that
prévoir to foresee
prier to beseech; **je vous en prie** you're welcome (14)
prière *f.* prayer; **prière de** (+*inf.*) please
primaire *adj.* primary; **école** (*f.*) **primaire** elementary school
primer to dominate; to take first place
prime: en prime as a free gift
principalement *adv.* principally
principe *m.* principle
printemps *m.* spring; **au printemps** in spring (5)
priorité *f.* priority, right of way; **en priorité** as a (matter of) priority
pris *p.p.* of **prendre**
prise *f.* hold, capture; **être pris**(**e**) to be taken, caught; to be busy
privé *adj.* private; **école** (*f.*) **privée** private school
privilège *m.* privilege
privilégié *adj.* privileged
prix *m.* price (6); prize; **hors de prix** outrageously expensive; **prix net** net price
probabilité *f.* probability, likelihood
probablement *adv.* probably
problème *m.* problem (15)
procédé *m.* process, method
prochain *adj.* next (4)
prochainement *adv.* soon, shortly
proche *adj.* near, close; **famille** (*f.*) **proche** close family

proclamer to proclaim
produire to produce
produit *m.* product; **produit intérieur brut** gross national product; **produits laitiers** dairy products
prof *m., f. fam. ab.* of **professeur**
professeur *m.* professor, instructor (0)
professionnel(le) *adj.* professional
profil *m.* profile
profiter to take advantage of
profond *adj.* profound, deep
profondément *adv.* profoundly
programmation *f.* programming
programme *m.* program, curriculum, plan
programmeur (-euse) *m., f.* computer programmer
progrès *m.* progress
progressiste *adj.* progressive
progressivement *adv.* progressively
proie *f.* prey
projet *m.* project, plan (4)
prolifération *f.* proliferation (15)
promenade *f.* walk, excursion; **faire une promenade** to take a walk (4)
promener to take out walking; **se promener** to walk (12)
promettre to promise (14)
promis *p.p.* of **promettre**
promotionel(le) *adj.* promotional
promulguer to promulgate
pronom *m.* pronoun
pronominal: verbe pronominal reflexive verb
prononcer to pronounce
prononciation *f.* pronunciation
prophète *m.* prophet
proportionnellement *adv.* proportionally
propos *m.* purpose; **à-propos** aptness; **à propos de** with respect to
proposer to propose
propre *adj.* clean (10); own; proper
propriétaire *m., f.* owner, proprietor
propriété *f.* ownership
prospecter to prospect
prospecteur (-trice) *m., f.* prospector
protecteur (-euse) *adj.* protective
protectioniste *adj.* protectionist
protéger to protect (15)
provençal *adj.* of Provence
provoquer to provoke, bring on
proximité *f.* proximity; **à proximité (de)** close by
prudemment *adv.* cautiously
prudent *adj.* careful
pruneau *m.* prune
psychique *adj.* psychological; psychic
psychologie *f.* psychology (1)
psychologique *adj.* psychological
psychologue *m., f.* psychologist
pu *p.p.* of **pouvoir**
public (-ique) *adj.* public (10); **le grand public** the general public; **opinion publique** public opinion (15); *m.* the public
publicitaire *adj.* advertising (13); *m., f.* advertising executive
publicité *f.* advertising (9)
publier to publish
puéril *adj.* childish
puis *adv.* then, next (6); **et puis** and then; besides
puissance *f.* power, strength
pull(-over) *m.* pullover (sweater) (2)
punissable *adj.* punishable
pur *adj.* pure
purée: purée (*f.*) **de carottes** mashed carrots
pyramide *f.* pyramid

quai *m.* quay, platform (*train station*) (8)
qualificatif (-ive) *adj.* qualifying
qualifié *adj.* qualified
qualité *f.* quality
quand *adv.* when (2); whenever, while; **depuis quand** since when; **quand même** nevertheless
quantité *f.* quantity
quarante *adj.* forty (0)
quart *m.* quarter; **et quart** quarter past (the hour) (5); **moins le quart** fifteen minutes before the hour (5)
quartier *m.* quarter, neighborhood, district (1)
quatorze *adj.* fourteen (0)
quatorzième *adj.* fourteenth
quatre *adj.* four (0)
quatrième *adj.* fourth
que *conj.* that, than; **ne... que** only (8); *pron.* whom, that, which, what (13)
Québec *m.* Quebec City (17); **le Québec** (province of) Quebec (17)
québécois *adj.* of or from Quebec (17); *n.* French Canadian (language) (17)
quel(le) *adj.* what, which (6)
quelque(s) *adj.* some, a few (16); **quelque chose** *pron.* something (8); **quelques-un(e)s (de)** some (of) (16)
quelquefois *adv.* sometimes (1)
quelqu'un *pron.* someone (8)
questionner (sur) to question (about)
quête *f.* quest; collection
qui *pron.* who, whom (13)
quinze *adj.* fifteenth (0)
quinzième *adj.* fifteenth
quitter to leave (7); **ne quittez pas** don't hang up (9); **se quitter** to separate, leave each other
quoi *pron.* which, what (12); **il n'y a pas de quoi** you're welcome (14); **quoi de neuf?** what's new? **quoi donc?** what did you say?
quoique *conj.* although, even though (17)
quotidien(ne) *adj.* daily (12); *m.* daily newspaper
quotidiennement *adv.* daily

racisme *m.* racism
raconter to tell, relate (9)
radiophonique *adj.* radio
rafraîchir to refresh; to cool down
raisin *m.* grape (16)
raison *f.* reason; **avoir raison** to be right (3)
raisonnable *adj.* reasonable (2)
ralentir to slow down
ramasser to gather, collect
randonnée *f.* hike (16)
rapidement *adv.* rapidly
rappeler to remind (9); **se rappeler** to remember (11)
rapport *m.* report; relationship
rapporter to bring back
raquette *f.* racket
rarement *adv.* rarely (1)
ras: au ras de level with; just above; close to
raser to shave; to raze; **se raser** to shave; *fam.* to bore, to irritate
rassembler to assemble
rassurant *adj.* reassuring
rater *fam.* to fail
ratifier to ratify
ravager to ravage
ravi *adj.* delighted (14)
rayon *m.* ray
RDA *ab.* of **République démocratique allemande** (East Germany)
réacteur *m.* jet engine; reactor
réaction *f.* reaction
réagir to react
réalisateur (-trice) *m., f.* director, filmmaker
réalisation *f.* realization
réaliser to realize; achieve *(an ambition)*
réalisme *m.* realism
réaliste *adj.* realistic (2)
réalité *f.* reality
reboisement *m.* reforestation
récemment *adv.* recently
récent *adj.* recent, new
réception *f.* reception desk
recette *f.* recipe
recevoir to receive (16)
réchauffement *m.* warming up
recherche *f.* research, search; **à la recherche de** in search of
recherché *adj.* much sought-after
récif *m.* reef
réciprocité *f.* reciprocity
récit *m.* account, story
réclamer to ask for
récolte *f.* harvesting
recommandation *f.* recommendation

recommander to recommend
recommencer to start over
reconnaître to recognize (15)
reconnu *p.p.* of **reconnaître**
reconquête *f.* recapture, recovery
reconstituer to restore, reconstitute
reconstruire to rebuild
recréer to recreate
recrutement *m.* recruitment
recruter to recruit
recteur *m.* rector; commissioner of education
reçu *p.p.* of **recevoir;** *m.* receipt (13)
récupérer to get back, recover
recyclage *m.* recycling (15)
recycler to recycle (15)
rédacteur (-trice) *m., f.* editor; **rédacteur en chief** editor-in-chief
rédaction *f.* drafting, writing
redécouvrir to rediscover
redevance *f.* dues, fees
réduire to reduce, lower
réduit *p.p.* of **réduire;** *adj.* reduced
réel(le) *adj.* real, true
réellement *adv.* really, truly
refaire to redo
référence *f.* reference
se référer (à) to refer (to)
réfléchir (à) to reflect (upon), consider (3)
reflet *m.* reflection
réflexion *f.* thought, reflection
réforme *f.* reform (15)
réformer to reform, improve
refus *m.* refusal
refuser (de) to refuse (14); to deny
regarder to look at, watch (1); **se regarder** to look at each other, oneself
régent *m., f.* regent
régime *m.* diet (5)
région *f.* region, territory
régional *adj.* local
règle *f.* rule (14)
régler to regulate
regretter to be sorry (15)
regroupé *adj.* grouped together
régulier (-ière) *adj.* regular
regulièrement *adv.* regularly
réhabilitation *f.* rehabilitation; restoring to favor
reine *f.* queen
rejet *m.* rejection
rejeter to reject
rejoindre to rejoin
rejouer to play again
relâché *adj.* loose
relais m. relay
relatif (-ive) *adj.* relatively
relativement *adv.* relatively
se relaxer to relax
relecture *f.* rereading
relier to connect, link
religieux (-ieuse) *adj.* religious
remarquable *adv.* remarkable
rembourser to repay, reimburse
remède *m.* remedy
remercier to thank (14); **je vous remercie** I thank you; **je ne sais pas vous remercier** I don't know how to thank you (14)
remettre to put back
remise *f.* delivery
remonter to go upstream
remous *m.* upheaval
remplacer to replace, substitute
remplir to fill (11)
rémunération *f.* remuneration
rencontre *f.* meeting (12)
rencontrer to meet; **se rencontrer** to meet each other (12)
rendez-vous *m.* rendezvous, appointment (1); meeting place; **prendre rendez-vous** to make an appointment
rendre to give back (4); to render, make; **rendre visite (à)** to visit (*a person*) (4); **se rendre** to go; to give up
renforcement *m.* reinforcement
renforcer to reinforce, strengthen
renommé *adj.* renowned
renoncer to give up
rénové *adj.* renovated
renseignement *m.* information
renseigner to inform, teach; **se renseigner** to ask for information
rentrée *f.* return, return to school (*in the fall*) (11)
rentrer to return, return home (8)
réorientation *f.* reorientation
répandre to spread
réparation *f.* repair
réparer to repair
repartir to set out again
repas *m.* meal (5)
répertoire *m.* repertory
répéter to repeat
répondeur: répondeur (*m.*) **téléphonique** answering machine
répondre to answer, reply (4)
réponse *f.* answer, reply
repos *m.* rest
reposer: se reposer to rest (11)
reprendre to take up again (11); to recover
représentant *m., f.* representative
représenter to represent
reprise *f.* renewal, resumption
se reproduire to recur
république *f.* republic
réputation *f.* reputation
réseau *m.* network, system
réservation *f.* reservation
réserve *f.* reserve
réserver to reserve, make a reservation
réservoir *m.* reservoir
résidence *f.* residence
résider to reside, dwell, live
résister to resist
résolument *adv.* resolutely
résolution *f.* resolution
résoudre to resolve, settle, solve
respecter to respect
responsabilité *f.* responsibility
responsable *adj.* responsible, accountable
ressemblance *f.* resemblance
ressembler (à) to be like, resemble
ressentir to feel
ressource *f.* resource; **ressources naturelles** natural resources (15)
restaurer to restore
restau-U *m.* university cafeteria
reste *m.* rest, remainder
rester to stay (4)
résultat *m.* result
résulter (de) to result (from)
résumer to sum up
retard *m.* delay; **en retard** late (8)
retenir to retain
retirer to take out (13)
retour *m.* return
retourner to return
retracer to relate, recount
retrait *m.* withdrawal
retransmettre to broadcast, relay
retrouver to recover, find again; to recognize
réunion f. meeting, reunion
réunir to unite
réussir (à) to succeed, pass (*a test*) (3)
réussite *f.* success (15)
revanche: en revanche on the other hand
rêve *m.* dream
réveil *m.* alarm clock
réveiller to awaken; **se réveiller** to wake up (12)
révéler to reveal
revendication *f.* demand, claim
revenir to come back, return (7)
revenu *m.* income, revenue
rêver to dream (1)
réviser to review (11)
revoir to see again (7); **au revoir** good-bye (0)
révolution *f.* revolution
révolutionnaire *m., f.* revolutionary
revu *p.p.* of **revoir**
revue *f.* review, magazine (3)
rez-de-chaussée *m.* ground floor
RFA *ab.* of **République fédérale d'Allemagne** (West Germany)
Rhin *m.* Rhine river
rhinocéros *m.* rhinoceros
Rhône *m.* Rhone river
rhum *m.* rum
rhume *m.* cold
ri *p.p.* of **rire**
riche *adj.* rich
richesse *f.* wealth
ridé *adj.* wrinkled
rideau *m.* curtain (3)

rien *indef. pron.* nothing; **de rien** you're welcome (0); **ne... rien** nothing (8)
rigolo (-ote) *adj.* funny
rire to laugh (14); *m.* laughter
risque *m.* risk
rite *m.* rite, ritual
rival(e) *m., f.* rival
rivalité *f.* rivalry
rive *f.* bank, shore; **Rive droite** Right Bank (of Paris) (10); **Rive gauche** Left Bank (of Paris) (10)
rivière *f.* river (tributary)
riz *m.* rice; **riz complet** brown rice
robe *f.* dress (2)
robuste *adj.* sturdy, strong
rocher *m.* rock, crag
rocheux (-euse) *adj.* rocky
rockeur (-euse) *m., f.* fan of rock 'n' roll
roi *m.* king (16)
rôle *m.* part, role; **jeu** (*m.*) **de rôle** role-play; **jouer un rôle** to play a role
romain *adj.* Roman (16)
roman *m.* novel (9); **roman policier** detective novel
romancier (-ière) *m., f.* novelist (17)
romantique *adj.* romantic
roquefort *m.* Roquefort cheese
rose *f.* rose; *adj.* pink (2)
roseau *m.* reed
rosier *m.* rosebush
rossignol *m.* nightingale
rôti *m.* roast (6); **dinde rôtie** roast turkey (5)
rouage *m.* machinery
rouge *adj.* red (2); **feu** (*m.*) **rouge** red (traffic) light
rouler to roll (along); to drive (8)
roulette *f.* roller; roulette (*game*)
roumain *adj.* Romanian
route *f.* road, route (7); **bonne route!** have a safe journey! **en route** on the road
routinier (-ière) *adj.* humdrum, routine
roux (rousse) *adj.* reddish, red-haired (3)
royaliste *adj.* royalist
royaume *m.* kingdom, realm
rue *f.* street (3)
ruine *f.* ruin; **en ruine** in ruins
ruisseau *m.* stream, brook
rumeur *f.* rumor
russe *adj.* Russian (1)
rustique *adj.* rustic
rythme *m.* rhythm

sa *adj. f.* his, hers, its
sable *m.* sand
sac *m.* bag; **sac à dos** backpack (2); **sac à main** handbag (2); **sac de couchage** sleeping bag (7)
saccagé *adj.* devastated
sacré *adj.* sacred
sage *adj.* wise
sagesse *f.* wisdom
Sagittaire *m.* Sagittarius
saignant *adj.* rare (*meat*)
sain *adj.* healthy
saint *adj.* holy; **Saint-Valentin** *f.* Saint Valentine's Day
saison *f.* season; **demi-saison** *f.* spring (*cool season*); **hors saison** out of season (5)
saisonnier (-ière) *adj.* seasonal
salade *f.* salad (5)
salaire *m.* salary, wages (13)
salarié *adj.* salaried
salé *adj.* salted, salty
salière *f.* saltcellar
salle *f.* room; theater; **salle à manger** dining room (4); **salle d'attente** waiting room; **salle d'eau** shower room; **salle de bains** bathroom (4); **salle de classe** classroom (0); **salle de séjour** living room (4); **salle de sport** gym
salon *m.* parlor
saluer to greet
salut *int.* hello, hi (0)
samedi *m.* Saturday (0)
sandale *f.* sandal (2)
sang *m.* blood
sang-froid; garder son sang-froid to keep one's cool
sanglier *m.* (wild) boar
sans *prep.* without (3); but for; **sans doute** no doubt, probably; **sans faute** without fail; **sans que** *conj.* without (17)
santé *f.* health; **bilan** (*m.*) **de santé** checkup (12)
santiag *m.* cowboy boot
Saoudite: Arabie (*f.*) **Saoudite** Saudi Arabia
sapin *m.* fir tree
sarcastique *adj.* sarcastic
satirique *adj.* satirical
satisfaire to satisfy
satisfait *adj.* content, pleased
Saturne *f.* Saturn
saucisse *f.* sausage
saucisson *m.* sausage, salami (6)
sauf *prep.* except for, save
saumon *m.* salmon
sauvage *adj.* wild
sauver to save (15)
saveur *f.* flavor
savoir to know (how) (10)
savoureux (-euse) *adj.* savory
scandale *m.* scandal
scandaleux (-euse) *adj.* scandalous
sceller to seal
scénario *m.* scenario
scène *f.* scene, quarrel; **mise** (*f.*) **en scène** staging, production
sceptique *m., f.* skeptic
schéma *m.* diagram
science: les sciences (*f. pl.*) **économiques** economics
scolaire *adj.* scholarly, of school; **congés** (*m. pl.*) **scolaires** school vacation; **fournitures** (*f. pl.*) **scolaires** school supplies
scolarité *f.* schooling
sculpter to sculpt
sculpteur *m.* sculptor
séance *f.* film (showing) (14)
sec (sèche) *adj.* dry; **fruit** (*m.*) **sec** dried fruit
sécession *f.* secession
sécher to dry; *fam.* to cut (*class*); **se sécher** to dry oneself (12)
secondaire *adj.* secondary (11)
secours *m.* help
secret (-ète) *adj.* secret
secrétaire *m., f.* secretary; *m.* writing desk
secteur *m.* sector, district
sécurisant *adj.* reassuring
sécurité *f.* security; confidence; safety
séduction *f.* seduction
séduire to seduce
seize *adj.* sixteen (0)
séjour *m.* stay; **salle** (*m.*) **de séjour** living room (4)
sel *m.* salt (5)
sélection *f.* selection
sélectionné *adj.* specially selected
selon *prep.* according to, depending on
semaine *f.* week (7); **fin** (*f.*) **de semaine** weekend
semblable *adj.* similar (16)
sembler to seem, appear; **il semble que** it seems that (15)
semestre *m.* semester
sénat *m.* senate
sénateur *m.* senator
Sénégal *m.* Senegal
sénégalais *adj.* Senegalese
sens *m.* meaning; **sens interdit** wrong way; **sens pratique** common sense
sensationnel(le) *adj.* sensational
sensibiliser to sensitize
sensiblement *adv.* markedly, appreciably
sensualité *f.* sensuality
senteur *f.* scent, perfume
sentier *m.* path
sentiment *m.* feeling, sentiment
sentir to sense; to smell (7)
séparément *adv.* separately
séparer to separate
sept *adj.* seven (0)
septembre *m.* September (3)
septentrional *adj.* northern
septième *adj.* seventh
séquence *f.* sequence
série *f.* series
sérieusement *adv.* seriously
sérieux (-ieuse) *adj.* serious (2); **prendre au sérieux** to take seriously
serre: l'effet (*m.*) **de serre** the greenhouse effect
serré *adj.* tight
sertir to set

serveur (-euse) *m., f.* waiter, waitress (6)
serviette *f.* napkin (5)
servir to serve (7); to help; **servir (à)** to be used (to, as)
ses *adj. pl.* his, hers, its, one's
seul *adj.* alone, sole, only (9)
seulement *adv.* only (7)
sévère *adj.* severe, grave
sexe *m.* sex
sexisme *m.* sexism (15)
shampooing *m.* shampoo
shopping: faire du shopping to go shopping
short *m.* shorts (7)
si *adv.* so (6); yes (8); *conj.* if, whether (6)
SIDA *ab.* of **Syndrome Immuno-Déficitaire Acquis** AIDS
sidérurgique *adj.* steel-making
siècle *m.* century (16)
siège *m.* seat, headquarters
sien(ne) *pron.* his, hers, its
sieste *f.* siesta; **faire la sieste** to take a nap
signalé *adj.* signal
signaler to indicate; to be a sign of
signalétique; fiche (*f.*) signalétique (police) identification sheet
signe *m.* sign, mark
signer to sign (13)
signifier to mean, signify
silencieux (-ieuse) *adj.* silent
similaire *adj.* similar
simplement *adv.* simply
simplifier to simplify
sincère *adj.* sincere, frank (2)
sincérité *f.* sincerity
singulier (-ière) *adj.* singular
sinon *conj.* otherwise, if not
sirop *m.* syrup; **sirop d'érable** maple syrup
site *m.* setting; site
situation *f.* position (*location*)
situé *adj.* situated
se situer to be situated
sixième *adj.* sixth
ski *m.* ski, skiing (7); **lunettes (*f. pl.*) de ski** ski goggles; **ski nautique** water skiing
skier to ski (1)
skieur (-ieuse) *m., f.* skier
slip: slip (*m.*) de bain (*man's*) swimsuit (7)
SMIC *ab.* of **salaire minimum interprofessionnel de croissance** guaranteed minimum wage
snob *adj.* snobbish, pretentious (2)
sociable *adj.* social
socialiste *m., f.* socialist
société *f.* society, association, company (13); **jeu (*m.*) de société** parlor game (14)
sociologie *f.* sociology (1)
sociologue *m., f.* sociologist
sœur *f.* sister (4)
soi: soi-même *pron.* oneself, himself, herself, itself
soie *f.* silk
soif *f.* thirst; **avoir soif** to be thirsty (3)
soigner to take care of
soigneusement *adv.* carefully, neatly
soin *m.* care
soir *m.* evening, night; **bonsoir** good afternoon; good evening (0); **du soir** P.M. (5); **tous les soirs** every night
soirée *f.* evening (*duration*) (7); party (1)
soixante *adj.* sixty (0)
sol *m.* ground; floor; soil
solaire *adj.* solar; **énergie solaire** solar energy (15); **huile (*f.*) solaire** suntan oil
soldat *m.* soldier
solde *f.* pay (*wages*); *m.* balance; sale
sole *f.* sole (*fish*) (6)
soleil *m.* sun; **faire du soleil** to be sunny; **il fait du soleil** it's sunny (5); **lunettes (*f. pl.*) de soleil** sunglasses; **prendre le soleil** to sunbathe
solidarité *f.* solidarity
solide *adj.* solid, strong
solitaire *adj.* solitary
sombre *adj.* dark, gloomy
somme *f.* sum
sommeil *m.* sleep; **avoir sommeil** to be sleepy (3)
sommet *m.* summit
son *adj.* his, hers, its, one's
sondage *m.* opinion poll
sonder to sound out
songe *m.* dream
sonner to ring (9)
sonnette *f.* bell
sophistiqué *adj.* sophisticated
sorbet *m.* sherbet
sorte *f.* sort, kind
sortie *f.* exit, outing
sortilège *m.* (magic) spell
sortir to leave; to go out (7)
souci *m.* care, worry
soudain *adv.* suddenly (10)
Soudan *m.* the Sudan
souffert *p.p.* of **souffrir**
souffle *m.* blow, puff
souffler to blow
souffrir to suffer (13)
soufre *m.* sulfur
souhaiter to wish, desire (15)
soulèvement *m.* uprising
souligner to underline
soupe *f.* soup; **cuillère (*f.*) à soupe** tablespoon, soupspoon
souper *m.* supper
souple *adj.* supple, pliable
source *f.* source, origin; spring (15)
sous *prep.* under, below (2); **sous forme de** in the form of; **sous terre** underground
sous-marin *adj.* underwater; **faire de la pêche sous-marine** to go underwater fishing; **plongée (*f.*) sous-marine** scuba diving
soutenir to sustain, support
souterrain *m.* underground passage
souvenir *m.* memory; **se souvenir de** to remember (11)
souvent *adv.* often, frequently (1)
souveraineté *f.* sovereignty
soviétique *adj.* Soviet
spacieux (-euse) *adj.* spacious, roomy
spécial *adj.* special
spécialement *adv.* especially, particularly
spécialisation *f.* specialization
spécialiser to specialize; **se spécialiser** to specialize in
spécialiste *m., f.* specialist
spécialité *f.* specialty
spécification *f.* specification
spécifier to specify
spectacle *m.* show, performance (14)
spectaculaire *adj.* spectacular
splendeur *f.* splendor
splendide *adj.* magnificent
spontané *adj.* spontaneous
sport: faire du sport to participate in sports
sportif (-ive) *adj.* athletic, sports-minded (2); **manifestation sportive** sporting event (14)
stade *m.* stadium
stage *m.* training period, training course
stagiaire *m., f.* apprentice
stationner to park; **défense de stationner** no parking
statut *m.* status
stéréo *adj.* stereo; **chaîne (*f.*) stéréo** stereo (system) (3)
stéréotype *m.* stereotype
stimuler to stimulate
stocker to stock
stratégie *f.* strategy
stressant *adj.* stressful
strophe *f.* verse, stanza
studieux (-ieuse) *adj.* studious
stupéfiant *adj.* stunning, astounding
stupide *adj.* stupid, foolish
stylo *m.* pen (0)
su *p.p.* of **savoir**
subir to be subjected to, undergo
subjonctif *m.* subjunctive mood
subsaharien(ne) *adj.* sub-Saharan
substantif (-ive) *adj.* noun, nominal
substituer to substitute
subtil adj. subtle
subventionné *adj.* subsidized
succès *m.* success
sucre *m.* sugar (5)
sud *m.* south; **au sud** to the south (8)
Suède *f.* Sweden
suffisamment *adv.* sufficiently, enough
suffisant *adj.* sufficient
suffrage: suffrage (*m.*) universel universal suffrage
suggérer to suggest

Suisse *f.* Switzerland (8)
suite *f.* rest; **à la suite (de)** after; **tout de suite** right away
suivant *adj.* following, subsequent
suivre to follow (11); **suivre un cours** to take a course, a class (11)
sujet *m.* subject
superbe *adj.* superb
superficie *f.* area, surface
superflu *adj.* superfluous
supérieur *adj.* superior, upper (11); **cadre** (*m.*) **supérieur** executive
superlatif (-ive) *adj.* superlative
supermarché *m.* supermarket
superstitieux (-ieuse) *adj.* superstitious
supplément *m.* supplement
supplémentaire *adj.* supplementary
supporter to support
supposer to suppose
sur *prep.* on, upon (2); **sur place** installed
sûr *adj.* certain, sure (15); safe; **bien sûr** of course
sûrement *adv.* certainly
surexploité *adj.* exploited
surprenant *adj.* surprising
surprendre to surprise
surpris *adj.* surprised (15)
surtout *adv.* above all, especially (9)
surveiller to keep watch over, supervise
survie *f.* survival
survivre to survive
survoler to fly over
suspecte *f.* suspect
suspens *m.* suspense
symbole *m.* symbol
symboliser to symbolize
sympa *adj. fam. ab.* of **sympathique** (2)
sympathique *adj.* congenial, likable, nice (2)
symphonie *f.* symphony
symptomatique *adj.* symptomatic
syndicat *m.* trade union; **syndicat d'initiative** tourist information bureau (10)
synonyme *adj.* synonymous
synthèse *f.* synthesis
Syrie *f.* Syria
système *m.* system, plan

ta *adj. fam.* your
tabac *m.* tobacco; tobacco counter; tobacco shop
table *m.* (0); **à table** at the table (5)
tableau *m.* picture, painting (16); **tableau d'affichage** notice board; **tableau noir** blackboard (0)
tabuler to tabulate
tâche *f.* task; **la tâche** by the piece
taille *f.* height, size; **de taille moyenne** of average height (3)
tailleur *m.* (*lady's*) suit (2)
tant *adv.* so much; **tant de** so much, so many (16); **tant pis** too bad (12)
tante *f.* aunt (4)
tantôt *adv.* shortly; now . . . , now (then); sometimes . . .
Tanzanie *f.* Tanzania
taper to type
tapis *m.* carpet, rug (3)
tard *adv.* late (7); **plus tard** later
tarif *m.* rate; **demi-tarif** *m.* half price
tarte *f.* pie (5)
tartine *f.* slice of bread (*with jam or butter*)
tas (de) *m.* heap, pile
tasse *f.* cup (5)
tatin: tarte (*f.*) **tatin** a kind of tart
taudis *m.* slum
Taureau *m.* Taurus
taux *m.* rate
taverne *f.* inn, tavern
taxe *f.* tax, duty
Tchécoslovaquie *f.* Czechoslovakia
Tchekhov *m.* Chekhov
technicien(ne) *m., f.* technician
technique *adj.* technical
technologie *f.* technology
technologique *adj.* technological
tee-shirt *m.* T-shirt (2)
teinté *adj.* tinted, tinged
tel(le) *adj.* such, like
télé(vision) *f.* television, TV (1)
télégramme *m.* telegram (9)
télégraphique *adj.* telegraphic
téléphone *m.* telephone (3); **au téléphone** on the telephone (9); **coup** (*m.*) **de téléphone** telephone call (4)
téléphoner (à) to telephone (2)
téléphonique *adj.* relating to the telephone; **cabine** (*f.*) **téléphonique** telephone booth; **conversation** (*f.*) **téléphonique** phone conversation; **répondeur** (*m.*) **téléphonique** answering machine
télescope *m.* telescope
téléspectateur (-trice) *m., f.* television viewer
téléviseur *m.* television set
télex *m.* telex
tellement *adj.* so, so much
tempérament *m.* constitution
température *f.* temperature
tempête *f.* storm
temporaire *adj.* temporary
temps *m.* weather; time (4); tense; **de temps en temps** from time to time (10); **en même temps** at the same time; **quel temps fait-il?** what's the weather like? (5); **tout le temps** all the time
tendance *f.* tendency
tendre *adj.* tender, new
tendrement *adv.* tenderly
tendu *adj.* tight, taut, tensed
ténébreux (-euse) *adj.* dark, gloomy
tenir to hold, to have (7); **se tenir** to be held; **tenir à** to hold dear; to be eager to (7); to anticipate
tennis *m.* tennis (2); *pl.* tennis shoes (7)
tentation *f.* temptation
tentative *f.* attempt
tente *f.* tent (7)
tenter to tempt; to attempt
terme *m.* term
terminer to end; **se terminer** to come to an end
terrain *m.* ground, field; **terrain de camping** campground; **terrain de jeu** playing field or court
terrasse *f.* terrace (4)
terre *f.* earth, land (2); property; **pomme de terre** *f.* potato
Terre-Neuve *f.* Newfoundland (17)
terreur *f.* terror; **la Terreur** the Reign of Terror
terrifiant *adj.* terrifying
terrine: terrine (*f.*) **du chef** chef's special pâté
territoire *m.* territory
terroir *m.* soil
terrorisme *m.* terrorism
tes *adj. pl.* your
tester to test
tête *f.* head (12); **avoir mal à la tête** to have a headache; **tête-à-tête** *m.* private conversation
texte *m.* text, passage
TF1 *ab.* of **Télévision Française Un** (French television channel)
TGV *ab.* of **train à grande vitesse**
Thaïlande *f.* Thailand
thalasso: cure (*f.*) **thalasso** sea water treatment
thé *m.* tea (5)
théâtre *m.* theater; **pièce** (*f.*) **de théâtre** play (14)
thème *m.* theme, topic
théorie *f.* theory
thèse *f.* thesis, dissertation
thon *m.* tuna
thym *m.* thyme
thyroïde *f.* thyroid
tien(ne) *pron.* yours
tiers *adj.* third; **Tiers Monde** *m.* Third World
tigre *m.* tiger
tilleul *m.* linden trees; lime trees
timbre *m.* stamp (9)
timide *adj.* timid
timidement *adv.* timidly
timidité *f.* timidity
tinque *m.* Q. tank
tir: tir (*m.*) **à l'arc** archery
tirer to pull out, pull on, tug
tiret *m.* dash, hyphen
tissage *m.* weaving
titre *m.* title
toi *pron.* you (11); **à toi** to you; **toi-même** yourself
toile *f.* cloth
toilette *f.* lavatory; **faire sa toilette** to wash and dress
toit *m.* roof

tomate *f.* tomato
tombeau *m.* tomb
tomber to fall (8); **laisser tomber** to drop; **tomber amoureux (de)** to fall in love (with) (12); **tomber en panne** to break down (8); **tomber malade** to fall ill
ton *adj.* your
tonne *f.* ton
tonnerre *m.* thunder
tonus *m.* muscular tone
topaze *f.* topaz
tordre to twist; **se tordre** to be doubled up (with pain, with laughter)
tort *m.* wrong; **avoir tort** to be wrong (3)
tortue *f.* tortoise, turtle
tôt *adv.* soon, early (8)
total *adj.* total; *m.* whole, total
toucher to touch; to affect; to concern (10); to cash a check (13)
toujours *adv.* always, still (1)
tour *m.* turn; tour; **à ton tour** (it's) your turn; **demi-tour** turnabout, U-turn; *f.* tower (10)
tourisme *m.* tourism
touriste *m., f.* tourist
touristique *adj.* touristic
tournage *m.* shooting (of a film)
tournedos *m.* tornado
tourner to turn (10)
tout (tous) *adj.* all, every, each (3); **à tout moment** continually; **en tout cas** in any case, however; *adv.* entirely, quite; **tout d'abord** initially; **tout à fait** completely; **tout à l'heure** just now; **toute de suite** immediately (4); **tout droit** straight ahead (10); **tout d'un coup** all at once (10); **tout en** + *present participle* while . . . , at the same time . . . ; **tout le monde** everyone (8)
tout *pron.* everything (8)
toutefois *adv.* yet, however
toxique *adj.* toxic
tract *m.* pamphlet
tracteur *m.* tractor
traditionaliste *adj.* traditionalist
traditionnel(le) *adj.* traditional
traduire to translate
tragédie *f.* tragedy
train *m.* train (8); **être en train de** to be in the middle of (*doing something*) (14)
traité *m.* treaty
traitement *m.* treatment
traiter to treat, discuss
traiteur *m.* caterer
tranche *f.* slice
tranquille *adj.* quiet, calm (3)
tranquillement *adv.* quietly, calmly
tranquillité *f.* tranquility
transformer to transform, change
transfuge *m., f.* renegade
transmettre to transmit
transmis *adj.* transmitted
transport *m.* transport, transportation
transporter to transport, move
travail *m.* work, industry (1); **Fête** (*f.*) **du Travail** Labor Day; **travaux pratiques** small group work or lab; **travaux publics** public works
travailler to work (1)
travailleur (-euse) *m., f.* worker, laborer (13); *adj.* hard-working (2); **travailleur indépendant** self-employed worker (13); **travailleur salarié** salaried worker (13)
travers: à travers across, through
traverser to cross (8)
traversin *m.* bolster
treize *adj.* thirteen (0)
treizième *adj.* thirteenth
tréma *m.* diaeresis
tremblement: tremblement (*m.*) **de terre** *m.* earthquake
trente *adj.* thirty (0)
très *adv.* very, very much (2); **très bien** very good (0)
trésor *m.* treasure
trésorier (-ière) *m., f.* treasurer
tribu *f.* tribe
tribunal *m.* tribunal; court of law
tricoter to knit
trimestre *m.* quarter (*three months*), trimester
triomphe *m.* triumph
triste *adj.* sad (9)
trois *adj.* three (0)
troisième *adj.* third
tromper to deceive; **se tromper** to be mistaken (11)
trop *adv.* too much, too; **trop de** too many (5)
tropiques *m. pl.* the tropics
trottoir *m.* sidewalk
trou *m.* hole
troublé *adj.* troubled, worried; confused
trouver to find; to think (1); **se trouver** to be (*located*) (11)
truc *m., fam.* whatsit, thing (17)
ttc *ab.* of **toutes taxes comprises**
tu *pron.* you
tué *m., f.* person killed, casualty
tuer to kill
tulipe *f.* tulip
Tunisie *f.* Tunisia (18)
tunisien(ne) *adj.* Tunisian (18)
turc (turque) *m., f.* Turkish
tuteur *m.* tutor
type *m. fam.* guy; type
typique *adj.* typical
typiquement *adv.* typically
tzigane *adj.* (Hungarian) gypsy

ultramoderne *adj.* ultramodern
ultra-rapide *adj.* ultrafast
Ulysse *m.* Ulysses
un *adj.* one, a, an, any (0)
uni *adj.* united
unifié *adj.* unified
unir to unite
unité *f.* unit
univers *m.* universe
universel(le) *adj.* universal
universitaire *adj.* academic, university; **cité** (*f.*) **universitaire** university living quarters, dormitory (1)
université *f.* university (1)
urbain *adj.* urban
urbanisme *m.* town planning
U.R.S.S. *f.* U.S.S.R. (*Soviet Union*) (8)
usine *f.* factory
ustensile *m.* implement
utile *adj.* useful
utilisateur (-trice) *m., f.* user
utilisation *f.* utilization
utiliser to use, employ
utopique *adj.* Utopian

vacances *f. pl.* vacation (4); **en vacances** on vacation
vacancier (-ière) *m., f.* vacationer
vacherin *m.* Vacherin cheese
vagabonder to roam
vaincre to defeat, vanquish
vaisselle *f.* dishes (4)
valeur *f.* worth, value
valide *adj.* valid
valise *f.* suitcase (8); **faire sa valise** to pack one's suitcase
vallée *f.* valley
valoir to be worth (15); **valoir la peine** to be worth the trouble; **valoir mieux: il vaux mieux** it is better
vanille *f.* vanilla
varié *adj.* varied
varier to vary
variété *f.* variety; **chanson** (*f.*) **de variété** popular song (14)
vaste *adj.* vast
vaudou *m.* voodoo (17)
veau *m.* veal (5)
vécu *p.p.* of **vivre**
vedette *f.* celebrity, star
végétal *adj.* vegetable
végétarien(ne) *adj.* vegetarian
véhicule *m.* vehicle
veille: à la veille de on the eve of; **la veille** the day before
vélo *m.* bike; **faire du vélo** to go cycling
vençois *adj.* of Vence (*in French Alps*)
vendange *f.* grape harvest
vendeur (-euse) *m., f.* sales clerk
vendre to sell (4)
vendredi *m.* Friday (0)
venger to avenge
venir to come (7); **faire venir** to send for; **venir de** to have just (7)
vent *m.* wind
vente *f.* sale (11)
ventre *m.* belly, abdomen (12)
Vénus *f.* Venus

verbe *m.* verb
verdure *f.* greenery
vérifier to verify
véritable *adj.* genuine, true
vérité *f.* truth (9)
verre *m.* glass (5)
vers *prep.* toward (16)
Verseau *m.* Aquarius
versement *m.* payment (by installments)
verser to pour
verso: voir au verso see other side
vert *adj.* green, hearty (2); **l'Europe** (*f.*) **verte** European agriculture; **poivron** (*m.*) **vert** green pepper
vertigineux (-euse) *adj.* vertiginous, breathtaking
vertu *f.* virtue
veste *f.* jacket (2)
vestige *m.* relic; trace
veston *m.* (man's) suit jacket
vêtement *m.* garment; *pl.* clothes (2)
vétérinaire *m., f.* veterinarian (13)
viande *f.* meat (5)
victime *f.* victim
victoire *f.* victory
vide *adj.* empty
vidéocassette *f.* video cassette
vidéoclip *m.* videotape (14)
vie *f.* life (1); **assurance-vie** *f.* life insurance; **gagner sa vie** to earn one's living
vieillesse *f.* old age
vierge *f.* virgin; **Vierge** Virgo
vietnamien(ne) *adj.* Vietnamese
vieux (vieil, vieille) *adj.* old, aged (6)
vigne *f.* vineyard, vine (16)
vigneron *m.* vine grower (16)
vignette *f.* (manufacturer's) seal; illustration
vignoble *m.* vineyard (16)
villageois *adj.* rustic, country
ville *f.* city (1); **centre-ville** *m.* downtown (10)
vin *m.* wine (5)
vinaigrette *f.* vinegar and oil dressing
vingt *adj.* twenty (0); **vingt et un** twenty-one (0); **vingt-deux** twenty-two (0)
vingtaine *f.* twenty or so, about twenty
vingtième *adj.* twentieth
violet(te) *adj.* violet (2)
violon *m.* violin
virage *m.* curve (*in the road*)
visage *m.* face (12)
viser to aim at, be directed at
visite *f.* visit (1); **rendre visite à** to visit (*a person*)
visiter to visit (*a place*) (1)
visiteur (-euse) *m., f.* visitor
vite *adv.* quickly, fast (5); **guéris vite!** get well soon! (12)
vitesse *f.* speed, gear; **à grande vitesse** at full speed
viticulteur *m.* viticulturist, wine grower
vivants *m. pl.* the living
vive... ! *int.* long live . . . !
vivre to live (11)
vocabulaire *m.* vocabulary (0)
voici *prep.* here is (are) (0); this is; these are
voie *f.* road, way
voilà *prep.* there is (are) (0); **voilà... que** it's been . . . since
voile *f.* sail; *m.* veil; **faire de la voile** to sail; **faire de la planche à voile** to go windsurfing
voir to see (7); **se voir** to see each other, see oneself
voisin(e) *m., f.* neighbor (7)
voiture *f.* car, vehicle (2)
voix *f.* voice
vol *m.* flight (8); robbery
volcan *m.* volcano
voler to fly; to steal
volet *m.* shutter
voleur (-euse) *m., f.* thief, robber
volontaire *m., f.* volunteer
volontairement *adv.* voluntarily
volonté *f.* will, wish
volontiers *adv.* gladly, with pleasure
vos *adj. pl.* your
voter to vote
votre *adj.* your
vôtre (le/la) *pron.* yours, your own
voué (à) *adj.* dedicated (to), devoted (to)
vouloir to want, desire (6); **je voudrais...** I would like (7); **vouloir bien** to be willing (6); **vouloir dire** to mean (6)
voulu *p.p.* of **vouloir**
voyage *m.* trip (4); **agence** (*f.*) **de voyages** travel agency; **chèque** (*m.*) **de voyage** traveler's check
voyager to travel
voyageur (-euse) *m., f.* traveler, passenger
voyant(e) *m., f.* seer, fortune teller
voyelle *f.* vowel
vrai *adj.* true, genuine (6)
vraiment *adv.* really
vraisemblable *adj.* probable, believable
vu *p.p.* of **voir**
vue *f.* view, sight; **point** (*m.*) **de vue** viewpoint
vulnérable *adj.* vulnerable

wagon *m.* car (*train*) (8)
wagon-lit *m.* sleeping car
wagon-restaurant *m.* dining car
week-end *m.* weekend (10)

y *adv. pron.* there, here (10); **il y a** there is (are) (0)
yaourt *m.* yogurt
yeux *m. pl.* eyes (3)
Yougoslavie *f.* Yugoslavia

Zaïre *m.* Zaire
zaïrois *adj.* Zairian
zèbre *m.* zebra
zénith *m.* zenith
zéro *m.* zero
zodiaque *m.* zodiac
zone *f.* zone, area; **zone (non) fumeur** (non) smoking area
zoologie *f.* zoology
zoologique *adj.* zoological; **jardin** (*m.*) **zoologique** zoo
zoologiste *m., f.* zoologist
zut *excl.* darn it!

Lexique anglais-français

This English-French end vocabulary includes all words needed to do the translation exercises, as well as the words in the active vocabulary lists of all chapters.

Abbreviations

adj. adjective
adv. adverb
f. feminine noun
m. masculine noun
pl. plural
pron. pronoun
p.p. past participle

a un, une
abdomen ventre *m.*
able: to be able pouvoir
abolish abolir
about vers; de
abroad (*in a foreign country*) à l'étranger
absolute absolu(e)
accept accepter
accomplishment réussite *f.*
account compte *m.;* **checking account** compte courant; **savings account** compte d'épargne
accountant comptable *m., f.*
accounting comptabilité *f.*
across: across from en face de
act agir
address adresse *f.*
adore adorer
ads (classified) petites annonces *f. pl.*
advertisement (advertising) publicité *f.*
advice conseil *m.*
advise conseiller
afraid: to be afraid avoir peur
after(ward) après
afternoon après-midi *m., f.*
again de nouveau
against contre
agent (*insurance*) assureur *m.;* (*advertising*) publicitaire *m.*
ago il y a; **two days ago** il y a deux jours
agreeable agréable
agreed d'accord
agricultural agricole
airplane avion *m.*
airport aéroport *m.*
algebra algèbre *f.*
Algerian algérien(ne)
all tout, toute, tous, toutes; **all the time** tout le temps
almost presque
alone seul(e)
a lot (of) beaucoup (de)
already déjà
also aussi
although bien que, quoique
always toujours
America Amérique *f.*
American américain(e)
amount montant *m.*
amusing amusant(e)
ancestor ancêtre *m.*
and et
angry: to get angry se fâcher
another un(e) autre
answer réponse *f.;* **to answer** répondre à
antique ancien(ne)
anymore ne... plus
anyone quelqu'un; **not . . . anyone** ne... personne
anything quelque chose; **not . . . anything** ne... rien
apartment appartement *m.*
appetizer hors-d'œuvre *m.*
apple pomme *f.*
apprenticeship apprentissage *m.*
approve approuver
April avril *m.*
architect architecte *m., f.*
arena arène *f.*
argue se disputer
arithmetic calcul *m.*
arm bras *m.*
around autour de
arrival arrivée *f.*
arrive arriver
artist artiste *m., f.*
as comme, si, que; **as much/many as** autant que... ; autant (de)... que, aussi... que; **as soon as** dès que, aussitôt que
ashamed: to be ashamed avoir honte
ask (for) demander (à); **to ask a question** poser une question
astronomy astronomie *f.*
at à, chez; **at the** au, à la, aux
athletic sportif (-ive)
atmosphere atmosphère *f.*
attend assister à
August août *m.*
aunt tante *f.*
author auteur *m.*
automatic teller distributeur automatique
automobile voiture *f.*
autumn automne *m.*
awaken se réveiller
aware: to become aware of s'apercevoir de
awful affreux (-euse)

baby bébé *m.*
backpack sac à dos *m.*
bad mauvais; **it's bad weather** il fait mauvais; **it is too bad that . . .** il est dommage que... ; **not bad** pas mal; **That's too bad!** Quel dommage! **Too bad!** Tant pis! **What bad news!** Quelle mauvaise nouvelle!
badly mal; **things are going badly** ça va mal
bakery boulangerie *f.*
balcony balcon *m.*
ball: masked ball bal masqué *m.*
bank banque *f.*
banker banquier (-ière) *m., f.*
bargain marchander
bar-tobacconist café-tabac *m.*
bathe se baigner
bathroom salle de bains *f.*
be être; **how are you?** comment allez-vous? **isn't it?** n'est-ce pas? **it is, that is** c'est; **there is, there are** il y a; **to be able** pouvoir; **to be eager** tenir à; **to be hungry** avoir faim; **to be afraid** avoir peur; **to be sleepy** avoir sommeil; **to be thirsty** avoir soif; **to be wrong** avoir tort
beach plage *f.*
beautiful beau, bel, belle, beaux, belles
beauty beauté *f.*
because parce que; **because of** à cause de
become devenir; **to become accustomed to** s'habituer à; **to become aware of** s'apercevoir de
bed lit *m.;* **to go to bed** se coucher
bedroom chambre *f.*

beer bière *f.*
before avant, avant de, avant que; **before** (*doing something*) avant de (+ *inf.*)
begin commencer, se mettre à
beginning début *m.*
behind derrière
believe croire, estimer; **to believe in** croire à
belong appartenir (à)
berth couchette *f.*
beside à côté de
best meilleur(e), mieux
better meilleur(e), mieux; **it's better that** il vaut mieux que; **we had better** nous devrions
between entre
bicycle bicyclette *f.*
big grand(e), gros(se)
bill addition *f.;* **bill** (*currency*) billet *m.*
bird oiseau *m.*
birthday anniversaire *m.*
black noir
blackboard tableau noir *m.*
blazer veste *f.*
blouse chemisier *m.*
blue bleu(e)
boarding pass carte d'embarquement *f.*
boat bateau *m.*
bocce ball pétanque *f.*
body corps *m.*
book livre *m.*
bookcase étagère *f.*
bookstore librairie *f.*
boot botte *f.*
bored: to be bored s'ennuyer
boring ennuyeux (-euse)
born né(e); **to be born** naître
borrow emprunter
both tous/toutes les deux
bottle bouteille *f.*
bowl bol *m.*
bowling (lawn) pétanque *f.*
boy garçon *m.*
brave courageux (-euse)
bread pain *m.*
break down (*vehicle*) tomber en panne
breakfast petit déjeuner *m.*
brief bref (brève)
briefly brièvement
bring apporter; **to bring** (*a person somewhere*) amener
brother frère *m.*
brown marron; **brown** (*hair*) châtain
brush brosse *f.;* **to brush** (se) brosser
budget budget *m.*
build construire; bâtir
building immeuble *m.*
bus autobus *m.*
business class classe d'affaires *f.*
but mais
butcher: butcher shop boucherie *f.;* **pork butcher's shop** charcuterie *f.*
butter beurre *m.*
buy acheter
by par, en

Cajun acadien(ne)
cake gâteau *m.*
call appeler, téléphoner (à); **telephone call** coup de téléphone *m.;* **who may I say is calling?** c'est de la part de qui? **who's calling?** qui est à l'appareil? **to be called** (*named*) s'appeler; **to call back** rappeler
calm calme *m.;* tranquille *adj.*
camera appareil-photo *m.*
camp camper
can (*to be able to*) pouvoir; **can** (*of food*) boîte de conserve *f.*
candy bonbon *m.*
capital capitale *f.*
car voiture *f.;* (*train*) wagon *m.*
care: I don't care Je m'en fiche
carrot carotte *f.*
carry porter; **to carry away** emporter
case cas *m.;* **in that case** alors
cash argent liquide *m.;* **cash a check** toucher un chèque
cash register caisse *f.*
cashier caissier (-ière) *m., f.*
castle château *m.*
cat chat *m.*
cathedral cathédrale *f.*
celebrate fêter
celebration fête *f.*
centime one 100th part of franc *m.*
century siècle *m.*
certain sûr(e), certain(e)
chair chaise *f.*
chance: to have the chance to avoir l'occasion de
change monnaie *f.;* **to change** changer (de)
channel (*TV*) chaîne *f.*
character personnage *m.*
cheap bon marché
check chèque *m.;* (*in a restaurant*) addition *f.*
checkbook carnet de chèques *m.*
cheese fromage *m.*
chemistry chimie *f.*
chest of drawers commode *f.*
chestnut (candied) marron (glacé) *m.*
chicken poulet *m.*
child enfant *m.*
Chinese chinois(e)
chocolate chocolat *m.*
choice choix *m.*
choose choisir
church église *f.*
citizen citoyen(ne) *m., f.*
city ville *f.*
civil servant fonctionnaire *m., f.*
class classe *f.*
classical classique
classmate camarade de classe *m., f.*
classroom salle de classe *f.*
clean propre
clear clair(e)
climb monter
close fermer; **close to** près de
clothes vêtements *m. pl.*
coat manteau *m.*
coffee café *m.*
coin pièce *f.*
cold froid; **it's cold** il fait froid
collect collectionner
colonist colon *m.*
colonize coloniser
color couleur *f.*
comb peigne *m.;* **to comb** (se) peigner
come venir; **to come down** descendre; **to come back** revenir
commercial publicité *f.*
company société *f.*
compartment compartiment *m.*
computation calcul *m.*
computer ordinateur *m.*
computer science informatique *f.*
concern toucher
condition condition *f.;* **on condition that** à condition que
conference conférence *f.*
conflict conflit *m.*
conformist *m., f.* conformiste
Congolese congolais(e)
conserve conserver
consider estimer
constant constant(e)
construct construire
continue continuer (à)
contrary: on the contrary au contraire
control contrôle *m.*
cook faire la cuisine
cooking cuisine *f.;* **to do the cooking** faire la cuisine
cool frais (fraîche); **it's cool** il fait frais
corner coin *m.*
cost coûter; **cost of living** coût (*m.*) de la vie *f.*
country(side) campagne *f.*, paysage *m.*
courageous courageux (-euse)
course cours *m.;* **course** (*meal*) plat; (*first of meal*) entrée *f.;* **of course** (*not*) bien sûr que oui (non)
cousin cousin(e) *m., f.*
cover couvrir
crab crabe *m.*
craftsperson artisan(e) *m., f.*
crayfish écrevisse *f.*
cream crème *f.*
create créer
credit card carte de crédit *f.*
crepe crêpe *f.*
croissant croissant *m.*
cross traverser
cult culte *m.*
cup tasse *f.*
curly frisé(e)
curtain rideau *m.*
customs officer douanier (-ière) *m., f.*
cycling cyclisme *m.*

daily quotidien(ne)
dancer danseur (-euse) *m., f.*
data processing informatique *f.*
daughter fille *f.*
day jour *m.*, journée *f.;* **day before yesterday** avant-hier; **one of these days (someday)** un de ces jours
dear cher (chère)
December décembre *m.*
decide décider

degree diplôme *m.*; **bachelor's degree** licence *f.*; **master's degree** maîtrise *f.*
delicatessen charcuterie *f.*
delighted ravi(e)
demand exiger
demonstrate manifester
departure départ *m.*
deposit déposer
describe décrire
desert désert *m.*
desire désirer, souhaiter
determined: to be determined (*to do something*) tenir à
detest détester
desk bureau *m.*
dessert dessert *m.*
destroy détruire
develop développer
development développement *m.*
dial (*a number*) composer un numéro, faire un numéro
dictionary dictionnaire *m.*
die mourir
diet régime *m.*
different différent(e)
difficult difficile
dinner dîner *m.*; **to have dinner** dîner
diploma diplôme *m.*
direct diriger
discover découvrir
discuss discuter (de)
disguise: to disguise oneself se déguiser
dish plat *m.*; assiette *f.*
dishes: to do the dishes faire la vaisselle
diskette disquette *f.*
disorderly en désordre
division (*academic*) faculté *f.*
do faire; **do-it-yourself work** bricolage *m.*
doctor médecin *m.*
doctorate doctorat *m.*
dog chien *m.*
door porte *f.*; **next door** (**to**) à côté (de)
dormitory cité universitaire *f.*
double room chambre pour deux personnes *f.*
doubt douter
down: to come down descendre; **down with** à bas
downtown centre-ville *m.*
dramatic arts art dramatique *m.*
drawing dessin *m.*
dream rêve *m.*; **to dream** rêver
dress robe *f.*; **to dress** (s')habiller; **to dress up in disguise** se déguiser
drink boisson *f.*; **to drink** boire
drive conduire
driver conducteur (-trice) *m., f.*
dry: to dry oneself se sécher
during pendant
dynamic dynamique

each chaque; **each** (**one**) chacun(e); **each other** l'un l'autre, les uns les autres
eager: to be eager (*to do something*) tenir à
ear oreille *f.*
early tôt
earn gagner
earth terre *f.*
east: to the east à l'est *m.*
easy facile
eat manger
eccentric excentrique
eclair (*pastry*) éclair *m.*
ecological écologiste
economics sciences économiques *f. pl.*
egg œuf *m.*
eight huit
elect élire
eleven onze
employee employé(e)
end fin *f.*
end up (**by**) finir par
endorse (*a check*) endosser
energy énergie *f.*
engagement les fiançailles *f. pl.*
engineer ingénieur *m.*
engineering génie civil *m.*
English anglais *m.* (*language*); anglais(e); **English-speaking** anglophone
enough assez (de)
enter entrer
enthusiastic enthousiaste
envelope enveloppe *f.*
environment environnement *m.*
errands: to do errands faire les courses
escape échapper (à)
essential essentiel; **it is essential that** il est essentiel que
estimate estimer
Europe Europe *f.*
even même; **even though** bien que, quoique
evening soir *m.*; soirée *f.*; **good evening** bonsoir
event événement *m.*; (*sporting*) manifestation sportive *f.*
every chaque; tout, toute, tous, toutes; **every day** tous les jours
everyday quotidien(ne)
everything tout *m.*
everywhere partout
evident évident(e)
exam examen *m.*
example: for example par exemple
exchange rate cours *m.*
excuse oneself s'excuser; **excuse me** excusez-moi
expense dépense *f.*
expensive cher (chère)
explain expliquer
eye œil *m.*; **eyes** yeux

face visage *m.*
fact fait *m.*; **in fact** en fait
fail échouer (à)
fair juste
fall automne *m.*; **to fall** tomber; **to fall asleep** s'endormir; **to fall in love** (**with**) tomber amoureux (-euse) (de)
false faux (fausse)
family famille *f.*
far ferme *f.*; **far** (**from**) loin (de)
farmer agriculteur (-trice) *m., f.*
fast vite, rapide
fat gros(se)
father père *m.*
fault: it's your fault, you know c'est de ta faute, tu sais
favor service *m.*
favorite préféré(e)
February février *m.*
feel sentir; **to feel badly** aller mal; **to feel like** avoir envie de
female femme; féminin
feminine féminin(e)
few: a few quelques *adj.*; quelques-uns (unes) *pron.*
field champ *m.*
fifteen quinze
fifties (*decade*) les années (*f. pl.*) cinquantes
fill (**in, up**) remplir; (*the tank with gas*) faire le plein
finally enfin
find trouver
fine: I'm fine ça va bien
fine arts beaux-arts *m. pl.*
finger doigt *m.*
finish finir (de + *inf.*); **to finish by** finir par
first premier (-ière); **first of all, at first** d'abord
fish poisson *m.*; **fish market** poissonnerie *f.*
fishing pêche *f.*
five cinque
flight vol *m.*
float (*parade*) char *m.*
flower fleur *f.*
fluently couramment
follow suivre
foot pied *m.*
football football américain *m.*
for pour, depuis, pendant; **for how long . . . ?** depuis quand... ? depuis combien de temps... ?
foreign étranger (-ère)
forest forêt *f.*
forget oublier
fork fourchette *f.*
former ancien(ne)
formerly autrefois
fortunate heureux (-euse)
four quatre
fourteen quatorze
free (*to do something*) libre
French français *m.* (*language*); français(e); **French-speaking** francophone
frequently fréquemment
fresh frais (fraîche)
Friday vendredi *m.*
friend ami(e) *m., f.*; **boy/girlfriend** petit(e) ami(e)
from de; **from the** de la, du, des; **from now on** à l'avenir
fun: to have fun s'amuser
funny drôle; amusant(e)
furious furieux (-ieuse)
furniture (*piece of*) meuble *m.*
future avenir *m.*; futur *m.*; futur(e) *adj.*

game match *m.;* jeu *m.;* (*of chance*) jeu de hasard *m.;* (*social*) jeu de société *m.*
garden jardin *m.*
gardening jardinage *m.*
generally en général
geography géographie *f.*
geology géologie *f.*
geometry géométrie *f.*
get recevoir, obtenir; **to get along** s'entendre; **to get dressed** s'habiller; **to get ready** se préparer; **to get up** se lever; **to go down from, get off** descendre (de)
gift cadeau *m.*
gifted doué(e)
girl jeune fille *f.*
give donner; **to give back** rendre
glad content(e), heureux (-euse)
glasses lunettes *f. pl.*
glove gant *m.*
go aller; **to go away/off** s'en aller; **to go down** (*south*) to descendre à; **to go home** rentrer; **to go out** sortir; **to go up** monter
goggles lunettes de ski *f. pl.*
gold or *m.*
good bon(ne); bien
good-bye au revoir
Gothic gothique
government gouvernement *m.*
grade note *f.*
granddaughter petite-fille *f.*
grandfather grand-père *m.*
grandmother grand-mère *f.*
grandparent grand-parent *m.*
grandson petit-fils *m.*
grape raisin *m.*
gray gris(e)
great grand(e); formidable
green vert(e)
green bean haricot vert *m.*
grocery store épicerie *f.*
ground terre *f.;* **on the ground** par terre
guess deviner
guidebook guide *m.*

habitually d'habitude
haggle (*over a price*) marchander
hair cheveux *m. pl.*
half: half past the hour et demi(e)
hall couloir *m.*
ham jambon *m.*
hand main *f.*
hand: to hand in rendre
handbag sac à main *m.*
handsome beau, bel, belle, beaux, belles
handwriting écriture *f.*
happen arriver; se passer; **It's what happens when . . .** c'est ce qui arrive quand... ; **what's happening?** qu'est-ce qui se passe?
happy heureux (-euse); content(e); **I'm happy for you** je suis content(e) pour vous
hard dur(e)
hardly peu
hard-working travailleur (-euse)
hat chapeau *m.*
hate détester

have avoir; (*to eat; to order*) prendre; **to have fun** (*a good time*) s'amuser; **to have just done** (*something*) venir de + *inf.;* **to have to** devoir; avoir besoin de, il faut...
he il, lui, ce
head tête *f.*
health santé *f.*
hear entendre
heavy lourd(e)
height taille *f.*
hello bonjour, salut; (*telephone*) allô
help (*someone do something*) aider (quelqu'un à faire quelque chose)
her (*personal pron.*) la, lui; (*possessive pron.*) son, sa, ses
here ici; **here is/are** voici
hi salut
high élevé(e)
highway autoroute *f.*
hike randonnée *f.;* marcher; **to take a cross-country hike** faire une randonnée
him le, lui; **to him** lui
his son, sa, ses
history histoire *f.*
hobby passe-temps *m.*
hold tenir; **please hold** (*telephone*) ne quittez pas
holiday fête *f.*
home maison *f.;* **at home** à la maison, chez nous; **to go home** rentrer
homework devoir *m.;* **to do homework** faire ses devoirs
horror horreur *m.*
hospital hôpital *m.*
hot chaud; **it's hot** il fait chaud; **to be hot** avoir chaud
hotel hôtel *m.*
hour heure *f.*
house maison *f.;* **at our house** chez nous
housework: to do the housework faire le ménage
how comment; **how are you?** comment allez-vous? (**for**) **how long?** pendant combien de temps? depuis quand... ? **how many . . . ?** combien (de)... ? depuis combien de temps... ? **how's it going?** ça va?
however pourtant
hunger faim *f.;* **to be hungry** avoir faim
hurry se dépêcher
hurt avoir mal
husband mari *m.*

I je, moi
ice glace *f.*
ice cream glace *f.*
idea idée *f.*
idealistic idéaliste
if si
ill malade
immediately tout de suite
impatient impatient(e)
improvement perfectionnement *m.*
in à, dans, en; **in order to** pour; **in front of** devant; **in French** en français: **in Paris** à Paris
increase augmentation *f.*

individualistic individualiste
industrial industriel(le)
inexpensive bon marché
insect insecte *m.*
inspect contrôler
instead plutôt
insurance agent assureur *m.*
intellectual intellectuel(le)
intelligent intelligent(e)
interest intéresser; **to be interested in** (*something*) s'intéresser à (quelque chose)
interesting intéressant(e)
interpreter interprète *m., f.*
invite inviter
island île *f.*
it ce, il, elle; le, la; **isn't it?** n'est-ce pas? **it is** c'est, il est
Italian italien *m.* (*language*); italien(ne)
Ivory Coast (**inhabitant**) ivoirien(ne)

jacket veste *f.;* **ski jacket** anorak *m.;* **(man's) suit jacket** veston
January janvier *m.*
Japanese japonais(e)
jeans jean *m.*
journalist journaliste *m., f.*
judge magistrat *m.*
juice jus *m.*
July juillet *m.*
June juin *m.*
just seulement; **to have just** venir de (+ *inf.*)

keyboard (*computer*) clavier *m.*
kindergarten école maternelle *f.*
kindly gentiment
king roi *m.*
kitchen cuisine *f.*
knapsack sac à dos *m.*
knife couteau *m.*
know (*how*) savoir; (*a person or place*) connaître
knowledge connaissance *f.*

lady dame *f.;* **young lady** jeune fille *f.*
lake lac *m.*
lamp lampe *f.*
land terre *f.*
landscape paysage *m.*
language langue *f.*
last dernier (-ière), passé(e); **last night** hier soir
late tard; en retard
laugh rire
law droit *m.,* loi *f.*
lawyer avocat(e) *m., f.*
lazy paresseux (-euse)
lead diriger
leaf feuille *f.*
learn apprendre
learning (*apprenticeship*) apprentissage *m.*
leave laisser, quitter, partir, sortir; **to leave each other** se quitter; **leave (behind)** laisser
lecture conférence *f.;* **lecture hall** amphithéâtre *m.*
left gauche *f.;* **on / to the left** à gauche

leg jambe *f.*
legacy patrimoine *m.*
legalization légalisation *f.*
leisure (*activities*) loisirs *m. pl.*
lend prêter
less moins (de); **less than** moins... que
letter lettre *f.*
lettuce salade *f.*, laitue *f.*
liberty liberté *f.*
library bibliothèque *f.*
life vie *f.*
lightning coup de foudre *m.*
like comme; **to like** aimer; **to like better** aimer mieux; **I (don't) like that** ça (ne) me plaît (pas)
likely probable; **it's not likely that** il est peu probable que
line ligne *f.*
linguistics linguistique *f.*
listen (to) écouter
literature littérature *f.*
little petit(e); **a little** un peu de (+ *noun*)
live habiter, vivre
living room salle de séjour *f.*
located: to be located se trouver
lodging logement *m.*
long long(ue)
look (at) regarder; **to look (like)** avoir l'air (de + *inf.*); **to look for** chercher
lose perdre
lot: a lot (of) beaucoup (de)
love aimer; adorer; amour *m.; **love at first sight*** coup de foudre *m.*, **in love, loving** amoureux (-euse); **to fall in love (with)** tomber amoureux (-euse) (de)
lucky: to be lucky avoir de la chance
luggage bagagerie *f.*
lunch déjeuner *m.*

Madagascar (inhabitant) malgache
magazine revue *f.*
mail courrier *m.;* **mailbox** boîte aux lettres *f.*
mail carrier facteur (-trice) *m., f.*
make faire; **to make the acquaintance of** faire la connaissance de; fabriquer
makeup maquillage *m.;* **to put on makeup** se maquiller
man homme *m.*
management (*business*) gestion *f.*
manager cadre *m.*
many beaucoup; **how many?** combien? **so many** tant (de)
map carte *f.*
March mars *m.*
market marché *m.;* **to go to the market** faire le marché
marriage mariage *m.*
marry se marier (à, avec)
marvellous merveilleux
masterpiece chef-d'œuvre *m.*
mathematics mathématiques (maths) *f. pl.*
matter: it doesn't matter (to me) ça m'est égal; **that doesn't matter** ça ne fait rien
May mai *m.*
me me, moi
meal repas *m.*
mean vouloir dire
meat viande *f.*
mechanical engineering mécanique *f.*
media média *m.s.* or *pl.*
medicine médecine *f.*
medieval médiéval(e)
medium moyen(ne)
meet (se) rencontrer; (*someone for the first time*) faire la connaissance de
meeting réunion *f.;* rencontre *f.;* rendez-vous *m.;* **to have a meeting** avoir rendez-vous
member membre *m.*
menu carte *f.;* (*fixed price*) menu *m.*
merchant commerçant(e)
middle milieu *m.;* **to be in the middle of** (*doing something*) être en train de (+ *inf.*)
Middle Ages moyen âge *m.*
midnight minuit *m.*
milk lait *m.*
mine le mien, la mienne, les miens, les miennes
mineral minéral(e)
Miss mademoiselle *f.* (Mlle)
mistaken: to be mistaken se tromper
mixture mélange *m.*
Monday lundi *m.*
money argent *m.*
monitor contrôler; (*computer*) moniteur *m.*
month mois *m.*
monument monument *m.*
more encore; plus de (+ *noun*); **more than** plus... que
morning matin *m;* matinée *f.*
Moroccan marocain(e)
most le (la) plus; **most (of)** la plupart (de)
mother mère *f.*
motorcycle motocyclette *f.*, moto *f.*
mountain montagne *f.;* **mountaineering** alpinisme *m.*
movie film *m.;* **movie theater** cinéma *m.*
Mr. monsieur *m.* (M.)
Mrs. madame *f.* (Mme)
much beaucoup; bien; **so much** tant (de); **too much** trop
museum musée *m.*
music musique *f.*
must devoir
my mon, ma, mes

naive naïf (naïve)
name nom *m.;* **first name** prénom; **to be named** s'appeler; **what's your name?** comment vous appelez-vous?
napkin serviette *f.*
national national(e)
near près (de); **near here** près d'ici
necessary nécessaire; **it is necessary** il faut
neck cou *m.*
need avoir besoin de
neighbor voisin(e) *m., f.*
neither . . . nor ne... ni... ni; **neither one** ni l'un ni l'autre
nephew neveu *m.*
nervous nerveux (-euse)
never jamais, ne... jamais
new nouveau (nouvel, nouvelle); neuf (neuve)
news (*information*) nouvelles *f. pl.;* **TV news** informations *f. pl;* **what bad news!** quelle mauvaise nouvelle!
newspaper journal *m.*
newsstand kiosque *m.*
next prochain(e); ensuite; **next door** à côté; **next to** à côté de
nice gentil(le); sympathique; **it's nice out** il fait beau
niece nièce *f.*
night nuit *f.*, soir *m.;* **last night** hier soir
nine neuf
no non; **no longer, no more** ne... plus
nobody, no one personne, ne... personne
noise bruit *m.*
nonsmoking section section non-fumeurs
noon midi *m.*
north: to the north au nord *m.*
nose nez *m.*
not ne... pas; **not at all** pas du tout; **not yet** ne... pas encore
notebook cahier *m.*
nothing rien, ne... rien
novel roman *m.*
novelist romancier (-ière) *m., f.*
November novembre *m.*
now maintenant
number numéro *m.;* (*digit*) chiffre *m.*
nurse infirmier (-ière) *m., f.*

obliged: to be obliged to devoir
obtain obtenir
occupied occupé(e)
ocean océan *m.*, mer *f.*
o'clock heure *f.*
October octobre *m.*
odd drôle
of de; **of course** bien sûr; **of whom, of which** dont
offer offrir
office bureau *m.;* (*administrative center*) secrétariat *m.*
often souvent
oh! ah!
okay d'accord
old ancien(ne); vieux (vieil, vieille, vieilles); **to be . . . years old** avoir... ans
on sur, dans, à; **on weekends** le week-end
one un(e); on
only seulement, ne... que
open ouvrir
opinion: in my opinion pour ma part, à mon avis
opportunity: to have the opportunity to avoir l'occasion de
optimistic optimiste
or ou
orange orange
order (*in a restaurant*) commander
order: in order that afin (que, de), pour que, pour
orderly en ordre
other autre
ought devoir
our notre, nos
outdoors en plein air

outside dehors
overseeing contrôle *m.*
over there là-bas
owe (*money*) devoir
oyster huître *f.*

pain: to have pain avoir mal
painter peintre *m.*, artiste *m.*, *f.*
painting tableau *m.*; peinture *f.*
palace palais *m.*
pants pantalon *m.*
parade défilé *m.*
pardon: pardon me pardon
Parisian parisien(ne)
park parc *m.*
partial partiel(le)
partner partenaire *m.*, *f.*
party parti *m.*; soirée *f.*
pass passer; (*exams*) réussir à
passenger passager (-ère) *m.*, *f.*
passport passeport *m.*
past passé(e)
pastry pâtisserie *f.*; **pastry shop** pâtisserie *f.*
pâté (liver) pâté (de foie gras) *m.*; **country pâté** pâté de campagne
patience patience *f.*
patient patient(e)
patrimony patrimoine *m.*
pay (for) payer
payment paiement *m.*
pear poire *f.*
pen stylo *m.*
pencil crayon *m.*
people on; gens *m. pl.*
pepper poivre *m.*
perceive apercevoir
perfect perfectionner
perfection perfectionnement *m.*
perhaps peut-être
period *(of history)* époque *f.*
permit permettre
person personne *f.*
personally personnellement
pessimistic pessimiste
pharmacy pharmacie *f.*
philosophy philosophie *f.*
phone téléphone *m.*; **on the phone** à l'appareil, au téléphone
physics physique *f.*
pie tarte *f.*
piece morceau *m.*
pilot pilote *m.*
pink rose
place endroit *m.*; lieu *m.*; **to place, put** mettre; **in your place** à votre place; **that's the place where . . .** c'est l'endroit où...
plan projet *m.*; **to plan** organiser
plane avion *m.*
plant plante *f.*
plate assiette *f.*
platform (*train station*) quai *m.*
platter plat *m.*
play pièce *f.*; **to play** (*a sport or game*) jouer à; **to play** (*a musical instrument*) jouer de
playwright dramaturge *m.*, *f.*
pleasant agréable, gentil(le)
please s'il vous plaît
pleased content(e)
pleasure plaisir *m.*
P.M. de l'après-midi
poem poème *m.*
poet poète *m.*
point (out) indiquer
policeman agent de police *m.*
police station commissariat *m.*, poste de police *m.*
polite poli(e)
politics politique *f.*
pollute polluer
pollution pollution *f.*
poor pauvre
pork porc *m.*
possible: it is possible that il se peut que..., il est possible que...
postcard carte postale *f.*
poster affiche *f.*
post office bureau de poste *m.*
potato pomme de terre *f.*
prefer préférer, aimer mieux
preferable préférable
prepare préparer
preschool école maternelle *f.*
pretty joli(e)
prevent empêcher
price prix *m.*
printer imprimante *f.*
probably probablement, sans doute
problem problème *m.*
process: in the process of (*doing something*) en train de (+ *inf.*)
professor professeur *m.*, prof *m.*
program programme *m.*; émission *f.*
proliferation prolifération *f.*
promise promettre
protect protéger
proud fier (fière)
provided that pourvu que
psychology psychologie *f.*
pupil élève *m.*, *f.*
purchase achat *m.*
purse sac à main *m.*
pursue poursuivre
put mettre
putter: puttering around bricolage *m.*

quarrel (se) disputer
quarter quartier *m.*; **quarter past the hour** et quart; **quarter to the hour** moins le quart
Québec Quebec *m.*; **from Quebec** québécois(e)
queen reine *f.*
question: to ask a question poser une question
quickly vite, rapidement
quiet tranquille
quite tout, assez

rain pluie *f.*; pleuvoir; **it's raining** il pleut
raincoat imperméable *m.*
rapid rapide
rarely rarement
rather plutôt; assez
read lire; *p.p.* lu
reading lecture *f.*
ready prêt(e); **ready to** (*do something*) prêt(e) à (+ *inf.*)
realistic réaliste
really: Oh, really? Ah? bon
reasonable raisonnable
receipt reçu *m.*
receive recevoir
recently récemment
recipe recette *f.*
recognize reconnaître
record disque *m.*
recycle recycler
recycling recyclage *m.*
red rouge; **red-headed** roux (rousse)
reform réforme *f.*
refundable remboursable
refuse refuser (de)
region région *f.*
regret regretter
relate raconter
relatives parents *m. pl.*
relax se reposer, se détendre
relaxation détente *f.*
remain rester
remember se souvenir de, se rappeler
rent louer
repeat répéter
require exiger
required obligatoire
rescue sauver
residence (*place of*) logement *m.*
resource ressource *f.*
rest se reposer
return retourner; **to return** (*something*) rendre; **to return home** rentrer; **to return** (*come back*) revenir; **return to schoolwork in September** rentreé *f.*
review (*for a test*) réviser
rice riz *m.*
rich riche
right droite(e) *adj.*; **right?** n'est-ce pas? **to the right** à droite; **to be right** avoir raison
ring bague *f.*; **to ring** sonner
river fleuve *m.*; **riverbank** rive *f.*
road route *f.*; chemin *m.*
roast rôti *m.*
Roman romain(e)
room pièce *f.*; chambre *f.*; **living room** salle de séjour *f.*; **dining room** salle à manger *f.*; **bathroom** salle de bains *f.*
roommate camarade de chambre *m.*, *f.*
rug tapis *m.*
run courir
Russian russe *m.*, *f.*

sad triste
sailboat bateau à voile *m.*
salad salade *f.*
salary salaire *m.*
sale vente *f.*
salt sel *m.*
same même
sandal sandale *f.*
sardine (*in oil*) sardine à l'huile *f.*
Saturday samedi *m.*
sausage (*dry*) saucisson *m.*
savannah savanne *f.*

save sauver; **to save (up) money** faire des économies
say dire; **that is to say** c'est-à-dire
scared: to be afraid avoir peur
schedule horaire *m.*
school école *f.;* scolaire *adj.;* **elementary school** école primaire *f.;* **first cycle of secondary school** collège *m.;* **second cycle of secondary school** lycée *m.*
screen (*computer*) écran *m.*
sea mer *f.*
search (for) chercher
season saison *f.*
second deuxième
secondary secondaire
section (*of Paris*) arrondissement *m.*
see voir; **see you soon** à bientôt; **to see again** revoir
seem avoir l'air; **it seems that** il semble que...
sell vendre
senator sénateur *m.*
send envoyer
Senegalese sénégalais(e)
sense sentir
September septembre *m.*
serious sérieux (-euse)
serve servir
settle: to settle down s'installer
settler colon *m.*
seven sept
seventeen dix-sept
several plusieurs, quelques
shame honte *f.*
sheet (*of paper*) feuille *f.*
shirt chemise *f.*
shoe chaussure *f.;* **tennis shoes** tennis *m. pl.*
shopping: to do the shopping faire le marché
short court(e); (*size*) petit(e); bref (brève)
shorts short *m.*
should devoir
show montrer; indiquer; (*movies*) séance *f.;* (*performance*) spectacle *m.*
sick malade
sign signer
similar (to) pareil(le) à; semblable à
since depuis; comme; **since when?** depuis quand?
sincere sincère
sing chanter
singer chanteur (-euse) *m., f.*
single: single life célibat *m.*
sink lavabo *m.*
sister sœur *f.*
sit s'asseoir
six six
sixteen seize
ski ski *m.;* **to ski** skier, faire du ski
skirt jupe *f.*
slave esclave *m., f.*
sleep dormir
sleeping bag sac de couchage *m.*
sleepy: to be sleepy avoir sommeil
slow lent(e)
small petit(e)
smell sentir
smoke fumer
smoking section section fumeurs *f.*
snack (*afternoon*) goûter *m.*
snail escargot *m.*
snobbish snob
snow neige *f.;* **to snow** neiger
snowman bonhomme de neige *m.*
so si, alors; **so that** afin que, afin de, pour que, pour; **so much, so many** tant (de)
sociology sociologie *f.*
sock chaussette *f.*
sofa canapé *m.*
software logiciel *m.*
some de la, du, des; en *pron.;* quelques; quelques-uns (unes)
someday un jour, un de ces jours
someone quelqu'un
something quelque chose
sometimes parfois, quelquefois
somewhat assez
son fils *m.*
song chanson *f.;* **popular song** chanson de variété
soon bientôt; **as soon as** dès que, aussitôt que
sorry désolé(e): **to be sorry** regretter; **I'm sorry for you** je suis désolé(e) pour vous
south: to the south au sud *m.*
space espace *f.*
Spanish espagnol *m.* (*language*); espagnol(e)
speak parler
spend: to spend (time) passer: **to spend** (*money*) dépenser
spoon cuillère *f.;* **soupspoon** cuillère à soupe *f.*
sport sport *m.;* **sports coat** veste *f.;* **sports-minded** sportif (-ive); **sporting event** manifestation sportive *f.*
spring printemps *m.*
square place *f.*
stamp timbre *m.*
stand: I can't stand . . . J'ai horreur de...
start commencer (à); se mettre à; **to start again** reprendre
state état *m.*
station (*train*) gare *f.;* **police station** commissariat *m.*, poste de police *m.;* **metro station** station de métro *f.*
stay rester
steak bifteck *m.*
stereo chaîne stéréo *f.*
steward steward *m.*
stewardess hôtesse de l'air *f.*
stick of chalk bâton de craie *m.*
still encore
stop (s')arrêter
storekeeper commerçant(e) *m., f.*
straight ahead tout droit
strange: it is strange that il est étrange que
strawberry fraise *f.*
street rue *f.*
stroll flâner
student étudiant(e) *m., f.*
studies études *f. pl.*
study étudier
stupid stupide
subject (*of study*) matière *f.*
suburbs banlieue *f.*
subway métro *m.*
succeed réussir (à)
success réussite *f.*
suddenly soudain, soudainement; tout d'un coup
suffer souffrir
sugar sucre *m.*
suggest suggérer
suit costume *m.;* (*woman's*) **suit** tailleur *m.*
suitcase valise *f.*
suit jacket (*man's*) veston *m.*
sum montant *m.*
summer été *m.*
sun soleil *m.;* **it's sunny** il fait du soleil
Sunday dimanche *m.*
sunglasses lunettes de soleil *f. pl.*
superior supérieur(e)
sure sûr(e), certain(e)
surely sûrement
surprised surpris(e) (*p.p. of* surprendre); **to be surprised** être surpris(e)
sweater pull-over *m.*
swim nager, se baigner
swimming pool piscine *f.*
swimsuit maillot de bain *m.* (*woman's*); slip de bain *m.* (*man's*)

table table *f.*
take prendre; **to take a walk** faire une promenade; **to take a hike** faire une randonnée; **to take out** (*food from a restaurant*) emporter; **to take out** sortir; **to take** (*someone*) emmener; **to take place** avoir lieu, se passer; **to take a course** suivre un cours; **to take again** reprendre; **to take an exam** passer un examen
talented doué(e)
talk parler
tall grand(e)
taste goûter
tea thé *m.*
teach enseigner
teacher professeur *m.*, prof *m.;* (*preschool and elementary*) instituteur (-trice) *m., f.*
teaching (*profession*) enseignement *m.*
team équipe *f.*
telegram télégramme *m.*
telephone téléphone *m.;* téléphoner à; **telephone call** coup de téléphone; **on the phone** à l'appareil, au téléphone; **telephone number** numéro de téléphone *m.;* **telephone book** annuaire *m.;* **telephone booth** cabine téléphonique *f.*
television télévision *f.;* **TV** télé *f.;* **television set** poste de télévision *m.;* **television news** informations *f. pl.;* **television channel** chaîne *f.*
tell raconter; dire
ten dix
tennis shoes les tennis *m. pl.*
tent tente *f.*
terrace terrasse *f.*
text examen *m.*

thank remercier; **I don't know how to thank you** je ne sais pas vous remercier
thank you merci
that que; ça; ce, cet, cette, ces
the le, la, les
theater théâtre *m.;* **movie theater** cinéma *m.*
their leur, leurs
them les, leur, eux
then puis, alors, ensuite
there y, là; **there is, there are** il y a
therefore donc
these ces
they ils, elles, on
thick gros(se)
thing chose *f.;* truc *fam.*
think penser, croire; **think (of, about)** réfléchir à, penser à; **to think of** (*have an opinion about*) penser de; **what do you think of that?** qu'en penses-tu?
third troisième
thirsty: to be thirsty avoir soif
thirteen treize
this ce, cet, cette
those ceux, celles
three trois
throat gorge *f.*
through par
throw lancer
Thursday jeudi *m.*
ticket billet *m.;* **ticket window** guichet *m.*
tie cravate *f.*
time temps *m.*, heure *f.;* (*occasion*) fois *f.*; (*once*) une fois; **a long time** longtemps; **from time to time** de temps en temps; **to spend time** passer du temps; **what time is it?** quelle heure est-il?
tip pourboire *m.*
tired fatigué(e)
to à, en; pour; chez
today aujourd'hui
tomorrow demain
tonight ce soir
too aussi; **too much** trop (de)
tooth dent *f.*
touch toucher
tourist touriste *m., f.;* **tourist class** classe économique *f.;* **tourist information bureau** syndicat d'initiative *m.*
toward (*a place*) vers
tower tour *f.*
town hall mairie *f.*
train train *m.;* (*car*) wagon *m.;* **train station** gare *f.*
travel voyager; faire un voyage; (*in a car*) rouler
traveler's checks chèques de voyage *m.*
tree arbre *m.*
trip voyage *m.;* **to take a trip** faire un voyage
truck camion *m.*
true vrai(e)
truth vérité *f.*
T-shirt tee-shirt *m.*
Tuesday mardi *m.*
Tunisian tunisien(ne)
turkey (*roast*) dinde rôtie *f.*
turn tourner; **to turn on** mettre
twelve douze
two deux

ugly moche
umbrella parapluie *m.*
unbelievable incroyable
uncle oncle *m.*
under sous
understand comprendre
unemployment chômage *m.*
unfair injuste
unfortunate pauvre; **it is unfortunate that** il est fâcheux que
unfortunately malheureusement
unhappy triste, malheureux (-euse)
United States États-Unis *m., pl.*
university université *f.;* universitaire *adj.*
unless à moins que, à moins de
unlikely peu probable
unpleasant désagréable
unsociable insociable
until jusqu'à, jusqu'à ce que
up: to go up monter
use utiliser, employer; **it's something that's used for . . .** c'est quelque chose qu'on utilise pour...
useful: it is useful that il est utile que
useless: it is useless that il est inutile que
usually d'habitude

vacation vacances *f. pl.*
veal veau *m.*
vegetable légume *m.*
very très, fort
veterinarian vétérinaire *m., f.*
videotape vidéoclip *m.*
view: in my view pour ma part, à mon avis
vine vigne *f.;* **vineyard** vignoble *m.*
violet violet(te)
visit visite *f.;* **to visit** (*a place*) visiter; (*person*) rendre visite à
voodoo vaudou *m.*
voter électeur (-trice) *m., f.*

wait (for) attendre
waiter serveur *m.*
waitress serveuse *f.*
wake up (se) réveiller
walk promenade *f.;* **to take a walk** faire une promenade; marcher
walking marche *f.*
wall mur *m.*
wallet portefeuille *m.*
want vouloir, avoir envie de
war guerre *f.*
warm: to be warm avoir chaud
wash se laver
washbasin lavabo *m.*
waste gaspillage *m.;* **to waste** gaspiller; **waste** (*material*) déchet *m.*
watch regarder
water eau *f.*
way chemin *m.*
we nous, on
wear porter
weather temps *m.;* **how's the weather?** quel temps fait-il?
Wednesday mercredi *m.*
week semaine *f.*
weekend week-end *m.*, fin de semaine *f.*
welcome: you're welcome de rien; il n'y a pas de quoi; je vous en prie
well bien; eh bien; **get well soon!** guéris vite!
west: to the west à l'ouest *m.*
what que, ce qui, ce que, quoi: que... ? quoi? qu'est-ce que? comment? **what is it?** qu'est-ce que c'est?
when quand, lorsque
where où
whether si
which quel, quelle, quels, quelles; **that which** (*subject of verb*) ce qui; **that which** (*object*) ce que; **to which** auquel, à laquelle, auxquels, auxquelles
while temps *m.;* pendant que
white blanc (blanche)
who qui? qui est-ce qui?
whom qui? qui est-ce que?
whose dont
why pourquoi; **why not?** pourquoi pas?
wife femme *f.*
willing: to be willing vouloir bien
win gagner
wind vent *m.;* **it's windy** il fait du vent
windbreaker blouson *m.*
window fenêtre *f.;* (*ticket*) guichet *m.*
windsurfing planche à voile *f.*
wine vin *m.;* **winemaker** vigneron *m.*
winter hiver *m.*
wish souhaiter
with avec
withdraw retirer
without sans, sans que
woman femme *f.*
wonder se demander
wonderful merveilleux (-euse); formidable
woods bois *m.*
word mot *m.*
work travail *m.;* **to work** travailler; (*function*) marcher; **work of art** œuvre d'art *f.*
worker ouvrier (-ière); travailleur (-euse); **salaried worker** travailleur salarié *m.;* **self-employed worker** travailleur indépendant *m.*
workshop atelier *m.*
worse pire
worth: to be worth valoir
write écrire
writing écriture *f.*
wrong: to be wrong avoir tort; se tromper

year an *m.*, année *f.;* **to be . . . years old** avoir... ans
yellow jaune
yes oui
yesterday hier
yet encore; pourtant
you tu, te, toi, vous
young jeune
your ton, ta, tes, votre, vos

zero zéro

Index

In this index, vocabulary topic groups are listed by individual topic as well as under the heading *Vocabulary*. **A propos** sections appear only as a group, under that heading.